THEY CRIED
TO THE LORD

❧

Then they cried to the Lord in their trouble,
and he delivered them from their distress.

Ps 107:6, 13, 19, 28

THEY CRIED
TO THE LORD

The Form and Theology of Biblical Prayer

PATRICK D. MILLER

Fortress Press   Minneapolis

THEY CRIED TO THE LORD
The Form and Theology of Biblical Prayer

Interior design: ediType
Cover design: Ann Elliot Artz Hadland
Cover art: "Hebrew Harpists," by Sandra Bowden, painter and printmaker, living in Clifton Park, N.Y. Used by permission of the artist.

Library of Congress Cataloging-in-Publication Data
Miller, Patrick C.
    They cried to the Lord : the form and theology of Biblical prayer
/ Patrick D. Miller.
      p. cm.
    Includes bibliographical references and index.
    ISBN 0-8006-2762-8 (alk. paper) :
    1. Bible—Prayers. 2. Bible—Prayers—History and criticism.
3. Prayer—biblical teaching. I. Title.
BS680.P64M55 1994
248.3'2'0901—dc20
                          94-10750
                          CIP

Manufactured in the U.S.A.   AF 1-2762
98   97   96   95   94   1   2   3   4   5   6   7   8   9   10

To
James L. Mays
Teacher, Colleague, and Friend

Summary of Contents

Contents

oↄ

Preface

❧

This study of biblical prayer arises from teaching seminary students, pastors, and lay people about the Psalms and, more broadly, about prayer in Scripture. All of these groups have taught me as I have taught them and thus have helped to shape this book in large and small ways.

Particular words of thanks are necessary, however, to a number of institutions and persons. Princeton Theological Seminary and its president, Thomas W. Gillespie, have provided a congenial atmosphere for teaching and writing and, more specifically, sabbatical time and financial support for the completion of this book. In addition, this book had its genesis in the 1987 Alumni Lectures at Princeton Theological Seminary, although its final form is far different from the original lectures.

Pittsburgh Theological Seminary and its president, Samuel Calian, graciously extended the invitation to present the 1993 Schaff Lectures at that institution and thus provided a platform for communicating parts of this study prior to publication. The Association of Theological Schools also provided financial support for a sabbatical that enabled me to finish writing the manuscript.

Parts of chapters 3, 5, and 9 have appeared in earlier form in the following essays: "Prayer as Persuasion: The Rhetoric and Intention of Prayer," *Word & World* 13 (1993) 356–62; "In Praise and Thanksgiving," *Theology Today* 45 (1988) 180–88; "The Blessing of God: An Interpretation of Numbers 6:22-27," *Interpretation* 29 (1975) 240–51. Chapter 6 was published first as "Things Too Wonderful: Prayers of Women in the Old Testament," *Gesellschaftliche Wandel und biblische Theologie: Festschrift für Norbert Lohfink S.J. zum 65 Geburtstag* (ed. G. Braulik, W. Gross, and S. McEvenue; Freiburg: Herder, 1993) 237–51. I am also grateful to colleagues at the universities of Lund, Hamburg, and Heidelberg, as well as Yale Divinity School, for the opportunity to present the material in chapter 6 in public lecture and for their helpful comments and warm hospitality.

While I am indebted to a number of colleagues at Princeton and elsewhere who talked with me about various aspects of this project, several persons merit special acknowledgment. Lillian Taylor, friend and former student, put the idea for the book in my mind. Parts of the book were read and criticized by Walter Brueggemann, J. Christiaan Beker, Gerald

Janzen, Ulrich Mauser, and J. J. M. Roberts. I am grateful for their suggestions, even those I did not follow. They have helped me think more clearly. My student Walter Bouzard Jr. gave superb assistance in reading the manuscript and in checking references and bibliography in the final stages, as well as in preparing the index. My thanks to all of these persons for their time and their interest.

Scripture citations are given according to the versification of the English translation and taken from the NRSV except when they are my own translation or a modification of the NRSV.

Introduction

No single practice more clearly defines a religion than the act of praying. Nor is there any religious practice more apt to take place on the part of those who otherwise are not religious at all. For those of every religious faith, prayer is one of the primary modes of relating the divine and the human, and for those of no faith at all, occasions of deep crisis often evoke a spontaneous cry for help from the lips of those who may not really believe there is anyone to hear or to help.

Prayer does assume, in most of its definitions and most of its practice, a higher power who is in touch with human life. It may arise out of such an assumption as a deep conviction of a person's life and faith, or it may be a momentary hope for one with little or no religious convictions. In like manner, prayer has been seen as a primary indicator of the practice of piety, but it is not only the pious who turn to God in the moments of deepest distress. Prayer is often a spontaneous outcome of life at its heights and depths whatever the religious grounding of the one who prays. It may be a painful, stuttering, reluctant expression. Or it may be a carefully formal, disciplined, planned communion with the divine.

Prayer is not, however, only a matter of spirituality and the practice of piety. It also has to do with faith, that is, with whom we trust and what we believe. Theologians have long maintained that theology is at least in part an outgrowth of prayer—*ut legem credendi statuat lex orandi* (so that the rule of worship should establish the rule of faith)— that it is not simply a matter of believing and then praying to God in the light of what one believes. That very belief is shaped by the practice of prayer. So prayer and theology exist in relation to each other in a correcting circle, the one learning from the other and correcting the other. Religious faith seeks not to think one way and to pray another but to come before God in a manner that is consistent with what we believe and profess about God and God's way and to think about God in a way that is shaped by the experience of actual encounter in prayer. Learning to pray teaches about God.

This book is written, therefore, in the conviction that prayer and faith are interwoven into a single whole. It seeks to demonstrate the inextricable connections between faith and prayer, exploring the character of prayer in Scripture and in so doing uncovering the structure and shape of biblical faith. Much can be learned from Scripture about the relation between the human creature and God and about the nature of that relationship as it takes active form in prayer. The Bible is at least one important teacher in "the school of prayer." The disciples' strange request to Jesus, "Lord, teach us to pray," suggests what others have discovered, that prayer is something about which we have questions, perplexities, and problems—both in doing and in understanding. The chapters that follow seek to understand prayer in the light of Scripture, to discern how the form and theology of prayer are bound together.

The aim of this book is to look fairly comprehensively and broadly at biblical prayer. The reader should know from the start, however, that the weight of discussion rests upon what we find in the Old Testament. There is an obvious and practical reason for that in the limitations of the author's expertise. But the Old Testament also provides a weight of data for the subject that justifies such a focus. Most of the praying recorded and alluded to in Scripture is there. But the New Testament, which itself has often been the focus of studies of prayer (see chap. 10), is not ignored in what follows. It is present in three ways. First, canonical assumptions are operative throughout this work, to wit, that the Bible is a confessional document, or Scripture, and also that there is one canon of Scripture and not two. Thus the theological framework provided by the unity of Old and New Testaments is the context for much of the theological interpretation that follows. Second, there are frequent references to and examples from the New Testament in the bulk of the work that is focused primarily upon Old Testament texts. And, finally, the concluding chapter explores the further witness of the New Testament both in its confirmation of what has already been laid out and in the ways it extends the Bible's instruction about prayer beyond (or different from) what has been discerned from the Old Testament. The placing of a chapter on the New Testament at the conclusion of the book should not, however, be taken as an indication that the approach taken in these pages is essentially historical. Quite the contrary. As the subtitle indicates, the focus of this study of prayer is on its form and theology. That is, I have sought to take a broad and detailed look at the shape of prayer, its primary features, structure, and content in its various forms, and in that context to discern something of the theology of prayer, but even more determinedly of the character of the God to whom these prayers are lifted, the human ones who utter them in joy and sorrow, and what we can discern from them about the divine-human relation. The volume, however, is not a theology of prayer in general. Such a work might look very different, as even a casual perusal of the literature indicates. It is the theology of biblical prayer that is at issue here.

The center of this treatment of prayer is found in chapters 3–5. There, I have laid out the movement that leads from the human cry for help to divine response, which, in turn, evokes a grateful reaction of praise and thanksgiving from the one(s) who cried out. Here is the heart of biblical prayer but also a divine-human dialogue or conversation that identifies the very structure of faith as it is lived out in the words and lives of those who walk the pages of Scripture. Time and again, prayer arises when people in need of various sorts turn to the source of their help, the Lord of Israel. The biblical story itself takes much of its movement and direction out of those cries—first heard when Abel's blood cries out from the ground for justice against a killing brother—and the power of such prayer to evoke a response from God, words of assurance and deeds to help and save. While such prayers are prominent in the Psalter, they are often heard along the course of the story of Israel and the church. When such a dynamic occurs, however, it is not the end of the matter. Those who have been recipients and beneficiaries of the divine impulse to help and to save have something further to say in this conversation of faith. Indeed, when the Scriptures come to an end, we hear the choirs of heaven and earth joined in echoing the praise and thanksgiving that are heard time and again throughout the story when the redeemed of the Lord give thanks and sing hymns to praise the one who has helped them.

While this movement is at the heart of biblical prayer, it is by no means all that needs to be said about the subject. The chapters that precede and follow lead into the center and flow out from it. Chapters 1 and 2 are prolegomena in several ways, laying the groundwork for what follows. The first chapter, a look at the modes and forms of prayer among Israel's neighbors, has to do with things that are "before" Israel and thus "before" those matters discussed in chapters 3–5. While it seems to be apart from biblical prayer, in fact it leads quite directly into it. The book models Israel's own experience with prayer at this point. That is, Israel's prayer grows out of the larger universal experience even as it contributes to it. So, in this book, that larger experience sets the stage for the particular focus that is the primary undertaking. In chapter 1, glimpses of what is to come are given. Lines are thrown out that will be picked up in the chapters that follow. From the start, the prayer of Israel and the church is seen to be a part of a larger whole. The particular is also universal. That is not without its implications for our understanding of either prayer or the faith that evokes it.

Chapter 2 then takes us directly into biblical prayer, but still in regard to matters other than the prayers themselves. Here we look at the terms and designations for prayer that one finds in the Old Testament as one way of gaining some understanding about the nature of prayer. But one also needs to pay attention to those matters that have to do with when, where, and how in order to see what they tell us about prayer, its form and theology.

Chapters 6–9 develop the central themes in particular ways. While the prayers of women (chap. 6) are not different in form and theology from other prayers, it is important in our time to lift them up and to ask after the particular ways in which women's experience and their faith join in the act of prayer. The chapters on confession and penitence (chap. 7), intercession (chap. 8), and blessing and curse (chap. 9) deal with forms of the prayer for help that is the subject of the third chapter. While each of these modes of prayer is a form of the cry for help, the particular focus of each merits a separate treatment.

The reader may note the absence of any extended definition of prayer. At this point, the book follows the Bible in not devoting attention to that question except as it looks at the terminology for prayer in the Old Testament and takes up the instruction on prayer in the New Testament. The assumption at work here is that on those occasions when human beings, at their initiative, address God with some sort of need and in hopes of divine response, prayer is in place. It is also present when individuals and the community respond to God's help by initiating words and songs of praise and thanksgiving.

This study of prayer is intended for a broad audience. It assumes that an examination of what the Bible shows and teaches about prayer is of interest to academics and church folk, scholars and pastors. While some topics will be more familiar to teachers and scholars, it is my hope that nothing here will be inaccessible to those persons among the laity and the clergy who wish to think at some depth and breadth about a subject that is a part of the life of faith for all of us. Even so, the explicit intent to speak here to a broader audience should not preclude the possibility that those more versed in these matters may also find here food for further thought. Because of who and what I am, it should be said at the start that these pages are written from faith for faith. The questions that arise and the perspective for viewing them are voiced and envisioned by one who is a part of the believing community and seeks to address that community quite directly. Others are most welcome to listen in.

1

"What Other Great Nation Has a God So Near to It?"

ISRAEL'S NEIGHBORS AT PRAYER

When Israel began to pray to the Lord, it did so in the midst of peoples whose arms had long been raised and whose heads had been bowed to the gods that directed their lives and delivered them from disaster. If the tradition of Scripture is correct that Israel's ancestors came from Mesopotamia, then it is likely that in some way the many stories of those ancestors at prayer (Genesis) have some continuity in form and content with the traditions and practices of prayer of the people of Babylonia and Assyria. Biblical history also places Israel early and late in direct involvement with Egypt and its religion. The land of the Canaanites and the Phoenicians became Israel's habitation. To what extent any of these religious traditions influenced Israel is always debatable. What is not debatable is that Israel's ancestors lived among them and shared a world of thought and religious practices in a very fundamental way even if on any particular matter there may have been sharp differences. Both the lines of continuity and the points of difference belong to the description of Israel at prayer. The picture of Israel's neighbors at prayer may help us see that Israelite picture in sharper profile, giving us a sense of both its universality and its particularity.

It certainly will help one become more aware of the historicality of what one finds in the Bible. The scriptural teaching comes out of a time and place, of a particular historical community that existed over a long period in ever changing forms and circumstances. That teaching, to the extent that one can discern it, is not simply *de novo*, without origin or antecedents, even when at times it is so depicted. It takes place in and out of history. One may not always be able to discern its particular origins, but the antecedents and the cultural context are everywhere apparent. Indeed within the Bible itself, there is explicit testimony to the centrality of prayer among Israel's neighbors (and enemies). One of the greatest conflicts between the worship of the Lord of Israel and the worship of other gods that we know of in the history of Israel's religion, Elijah's encounter with the prophets of Baal on Mount Carmel (1 Kings 18), centers around prayer to the deities, Yahweh and Baal, and the ability of those deities to respond to the prayers of their adherents. And the final and climactic episode of Samson's life, his destruction of the Philistine temple, takes place on an occasion of Philistine praise, thanksgiving, and sacrifice that is very similar to what we encounter in Israel's praise (Judg 16:23-24).

There is thus a contextual and cultural shaping of the religious life that is the revelatory matrix of Scripture. To take a look at that cultural context is to gain some sense of *wherein*—literally—Israel came to pray as well as to open up some of the issues, direction, and questions that belong to the discussion of biblical prayer. Knowledge of the forms and practices of prayer in that religious world may help flesh out and clarify what one encounters in Scripture. To that end, this chapter will take a glimpse into that religious world, not in an exhaustive sense, but hopefully without misunderstanding. The subject and the materials are too vast to be comprehensive. The primary focus of the following discussion, therefore, will be upon Mesopotamia, but a sampling of Egyptian prayer texts will be included[1] as well as appropriate Canaanite materials where available—and they are surprisingly sparse. In chapter 4, further texts from the religious life of Israel's neighbors will be taken up in relation to the question of how the deity responds to prayers for help.

A caveat should be registered at the beginning. In the realm of prayer, the public cultus is a prominent dimension, as are the prayers of the leaders of the community. But there is also a large dimension of prayer that is quite nonpublic, individual, private, oral, and spontaneous (see appendix 1). Such prayers of the people, like all aspects of popular religion, are less preserved and protected in the tradition. With this subject probably more than others, one needs to be reminded that the very subject itself insures that there are large gaps in our knowledge that can never be filled. The picture that follows, therefore, is both partial and inevitably distorted by the available data as well as the possible interpretive misunderstandings. What is there, however, will help one to enter Israel's world with some awareness and familiarity, a readiness to understand that is reinforced by the universality of prayer, not only across contemporary cultures but across the millennia as well. In this subject as much as any, the student of Israel's world will have a sense of being at home with strangers. Familiarity and strangeness will intermix.

TERMINOLOGY

The language for prayer and the activities or expressions associated with it were as common and varied in Assyria and Babylonia as in Israel. Technical terms for "prayer" and the act of praying existed.[2] One could "speak," "pray," "bring," or "cry out" a prayer, and prayers were "received" or "heard" by the deity or deities. Sometimes they were not received. Of particular interest are the two Akkadian terms *aḫulap* and *šigû*. Both of these terms functioned as interjections or outcries for help, although the second term came to designate a particular type of penitential prayer. Texts speak of "crying *šigû*" or "entering to *šigû*," which may have referred to an actual formal prayer but may also have simply indicated the act of crying out. The term *aḫulap* has been translated "it is enough!"[3] While both terms are cries for pity to elicit divine compassion, *aḫulap* seems to be a more general cry for help while *šigû* implies a plea for pardon. The expression *šigû šasû* seems to mean in effect "to cry for mercy."[4] In such expressions, one may see the antecedents to the Hebrew exclamatory "Violence!" (*ḥāmās*) but more especially to the frequent reference to "crying out" (*ṣā'aq, zā'aq*), which becomes almost technical terminology for the cry for help (chap. 2, below).

POSTURES OF PRAYER

Both texts and iconography reveal the attitudes and postures of prayer. Prayers are offered in postures of standing, kneeling, and falling down before the deity, as in the case of Sumerian and Babylonian suppliants, or before the image of the deity, as in the case of Assyrian suppliants.[5] The latter mode of supplication may be manifest in a Palestinian context in the stela found in a shrine at Hazor depicting up-raised arms directed toward a crescent with a sun disk within.[6] It also may be reflected in the Deuteronomic notion of praying toward the temple where God has said, "My name shall be there" (1 Kings 8). On some of the reliefs or statues, the suppliant with one hand raised is led before the deity by another figure who may be a priest or a lesser or personal deity. The imagery of mediation or intercession is clearly suggested by these figures. Prostration and kneeling before the deity are probably positions of humility. The lifting of the hands may be in greeting, as seems to be the case in some instances of the raising of the right hand as the suppliant is led before the deity, or in manifestation of a beseeching, imploring manner, as seems to be the case when both hands are raised with the palms inward, a gesture that is known from visual representations in Palestine also[7] and is clearly a universal attitude and gesture of prayer.[8] In Mesopotamian texts there is not infrequently a reference to "touching the nose" in relation to prayer. For example:

> Prayer, supplication, and "touching of the nose"
> Offer him daily, and you will get your reward.[9]

and: "With 'touching of the nose' and prayer I followed my goddess."[10]

This expression customarily has been understood as touching the nose to the ground, that is, proskynesis or prostration.[11] While that may be the proper interpretation, it is more likely that this refers to the touching of the hand to the nose, a gesture of obeisance illustrated on the Hammurabi stela.[12]

The characteristic Egyptian attitude of prayer has the arms raised with the palms facing outward. This has been understood as possibly being exorcistic in its original purpose. Othmar Keel explains its varying meanings as follows:

> Subsequently, depending on the circumstances, it developed a defensive, aversive significance or a sense of protection, blessing, and praise.... The gesture of raised arms with palms forward is as appropriate to aversion as to veneration. In the final analysis, it expresses the attempt to restrain a superior, numinous opposite by means of conjuring, thus rendering it serviceable or averting it.[13]

He goes on to point out that only rarely did the Egyptian approach a deity with direct requests. Usually one came before the god with praise and blessing even if petition was the eventual intention. But the petition came only in a concluding statement indicating why all the praise had come forth. Even, therefore, in asking or petitioning the deity, an Egyptian would stand before the deity in an attitude of praise.[14]

MODES OF PRAYER

With regard to the actual character and form of Mesopotamian prayer, like the later Israelite prayer literature, the "older religious literature shows a basic division into works of praise...and works of lament."[15] Thorkild Jacobsen summarizes the fundamental aims of these two kinds of literature—which are at the heart of our discussion of biblical prayer in the following chapters—in a way that serves well to introduce discussion of some of their particular forms and characteristics:

> The literature of praise included hymns to gods, temples, or deified human rulers, as well as myths, epics, and disputations. It activated power already present or at least near at hand. The literature of lament, on the other hand, was directed to powers lost,

difficult or impossible to regain: the dead young god of fertility in the netherworld, the destroyed temple, the dead king or ordinary human. In the lament the vividness of recall and longing was an actual magical reconstitution, an attempt to draw back the lost god or temple by recreating in the mind the lost happy presence. Progressively, however, under the influence of sociomorphism, the aspect of magical forcing seems to have lessened, yielding in the classical periods to petition. In its new aspect praise literature was primarily aimed at blessing the ruling powers and thereby making them favorably inclined to human petition. The laments were aimed at influencing and swaying the divine heart by reminding the god of past happiness, rather than by magically recreating that past.[16]

Name Prayers

Both kinds of prayer are reflected in the simplest and shortest of prayers in the ancient world—the personal name, in which one often encounters prayers of praise or petition.[17] Thus one finds prayer names such as "Assur is great," "Sin heard my prayer" (cf. biblical Ishmael), and "My God has dealt compassionately with me."[18] All of these are names given to children as expressions of thanks and praise to the deity for the gift of the child, for having heard the prayer for a child—much like several of the names of Jacob's sons (Genesis 30). But names can express aspects of petitionary prayer also. So one encounters such names as "I have become weary, O my God," "My God, I am alone," "Where is my God?" "Enough for me, O Eštar!" and "How long, O my God?"[19] expressing elements of complaint or lament.[20] There are petitionary names, such as "Sin, deliver me!" "Turn to me, my God!" "Sin, remove my burden!" "Stand with me, O my God," "May I not be ashamed, O my God," "May I see/experience the grace/kindness of Sin," or a more complex petition, "Nabu you have caused him to be, may he prosper."[21] Expressions of trust that are frequent in petitionary prayers also become the names of children: "Nabu, I called to you and was not ashamed," "I trust in Šamaš," "I trust in Bel's word," "I wait on God."[22] Finally, there are names that correspond to the expression of thanks or praise at the end of petitionary prayers: "I will praise Sin," "I will praise Enlil."[23] One sees, therefore, that virtually every aspect of prayer is capable of being transformed into a permanent prayer, not in this instance on a votive object left at a sanctuary, but in the name of a walking and living human being. Such indirect but dynamic forms of prayer were as common among Israel's neighbors as they were in the names that Israelites themselves bore.[24]

Prayers of Lament and Petition

In the earliest period, prayer to the deity was most often found on votive objects deposited in the sanctuary near the statue of the deity to whom they were addressed. These could be all sorts of objects—bowls, tools, weapons, and statues of the deity. They were inscribed and left at the sanctuary on permanent deposit. "Such inscribed votive objects were, then, considered as taking the place of the suppliant, and relieving him of the need to proffer his prayer in his own person, orally and perpetually."[25]

For economic reasons at least, one is not surprised to see the development of this practice into prayers that were inscribed in simpler, less costly modes. This took the form of what have come to be called "Letter Prayers" or "Letters to Gods" because they are prayers originally modeled on the letter form. These letters were written and then left at the temple at the feet of the statue of the deity or in his or her sacred area.[26] They are sufficiently representative of the character of private prayer in Mesopotamia[27] from earliest stages on that a close look at them will be indicative—though not exhaustive—of the character of individual prayer in the Sumero-Akkadian tradition.[28] In the following discussion, the letter prayers form a base for analysis, but other types of prayer are drawn upon extensively.[29]

A single, long letter prayer to Enki, the personal god of the writer, Sin-šamuḫ, a scribe, provides a model to examine in some detail with reference to other similar prayers:[30]

i

1. To Enki, the outstanding lord of heaven and earth whose nature is unequalled

   Speak!

2. To Nudimmud, the prince of broad understanding who determines fates together with An,

3. Who distributes the appropriate divine attributes among the Anunnaki, whose course cannot be [reversed]

4. The omniscient one who is given intelligence from sunrise to sunset,

5. The lord of knowledge, the king of the sweet waters, the god who begot me,

   Say furthermore!

ii

6. (This is) what Sin-šamuh the scribe, the son of Ur-Nin [...],

7. your servant, says:

8. Since the day that you created me you have [given] me an education.

9. I have not been negligent toward the name by which you are called, like a father [...].

10. I did not plunder your offerings at the festivals to which I go regularly.

iii

11. (But) now, whatever I do, the judgment of my sin is not [...]

12. My fate has come my way, I am lifted onto a place of destruction, I cannot find an omen.

13. A hostile deity has verily brought sin my way, I cannot find(?) its side.

14. On the day that my vigorous house was decreed by Heaven

15. There is no keeping silent about my sin, I must answer for it.

iv

16. I lie down on a bed of alas and alack, I intone the lament.

17. My goodly figure is bowed down to the ground, I am sitting on (my) feet.[31]

18. My [...] is lifted from (its) place, my features are changed.

19. [...] restlessness is put into my feet, my life ebbs away.

20. The bright day is made like an "alloyed" day for me, I slip into my grave.

v

21. I am a scribe, (but) whatever I have been taught has been turned into spittle(?) for me

22. My hand is "gone" for writing, my mouth is inadequate for dialogue.

23. I am not old, (yet) my hearing is heavy, my glance cross-eyed.[32]

24. Like a brewer(?) with a junior term(?) I am deprived of the right to seal.

25. Like a wagon of the highway whose yoke has been broken(?) I am placed on the road

vi

26. Like an apprentice-diviner who has left his master's house I am slandered ignobly.

27. My acquaintance does not approach me, speaks never a word with me,

28. My friend will not take counsel with me, will not put my mind at rest.

29. The taunter has made me enter the tethering-rope, my fate has made me strange.

30. O my god, I rely on you, what have I to do with man?!

vii

31. I am grown-up, how am I to spread out in a narrow place?

32. My house (is) a plaited nest, I am not satisfied with its attractiveness.

33. My built-up houses are not faced with brick(?)

34. Like little (female) cedars planted in a dirty place, I(?) bear no fruit.

35. Like a young date palm planted by the side of a boat, I produce no foliage.

viii

36. I am (still) young, must I walk about thus before my time? Must I roll around in the dust?

37. In a place where my mother and father are not present I am detained,

38. who will recite my prayer to you?

39. In a place where my kinsmen do not gather I am overwhelmed,

40. who will bring my offering in to you?

ix

41. Damgalnunna, your beloved first wife,

42. May she bring it to you like my mother, may she introduce my lament before you

43. Asalalimnunna, son of the abyss,

44. May he bring it to you like my father, may he introduce my lament before you.

45. May he recite my lamentation to you, may he introduce my lament before you.

x

46. When I have verily brought (my) sin to you, cleanse(?) me from evil!

47. When you have looked upon me in the place where I am cast down, approach my chamber!

48. When you have turned my dark place into daylight,

49. I will surely dwell in your gate of Guilt-Absolved, I will surely sing your praises!

50. I will surely tear up my sin like a thread, I will surely proclaim your exaltation![33]

xi

51. As you reach the place of heavy sin, I will surely [sing your] praises.

52. Release me at the mouth of the grave, [save me] at the head of my tomb!

53. (Then) I will surely appear to the people, all the nation will verily know!

54. Oh my god, I am the one who reveres you!

55. Have mercy on the letter which I have deposited before you!

xii

56. May the heart of my god be restored!

The prayer begins with a salutation or address to the deity. Most of the named deities on such letter prayers have to do with either the underworld or healing, suggesting the threat of death or the predicament of sickness on the part of the one praying. In this prayer to Enki, the complaint in lines 16–20 is couched in the language of sickness and the ebbing of life. Here, however, as with the biblical prayers, the imagery of sickness and death may be metaphorical, a way of speaking about the disintegrating condition of the praying one, whose actual problem may be something else.[34] Some prayers are simply addressed to "my God," as in the Psalms, or in later prayer formulations, "my Lord/my Lady." What is immediately noticeable about the address in Sin-šamuḫ's prayer is that it is extended, both by appearing in a second form and, even more importantly, by a succession of laudatory appellations or appositional clauses. The deity is addressed by honorific titles and by more extended hymnic expressions of praise. Such elements of praise at the beginning of prayers are common in the prayers of Mesopotamia.[35] They are generally found not only in the letter prayers but also in the later Sumerian *eršaḫunga* prayers, which are clearly complaint or lament in character, as well as in the Sumerian and Akkadian incantation prayers of complaint/petition known as *ki'utukam* and *šu-illa* (a prayer of "the raising of the hand"), respectively. Even the very brief prayers found on Cassite seals, some two to five short lines on the average, include hymnic expressions of praise.[36] The more strictly penitential Akkadian *dingiršadibba* prayers have a much more restricted address and in that regard are more like the biblical prayers for help.[37]

The praise occurring in these prayers in more or less extended form addresses the deity particularly in terms of power, righteousness, and compassion. Recognition of the creative power and rule of the deity, as in line 1 of the prayer above, is common. Assertions of his or her protection of subjects and administration of righteous judgment are also frequent.[38] The deity is praised with regard to virtues and magnificence and characteristics that belong to deity, as, for example, in lines 1–4 of the prayer above, as well as in terms of the relationship with human beings or beneficent acts toward them, including the petitioner, as, for example, in line 5 above where the final element of praise is the expression "the god who begot me." Similar modes of address may be observed in Egyptian prayers, as, for example, the following excerpt from Neb-Re's prayer of thanksgiving upon deliverance of his son from illness by the god Amon-Re:

> Amon-Re...the august god, he who hears the prayer, who comes at the voice of the poor and distressed, who gives breath (to) him who is weak.[39]

Like the Lord of Israel (see chap. 3, below), Amon-Re is seen as the one who hears the cry of the sufferer and the poor.

While all this hymnic elaboration may have something to do with correct protocol in the relation with the deity,[40] it serves also "to remind them [the deities] of their special attributes, whose exercise may have caused the distress of the worshipper or may be the cause of salvation later to be invoked in the prayer."[41] In this respect, the hymnic address is not unlike the motivation clauses that pervade the Mesopotamian and Israelite prayers. Indeed, these hymnic elements may occur again in connection with the petition, for example, precisely to urge the deity to act in accord with his or her nature.[42] While this introductory praise, as it occurs in the various genres of Mesopotamian prayers, may be very general and sweeping in its description of the deity, as in the prayer above, not infrequently there may be an assertion about the deity that is designed to address the god as one able to deal with the particular problem of the one praying. William Hallo has noted this for the Sumerian letter prayers:

> The epithets applied to the various addressees in all these letter-prayers are drawn freely from all the rich storehouse of attributes available for embellishing Sumerian religious and monumental texts in general. But the choice was not wholly a random one, for in most instances there was a decided emphasis on those qualities of the addressee which were crucial for the substance of the petition that followed in the body of the letter. Thus the letters which prayed for the restoration of health praised the healing goddess for her therapeutic skills...; one which asked for legal redress stressed the unalterableness of the divine command....[43]

In the letter prayer of Sin-šamuḫ (above), the petitioner, who is concerned with scribal problems, addresses Enki—appropriately, under the circumstances—as prince of broad understanding and lord of knowledge or wisdom (ll. 2 and 5). The hymnic introduction indeed concludes with reference both to the attribute that fits the problem ("lord of knowledge") and to the relationship between the deity and the petitioner ("the god who begot me"). Both of these elements are then immediately picked up in line 8 as one moves into the body of the letter prayer: "Since the day that you created me you have [given] me an education."

Within the varied types of Mesopotamian prayers, there is often a fairly extensive elaboration of complaint and lament, describing the petitioner's condition in terms of causes and consequences.[44] Like the biblical psalms, the sufferings or miseries of these prayers fall generally into three categories: (1) physical and mental or emotional distress, (2) external or social adversity, and (3) divine disapproval.[45]

In part iv of Sin-šamuḫ's prayer above, the scribe describes a situation of both physical and emotional distress, of the body drooping to the ground, life ebbing away and slipping into the grave. He notes ailments of hand, mouth, ear, and eyes that incapacitate him for his scribal activity (ll. 21–23). Other prayers speak of headache, fever, and stiffness.[46] Crushed bones and limbs wasting away are characteristics of persons who pray these prayers. It should not be assumed that in all cases physiological sickness is the condition of the petitioner or that the language of sickness always comes into the complaint. Sometimes there is no specific reference to physical sickness. Nearly all the complaints do give some signs of emotional and mental distress, psychological malady of some sort. They speak of gloom, of languishing, of grief, pain, and sorrow, of being crushed in heart. Loneliness, anxiety, and weeping are manifestations of the suffering of the praying one. In one instance, the petitioner eats food and drinks water with tears and sighing (cf. Pss 42:3 and 102:9)[47] and speaks of falling into the mud, in imagery anticipatory of the various biblical complaints that speak of being in a pit or falling into a pit (cf. Pss 28:1; 30:3; 69:15):[48]

> The food I found I ate with sighing,
> The water I found I drank with sighing.
> Like one who goes down in the marshes,
> I have fallen in the mud.[49]

In these complaints, one hears the voice of those who are afraid, anxious, and in panic, of persons who are embarrassed and ashamed.[50] E. R. Dalglish summarizes the self-described plight of the lamenting one as follows:[51]

> [T]he penitent is "deaf," "dumb," "crushed," "in pain," "covered with gloom," in "dire straits," "oppressed," in "anguish," "weary from trembling," "bound," even from the days of his youth, "trodden down"; consequently, the penitent does not see, he "staggers like a reed in the whirlwind"; his "hand is weary from trembling"; and his lips are "muzzled"; his face is darkened; fear is in his body and over the land and people; he "faints" in misery, is "enfeebled," cannot eat; his soul is not cheerful; daily he is filled with crying and moaning; his mood is embittered; in sorrow of heart he utters wailing; he weeps and ceases not to lament; his breast is like a reed-flute echoing with the sound of lament; he has no confidence and has been treated as a faithless child.[52]

Sin-šamuḫ's prayer above shows also the complaint against external forces and social suffering. In part vi, the petitioner complains of being slandered ignobly, of being abandoned and rejected by friends and taunted by others. Again, one hears anticipations of the biblical psalms, whose complaints speak often of those who taunt or reproach (e.g., Psalm 69) and of friends who reject and taunt the praying one (e.g., Pss 22:6-8; and 55). Karel Van der Toorn lists among the social and economic aspects of the adversity lifted up in these prayers: financial setback, expenses, losses, privation and diminution, death of wife and children, hostility of friends and peers, quarrels at home and bickering in the streets.[53] One's place in the community is threatened in all sorts of ways in these prayers, and the distress is visible to others in the community.

The complaint against the god being addressed has several dimensions in these prayers. The suffering one may have experienced the deity's wrath because of sins committed. That is not spelled out in Sin-šamuḫ's prayer, but there are frequent indications of his sin, and, in part, he ascribes it to a hostile deity (l. 13). Communication with the deity through signs and omens has been lost, or evil signs may have come to him or her. In line 12 of Sin-šamuḫ's prayer, he complains that "I cannot find an omen." Yet another misery of the praying one may lie in the fact that the personal god has withdrawn protection, or the gods do not hear the cries of the petitioning one.[54] Jacobsen summarizes Sin-šamuḫ's prayer in this regard as follows: "He complains that his case has not been looked into and judged; that he is suffering for trespasses he has not committed; that he is abandoned [with reference to l. 25]."[55]

The petitions of the prayers are both general and specific. They may ask the deity to turn to the petitioner, as in the *eršaḫunga* translated below, to hear or accept the prayer, to be gracious, to destroy one's enemies, and to grant protection.[56] Sometimes, however, they seek specifically the healing of the sickness that is the reason for the lament,[57] release from debt slavery, confirmation of claims to one's patrimony, and, of course, release from sin and its consequences (see below).[58]

One could categorize the petitions in terms of those that have to do with the god's disposition, those dealing with the relationship between petitioner and deity, and those that have to do with specific interventions in behalf of the petitioner.[59] The most detailed organization of the petitions in terms of substantive categories, however, is that of W. Mayer and is as follows:

1. Petitions for the god's turning and hearing, for the deity's interest;

2. Petitions for the determination of one's destiny or fate;

3. Petitions for help couched in idioms from the language of law and the juridical process;

4. Petitions for compassion and grace, for mercy and deliverance;

5. Petitions for words that bring happiness to the one praying, that is, for words of blessing;

6. Petitions for the mediating intervention of the deity (see below on the mediation or intercession of deities);

7. Petitions for lifting the estrangement, for reconciliation, for reestablishment of friendly relations between deity and petitioner;

8. Petitions for one to be accompanied by "good forces" (protecting deities and spirits);

9. Petitions for the right word, well-received, and for obtaining one's wishes (the one praying wishes that what he or she says is heard and receives a quick corresponding response);

10. Petitions in reference to the surrounding environment, the public (the desire to have a place in one's community, to be able to walk without shame and have others speak well of him or her);

11. Petitions to become "pure" (that is, to become free of that which binds and hinders one: sickness, demons, sins, dangers announced through omens, and the like);

12. Petitions for deliverance from evil and bad things (sickness, demons, sorcery, enemies, sins, ominous omens, and the like);

13. Petitions relating to "signs" (against threatening signs or omens and in behalf of good signs);

14. Petitions for life and life's goodness (health, long life, prosperity, the joy of life).[60]

The petitions are as broad in scope as those of the biblical prayers though they include in prominent fashion some dimensions that are not common or present in the Bible, such as, signs and deliverance from sorcery (cf. the petitions in the *eršaḫunga* translated below).

Along with the complaint and petitions, there are often protestations of innocence or ignorance, or claims of past merit or desert. In lines 9–10 of Sin-šamuḫ's letter prayer to Enki, he claims not to have been negligent toward the divine name nor to have plundered the deity's offerings. Cultic piety, devotion to the deity, one's standing or status— all of these can be put forth as reasons to motivate the deity to help, to encourage the god to look favorably upon the petitioner.[61] Particular attention should be called to the claim of ignorance. The claim not to know the sin that has been committed is ubiquitous in the prayers. The system of diagnosis with omens and the like did not always uncover the particular sin that was regarded as evoking the divine wrath. The petitioner assumed that acknowledgment of guilt along with the claim of incapacity to discover the sin committed would mitigate the punishment. The claim of youthfulness is often given, also on the assumption that some leeway will be given to youthful ignorance.[62] The uncertainty and ignorance can lead to an accusation against the gods and on occasion to expressions that suggest that everyone has sinned.[63] But the claim of ignorance or innocence cannot eliminate guilt. Van der Toorn has summarized in this way:

> [The one] who is indicted of sin by a misfortune sent by the gods cannot but confess his crime. The audacious denial of guilt would be out of place in view of the severe limitations of conscience and memory and the uncertainties about the divine will. Self-absolution was considered a grave offence by the Babylonians, who held that

the humble acknowledgment of misbehaviour was an essential step towards reconciliation.[64]

These claims of innocence or ignorance or past good behavior serve in some sense as efforts to motivate and encourage the deity to respond to the petitions. Indeed most of what goes on in these prayers of supplication and petition plays some part in giving grounds for the deity to act benevolently. That is true of the lament itself as well as of the extended praise elements of the address. Within the petitions or the complaints there are often appeals to the character and nature of the deity as grounds to encourage positive response from the god. Invoking the biblical language, Hallo properly sees this as seeking "to persuade the deity or king to act, as it were, 'for the sake of thy name.' "[65] He cites examples from the Sumerian letter prayers, where the petitioner says, "If my queen is truly of heaven..." or "If my king is truly of heaven...." In other types of prayers, the petitioner may turn to the deity for help, "because you are gracious" or "because you are merciful."[66]

The common conclusion of Mesopotamian prayers in vows and expressions of praise and thanksgiving is also a part of the effort to evoke a positive response from the deity. In the letter prayer of Sin-šamuḫ, he promises to sing praise to the deity and exalt him when Enki has "turned my dark place into daylight" (see ll. 46–51).[67] The vow of praise includes an expression of confidence in the deity's will to help. Note also that the act of praise, as is often the case, is to be done in public before all the people (l. 53). Various expressions in the prayers indicate the extent of the praise, both spatially and temporally. Praise of the deity shall be proclaimed to "all people," to "the widespread people," to "all living on earth." It is to be rendered "for all time," "as long as I live," "daily," "day and night," "continuously."[68] There are also frequent expressions calling upon others than the petitioner to praise the deity. That is, not only does the praying one proclaim the goodness of the deity to others, but he or she also calls upon others—those in immediate relationship, the land, all people, heaven and earth, and other deities—to proclaim the greatness and the wonderful works of the god who will deliver, an aspect of praise and thanksgiving that is widespread in the biblical hymns and songs of thanksgiving (see chap. 5, below).[69]

Not infrequently the petitioner asks the deity for life or health or wholeness so that he or she can render praise and thanks to the deity. The one who prays seeks a circumstance wherein praise is possible. That inevitably means deliverance and restoration. The deity seeks the praise of the petitioner, and that, of course, requires the positive response of the god to make sure that the petitioner will be able to render praise.[70] In addition to rendering praise or vowing to do so, the petitioner may make other offers or vows. In a letter prayer, the praying one says, "I will surely be your slave-girl, will serve as court sweeper of your temple, will serve in your presence."[71] The vows and praises serve both to push the deity to respond[72] and to express the exuberant joy and gratitude of the one who is to be delivered.

Before turning to the Mesopotamian hymnic tradition, however, it should be noted that increasingly, in the history of Mesopotamian religion and piety, the concern for sin, guilt, and penitence comes to the fore. While that is not as prominent in the letter prayer of Sin-šamuḫ translated above, it becomes the center of attention in later prayers.[73] It is present in the Sumerian *eršaḫunga* prayers[74] that come after the letter prayers and especially in the Akkadian *šigû*[75] and *dingiršadibba* prayers,[76] which focus more upon the issues of sin and guilt than do the *namburbi* and *šu-illa* prayers, which deal more generally with broad-ranging circumstances and threatening situations or the particular problems of omens, sickness, demons, and sorcery.[77]

A fairly representative *eršaḫunga*[78] has been translated by Michalowski:

> You have smashed the sanctuaries in their places,
> you have sent my treasures abroad.
> Oh, my god, when will you return to me?
> May your angered heart be reconciled for me,
> May your furious heart be reconciled for me,
> May my supplication be my gift, I shall present it to you,
> the (very) tears of my eyes shall be my offering, you will receive them.
> During the daily offering may it be a prayer, by night may it be an offering.
> May you, (oh) *messenger,* accept my offering (and) to judge my case,
> . . . .
> May he enter into my temple in which the life of the land has been deposited,
> May he enter into my temple in which the life of all the foreign lands has been deposited.
> . . . .
> His sin which is sevenfold—release it!
> That humble man, in prayer...
> Like the heart of a mother, may your heart return to its place for me,
> Like a natural mother and a natural father may you return for me![79]

The petitioner comes in penitence seeking reconciliation and release of sin and its consequences from the deity, who is angered because of some action by the praying one that is not specified in the prayer (see Ps 6:1). The confessional part of the *eršaḫunga* prayers contains a certain restraint with regard to the mention of specific sins, as is true of the earlier letter prayers as well as of the later biblical Psalms.[80] In other penitential prayers, the confession of sin is much more elaborate and reiterated, with earnest pleas that the anger of the deity may be calmed and the penitent absolved and released from guilt and punishment.

It has been suggested that in the history of Mesopotamian religion there is a gradual shift from focus upon the afflictions and disasters encountered at the hands of the divine powers to a concentration upon the underlying sins that caused these.[81] Jacobsen sees in this shift an increasing move toward a focus upon the person and the personal relation to the deity. Whether or not this is the case, the extended and elaborate penitential prayers identify the confession of sin and the appeasement of an angry deity as a central concern of Mesopotamian prayer.[82] It seems, however, "to have remained an individual attitude and not decisively to have come to dominate public religion and shape the relation of the nation to the national gods."[83] That does not mean that there were no communal or corporate prayers of lament and petition. There were. But before turning to them, two matters need to be looked at briefly: the ritual setting of the prayers and the place of the intercessory deity.

Ritual acts. It is not necessary in this context to go into detail about the ritual around these prayers. The important thing is to recognize that they usually occurred in the context of ritual or liturgy of some sort, but there were many forms that it could take.[84] For the Sumerian letter prayers, we do not have liturgical directions and indications. Hallo, however, has noted that references in one of the prayers to depositing the letter with the deity and the fact that it is addressed to a statue show clearly that the letters "reflect a practice of leaving petitions in the temple, at the feet of the cult statue or at least in its own cella."[85] Many of the prayers, we may assume, belonged to ritual ceremonies in the temple, and a number of them were used most frequently in rituals associated with the king. A large number of the Mesopotamian prayers were associated with incantation rites, the setting of which was often, if not usually, not so much the official cultus of the temple as it was the primary group, such as the family, in which the petitioner lived. In these cases, the ritual could take place in the temple or the house of the sick person or in some other location, usually at night.[86] It was supposed to take place before the image of the deity, but this did not necessarily mean that the prayers and ritual were in the temple at the cella of the deity. More often, the images were probably simple statues of deities constructed for the occasion and taken to wherever the incantation or healing ceremony took place.[87] When the petitioner turned toward the deity in the form of the divine statue, he or she also was addressing the deity "in heaven." In many cases, the deity is addressed as being both in heaven and in the cult center.[88]

Erhard Gerstenberger suggests that there are four main types of ritual activity associated with incantation-based prayers: (1) Preparatory acts that have to do with making sure that the place is suitable for the healing activities. These include various purification and sanctification activities such as bathing and washing. Both liturgist, or ritual expert, and patient needed to be pure, consecrated, so that the gods would not reject the petitioner. (2) Bringing of gifts or performance of certain acts to soften up the deity, to move him or her to a good relation with the petitioner again, and to help bring the disturbed relation between petitioner and deity back into good shape. These gifts include food and drink, salt, honey, wine, beer, and the like. (3) Ritual activity with apotropaic or protective purpose or to exorcise the evil power at work. This may include such things as washing and anointing activities, the use of amulets, and putting blood on the house. (4) Finally, ritual activities that belong to the conclusion of the incantation ritual, making sure that things are done in order up to the end, that cultic apparatus is properly put away or disposed of, that things in some way related to the evil being exorcised be gotten rid of. They may be burned, buried, or thrown away.[89]

Intercession. One of the common features of the Mesopotamian prayers is the intercession of one deity before another deity in behalf of the petitioner. Not infrequently a suffering person will pray to his or her personal god to intervene in his or her behalf to one of the high gods. So the following statement of the ruler Entemena:

> May his personal god, Shul-utula, forever stand before Ningirsu in Eninnu (praying) for his (i.e., Entemena's) life.[90]

It may be, however, that the petitioner will appeal to a higher god to intercede to the personal god. The trouble is perceived as the anger or withdrawal of the personal, protecting deity, and so the sufferer appeals to a higher god to help restore relation with the protecting deity. Sometimes the spouse of a deity is asked to intercede with that deity, assuming, as in the court, that family members would have influence with the ruling figure.[91] The intercessory formulas are of various sorts. The deity may simply be asked to "intercede for me" or to "speak good for me." The deity may be asked to intercede with a particular deity, as in the case of Tašmētu, who is asked to

> intercede with Nabu your spouse that he may hear my words, at the command of your mouth accept my entreaties, get to know my prayers; at his weighty word may god and goddess become friendly with me again.[92]

In this case, as A. Leo Oppenheim has suggested, "The supplicant turns
to the specific intercession deities presumably because they provide in
some magical way an immediate contact with the great gods whose re-
actions then affect his personal protective gods either directly or through
some message or command."[93]

In a few prayers, the petitioner "sends" the addressed deity to his
or her protecting, personal deity and other addressees who are alienated
from the petitioner and have made life difficult for that person. This is
done in order to bring about reconciliation between petitioner and deity.[94] Oppenheim notes in this connection: "These and similar passages
show that the suffering individual felt himself more immediately dependent upon the good graces of what we call his personal protective spirits
than upon the great gods and that he seems to have called upon the
latter primarily to influence his protectors."[95]

In Egyptian religion, petitioners also approached the deity through
intermediaries, though in that case the intercession was tied to statues
and images of deified kings or important office bearers that were erected
in the temple precinct. These figures were to be the messengers bearing
the prayers to the god. One statue of Amenophis, son of Hapu, who was
a scribe of recruits during the reign of Amenophis III, has the following
inscription:

> Ye people of Karnak, ye who wish to see Amon, come to me! I
> shall report your petitions (*sprwt*). [For] I am indeed the messenger
> of this god. [The king] has appointed me to report the words of the
> Two Lands. Speak to me the "offering spell" and invoke my name
> daily, as is done to one who has taken a vow.[96]

In another case, an inscription inscribed on a statue of a person of
similar rank reads:

> I am the messenger of the mistress of the sky [i.e., Isis of Coptos],
> I belong to her outer court. Tell me your petitions so that I can
> report them to the mistress of the Two Lands, for she hears my
> supplications.[97]

Congregational laments. There are within the Sumerian literary tradition several laments over cities or important cult centers.[98] The most
famous of these is the Lament for the Destruction of Ur. In comparing
these congregational laments with the similar laments in the Psalms and
in the book of Lamentations, Hallo observes:

> In both cases, it is clear that real historic events, and more specifi-
> cally national disasters, inspired the compositions. But both tended
> to sublimate the events into vague and involved allusions to the
> flight of the divine presence or the breakdown of cultic processes.

As a result, there is sometimes uncertainty in both as to just what historic event is intended, the more so as there seems to have been no great reluctance about applying older allusions to more recent events. On the Mesopotamian side, it is clear from the number of Sumerian examples; from their intricate strophic structure and liturgical glosses; and from their survival in other forms into later periods, that the public laments represented a thoroughly institutionalized, temple-centered response to the recurrent trauma of wholesale destruction which was visited on the Mesopotamian city-states and empires throughout their history.[99]

In many respects, these are true lamentations or dirges over cities destroyed and having to be rebuilt.[100] They bewail the destruction and ask, "How long?" In the Lament for Ur, much of the text is occupied with recounting how Ningal sought to prevent the destruction of the city by the gods and how it was destroyed. Even in the later and more stereotyped congregational city laments, there is some appeal to the deity to restore or look with favor or "turn around and look at your city."[101] But their function as prayers, in the sense of the individual prayers discussed above, is less central in these texts. At the end of the Lament for Ur, however, there is a moving prayer to Nanna to absolve the people of their guilt and restore the city to its former state:

> The personal god of a human
>   has brought you a greeting gift,
> a (human) supplicant is beseeching you.
> O Nanna, you having mercy on the country,
> O Lord Ash-im-babbar, you having,
>   according to what your heart prompts,
> absolved, O Nanna,
>   the sins of that man,
> the man who beseeches you, an anointed one,
>   may bring your heart
>   to relent toward him,
> and having looked truly upon the supplicant
>   who stands here for them,
> O Nanna, whose penetrating gaze
>   searches the bowels,
> may their hearts,
>   that have suffered (so much) evil
>   appear pure to you,
> may the hearts of your ones who are in the land
>   appear good to you,
> and, O Nanna!—in your city again restored
>   they will offer up praise for you![102]

Jacobsen points out that in the later periods of Mesopotamian history (the Lament for Ur is around 2000 B.C.) "though we hear of human misdeeds calling forth divine punishment on a national scale and about national gods temporarily angry with their people and leaving them—we find little talk of nationwide repentance and self-abasement as a means of regaining divine favor." He suggests that we have to turn to Israel to see this character of personal religion with its moral sense and openness to penitence, its desire for forgiveness, moved from an individual level to a national level.[103]

Hymn and Thanksgiving

We have already noted that praise is a significant element in the prayers and petitions of Mesopotamia. It often paves the way for the petition that follows in the many different types of prayers found there. But there are also texts that are more strictly and entirely hymns, as is true also of Egypt. These hymns tend to exalt the deity, sometimes calling for praise in an imperative tone, but more often rendering it in an indicative mode. A representative example is the Hymn to Ishtar:

> Praise the goddess, the most awesome of the goddesses.
> Let one revere the mistress of the people, the greatest of the Igigi.
> Praise Ishtar, the most awesome of the goddesses.
> Let one revere the queen of women, the greatest of the Igigi.
>
> She is clothed with pleasure and love.
> She is laden with vitality, charm, and voluptuousness.
> Ishtar is clothed with pleasure and love.
> She is laden with vitality, charm, and voluptuousness.
>
> In lips she is sweet; life is in her mouth.
> At her appearance rejoicing becomes full.
> She is glorious; veils are thrown over her head.
> Her figure is beautiful; her eyes are brilliant.
>
> The goddess—with her there is counsel.
> The fate of everything she holds in her hand.
> At her glance there is created joy,
> Power, magnificence, the protecting deity and guardian spirit.
>
> She dwells in, she pays heed to compassion and friendliness.
> Besides, agreeableness she truly possesses.
> Be it slave, unattached girl, or mother, she preserves (her).
>
> One calls on her; among women one names her name.
> Who—to her greatness who can be equal?
> Strong, exalted, splendid are her decrees.

Ishtar—to her greatness who can be equal?
Strong, exalted, splendid are her decrees.

She is sought after among the gods; extraordinary is her station.
Respected is her word; it is *supreme* over them.
Ishtar among the gods, extraordinary is her station.
Respected is her word; it is *supreme* over them.

She is their queen; they continually cause her commands to be
    executed.
All of them bow down before her.
They receive her light before her.
Women and men indeed revere her.

In their assembly her word is powerful; it is dominating.
Before Anum their king she fully supports them.
She rests in intelligence, cleverness, (and) wisdom.
They take counsel together, she and her lord.

Indeed they occupy the throne room together.
In the divine chamber, the dwelling of joy,
Before them the gods take their places.
To their utterances their attention is turned.

The king their favorite, beloved of their hearts,
Magnificently offers to them his pure sacrifices.
Ammiditana, as the pure offering of his hands,
Brings before them fat oxen and gazelles.

From Anum, her consort, she has been pleased to ask for him
An enduring, a long life.
Many years of living, to Ammiditana
She has granted, Ishtar has decided to give.

By her orders she has subjected to him
The four world regions at his feet;
And the total of all peoples
She has decided to attach them to his yoke.[104]

Frequently the hymn will conclude, as did this one, with a very short
prayer for the king.[105] Such hymns are often filled with epithets and
names of the deity. They describe the attributes and activities of the deity, in relation to other gods and in relation to human beings. What is
especially noticeable about the Mesopotamian hymns of praise is that
there is very little thanksgiving by an individual for the deity's deliverance of that person in a particular moment. They are almost entirely
general descriptive praise of the deity. There are some exceptions, as
Hermann Gunkel noted long ago.[106] And the Egyptian thanksgiving

inscriptions of Neb-Re (late thirteenth century B.C.) and Nefer-Abu (thirteenth or twelfth century B.C.) have been compared with the psalmic songs of thanksgiving, such as Psalm 30.[107] Neb-Re gives thanks to Amon for delivering his son from illness and near death after he had prayed to him:

> Thou art Amon, the lord of the silent one [i.e., humble], who comes at the voice of the poor one. If I call to thee when I am distressed, thou comest and thou rescuest me. Thou givest breath (to) the one who is weak; thou rescuest the one who is imprisoned.[108]

The joining of adoration and praise in the prayers of petition, which is standard in the Mesopotamian petitionary prayers, is suggested in this song of thanksgiving when Neb-Re says:

> Adorations were made for him in his name, because of the greatness of his strength; supplications were made to him before his face and in the presence of the entire land.[109]

In the praise and thanksgiving that begin this prayer of thanksgiving, Neb-Re bears testimony to the power and mercy of the deity:

> Giving praises to Amon. I make him adorations in his name; I give him praises to the height of heaven and to the width of earth; [I] relate his power to the one who travels downstream and to the one who travels upstream. Beware ye of him! Repeat him to son and daughter, to great and small; relate him to generations of generations who have not yet come into being; relate him to fishes in the deep, to birds in the heaven; repeat him to the one who knows him not and to the one who knows him! Beware ye of him![110]

The similarities to biblical songs of thanksgiving or the praise and thanks section of Psalm 22 will be evident as we look more closely at the songs of thanksgiving of Israel in the chapters to follow.

There are also examples of hymns to temples and sacred cities that remind one of the Zion hymns of the Psalter, such as Psalm 122 where Jerusalem is praised.[111]

PRAYER IN SYRIA-PALESTINE

This treatment of Israel's neighbors at prayer has been confined primarily to Mesopotamia with some reference also to Egypt. One would expect that such a discussion would focus more on the immediate geographical environment of Israel, the peoples of Syria-Palestine, Canaanites, and others. Unfortunately, there is not a significant corpus of prayer texts from that area to tell us very much. There are a number of Phoenician and Aramaean votive inscriptions that speak of the deity hearing the prayer the petitioner uttered.[112] We also have the eighth-century Aramaean stele of Zakir, king of Hamat and Lu'ash, which J. Greenfield has properly compared to the biblical prayer genre of the song of thanksgiving.[113] The king speaks of himself as a humble (*'nh*) man (see Ps 34:6: "This poor soul [*'ānî*] cried, and was heard by the LORD, and was saved from every trouble"). He then narrates how he was besieged by a group of ten kings. "But I lifted up my hand to Be'elshamayn, and Be'elshamayn heard me. Be'elshamayn [spoke] to me through seers and through *diviners*. Be'elshamayn [said to me]: Do not fear, for I made you king, and I shall stand by you and deliver you from all [these kings who] set up a siege against you. [*Be'elshamayn*] said to me: [*I shall destroy*] all these kings. . . . "[114] The king thus reports his trouble and how he prayed to the deity, who responded with an oracle of salvation (see chap. 4, below) that announced deliverance from the king's enemies. In the self-characterization of the petitioner, the narrated report of the troubles, and the declaration that the deity heard the prayer and delivered the petitioner out of his troubles, the Zakir stele is very close to the song of thanksgiving that follows the experience of having one's prayers for help answered.

Much earlier in time, there is within the large corpus of Ugaritic texts from northern Syria in the mid– to late second millennium a report of King Kirta, in grief over the death of his family, going up to the top of a tower, lifting his hands to heaven, and sacrificing to El and Baal. No prayer is reported, but the narrative obviously intends to portray the king praying for divine help before going off on an expedition to find a new wife.[115] One important prayer to Baal is preserved in the Ugaritic corpus (*KTU* 1.119.26'-35'):[116]

> When a strong one has attacked your gates,
> > a warrior your walls,
> > > your eyes to Baal you shall lift up:
>
> O Baal,
> > if you will drive the strong one from our gates,
> > > the warrior from our walls,
> > a bull, O Baal, we shall consecrate,
> > > a vow, O Baal, we shall fulfill,
> > a male animal, O Baal, we shall consecrate,
> > > a sacrifice, O Baal, we shall fulfill,
> > a libation, O Baal, we shall pour out.
> > To the sanctuary of Baal we shall go up,
> > > the paths of the house of Baal we shall traverse.
> > So Ba[al has hea]rd your prayer.

He will drive the strong one from your gates,
the warrior from your walls.

While formally a vow, the prayer has affinities with the biblical laments
or prayers for help. The latter only report the vows while the plight
and petition are elaborated. In the prayer above, the reverse is the case.
The narrative bracket around the prayer, in which the community is instructed to pray and then told that Baal has heard and will respond,
is probably a priestly instruction that serves to identify the situation of
crisis and also to report the response and deliverance by the deity. The
latter has the characteristic elements of the divine response to laments as
one often encounters them in the prayers for help and the oracles of salvation (see chap. 4, below). In the story of Hannah's prayer for a child
in the sanctuary at Shiloh (1 Samuel 1), she utters a vow, but it is in
the context of supplication and weeping, that is, a prayer for help, even
as the vow of *KTU* 1.119 is described at the end as "prayer." In both
cases, the prayer is granted by the deity and that word is brought by
the priest. One notes further that the prayer to Baal is placed in a larger
literary context (not quoted above) describing and prescribing regular
ritual, even as Hannah's prayer takes place at the occasion of the regular festival visit to the central sanctuary. In both cases, prayer for the
deity's help in a quite specific situation of trouble is placed in the context
of recurring sacrificial activities. As in the biblical prayers, sacrifice and
going to the shrine are critical or primary dimensions of the vows or the
response to the deity hearing the prayer (cf. Ps 66:13ff.).[117]

CONCLUSION

While detailed discussion of the prayers and hymns of Israel belongs
to the pages that follow, it is appropriate to anticipate that discussion
further by identifying some broad lines of comparison or contrast between those biblical prayers that are the primary subject matter of this
book and the ones under discussion in this chapter. J. J. M. Roberts
has suggested that some of the immediately discernible differences between these bodies of prayer literature are due to the difference between
a monotheistic and a polytheistic religious structure as a context for
praying.[118] The hymns and complaints tend to invoke and praise the
deity in fairly extended fashion. The often long introductory sections
of praise in the petitionary and penitential prayers contrast rather obviously with the relatively simple or short invocations of the God of
Israel. One notes further, for example in the Neo-Babylonian incanta-
tional lament to Ishtar,[119] that the forty-line invocation speaks of the
goddess heavily, if not primarily, in relation to the divine world, the

world of the gods. The Psalms, as we shall see, invoke the deity primarily either by simply calling the name or in relational language claiming the relationship between the one praying and the deity. This is not absent in the Mesopotamian prayers, as one can see from the prayer of Sin-šamuḫ above and the hymn to Ishtar. But in general, as these two examples illustrate, that is secondary to the appeal to the deity in relation to the divine world.[120] As Roberts has indicated, this probably has to do with clearly specifying the god who is being invoked,[121] but it also implicitly recognizes that the gods have their history[122] and their primary story among the other gods whereas the Lord's story is with Israel and the world in which it lived.[123] That is further indicated by the fact that the hymnody of Mesopotamia tends to involve general descriptive praise of characteristics of the deity relative to either the other gods or humankind rather than specific praise and thanksgiving for particular help by the deity in crisis, which is more common in Israel.

The difference between the polytheistic and monotheistic religious structures and conceptions is also reflected, Roberts suggests, in two other ways:

> The motif in Mesopotamian prayers of calling upon one god to intercede with another god is obviously rooted in polytheism, and the pervasiveness of the set formulae that occur in many Mesopotamian prayers expressing fear over bad omens or blaming one's suffering on the work of sorcerers owes a great deal to the multiplicity of independent powers in a polytheistic universe.[124]

Intercession is a fairly common form of prayer in the Bible. In the Old Testament, however, this stays entirely on the human plane as persons such as Abraham, Moses, and Samuel, persons who stand in a particularly close relationship to the Lord, are those who make intercession, usually for the community as a whole. The New Testament draws these two intercessory modes together in the notion of the intercession of Christ, which is something taken up by the earthly Jesus and by the heavenly Christ. The New Testament sees some antecedent to that christological intercession in the work of the suffering servant who "made intercession for the transgressors" (Isa 53:12).

In thinking about Israel's prayer in comparison with the prayer of its neighbors, one must be careful about false dichotomies. One of these is the assumption that in Israel, prayer was truly prayer, in which petitions were lifted up to God, who was totally free to respond in whatever way God desired, whereas in Mesopotamia prayer was more a magical act to manipulate and control the deity to bring about the desired end. But many of the aspects of Mesopotamian prayer that are viewed as manipulative, for example, the flowery layering of epithets and good words on the deity or the presentation of gifts and sacrifices, do not necessarily demonstrate a lower spiritual level on the part of Israel's neighbors at that point. As we shall see, Israel had various ways of seeking to push God into action in behalf of the petitioner.

While the discussion above has focused upon the content of the prayers, enough indication has been given of their connection to ritual to make it clear that prayer and ritual, or complex liturgy, are often—not always—closely bound together in Mesopotamia and in the communal prayer-vow from Ugarit. Again, the difference between these prayers and Israel's practices may be more apparent than real, as the following comments indicate:

> Akkadian *shu-illa* prayers are typically accompanied by ritual directions following a ruled line at the end of the prayer. These normally indicate that the prayer was to be recited several times as accompaniment to a sacrificial offering. Biblical Psalms lack such ritual directions, but it is clear from references in the Psalms and the historical books that the biblical laments and thanksgiving songs were also accompanied by sacrifice. In fact, the same Hebrew term, *todah*, designates both the thanksgiving song and the thanksgiving sacrifice. It is important to remember that, both when studying the Psalms and when studying the rules for sacrifice in Leviticus. The relative separation of cultic word and ritual act in the biblical sources is a literary phenomenon that does not reflect what actually went on in the cult.[125]

What is increasingly apparent in the following pages is the high degree of formal similarity, the many common motifs and images in both contexts, and the development of set prayers that could be used again and again by different individuals. That is clearly the case with the Psalms, but it is also true of the Mesopotamian prayers. Roberts points to the occurrence in those prayers of the formula identifying the speaker in the form "I so-and-so, the son of so-and-so...," which meant that these prayers "were obviously intended for repeated use by different individuals; the supplicant needed only to insert his [or her] own name at the appropriate place."[126]

The commonality that does exist between Israel's prayers and those of its neighbors suggests structures and modes of prayer that are not precisely identical but sufficiently related that we can assume there is something universal here, that it is in the shared and common history that we learn what God seeks in prayer, that the modes receive a confirmation in part because they seem to be common human ways belonging to the creatureliness of every human being and the imperfect and partial effort on the part of the creature to communicate with the divine.

2

"Whenever We Call"

PRAYER BY ANY NAME

&

While the character of prayer is determined primarily by its form and substance, there are also clues to the nature of prayer both in the ways it is described or designated, that is, the language or terminology for prayer, and in the manner in which it is carried out, the activities and movements, the posture and demeanor of those who pray. In this chapter, we will explore some of those ways of describing and doing prayer, with primary reference to the Old Testament, not in order to uncover from Scripture some primary or all-encompassing definition or some "correct" way of praying but to grasp the significance of the varied terms for prayer and the many ways it may take place. What is being suggested or conveyed in the different ways of speaking about prayer? What do the different modes and postures of those who pray express about what is going on in the activity of prayer?

TERMINOLOGY

General Words for Communicating with the Deity

At least two types of very general terms are used frequently to introduce prayers or to refer to prayers.[1]

1. The first of these is the use of the verb "say" or its equivalent, "speak." A number of the prayers of the patriarchs, for instance, are introduced simply by, "And so-and-so said to God/the Lord." For example, we have Abraham's prayer for Ishmael: "And Abraham said to God, 'O that Ishmael might live in your sight'" (Gen 17:18); the prayers of Eliezer, first for divine guidance: "And he said, 'O LORD, God of my master Abraham, please grant me success today...'" (Gen 24:12), and then in gratitude: "The man bowed his head and worshiped the LORD and said, 'Blessed be the LORD, the God of my master Abraham...'" (Gen 24:26-27); Jacob's prayer for God's deliverance before meeting

Esau: "And Jacob said, 'O God of my father Abraham...'" (Gen 32:9). But such "saying" to God as a way of speaking of prayer is not confined to these early texts. It is a common way of designating prayer elsewhere.[2]

It is clear from the texts cited above that this ordinary language for saying or speaking turns out to be a very common way of introducing the prayers of Scripture: petition, intercession, thanksgiving, and blessing. There is even a royal hymn of praise or thanksgiving in the Psalter, Psalm 18 (= 1 Samuel 22), that is given a narrative introduction in both settings without reference to any category of prayer: "David spoke to the LORD the words of this song on the day when the LORD delivered him from the hand of all his enemies, and from the hand of Saul" (2 Sam 22:1). Such common uses of the simple "He said..." or "She said..." without any technical language for prayer raises the problem of the definition of prayer. In a number of these cases, there is no explicit reference to prayer in any technical sense in the context. Does this mean that all human effort at communication with the divine as we find that in Scripture is to be regarded as prayer? Not necessarily so. A number of conversations between God and human beings in Scripture are initiated by God and are not prayerlike in any form. It is the case, however, that most of those situations in which God is addressed by human beings at their initiative, whatever language is used to describe the act, will be seen by the reader as prayerlike in some form or other.

Use of the nontechnical language for saying and speaking thus presses one toward a broader rather than a narrower definition, to a way of speaking about prayer that we use in common parlance in a more popular way, that is, *conversation with God*. In some sense, therefore, almost any address to God functions as prayer. And, as is clear in the reading of the texts, virtually every such address is perceived as receiving either an explicit or implicit response from God—thus conversation or dialogue is effected in this act, sometimes, at sufficient length or back and forth enough that the reader may forget that the conversation is a prayer in its basic character or initiating moment (e.g., Gen 18:23-33). This kind of language for prayer also suggests the possibility of spontaneity and flexibility. Many of the cases where someone "says" something to God are spontaneous, noncultic, occurring in the immediate situation (e.g., Eliezer in Genesis 24).

So here is a way of speaking of prayer that places it in the category of ordinary discourse, often in situations of daily existence, some more critical than others. While prayers can be introduced simply by "She said..." in a more cultic or specifically religious or formal setting, this language invites a sense of the ease of communication, less formal or set contexts for prayer. That is true of the language of speaking and saying on the human scene; by analogy it is also true of divine-human intercourse.

2. A second type of general vocabulary regarding human address to God and belonging in different ways to the language of prayer is that cluster of words that have to do with "seeking," "asking," and "inquiring." All of these words are used in synonymous or overlapping ways in English. To some extent that is the case in Hebrew. But it is also clear that they have some particular uses that may be identified and contribute to our understanding of modes of approach to the deity.

While the differentiation cannot be complete, in the following discussion, the word "seek" will refer to the Hebrew verb *biqqēš* and its cognates, the word "ask" will refer to the Hebrew verb *šāʾal* and its cognates, and the word "inquire" will refer to the Hebrew verb *dāraš* and its cognates.[3]

The expression "to seek [*biqqēš*] God" is used infrequently in the Old Testament to refer to a one time act. David "seeks" the Lord for the life of Bathsheba's child (2 Sam 12:15). In three instances, the community gathers to "seek" the Lord in a situation of distress, and prayer is either offered or referred to.[4] In 2 Sam 21:1, David "seeks" the face of the Lord with regard to a famine, and the Lord responds with an explanation. Daniel also "seeks [*biqqēš*] an answer by prayer and supplication" (Dan 9:3). This may be an act of formal prayer, or it may be a matter of oracle inquiry (see discussion of *dāraš,* below). There are some thirty times in the Old Testament, however, where the expression "seeking God" does not mean seeking in a particular instance, a specific reference to seeking God in prayer as in the examples above where the word "say" is used, but refers to the God-human relationship and has to do more with status and relationship than with act. Acts of prayer and devotion may have something to do with this relationship, but the use of the expression is more general. Those who "seek God" are the pious faithful members of the community:

> May all who seek you rejoice and be glad in you.
>
> > (Ps 40:16)
>
> Seek his presence continually.
>
> > (Ps 105:4)
>
> [T]he hand of our God is gracious to all who seek him, but his power and his wrath are against all who forsake him.
>
> > (Ezra 8:22)
>
> Afterward the Israelites shall return and seek the LORD their God, and David their king; they shall come in awe to the LORD and to his goodness in the latter days.
>
> > (Hos 3:5)

> The evil do not understand justice,
> but those who seek the LORD understand it completely.
>
> (Prov 28:5)

Thus, the language of "seeking God," while it may on occasion refer to prayers of petition, has in mind the broader reality of a life lived in relationship with the Lord, involving the full devotion of prayer, obedience, and righteousness. The specific act of prayer at times is seen as part of such "seeking," but it does not exhaust that relationship.

The notion of "asking God" (*šā'al*) is a rather different matter. The verb referred to here would be better translated—and often is—as "inquire." For it plays its part in a quite specific activity, the request for a decision on the part of community or individual about an important matter or crisis that is at hand. The priest places the inquiry before God by casting lots (or by some similar device), and God responds by the way the lot falls. Here one is normally after a simple and decisive yes or no from God. Such inquiry of the deity takes place primarily in regard to war. It was a way of asking the strategic question of the next step in holy war, either on the way or in the battle itself (e.g., Josh 9:14; Judg 1:1).[5] The customary divine response was a word to the effect that God was handing the enemy over into Israel's hands together with God's command to go into battle (e.g., Judg 1:1). Such an inquiry of God came to an end, however, during the early years of the monarchy, at least as a regular practice. The frequent references to the inquiry of God in 1 Samuel may be an indication of its increasingly problematic character. In any event, in 2 Sam 16:23 we hear:

> Now in those days the counsel that Ahithophel gave was as if one consulted [*šā'al* = "inquired"] the oracle [or "word"] of God; so all the counsel of Ahithophel was esteemed, both by David and by Absalom.

The inquiry of God has ceased and been replaced by the consultation of a wise man or counselor.

Thus, one of the most obvious or expected terms for petitionary prayer is not all that common in the Old Testament, and where it does occur it is in a very specific institutional context that did not continue far into the history of Israel. The notion of prayer as a general *asking* of God is not carried through with that language in an extensive way. Where we encounter it in a particular period in Israel's history, such asking or inquiry has to do with *seeking direction or instruction* rather than with a general asking. In other words, we are talking about inquiry and consultation of the deity rather than petition.

Another kind of inquiry expressed by a different Hebrew verb, *dāraš,* comes into play after this early period and to some extent alongside it.

It is an inquiry of God through a prophetlike figure who was able to give the direction of God, often more than just a yes or no type answer. A good example is 1 Kgs 22:5. Jehoshaphat inquires (*dāraš*) for the word of the Lord from the four hundred prophets. It is the typical query before battle: "Shall I go to battle against Ramoth-gilead, or shall I refrain?" The prophets say, again in typical fashion for such inquiry: "Go up; for the LORD will give it into the hand of the king." But skeptical Jehoshaphat asks if there is another prophet through whom inquiry of the Lord may be made. Micaiah is brought on the scene. At first, he offers the typical answer to such inquiry; when pushed, however, he gives an alternative response, which is an elaborated report from the divine council of the Lord's plan to deceive the kings of Israel and Judah.[6] In several cases, the inquiry of the Lord through a prophet involves military or political situations such as the above.[7] But it may also take place in cases of personal need, such as illness, when inquiry of the Lord is to discern how to bring about healing.

But then, in the later period, a use of the term *dāraš* develops that is no longer tied to institutions of prophet or priesthood (or diviner, e.g., 1 Samuel 28), but is like the "seeking [*biqqēš*] of the Lord" discussed above. It is now a matter of relationship, an unmediated relationship to God, and often in places where the holding to a relationship to God is characterized according to its intensity, for example, Deut 4:29: "If you search after him with all your heart and soul..."; or Jer 29:13: "[I]f you seek me with all your heart...."[8] The sequence of texts in Amos 5:4-6, 14-15 in which *dāraš* is used is instructive, for there it seems as if the expectancy is that seeking the Lord involves coming to the sanctuary for worship or inquiry, but Amos makes clear that the true seeking of the Lord involves a mode of moral conduct that is absent among the people.[9]

The examination of this second category of general terminology for communicating with the deity leads to the following conclusions.[10] The term *biqqēš,* "seek," for the most part stays on the most general level. Indeed it has to do primarily with the totality of the relationship with God that may, at particular moments, involve prayer. The two terms *šā᾽al,* "ask," and *dāraš,* "inquire," however, would seem to be general in their meaning but in fact are used in a fairly technical way. These two words identified two different kinds of inquiry or questioning of God. They existed together in an institutional sort of way and eventually came to an end or, at least, according to the textual evidence, declined in frequency. The inquiry by lots (*šā᾽al*) was essentially a premonarchical institution. The inquiry of God by a prophet (*dāraš*) continued down to the exile. During this period the God-directed questioning was an essential part of the relationship to God. Questioning or inquiry in the sense of seeking some sort of direction from the Lord was a part of the divine-human relationship. It was presumed that God is within the sphere of human inquiry.

When these institutions fell with the failure of the kings and the people, did that mean that direct inquiry of God was no longer possible? Not exactly. What it meant was that increasingly the query for a divine decision or a word of direction from God came in different ways. It was probably present in the personal prayer for God's direction, but more indirectly the divine prayer comes from the inquiry of Scripture. In the later period, increasingly we find Israel's inquiry of the Lord related to their paying close attention to the Lord's torah, God's law or instruction. That is probably what is involved in the Deuteronomistic promise that if exiled Israel seeks the Lord with the whole heart, they will find the Lord (Deut 4:29). In light of what Deuteronomy says about the presence of the Lord being connected to the law and the commandments (4:7-8; 30:11-14), it is likely that what is meant here is that Israel will come into relationship with the Lord and find understanding of God's direction and way by the inquiry and study of the divine instruction. A similar perspective is found in the Chronicler:

> [Asa] commanded Judah to seek [*dāraš*] the LORD, the God of their ancestors, and [or "that is"] to keep the law and the commandment. (2 Chr 14:4)

> And all the work that he undertook in the service of the house of the LORD and in the torah and in the commandment to seek [*dāraš*] his God, he did with all his heart; and he prospered.
> (2 Chr 31:21; my trans.)

The combination of personal prayer and attention to the Scripture as a way of discerning the Lord's will is seen at length in Psalm 119.[11]

Where, therefore, the community of faith asks after the next step on its way, where it has to make decisions that are required by new situations, everything depends upon the fact that the request to God for direction stands in living unity with the interpretation of Scripture.[12] The "asking" of God belongs now to the interaction of prayer and listening to Scripture. The "seeking" of God describes now—as it had to a large extent earlier—a total relation to God that is confirmed in the doing of justice, the seeking of good in the human community.

In this instance, one should note the tenacity of the earlier practices in a much later time. One of the clearest biblical instances of prayer for the purpose of seeking divine guidance and instruction is the gathering of Jesus' disciples, after his departure, for the purpose of choosing a successor to Judas. The account of that event reads:

> Then they *prayed* and said, "Lord, you know everyone's heart. Show us which one of these two you have chosen to take the place

in this ministry and apostleship from which Judas turned aside to go to his own place." And then they *cast lots* for them, and the lot fell on Matthias; and he was added to the eleven apostles.

(Acts 1:24-26)

Prayer and the casting of lots are not deemed incompatible in the desire for divine guidance here in the New Testament. The latter does not take place without the former. Nor does the casting of lots play any further part in the activity of prayer in the New Testament. Even in the choosing of the seven apostolic assistants in Acts 6, there is no reference to lots. Rather, it would seem that the choice is made on the basis of characteristics of the individuals chosen, as, for example, in Deut 1:9-18. Prayer takes place in this instance after the choice is made and as a part of the commissioning and dedication of seven. The same would seem to be the case also in Acts 13:2-3, when Barnabas and Saul are "set apart" by God, as well as in 14:23, when Paul and Barnabas appoint elders in each of the churches and with prayer and fasting entrust them to the Lord. And at the Jerusalem council nothing is said about prayer at all in the choosing of representatives to accompany Paul and Barnabas to Antioch, but attention to Scripture is very much a part of the debate in the council over the keeping of circumcision and the law.

Technical Terms for Prayer

There are a number of terms that belong explicitly to the vocabulary of prayer and in that sense are technical terms for prayer of various sorts. The comments here are confined to three that belong to the prayer of petition.

1. The term that is most often translated in English as "pray" (*hitpallēl*) or "prayer" (*tĕpillâ*) is rooted in notions of estimating, calculating, and assessing.[13] The basic connotation of the ground form of the verb, *pālal,* is to estimate or assess. The particular conjugation of the verb that is used to express the notion of praying can often mean "to seek what the simple stem or ground form designates," thus, in this case, "to seek an assessment, consideration." Inherent in the word, therefore, is the notion of prayer as *the placing of a case, a situation, before God for consideration, for God's assessment.*[14] This is done in the conviction that the situation is worthy of God's attention and consideration. When one looks at the contents of many of the "prayers," that is, those prayers that are designated by some nominal or verbal form of this root *pālal,* one can see they are often uttered out of a sense that the particular situation or case has not been considered by God, has not been assessed, else God would act. At other times—and sometimes with the same prayer— the sense is that what is happening is the kind of thing that the Lord,

the one whom the petitioner can truly call "my God," would consider and assess in positive ways, and so the request for God's assessment is fitting. It is appropriate, therefore, to the situation, to what this God is like, and to the relationship between God and the one praying to lay out this situation for God's consideration. What that situation may be is quite open. The noun "prayer" (*těpillâ*) as well as verbal forms of this root (*hitpallēl*) are used of prayers for help or laments. Psalm 17 is called "a prayer [*těpillâ*] of David." And it is indeed a prayer in which a case is set before God for God's assessment:

> Hear a just cause, O LORD; attend to my cry;
> > give ear to my prayer from lips free of deceit.
> From you let my vindication come;
> > let your eyes see the right.
> If you try my heart, if you visit me by night,
> > if you test me, you will find no wickedness in me;
> > my mouth does not transgress. (vv. 1-3)

Psalm 102 is also so designated in its superscription, and in the communal prayer for help, Ps 80:4, the people ask the Lord, "[H]ow long will you be angry with *the prayer of your people* [*těpillat 'ammekā*]?"—a phrase that probably is the Old Testament designation of a community lament or prayer for help.[15] At the conclusion of book 2 of the Psalter, the notation is made that "the prayers [*těpillôt*] of David are ended," indicating that the first half of the Psalter is a collection of this sort of prayers. And indeed the great majority of those psalms are individual laments or prayers for help in which those in trouble or suffering of some sort appeal to God and lay out their case, identifying in general but powerful terms their plight, sometimes claiming their own innocence, often laying out reasons that God should help, and appealing to the righteousness of God in confidence that that will mean vindication and deliverance. In the expression of confidence at the beginning of the long lament in Psalms 9–10, the psalmist specifically recalls that God has maintained his or her just cause in the past:

> For you have maintained my just cause;
> > you have sat on the throne giving righteous judgment.
> > > (Ps 9:4)

> But the LORD sits enthroned forever,
> > he has established his throne for judgment.
> He judges the world with righteousness;
> > he judges the peoples with equity. (Ps 9:7-8)

In some of the narrative prayers, one can also see the petitioner laying out a case. Hezekiah prays (*wayyitpallēl*—2 Kgs 19:15) for God's deliverance when surrounded by Sennacherib's army:

> O LORD the God of Israel, who are enthroned above the cherubim, you are God, you alone, of all the kingdoms of the earth; you have made heaven and earth. Incline your ear, O LORD, and hear; open your eyes, O LORD, and see; hear the words of Sennacherib, which he has sent to mock the living God. Truly, O LORD, the kings of Assyria have laid waste the nations and their lands, and have hurled their gods into the fire, though they were no gods but the work of human hands—wood and stone—and so they were destroyed. So now, O LORD our God, save us, I pray you, from his hand, so that all the kingdoms of the earth may know that you, O LORD, are God alone. (2 Kgs 19:15-19)

Hezekiah appeals on the grounds that the Lord is "the God of Israel" and so is the one to pay attention to and to do something about this case; but he goes on to acknowledge God as lord of *all* the nations and creator of the earth. So here is the appropriate power to consider and act in this situation. In verse 16, the king asks for consideration of the facts of the matter, calling upon God to look and listen to what is going on. Then the case is laid. It is essentially an appeal on the grounds that the Assyrian king has taunted and mocked the living God, the Lord of Israel, consistent with his policy with other nations when he has taunted their gods by hurling their idols or gods into the fire. In the final verse, Hezekiah draws what he sees as the appropriate implication of an assessment of the case he has laid out: "So now . . . save us from his hand." Such an action, the king claims, will be a vindication of the Lord's power before all the nations. In other words, the prayer appeals on the grounds that God's reputation and power are at stake in this situation, and when that is considered, God will act.

In similar but briefer fashion, the same king lays out his case in another prayer, this time for God's deliverance from his sickness unto death (2 Kgs 20:1-3). This is an abbreviated individual prayer for help (note: "Hezekiah wept bitterly" [v. 3]) in which Hezekiah "prayed" (*wayyitpallēl*) to the Lord:

> Remember now, O LORD, I implore you, how I have walked before you in faithfulness with a whole heart, and have done what is good in your sight.

The case Hezekiah presents is simply his faithful life. When God considers that, then there should be sufficient reason for God to intervene with healing power—which is exactly what happens (vv. 5-6).

Twice Jonah "prays" (2:1 and 4:2). On both occasions, he lays out reasons for his appeal. In one instance (2:4), he prays for help because he is driven away from God's sight, and if that continues to be the case, he can never look again upon "your holy temple." In the other instance

(4:2), the prophet angrily argues that he knew God was gracious and that was why he fled the first time; so that being clearly the case, there is no reason for him to keep on living.

Elsewhere, when prayers call upon God to "look" or to "see" the situation, it may be assumed that in some sense God is being asked to assess it. So, for example, Peter and John, when threatened by the chief priests, rulers, and elders in Jerusalem, pray, "Lord, look at their threats" (Acts 4:29), that is, take note of how they are opposing and threatening them. Such notice should justify a response by God emboldening them against such opposition.[16]

Daniel 9 and 1 Kgs 8:30 indicate that the term "prayer," seeking God's consideration, is appropriate also to that communication whose basic thrust is *penitence and the seeking of forgiveness*. It is also the standard term to refer to *acts of intercession*. In this regard, 1 Sam 2:25 is instructive:

> If someone sins against another, God will arbitrate [*ûpillô*] it [or "for that one"], but if it is against the LORD that one sins, who will intercede [*yitpallēl*] for such a one?

In Deut 9:26ff., Moses prays (*hitpallēl*) to the Lord for the people and lays out a case that he believes should convince the Lord that the people should be spared.[17]

2. A second technical term for prayer is *'ātar,* which is sometimes the word behind the English term "entreat," at least in the RSV/NRSV. But in those translations it has no single English equivalent, sometimes being translated as "entreat," at other times "pray" or "make or heed supplication." The root appears only in verbal forms. It functions in ways not dissimilar to nominal and verbal forms of *pallēl* (see above). Several aspects of its usage should be noted.

a. Unlike the forms of the root *pallēl,* this verb always refers to prayer to God. It has no usage in the interhuman sphere.

b. The basic form of the verb may be used generally to refer to prayer of any sort, such as petition, for example.[18]

c. In that sense, however, the verb often appears in a conjugation that puts the force on God hearing the prayer or entreaty.[19] Instructive in this regard are 2 Chr 33:13 and 19, referring to the prayer of Manasseh for restoration. In both verses, the text distinguishes between Manasseh "praying" (*hitpallēl* and *těpillâ*) and "God granting his entreaty" (*nē'ātar*):

> He prayed [*wayyitpallēl*] to him, and God received his entreaty [*wayyē'āter lo*], heard his plea, and restored him again to Jerusalem and to his kingdom. (v. 13)

His prayer [*tĕpillātô*], and how God received his entreaty [*hē'āter-lô*], all his sin and his faithlessness...these are written in the records of the seers. (v. 19)

d. In several contexts, the term specifically refers to the entreaty of one person in behalf of another. Isaac's prayer for Rebekah because she is barren is recounted using a form of *'ātar* (Gen 25:21).[20] In this usage, *'ātar* (= entreaty) often has a more formal character. The entreaty can be a requested one; it may be done publicly; and it can be and is made at set times. That is seen particularly in two contexts. In Exodus 8–10, *'ātar* is regularly used for Pharaoh's plea to Moses to pray to the Lord to remove the plagues.[21] Pharaoh makes the request; Moses asks when he is to do this; and he always goes out from Pharaoh to make the entreaty of God.

e. The other context in which *'ātar* is used with reference to entreaty to God in behalf of others is in the David stories. There also the entreaty seems to be of a very formal sort, *accompanied by ritual activities*. In 2 Samuel 21, there is a famine in the land. When David goes to seek the face of God,[22] he is told there is blood guilt on Saul and his house because he put the Gibeonites to death. So David gives the sons of Saul to the Gibeonites and they hang them. At the end of the story, it is said: "[T]hey did all that the king commanded. After that, God heeded supplications [*wayyē'āter*] for the land" (v. 14). The "after that" suggests that certain actions need to take place to make the supplications effective. In like manner, after David makes a census of the land in 2 Samuel 24 and God sends a pestilence on Israel, David confesses his sin, and the prophet Gad tells him to erect an altar on the threshing floor of Araunah. The story then concludes:

> David built there an altar to the LORD, and offered burnt offerings and offerings of well-being. So the LORD answered his supplication [*wayyē'āter*] for the land, and the plague was averted from Israel.
>
> (v. 25)

Again, the divine response to the entreaty for the land seems to be tied to the building of the altar and the sacrifices.[23]

With *'ātar*, therefore, one encounters an apparently quite specific term that has to do with *intercession* and focuses attention particularly upon *the divine response* as well as upon its character as often a rather *formal, public act,* sometimes, if not often, accompanied by formal acts of ritual and sacrifice. But this specific term, like the various forms of *pallēl,* also functions, and especially in the later period (see Job, Chronicles, and Ezra), as a more general term for prayer—confession or petition for deliverance—as well as an indication of intercession for others. Because this single term is capable of serving in various forms for both the entreaty and the divine response, this sphere of terminology points the reader toward the dialogical character of prayer. It also focuses attention both upon the frequent entreaty of an individual—probably a leader of some sort (see chap. 8, below)—in behalf of another who suffers under divine affliction as well as upon the place of prayer in a matrix of acts having to do with encountering the divine and confirming the relationship in public and formal ways. With this language, one is less in the everyday conversation with God, or in the prayer closet, and more in the domain of prayer within and for the community, persons in the community, and even the land itself.

3. The third specific or technical term for prayer as petition and supplication is the one most often translated as "supplication" or "plea" in the RSV/NRSV translations. It is the root *ḥānan*, which as a verb appears in the *hithannān* conjugation and as a noun in the forms *tĕḥinnâ* and *taḥănûn*. The forms work on analogy with the forms of the root *pallēl*. Like *hitpallēl*, the verbal forms of *ḥānan* are in a derived stem or conjugation, *hithannān*. The primary nominal form is *tĕḥinnâ*, analogous to *tĕpillâ*. The basic meaning of this verb is "to be gracious, kind, merciful," "to show favor." So the derived form, that is, "make supplication," "plea," means *to ask or seek for oneself grace, kindness, mercy, favor*. It is to appeal to God as one whose very nature is gracious (*ḥannûn*). The theological ground for the use of these forms and this understanding of prayer is found in Exod 33:19 and 34:6-7. Here is one of the oldest confessional formulas about the nature of God: "I will be gracious to whom I will be gracious" (33:19), and "The LORD, the LORD, a God merciful and gracious [*ḥannûn*]" (34:6). The Psalms frequently draw on this confessional language (e.g., Pss 103:8; 116:5), and the appeal to God in the laws is grounded in the compassion or grace of God (Exod 22:27b). In Isa 30:19, the prophet assures the people that when they cry out (*zā'aq*), that is, utter a prayer to the Lord for help,[24] God "will surely be gracious" and will answer them. In Isa 33:2, a prayer of supplication by the people begins: "O LORD, be gracious to us; we wait for you." Similarly, the psalmist says:

> To you, O LORD, I cried,
>   and to the LORD I made supplication ['*ethannān*]. (Ps 30:8)

Then, when the actual petition is given in the following verses, it is:

> Hear, O LORD, and be gracious to me [*wĕḥānnēnî*]!
> O LORD, be my helper. (Ps 30:10)

Here, therefore, prayer is understood as appealing to God as the deliverer and helper, whose inclination is to show mercy and favor, to be gracious, even when the petitioner has sinned and done wrong.

The usage of this category of terms is consistent with this analysis. Forms of the root *ḥānan* in the context of prayer are relatively late in Israel's history. The only clear usage as early as the eighth century is Hos 12:5, where the verb appears in reference to Jacob's pleading with the "man" at the Jabbok (Genesis 32). All other uses are in Deuteronomistic material, Jeremiah, the Chronicler, Job, Daniel 9, and the Psalms, plus one occurrence in Zechariah.[25] In the Psalms and Job, the forms of the root have a general use, analogous to and sometimes parallel to or in collocation with forms of *pallēl*. The heaviest use of the root is in two places: 1 Kings 8–9, the prayer of Solomon at the dedication of the temple, where there are twelve occurrences,[26] and Daniel 9.[27] In these instances as well as in several others,[28] the root is directly connected with prayers in which sin and confession of sin are at the center. Such prayers, therefore, are appeals to the mercy and compassion of God, who will show kindness to the people and forgive their sins.[29] A similar type of prayer language is found in the idiom *ḥālâ pĕnê yhwh*, "entreat the favor of the Lord." The idiom is used several times as a general expression for prayer to seek God's help.[30] Most often, it is used in situations where there has been some sinful act or something displeasing to the Lord,[31] and the petitioner is seeking, almost literally, "to make the face of the Lord pleasant" rather than angry. Confession of sin and guilt is normally to be inferred, and sometimes it is explicit in the text.

General Terms That Become Virtual Technical Terms for Prayer for God's Help

In this category belong certain terms for crying out and calling out to the deity, specifically the roots *qārā'*, "call," and *ṣā'aq/zā'aq*, both of which mean to "cry out." One may call (*qārā'*) upon the name of the Lord in worship, but here we have in mind the calling to God that is essentially a cry for help of some sort and thus a prayer. Twice, for example, Samson "called on the Lord," once when he was thirsty after battling the Philistines (Judg 15:18) and then at the end of his life when he prayed for strength to pull down the pillars of the house of Dagon and thus pay back the Philistines for blinding and imprisoning him (Judg 16:28). Deuteronomic laws warn against mistreatment of the poor on the grounds that "they might cry [*qārā'*] to the LORD against you, and you would incur guilt" (Deut 15:9; 24:15; cf. 4:7). Here and elsewhere, especially in the Psalms, the calling out seems to be the cry for help of a victim of suffering of some sort and often the oppression of others. The "call" to God for help is certainly frequent in the Psalms in the context of the lament prayers.[32]

In like manner, "crying out" (*ṣā'aq/zā'aq*)[33] to God is most often a plea for help on the part of the innocent and the victim. While an angry

Samuel may "cry out" to the Lord (1 Sam 15:11), the frequent uses of these verbal roots and their nominal formations are in the context of the plea of marginal persons to a higher power when they cannot get justice or help in the ordinary structures of life or when they are done in by the oppression of others, even if that is the judgment of God.[34] Abel's blood "cries out" to God from the ground as a victim of injustice (Gen 4:10). God hears and responds to the "outcry" against Sodom and Gomorrah.[35] The outcry of the Hebrews against Egyptian oppression precipitates the redemptive response of God.[36] During the period of the Judges, when the Israelites come under outside oppression, they cry out to God, who sends a deliverer.[37] In the Book of the Covenant, the crying out of the poor, widow, and orphan who are not dealt with justly will be heard by a compassionate God.[38] The sailors with whom Jonah seeks to flee to Tarshish cry out to the Lord in the midst of the storm (Jonah 1:14). Several times in the Psalms, individuals or groups in trouble cry out to the Lord.[39] From the cross, Jesus "cried with a loud voice, . . . My God, my God, why have you forsaken me?"[40]

This crying out of people in trouble and suffering is one of the thematic threads of the Scriptures. Only rarely are the actual words or prayers of those who cried out given, as, for example, in Jonah 1:14; it is likely that the prayers for help of the Psalter best represent the articulation of this outcry (see chap. 3, below). In addition, there are two instances in which the outcry is a single exclamation: "Violence!" (*ḥāmās;* Job 19:7; Hab 1:2). One is reminded of the Mesopotamian exclamation prayer *aḫulap* (see chap. 1, above). The prayer of complaint or the prayer for help can be reduced to a single note. There is violence in the human community, and when that is lifted before God by the victims, then it becomes a prayer for help, and the ears of God are alerted to such cries.[41]

Such lament or complaint prayers are also indicated by another set of vocabulary, that is, verbal and nominal forms of the root *šiwwaʿ,* all of which indicate cries for help, regularly by those who are identified as poor, oppressed, weak, or occasionally by those who cry for healing (e.g., Ps 30:3). Not surprisingly, the root appears most often in Job[42] and the Psalms.[43] The occasional other uses are consistent with the general picture.[44]

Finally, there is the less frequent but specific use of the root *śîaḥ,* with the meaning "complain/complaint." Here, as with *šiwwaʿ,* we have a technical term but one that shares with *qārāʾ* and *ṣāʿaq/zāʿaq* the context of oppression and suffering and the purpose of praying to God in complaint and petition. After her prayer in the sanctuary, Hannah tells Eli that she has been speaking out of "the greatness of her complaint" (1 Sam 1:16). As with *šiwwaʿ,* the primary usage of *śîaḥ* in verbal and nominal forms is in Job[45] and the Psalms,[46] the former to refer to Job's complaint against God and over his suffering, the latter most often to refer to the psalms of lament or complaint, the prayers for help of the Psalter.[47]

With this last term or root (*śyḥ*), however, we encounter another dimension of prayer that is not generally a part of the discussion of biblical prayer. For forms of this root, as well as instances of the root *hāgâ,* can refer to a meditation or musing that seems related to prayer. Virtually all of the instances of such meditating are in the Psalter and thus in the context of prayers themselves. So in prayers for help,[48] as well as frequently in Psalm 119,[49] in part, at least, a prayer for help, the petitioner speaks of meditating. This may or may not be a musing in silence. Presumably in some cases it is. But the verb *hāgâ* often refers to a speaking act, and so the meditation in this instance may be verbal. At times, it seems to be accompanied by moaning and groaning (Ps 77:3). In a couple of instances, such meditation takes place at night, when one is in bed, and may be a part of the prayer for help that often seems to belong to the nighttime before God's help comes in the morning.[50] Such meditation is not generalized or empty thinking. While we are not always given an object of meditation, in most cases it is clear. The psalmist meditates on God,[51] on God's wonderful works,[52] or on God's instruction or law.[53] Psalm 19:14 concludes with a prayer and then these words:

> Let the words of my mouth and the meditation of my heart be
> acceptable to you,
> O LORD, my rock and my redeemer.

The "meditation of my heart" may refer to the immediately preceding prayer, but one notes that the rest of the psalm is about God's wonderful works in nature and God's law. The psalm is itself a meditation on these things.[54]

Conclusion

While there are other important terms that have to do with human address to God, specifically those regarding praise and thanksgiving, their meaning is so tied up with form-critical questions about the types of psalms involved that those terms will be discussed in the context of the larger presentation of thanksgiving, praise, and blessing (see chap. 5, below). At this point, however, it is appropriate to bring together the significant results of the detailed analysis given thus far in this chapter:

1. Some of the vocabulary regularly associated with prayer suggests its character as a *conversation or dialogue with God.* Prayers are often "said" or "spoken" without reference to their character as prayer and without reference to any cultic activity or locale.

2. Other terminology sets prayer in a more formal activity associated with shrines, with ritual acts of sacrifice and offering (*'ātar*). The language of prayer, therefore, is highly varied relative to the question of formality and informality, liturgical and nonliturgical context, sanctuary or commonplace setting. It designates prayer as an occurrence in the midst of the affairs of life and without special accoutrements, simply as human communication with the divine; but it also speaks of the phenomenon of prayer with language that designates it as a particular speech-act and may at times point to prayer as an occurrence accompanied by varied acts of worship and ritual.

3. Sharp distinctions in terminology between types of prayer—apart from the different sets of vocabulary belonging to petition and to praise—do not exist. Intercession, petition, complaint, and confession may all take place under a variety of designations.

4. It is the case, however, that prayers for help by those in suffering, particularly as victims of oppression, are identified in a number of cases by a particular set of terms that all have to do with "crying out" or "calling out" for help (*qārā'*, *ṣā'aq/za'aq*, and *šiwwa'*). Frequently the content of the cry is not included. Sometimes it is simply the exclamation, "Violence!" One may presume that a more detailed articulation of these cries is to be found in the prayers for help of the Bible, particularly the Psalms, Job, and Lamentations. The one term that seems specifically to refer to a type of psalm or prayer is the relatively infrequent *śîaḥ*, "complaint." In all of these cases, prayer is found in the cry of hurt of the victim and sufferer.[55]

5. In two of the terms or roots for prayer (*hitpallēl/tĕpillâ* and *hithannān/tĕhinnâ*), two of the primary characteristics and images of God as God is portrayed in Scripture come together as the ground for appeal to God to deal with the human plight. These are God as *righteous judge* who assesses the human situation and determines the right, insuring that it will be done, and God as *gracious deliverer* whose every inclination is to deal kindly with creatures in trouble, exercising compassion where it is either unexpected or unprovided for in the human structures. Such grounds for the appeal or plea of prayer are uncovered by a look at the terminology for prayer. It is corroborated over and over again by the actual content of the prayers as various appeals either to the justice of God or to the mercy of God—or often both—occupy much of the formal pleas that are expressed. The crying out of the oppressed is specifically grounded in God's own claim to be compassionate, and the frequent supplications (*tĕhinnâ*) of the Psalms and elsewhere often have at their center the plea to God to be gracious or compassionate (*ḥannûn*).

6. Finally, some of the terminology for prayer has to do with seeking direction or instruction from God. There one can see historical develop-

ment or movement as such inquiry of God moves from technical (the casting of lots) and professional (consultation of prophetic figures) to the prayerful study of the instruction that is already given in the torah or law. At the same time, the notion of seeking God is seen to incorporate the whole of one's relationship with God and not simply the act of prayer. Devotion, worship, and moral goodness all belong to the act of "seeking" the Lord.

The Time and Place of Prayer

Both narrative and psalmic texts indicate considerable openness about when and where people prayed in ancient Israel. Prayers for help in crisis and threat, or even without such circumstances, could take place at any time. Often there is no indication of the time of day or night. So one needs to be careful not to assume any restriction or precise definition of appropriate times of prayer. But there are indications of prayers in the nighttime, and it has been suggested that that was often the time when persons in trouble of some sort prayed to the Lord. Psalm 134:1 speaks explicitly of the servants of the Lord "who stand by night in the house of the LORD," identifying possibly both a time and a place of prayer, although the psalm is not specific about what happens at night in the temple.[56] One may assume that this reflects some period in Israel's history when nighttime prayer in the temple was customary. Psalm 42:8 may confirm this as the psalmist says:

> By day the LORD commands his steadfast love,
>> and at night his song is with me,
>> a prayer to the God of my life.

The reference here to night, however, may be an example of a merismus, that is, night and day meaning all the time.[57] Other places in the Psalms may point to the nighttime as a time of anguished prayer.[58] A song at night is referred to also in Isa 30:29, in connection with one of the festivals. There is a clear reference to prayer for help at night in Samuel's crying out to the Lord "all night" when he was angry at Saul's disobedience and the Lord's rejection of his rule over Israel (1 Sam 15:11). In Ps 88:1-2 the psalmist says,

> O LORD, God of my salvation,
>> when, at night, I cry out in your presence,
> let my prayer come before you;
>> incline your ear to my cry.

And in verse 13, the same petitioner says,

> But I, O LORD, cry out to you;
> in the morning my prayer comes before you.

This psalm indicates more straightforwardly what others suggest, to wit, that the night is often a time of praying. The fact that God's help often comes in the morning tends to confirm the assumption that the night was especially a time of praying in distress for God's help.[59]

We should note, in this context, that in the later parts of the Old Testament as well as in the New Testament, we begin to hear of set hours and times of prayer. It is reported of Daniel that he "continued ... to get down on his knees three times a day to pray to his God and praise him" (Dan 6:10). Peter and John are also depicted as "going up to the temple at the hour of prayer" (Acts 3:1), and the vision of the centurion Cornelius takes place when he is praying at the afternoon hour for prayer, three o'clock.[60] In these texts, we encounter the development within Judaism of such set times for prayer—morning, afternoon, and evening—a development attested in Old Testament texts and carried over into the prayer life of the early Christian community.

Several of the texts already cited indicate that the one praying in these psalms was in the temple. Certainly that was the case for the prayers of thanksgiving that accompanied thanksgiving offerings and the hymns of praise (see chap. 5, below). Other texts speak of an individual entering into a sanctuary to pray for help as well as to give thanks. Hannah does so when she weeps bitterly and vows her son if God will only undo her barrenness (1 Sam 1:9-12). But one must not assume that all such laments or prayers for help were confined or restricted to a sanctuary. In fact, Erhard Gerstenberger has argued the opposite case, suggesting that it was not necessary for individuals to be in the sanctuary to pray, as was Hannah.[61] Many were sick and unable to be there.[62] Healing ritual seems to have taken place often outside the sanctuary.[63] Some psalms suggest that the petitioner was far from the sanctuary.[64] And in the stories of the early Christian community in Acts we hear of praying in the temple and in places of prayer but also in many instances of prayer in homes and by sickbeds as well as in prison.[65] Jesus' instruction about going into your room and shutting your door to pray (Matt 6:6) as well as his own experiences of withdrawing for prayer and praying in agony in the Garden of Gethsemane show the freedom of location in prayer, the possibility of prayer in a nonholy place being as valid and desirable as the prayer in the sanctuary.

So while the gathering of the community for praise and thanksgiving, and often the prayer of an individual for help in trouble, had their setting in a holy place, that was not required in prayer. The formal appearance of a petitioner before God in a sacred place is well recognized. But prayers were offered and heard in all sorts of places and contexts. Nor should one assume that there was no ritual accompanying prayer except in the sanctuary. We find prophetic and other figures laying hands, or even whole bodies, on the sick in prayer wherever they are.[66] Holy place and private room, sanctuary and sickbed are all places of prayer. Set times and any time, morning and night are all times of prayer. The Scriptures identify prayer as an act that could be set in particular moments and places and routinized in definite ways.[67] But it was not confined to such settings. Formality and fixity interchange with openness and freedom in the time and place of prayer.

GESTURES AND ACTS OF PRAYER

Praying is so much a verbal act, even if only in the mind, that one is inclined to neglect the nonverbal dimension that is frequently indicated in the texts. But in ancient times as much or more than in the present, dimensions of prayer were expressed with the body and in acts, movements, and gestures as well as with words. Affective and symbolic aspects of the activity of prayer contribute to the wholeness of the "act." There are various stances, for example, in which prayer may take place. David is recorded as having gone in and "sat before the LORD" when he asked for God's blessing upon his house in 1 Samuel 7. Sitting in prayer, however, is less common[68] than standing[69] or being prostrate. The last position would seem to have been the most common. There are numerous instances of persons falling on their face or lying prostrate in prayer before the deity.[70] Sometimes such action happens after prayer and the divine response.[71] Elijah's stretching himself out upon a sick child in prayer for healing may be a related action (1 Kgs 17:21). The bowed head as well as kneeling may accompany prayer.[72] All such actions place prayer in the context of the worship of God, conveying in body language the sense of humility before God, that the conversation is not ordinary conversation, but communication with the holy God.

One of the most common gestures in prayer—and one often seen in visual presentations of prayer[73]—is the upraising of the hands of the petitioner. The psalmist says: "I stretch out my hands to you" (Ps 143:6). Elsewhere we read:

> Hear the voice of my supplication,
>   as I cry to you for help,
> as I lift up my hands
>   toward your most holy sanctuary. (Ps 28:2)

And in Lam 2:19 Jerusalem is told:

> Lift your hands to him
>   for the lives of your children,

> who faint for hunger
> at the head of every street.

When Solomon prays at the dedication of the temple, he does so with hands outstretched toward heaven (1 Kgs 8:22, 54), as does Ezra in his great prayer of confession (Ezra 9:5). Here the gesture of prayer is clearly one of imploring and beseeching, of reaching out toward God. The urgency that is so often heard in the imploring, urging words is conveyed also in the gesture of raising or stretching out the hands. Such action, however, also may accompany the praise and blessing of God as the ones who sing praise to God lift their hands not to beseech but in exaltation (Ps 134:2). In both petition and praise, the outstretched hands again convey a sense of the transcendent, that prayer is directed beyond oneself and this world to the God who is in heaven (1 Kgs 8:22, 54, and passim). The gestures of the hands are, therefore, a way also of directing the prayer, as is specifically indicated by those references to lifting the hands toward the sanctuary (Ps 28:2; 1 Kgs 8:29-30, 44, 48). Symbolically as well as in words, prayer becomes a communication with the divine, a reaching out beyond the ordinary confines of human life to a power that is accessible but not confined or contained within the visible natural order and the human structures. The outstretched hands are one of the symbols of heaven in the midst of the mundane. They are the permissible way of reaching to heaven, not to grasp but to implore and to praise.

All these gestures and actions serve to recognize that the act of praying to God, of setting one's case before God or presenting prayers in behalf of another in need, is not simply a routine action. In some sense, one moves one's whole being into a stance of prayer. There is a break from whatever is happening, an acknowledgment that now one is coming before God. One sees this sharply in Moses at the burning bush where he has to take off his shoes because he is on holy ground before God. Not all praying assumes a specifically holy ground, but this kind of action is not done matter-of-factly, and the reaching to heaven or to the holy place, the sanctuary, symbolizes that fact, that the very act of prayer takes one into another world, reaches out toward the transcendent. Such bodily movements embody what is meant by "turning to God in prayer."[74]

Specific mention should be made of those extreme gestures and acts that accompany the confession of sin, particularly, but may be present in other contexts, especially when the community cries out to the Lord in its distress. The prayer of confession in the Old Testament is present primarily in the accounts of the life of the later, postexilic community. In Ezra 9, Ezra hears from the officials that the people have engaged in mixed marriages with the surrounding peoples and prays a long prayer of confession (vv. 5-15). Before he begins the prayer, he tears his clothes and pulls hair from his head and beard, fasts, and falls on his knees with "his hands to the LORD my God" (v. 5). And his prayer takes place at the evening sacrifice. Later reference to the prayer in 10:1 tells of Ezra praying and making confession, "weeping and throwing himself down before the house of God," and indicates that all this happened in front of the gathered congregation, also weeping bitterly. The praying before the house of God conforms to the Solomonic prayer of dedication beseeching God to hear when the people pray toward the house of God. The prayer is directed toward the throne of God, toward the Holy One who alone can forgive. The other acts of Ezra, which are partly ritual in character and may also be partly spontaneous, are appropriate to the act of confession of sin. In powerful visual, symbolic ways, they express the contrition and humility of the one who confesses in behalf of the community, and the community joins in (10:1). In similar fashion, Daniel "prayed to the LORD my God and made confession" (Dan 9:4), "with fasting and sackcloth and ashes" (9:3). Like Ezra, the consciousness of sin before the Lord is expressed in concrete, visible ways through gestures of contrition and humility.[75]

These more extravagant acts of weeping, fasting, putting on sackcloth and ashes, and even tearing the clothes, which clearly are appropriate for the confession of sin, seem, however, to have accompanied other instances of individuals and the community crying out to God when confession of sin was not necessarily the primary fact or was a dimension of the cry for help. Nehemiah "sat down and wept, and mourned for days, fasting and praying before the God of heaven" (Neh 1:4). His prayer begins in confession of sin, but it is aimed at seeking God's help in giving him "success" when he goes before the Persian king, asking him to let him go back to Jerusalem to rebuild it (Neh 2:4-5). And it is the "trouble and shame" (1:3) of the survivors in Jerusalem that have precipitated his crying out in prayer to the Lord. This "shame," more literally, "taunting," is typically a symptom of the trouble felt by those who cry out in the laments of the Psalter, usually being taunted and mocked that God has abandoned them or is unwilling to come to their aid (e.g., Pss 69; 74), sometimes claiming that the taunts and insults are in fact against God (e.g., Ps 69:6-12). Nehemiah's actions, therefore, are not simply those of one who speaks primarily out of the awareness of sins committed and with the primary aim of forgiveness (as, e.g., in Psalm 51). He prays to God for help because of the awareness of the trouble of his comrades in Jerusalem. Similarly, Joshua prays a prayer of complaint after the men of Ai have routed the Israelite warriors. According to the story, "Joshua tore his clothes, and fell to the ground on his face before the ark of the LORD until the evening, he and the elders of Israel; and they put dust on their heads" (Josh 7:6). The narrative goes on to indicate quite clearly that the Lord is angry because the people have sinned; but that is given as a response to Joshua's complaint, which is not itself a confession of sin. It is a powerful complaint against God with its "Why have you done this?" character and its claim that God's actions will destroy both Israel's name and God's name. So here, as in Nehemiah's case, the leader's gestures of tearing the clothes and putting dust on the head are in the context of the cry to and against God and not simply confession of sin.

In Joel 1–2, there is extended communal lament. Priests and elders are told to declare a fast and a solemn assembly, to weep and put on sackcloth, to cry to the Lord because of the great devastation that has come upon the Lord (Joel 1:13-14, 19). The destruction is understood to be the Lord's doing, and the people are called to "turn" or "return":

> Yet even now, says the LORD,
>   return to me with all your heart,
> with fasting, with weeping, and with mourning;
>   rend your hearts and not your clothing. (Joel 2:12-13)

Here, therefore, the weeping, fasting, and sackcloth, as well as the implied tearing of the clothes presume some confession of sin. But in the actual prayer that is uttered, we do not in fact hear such confession. Instead there is the abbreviated form of the typical communal lament of the Psalms:

> Between the vestibule and the altar
>   let the priests, the ministers of the LORD, weep.
> Let them say, "Spare your people, O LORD,
>   and do not make your heritage a mockery,
>   a byword among the nations.
> Why should it be said among the peoples,
>   'Where is their God?' " (Joel 2:17)

The strong gestures of contrition and humility occur again, not simply in confession of sin, but in forthright complaint to God and outcry for help. The Psalms also show the outcry of the individual petitioner in trouble accompanied by fasting and the putting on of sackcloth as well as mourning.[76]

All of this suggests that the dramatic demonstration of contrition and humility belongs not only to the act of confession of sin, where one might readily expect it, but to any crying out in anguish to the Lord. Confession of sin and complaint against God may go together, as Joel 1–2 suggests, but the fasting and tearing of clothes, the weeping and sackcloth accompany forthright complaint and cry for help and not just confession. One notes, therefore, the apparent contrast between the presented humility in acts and gestures and some of the words of the prayers that express strong complaint and protest, frustration and deep anguish, not simply about one's sinfulness but about one's condition of suffering. Humility, which is strongly indicated in the acts of the penitent, is also the stance of those who petition and intercede, indeed of those who may complain quite loudly. The anger and anguish of the complaints, the open confrontation of God that one finds in these prayers, are often uttered by those who may demonstrate their anguish in weeping and tearing of clothes but who also, in sackcloth and fasting, show their humility before the holy God. However direct the encounter of prayer may be, however open and assertive may be those who cry out and complain, there is no doubt that these are prayers of creature before creator, that anguish and anger do not belie the relationship. The angry, human, understandable complaints of Job conclude with these words:

> Therefore I have uttered what I did not understand,
>   things too wonderful for me, which I did not know.
> . . . .
> I had heard of you by the hearing of the ear,
>   but now my eye sees you;
> therefore I despise myself,
>   and repent in dust and ashes. (Job 42:3, 5-6)

Job has come to an understanding that all his justified anger has been addressed to the holy transcendent one before whom he is but creature. The gestures and acts of prayer demonstrate that is *always* the case, however bold may be the creature's address to God.[77]

3

"They Cried to You"

PRAYERS FOR HELP

✦

Address to God in the Bible and in human life generally moves back and forth between plea or petition and praise or thanksgiving.[1] In that movement, one is at the heart of what prayer is all about. The biblical story as a whole and in many of its parts may be charted along that movement also. It begins in human address that is the cry of a suffering one (Gen 4:10), and it ends when those cries have ceased (Rev 21:1-4) and the world is filled with the praise of God (Psalm 150 and Revelation 19). That movement, however, from plea to praise happens only because between those words to God things happen to transform the human situation or attitude and turn weeping to joy, tears to laughter. In the chapters that follow, we will seek to lay out and explicate this movement, which not only opens up the nature of prayer but also places us within the very structure of faith in relation to God as that is uncovered in the pages of Scripture.

Prayer as it is most commonly understood, as a plea to God for help, is the focus of this chapter. The largest number of the psalms are prayers of this sort. But there are also many prayers in the narrative and prophetic books of the Old Testament that are prayers to God for help. All of these need to be considered in thinking about the character and circumstances of human pleas to the Lord.[2] Form-critical study of the psalms has distinguished between individual prayers and community prayers. That distinction will be observed here while recognizing that in many respects both types of prayer are similar and so may be looked at together. Form-critical analysis has also led us to designate the prayer of the Psalter as "lament," that is, "individual lament" and "community/communal lament."[3] Sometimes the term "complaint" is used instead of "lament." That is not altogether inappropriate, but it may lead to some confusion. Complaint about one's situation is a significant part of many of the prayers for help, but it is not always present. Nor does "complaint" exhaust the content and purpose of prayer, as the use of the term as an overall rubric might suggest. More appropriate in terms of the purpose of prayer would be the use of the terms "plea" or "petition," as some interpreters have chosen to do. There are prayers of complaint that seem to do nothing but protest the situation, but it is rare that petition is not at least implied even in these prayers.

It is also unusual to find prayers for help that do not represent situations of distress of some sort. They are virtually nonexistent in the Psalms. In narrative texts, there are some prayers for God's help or direction that do not appear to belong to a setting of crisis or trouble.[4] Most of these, however, in fact, do reflect a situation of stress of some sort. In Genesis 24, Eliezer, Abraham's servant, having been sent to find a wife for Isaac from Abraham's kin, prays to God a quite specific prayer for help in that process: "O LORD, God of my master Abraham, please grant me success today and show steadfast love to my master Abraham" (v. 12). Then in his prayer he proposes a way that he wants God to identify for him the one divinely appointed as Isaac's wife and says: "By this I shall know that you have shown steadfast love to my master" (Gen 24:13-14). When the plan has worked, the servant then prays: "Blessed be the LORD, the God of my master Abraham, who has not forsaken his steadfast love and his faithfulness toward my master. As for me, the LORD has led me on the way to the house of my master's kin" (Gen 24:27). While there is no personal threat to the servant, the prayers at the beginning and at the end are couched as prayers in Abraham's behalf, and it is made clear that the faithfulness of God is at stake in this little episode.[5] The servant calls upon God's steadfast love and regards the Lord's positive response as an indication that Abraham has not been abandoned by God, precisely the fear or reality that is so prevalent in the complaint psalms. In other words, Abraham is in genuine need. The realization of the divine promise to him is at issue in this enterprise, and the servant knows it.[6]

In the wilderness, Moses asks God to appoint someone over the congregation in his place, "so that the congregation of the LORD may not be like sheep without a shepherd" (Num 27:16-17). Here again the prayer itself does not suggest a context of trouble or crisis, but what has just happened points in that direction. Moses' prayer arises out of the divine word that he is going to die without going into the promised land because he rebelled against the Lord's word in the wilderness (vv. 12-14). While nothing is said of Moses' reaction, the situation is indeed one of distress and crisis. The prayer is made in the face of divine judgment and in order to save the people.

Gideon's prayer in Judg 6:36-37, 39 is more of an oracle inquiry before battle than a distinctive prayer for help. But it is made in order to seek an assurance of God's help against the dire threat of the Midianites. The prayer of Manoah for instruction about how he and his wife are to raise their son Samson (Judg 13:8) and David's long prayer of praise and petition in 2 Sam 7:18-29 are both instances of prayer to God in which there is little immediate indication of a situation of distress.[7]

But these are clearly the exception to the rule. Where they occur, they tend to be prayers for divine direction and instruction, for help in dealing with a situation that may not be immediately threatening. Petitionary prayers of the Old Testament, however, ordinarily assume a circumstance of trouble and distress, of personal or corporate threat that will undo the individual or the community that prays if God does not respond and act to help.[8] A look at such prayers will take us into the heart of biblical prayer.

The many prayers for help show both variety and consistency. That is, they are rarely precisely alike, though repeated formulas are not uncommon, especially in the Psalms; and they may vary significantly in their length and the degree of elaboration of their component parts. Some are very succinct[9] while others are extended in one or more of their basic elements. Some do not contain all the elements that other prayers do. Nevertheless, the basic form of the petitionary prayer is fairly consistent. It consists of *address* to the deity, *petition,* and *motivation* clauses.[10] Elements of *lament about one's situation* and *expressions of confidence or trust* are regularly enough present to be included in the basic form, especially for the psalm prayers. In the prose prayers, both lament and expressions of confidence are less frequent. Where the prayer contains lament, it is primarily in the form of complaint against God. Where the prayers within narratives express confidence and trust in God, it is in the context of praise elaborations of the address. In the psalm prayers, however, the statements of confidence are a constitutive part of the prayer, and the lament may involve complaint against God but also may involve lament about the self as well as about others, especially the enemies of the one praying.[11] In addition to these elements, one may encounter in the psalm prayers some sort of *offer* or *vow* on the part of the petitioner. Each of these elements needs to be looked at with some care in order to understand what takes place in these prayers as a whole.

In order to facilitate ease of analysis, appendix 1 provides a simple structural analysis of most of the prose prayers for help,[12] including some that will be looked at more closely in other chapters (e.g., intercession) but omitting others dealt with elsewhere (e.g., confession).

ADDRESS TO GOD

Forms of Address

While address to the deity is characteristically a part of prayer in the Old Testament, there are a few instances in the prose prayers where no address is given. These have the character of conversation in some instances,[13] which may account for the absence of the address. A very few prayer psalms[14] contain no explicit calling on the name of the deity. That may be explained by the fact that these psalms, like Psalm 23, are as much expressions of trust as they are prayers for help. Most of the prayers for help do address the deity directly and call God by some form of address. In the prose prayers, this is nearly always at the beginning, though further terms of address may appear in the prayer on occasion. That is true generally of the psalm prayers also, but there the address sometimes may not appear until the middle of the prayer (e.g., Psalm 142). Often God is addressed by name or epithet at the beginning and at the end (e.g., Ps 55:1, 23) or as many as three or four times throughout the psalm.[15] Such frequent address reinforces the highly personal character of the plea and the urgency with which it is uttered. The reference to God may be of the simplest sort, either "O God"[16] or "O LORD"[17] or "O Lord GOD" (*'ădōnāy YHWH*).[18] Such straightforward calling on the name of God is the most common mode of address in prose prayers and in the Psalms. Not infrequently, however, the address may be of another sort, or the address to God/the Lord is expanded. Such expansions are of several sorts. They may be alternative names or epithets familiar from the biblical tradition in other contexts, for example, Most High, God/Lord of Hosts, the Holy One of Israel, and the God of Israel.[19] In such epithets, God is appealed to particularly in terms of majesty and transcendence, the Most High God who rules the universe, the one accompanied by all the hosts of heaven, the one who is holy and thus wholly other. The human predicament as articulated in the prayer is overcome only by one who transcends the present situation and its reality and is able to redeem precisely because God is the Most High, the ruler of the universe.

As the last two epithets referred to above indicate, however, the direct appeal to God is even more often in highly relational terms, identifying or claiming a relationship to God that is an implicit but significant ground for the appeal. One of the most common of these appeals, especially in the psalm prayers, is the simple, "my God" or "O LORD my God."[20] The body of the psalmic prayer itself will often contain reference to "my God,"[21] so that the claim that is there in the address is asserted in the dialogue. The interplay of the address to the one who is the personal God of the petitioner and the assertion of that intimate relationship as the ground of trust is well illustrated in Psalm 22, where the repeated, and thus emphasized, "My God, my God" of verse 1, echoed again in verse 2, is the strong claim on the close relationship between the sufferer and God precisely in the context of the cry of abandonment, the terrible sense of the absence, the distance, and the silence of God. There is an almost unbearable sense of contradiction between the roaring cry of dereliction and the address that repeatedly insists that the silent, forsaking, distant God is *"my* God." The psalmist claims in the present what present experience has denied. But there is a larger experience that validates the assertion of the address, and it is seen in the verses that follow, explicitly stated in verse 10:

> On you I was cast from my birth,
>   and since my mother bore me
>   you have been *my God.*

The suffering and praying one in Psalm 31 recites the woes of personal distress and the oppression of external foes at some length and then begins to turn in hope and expectation in a series of petitions that begin with the claim (v. 14):

> But I trust in you, O LORD;
>   I say, "You are *my God.*"[22]

So also the oppressed petitioner of Psalm 140 grounds his or her petition as follows:

> I say to the LORD, "You are *my God;*
>   give ear, O LORD, to the voice
>   of my supplications." (v. 6)

Then follows the appeal, "O LORD, my Lord, my strong deliverer" (v. 7). In similar fashion, the psalmist prays for help in Ps 86:2 because "You are *my God"* and then in confidence says: "I give thanks to you, O LORD *my God,* with my whole heart" (Ps 86:12).[23] The prominence of this appeal is seen also in its being quoted as the appropriate form of prayer of one who cries out in trouble, first in Psalm 91 and then in 102:

> The one who lives in the shelter of the Most High,
>   who abides in the shadow of the Almighty,
> will say to the LORD, "My refuge and my fortress;
>   *my God,* in whom I trust." (91:1-2)

> "O *my God,*" I say, "do not take me away
>   at the mid-point of my life." (102:24)

In 2 Chr 14:11 a communal prayer is recorded that also addresses God in this personal way, "O LORD *our God,*" and then immediately claims, "You are *our God.*"

As Ps 91:2 reveals, the fundamental claim that the Lord is the personal God of the one who prays takes shape in other forms of address as well. There is a whole stock of expressions asserting that personal relationship but also appealing to God as one whose strength or protection is available to the praying one. The royal song of thanksgiving in Psalm 18, which recounts the near-death experience of the singer, begins with a string of such expressions:

> I love you, O LORD, *my strength.*
> The LORD is *my rock, my fortress,*
> and *my deliverer,*
> *my God, my rock* in whom I take refuge,
> *my shield,* and the horn of *my salvation,*
> *my stronghold.* (vv. 1-2)

In the rest of the song, these divine characteristics that are experienced by the psalmist are referred to as he recounts how God delivered and protected him:

> to *my God* I cried for help (v. 6)
>
> the LORD, *my God,* lights up my darkness (v. 28)
>
> and by *my God* I can leap over a wall (v. 29)
>
> he is a *shield* for all *who take refuge in him* (v. 30)
>
> who is a *rock* besides our God? (v. 31)
>
> the God who girded me with *strength* (v. 32)[24]
>
> you have given me the *shield of your salvation* (v. 35)
>
> you girded me with *strength* for the battle (v. 39)[25]
>
> Blessed be *my rock,*
> and exalted be the God of *my salvation* (v. 46)

Such expressions appear frequently in the address to God of the petitionary prayers of the Psalms: my rock, God of my salvation, my help, my strength, God of my right, faithful God, our shield.[26] The community prayers for help sometimes address God in the same way: my God, our God, God of our salvation.[27] In all of these instances, God is not appealed to in general ways but is seen by the troubled pray-er as being *pro me* and able to deliver in the situation of dire threat or provide protection and security. The list above suggests several ways in which the character and way of God in personal relationship provide a ground for hope: (1) God's power and willingness to help and save me out of the trouble; (2) God's inclination always to vindicate and support the righteous or innocent; (3) God's protecting and guarding of me in the midst of trouble, so that I am not undone by it; and (4) God's faithfulness that will not leave me abandoned in my distress.

The faithfulness of God, which is not often explicitly cited in the petitionary addresses to God, is nevertheless implicitly present in a quite specific way in the address to God of some of the prose prayers where the relational assumption is also explicitly indicated. When Eliezer, Abraham's servant, prays for God's help in finding a bride for Isaac, he begins his prayer, "O LORD, *God of my master Abraham*" (Gen 24:12). The address to God is equivalent in function and meaning to the "my God" of the Psalms. The errand is in behalf of Eliezer's master, Abraham, and so he prays to the one who is the personal god of his master. That such appeal is to God's faithfulness, an implicit assumption about the various examples mentioned earlier, is made explicit in what follows the address in Eliezer's prayer: "Please grant me success and show steadfast love to my master Abraham" (v. 12). This assumption that the appeal for God's help is an appeal to the faithfulness of God toward one with whom the Lord stands in intimate personal relationship is then confirmed in Eliezer's prayer of thanksgiving after the prayer has been heard and divine help received: "Blessed be the LORD, *the God of my master Abraham, who has not forsaken his steadfast love and his faithfulness toward my master*" (Gen 24:27).

A similar address appears on the lips of Jacob when he prays for God's help at the Jabbok River before meeting Esau on his return home: "O God of my father Abraham and God of my father Isaac, O LORD . . . " (Gen 32:9). The appeal is to the personal God of Abraham's ancestors. As in every prayer, such an appeal is in part to identify the one to whom the plea is addressed, but here the identification also recalls the continuing relationship to the ancestors and to the clan. Implicitly, such an address calls upon God to be with and for Jacob as God was with and for Abraham and Isaac. That such an appeal is fundamentally a call for God's faithfulness is confirmed in the rest of the address, which is more extended than in many prayers: "O LORD, who said to me, 'Return to your country and to your kindred, and I will do you good.' " The prayer is a call for God to follow through on the promises made long before. In a double way, the address anticipates the fundamental petition of the prayer ("Deliver me . . . ") as it appeals to the clan deity, the God of the ancestors who has guided the destiny of the clan and its leaders in the past, and as it appeals to God as one who has made promises of good and can be counted upon to keep the promises made.

Such address to the God who has guided and delivered the ancestors in the past is found at a much later time also in Elijah's prayer on Mount Carmel in the conflict with the prophets of Baal when he prays: "O LORD, God of Abraham, Isaac, and Israel . . . " (1 Kgs 18:36). This prayer suggests that when Solomon three times prays, "O LORD, God of

Israel," in the dedicatory prayer after the building of the temple[28] and Hezekiah prays for God's deliverance in the face of the Assyrian threat, "O LORD the God of Israel" (2 Kgs 19:14), their prayers, in their very address, not only claim the relationship between God and people (Israel), but also hark back to the faithfulness of God to the ancestor Israel (Jacob) as demonstrated in stories such as that of Jacob meeting Esau at the Jabbok (Genesis 32). In the case of both Solomon and Hezekiah, the character of the address as claiming an intimate relationship between the one(s) praying and the God addressed is confirmed by the fact that in the first instance, there is a further address, "O LORD *my God*" (1 Kgs 8:28), and in the second instance, Hezekiah, later in the prayer, addresses God, "O LORD *our God*" (2 Kgs 19:19). This mode of address appealing to God as God of the ancestors and also "our" God is found another time in the prayer of Jehoshaphat in 2 Chr 20:5-12 when the king begins the prayer, "O LORD, God of our ancestors" (v. 5) and then addresses God two more times as "O *our God*" (vv. 7, 12).

A particular and somewhat unusual form of address appears twice, both times in Numbers in the Priestly stratum of the Pentateuch. In his plea to God not to destroy the congregation after Korah's rebellion (Num 16:22) and then again in his prayer asking God to appoint a leader to help carry the burden of the people (Num 27:16), Moses appeals to "the God of the spirits of all flesh." In contrast to the various kinds of appeal that stress the particular and personal relation of petitioner to the deity, Moses' appeal here is to God as the source of all life. In the first instance, it appears that the appeal is in relation to God's power over life, capable of destroying it as well as creating it. It is at least an acknowledgment of that power that is now so real and threatening to the whole people. The address may also imply that the one who is the God of all life should protect it and not destroy it. Rabbinic tradition understood this in terms of God's discernment of those who had sinned and those who had not and thus God's right to determine who is to live and who to die.[29] In similar fashion, the Rabbis suggested, the second use of this address refers to God's discernment, as the creator of all flesh, of the right person out of "all flesh" to lead the people.[30]

The address to God, therefore, plays a fundamental role in the act of prayer. It identifies the one to whom the prayer is addressed, the Lord of Israel, whose character and way with those who pray and worship are well known. As a direct address, it assumes a personal relationship with the deity. That is specifically elaborated in various ways as those who pray speak to "my God" and claim that such a personal relationship is the ground of hope and expectation for deliverance. It is rooted in the faithfulness of God to those who have gone before, and the address frequently is directed toward the God of the fathers and mothers of Israel, who guided their destiny and kept them from all harm. In other prayers and less frequently, however, it is the transcendent and holy God who is seen as the one who is able to deliver. That does not mean there is no sense of a personal relationship. But with equal force the praying one calls on the Lord of the universe, who has the power and whose way is holy, to help the one who is powerless to overthrow the present danger.

Address and Praise

Another dimension to the address to God appears in a number of prose prayers but is not consistent enough to be identified as a regular feature of the prayer for help. It also shades off frequently into being motivation and so needs to be considered in relation to that part of the prayer structure also. It is the presence of an element of *praise* in the process of addressing God and encouraging God's response.[31] When, for example, Moses entreats the Lord to let him cross over the Jordan into the land, he follows the address, "O Lord GOD" (*'ădōnāy YHWH*), with an implicit praise or acknowledgment of God's greatness and strength: "You have only begun to show your servant your greatness and your might [lit. mighty hand]" (Deut 3:24; see appendix 1). The reference to God's greatness and mighty hand is typical of Deuteronomy and especially in reference to the deliverance from Egypt. The word for "greatness" here is used of God only in Deuteronomy except for one reference to God's mercy in Moses' prayer in Num 14:19 and two references in the Psalms (79:11 and 150:2).[32] In both Deut 32:3 and Ps 150:2, allusion to God's "greatness" is explicitly part of hymnic praise of God. The hymnic character of the second sentence of Moses' address in Deut 3:24 is even more evident: "Who is God in the heavens and on earth who can perform deeds and mighty acts like yours?" Rhetorical questions declaring the incomparability of God are standard features of hymnic praise.[33] The address of Moses thus serves to exalt God as the one whose greatness and power are beyond compare and thus able to do whatever God wishes. As it serves to claim that "you have only begun to show your servant your greatness and your might," the praise here becomes motivational also, inviting yet further demonstration to Moses of that greatness and might through God's positive response to Moses' plea.

The most extensive declaration of praise in the context of address to God in prayer occurs in 2 Sam 7:18-24 (see appendix 1). The long statement of David at the beginning of the prayer (vv. 18-24) is essentially—like Deut 3:24—an exaltation of the greatness of God as manifest in what God has done. In this case, those mighty deeds are two: the establishment of David and the promise of the Davidic royal line (vv. 18-21) and the redemption and establishment of Israel as a nation and the Lord as their God (vv. 23-24). Set between David's recitation of those two divine acts is the pivotal expression of praise that declares—again like Deut 3:24—the incomparability of God's greatness (v. 22):

> Therefore you are great, O Lord GOD; for there is no one like you,[34] and there is no God besides you, according to all that we have heard with our ears.

While the praise may be motivational to some extent, as indeed may be the case with praise of God in any prayer for help, David's praise seems to serve primarily to express thanksgiving and give glory to God. That the prayer is less a cry for help than most prayers may be a determining factor, for several of the prose prayers that include a dimension of praise are less explicitly prayers for help in time of trouble.

Other examples are the two prayers of Solomon in 1 Kings. When the Lord speaks to him at Gibeon and invites his request, Solomon responds first with praise-thanksgiving not unlike David in his prayer (see above). He praises God for the great and steadfast love that God has shown to David and now to him (1 Kgs 3:6). Then in his prayer of dedication at the temple, which includes anticipatory petitions in time of trouble but is itself not prayed in crisis but in celebration, Solomon begins the prayer with hymnic praise as a part of the address. The formulation is similar to 2 Sam 7:22: "O LORD, God of Israel, there is no God like you in heaven above or on earth beneath" (1 Kgs 8:23). This is followed by a typically hymnic active participle describing some praiseworthy characteristic of God: "keeping covenant and steadfast love for your servants . . ." Here, as in Solomon's prayer at Gibeon and David's prayer in the sanctuary, the praise is more a part of the address to God than it is an encouragement for God to act on a particular petition.

In two of the Chronicler's prayers, however, the praise clearly has a motivational force. Not surprisingly, these prayers are cries for help in a situation of extreme national distress. When Asa prays, "O LORD, there is no difference for you between helping the mighty and the weak" (2 Chr 14:11), his address renders praise to God for an unbiased and equitable openness to help. But in the face of an army twice the size of his, the king clearly is appealing to God's inclination to help "the weak" (see below on motivation clauses), which is how he views his army in comparison with that of Zerah the Ethiopian.[35] Jehoshaphat's prayer in the face of the Moabites and Ammonites (2 Chr 20:5-12) is uttered explicitly in an attitude of fear (v. 3). He follows the address, "O LORD, God of our ancestors," with the questions:

> Are you not God in heaven? Do you not rule over all the kingdoms of the nations? In your hand are power and might so that no one is able to withstand you. Did you not, O our God, drive out the inhabitants of this land before your people Israel, and give it forever to the descendants of your friend Abraham?

His words not only render praise to God as God in heaven, ruler of all nations, full of power and might, deliverer of Israel, and the like. They also serve in some sense both as complaint and motivation. The putting of questions to God (in effect asking: If all these things are true, why is this going on?) is a common form of complaint. Such praise also serves as a reminder to God of God's character and promises (see also v. 9) as a ground for the appeal for deliverance now.

Jacob's prayer in Gen 32:9-12 includes a dimension of praise and thanksgiving as he says:[36]

> O LORD who said to me, "Return to your country and to your kindred, and I will do you good," I am not worthy of the least of all the steadfast love and all the faithfulness that you have shown to your servant, for with only my staff I crossed this Jordan; and now I have become two companies.

As in the prayers of the Chronicler, the praise or thanksgiving is tied to the address and set in a context of fear and a serious plea for help. Like Asa's prayer, it also is clearly motivational in its appeal to God's inclination toward the weak.

When Jeremiah—with the Babylonian king at the gates—is told to buy land at Anathoth, his prayer contains extended praise after the initial address (Jer 32:17-23). It is quite likely that some or all of this is the result of literary expansion,[37] but in its content it is not unlike other praise elements as it praises the power of God in and over creation:

> It is you who made the heavens and the earth by your great power and by your outstretched arm! Nothing is too hard for you. (v. 17)

The rest of the extended praise points to God's omniscience over all the ways of human beings and the power of God manifest in deliverance and judgment.

When one looks at the number of prose prayers for help, it is clear that elements of praise are infrequent but may sometimes occur, either as an elaboration of the address to God and/or as a motivational factor in the prayer. One also notes that the tendency to include an element of praise is most common in the prayers of the Deuteronomistic Historian[38] and the Chronicler.[39] With regard to the prayers of Jacob and Jeremiah (Jeremiah 32), the praise element may also be the result of Deuteronomistic or other forms of expansion.

The place of praise in typical prayers of those in trouble is, therefore, as generally thought, fairly minor. It belongs more to the literary-theological construction of the Deuteronomists and the Chronicler than to standard forms of oral prayer. That tendency in the later material to include dimensions of praise and thanksgiving in relation to the address of prayer is carried forward, as we shall see, in the long confessional prayers of Daniel, Ezra, and Nehemiah. One recognizes, therefore, in the history of prayer in the Old Testament some movement toward the incorporation of praise within the prayers for help and not simply as a response to the help that has been received, which is the more typical pattern or movement. Insofar as these prayers serve as models, the biblical evidence is open at this point. Praise in the context of complaint and petition for help is not a standard feature, but it became increasingly a part of the form of prayer.

The prayers for help, or lament psalms, of the Psalter tend to reflect the same pattern.[40] Praise in any extended fashion does not seem to accompany the address very often although there are exceptions, such as, "O savior of those who seek refuge from their adversaries at your right hand" (Ps 17:7), or "I cry to God...who fulfills his purpose for me" (Ps 57:2), or "O LORD, my Lord, my strong deliverer, you have covered my head in the day of battle" (Ps 140:7). In some cases, praise may break forth at various points in the psalm prayer as expressions of confidence or trust tied to address and petition, as, for example, in Psalm 71, which is largely an interplay of petition and expressions of confidence in the form of praise that both glorifies and gives thanks to God and also grounds the petitions in pressing God to act now as God has acted in the past.[41] One sees this interplay in verse 3:

Petition Be to me a rock of refuge,
     a strong fortress, to save me,

Praise   for you are my rock and my fortress.

The psalmist praises God as rock and fortress as a basis for appealing to God to be that now in time of trouble. Again in verses 4-6:

Petition Rescue me, O my God, from the hand of the wicked....

Praise   For you, O LORD, are my hope,
     my trust, O LORD, from my youth.
    Upon you I have leaned from my birth;
     it was you who took me from my mother's womb.
    My praise is continually of you.

Several times the psalmist speaks explicitly of praising God[42] and in so doing declares the mighty deeds of God or asks the familiar hymnic rhetorical question about God's incomparability: "O God, who is like you?" alongside the declaration: "You have done great things" (v. 19).

In such a prayer, we see what often happens as elements of the prayer function in more than one way. Here address, petition, motivation, and confidence are all expressed via declarations of praise. There is little doubt that such praise is an example of the expressions of trust that are so much a part of the psalm prayers. But in verses 3 and 5, the presence of the conjunction "for" at the beginning of the clauses and the placing of these causal clauses immediately after petitions make it equally clear that they serve to motivate the deity as they appeal to the character of God and the past way of God with the individual as the ground for present help (see the section below on motivation). Yet, at every point, praise of God comes forth from the psalmist—in the course of address, as the ground for petition, and as the basis of confidence and hope for God's action.

Psalm 86 is similar to Psalm 71 in this regard. It begins with a series of petitions ("Incline your ear...preserve my life...save your servant...be gracious to me...gladden the soul of your servant...") and then in verse 5 provides a basis for the plea in language that acknowledges the way God is and can be counted upon and thus is also an expression of trust:

> For you, O LORD, are good and forgiving,
>   abounding in steadfast love to all who call on you.

Such a sentence has a complex function, doing several things at the same time. So also verse 15, which draws on ancient confessional language:[43]

> But you, O LORD, are a God merciful and gracious,
>   slow to anger and abounding in steadfast love and faithfulness.

The praise and confidence expressed here are an explicit basis for the petition that follows:

> Turn to me and *be gracious* to me. (v. 16)

In the middle of the prayer, immediately after the psalmist expresses confidence that he or she will be heard by God, the praying voice breaks forth into extended hymnic praise, reminiscent of expressions seen in some of the prose prayers:

> There is none like you among the gods, O LORD,
>   nor are there any works like yours.
> All the nations you have made shall come
>   and bow down before you, O LORD,
>   and shall glorify your name.
> For you are great and do wondrous things;
>   you alone are God. (vv. 8-10)

Within the Old Testament prayers for help, therefore, an element of praise may be present in relation to the act of addressing God (as distinct from vows of praise at the end in anticipation of God's help), whether the prayer is encountered in a prose or narrative context or in the Psalms. It is not a regular part of prayer and often seems to belong to the literary development of prayers where it does occur. Such praise at the beginning of petitionary prayers may in some instances function largely as an exaltation of the deity, but a number of examples suggest that it served to express or strengthen the confidence of the petitioner while also urging action on the part of God, giving reasons, either explicitly or implicitly, for God to help.[44]

It has been suggested by some that one of the significant distinctions between the prayers of Israel and those of its neighbors lies at this point, both in the degree of praise in addressing the deity and in its function. The Mesopotamian prayers are said to be full of praise in contrast to its absence or infrequent appearance in Israelite prayer. Such extended praise is presumed to be flattery, "the sole purpose of which is to persuade the deity to grant what is prayed for."[45] Or it is claimed that the Babylonian prayer psalms "primarily praise the one who exists, the god who exists in his world of gods,"[46] whereas Israelite prayer praises God for wonderful interventions in the history of individuals or people. Such sharp contrasts are not finally satisfactory. As one can see from the above discussion, praise does appear a number of times in Old Testament prayers addressing the deity. While one would not in every—or perhaps any—instance say that the sole purpose is to persuade God to grant what is prayed for, that is significantly a part of what goes on when such praise is uttered. Furthermore, by looking at the prayers of Israel's neighbors, one may see that they do indeed praise deities for things that have to do with the interrelationships of the gods, as one might expect in an explicitly polytheistic religion. But they also manifest exaltation of the deity as ruler of heaven and earth or assert a god's incomparability in a fashion similar to what happened in Israelite prayer. Further, such forms of address as "the lord of knowledge, the king of the sweet waters, the god who begot me" manifest a clear sense of the involvement of a deity in the personal life of the one who prays. Here, and in other prayers, the praise may address the deity, precisely as in Israelite prayer, in terms of attributes or characteristics that are crucial for the particular situation or the substance of the petition. Furthermore, these words of praise may express or strengthen the confidence of the petitioner in much the same way that happened in Israelite prayer.

LAMENT OVER DISTRESS

While both the terms "lament" and "complaint" have been used to categorize in general the prayers of those crying for help, neither term sufficiently describes the various and numerous such prayers in Scripture. Both terms identify a dimension of these prayers, but they require a more precise use than is often the case. Some clear distinctions exist in the way in which complaint and lament are present as one moves from prose prayers embedded in narrative contexts to formal prayer psalms set for use in the sanctuary or in some form of ritual activity to overcome the threat, or as one moves from individual prayers for help to communal prayers. These distinctions have not been recognized generally in the treatments of prayers or laments and so require some brief explanation.

Within the prose prayers, there is little extended lament in the sense that Hermann Gunkel, Claus Westermann, and others have described it in the Psalms.[47] Where it is present, it is almost entirely in the form of *complaint* to or against God. The Psalms, however, are different. Complaint against God is a fairly common feature, but it may be a part of *a more extended lament* about one's plight that also describes personal undoing and/or the effects of the words and deeds of others on the one who is in trouble.[48] This dimension of personal lament or lament about others (usually enemies) is very rare in the narrative or prose prayers. To the degree that it is present, it seems to be a part of the complaint against God, or part of the petition, or one of the motivating factors urging God's help.[49] In the communal laments of the Old Testament, the complaint element, or God lament, as it is sometimes called,[50] is especially strong, which is not surprising in light of the fact that the complaint element is most prominent in prose prayers that are prayers of leaders despairing over the plight of the people or some person in the community,[51] and thus have some relation to the communal laments.

Recently, with regard to the psalm prayers, it has been proposed to distinguish between psalms of complaint, that is, those in which the God lament is prominent,[52] and psalms of plea, that is, those psalms in which there is no protest against God about one's plight, only petition in the context of praise and confidence.[53] The recognition of the significance of the complaint against God and its prominence in certain psalms, as well as its absence in others, is helpful in our understanding the nature and character of the psalmic prayers. The easy assumption that complaint against the deity is always present is seen to be invalid. Many of the psalms of plea or petition, that is, prayers for help, do not complain. They speak of God only in terms of confidence and trust. But the sharp separation of complaint psalms from all others is not satisfactory either. The complaint against God does in fact belong to the dimension of lament generally; that is, it is a part of the praying one's characterization of his or her plight. Psalms containing clear and indisputable complaint against God usually have the other dimensions of personal lament (over internal disintegration) and lament about enemies also. Furthermore, a number of psalms that might be, or are, regarded as lacking the God lament or complaint and so belonging to the category of psalms of plea have implicit or indirect signs of complaint against God, thus blurring any sharp line that one might attempt to draw between psalms of complaint and psalms of plea.

In the following analysis, we will assume that the prayer component under discussion is some characterization of the plight or situation of the one who prays, that is, lament about one's situation of distress. Because of the presence of the God lament or complaint against God in the prose prayers without other dimensions of lament, except on rare occasions, and because of the prominence of the complaint against God in some psalm prayers, we will look first at that aspect of the prayers for help[54] and then turn to examine the other dimensions of the lament (personal lament and lament about others).

Complaint against God

When one looks at the *formal* character of the complaint against God as it is present in both prose prayers and psalms, the most obvious feature is the consistent presence of *questions directed to God*.[55] All of the complaint psalms listed by Craig C. Broyles,[56] except Psalm 102, have questions addressed to God in which God's attitudes and actions toward the praying one are questioned and challenged. The same pattern is present in the prose prayer texts as well as in the poetic complaint prayers of the prophets.[57] This is true whether the prayer is that of an individual or a prayer of or for the whole community. A sample of the questions gives their flavor. First, from the prose prayers, where, because of their rootage in a context, the questions have a specificity lacking in the psalm prayers:

What will you give me for I continue childless . . . ? (Gen 15:2)

Why have you done evil to this people? (Exod 5:22)

Why did you ever send me? (Exod 5:22)

What shall I do with this people? (Exod 17:4)

Why does your wrath burn hot against your people? (Exod 32:11)

Why have you treated your servant so badly? (Num 10:11)

Shall one person sin and you become angry with the whole congregation? (Num 16:22)

Why have you brought this people indeed across the Jordan to give us to the Amorites to destroy us? (Josh 7:7-9)

If the LORD is with us, why then has all this happened to us? And where are all his wonderful deeds that our ancestors recounted to us, saying, "Did not the LORD bring us up from Egypt?" (Judg 6:13)

Am I now to die of thirst and fall into the hands of the uncircumcised? (Judg 15:18)

Why has it come to pass that today there should be one tribe lacking in Israel? (Judg 21:3)

Have you brought calamity even upon the widow with whom I am staying, by killing her son? (1 Kgs 17:20)

Is this not what I said while I was still in my own country?... [F]or I knew that you are a gracious God... (Jonah 4:2)

Exodus 14:10-12 contains a series of questions by the fleeing Israelites as they see the Egyptians advancing on them. They are addressed to Moses but are in fact a complaint to God ("In great fear the Israelites cried to the LORD") "channeled through Moses":[58]

Was it because there were no graves in Egypt that you have taken us away to die in the wilderness? What have you done to us, bringing us out of Egypt? Is this not the very thing we told you in Egypt, "Let us alone and let us serve the Egyptians"? For it would have been better for us to serve the Egyptians than to die in the wilderness.[59]

The questions of complaint are varied, but all of them are a direct challenge to the way God has acted or threatened to act—the failure to provide promised offspring to Abraham, delivering the people from slavery only to let them die at the hands of others, allowing faithful servants to be victims or bearers of evil (Moses and Elijah), a lack of compassion and forgiveness. The present circumstances of distress seem to indicate to the ones praying a terrible inconsistency on the part of God. The Lord seems to have caused or allowed things to happen in a way inappropriate to the faithfulness and compassion that are characteristic of the Lord of Israel. The fundamental query of all these complaining questions is: Why are you doing this or allowing this to happen? They are a protest, not a request for information.

In the psalm prayers, the questions of complaint, more generalized because of the more formal character of the prayer, are just as numerous:

Why do you hide your face?
Why do you forget our affliction and oppression?
(Ps 44:24; cf. 13:2; 88:14)

How long, O LORD? Will you forget me forever?
How long will you hide your face from me?
(Ps 13:1; cf. 89:46)

How long, O LORD, will you look on? (Ps 35:17)

Why do you sleep, O LORD? (Ps 44:23)

My God, my God, why have you forsaken me?
  Why are you so far from helping me, from the words of my
  groaning? (Ps 22:1)

O God, why do you cast us off forever?
  Why does your anger smoke against the sheep of your pasture?
                                                    (Ps 74:1)

How long, O God, is the foe to scoff?
  Is the enemy to revile your name forever?
    Why do you hold back your hand;
  why do you keep your hand in your bosom? (Ps 74:10-11)

Will the LORD spurn forever
  and never again be favorable?
Has his steadfast love ceased forever?
  Are his promises at an end for all time?
Has God forgotten to be gracious?
  Has he in anger shut up his compassion? (Ps 77:7-9)

The juxtaposition of the two questions "How long?" and "Why?" in
Psalm 74 reflects the centrality of those questions in the many protests
against God. They are at the very heart of the human rage against
heaven. When one is in distress and trouble, the questions that always
come roaring to the forefront of the mind and heart—and here articulated in prayer—are "*Why* is this happening?" or, to God, "*Why* are
you doing this (letting this happen, etc.)?" and the complaining query,
"*When* is this going to end?" or "*How long* do I have to endure this
suffering?" The complaint to God in these prayers thus gives voice to
the most fundamental of human questions when life is threatened and
falls apart.

Within the prophetic prayer texts, the questioning tone is readily evident. The two short prayers in Ezek 9:8 and 11:13 are nothing but
questions complaining to God:

Ah Lord GOD! will you destroy all who remain of Israel as you
pour out your wrath upon Jerusalem? (9:8)

Ah Lord GOD! will you make a full end of the remnant of Israel?
                                                    (11:13)

Jeremiah lays charges against God and queries the Lord in his laments:

Why does the way of the guilty prosper?
  Why do all who are treacherous thrive? (12:1)

Why is my pain unceasing, my wound incurable,
  refusing to be healed? (15:18)

So also do the people in their laments recorded in Jeremiah:

> Why should you be like someone confused,
>> like a mighty warrior who cannot give help? (14:9)

> Have you completely rejected Judah?
>> Does your heart loathe Zion?
> Why have you struck us down
>> so that there is no healing for us? (14:19)

Habakkuk's anguished prayers are almost nothing but complaint to God in challenging questions:

> O LORD, how long shall I cry for help,
>> and you will not listen?
> Or cry to you "Violence!"
>> and you will not save?
> Why do you make me see wrong-doing
>> and look at trouble? (Hab 1:2-3a)

> Why do you look on the treacherous,
>> and are silent when the wicked swallow
>> those more righteous than they? (Hab 2:14b)

These questions explicitly complain to and against God. But that complaint can be found implicitly in another form, that is, in *quotations* of comments others make, comments that seem to question God's involvement or concern about the plight of the one who prays. Such quotations may be followed by assertions of confidence in God on the part of the one who prays, but so also are many of the quotations cited above.[60] Psalm 3 begins:

> O LORD, how many are my foes!
>> Many are rising against me;
> many are saying to me,
>> "There is no help for you in God." (vv. 1-2)

The comment of the enemies is an implicit complaint against God as they verbalize the fear that the psalmist has in light of the affliction and oppression encountered. As in the most powerful of the complaint psalms, Psalm 22, such complaint is followed immediately by a strong expression of confidence: "But you, O LORD, are a shield around me" (Ps 3:3). Psalm 22 begins with the strongest questions and assertions about God's distance and abandonment in verses 1-2 (see above), followed immediately by the sufferer's expression of confidence: "Yet you are holy" (v. 3). Then in verse 8, the psalmist's fears and hopelessness take the form of an indirect complaint against God as she or he quotes those who mock and say:

He committed his cause to the LORD; let him deliver him,
let him rescue him, for he delights in him! (v. 8; RSV)

Such taunts suggesting God's inability or disinterest in helping a faithful
but suffering member of the community articulate the psalmist's predicament, that he or she has trusted in the Lord but to no avail in time of
trouble. That expression, however, is immediately met—in a kind of internal dialogue going on in the prayer—by a renewed statement of trust:
"Yet it was you who took me from the womb" (v. 9). Such confidence
does not last long in this prayer because the psalmist is thrust into the
pit of despair again in an extended lament about the physical and mental
disintegration of the psalmist beset and hounded—the animal metaphor
is prominent—by foes on every side (vv. 12-18). The complaint against
God then appears in an indirect sense in another form: petitions that ask
God not to be distant, hidden, not to cast off or reject (see below): "But
you, O LORD, do not be far away" (v. 19).

The same sort of movement back and forth between complaint—in
the form of both questions and quotations—and trust is found in Psalms
42–43. Near the beginning of Psalm 42, the praying one expresses the
longing for God and asks: "When shall I come and behold the face of
God?" (v. 2). Then comes the quotation:

My tears have been my food day and night,
while people say to me continually,
"Where is your God?" (v. 3)

Immediately the psalmist remembers past times of coming to the sanctuary, which serve to encourage. Later the psalmist questions God:

I say to God, my rock,
"Why have you forgotten me?
Why must I walk about mournfully
because the enemy oppresses me?" (v. 9)

Then comes again the quotation of the enemies' taunts:

As with a deadly wound in my body, my adversaries taunt me,
while they say to me continually,
"Where is your God?" (v. 10)

Psalm 10 begins with strong questions of complaint against God:

Why, O LORD, do you stand far off?
Why do you hide yourself in times of trouble? (v. 1)

Four times in the rest of the psalm, the adversaries of the psalmist are
quoted as saying things that clearly suggest God's noninvolvement or
indifference to the plight of the one who prays:

In the pride of their[61] countenance the wicked say,
  "God will not seek it out";[62]
All their thoughts are, "There is no God." (v. 4)

They think in their heart, "We shall not be moved;
  throughout all generations we shall not meet adversity." (v. 6)

They think in their heart, "God has forgotten,
  he has hidden his face, he will never see it."[63] (v. 11)

Why do the wicked renounce God,
  and say in their hearts,
"You will not call us to account"? (v. 13)

The quotations again give voice to the complaint of the psalmist, which is spoken directly in the questions at the beginning of the psalm. Similar such quotations of the wicked's assumption of God's indifference or inability to perceive the trouble of the praying one and deliver are found in other psalms.[64] In Psalms 59 and 64, the quotations are followed by assertions of confidence, but not in Psalm 73, although they are there elsewhere in the psalm. Psalm 94 not only quotes the challenge of the wicked, but begins with the complaining questions of the psalmist:

O LORD, how long shall the wicked,
  how long shall the wicked exult? (v. 3)[65]

Psalm 31:22 quotes the psalmist's own complaint before asserting that the complaint was heard:

I had said in my alarm,
  "I am driven far from your sight."
But you heard my supplications,
  when I cried out to you for help.

Jeremiah quotes the people as saying, "He is blind to our ways" (12:4).

The complaint against God also takes other forms in assertions or petitions that refer either to God's hiding the face, forgetting, abandoning, being far off, rejecting, and casting off[66] or to the praying one being shamed, taunted, reproached, and mocked, acts that also are directed against God. They are present in the obvious God laments or complaints, such as:

Do not forget the oppressed. (Ps 10:12; cf. Ps 74:19, 22)

Do not be far from me. (Ps 22:11; cf. v. 19a)

You have seen, O LORD; do not be silent!
  O LORD, do not be far from me! (Ps 35:22)

> Yet you have rejected and abased us,
>> and have not gone out with our armies. (Ps 44:9; cf. vv. 10-12)

> O God, you have rejected us,
>> broken our defenses. (Ps 60:1)

> [I am] like those whom you remember no more,
>> for they are cut off from your hand. (Ps 88:5)

Psalm 88 follows up the questions complaining to God (v. 14) with even stronger assertions of God's wrath and hostility doing in the psalmist:

> Wretched and close to death from my youth up,
>> I suffer your terrors; I am desperate.[67]
> Your wrath has swept over me;
>> your dread assaults destroy me.
> They surround me like a flood all day long;
>> from all sides they close in on me.
> You have caused friend and neighbor to shun me;
>> my companions are in darkness. (vv. 15-18)

The community prayer for help in Jer 14:19-22 begins in questions that lead into assertions of complaint:

> Have you completely rejected Judah?
>> Does your heart loathe Zion?
> Why have you struck us down
>> so that there is no healing for us?
> We look for peace, but find no good;
>> for a time of healing, but there is terror instead.

And Jeremiah's own complaining question, "Why is my pain unceasing...?" is followed up by the straightforward accusation, "Truly you are to me like a deceitful brook" (Jer 15:18; cf. 4:10).[68]

But one hears such sentiments in other cries for help where the explicit questioning of God is not present:

> Do not forsake me, O LORD;
>> O my God, do not be far from me. (Ps 38:21)

> Do not hide yourself from my supplication. (Ps 55:1)

> Do not hide your face from your servant. (Ps 69:17)

> Do not cast me off in the time of old age;
>> do not forsake me when my strength is spent.
>>> (Ps 71:9; cf. vv. 12, 18)

> Do not hide your face from me. (143:7)

In Psalm 27, which begins with a song of trust, the lament that follows includes a sequence of four petitions expressing the fear that the psalmist has been rejected by God:

> Do not hide your face from me.
> Do not turn your servant away in anger....
> Do not cast me off, do not forsake me. (v. 9)

The assertions that God has "forgotten" or "cast me off" and the like are characteristic of the explicit complaint psalms where questions challenge God and often in these terms. But the petitions asking God not to do or let such things happen, which are present more widely in prayers for help, are also an implicit articulation of the fear and complaint that God has turned away from or cast off the one who is in trouble and yet trusts in God. The challenge is not as sharp in the petitions as it is in the questions, but the questions are often followed by just such petitions. Where the latter occur by themselves, one may assume that there is some sense of rejection, an alienation from God that is lifted up in prayer with some urgency that God might turn toward and be near as God has been in the past.

The expressions of shame, the humiliation of taunts and mockery, are another facet of the complaint against God. They appear less in the form of questions, but they are clearly present in the God laments. Jeremiah puts his shame in the form of a question:

> Why did I come forth from the womb
> to see toil and sorrow,
> and spend my days in shame? (Jer 20:18)

In Ps 39:8, the praying one says: "Do not make me the scorn of the fool." This is immediately followed by the statement:

> I am silent; I do not open my mouth,
> for it is you who have done it.
> Remove your stroke from me;
> I am worn down by the blows of your hand. (vv. 9-10)

It is precisely because of what God has done that the psalmist fears the scorn (*ḥerpâ*) of the fool. Psalm 22 shows the shame and humiliation of the sufferer. The movement of the psalm makes it clear how that sense of shame is an implicit complaint to God. The explicit complaint, in the form of questions about why God has forsaken, is distant and absent, comprises the first segment of the psalm. The psalmist then rises from the pit of despair in an expression of trust as he or she recalls how "our ancestors" trusted—the verb appears three times in two verses—and "*were not put to shame*." But it is just that recollection that sends the psalmist back into despair:

> But I am a worm, and not human;
> scorned by others, and despised by the people. (v. 6)

The one who cries out here goes on to quote the mockery of others, implicitly but clearly suggesting, in effect, that "my fathers and mothers trusted and were not ashamed, but *I* am terribly ashamed because you are far off and do not answer."

Such shame at the taunts of others is clearly set at God's doorstep in Psalm 44, a community prayer:

> You have made us a taunt [*ḥerpâ*] of our neighbors,
> the derision and scorn of those around us.
> You have made us a byword among the nations,
> a laughingstock among the peoples.
> All day long my disgrace is before me,
> and shame has covered my face
> at the words of the taunters [*mēḥārēp*] and revilers,
> at the sight of the enemy and the avenger. (vv. 13-16)

Such experience of shame because of the torment and taunts of others is found in other prayers where the God lament is less directly present but implicit in the voicing of this shame, for example, Psalm 69:

> It is for your sake that I have borne reproach [*ḥerpâ*],
> that shame has covered my face. (v. 7)

> The insults [*ḥerpôt*] of those who insult you [*ḥôrĕpeykā*]
> have fallen on me. (v. 9b)

> When I humbled my soul with fasting,
> they insulted [*laḥărāpôt*] me for doing so. (v. 10)

> You know the insults [*ḥerpātî*] I receive
> and my shame and dishonor;
> my foes are all known to you.
> Insults [*ḥerpâ*] have broken my heart,
> so that I am in despair. (vv. 19-20)

The community prayers for help, where the complaint against God is especially prominent, manifest a strong sense of shame as a part of that complaint and, like Psalm 44, see the mockery and shame directed both at God as well as at the people.[69]

The experience of being taunted and the shaming that comes from it are seen to be in some sense challenges or complaints to God not only because, as in several cases above, the taunts received by the psalmist are explicitly said to be directed toward God but also because the shame of the faithful sufferer suggests God's indifference or powerlessness in the situation. The one who prays complains that the reproach of God has fallen upon him or her (Ps 69:9). The character of the taunt as a challenge to God by the mockers that becomes an implicit complaint by the praying one is further clarified with the realization that the term *ḥerpâ*, "reproach," "taunt," "insult," and its related verbal forms regularly refer to a challenge of the power of the one being taunted or of his or her god. The characteristic form of the insult is, "Where is your God?"[70]

Thus, in sharp questions to the deity, beleaguered statements about the Lord's undoing of the sufferer, quotations of those who mock the one praying because of his or her trust in God, and urgent petitions asking God not to hide or reject or be far off, the prayers that cry out for help frequently complain to God about God's indifference or active hostility to the sufferer. The sense of abandonment and rejection by God and the sense of shame at being exposed to the taunts of others are the primary feelings set forth in these complaints.[71] The justice of God and the power of God are both at risk according to these complaints. God's way is not just in that the righteous are wrongly or unduly punished and the wicked thrive, or God's willingness and ability to help the suffering ones, those in distress, is not demonstrated in the world.

Personal Lament

As noted earlier, the lament about one's personal condition is not a significant part of the prose prayers for help. Personal discomfort in those contexts is alluded to only briefly inasmuch as the lament dimension of prayer is generally not extensive and is apparent most clearly in the questions of complaint. It is suggested in Hagar's weeping and her plea, "Do not let me look on the death of the child" (Gen 21:16; see chap. 6, below), as well as in Jacob's words, "I am afraid," as he prays for God's deliverance from the hand of Esau (Gen 32:11). Moses complains to God on one occasion that the people are about to stone him (Exod 17:4) and on another occasion speaks of his "misery" (*rā'ātî*) because he is overburdened with the responsibility of leadership (Num 11:10-15). Gideon points to the people's experience of fear when he complains because "all this has happened to us" (Judg 6:13). The fear of death is there in the petition of the sailors on Jonah's boat: "Do not let us perish on account of this man's life" (Jonah 1:14). The most explicit expressions of personal distress are in Samson's words: "Am I now to die of thirst...?" (Judg 15:18) and Baruch's lament: "I am weary with my groaning and find no rest" (Jer 45:3), an expression of lament over the self similar to those of the psalm prayers.[72]

In all of these cases, one encounters the fear of death or personal anguish and suffering over the circumstances in which the petitioner is caught. But it is in the psalm prayers that this dimension is elaborated at greater length and often with the vivid imagery that comes in poetic speech. The prayer for help could always include some lifting up of the personal distress. The form of that prayer that is present in the lament psalms provides a vehicle for a more elaborated and explicit openness of the self and its disintegration to God.

While the poetic form of these prayers means that we may not view their depictions simply literally, they are, for that very reason, vivid presentations of internal, physical, mental, and spiritual anguish. Tears and weeping often accompany these prayers.[73] Loneliness and alienation or estrangement from others may be the experience of the one praying as well as terrible weariness.[74] This may involve either physical weariness or emotional exhaustion.[75] Frequent expressions of physical dissolution and disintegration reflect the I-lament of the psalmist.[76] The language of sickness[77] is naturally prominent and may be recognized as reflecting the facts that these prayers are offered in times of sickness and that the language and imagery of sickness and healing are a rich resource for depicting distress and relief of various sorts. Indeed we speak of sicknesses of the body, mind, and spirit and understand the category of illness in the broadest sense possible. No less was that the case with those who prayed these prayers of Scripture.

The strong sense that death is imminent is closely tied to the language and imagery of sickness (Ps 6:2-5). Psalm 88 sets forth this predicament at length:

> My life draws near to Sheol.
> I am counted among those who go down to the Pit;
>   I am like those who have no help,
> like those forsaken among the dead,
>   like the slain that lie in the grave,
> like those whom you remember no more,
>   for they are cut off from your hand.
> You have put me in the depths of the Pit,
>   in the regions dark and deep. (Ps 88:3b-6)

Not infrequently, as here, the experience of imminent death is seen as a result of God's activity,[78] but it also may be due to the hostile acts of an enemy or enemies.[79] The experience of personal distress that threatens to do in the sufferer is conveyed powerfully by the imagery of flood or overwhelming waters, especially in Psalms 42, 69, and 88.[80] This sense of drowning and being overcome by deep or raging waters may be attributed to God's doing, as in Ps 42:7 and Psalm 88, or it may be the effect of others. Psalm 69 pictures the praying one as in a deep pit or cistern with waters up to the neck and about to drown. In Psalms 42 and 88, the waves of God's anger or judgment roll over the psalmist. While the particular situation that may elicit any one of these prayers can be different, the imagery is a powerful expression of the personal sense of drowning under the weight of burdens and stresses beyond one's control. It is a universal image for the sense of distress that is too much to handle and under which one sinks as if to rise no more. The plea to God may be couched in that same language, asking God to extricate the sufferer from the pit and to rescue from drowning.

One of the ways in which the individual or the community experiences distress is in a sense of shame that comes upon them, especially in the face of the taunts and mockery of others. This has already been identified as a significant part of the God lament or complaint in the psalmic prayers, but it is experienced as a personal humiliation and so testified to again and again in the Psalms. Embarrassment and shame because of the situation in which one finds oneself, whether sickness, false accusations, or the hostilities of others, or because of the explicit taunts of others, are a constant feature of these prayers.

While it is not a prominent feature of the prayers for help, there are several instances in which the personal distress of the one who prays is seen to be the burden of sin or the experience of God's wrath evoked by sinful deeds. Those psalms known in the tradition of the church as the Penitential Psalms[81] particularly show the psalmist praying to God beset with a sense of sin, but in other prayers also one encounters a confessional dimension.[82] These prayers will be looked at more closely in chapter 7.

Lament about Enemies and Others

The third dimension of the lament, already touched upon above, is the lament over the hostility, oppression, and affliction directed toward the praying one by others. This element of voiced affliction is not always present in the prose prayers, but where it is, the "third party" is usually identified, and the context makes clear the way in which that party has contributed to the distress.

For Jacob, the source of his distress is his brother, Esau, who, he fears, will kill his whole family in revenge for Jacob's earlier acts. Moses, complaining to God over the complaints of the people, laments, "They are almost ready to stone me" (Exod 17:4). Samson, fearing death, laments that he may "fall into the hands of the uncircumcised," that is, his archenemies, the Philistines, who are also present in the motivation for his final prayer at the end of his life (Judg 16:28). Gideon's complaint ends in the fear that because God has cast the people off, they will fall now into the hands of the Midianites (Judg 6:13), a lament comparable to that of Joshua, who fears that "the Canaanites will hear ... and surround us and cut off our name from the earth" (Josh 7:9), as well as Jehoshaphat's lament over the threat of Ammon, Moab, and Edom, "who are coming to drive us out ... " (2 Chr 20:11). The prayer of the people rebuilding the walls of Jerusalem in the face of the mockery of Sanballat and Tobiah laments their activity in language that echoes the laments of the psalm prayers: "For they have hurled insults in the face of the builders" (Neh 4:5). Taunts and insults, we have seen, are primary manifestations of the distress created by enemies. The threat of death at the hands of others, even those within the community (e.g., a brother, the people), evokes as well the lament of prayer.

In the psalm prayers, the external threats are often characterized as "enemies," and frequently "the wicked," "evildoers," "those who hate me," "workers of evil," and the like.[83] Rare is the prayer in the Psalms and Prophets that does not mention some external group or person as contributing significantly to the distress of the one praying. If the complaint against God and the lament over the self make us aware of the way in which these prayers identify the human situation in theological, spiritual, and psychological or psychophysical terms, the lament about the enemies, which is the most pervasive of all, identifies the problem prayer lifts up as very much a *social* one. Not all the prayers for help in Scripture arise out of the experience of oppression and hurt by others, as one can see from the prose texts, but the stories of Scripture and the prayers of the Psalms inform us of this experience as a primary impetus for much of the praying that is recorded in the Bible.

The enemies and evildoers and their actions are depicted in vivid language and with various images. Psalm 22 portrays the enemies of the psalmist as animals who have surrounded the psalmist "like a ravening and roaring lion." Both the imagery of the enemies as wild animals threatening the praying one and the sense of being surrounded and hemmed in are regular features of the prayer language of these cries for help.[84] It is not surprising, therefore, that one of the things that is desired or for which one gives thanks is that God provides space and elbow room for the psalmist.[85] In a similar fashion, the one in distress will lament that he or she is caught in a net by the enemies or has fallen into their pit or trap.[86] The particular nature of the persecution by others is not easy to tell. The metaphorical and open character of the language inhibits determining a single mode of oppression. But one notes that often the persecution is an act of the tongue, or speaking. Slander, lying, accusations, and insults are modes of attack on the afflicted one,[87] and the one who prays feels them as violence:

> False witnesses have risen against me,
> and they are breathing out violence. (Ps 27:12)

Secret plots and schemes of various sorts threaten the one who prays.[88] Deceit and treachery are characteristic of the attacks on the afflicted.

It is as difficult to discern the specific character of the attacks of the enemies as it is to figure out what personal and physical maladies may be reflected in the lament over the self. Certainly, one may assume that at times there were false accusations in the courts or that economic injustice was practiced by deceit and conspiracy. But the poetic form of these prayers for help leaves them open for various particular circumstances to be brought to God in their words. Some clues to possible experiences of persecution and external threats may be gleaned from two sources. One of these is the superscriptions at the beginning of the psalmic prayers. While they may not be read to identify the precise situation in which the prayer was first composed, they indicate how the community of faith and those responsible for the transmission of these prayers associated them with varying human predicaments, primarily in the life of David. His story, therefore, is given in these prayers as exemplary of human life. The elusive and open language of the prayers gains a specificity in reference to the life of David, and David's life is given a universality of reference as various prayers are associated with particular distresses that he underwent.

The foes who "are rising against me" in Psalm 3 are seen to be the forces who supported Absalom and made David flee from Jerusalem for his life and his throne. Likewise, 1 Samuel 15 reports a growing conspiracy against David and the increase of strength of Absalom's support until David receives the word that the hearts of the Israelites have gone after Absalom. At that point, he tells all his officials that they must flee or there will be no escape and disaster will come upon them. In such circumstances of political intrigue, conspiracy, and threat, Psalm 3 is seen as the prayer David would have prayed. The theme of the "many" set against the praying one is appropriate to David's flight from Absalom.

Psalm 18 is a song of thanksgiving rather than a prayer for help. But it alludes to the previous prayer for help (v. 6), and the superscription sees this as a prayer of thanksgiving by David when delivered from Saul and from all his enemies. The prayer is thus broadened to encompass any such event in David's life. Two psalms are associated with David's efforts to hide from Saul's threats to kill him (Psalms 52 and 54). It is not surprising to hear in one of them that "the ruthless seek my life" (Ps 54:3). In this instance, the fear is a literal one and the prayer a cry for help in face of the possibility of capture and death. When Psalm 59 is said to be a prayer "when Saul ordered his [David's] house to be watched in order to kill him," the consonance of the prayer with the circumstances is made clear by the words of the prayer:

> Even now they lie in wait for my life;
> the mighty stir up strife against me. (v. 3)

Some of the prose prayers also speak of enemies that threaten the king and the army, though in those prayers the enemies are specifically identified and not spoken of in generalities or with the rhetoric of lament that is so common to the prayers of the Psalms (2 Kgs 19:14-19; 1 Chr 20:5-12).

One must not assume, however, that all such prayers belong only to the persecutions and afflictions of military leaders, kings, and armies. Other stories and contexts suggest the way in which the language of lament fits different personal and individual circumstances. Jeremiah provides a good example. In his prayers to God, he laments about those who devise schemes against him and would "cut him off from the land of the living" (Jer 11:19). The narrative material around these prayers shows that such schemes and threats to his life were real. Indeed the members of his own family "seek his life" (Jer 11:21). The leaders of the community plot against him to throw him in jail or kill him. He is taunted by members of the community: "Where is the word of the LORD? Let it come!" (Jer 17:15). This is similar to the taunt found in the psalm prayers and elsewhere: "Where is your God?"[89] But the form of the taunt in Jeremiah's prayer is appropriate to his particular context where the issue of true and false prophecy and the credibility of the prophetic word is very much to the fore. His reference to the enemies digging a pit for his life is in this instance not simply metaphorical as it may be in some of the psalm prayers. On one of the worst occasions of his particular persecution, Zedekiah has him put in a dungeon and from there lowered into a cistern where he sinks into the mire (Jeremiah 37–38). Jeremiah's complaints about his loneliness reflect his true isolation in the community, from family and friends. His complaint against God as one who has deceived him and on whose account he has suffered insult (Jer 15:15-18) is an authentic reflection of his predicament as one who has been isolated and taunted and threatened because of his following the divine call and proclaiming the divine word.

The narratives of the historical books manifest resonances with these prayers of the Psalms and suggest various kinds of situations of distress and affliction. Not all of them are literally life-threatening as seems to be the case often in the Psalms and in Jeremiah's experience. In 1 Samuel 25, while David is out in the wilderness, he seeks food for his young men from a man named Nabal (lit. "fool"). The response is an insulting refusal. When later in the story Nabal has died, David praises God for judging the case of "Nabal's insult [*ḥerpâ*] to me" (1 Sam 25:39). One hears echoes of the Psalms:

> Rise up, O God, plead your cause;
>   Remember your insult [*ḥerpâ*] from a fool [*nābāl*]. (Ps 74:22)

> Do not make me the scorn [*ḥerpâ*] of a fool [*nābāl*]. (Ps 39:8)

The enemy here is not a hostile political force or those plotting against David's life. It is one who has refused hospitality and mocked David.

The injustice and "evil-doing" (1 Sam 25:39) are recognized and so described by both Nabal's workmen and his wife Abigail, who pointedly notes that Nabal's name equates him with the "fool," that is, the one against whom the lamenting prayers cry out, the fool who is also the wicked (see Psalm 14).

A quite different situation of wicked foolishness and insult in the midst of oppression is found in the words of David's daughter Tamar when her half-brother Amnon begs her to sleep with him. She answers him: "No, my brother, do not force me; for such a thing is not done in Israel; do not do this folly [*nĕbālâ*]. As for me, where could I carry my shame [or 'insult' = *ḥerpâ*]? And as for you, you would be one of the fools [*nābāl*] in Israel" (2 Sam 13:12-13). Amnon's response is to rape her and then to treat her with loathing. She goes away, ashes on her head, tearing her robe, and crying. The last word we hear of her is that she "remained a desolate woman in her brother Absalom's house" (2 Sam 13:20). Here, therefore, we encounter a terrible story of the oppression by the wicked = fool and its consequences of personal distress and suffering, one that would fit not only the psalms mentioned above (14, 39, and 74) but many of the laments that speak of the enemy rising up against the sufferer, of taunts, insults, and violence, of personal disintegration and distress. One may imagine without much fear of contradiction that such prayers for help as one finds in these psalms were on the lips of Tamar in the midst of her suffering.

The story of Hannah in 1 Samuel 1 is yet another instance of the circumstances in which lament in prayer to God comes forth. The complaint against God, the lament over personal distress, and the affliction of personal enemies are all present explicitly or implicitly in the story. Her prayer in the sanctuary is not directly given except for the vow at the end. But the narrative uncovers God's involvement in her distress when it twice reports that "the LORD had closed her womb" (1 Sam 1:5-6). The story assumes that the distress has to do with God. It is felt in the personal experience of barrenness and the concomitant weeping, depression, and refusal to eat. In this narrative, we encounter quite directly one of God's suffering ones who cries out for help in prayer, knowing the affliction of God's hand and psychological, mental, and physical suffering. She also is persecuted by her enemies. Here they are not the violent perpetrators of rape, economic injustice, and death. Hannah's enemies are present in a rival (i.e., adversary) wife, Peninnah, who is blessed with children and vexes and taunts Hannah because she has none. But the narrative lets the reader know that her suffering is theological, personal, and social. One may assume that a prayer such as Psalm 6, or one of the other individual prayers for help, would be appropriate on the lips of Hannah in her deep distress.[90]

The narrative superscriptions of the Psalms provide a kind of hermeneutical and literary bridge for suggesting a consonance between the psalm prayers and such occasions and figures as mentioned above. In doing so, however, one must remember that the actuality of praying in any such case may have been quite different, at least vis-à-vis the lament part of the prayers. For as we have noticed in the many prayers for help that appear in the narrative texts and on the lips of such figures as those mentioned above, the element of lament is less regularly a feature than the other component parts of the prayer for help. Where it does appear, it is present most often in complaint against or toward God (see above). This difference may represent, as Claus Westermann has suggested, different stages in the history of prayer: an early stage in which appeals to God were brief prayers arising directly from a situation and reported in the narrative account; a second stage represented by the Psalms, which involved collecting together in worship many elements of prayer from such occasions as the narratives report into prayers for use by the community in worship;[91] and a third stage represented by the long prose prayers such as 1 Kings 8, Ezra 8, and Nehemiah 9, which are clearly literary constructions although they may have had some place in liturgy or prayer.[92] It is important in this connection, however, to keep in mind Westermann's claim that "the middle stage...represented by the psalms...is closely connected with the first stage."[93] This is less a sharp historical difference than it is a difference in function and setting. In that sense, one may connect with the distinction that Moshe Greenberg makes between the "unmediated, direct forms of popular piety" present in the prose prayers (Westermann's first stage) and the "mediated" and "refined" piety of the populace present in the Psalms (Westermann's second stage).[94] The refinement that takes place tends to lift up lament over the self and enemies and assertions of trust in the elaboration and elongation of the prayer form. Address, complaint, petition, and motivation are thoroughly a form of these prayers for help in every form and context.

PETITION

At the heart of the prayer for help in the Bible is the petition, the specific or general plea for God to help. There are some prayers where the petition is in effect replaced by a complaint, but even there the petition is often implicit in the complaint. The frequent designation of the psalmic prayers for help as "lament" or "complaint" tends to create a sense that the primary function of the prayer is to complain or lament. In all the prayers under study in this chapter, however, the fundamental aim is to seek help from God. So the petition or plea is where one discerns the basic intention of the prayer for help. All of the language of complaint or lament serves to ground the petition and, like the more explicit motivation sentences (see below), to encourage and justify, from the angle of the one praying, the intervention of God as a necessary and appropriate step to overcome the suffering or distress. Within those prayers set in narrative texts and in relation to particular events, the petition is quite specific and directed toward the identifiable source of distress. Within the psalmic prayers, loosed from a particular occasion and created for the community at worship or some other occasion of presenting one's situation to God to receive deliverance or healing, the petition is quite general and stereotyped around the various ways of entreating God's help, deliverance, or healing. We shall look at the petitions in both of these contexts.[95] In all of this discussion we are, in effect, asking the question: For what did the needy and afflicted of the Old Testament—or their representatives—pray? What did people in trouble seek from God in prayer?[96]

Petitions in Narrative Prayers

Hear. In three of the prose prayers, the specific petitions addressing the need of the ones praying are preceded by the general petition to hear or heed the prayer. This is at the heart of the long Deuteronomistic prayer of Solomon at the dedication of the temple (1 Kings 8). The general plea in verses 27-30 makes this petition in several different ways. The particular circumstances and petitions that follow are all manifestations of God's willingness to hear when the people pray toward the temple. Hezekiah's prayer to God in the face of the Assyrian threat begins with a petition to "incline your ear ... and hear," to "open your eyes ... and see" (2 Kgs 19:16), and then moves to the particular need, "save us" (v. 19). So also Nehemiah begins his prayer in Neh 4:4-5 with the plea, "Hear," and then turns to the specific petitions directed against his foes. The narrative prayer, therefore, suggests that the prayer for help may begin with the plea that God will turn toward the petitioner, will pay attention to the plight and the plea. There is an implicit assumption that God's attention means God's help. To catch God's ear and eye—to use one of the Bible's anthropomorphic phrases—is to be able to expect God's help.[97] The stories of Scripture confirm that. When the outcry of the victims of Sodom comes up to God, the Lord responds: "I must go down and *see* whether they have done altogether according to the outcry that has come to me" (Gen 18:21). God confronts Cain because "your brother's blood is crying out to me from the ground" (Gen 4:10). When the Israelites' "cry for help rose up to God" from Egyptian slavery (Exod 2:23), God says to Moses: "I have seen the affliction of my people who are in Egypt, and I have heard their cry on account of their taskmasters" and then goes on to say, "and I have come down to deliver them" (Exod 3:7—my trans.; cf. Exod 2:24-25). This occasion, which functions as a kind of paradigm of God's response to the cry for help of God's people, is reflected precisely in the prayer of Hezekiah above when he asks God to hear the prayer and save them from the Assyrians. We see it again and again in the prayers for help of the Psalms (see below), as well as in one of Jeremiah's laments where the prophet asks God to listen not only to him but also to what his adversaries say, that is, to their plots against him that have been quoted in the immediately preceding verse (Jer 18:18-19).

Release by death. While not a common petition in the narrative prayers, there are a few instances where the afflicted one asks God, in effect, to put the petitioner out of the misery of present circumstances by death. So Moses twice makes such a plea. Once in a case of the people's sin, Moses asks God to "blot me out of the book" (Exod 32:32). In another instance, when burdened by the heavy duties of leading the people, he says: "Put me to death at once—if I have found favor in your sight—and do not let me see my misery" (Num 11:15). A petition similar to that last part is uttered also by a weeping Hagar over a dying Ishmael: "Do not let me look on the death of the child" (Gen 21:16). In each of these instances, the present situation is so bad that the praying one would rather not continue in life this way. That is explicit in the case of Moses and implicit in Hagar's prayer.[98]

The latter, however, is somewhat cryptic in this regard, and the former prayers contain other elements of the petition that indicate the one pleading really seeks deliverance and not death. Moses' complaint about the burden of the people asks for death only "if this is the way you [i.e., God] are going to treat me." It is clear that what he wants is some relief from the burden, and he receives it.[99] In the case of his intercession over the sin of the people, his plea to be blotted out is qualified first by asking for God's forgiveness, and only if that is not forthcoming does he ask for death. One may assume that in Hagar's case also, the petition is as much a plea for deliverance of the child from death as it is a plea to die that she may not see her child die. The plea for release from suffering by death is not, therefore, what the afflicted in fact seek. It is only a last resort if God will not provide the deliverance from trouble that is really sought.

There are two exceptions to the above conclusion. One is Elijah's prayer at Horeb to "take away my life" (1 Kgs 19:4). The prayer is succinct and unqualified. "He asked that he might die" (v. 4a). Elijah is afraid and has fled for his life from Jezebel. In his explanation to God, he twice speaks in a way that anticipates the language of the psalmic prayers about the enemies: "They are seeking my life, to take it away"

(vv. 10, 14).[100] What is implicit but clearly apparent in this instance is that the petition is not regarded by God although Elijah's fear is. He is nourished with food and not allowed to starve to death. He is challenged by God ("What are you doing here, Elijah?") and ultimately sent back into the fray. While the petition is a genuine one out of a clear case of persecution and fear for his life, it is also seen as an unacceptable way out of the prophetic task. Like Jeremiah, Elijah is required to continue the work for which he was sent as a prophet.

The same analysis is even more appropriate to Jonah's plea at the end of his mission to Nineveh: "And now, O LORD, please take my life from me, for it is better for me to die than to live" (Jonah 4:3). Twice the Lord challenges his anger that takes form in depression and self-pity. The petition is not authentic. Jonah's prayer is not as genuine as that of the Gentile sailors. It is not affliction and suffering that evoke this petition, but anger at mercy and deliverance. Rather than listening to the petition, the Lord challenges its very grounds.

Heal. The shortest and simplest of all the prayers is Moses' outcry to God to heal Miriam's leprosy: "O God, please heal her" (Num 12:13). In the Hebrew, the sentence is marked by particles of urgency as much as by the content of the petition. The illness is real and the only petition that matters is healing. Elijah also "cries out" to God for healing for the son of the widow with whom he is staying. The situation is clearly one of sickness, but in this instance it is also the kind of near-death experience that one often sees articulated in the Psalms. The prayer for healing is a prayer to revive the dying child. When Hezekiah is sick and near death, his plea is that God will remember how he has been faithful, but the response of God explicitly promises healing for Hezekiah (2 Kgs 20:3 || Isa 38:3). It is worth noting that whereas some of the prayers of the Psalms that use the language of sickness may have a broader possibility for use than simply occasions of illness, here is a prose prayer arising explicitly out of the king's illness that makes no direct reference to that illness in the petition. In this respect, the prose prayer is not unlike some of the psalmic prayers for help in that the particular situation of affliction that evokes the prayer is not identified in the prayer itself. One notes, further, that there is nothing in the prayer to identify the petitioner as a king, suggesting the possibility that other prayers for which no context is given may be the prayer of a faithful king seeking God's help in varying situations of distress.

In a somewhat reverse sort of way, Jeremiah, in one of his lament prayers, prays to God to "heal me . . . and I shall be healed" (Jer 17:14); here the circumstances, as well as they can be reconstructed from the biographical notations concerning Jeremiah's life, do not suggest that actual sickness was his plight. Indeed the following line, which entreats "save me, and I shall be saved," suggests a broader situation, as do the rest of the lines of this lament. The use of the healing petition may suggest that Jeremiah's laments are not to be connected specifically with his life, but are stereotyped examples of prayers for help, like the lament psalms. It indicates as well what one may infer from those same psalms, that the healing language and imagery may be associated with all sorts of predicaments and not only with situations of literal illness.

A somewhat unusual brief prayer of Hezekiah recorded in Chronicles should be mentioned in this context. It is a prayer for pardon of those people who have come to partake of the Passover even though not being cleansed (2 Chr 30:18-20). The divine response in this instance is simply: "The LORD heard Hezekiah and healed the people." Here, therefore, is a narrative prayer in which, like some of the psalms, healing can be a way of understanding what God does in response to the prayer for pardon. The connection between forgiveness and healing is apparent, as it is elsewhere in the prayers of the Psalms.

Forgive. Most of the prayers for forgiveness are intercessory and are examined in more detail in chapter 8. These are not individual prayers for forgiveness as we seem to find in the Psalms. They are the petitions of one of the leaders or representative figures—Abraham, Moses, Solomon, Amos. Their primary intent is to divert the divine anger at the sin of the people, as, for example, Abraham does for Sodom and Gomorrah, Moses for the sinful community in the wilderness, Amos for the sins of the Northern Kingdom. The prayer may simply ask for forgiveness, as Moses does in Exod 32:31-32. More often some sort of case is made to justify the change of God's mind. Indeed, particularly in these prayers, one sees explicit indication that the plea is designed to have an effect on God. The petition of Moses in Exod 32:11-13 asks that God will turn from the divine wrath and "repent," that is, exercise a change of mind, and the response to the prayer indicates that is exactly what happened.

In such instances, the motivation clauses (see below) are a prominent ingredient. Abraham appeals to the justice and righteousness of God: "Will you indeed sweep away the righteous with the wicked? . . . Shall not the Judge of all the earth do what is just?" (Gen 18:23, 25). Moses does the same when—at Korah's rebellion—he asks if God is going to punish the whole congregation because of the sin of one man (Num 16:22). But Moses also appeals to the promises to the ancestors (Exod 32:11-13; Deut 9:25-29) as well as to the character and consistency of the divine action (Num 14:13-19). Amos seeks God's forgiveness on the grounds of the smallness (and thus weakness) of Israel. In most of these cases, therefore, the motivation clauses provide an implicit petition accompanying the prayer for forgiveness or the removal of divine wrath. In some instances, the prayer implicitly asks for the justice of God in behalf of the innocent or righteous (Genesis 18; Numbers 16). In other cases, the leader asks God to keep the promises God has made (Exodus 32; Deuteronomy 9). And in Amos's prayer, he asks, implicitly, for God's protection of the weak and helpless, the "small" (Amos 7:2). Only once is the mercy of God an implicit object of the petition (Numbers 14).

The extended Deuteronomistic prayer placed on the lips of Solomon in 1 Kings 8 places God's forgiveness at the heart of the petitions that are uttered there. It assumes that the fundamental problem of the future, manifest in various ways, will be the sin of the people. In the opening general petition, even when a specific circumstance or need has not been identified, Solomon asks that God would hear in heaven and forgive (v. 30). Then, in several particular circumstances, the petition that may be directed toward the particular circumstance, for example, bringing the people back into the land (v. 34), granting them rain in time of drought (v. 36), or granting them compassion in the sight of their captors (v. 50), is accompanied by a prior petition that God would forgive the people their sin. The communal distress and affliction are understood to be consequences of the sin of the people.

Deliver/save/help. The petition for God's deliverance comes in varying circumstances. It is Jacob's plea when he is afraid of his brother Esau: "Deliver me from the hand of my brother" (Gen 32:11), and it is Moses' implicit petition when he complains to God that "you have done nothing at all to deliver your people" (Exod 5:23). In the Deuteronomistic confessional prayer of Judg 10:10, 15, the people cry out to God to "deliver us today." Hezekiah, in the face of the Assyrian threat, prays: "So now, O LORD our God, save us, I pray you, from his hand" (2 Kgs 19:19). The same king's petition to God to "remember" in the face of his sickness and imminent death is answered by an oracle of salvation in which God promises that "I will deliver you and this city out of the hand of the king of Assyria" (2 Kgs 20:6). Jeremiah follows up his plea to "heal me" with the petition "save me," contextually to be understood as a plea for God's deliverance from the threats against him by his enemies (Jer 17:14).

There is one prayer petition seeking God's "help" (2 Chr 14:11). Facing the Ethiopian army, King Asa prays: "Help us, O LORD our God." This single example of a quoted prayer explicitly for "help" in the narrative prayers is deceptive if it suggests that the pleas of the prayers are for something other than God's "help." Not only are the prayers for salvation and deliverance another form of the prayer for "help," but the psalmic prayers include frequent petitions for help, and the narratives and other texts contain instances of persons or communities who "cry" to God and receive "help":

And when they received *help* against them, the Hagrites and all who were with them were given into their hands, for they *cried* to God in the battle, and he granted their *entreaty* because they trusted in him. (1 Chr 5:20)

And Jehoshaphat *cried* out, and the LORD *helped* him.
(2 Chr 18:31)

> Because I delivered the poor who *cried,*
> and the orphan who had no *helper.* (Job 29:12)

Judge. Not surprisingly, in light of the above petitions for deliverance or help on the part of kings as they faced opposing armies, other such occasions elicited similar petitions in other language.[101] So Jehoshaphat asks God to "judge" or "execute judgment" (so the NRSV) against the Moabites, Ammonites, and Edomites arrayed against the Judaean army (2 Chr 20:12). The call for God to act as judge, which may be a plea for God's justice in the face of any one of many forms of oppression or injustice, is here specifically uttered before an overwhelmingly superior military force that has come to drive the Judaeans out of their land and has struck fear in the heart of the king (2 Chr 20:3).

The prayer for God's judgment and vindication of the right and the innocent is also an element in the Deuteronomistic prayer of Solomon at the dedication of the temple (1 Kings 8). In the first particular petition of that prayer, which deals with an oath sworn at the altar by someone who has sinned against a neighbor, Solomon asks God to *"judge your servants, condemning the guilty* by bringing their conduct on their own head, and *vindicating the righteous* by rewarding them according to their righteousness" (v. 32). Then in the sixth particular circumstance, having to do with battle against the enemy (v. 45), Solomon's plea is that God will hear their prayer (*tĕpillâ*) and their plea (*tĕḥinnâ*) and "maintain their cause." These two petitions again demonstrate that the prayer for God's judgment, or, perhaps better, for God's justice, a notion that is inherent in the very term *tĕpillâ,* "prayer" (see chap. 2, above), ranges across varying circumstances and is a fundamental appeal of those in distress, whether in relation to an immediate neighbor or as a part of a community under assault and persecution.

Two of Jeremiah's petitions for help are probably to be brought into connection with this plea to God to act as judge. When in Jer 11:20 the prophet pleads, "[L]et me see your retribution [vengeance] upon them," he introduces that petition with the address:

> But you, O LORD of hosts, who judge righteously,
> who try the heart and the mind...

The petition for retribution or vengeance is itself a plea for the vindication of the right by the righteous judge. In like manner, the prophet seeks retribution against his enemies in 12:1-4 by addressing God:

> You will be in the right, O LORD,
>   when I lay charges against you;
>   but let me put my case to you. (v. 1)

He then says (v. 3), "[Y]ou see me and test [or 'try'] me," using the same verb as in 11:20 for describing God as judge. Such petitions as these need to be kept in mind when we think about the imprecations against enemies that are found so regularly in the Psalms. Jeremiah's petitions here suggest what is surely the case there also, that such curses are petitions for the justice of God, for the vindication of God's righteous nature and purposes (see chap. 9, below).[102]

Remember. We have already taken note of Hezekiah's plea to God: "Remember now, O LORD, I implore you, how I have walked before you in faithfulness with a whole heart and have done what is good in your sight" (2 Kgs 20:3). The situation that evokes the prayer is the king's sickness unto death. The petition is a protestation of innocence that beseeches God to remember the righteousness of the king on the assumption that God will not punish with death one who has been faithful. The plea is for the justice and faithfulness of God. If they can be counted upon as operative in this situation, then the king knows that he will be healed.

On another occasion, one of the prose prayers is essentially a prayer to God to "remember." That is Samson's prayer at the end of his life when he asks God to "remember me and strengthen me" so that he may have the power to pull down the pillars of the temple of Dagon (Judg 16:28). The content of the remembering is not specified. It may be a call to God to remember Samson's faithfulness in the past or to remember his present affliction. Or it may be a prayer for God's justice in remembering the oppression done to Samson by the Philistines. As in the case of Hezekiah, the petition is a way of seeking God's particular help, in this case specifically indicated by the second petition, "strengthen me." If God remembers, then God will give the strength necessary to carry out this final act of vengeance against the Philistines.

Moses' intercession in behalf of the people after they have sinned in making the golden calf also includes a petition to God to remember (Exod 32:11-13; Deut 9:25-29). In this instance, there is no doubt what Moses wants God to remember. It is the promises to the ancestors, Abraham, Isaac, and Jacob. The appeal to the divine memory is an appeal to the faithfulness of the God who keeps promises. The prayer assumes, therefore, that the faithfulness of God is a more controlling dimension of the divine character than the wrath or even the justice of God. The outcome of the prayer—"And the LORD changed his mind about the disaster that he planned to bring upon his people"—suggests that Moses' perception is accurate. In this prayer, therefore, one gains a clue to the fundamental ground of many of the prayers of Scripture. The faithfulness of God can be counted upon, so prayer to seek God's response of faithfulness is appropriate. Needless to say, this prayer suggests that the prayer of the faithful participates in the divine decision, that the appeal evokes from God the characteristic response and indeed helps to shape that response in the face of other legitimate and appropriate options for the divine activity.[103]

Several times in the book of Nehemiah, brief prayers are inserted into his ongoing memoir. Once, when he perceives the effort of his enemies as directed toward frightening the people so that "their hands will drop from the work," he prays: "But now, O God, strengthen my hands" (Neh 6:9). Most of the time, however, the prayer is a simple petition to God to "remember," with varying objects:[104]

Remember for my good, O my God, all that I have done for this people. (5:19)

Remember Tobiah and Sanballat, O my God, according to these things they did, and also the prophetess Noadiah and the rest of the prophets who wanted to make me afraid. (6:14)

Remember me, O my God, concerning this, and do not wipe out my good deeds that I have done for the house of my God and for his service. (13:14)

Remember this also in my favor, O my God, and spare me according to the greatness of your steadfast love. (13:22)

Remember them, O my God, because they have defiled the priesthood, the covenant of the priests and the Levites. (13:29)

Remember me, O my God, for good. (13:31)

These are hardly formal prayers. But they are petitions with divine address that, like the other prayers, invoke the memory of God as grounds for positive regard for the petitioner or negative regard for his enemies. The appeal to divine memory carries with it, therefore, an assumption that God's remembering is not simply a favorable attitude but involves activity for or against the objects of memory, as in Exod 2:23-25:

The Israelites groaned under their slavery, and cried out. Out of the slavery their cry for help rose up to God. God heard their groaning, and God remembered his covenant with Abraham, Isaac, and Jacob. God looked upon the Israelites, and God took notice of them.

The same notion is present in Jeremiah's appeal to God to "remember me and visit me" and "bring down retribution for me on my persecutors" (Jer 15:15) as well as in his petition: "Remember how I stood before you to speak good for them" (Jer 18:20). God's remembering of Jeremiah will take shape in the overthrow of those who plot against him and persecute him.

Teach and guide. While most of the prose prayers are cries for help in some situation of distress, there are times when the help that is needed is divine instruction and guidance. That is what Manoah needed when his barren wife received word of the child she would bear and the peculiar life he would have to leave. One senses from the text that the entreaty of Manoah is heartfelt, that the gift of a child had laid a large burden upon him, for which he needed help. So also, according to the book of Kings, the young Solomon, as he begins his reign, senses the great burden he takes up with the rule of the kingdom and his own inadequacy without divine direction. He prays: "Give your servant therefore an understanding mind to govern your people, able to discern between good and evil" (1 Kgs 3:9). The prayer is not simply a general prayer for guidance. It is the plea of one who senses, according to the text, a large inadequacy—"I am only a little child; I do not know how to go out or come in" (v. 7)— in the face of the very difficult task of ruling the kingdom and having to follow the great King David, his father.[105]

Bless. On two occasions, the petitioner seeks God's blessing. David's prayer in 2 Samuel 7 is not really a prayer of distress. It is a prayer for God to confirm the promise made to David and his line and to bless the house of David so that it may continue forever. The brief prayer of Jabez (1 Chr 14:10), which does seem to presupposes some situation of pain, seeks among other things that God would bless him and indicates specifically what that means, the enlargement of his borders. The prayer for God's blessing is not a common one in the prose prayers for help of the Old Testament, but it may arise in very different situations. The divine blessing may, therefore, take different forms, depending upon the circumstances in which the prayer is uttered.

Other petitions. A number of the petitions manifest such particularity that they resist categorization. Samson, after his slaughter of the Philistines, cries out to God that he is near death of thirst, and the Lord provides water. While there is no explicit petition, the same situation evokes Moses' complaint in the wilderness over the grumbling of the people (Exod 17:4). Again the petitioner interprets the occasion as a near-death experience ("They are almost ready to stone me"), and God responds by providing water.

God's forbidding Moses to enter the land evokes two prayers. One is the simple petition to be allowed to cross over and see the good land, which God denies because of his anger with the people (Deut 3:23-25). The other is a prayer for God to appoint a leader in his place, and Joshua is designated (Num 27:16-17).

Fleeing for his life before Absalom, David prays the prayer appropriate to his particular need that God would turn the counsel of the wise man Ahithophel, who is Absalom's adviser, to foolishness. Elijah, in conflict with the prophets of Baal on Mount Carmel (1 Kings 18), prays that God would let it be known that the Lord is God in Israel by answering him. The specific need is not indicated in the prayer but in the narrative, that is, the burning of the sacrifice on the altar by a fire from heaven ("[T]he god who answers by fire is indeed God" [v. 24]). One sees, therefore, in the prayer, that the petition may be simply a request to be heard and answered by God. It is necessary to know the circumstances of the prayer in order to know the nature of the "answer." In the psalmic prayers, we encounter just such prayers or indication that the prayer has been "answered" without being told the specifics of the circumstances.[106] They are determined by the context in which the prayer is uttered.

In 2 Kgs 6:17-18 and 20 we have a quite particular prayer whose three petitions having to do with two different parties all relate to seeing and not seeing. The first plea of Elisha is that his frightened servant "may see," that is, may see the armies of heaven surrounding and protecting Elisha against the Aramaean army. The second plea, then, is that the Aramaeans may be struck with blindness. And the third petition is that the eyes of the ones struck blind may be opened so that they will see they are now caught within the city.

Finally, two quite specific prayers arising out of particular contexts anticipate the petitions of the noncontextual prayers for help of the Psalms. Nehemiah's plea in the face of the mockery of Sanballat and Tobiah is that God would "turn their taunt back on their own heads and give them over as plunder in a land of captivity" (Neh 4:4-5). The petition is directed at the taunts of enemies[107] and seeks for them the fate that the ones they persecute have undergone.

The prayer of the sailors in the storm (Jonah 1:14) is a simple but anguished plea: "Do not let us perish on account of this man's life." It is followed by a prayer that is, in effect, a plea for God's justice: "Do not make us guilty of innocent blood." We here anticipate the tormented petitions for deliverance from death and the protestations of innocence that are both heard frequently in the prayers of the Psalter.

Petitions in Psalm Prayers

The prayers for help in the Psalms manifest a much greater number and variety of forms and content of petition, but they do not differ in any fundamental way from the pleas of the narrative prayers except in two respects.[108] In the Psalms, petitions against the enemy or enemies and negative petitions occur more frequently than in the narrative prayers (see below). Some of the petitions appear with much greater frequency, not surprisingly in light of the number of prayers in the Psalter. The petitions are so abundant and repetitive that it would be too large—and unnecessary—a task to recount or categorize all of them here. An overview will give a sense of the main concerns and characteristics of the petitions in the prayers for help or laments, as they are often called. Where the force and meaning of the particular petition have already been dealt with in the discussion of the narrative prayers, it is not necessary to repeat that in examining the psalm prayers.

Petitions that seek God's attention. The call to God to "hear," to "give ear," or to "attend = heed" is sounded often in the Psalms, as well as, but less frequently, the plea to "see" or to "consider."[109] In the former case, it is of course the voice or prayer of the praying one that God is asked to hear;[110] in the latter cases it may be the petitioner, the predicament, or no object at all that God is to consider. Presumably, God is to "see" and consider the petitioner, the plight, the enemies—everything.

The plea to be heard or to be seen is usually accompanied by other petitions that lay out before God the need and what the one in trouble wants God to do. But this call for a hearing is fundamental especially in those frequent situations when the psalmist feels that God is hidden or silent, when God has forgotten or forsaken the one in trouble. Getting God's attention is the crucial turning point. It is not surprising that in Psalm 88—the most relentless of all the prayers for help in its lack of any expressed confidence in God's help, any expectation of God's deliverance—the petitions of the prayer are entirely pleas to be heard. It is indeed a prayer for help in time of trouble, but inasmuch as God is a significant part of the problem, no way out is possible unless God receives the prayer.

Closely related to these appeals to "hear" and, less often, to "see" are the several instances of the petition to God to "answer me."[111] Often the appeal for an answer occurs in close proximity to the plea to God to "hear" or to "listen."[112] It is possible that such a petition seeks a specific divine word of assurance, an oracle of salvation. Certainly there are prayers where such seems to have come as God's "answer." But, as Anneli Aejmelaeus has pointed out, the plea for an answer is even broader than the petition to hear. In the one narrative context where such a petition comes forth, the prayers of Elijah and the prophets of Baal, the answer sought is not a word but a deed, fire on the altar.[113] In Ps 81:7, a divine oracle is heard wherein God speaks of having "answered you" when "in distress you called." The parallel to "answered you" is "rescued you," again a deed more than a word. The "answer" sought, therefore, is either a divine word of salvation that serves to assure the petitioner that God will help or the deed of help and deliverance itself.

The plea for a hearing in God's ears or for an answer from God is reflected in other ways in the structure of biblical prayer. While not universal, the certainty that God will hear or has heard is one of the common features of the prayers for help in the Psalms and the songs of thanksgiving that follow God's help.[114] That is true also of the prayer for God to answer.[115] In expressions of trust and confidence, those in pain know that the Lord listens to the cry of the sufferer, answers the prayers of the innocent and oppressed, those in mental and physical pain. They anticipate that God will do so in their case. Twice God speaks of answering the cry of distress (Pss 81:7; 91:15), and God is praised as "you who answer prayer."[116] In some instances, one may assume that the one who prays has actually received a divine word or oracle of salvation[117] in response to the prayer and gives praise to God even in the prayer itself.

Pleas for God's attention occur in other forms also. The psalmist may call out to God to "turn to me."[118] One notices immediately that this petition is always followed immediately by other petitions, particularly "be gracious" (see below), indicating its character as a plea for God's attention and involvement, the substance of which is then spelled out in further pleas. Psalm 69:16-17 is an instructive example of the heaping up of appeals for a hearing, for God to turn toward the sufferer, appeals that move toward pleas for help:

> Answer me, O LORD, for your steadfast love is good;
>   according to your abundant mercy, turn to me.
> Do not hide your face from your servant,
>   for I am in distress—make haste to answer me.
> Draw near to me, redeem me,
>   set me free because of my enemies.

The one in deep distress calls for God's positive attention ("answer," "turn to me," "do not hide your face," "draw near to me") and then for God's saving intervention ("redeem me," "set me free").[119]

It should be noted, however, that the movement described in these instances—from God's turning and attention to God's intervention and help—does not mean that the petitioner cannot simply cry out immediately for help or deliverance. Indeed, in Psalm 69, the first words of the prayer are "Save me!" It does mean that there are a number of petitions whose function in the structure of prayer is to gain a hearing of the predicament by the Lord of Israel, a consideration by the one who weighs every deed and circumstance and makes just judgments and who is compassionate and gracious to the weak and helpless,[120] so that the supplicant can then go on to ask specific help for the present distress.[121]

Two other examples of such petitions should be noted. They are in a sense calls for action on God's part and are usually followed by other petitions or elaborations. Frequently, the psalmist will cry out to God to "arise/rise up" or to "awake." These are calls for God's initiative, sometimes simply, "[R]ise up to help";[122] in other instances they are followed by further petitions for action against the enemy.[123] The implicit assumption is that God is asleep or inactive and the petition seeks God's arousal. While Psalm 121 expresses the confidence that God never slumbers or sleeps, a conviction central to biblical faith, the petitioner in distress experiences God as quiescent and calls for action.[124]

In like manner, the psalmist in distress may plead "Hasten!" Here, also, the prayer does not usually stand by itself but is followed most often by the phrase "to my help" and twice simply by "to me."[125] In Ps 70:5, the prayer, "[H]asten to me, O God," is followed immediately by "you are my help and my deliverer," so that it is, in effect, also a prayer specifically for God to make haste in order to help.

We should not leave this particular category of petitions without recognizing their reflection in the oracle of salvation. Such an oracle is often the word of assurance, "Do not be afraid," that turns prayers of weeping into songs of praise and thanksgiving (see chap. 4, below). One of the grounds for that assurance is God's turning toward the petitioner, God's claim to be present, to be in relationship with the sufferer who cries for help, expressed in such declarations as "I am with you," "I am your God," "I am your shield." Like the petitions for God's hearing, God's attention and arousal, this basis of assurance is often followed by a further word of divine intervention and action: "I will help you," "I will deliver you," and the like. The needs voiced in the prayer are responded to by the God who turns and hears and hastens to the help of the sufferer.

Petitions that arise out of complaint and lament. It is certainly to be expected that expressions of the distress and plight of the one who prays would be reflected in the petitions themselves, and indeed they are. Those that are closely tied to the complaint against God, or the God lament, are often formulated negatively and are like the previous category in seeking the response of a seemingly unresponsive God or in averting the negative actions of a God whose hand is heavy.

Several examples will show how the complaint against God or the lament over one's condition has its corollary in a petition for God's help:

(1) Complaint:	Why are you *so far* from helping me, from the words of my groaning? (Ps 22:1; cf. Ps 10:1)
Petition:	Do not be *far* from me, for trouble is near.... Do not be *far away*. (Ps 22:11, 19; cf. 35:22; 38:21; 71:12)[126]
(2) Complaint:	There is no one to *help*. (Ps 22:11; 'ên 'ōzer)
	I am like those who have no *help*. (Ps 88:4; 'ên 'ĕyāl)
Petition:	O my *help* ['ĕyālûtî], come quickly to my aid ['ezrātî]. (Ps 22:19)[127]
(3) Complaint:	Why have you *forsaken* me? (Ps 22:1)
	...whom God has *forsaken*. (Ps 71:11)
Petition:	Do not *forsake* me. (Ps 71:9, 18; cf. 27:9; 38:21)
(4) Complaint:	There is no one to *deliver*. (Ps 71:11)
Petition:	In your righteousness, *deliver* me. (Ps 71:2;[128] cf. 7:1; 22:20; 25:20; 79:9, etc.)
(5) Complaint:	Why do you *hide your face* from me? (Ps 88:14; cf. 10:11; 13:1; 44:24)[129]
Petition:	Do not *hide your face* from me. (Ps 27:9; cf. 69:17; 102:2; 143:7)
(6) Complaint:	Why have you *cast me off*? (Ps 43:2; cf. 74:1; 88:14)
Petition:	Do not *cast me off*. (Ps 27:9; cf. 44:23)
(7) Complaint:	God has *forgotten*. (Ps 10:11; cf. 42:9; 13:1; 44:24; 77:9)
Petition:	Do not *forget* the oppressed. (Ps 10:12; cf. 74:19)[130]
(8) Complaint:	*Shame* has covered my face. (Ps 44:15; cf. 4:2; 69:7, 19; 89:45)[131]
Petition:	Do not let me be put to *shame*. (Ps 25:2; cf. 25:3, 20; 31:1; 69:6; 71:1, etc.)

In this last case, the petitions go a step further and overlap with another category as they frequently pray for the enemy to be shamed.[132] The rhetoric of the prayer thus creates a call for poetic justice, which is a way of saying that as the plea is appropriate to the need, so the judgment upon the persecutors should be appropriate to their sin.[133]

The above examples indicate that while the correspondence of complaint/lament and petition may be across different prayers, not infrequently it appears within the same prayer. A good example of this, not immediately apparent in translations, is found in Psalm 3:

(9) Complaint: Many are saying to me,
                "There is no *salvation* [*yĕšû'ātâ*] for you in God."
                (v. 2; my trans.)

    Petition: Rise up, O LORD!
                Save me [*hôšî'ēnî*], O my God! (v. 7)[134]

Several examples show how petitions may overlap the categories laid out in these pages. It is not surprising, for example, that the prayers for a hearing, for consideration and attention, arise out of complaints over God's inattention, God's silence and inactivity. In Psalm 44, a community prayer for help, the people complain, "Why do you sleep, O LORD?" (v. 23), and then immediately plead: "Awake." In the prayer contained in Psalms 9 and 10, the quoted words, "he will never *see* it" (10:11), serve as part of the complaint while the petition goes up: "*See* what I suffer from those who hate me" (9:13).[135] The frequent petitions to God to "answer" echo the complaint of the sufferer in Ps 22:2: "O my God, I cry by day, but you do not answer."[136] The complaint, "no refuge remains to me" (Ps 142:4), is converted into the petition: "Be a rock of refuge for me" (Pss 31:2; 71:3).

Reflection of the complaint in the petition is not always as linguistically precise as in the above examples. But the correspondence may be just as clear and eloquent. The frequent petition, "Do not be silent," is a negative form of the positive petition, "Answer me,"[137] and so reflects the complaint of Ps 22:2, referred to above, that God is silent and there is no answer when the cry for help goes up. The frequent lament about the enemies that they have caught the sufferer in a net or trap,[138] that they wait in ambush or plot secretly, has its correlate in the petitions: "Take me out of the net that is hidden for me" (Ps 31:4); and "Keep me from the trap that they have laid for me, and from the snares of the evildoers" (Ps 141:9).

A poetically beautiful interplay of lament and petition is found in the prayer of Psalm 69. The powerful image of one sinking and drowning in water, flood, and deep mire is the vehicle of the personal lament at the beginning. It is the cry of one who is "going under," overwhelmed by the forces of oppression and unable to stand before them:

        Save me, O God,
           for the waters have come up to my neck.
        I sink in deep mire,
           where there is no foothold;

> I have come into deep waters,
> and the flood sweeps over me. (vv. 1-2)

When the prayer moves to petition and pleading, it is just this terrible sensation and reality from which the one who prays seeks deliverance:

> But as for me, my prayer is to you, O LORD.
> At an acceptable time, O God,
> in the abundance of your steadfast love, answer me.
> With your faithful help rescue me
> from sinking in the mire;
> let me be delivered from my enemies
> and from the deep waters.
> Do not let the flood sweep over me,
> or the deep swallow me up,
> or the Pit close its mouth over me. (vv. 13-15)

The petition for deliverance is couched in the same language of sinking in mire, deep waters, and sweeping flood that so accurately describes the distress of the sufferer. The metaphor unifies the prayer at its "deepest" point.

Petitions for grace and mercy. The frequency of the petition, "Be gracious to me," or "Be merciful to me," sets it off as one of the basic pleas of the prayer for help.[139] Indeed, the root *ḥānan*, "be gracious," provides one of the primary words for prayer discussed in chapter 2, *těḥinnâ* and *taḥanûn*, "supplication" or "plea." As was noted there, this plea is rooted in the ancient Israelite confession, "The LORD, the LORD, a God *merciful* [*raḥûm*] and *gracious* [*ḥannûn*], slow to anger, and abounding in steadfast love and faithfulness" (Exod 34:6),[140] an affirmation that appears in various forms several times in the Psalter.[141] The character of God as revealed to the people Israel in the foundational events of their history is the ground of the petition for God to be gracious.[142] It is one of the most elemental of all pleas, appealing to the inclination of God to be compassionate, to look with favor upon those in trouble, to forgive sins, to help when someone is undone by oppressive forces. It is a form of the prayer for forgiveness,[143] but it encompasses potentially any situation of distress.

There are explicit petitions for forgiveness in the Psalms, but they are relatively infrequent.[144] Not surprisingly, most of them are in the great penitential prayer, Psalm 51: "Blot out my transgressions" (v. 1); "wash me thoroughly from my iniquity" (v. 2); "cleanse me from my sin" (v. 2); "hide your face from my sins" (v. 9); "blot out all my iniquities" (v. 9). The brief prayer concluding Psalm 19 includes the petition: "Clear me from hidden faults" (v. 12). This, however, is less a prayer of forgiveness for sins committed than it is the plea of one who keeps God's law with joy but knows there will still be hidden errors and sins that God will need to forgive. Psalm 25, not traditionally regarded as a penitential psalm, includes specific petitions for forgiveness (vv. 11, 18) and, at one point (vv. 6-7), does so by appealing to the mercy of God as confessed in the ancient formula of Exodus 34 (above). The focus here seems to be more on the sins of the past (v. 7) than the present.[145] Psalm 79, a community prayer for help, contains a plea for forgiveness (v. 9) in the context of a call for the compassion or mercy of God (v. 8), but, somewhat surprisingly, such a plea is infrequent in this type of prayer in the Psalms.[146] The grace and mercy of God encompass the plea for forgiveness in Israel's prayers, but that particular plea is not a characteristic part of the individual prayers for help in either the narrative texts or the Psalms. Its presence is more evident in the intercessory prayers of the leaders and in the great prose prayers of the postexilic period (see chap. 8, below).[147]

It is worth noting that a simple prayer of this sort, also drawing upon Exod 34:6ff., has been found inscribed upon a cave in the region of Samaria. It is part of a group of brief "prayers in time of crisis" accompanied by drawings of figures with hands upraised in prayer.[148] It reads:

> *pqd yh 'l ḥnn*
> *nqh yh yhwh*
> Be mindful, Lord, Gracious God;
> Absolve, Lord, Lord.

All of the words in this brief prayer are reflected in some way in the confessional formula of Exodus. God is addressed as the "gracious" or "compassionate" Lord, as in that text, and the verbs of petition are found in the references to not "clearing" (*nqh*) the guilty and "visiting" (*pqd*) the iniquity of the parents upon the children (Exod 34:7). In this instance, however, the petitioner stands the formula on its head, asking God not to "visit [*pqd*] iniquity" but to "visit" in the sense of "pay attention," claiming an innocence before God and seeking indeed to be cleared or absolved (*nqh*). We do not know the circumstances of this prayer. It appears to have been inscribed in the late sixth century around the time of the Neo-Babylonian invasion, though some have suggested it is a century older. It is probably the prayer of someone or some group fleeing from Samaria and hiding for their lives in the cave at Khirbet Beit Lei.[149]

Petitions for salvation, deliverance, and help. Certainly the heart of the prayer for help is the petition that asks for just that—help, deliverance, rescue, salvation, redemption by God. The largest number of petitions fall into this category and encompass the whole of the vocabulary of words for help and deliverance.[150] The dominance of these petitions, together with the actual content of many other pleas, pushes us to recognize the fundamental character of the psalm prayers as *prayers for help.*

Often two or more of the terms for help will appear in a cluster of petitions.[151] As one would expect, the plea is often made with particular reference to the self: "save me," "deliver me," "help me," and without reference to the plight of the one praying.[152] One of the inscriptions carved on walls of the cave at Khirbet Beit Lei (see above) is a one-line prayer comprised of just such a petition:

> *ḥwš' [y]hwh*
> Save, O Lord!

Psalm 69 begins with essentially the same prayer:

> Save [*ḥwš'*] me, O God! (v. 1)

Its conclusion is similar in language and function to one of the other inscriptions in the cave (see chap. 4, below).

Other prayers speak of the trouble from which the sufferer seeks deliverance:

> Deliver me from my enemies. (Ps 59:1; cf. 143:9)

> Deliver me from those who work evil;
>   from the bloodthirsty save me.
>   (Ps 59:2; cf. 17:13; 71:4; 140:1)

> Save me from my persecutors. (Ps 142:6; cf. 7:1; 31:15)

> Bring me out of prison. (Ps 142:7; cf. 25:17)

> Redeem me from human oppression. (Ps 119:134)

> Rescue me from sinking in the mire;
>   let me be delivered from my enemies
>   and from the deep waters. (Ps 69:14)

> Deliver me, O Lord,
>   from lying lips,
>   from a deceitful tongue. (Ps 120:2)

> Rescue me from the mighty waters, from the hand of aliens.
>   (Ps 144:7; cf. v. 11)

> Deliver my soul from the sword,
>   my life [or "my only one"] from the power of the dog!
> Save me from the mouth of the lion. (Ps 22:20-21)

While the imagery of water and mire plays a part in some of these petitions, they all have to do with a cry for help against inimical forces, persecutors and oppressors who threaten the life or well-being of the one who prays. The trouble is real and threatening. The cry for help arises out of suffering and oppression that may be foreign nations against a king and a people,[153] false accusations against an innocent person, possibly prison as a result of the plots of the wicked. Situations of illness or personal suffering may evoke the cry for help and deliverance, but most of the petitions for deliverance that *identify* the distress speak of a situation of external threat. It is the cry of the innocent and the poor, the weak and the helpless, in a world where the strong, the rich, and the powerful use those characteristics as weapons against others. The language is stereotypical and imaginative, but it can hardly be understood apart from the real presence of such hostile forces.

More often the cry for help is quite general, and the petitioner simply asks God to save or deliver or help.[154] The plight may be illness, guilt, abandonment, hostile enemies, or whatever. Extrication from the distress, God's help to alleviate the situation, is the primary aim of all these prayers, and so time and time again the suffering ones will call out for help and deliverance. The prayers arise because "trouble is near and there is no one to help." Human power is inadequate (Ps 146:3) or marshalled against the one who prays. Only God can help.[155] "Deliverance belongs to the LORD" (Ps 3:8).

Petitions for protection. A form of the prayer for help is the explicit cry to God to protect the suppliant from harm, to keep or guard the one whose life is somehow threatened or in danger.[156] Such pleas are rooted deeply in the conviction that God is a sure refuge in the midst of personal, natural, and political or social threats and catastrophes (Psalm 46), that the Lord is the one who keeps and watches over the community and each member of it (Psalm 121). If the previous category suggests the desire to be extricated and freed from the predicament or distress of the sufferer, these petitions seek God's protection in the face of and in the midst of the trouble, a place of hiding from the "beasts" and persecutors who lie in wait and set traps, from "the dread enemy" and "the scheming of evildoers," when "evils have encompassed me without number."[157] So the imagery of God as rock and fortress joins with the imagery of God as hiding place and a bird under whose wings one may take refuge to provide the ground for the many petitions for God to protect the person(s) in trouble.[158] In several instances, the cry for protection, and indeed other petitions, are explicitly connected to the conviction that the Lord is a refuge or that one may take refuge in God.[159]

The plea for protection, like the cry for deliverance and help, may go up also as a petition for God to guard and protect from the power of death. That is, of course, implicit in many of the threats cited above. At times it becomes explicit in the text as the cry for help is a call to "preserve those doomed to die" or to "preserve my life."[160] "Do not take me away at the mid-point of my life," says the one afflicted (Ps 102:24); "[S]ave my life;...for in death there is no remembrance of me" (Ps 6:4-5). The distress that evokes these prayers for help is often a near-death experience,[161] whether through sickness or national disaster, the accusations of enemies that could lead to a judgment of death or the judgment of God for the sins of the supplicant. It is characteristic of the psalmic prayers for help, as is frequently the case in the narrative prayers, that they are prayed in extremis, where life is perceived as in the balance, and only the protection or help of God can "preserve my life." One cannot single out any particular kind of petition as a plea to be saved from death. That comes in many forms, including the cry to God to do in the enemies, to let them be caught in the traps that they have set to take the life of the petitioner. These prayers for help should not be understood as always arising out of the imminent danger of death. Sometimes the imagery and language suggesting the threat of death represent the powerful suffering of one whose actual life may not be threatened but who experiences life as so on the brink that the cry "Save my life" is authentic expression of where the sufferer really is.[162]

Petitions against the enemy. The appeals to God to do something to or against persons who persecute and oppress the individual crying out in the psalmic prayers are many and varied. They probably outnumber any other single category of petitions. These prayers against the enemies and the wicked, often expressed in third-person form as wishes for their destruction and thus commonly regarded as curses or imprecations, are dealt with more directly and theologically in chapter 9, on prayers of blessing and curse. But we would be remiss in looking at the character of the petition in the prayer for help in the Psalms if we did not take some brief account of them along with the other petitions.

To begin, it is to be recognized that many of the petitions already discussed are appeals for deliverance from persecutors and enemies. In Psalm 17, the afflicted psalmist asks to be *guarded* and *hidden* from the "wicked," "my deadly enemies" (vv. 8-12), and to be *delivered* from them (vv. 13b-14). In that same psalm, the petitioner also makes a direct call for God to "confront them, overthrow them" (v. 13a) and then expresses several strong wishes to God against them and their children:

> May their bellies be filled with what you have stored up for them;
>   may their children have more than enough;
>   may they leave something over to their little ones. (v. 14b)

Two things are evident from this particular example. One is that the petition against the enemies is another form of the cry for help. The destruction of the enemies is the way of delivering the persecuted one who prays. It is only as they are undone that the psalmist can be saved and protected. These petitions and wishes are, therefore, not self-standing vindictive calls against other persons. They are part and parcel of the cry for help, indeed a form of that. The depth of emotion, despair, agony, and rage that is present in many of the complaint and lament elements, as well as in the urgent, beseeching petitions, is evident here also. These are the forces that threaten the life and well-being of the psalmist. His or her only hope for help and deliverance is as they are restrained and put to naught.

The second important observation to draw from the example of Psalm 17, which is quite representative, is the poetic equation of the *enemies* and *persecutors* of the psalmist with the *wicked* and the *evildoers* (cf. Ps 3:7).[163] In other words, the persons against whom these petitions are directed belong to two categories at the same time. They are perceived as those who "rise" or "set themselves against me" (i.e., the praying one),[164] "my pursuers."[165] That is, they are identified in *personal* terms, vis-à-vis their hostile attitude toward the one crying out. But they are also called the "wicked," and the manifestation of their wickedness is sometimes spelled out at great length.[166] Their actions are characterized by lying,[167] slander, and oppression of the weak and the poor (see again Psalm 10). The enemies in these prayers, therefore, are identified not only in personal terms, but also in *moral* terms. They are persons who violate the commandments and statutes of the Lord. The manifestation of that violation is against the afflicted one who prays or the group of persons he or she belongs to and represents in the prayer. As the one who prays is "innocent" and thus "righteous," so the persecutors are in their actions "guilty" and thus "wicked." Furthermore, it is clear that the wickedness is social and not just individual. The recipient may experience the oppression as one of the weak and the poor, a victim of the legal and illegal acts of others. But even if not one of the poor, the afflicted petitioner often appeals to God as a victim of injustice whose cry against "my foes" is a cry for justice. It will be found and help obtained as the enemies/wicked and their unjust schemes and acts are brought to naught.

The understanding of the petitions against the enemies as pleas for justice is reinforced by the number of times that they manifest a call for God to repay the enemies according to their evil deeds (e.g., Ps 28:4) or to see that the schemes and plots they hatch become their undoing, that they are caught in their own net or pit or snare.[168] The correspondence of sin and judgment, of deed and consequence, suggests a notion of justice, either in the sense of a punishment appropriate to the crime or a

poetic justice effected by the hand of God that turns the sin against the
persecuted one into a punishment of the persecutors.[169]

Petitions for healing. While most of the appeals to God in these prayers
are of a more general nature, the specific plea to be healed occurs a few
times in the psalm prayers,[170] reflecting the fact that illness of some sort
is often portrayed as the cause or manifestation of suffering. As we have
noted, the frequent language of sickness in the complaints and laments
may be a metaphorical way of speaking of personal disintegration in
the face of affliction from external sources. It is likely, however, that the
predicament lying behind some of these prayers was indeed some sort
of physical or mental illness.[171] Even prayers that do not suggest sickness in their language may have been prayed by or for the seriously ill.
Whether literal or figurative, however, the language of sickness evokes,
at times, the specific cry for healing, the renewal of body and mind, deliverance from the threat of death that was always present in sickness in
the ancient world, and indeed up to modern times. God's help in such
instances is both therapy and absolution. For these prayers for healing,
whether the specific petition is there or not, often carry an acknowledgment of sin and see in the illness the judging hand of God.[172] They are
implicit, if not actual, prayers for forgiveness as well as healing, assuming a unity of body and soul, and believing that God is the one who
"forgives all your iniquities, who heals all your diseases" (Ps 103:3),
who heals the broken of heart and mind as well as those with broken
bodies (Ps 147:3).

Petitions for judgment and vindication. The plea for God's judgment is
one of the more common petitions of the psalm prayers and the particular focus of some psalms.[173] The appeal of the suppliant in most of these
instances is for a judgment upon the wicked, the enemies who threaten
the life of the one praying, and for his or her vindication as innocent
before the accusations and assaults of the evildoers.[174] We may assume
that lying behind these petitions is often some accusation, formal or in-
formal, against the psalmist. The only way out of the predicament is for
God to sustain the innocence of the petitioner and render the accusers
guilty for their oppressive deceit.

   If the prayers for healing belong more in the sphere of the personal
and individual experience of health and wholeness, the prayers for vindication and judgment belong more in the social experience of justice
and injustice. The enemies of the sick are more those who abandon and
taunt the sufferer, who hope the one who is ill will die, and who may
gain in some fashion by his or her death. The plea for judgment and
vindication is against enemies whose hostility is manifest in oppressive
acts of deceit and treachery. They are probably the same persons against

whom Amos and other prophets of the eighth century inveighed because they used the courts to oppress the weak and the poor, to gain land and property by the manipulation of the courts. The prayer for healing may be, and often is, uttered by a person who has some sense of guilt and confesses that sin. The prayer for vindication in its explicit and implicit forms is the prayer of one who is innocent and cries out for justice against those who are guilty of oppression.

That is why one hears in these prayers a frequent protestation of innocence by the petitioner,[175] a claim of righteousness that sounds strange to those shaped by the strong emphasis on the universality of sin within the Western tradition of Christianity. The conviction of sin places everyone under fear of judgment. But in these prayers, the specific plea for salvation and deliverance is in fact a plea for *judgment*. Indeed, it is, again somewhat surprisingly, "Judge *me*." The judgment against the enemies is called for in the many pleas and wishes against the enemy expressed in various ways and discussed above. But the oppressed sufferer places herself or himself before God's judgment as one who is truly innocent, the victim of injustice, and thus righteous in this situation, not guilty. So the translations that in most instances render the forms of the roots *špṭ* and *dîn* as "judge" or "judgment" in reference to God's activity as judge of the earth and its inhabitants often translate the same roots as "vindicate" in these individual pleas for judgment.[176] Rather than the understanding of God as judge being a negative image for the righteous, it is the only hope, the court of last resort. When the human systems of justice and its administration fail to deliver the oppressed, they cry out for help and vindication, for a right judgment by God that will sustain them before the plots and deceits of others. We are not altogether sure what that process may have been. It may have involved refuge in the sanctuary, trial by ordeal, appearance in the sanctuary before a special court or for a divine verdict in the same fashion that an oracle of salvation may have been given by God through a priestly figure.[177] Perhaps the prayer came even before the court in the gate of the city had carried out its justice. Whatever the procedures, the petitioner pleading for vindication seeks God's intervention in the human situation to establish the innocence of the one praying, who sometimes makes his or her own case before God and is willing to be checked out by God, to be tested and proved (Pss 26:2; 139:23).

Such petitions, therefore, challenge the assumption that because "all have sinned" everyone comes before God in the same way. There are persons for whom and situations in which the conviction of sin is not an assumption on the part of the petitioner. Quite the contrary. In the face of human oppression, the innocent victim appeals to a righteous judge in heaven (Ps 7:11) to confirm that innocence, to render a fair verdict, and to preserve the life and well-being of the one who has been done in by the forces and agents of injustice, malicious witnesses,[178] the ruthless (Ps 54:3), and the bloodthirsty (Ps 26:9), people whose hands are "full of bribes" to manipulate the human machinery of justice.[179]

The social and theological picture thus described is well presented in Ps 7:8-11:

> The LORD judges the peoples;
> judge me, O LORD, according to my righteousness
> and according to the integrity [or "blamelessness"] that is in me.
> O let the evil of the wicked come to an end,
> but establish the righteous,
> you who test the minds and hearts,
> O righteous God.
> God is my shield,
> who saves the upright in heart.
> God is a righteous judge,
> and a God who has indignation every day.

The assumption that God is judge of all peoples leads the psalmist to call upon God to "judge me." It is a cry for help, for salvation. The hopefulness that is in the appeal is in the psalmist's claim of innocence and uprightness (v. 8b; cf. vv. 3-5). The plea is repeated in verse 9 as a plea for judgment of the wicked, who are those enemies referred to earlier in the psalm, and establishment of the righteous, that is, the innocent, among whom the petitioner is to be counted. The submission of the petitioner to God's test is assumed then in verse 9b. The rest of the passage consists of statements of confidence in God's judgment because *God* is righteous and stands in behalf of the right.[180] It closes with a particularly powerful image of God's continuing indignation over the injustice and the oppression of the innocent and righteous. The psalmist declares what is evident time and time again, that the oppression of the weak and the innocent by the wicked is something that arouses a reaction in God. The divine pathos at work in the world will overthrow the wicked and bring about a vindication for the oppressed and suffering who cry out for help. That cry is heard by a God who is *'ēl zō'am*, perpetually indignant, constantly upset at the presence of injustice in the world. The same Lord who "forgives all your iniquity" and "heals all your diseases" is the one who "works vindication and justice for all who are oppressed" (Ps 103:3, 6).

Petitions to remember. As in the narrative prayers for help, the plea to God to "remember" occurs several times in the Psalms, albeit not generally in the individual prayers.[181] It appears primarily in community prayers for help and prayers for the king.[182] Three sorts of appeals seem to be present in asking God to remember. One is a negative request, that is, for God *not* to remember the sins of the those who cry out (Ps 25:7) or the sins of their ancestors. In the first instance, the plea is another form of the prayer for forgiveness, for God to set aside the petitioners' sins and not keep them in mind. In Psalm 79, the people ask God not to punish them for the sins of their fathers and mothers, mindful of God's judgment as extending across the generations. The cry of the people in this prayer is precisely not a plea for forgiveness. It is a call for God's compassion in not punishing them for the sins of others. In both of these cases, however, the plea is, in effect, for God to forget the sins that would bring divine punishment.

What God needs to call to mind, according to these urgent cries, are two things. One is the deeds and words of the enemies, their taunts and insults as well as their destruction of Jerusalem.[183] Explicitly and implicitly this cry suggests that what needs to be remembered is that these taunts and attacks were against God as well as the people, that, remembering what they did—scoffing and reviling "you," "your name," and "your servant"[184]—God will come to save the king and the people against the enemy and will destroy them. Once again, the appeal is to the safety of the Lord's reputation.

These prayers also call for God to remember both God's way and character and covenant and also what the ones who petition have done by keeping faithful to that way and that covenant. In their prayer in Psalm 74, the people appeal to God to remember that this "congregation" are those created and redeemed by God long ago, the Lord's heritage and special people, and also to remember Zion, which was the place that the *Lord* chose as a dwelling place. So also the prayer in Psalm 25 is for God to remember "your mercy" and "your steadfast love" (v. 6; cf. v. 7b), calling upon God to act according to the character revealed in the ancient confessional formula of Exod 34:6.[185] Paired with these petitions are those that appeal to God to remember the faithful acts of the king for whom the prayer is lifted (Pss 20:3; 132:1), similar to Jeremiah's plea: "Remember how I stood before you to speak good for them, to turn away your wrath from them" (Jer 18:20). Here, therefore, as we saw in the narrative prayers, the plea to "remember" is really a call upon the faithfulness of God, both to the way that God has determined to be in the world and to those who have kept the covenant and lived by the divine instruction. Such a plea is present in another form in those prayers that ask for God *not to forget*, that is, to remember "the oppressed" (Ps 10:12) and "the life of your poor" (Ps 74:19).[186] Not only are these *your* poor, so that "your" power and reputation are at stake in their fate, but God has made it clear time and time again that it is in God's very being to be inclined and compassionate toward the weak and the poor.[187]

Petitions for blessing. As in the prose prayers, the particular prayer for God to "bless" the individual petitioner or the people is not a common plea. In most of its occurrences, it is a benediction in behalf of the people.[188] One probably encounters in this prayer for blessing a reflex of the Priestly Blessing in Num 6:22-27.[189] That is further suggested by the way in which Psalm 67, which has opening and closing petitions for God to bless, appropriates the words of the Priestly Blessing. The prayer of blessing over the people, to be prayed or "put" by the Aaronic priests, echoes in many places in the Old Testament.[190] Its particular character and content as prayer are discussed in chapter 9, below.

In the three cases where the prayer for God to bless occurs in individual prayers for help, it is paired in some way with the plea for deliverance or salvation.[191] The combination is an all-encompassing prayer for God's help. Salvation is God's act in particular situations to help or to deliver from trouble, danger, suffering. Blessing is God's providence, a provision of the continuing needs of life, the "help" of God that keeps the creation and human existence going, builds continuity into the life of the world and the people.[192] It is not surprising that in the individual prayers there are far more petitions of various sorts for God's help and salvation than there are for blessing. They arise out of particular moments and experiences of distress and affliction, and the petitioner seeks to be freed from *that* affliction and given new life. When the prayer for blessing is joined with the prayer for salvation, the help sought from God is extended in the broadest way possible, beyond the present danger and suffering into the ongoing provision of a context for life from day to day (see chap. 9, below).

Petitions for instruction and guidance. Unlike the prose prayers, the prayers for help of the Psalter include a number of petitions for God to teach and to guide. In them, we hear a different sort of prayer than the more customary plea for deliverance related to a crisis or danger that threatens the psalmist. The one who prays these petitions seeks instruction and guidance in the Lord's way. Such requests may be accompanied by other prayers for help,[193] but the prayer to be taught and led is, like the prayer for blessing, a plea for an *ongoing* work of God, a continuing direction for life, instilling in the petitioner an understanding of God's will and God's way. What is important to note, however, is that such a "different" plea appears not in a different type of prayer, but almost exclusively in the context of prayers for help. When the prayer for instruction and guidance in the way is thus set in the context of the prayer for deliverance from enemies (as, e.g., in Pss 5:8 and 27:11), a direct connection is made between God's help and God's instruction. The one praying perceives a salvific effect in God's guidance. That is not spelled out, but the psalmist knows that the Lord's way is in some sense a way out of the predicament. Persistence in the way of righteousness will bring a vindication against the unrighteous enemies.

This association of prayer for help and prayer for guidance is the key to the character of the long Psalm 119 and the difficulty of neatly categorizing it. It has been understood as a torah psalm, a psalm exalting the law of the Lord, a reflection of torah piety and the stimulus of wisdom teaching.[194] And so it is. Nowhere in Scripture is there more explicit comment on the instruction of God and the importance of attending to it. Eight different words for that instruction are used regularly in the psalm. Its familiar exclamation, "O how I love your law! It is my meditation all day long," is an accurate window into this psalm.

But Psalm 119 also clearly is an individual prayer for help with its reference to "those who taunt me" (v. 42), "the cords of the wicked" (v. 61), "the arrogant" who "have subverted me with guile" (v. 78), and "the wicked who lie in wait to destroy me" (v. 95).[195] The psalmist complains against God as explicitly as any other prayer for help (vv. 82-84), protests his or her innocence (v. 86), and cries for help (v. 86) and God's judgment against "those who persecute me."

How does all of that hold together? It may be a late psalm, as various features of the text—but not all—suggest, and certainly it is a literary construction with its carefully worked out alphabetic acrostic using the different words for law and instruction. As such, it resists easy definition or locus in a setting in life. But the very combination of basic themes observed here—law and prayer—indicates that it claims a connection between God's guidance in the course of life by means of the law and God's help in time of trouble. There are various clues to the connections in the psalm. The instruction found in God's law, precepts, commandments, and the like has sustained the sufferer in distress (v. 93). They are the ground on which the claim of innocence can be made and the judgment for the psalmist and against the wicked can be rendered (vv. 84, 126). In them, the petitioner hears the promises of God to be gracious (vv. 58, 76) that are the basis on which the plea for help can be uttered. The plea to "remember" is particularly directed toward all this instruction and guidance:

> Remember your word to your servant,
>   in which you have made me hope. (v. 49)

The faithfulness of God that is the ground of the appeal and the hope of the psalmist is made known in the law, the teaching of the Lord. In the midst of "trouble and anguish" the commandments of the Lord are a "delight" (v. 143). That is, the psalmist finds a kind of solace, a refuge in the midst of trouble, in God's law. Here one may associate the claim of the psalmist with the sort of confidence that is expressed in Psalm 46 but with a Deuteronomic twist.[196] For Deuteronomy is where one begins to hear that the presence of God is to be found in the presence of God's teaching and instruction in and among the people, even when they are far from the normal places with which God's presence is associated, when they are in exile and distress.[197] Indeed a psalm such as this one may express exactly what Deuteronomy is getting at, the prayer of an exile who has lost everything and complains to God while constantly listening to and being guided by all of God's teaching so that the comfort and refuge of God's presence are found within it. It is not surprising, therefore, to hear in the middle of the psalm the familiar cry of the individual in trouble, "Help me" (v. 86), echoed again near the end, "Let your hand be ready to help me" (v. 173), and taking its final form in the concluding appeal of the psalm:

> Let me live that I may praise you,
>   and let *your ordinances help me.*
> I have gone astray like a lost sheep; seek out your servant,
>   for I do not forget your commandments. (vv. 175-76)

Two things have happened by the end of the psalm, but they are well anticipated all the way through. The cry for God's help has become a prayer for God's *law* to help. The guidance of God in Scripture is able to help the person in distress. The prayer for help and the study and attention to God's teaching in the law have now become the way of "seeking" God (see p. 37, above). But God also seeks out and finds the faithful servant in the teaching of the law and the commandments. The one who confesses to having gone astray and who seeks God's help knows that help will be manifest as God "seeks out your servant" and finds him or her through the words of all the precepts and ordinances. They will return the afflicted and wandering servant to the right and safe path.[198] The cry for help is still an earnest prayer of a human being in trouble, but in this context that prayer is all tied up with righteous living.[199]

MOTIVATING AND URGING GOD

One of the most prominent features of the prayers for help is the regular presence, in a variety of forms, of *reasons* set before God as grounds for seeking and expecting help, a feature of biblical prayer that has come to be called the *motive* or *motivational* clause.[200] There is some sense in which most of the prayer functions in this fashion. Certainly the description of the plight of the petitioner, the lament over trouble and affliction, can be understood as evoking or eliciting the sympathetic response of God. So also the various expressions of confidence or trust (see below) tie the petitioner to the deity, presenting oneself as trusting in God and so acting as God would expect and seek. The first half of Psalm 22 is an obvious example of the way in which the plight and the trust interact and together implicitly ground the claim on God's response. In verses 3-5, the psalmist affirms the character of God as holy and the history of the people as a demonstration of the positive response of God to those who cried out in trust. Such recollection joins the psalmist with that company but also implicitly contrasts the present condition of the psalmist who trusts with the fathers and mothers who trusted. The recital is thus a reminder of the way God has been in order to evoke a similar response in the present situation.[201] The next three verses (6-8) carry that process of implicit motivation further as the psalmist now presents his or her plight, in effect suggesting that whereas "my" ancestors were not put to shame when they trusted and cried out for help, "I" am greatly ashamed and ridiculed because God does not help. That description of personal affliction again is an implicit way of presenting reasons for God to act. In this case, it involves the suggestion that God's way is not consistent unless the psalmist is helped and also that the taunting of the psalmist is at the same time a mockery of God that God should set to rest. In verses 9-10, we encounter the same type of motivating act as in verses 3-5. Only this time, it is the recollection of the psalmist's own history that presents a contrast with the present and suggests, therefore, that God, who has been "my" God throughout life, needs to act in this moment as "my God," that is, "keep me safe" now as you "kept me safe on my mother's breast." The history of the personal relationship with God presents implicit reasons for God to help now.

And so, in verse 11, the psalmist cries out for help to the one who has helped in the past when such cries went up. Then the afflicted one returns to a powerful description of the near-death condition and weakness, again to present to God a plight that should evoke the compassion of God and thus deliverance. This leads once more into a plea for help, all the prayer virtually serving as a basis of the plea, a presentation of the case that should serve to elicit a response that will save the psalmist. Other features of prayer already identified function to give reason for God's intervention. Protestation of innocence by the petitioner clearly is designed to make a case to justify God's help. Psalm 17 is an excellent example. The prayer begins with initial pleas such as, "Hear a just cause, O LORD," "[L]et your eyes see the right" (vv. 1-2), and returns to petition in verses 6ff. In between those petitions, the psalmist proceeds to make the case that his or her cause is just:

> If you try my heart, if you visit me by night,
>   if you test me, you will find no wickedness in me;
>   my mouth does not transgress.

> As for what others do, by the word of your lips
> I have avoided the ways of the violent.
> My steps have held fast to your paths;
> my feet have not slipped. (vv. 3-5)

In all these words, the suppliant is justifying, in direct address to God, why the Lord should intervene in this situation to protect the psalmist (vv. 8-9) and overthrow the enemies who have brought false accusations (vv. 13-15).

This way of perceiving the prayers for help as the presentation of a case to provide the grounds for God to act can be demonstrated in many if not most of them. In the following discussion, however, we will focus primarily on the more explicit and direct motivational expressions of these prayers. They work in much the same fashion as the implicit urgings, and often what happens is that implicit motivation simply becomes explicit, frequently in the form of clauses appearing in close proximity to petitions and usually with some syntactic indicator, such as "for/because," "for the sake of," "so that," or "lest." Implicitly or explicitly, we are confronted with a significant element of biblical prayer, the persistent and reasoned urging of God to act. What are the grounds for expecting God's help, and what is involved in urging God in prayer?

If most of the prayer for help can be understood as having a motivational function, it is also the case that the explicit motivational clauses and sentences are themselves so numerous in prose prayers and the psalms and prophetic prayers that cataloguing or reviewing all of them is too large and unproductive a task. Here we shall look at representative examples of motive clauses to see the primary grounds they present for God's response. In the broadest sort of way, they tend either to draw attention to some feature of *God's nature and character* or to lift up some aspect of *the situation of the petitioner(s)*. There are also a number of motive clauses that point to *the relationship between God and the petitioner(s)* as a reason for God's response. These categories help identify the primary things that are going on in the motive clauses, but one must be always conscious of the fact that they are really different angles on a single reality. Something about the character of God is a basis for urging divine action in a particular situation. Sometimes, it is the character of God that is called upon. At other times, it is the situation that is lifted up. And always the one praying assumes the relationship as a ground for appeal, sometimes explicitly calling attention to it as a way of urging God's attention. In many prayers, all three of these "angles" may be recognizable in very explicit fashion.[202]

An example of the complex interrelationship of these ways of urging divine action is Jacob's prayer to God just before his meeting, after many years, with his brother Esau:

O God of my father Abraham and God of my father Isaac,
O LORD who said to me, "Return to your country and to your
kindred, and I will do you good," I am not worthy of the least of
all the steadfast love and all the faithfulness that you have shown
to your servant, for with only my staff I crossed this Jordan; and
now I have become two companies. Deliver me, please, from the
hand of my brother, from the hand of Esau, for I am afraid of
him, he may come and kill us all, the mothers with the children.
Yet you have said, "I will surely do you good, and make your offspring as the sand of the sea, which cannot be counted because of
their number." (Gen 32:9-12)

As we have noted, the address itself offers implicit motivation for God's
response; that motivation is grounded in the relationship identified by
the reference to the Lord as the God of Jacob's ancestors. That relationship stakes a claim for calling upon God. Jacob's plight is placed
as a further ground when he says, immediately after the petition, "for I
am afraid of him." The potential threat is the situation of distress that
evokes this prayer and is here given as a basis for God to deliver. Within
that explicit identification of the plight of the petitioner as a motive for
God's action is an implicit drawing upon something in the very nature
of God. The characteristic way in which God responds to cries for help
is with the word of assurance, "Do not be afraid" (see chap. 4, below).
It is God's way to be the one who comes to people with such assuring words and deeds to help them out of their distress (cf. Gen 35:3).
Yet another statement of Jacob's has a motivational function: "I am not
worthy of the least of all the steadfast love...." He is saying, literally, "I
am too insignificant for all the kindnesses...." As such, the prayer expects to "move" God because the Lord is known as one who responds to
the plight of the small, the weak, the insignificant in the world. Finally,
the further reason set forth to urge God's help is the reminder of the
promise that God made. Here both the faithfulness of God and the relationship between Jacob and God are the implicit ground on which Jacob
appeals. The Lord has created a perduring relationship with Jacob and
his posterity, and God keeps promises.

A broader look at the prose and psalmic prayers will demonstrate
the way in which these categories or "angles" of motivation are present
in the prayer for help.

God's Nature and Character

One would expect that a prayer appealing for help and giving reasons
for it would explicitly invoke God's *justice and righteousness* as a sufficient ground. The supreme example of this is Abraham's prayer for

Sodom and Gomorrah. He asks God, "Will you indeed sweep away the righteous with the wicked?" and then goes on to ask a further question, whose motivational character is self-evident in its content: "Shall not the Judge of all the earth do what is just?" The appeal to God's sense of justice works, for God replies, "If I find at Sodom fifty righteous in the city, I will forgive the whole place for their sake" (Gen 18:25-26). A more implicit motivation of the same sort, but in behalf of God's just punishment, is made by Jeremiah in one of his prayers:

> But you, O LORD of hosts, who judge righteously,
>   who try the heart and the mind,
> let me see your retribution upon them,
>   for to you I have committed my cause. (Jer 11:20)

If God is a just judge, and Jeremiah knows that is true of God, then the prophet assumes God will want to act in deliverance of the one who has remained faithful and in judgment or retribution against the ones who have persecuted him. All those complaints that seek to establish the injustice and unrighteousness of the enemies and the innocence and faithfulness of the petitioner are giving a reason, implicitly or explicitly, for a just and righteous God to help, hoping thereby to move God to intervene in behalf of the just and innocent petitioner.[203] Here is where one sees clearly the overlap between the situation of the suppliant and the nature of God. It is precisely the injustice in the human situation that is lifted up, implicitly appealing to the justice of God. Or the reverse happens: a just God is called upon to act in a situation self-evidently oppressive and unjust.

In a similar fashion, one may appeal, like Jacob in Genesis 32, to the *faithfulness of God,* the consistency of God's way in the world as reflected in God's promises or previous behavior with individuals and the people. When God threatens to strike the people in the wilderness with pestilence because of their complaining, Moses says:

> And now, therefore, let the power of the LORD be great in the way
> that you promised when you spoke, saying,
>> "The LORD is slow to anger,
>> and abounding in steadfast love,
>> forgiving iniquity and transgression,
>> but by no means clearing the guilty,
>> visiting the iniquity of the parents
>> upon the children
>> to the third and the fourth generation."
> Forgive the iniquity of this people according to the greatness of
> your steadfast love, just as you have pardoned this people, from
> Egypt even until now. (Num 14:17-19)

The appeal is in part that the Lord will be faithful in several ways: in keeping the promise,[204] in acting in character (forgiving iniquity), and in being consistent by pardoning the people of their sins now as God has done through all the time up to the present. But, of course, this is not only an appeal to God's faithfulness. Moses is also urging God to act in accordance with that *mercy* or *steadfast love* that is so characteristic of the Lord and is explicitly made the identifying feature of the Lord's character in the confessional formula Moses cites. It is God's nature to be faithful, and it is God's nature to be merciful, to manifest a gracious love and forgiveness even against God's own inclination to reward faithlessness with justice instead of mercy. The appeal to the mercy or steadfast love of God is even more frequent in the biblical prayers, as an explicit motive, than the appeal to justice, and for good reason. God's justice may be the hope of the petitioner, but it also may be his or her downfall. So, remembering God's compassionate nature, as confessed in the ancient formula and in many other ways, the one who prays will repeatedly ask God to act "according to your steadfast love" and "your mercy."[205] In similar fashion, the petitioner may ask God to act "for your *goodness'* sake" (Ps 25:7; cf. 86:5), again consistent with Israel's experience of God as attested in its paradigmatic song of praise and thanksgiving: "O give thanks to the LORD, for he is good. His steadfast love endures forever."[206] The ground of Israel's praise is the ground of its plea.

Samson's prayer at the end of his life contains a motive clause that seems apparently to have nothing to do with the character of God but in fact does:

> Lord GOD, remember me and strengthen me only this once, O God, so that I may be avenged upon the Philistines for one of my two eyes. (Judg 16:28)

The prayer is one of self-interest and seems characteristic of Samson's violent ways. But his prayer for "vengeance" (*nqm*) is addressed to the God of vengeance,[207] the one who properly works out retribution in the world, "the ultimate redressing of all wrongs."[208] The way in which Samson's plea appeals to God's nature is well described by Greenberg:

> [God] may commit his *nqm* into human hands, in which case his cause and that of those humans are identified (e.g., Num 31:2, 3). More especially, mortals doing God's work may exact *nqm* on their own (Josh 10:13; 1 Sam 14:24; 18:25). Here Samson, beyond all hope of ever seeing procedural justice done him for his injuries, entreats God to empower him to exact extraordinary retribution for himself—for him, there can be no other kind; and the God of *nqm* complies.[209]

The urging of God by appealing to the divine nature and character has two other quite specific dimensions. One is the use of motive clauses that base the divine response in *God's desire to be praised and worshiped or feared*. The plea for God's protection in Ps 5:11 is "so that those who love your name may exult in you," and in Ps 9:14, the afflicted one asks the Lord to be gracious "so that I may recount all your praises."[210] In Ps 61:4-5, the psalmist prays for refuge "for you, O God, have heard my vows"; that is, God has heard the vows of the psalmist to render praise and thanksgiving when help is given. That vow is itself uttered at the end of the psalm:[211]

> So I will always sing praises to your name,
> as I pay my vows day after day. (v. 8)

At two points in Solomon's prayer of dedication of the temple, he pleads for God's forgiveness when it is sought in the future "so that they [Israel] may fear you" (1 Kgs 8:40) and indeed that "*all the peoples* of the earth may know your name and fear you, as do your people Israel" (v. 43). A particular form of this motivational ground is the claim that the death of the afflicted petitioner means that he or she cannot render praise to God:

> For in death there is no remembrance of you;
> in Sheol who can give you praise? (Ps 6:5; cf. 30:9)

In all of these instances, we come upon Israel's conviction that praise was owed to God and was indeed sought and desired by the Lord. (That claim will be examined further in chapter 5.)

The other way in which God is appealed to as God is by intimating, in more or less direct terms, that *God's reputation is at stake* in what happens to those servants of the Lord who cry out in affliction and oppression. One of the ways this is done is by the frequent urging of God to help "for your name's sake."[212] In one sense, such a reason is a call to God to act in the way identified with the Lord's name, a way demonstrated from the revelation of the name in the exodus until now. But even more, this is a call to God to live up to God's name, that is, to God's reputation. The petitioner claims thereby that an act of deliverance of one who is a servant of the Lord is appropriate, if not necessary, for God's reputation as a faithful and merciful God. The claim of God to be exactly the kind of deity indicated in the other motive clauses is at stake in this situation. In the community prayer of Psalm 79, the people cry out:

> Help us, O God of our salvation,
> for the glory of your name;
> deliver us, and forgive our sins,
> for your name's sake. (v. 9)

That petition with its concluding motive clause is followed by a question that identifies it as a matter of God's reputation quite clearly:

> Why should the nations say,
>   "Where is their God?" (v. 10a)

The question of the nations is really a challenge to the power of Israel's God. Their plight demonstrates to the world, it is suggested, that the Lord is ineffective or indifferent to those in God's care. That is why at the end of the prayer, the people plead:

> Return sevenfold into the bosom of our neighbors
>   the taunts with which *they taunted you,* O LORD! (v. 12)

God's reputation is at stake in Israel's fate. Their mockery of the people is really a mockery of the God whose people they are.[213]

It is not surprising, therefore, that this theme should be a strong motive in prayers for the people. In the community prayer of Jer 14:7-9, the people not only cry out, "Act, O LORD, for your name's sake," at the end of the brief prayer, but they also preface the final petition, "[D]o not forsake us," with the words: "We are called by your name." And in the later prayer of that same chapter, the people plead:

> Do not spurn us, for your name's sake;
>   do not dishonor your glorious throne. (Jer 14:21)

The first of those petitions is the real plea. The second one, growing out of the clause, "for your name's sake," is an effort to move God to act by suggesting that attending to their plight is a matter of divine honor.

Moses' prayer in behalf of Israel in the wilderness argues this way in a quite direct fashion. When God threatens to disinherit the people, Moses says:

> They [the inhabitants of the land] have heard that you, O LORD, are in the midst of this people; for you, O LORD, are seen face to face, and your cloud stands over them and you go in front of them, in a pillar of cloud by day and in a pillar of fire by night. Now if you kill this people all at one time, then the nations who have heard about you will say, "It is because the LORD was not able to bring this people into the land he swore to give them that he has slaughtered them in the wilderness." And now, therefore, let the power of the LORD be great in the way that you promised.
> (Num 14:14-17; cf. Deut 9:28)

The tactic of Moses is blatant. He seeks—and does so successfully— to change God's plan by appealing to the divine reputation. The whole extended prayer is a plea for forgiveness set forth in one long speech giving reasons for God to act according to God's nature (see above) and for the sake of God's reputation before the world (cf. 1 Kgs 8:51, 53).

The appeal to God's power or the reputation of God's power has a much later echo in a very different context. Jesus' prayer in the Garden of Gethsemane just prior to his arrest and execution is a cry for help: "Remove this cup from me" (Mark 14:36). That petition is preceded by a motivating clause appealing to God's power, "Father, for you all things are possible." Jesus grounds his plea for help in a reminder to God of God's omnipotence, seeing in his own predicament a situation in which God's great power can be manifest. Before the prayer is finished, however, Jesus places his appeal to God's power in his behalf in subordination to the divine purpose and will (cf. Isa 53:10) and Jesus' own self-submission to that will.[214]

When Joshua complains after the defeat at Ai, his plea is implicit: "The Canaanites and all the inhabitants of the land will hear of it, and surround us, and cut off our name from the earth." Then he connects the fate of Israel's name and reputation with the fate of God's: "Then what will you do for your great name?" (Josh 7:9). David asks God to confirm the promise to him so that "your name will be magnified forever in the saying, 'The LORD of hosts is God over Israel' " (2 Sam 7:26). Elijah praying for fire on the altar on Mount Carmel pleads with God to answer him, "so that this people may know that you, O LORD, are God" (1 Kgs 18:37). The same reason is put to God by Hezekiah when Sennacherib is at the gates, only it is expanded by elaborating how the Assyrian king has mocked "the living God" and thrown the gods of other nations into the fire. The opening address of this prayer, praising God as the one who alone has made the heavens and the earth, is an implicit urging of God to respond to the mockery of the king and live up to the divine nature and reputation.[215] In a similar way, Jehoshaphat begins his prayer for help against the Moabites and Ammonites with the words, "Are you not God in heaven? Do you not rule over all the kingdoms of the nations?" (2 Chr 20:6), and Asa concludes his prayer for help by saying, "You are our God; let no mortal prevail against you" (2 Chr 14:11). The effectiveness of such motivating clauses is indicated in God's response to Hezekiah.[216]

The Situation of the Petitioner(s)

While any motive clause assumes something about God as a part of its appeal, a number of them are formulated primarily with reference to the one who prays. The most obvious way that happens is by referring, in brief or extended fashion, to the distress and affliction of the petitioner. So Jacob says of Esau, "I am afraid of him; he may come and kill us all, the mothers with the children" (Gen 32:11), and Jeremiah prays that his enemies may be done in "for they have dug a pit to catch me" (Jer 18:22). Time and again the afflicted individual who prays in the Psalms urges his or her petition by saying, "for I am languishing, . . . for my bones are shaking with terror" (Ps 6:2), or "for trouble is near and there is no one to help" (Ps 22:11), or "for I am in distress" (Pss 31:9; 69:17).[217] The petition may be reinforced by asking for God's deliverance lest something happen to the one praying.[218] A number of times allusion is made to the danger posed by the enemies.[219] There are even times when petitions are grounded in presentation of the plight as the result of divine affliction.[220]

In all such motive clauses, the fundamental ground of prayer, the responsiveness of God to the cry of human need, is lifted up. All the description of the plight of the afflicted, wherever it occurs in the prayer, assumes God's care and compassion, especially for those in distress. Here again the appeal is implicitly to "the LORD, gracious and merciful," the one who has promised to heed the cry of the afflicted "for I am compassionate" (Exod 22:21-27). These specific motive clauses express the basic assumption of the prayer, that human suffering is something to which God will pay attention. So by laying that case out, they provide the grounds for the appeal. In one instance, the petitioner may call attention to God's nature; in another to the situation that allows, if not indeed pushes, God to act according to that nature.

A particular variation of this reference to the distress of the suppliant is an underscoring of the weakness and lowliness of the one who prays. So Jacob says, "I am too insignificant" (Gen 32:10), and Moses says of the people, "for they are too heavy for me" (Num 11:14). In a prayer for help that does not arise out of distress, Solomon nevertheless appeals for "an understanding mind to govern" on the grounds that "I am only a little child" and "[W]ho can govern this your great people?" (1 Kgs 3:7, 9). His weakness and lowliness for the task are the bases of his appeal for help. Perhaps the clearest example of this sort of motive clause is in Amos's two intercessions for the people asking God to forgive and stop the impending judgment. "Forgive, . . . cease," he implores, "How can Jacob stand? He is so small!" The judgment is averted by prayer that pleads on the basis of the lowliness of the one who has sinned. The fact that God is "moved" by such an appeal is evident from the response to the prayers. In both cases, the Lord relented.[221]

A further possible way of presenting the situation of the petitioner as a reason for God to act benevolently is by calling attention to the faithfulness and loyalty of the one who prays. Twice, Jeremiah pleads for God, as righteous judge, to let him see divine retribution (*nqm*)[222] against his enemies because "I have committed my cause to you" (Jer 11:20b; 20:12). In the testing of Jeremiah and his enemies by the divine judge, Jeremiah will be found faithful and so legitimately able to claim

God's help. Hezekiah's plea for healing when at the point of death is in fact a prayer that God will remember how faithful he has been (2 Kgs 20:3). The psalmist may claim to have walked in integrity and faithfulness and trusted in the Lord as a basis for praying for God's vindication. When the kings Asa and Jehoshaphat seek God's help against their enemies, they make a point of indicating their reliance on God (2 Chr 14:11; 20:12). So also, the individual prayers in the Psalms will often give as a reason for God's response, "for I take refuge in you."[223] At the end of the prayer in Psalm 143, the petitioner in distress pleads for help, first on the grounds of God's righteousness and steadfast love and "for the sake of your name," and then because "I am your servant" (vv. 11-12). The character of God and the loyalty of the suppliant are both grounds for expecting help and for "moving" God to do so.

The Relationship between God and the Petitioner(s)

Finally, we note those cases where the relationship between the one who prays and the God to whom that one prays is explicitly lifted up as a basis for urging God's help. That has been implicit in all the other motivating statements, but in some instances it is the focus. The relationship between God and Israel is the fundamental claim that grounds the prayer of Moses in Exod 32:11-13. It comes to the fore also in Deut 9:25-29. Moses pleads with God not to destroy "the people who are *your very own possession,* whom *you redeemed* in your greatness, whom *you brought out of Egypt* with a mighty hand. Remember *your servants, Abraham, Isaac, and Jacob. . . .* For they are the people of *your very own possession,* whom *you* brought out by *your* great power and by *your* outstretched arm." The whole purpose of the prayer is to identify this people as *"your* people," to lift up in the strongest way possible the continuing relationship God has with Israel as a basis for asking God not to destroy the people.

To the same end, Asa asks for help and says "[Y]ou are our God" (2 Chr 14:11), and the people in Jer 14:9 remind God that "we are called by your name." The appeal to the relationship runs all through the Psalms, not only in the language of address, such as "my God," but also in some of the explicit motive clauses, such as, "for you are the God of my salvation" (Ps 25:5) or "for you are my rock and my fortress" (Ps 71:3). The latter clause both claims the relationship and points to the nature of God as a secure protector to ground the petition.

This claim on the relationship as a reason for God to help is especially prominent in the communal prayers for help, particularly in the way the people identify or refer to themselves. In Psalm 74, the people pray:

Why does your anger smoke against the *sheep of your pasture?*
Remember *your congregation, which you acquired long ago,*
  which you redeemed to be *the tribe of your heritage.* (vv. 1b-2a)

Do not deliver the soul of *your dove* to the wild animals;
  do not forget the life of *your poor* forever. (v. 19)

At the center of the plea in Psalm 80 is a rehearsal of God's deliverance
of the people as a ground for their plea for help in the present. The plea
is couched in the metaphor of a vine planted by the Lord:

You brought a vine out of Egypt;
  you drove out the nations and planted it.
You cleared the ground for it;
  it took deep root and filled the land....
Turn again, O God of hosts;
  look down from heaven, and see;
have regard for this vine,
  the stock that your right hand planted.
                                    (vv. 8-9, 14-15)

It is not difficult to see why such community prayers would place such
great weight upon the relationship between God and the people. The
covenantal bond and their history with God have given them strong
reasons to see in that relationship their whole reason for being and a
particular purpose that God has with them. They have known themselves to be God's "special treasure," a people holy to the Lord.[224] In
these prayers, they remind God of that fact in various ways in order to
claim God's present protection and help.

The motivational dimension of these prayers is comprehensive and
broad-reaching. It pervades the prayers and suggests that one of the primary aims of the prayer for help is to urge and reason with God. Rarely
does a prayer not seek to lay a claim on God in some way. Petitions do
not go up unattended by implicit rhetoric and explicit reasons to evoke
a positive response from God. There is a kind of disturbing suggestion
here that if the petitioners do not lay out reasons and make a case, God
will not respond. Clearly there is no assumption that prayer is a mechanical matter of simply asking for help and receiving it. On the contrary,
if, as the terms *tĕpillâ,* "prayer," and *tĕḥinnâ,* "supplication," suggest,
prayer is a matter of laying a case before God (so *tĕpillâ*) or appealing
to God's grace and mercy (so *tĕḥinnâ*), that is truly what happens in
the motive clauses and rhetoric of prayer. God may not be coerced, but
God can be persuaded. The prayers do not assume that things are cut
and dried, either God answers prayer or does not. They seek to evoke
a response, not just in the petitions themselves but in all dimensions of

the prayer and especially those sentences and clauses that suggest reasons why God should act, results that can be accomplished or prevented by God's intervention. The impassibility of God and the immutability of God were not a part of Israel's understanding of prayer. In form and content, the prayer for help assumes that God can be moved and that God can be persuaded to act in the situation so that it is changed for good, even if that means that God changes. Those several places in the Bible where God relents and does not do what God had planned are regularly in response to prayer and the human insistence that there are reasons why God should act to help (see chap. 8, below).

The character of prayer in Scripture harbors a powerful suggestion that the one who prays can truly engage the deity, can urge reasons upon God for acting in behalf of the one in need, just as God, in giving the law, urges reasons upon the people for responding and obeying. Prayer was the point at which the human creature dared to approach the transcendent, holy deity with no restrictions on what could be expressed and free not only to cry out in rage, anger, despair, and hate, as in the lament part of the prayer, but also to beseech, urge, and persuade. We have placed the emphasis on the petitionary dimension of the prayer for help, but these motive clauses indicate persuasion is as much the heart of the prayer as plea. The mind and heart of God are vulnerable to the pleas *and the arguments* of human creatures.

It is important, however, to keep in mind the nature of the arguments. They appeal to God to be and to act as God would be and act. Here clearly prayer is not simply "thy will be done." Indeed the petitioner is at pains to impress his or her will, that is, one's need and sense of what God should do, upon the deity. And yet, in another sense, the prayer for God to act "according to your steadfast love" or "for your name's sake" is in the profoundest way possible a call upon God to help, *because that is God's will.* The motive clauses are, in effect, a way of indicating that God's response to the cry for help should be a manifestation of mercy and love, a demonstration of God's just dealings in the world, a compassionate response to the sufferer in pain or to the weak and powerless in the community, an act of righteousness in that God's help will be appropriate to the relationship established between God and the people. But those reasons, articulated by the suppliant in distress, have been found to be precisely the will and way of God as demonstrated in the long experience of God's way with Israel. It is in the very nature and structure of the relationship between God and the human creature that the deliverance from pain and suffering, the overcoming of affliction, guilt, and oppression by others, can be counted upon—which is why prayers of pain and suffering are so regularly full of confidence and trust, a feature of the prayer for help to which we now must turn.

EXPRESSIONS OF CONFIDENCE AND TRUST

Particularly in those prayers we find in the Psalms, the expression of confidence in God's help is about as widespread as the laments over the situation.[225] That is not the case with the prose prayers, where assertions of trust do not occur as a separate element but may be implicit in words of praise (see appendix 1).[226] Indeed, the line between expressions of confidence and words of praise is very narrow.[227] In the psalm prayers, however, one often encounters assertions of trust in God that are set over against the realities of the present situation and the terrible plight that has been described.

Some of the assertions of confidence in God may arise out of the experience of having received some word of assurance (see chap. 4, below), but that is not necessarily the case. Nor is it always easy to determine whether or not that is so for any particular psalm. In nearly all of the prayers for help in the Psalms, some expression of confidence occurs, but its location in the written prayer or in the experience of praying may vary considerably. The dimension of trust and confidence so permeates some prayers that it becomes their primary subject matter, so much so that they have come to be known as songs or prayers of trust.[228] Like the motive clauses, the declarations of trust tend to be either *a statement about God* in which some characteristic or quality or way of God's being and doing is lifted up in relation to the psalmist or *a straightforward confession of trust in God* on the part of the psalmist.

Not infrequently, confessional statements are marked in the prayer by an initial, "but you..." or "but I..." or its equivalent ("yet," "nevertheless").[229] This may not necessarily be the first expression of trust in the prayer, but in these instances it is clearly an assertion over against something else, either the harsh realities of the distress (e.g., Ps 3:2), or the lack of faithfulness on the part of the psalmist previously (e.g., Ps 73:23), or the faithlessness of others manifest in their wickedness (e.g., Pss 5:7; 31:4). When the assertion is about God, it may be the simple claim that "you are my God."[230] Or it may characterize God in some way that identifies what is sought in the prayer: God is my shield, my help or the helper of the helpless, my rock or strength, merciful and gracious, the one who lifts up my head or upholds my life.[231] Frequently the expressions of confidence point to God's salvation and may refer to such deliverance experienced in the past.[232] Confidence in God's opposition to the wicked and evil is expressed in these prayers, as well as the conviction of God's protection against the forces of wickedness and oppression and the enemies of the suppliant.[233]

When the focus of the expression of confidence is on the one praying,[234] it is nearly always a straightforward declaration of trust:

> O my God, in you I trust. (Ps 25:2)

> When I am afraid, I put my trust in you.
> In God whose word I praise,
>   in God I trust; I am not afraid;
>   what can flesh do to me? (Ps 56:3-4; cf. v. 10)

> But I trust in you, O LORD;
>   I say, "You are my God."
> My times are in your hand. (Ps 31:14-15a)

> But I trusted in your steadfast love. (Ps 13:5)

Such words of trust in God in the face of terrible trouble may be elaborated in other ways:

> I lie down and sleep;
>   I wake again, for the LORD sustains me.
> I am not afraid of ten thousands of people
>   who have set themselves against me all around.
>   (Ps 3:5-6; cf. 4:8)

> This I know, that God is for me. (Ps 56:9)

The conviction expressed in this last example catches up what all of these statements are about. Even when the questions are raised to God and the sense of abandonment, of being forgotten by God, is strong, there is an underlying assumption that is the fundamental basis of all the prayers for help: God is for me. On that ground, the petitioner can ask for any help.

Characteristically, the expressions of confidence of both sorts—statements about God and confessions of trust in God—echo expressions heard in the laments and in the petitions:

Complaint: Why have you forsaken me? (Ps 22:1; cf. 71:11)

Petition: Do not forsake me. (Ps 71:9, 18; cf. 27:9; 38:21)

Confidence: The LORD will not forsake his people. (Ps 94:14; cf. 9:10)

Complaint: Has God forgotten to be gracious?
             Has he in anger shut up his compassion [or "mercy"]?
             (Ps 77:9)

Petition: Be gracious to me. (Ps 86:3, 16; cf. 6:2; etc.)

Confidence: But you, O LORD, are a God merciful and gracious.
             (Ps 86:15)

Complaint: Shame has covered my face. (Ps 44:15; cf. 4:2; 69:7, 19;
             89:45)

Petition: Do not let me be put to shame. (Ps 25:2; cf. 25:3, 20; 31:1; 69:6; etc.)

Confidence: He will put to shame those who trample on me. (Ps 57:3; cf. 6:10; 22:5)

In some instances a single prayer will reflect in its expression of trust confidence over just that which was the subject of lament or petition. Psalm 3 is an example:

Complaint: Many are saying to me,
                "There is no deliverance [yšʿ] for you in God." (v. 2)

Petition: Deliver [yšʿ] me, O my God! (v. 7)

Confidence: Deliverance [yšʿ] belongs to the LORD. (v. 8)

So in Psalms 9–10, the central concern of the prayer is reflected in this sort of reiteration. The lament describes the oppression of the helpless at length and quotes the wicked and oppressors saying, "God has forgotten" (Ps 10:7-11); the plea arises, "Do not forget the oppressed" (v. 12); and then the psalmist says,

> But you do see! Indeed you note trouble and grief,
>   that you may take it into your hands. (v. 14)
>
> You will incline your ear
>   to do justice for the orphan and the oppressed.
>   (vv. 17-18)

Psalm 31 joins the statement of confidence immediately to the petition it reflects:

> Be a rock of refuge [māʿôz] for me,
>   a strong fortress [měṣûdâ] to save me.
> You are indeed my rock and my fortress [měṣûdâ];
> . . . .
> For you are my refuge [māʿôz]. (vv. 2-4)

And Psalm 70 creates an inclusio or envelope around the prayer by echoing in the statement of confidence at the end the pleas of the petition at the beginning:

> Be pleased, O God, to deliver me [nṣl].
> O LORD, make haste to help [ʿzr] me! (v. 1)
>
> You are my help [ʿzr] and my deliverer [plṭ]. (v. 5)

While we have noted the general absence of the statement of confidence in the prose prayers, there is at least one instance of such a prayer for help that is structured like the example of Psalm 70 above. When

Abraham's servant, Eliezer, prays for help in finding a wife for Isaac, he begins: "Please grant me success today and show steadfast love to my master Abraham" (Gen 24:12). At the conclusion of the prayer, he makes a declaration that functions in effect as a statement of confidence echoing the petition: "By this I shall know that you have shown steadfast love to my master" (Gen 24:14).[235]

All these examples suggest the place and meaning of such expressions of confidence in the prayer for help. The statements about God serve, implicitly, to give praise to God, but that is not their only function, if indeed it is the primary one. They also declare at every point that the one who cries out does so in trust that this prayer is an act of faith and faithfulness. Declaring what "I know" (Ps 56:9), the psalmist places himself or herself where he or she properly and always belongs—in a relationship of trust toward God, a position vis-à-vis God that does not negate or vitiate the depth of despair or the intensity of complaint, even the complaint against God. Indeed the confidence is often focused on just those things that are at the heart of the lament and the plea. The one who cries out in pain is a creature of trust (Ps 22:4-5).

Furthermore, these declarations of confidence are reminders to the one praying that the act is not a foolish and fruitless endeavor, a casting of one's cry into the void, or, perhaps more precisely, toward a capricious God who may or may not be counted upon. Whatever despair and anguish may be present in the lament, even in the complaints against God, the expressions of confidence underline what is implicit in the petition: God may be the problem, but God is, even more, the only way out, the one possible help in a situation of helplessness, the solid rock when everything teeters on the verge of destruction or oblivion. Nowhere does the anguish and Godforsakenness of the afflicted one sound more than in the opening verses of Psalm 22. But those cries and questions about God's absence and silence are followed by a recollection of the community's story in the past when they trusted, that is, when they cried to God and were saved (vv. 4-5). This psalm, therefore, suggests that the expressions of confidence are also part of a dialogue with the self as despair is fought and countered by memory and trust.[236] That dialogue toward trust does not always happen, witness Psalms 39 and 88, but it is meant to. Even the outcry itself is an incipient and important act of trust. In the structure of faithful prayer, it is—most of the time—undergirded with declarations of faith in the Lord of Israel.

Vow of Praise

Once again, we encounter a dimension of biblical prayer that is characteristic of the formal prayers of the Psalms but not of those prayers embedded in narrative and prophetic contexts (see appendix 1).[237] In the vow of praise, we have a suggestion that these psalmic prayers belonged to the experience of worship and ended in vows of the petitioner to conclude the act of praying by praise and thanksgiving and sacrifice before the gathered community in the sanctuary. The vow is not altogether absent from the prose prayers. Indeed, in one instance of a clear prayer for help arising out of a situation of great distress, the only part of the prayer retained in the text is the vow, and for obvious reasons. It is Hannah's vow to commit her child to the service of the sanctuary, which she later does when Samuel is born (1 Sam 1:11, 26-28). The narrative also reports that Hannah brought sacrifices (flour, wine, a bull) to the house of the Lord (vv. 24-25). Her song of thanksgiving on this occasion is also recorded. This narrative account, therefore, gives us a clue to what goes on in the psalm prayers when they conclude with vows of praise and sacrifice and suggests that those we find in the Psalms were likely to have been prayers uttered in the sanctuary. Many of the prose prayers are extemporaneous, uttered in the situation of need and therefore lacking specific reference to coming into the sanctuary with sacrifice and praise. The absence of the vow in the prose prayers, however, should not lead one to think that the anticipation of praise and thanksgiving had no part in them. At least a few of them tell of thanksgiving being given after the prayer was heard.[238]

Within the more formal and sanctuary-oriented prayers for help that are in the Psalter, the vow[239] of praise and thanks is more common.[240] Its most typical expression is a declaration of the individual[241] that "I will praise/give thanks." An example is the vow at the conclusion of Psalm 7:

> I will give to the LORD the thanks due to his righteousness,
> and sing praise to the name of the LORD, the Most High. (v. 17)

Most of the time, that is, there is some explicit statement of commitment on the part of the petitioner to give praise and/or thanks to God for the deliverance that is anticipated or already experienced in the process of the prayer.[242] The petitioner may indicate, explicitly, that the praise and thanksgiving will take place in the midst of or before the congregation.[243] The loneliness and abandonment that are often the symptoms, if not the manifestations, of the distress are overcome as the suppliant stands in the midst of the whole community. Here we can see the appropriateness of the claim that one of the purposes of the individual prayers for help—and whatever ritual accompanied them—was the restoration of the afflicted individual to full participation and acceptance in the community.[244] The creation of community is one of the primary effects of praise and thanksgiving—but more of that in chapter 5. Frequently, the suppliant makes explicit reference to singing and music as the expression of praise, less frequently to offerings and sacrifices as well as proclamation of God's deeds.[245] The last may be assumed in many of the other expressions even though it is not explicitly mentioned.

That is not the case, however, with sacrifice and offering. Because of the specific references to it and the examples from prose texts, such as Hannah's offering of sacrifice after Samuel was born, there is no doubt that the vow could include sacrifice. But it did not do so automatically. There are instances where the vow explicitly excludes sacrifice in the conviction that the Lord desires the expressed words of praise from the heart rather than the symbolic act of sacrifice.[246] It is likely that such formulation of the vows represents a movement toward a postcultic use of the psalms in their later history.[247] That is, as they came to be sung in a context that did not actually include extensive sacrificial activity and in relation to criticism of the sacrificial cult on the part of some members of the community, the vow of praise was confined to words and songs. This was a kind of spiritualizing that did not vitiate the authentic expression of thanks to God by means of offering, a practice that continues down to the present in most religious communities.[248] At the same time it gave expression to the conviction, there from the beginning, that symbolic acts may not substitute for the commitment of the heart and the will, given voice in praise and testimony and also in acts of obedience. While it is possible for words to be as empty as sacrificial acts,[249] it is difficult for expressions of singing and music that glorify God to be utterly without conviction. But more of that also in chapter 5.

The vow of praise is directly related backward to the expressions of confidence and forward to the songs of thanksgiving and hymns of praise. The forward movement is made explicit in one of the thanksgiving songs, which looks back to the prayer for help:

> I will come into your house with burnt offerings;
>   I will pay you my vows,
> those that my lips uttered
>   and my mouth promised when I was in trouble.
> I will offer to you burnt offerings of fatlings,
>   with the smoke of the sacrifice of rams;
> I will make an offering of bulls and goats. (Ps 66:13-15)

So also the hymn of praise in Psalm 65 begins:

> Praise is due to you,
>   O God in Zion;
> and to you shall vows be performed,
>   O you who answer prayer! (Ps 65:1-2a)

But the vow is also a powerful way of further expressing confidence in God's power and willingness to deliver.[250] In some instances, it is difficult to tell whether the declaration of praise at the end of the prayer is a vow in anticipation or the words of praise uttered upon receipt of a divine word of assurance or God's intervention to help. That reflects the way in which the psalm prayers for help are themselves open, some seeming to indicate a certainty that God will hear or some divine word of assurance actually having been given (see chap. 4, below), others anticipating and expressing confidence, including the vow of praise, and a few not moving even that far in the dialogue with God.[251] The last are quite rare, but the elements of confidence and vows of praise are not always present even in psalm prayers, a fact that tends to suggest what we have indicated earlier, that the heart of all the prayers for help is the address, the lament/complaint, the petition, and the motive clauses. But in those prayers for help that were set, if not created, for the continuing use of the people, the psalm prayers, the move toward praise, already there in the expressions of trust, is apparent and reinforced by the prayer of praise and thanks.

CONCLUSION

The Old Testament prayers for help are many. Each one is unique, and some marked differences may be found among them. All of them arise out of the structure of faith that assumes the ears of God are open to the cries of people in distress and need of help. Such prayers reveal that the relationship with God is highly dialogical. It is a most frank and straightforward conversation. No holds are barred, no questions or feelings taboo. Pain and suffering of various degrees lie behind many, if not most, of the prayers.

That affliction has theological, physical, psychological, and social dimensions. The experience of personal distress and often of personal disintegration, the "sickness unto death," is not prominent in the prose prayers, but it pervades the prayers of the Psalter. The threat from external forces who taunt, oppress, persecute, abandon, and threaten to kill is everywhere present. But at its deepest roots, the problem often has to do with God. The questions at the beginning of Psalm 22 and many prayers like it speak out of the sense of the abandonment of God, the distance or absence of God, the silence of God, and often the blow from God's hand. Here is human pain at its deepest hurt, whatever the actual situation of distress or affliction. The questions to God are really questions about the presence and power of God. The structure of faith does not *require* such questions. Often prayer arises out of a faithful trust that does not question God, knowing from beginning to end, even before the plea is uttered, that "God is my helper" (Ps 54:4). But the prayer of faith *permits* such questions and, usually, cannot avoid them. Sometimes they are veiled, implicit. Underneath they are there, and more often than not they surface. Is the human predicament—whether it is experienced as vast or small, by one or by many—a testimony to the absence of God from the world and human life, the disinterest or the rebuke of God? Some of these prayers suggest that it was often so felt and perceived even in the midst of a dialogue that assumed a hearing and responding God.

Such praying reveals an inherent tension that has been evident in our walk through these prayers. On the one hand, the prayer for help can so question God in the face of the human condition that it becomes almost an assault against God and a laying of all the pain at God's door while, on the other hand, it reveals a trust and confidence in the power and inclination of God that openly asks anything in the expectation of God's deliverance. The questioning and lamenting dimensions of the prayer for help arise out of an all-too-real experience of suffering, one that suggests the absence of God's will and power to save, if not the active judgment of God that has brought about the suffering. The earnest pleas and petitions, however, assume God's will and desire to help. So also the many expressions of confidence, the personal and relational modes of address, and the vows of praise reflect a trust and expectancy that stand in a sharp tension with the explicit and implicit ways the prayers urge and push God, as if there would be no response without such "pressure" being exerted.

Such tensions belong not simply to the structure of the prayer for help in a formal sense. They reflect the very nature of life under God, revealing a theological understanding of human existence lived in the tension between fearfulness and despair in the face of the contingency of life—Jacob says, "I am afraid" (Gen 32:11), and the psalmist says, "I am like those who have no help" (Ps 88:4)—and trust in the ground of our being, that God's providential blessing and God's saving help in time of trouble can be counted on; "This I know, that God is for me" (Ps 56:9).

If the prayer for help is conversational and dialogical, and if it often ends in expectancy, then one must assume a response of some sort, a word or reaction from the other voice in the dialogue, the conversation partner who is addressed in this very direct fashion. The prose prayers make it clear that the dialogue did indeed continue, that response was usually forthcoming from the conversation partner, the Lord of Israel. The prayers of the Psalter also suggest that God responded to the prayers, and the suppliant's need, in some fashion, was met. A movement has taken place, from plea to praise, from weeping to laughter. That response and that movement are the subject of the next two chapters.

4

"Do Not Be Afraid"

THE RESPONSE OF GOD

✍

The fundamental question of prayer is: Does anything happen? Does God answer prayer? If these are prayers for help, does help come? That perduring question is as appropriate for the biblical prayers for help as it is for contemporary ones. In its various forms, the question usually has two parts to it. One is the specific question about whether anything happens to change the external situation of the one praying. Whatever the situation of distress or need, is the petitioner extricated from the distress and is the need met? The other dimension to the question is whether anything happens internally to the one who prays so that the fear and anxiety are taken away. In other words, does the situation change and/or does the person change? It may be that only one of those things happens, or they both happen in a single whole. But whatever the case, the basic question is: Does prayer change things?

That question, however, is not asked in Israel in that general sort of way, in the way that one might (as has been done) test it out by growing plants and then praying over some of them to see if they grow better or faster than others. It is, in the Old Testament, always a question raised with reference to the prayer of some one or group in need of help and who, in many cases, has nowhere else to turn for help. This is no scientific exercise. It is a cry, a plea, an argument, a voice raised in anguish and quiet—or noisy—desperation. So the issue is not whether prayer changes things, but whether God hears *this* prayer and does something about *this* situation and for *this* person or group.

In previous chapters, it has been suggested that prayer is dialogical and conversational in the Bible. The aim in this chapter is to show how the conversation continues, becomes in fact a dialogue and not an unattended monologue, which is always the fear of the one praying—that there is no one to hear; that God will not answer. What are the indications that something happened and the cries were heard when the people of Scripture prayed, and what may be discerned about the process of change and divine response?

PRAYERS HEARD AND ANSWERED

There are many indications that the prayers are heard and answered. Sometimes this is a matter of direct testimony, particularly in the psalm prayers where there is no context to discover the outcome of the prayer except as it is conveyed within the prayer itself or in the song of thanksgiving that follows the prayer. Indeed it is in such testimony that the close connection of the song of thanksgiving to the prayer for help is indicated. One such song, Psalm 34, provides a kind of paradigm of the structure of prayer in Scripture and enables us to see the movement that is initiated in the relationship between God and the person in need when a cry for help goes up, when prayer is uttered:

> I sought the LORD, and he answered me,
>   and delivered me from all my fears.
> Look to him and be radiant;
>   so your faces shall never be ashamed.
> This poor soul [i.e., afflicted] cried
>   and was heard by the LORD,
> and was saved from every trouble. (vv. 4-6)[1]

The one who prayed is identified as an "afflicted" person. The term may have to do with humility and meekness, but, in the context of the prayers for help, it is also to be understood as an indication of the distress of the suppliant—literally poor and weak, afflicted or oppressed. That poverty and distress may be of the soul and spirit,[2] or it may be more physical and social. The psalm is very open at that point. But that the prayer was uttered in extremis is indicated by the other references to the situation of the petitioner, "my fears" and "his [lit.] troubles." The prayer for help has been a cry "out of the depths." Trouble evoking fear characterizes this situation and most of the ones in which people cry out for help.

The prayer is referred to in the verbs "sought" and "cried."[3] God's positive response is then indicated in two parts. The first is found in the verbs of hearing and answering and the second in the verbs of delivering and saving. In looking at the petitions, we have seen that there is often a two-part structure to the plea—a call for God's attention or turning toward the one in trouble, and a plea for help, that is, God's active intervention to save. That twofold plea is represented here also in the testimony that God has responded: God "answered" and "delivered"; God "heard" and "saved." The claim is simple and clear. When the cry went up in prayer, God heard and helped. The nature of that "answer" or of the salvation/deliverance is not indicated, but that it happened is the point of the song. Further, the frequent experience of shame is overcome by "looking to him," that is, by prayer. The experience of the psalmist is then made into a general claim about God's way and what happens when those in trouble cry for help:

> When they[4] cry for help,[5] the LORD hears,
>   and rescues them from all their troubles. (v. 17)

Again the two-part response is indicated: God hears and rescues. The song of thanksgiving testifies that in *this* situation God heard and saved *this* poor soul but also that what happened on this occasion is what God does when the cry for help goes up to heaven.

Support for that claim is given in other songs of thanksgiving.[6] Psalm 40:1-2, part of a thanksgiving for deliverance, is instructive in this regard:

> I waited[7] for the LORD,
>   he inclined to me and heard my cry.
> He drew me up from the desolate pit,
>   out of the miry bog,
> and set my feet upon a rock,
>   making my steps secure.

The psalmist testifies to an intense waiting and expectation of help, which came. The two-part movement of hearing and helping is indicated, and the particular act of help is described in powerful figurative language of extrication from mire and pit, from the quicksand into which the petitioner has sunk and threatens to go under, from the morass of trouble and woe. That figure is continued with the image of firm footing, the secure rock on which the afflicted one now stands because of God's help. The world of the suppliant no longer threatens to crumble underneath and fall apart. The persecutors and the troubles can no longer pull this sufferer under. The Lord has helped.

The king also gives thanks to God for hearing his cry:

> In my distress I called upon the LORD;
>   to my God I cried for help.
> From his temple[8] he heard my voice,
>   and my cry to him reached his ears. (Ps 18:6)

The song then continues with a long description of the appearing of God in the phenomena of a great storm, after which the king moves from the hearing of the prayer to God's deliverance:

> He reached down from on high, he took me;
>   he drew me out of mighty waters.
> He delivered me from my strong enemy,
>   and from those who hated me;
> for they were too mighty for me.

> They confronted me in the day of my calamity;
>> but the LORD was my support.
> He brought me out into a broad place;
>> he delivered me, because he delighted in me.
>> (vv. 16-19)

The imagery is reminiscent of Psalm 40 and of elements of the laments in the prayers for help.[9] God has extricated the king from the waters that overwhelmed him and has brought him out into a place to stand.[10] In this case, however, the deliverance is spelled out more specifically. The Lord has delivered the king from his enemies and so has made him secure against the dangers and foes that threatened to do him in.

In several instances, the afflicted one who prays for help testifies within the prayer itself that God has heard the prayer:[11]

> The LORD has heard the sound of my weeping.
> The LORD has heard my supplication;
>> the LORD accepts my prayer. (Ps 6:8-9)

The anguished prayer for help in Psalm 22, which later becomes a clue to the meaning of the passion of Christ, culminates in an extended song of thanksgiving at the end of the prayer, in which the psalmist testifies to the congregation that God heard "his" prayer (v. 24).

Lamentations 3:55ff. provides a formulation of the structure of prayer very much like what we saw in Psalm 34, only this time within the prayer for help itself:

> I called on your name, O LORD,
>> from the depths of the pit;
> you heard my plea, "Do not close your ear
>> to my cry for help, but give me relief!"
> You came near when I called on you;
>> you said, "Do not fear!" (vv. 55-57)

The prayer then goes on in several statements in perfect-tense form to express what God has done:

> You have taken up my cause, O LORD,
>> you have redeemed my life.
> You have seen the wrong done to me, O LORD.
>> (vv. 58-59)

The suppliant tells of the prayer "from the depths" and actually quotes it. Three things follow that cry. As in Psalm 34, there is a turning to the petitioner—"You came near. . . . " And there is God's active help to redeem and deliver the one who has cried out. The third element, not mentioned in Psalm 34, is the divine response, "Do not fear." That is a feature of God's hearing that is quite central and important; we shall look at it in some detail further on in this chapter.

Along with these explicit references to God hearing the prayer, there are other indicators of God's positive response to the prayers. In Ps 27:6, the petitioner says, "Now my head is lifted up above my enemies all around me," and then goes on to make a vow of praise and sacrifice, certain of God's help. The reverse move takes place in Ps 56:13. Following a vow to praise and sacrifice, the suppliant says:

> For you have delivered my soul from death,
> and my feet from falling.

Psalm 3 concludes with the declaration:

> For you have struck all my enemies on the cheek;
> you have broken the teeth of the wicked. (v. 7b)[12]

The prayer for the king in Psalm 20 contains an indication of God's answering help in verse 6:

Now I know that the LORD will save [NRSV: help][13] his anointed;
he will answer him from his holy heaven.

Because they provide a context not available for the psalm prayers, the prayers embedded in prose and prophetic texts often tell us more specifically about the outcome. In these cases, the texts give an explicit, and usually immediate, indication that the prayer has been heard and answered either in a report that God heard and/or helped in some way[14] or by means of a divine speech in response to the prayer.[15] At other times, the continuation of the story will give some indication of God's positive response to the prayer.[16] There are also occasions when the prayer itself is not recorded in the text, but some indication is given of God's positive response.[17]

The answer is not always positive. Or it may be only partially so. This may have implications for the psalm prayers also. That is, the prose prayers are uttered in similar situations of distress and need by faithful and trusting servants of the Lord. The mixed responses to the prayers in narrative texts may be indicative of mixed responses also to the more formal prayers of the Psalter. One has to be careful at this point, however. The negative responses tend to be of two sorts. In some instances, the purpose of God is carried out in another fashion than according to the petition. For example, Abraham's great distress is his lack of an heir. When he prays, "O that Ishmael might live in your sight!" the Lord answers, "No, but your wife Sarah shall bear you a son" (Gen 17:18-19). The prayer is indeed heard, and the negative answer is in behalf of an even greater positive response to the prayer. Elijah pleads to God to let him die, but instead the Lord rejuvenates him and sends him back to his calling as the prophet of God (1 Kgs 19:4-18). Jonah makes the same plea and is refused as a way of demonstrating the Lord's inclination toward mercy more than judgment (Jonah 4:2-11).

More often, the negative response is tied to the Lord's intention to punish the people for their faithlessness.[18] Here the tension between the justice and mercy of God is felt, pulling toward God's insistence on an obedience that cannot lightly be dismissed. We shall look at the prayers of intercession, the prayers of the mediator, more in chapter 8. When we do, we shall see the constant tug in the mind of God between a relenting mercy and a just punishment, between the divine will to forgive and the divine intention to create a faithful community to do the Lord's will in the world. One example of such a tension may be cited in this instance in relation to a prayer of Moses for the people.[19] When he pleads for God's forgiveness of the people in Num 14:19, that is granted; but the Lord goes on to prohibit any but Caleb from entering the land (vv. 21-24). Here it is likely that the response is to be understood as answering Moses' prayer by granting forgiveness, which was the specific petition of the prayer. The Lord's answer, however, also shows God's intention to bring into the land a people of "a different spirit" who will "follow me wholeheartedly."

This survey of the prayers of the Bible has made it clear that there are many indications, in the prayers themselves, in the songs of thanksgiving, and in the accounts of people praying, that God heard the prayers and responded in some fashion to help. One expects that would be so in the stories, for the record of the prayer is likely to be preserved precisely because the prayer was heard. But that, of course, is just the point. Time and again in the story, the people cried out to God and God responded. It is one of the primary threads binding the whole together. When the people, in one voice or in many, cry out for help, the ears of God are open,[20] and God responds in ways to deal with their situation, to provide the help that is needed. The narrative contexts reveal what the psalm prayers suggest, that the prayer for help is often in a situation of such desperation that no other help is available or possible. The human structures cannot help or have broken down, whether they are political,[21] judicial,[22] familial,[23] or whatever. So another structure takes over. It is the structure of human pain and divine compassion, a framework of existence that takes shape in prayer and God's response. We need to look more closely at the substance of that response, what happened when God heard and acted.

THE ORACLE OF SALVATION

When the community prays for help in the words of Psalm 85, its questions of complaint (vv. 5-6) are followed by a petition (v. 7):

> Show us your steadfast love, O LORD,
> and grant us your salvation.

Then a voice says these words (v. 8):

> Let me hear what God the LORD will speak,
> for he will speak peace to his people.

The psalm thus suggests that at some point in the midst of the prayer for help, or whatever ritual or liturgy may have accompanied it,[24] those praying expected a specific word of response from God communicated to them in some manner. The particular content or character of that response is peace, *šālôm*—well-being, safety, security.

Two of the prayers for help that appear without context to tell us anything of God's response also give us some indication of a quite specific word that was desired or received by the one who cried out. The paradigmatic prayer of Lam 3:55ff., referred to above, includes in it a report of what God said in answering the prayer:

> You came near when I called on you;
> you said, "Do not fear!"

In the midst of various petitions at the beginning of Psalm 35, the psalmist says:

> Say to my soul, "I am your salvation." (v. 3)

These explicit quotations of God's response to prayer, contained within the prayers themselves, give us a clue to the basic word of assurance that was the primary response desired (so Psalm 35) and received (so Lamentations 3) by those afflicted souls who lifted their prayers of pain to God. They do not exhaust the possible responses of God. Many of the prayers in the narrative texts have a quite specific word from God or act of help, and we shall look at these further. In some instances, the help needed was of a different sort altogether, direction and instruction. But these two quotations are indicative of what was at the heart of the matter when people were in trouble and sought God's help. They are echoed again and again in the course of Scripture and give us our best clue to God's response to prayer.

The two statements of God in Lamentations 3 and Psalm 35 give us the main parts of a form of divine speech that we hear frequently in the Old Testament and also in the New. It has come to be called the oracle of salvation, though that is merely a modern designation.[25] It means that a divine speech is transmitted through some agency, that is, an oracle, and its basic character is an announcement of salvation and deliverance. It is fundamentally a word of assurance, and we will also use that way of referring to this divine speech.

The Form of God's Response

Among the places where we hear this oracle of salvation best and in some detail is the prophecy of the Second Isaiah (Isaiah 40–55), who announced to weary, despairing, and complaining exiles that God would deliver them. We shall look at the oracle there, where it is not directly associated with prayer, before turning to examine its presence in the context of prayer. One such salvation oracle, a divine speech through the mediation of the prophet, is found in Isa 41:8-13:

> [8] But you, Israel, my servant,
>   Jacob, whom I have chosen,
>   the offspring of Abraham, my friend;
> [9] you whom I took from the ends of the earth,
>   and called from its farthest corners,
>   saying to you, "You are my servant,
>   I have chosen you and not cast you off";
> [10] do not fear, for I am with you,
>   do not be afraid, for I am your God;
>   I will strengthen you, I will help you,
>   I will uphold you with my victorious right hand.
> [11] Yes, all who are incensed against you
>   shall be ashamed and disgraced;
>   those who strive against you
>   shall be as nothing and shall perish.
> [12] You shall seek those who contend with you,
>   but you shall not find them;
>   those who war against you
>   shall be as nothing at all.
> [13] For I, the LORD your God,
>   hold your right hand;
>   it is I who say to you, "Do not fear,
>   I will help you."

The characteristic features of the oracle of salvation appear in these verses. They do not have to appear in any particular order. Some of them may be repeated, as they are in this case, and some of them may be abbreviated, as they are in other instances. Those features are as follows:

1. The divine speech is couched as a *direct address* to the one who prayed. It is not a generalized response, although it is the same word

over and over again. In each instance, it comes directly as God's word to a particular individual or community. That is seen sometimes in specific naming of the recipient of the oracle, in this case "Israel" or "Jacob,"[26] but even more in the frequent use of the singular second-person pronoun, "you" and "your," in this case over twenty times. This direct address is reinforced in this particular instance with such expressions as "my servant," "whom I have chosen," and "my friend." The oracle of salvation thus has a highly personal character. It assumes and speaks out of a relationship that is understood and couched in very personal terms. What in the prayer is so much up for grabs or under question, particularly in the complaints, is here made firm. The questions about whether in fact the relationship with God is sure, questions the suppliant seeks to answer for himself or herself in the expressions of trust and confidence, are here answered by God in the deeply personal tone and language of the oracle of salvation.

2. Some *intimation of the lament* or complaint may be present in God's word of response. That is, there is an allusion to the plight as it is understood by the one who prays. Here God says to exiled Israel, "I have not cast you off" (*m's;* v. 9). These words echo the complaint of the people over the destruction of Jerusalem in Lamentations that concludes that series of laments and prayers:

> Renew our days as of old—
>   unless you have utterly rejected us [*m's*],
> and are angry with us beyond measure. (Lam 5:22)

The oracle of salvation addresses the people precisely in their own self-understanding and deepest fear, that they have been rejected by God. The oracle that follows in Isa 41:14-16 is a divine speech of a similar sort, which addresses the people as "you worm, Jacob," a strange term, not meant as a divine denigration of the people, as might appear on the surface. That could hardly be so, following immediately after the words, "Do not fear." It is rather a reflection once more of the self-understanding of the afflicted one. We see the term exactly in that context in Ps 22:6: "But I am a worm." Those who see themselves as nothing but worms are given a word of assurance that comes to them in full awareness of that self-denigration, the low self-esteem of one in suffering and pain.[27] So also, the one who is overwhelmed by the mighty waters (e.g., Ps 69:1-2, 14-15) is addressed in that circumstance: "When you pass through the waters ... " (Isa 43:2). Those who feel forsaken and ashamed are spoken to in their shame and forsakenness with words assuring them that they will not be ashamed and forsaken.[28] The salvation oracle at one point in this kind of address even accounts for the tension between the experience of God-forsakenness and the promised grace of God with an explicit indication that the sense of abandonment was true to reality but not enduring:

> For *a brief moment* I abandoned you,
>   but with great compassion I will gather you.
> In overflowing wrath *for a moment*
>   I hid my face from you,
> but with *everlasting love* I will have compassion on you,
>   says the LORD, your Redeemer. (Isa 54:7-8)

That word of assurance is addressed to exiles and is consistent with the biblical story that sees them as the objects of God's wrath and "abandoned" to exile, but only for a brief period. It is the purpose of the prophet's words in Isaiah 40–55 to announce that the "moment" is over and the "everlasting love" continues. Such an understanding of the momentary wrath and the perduring love, however, is not confined to the exilic and prophetic context. In one of the most eloquent of all the songs of thanksgiving, just that point is made by the one who gives thanks for having been healed and restored to life:

> For his anger is but for a moment;
>   his favor is for a lifetime.
> Weeping may linger for the night,
>   but joy comes with the morning. (Ps 30:5)

3. The heart of the oracle of salvation and its effective and performative word is the simple *assurance, "Do not fear."* It occurs in most of the salvation oracles[29] and is the most characteristic single feature of this divine word. Lamentations 3:57, as we noted above, identifies these words, "Do not fear," or "Fear not," as the response of God to the prayer for help:

> You came near when I called on you;
>   you said, "Do not fear!"

This word of assurance is often repeated poetically, "Do not be dismayed," or "Do not be discouraged." Its performative character is suggested in the way that these assuring words have the capacity to remove the fear and anxiety that are at the center of the trouble and distress of those who cry out to God. Over and over again the prayers of the Psalms express the fear of death or the terror in the mind and heart of the petitioner in the face of enemies. In the expressions of trust and confidence or songs of thanksgiving, the afflicted one bears witness to the power of this word of assurance to quell the fear that has evoked the prayer.[30] It is no accident that in the summary structure or paradigm of prayer that we noted in Psalm 34, this particular point is made quite directly:

> I sought the LORD, and he answered me,
> and delivered me from all my fears. (v. 4)

4. That fundamental word of assurance is then given a *basis,* a reason for not being afraid.[31] It takes form in one or two ways typically, and sometimes both types of reasons will be present:

a. The first is a nominal sentence expressing God's turning to the person and assurance that the relationship continues. The most common form of this is, "I am with you."[32] Its frequency is tied to the way it addresses the fundamental fear of those who cry out, that God has abandoned or forsaken them, that the enemies and wicked are correct when they say, "Where is your God?" or "God has forgotten." The prayers for help identify the presence of God as one of the key issues raised by the trouble and affliction. The oracle of salvation speaks directly to that issue, assuring those in trouble that God is indeed with them. Other such expressions also occur, affirming on God's part the perdurance of the relationship as sufficient reason not to be afraid any longer: "I am your God" (Isa 41:10); "I am the LORD your God, the Holy One of Israel, your Savior" (Isa 43:3); "[Y]our Redeemer is the Holy One of Israel" (Isa 41:14; 54:5); "[F]or your Maker is your husband" (Isa 54:5). It is exactly one of these divine words for which the psalmist prays in Ps 35:3, that prayer where we began to see intimations of the oracle of salvation in the prayer for help:

> Say to my soul,
> "I am your salvation."

The one who "speaks peace to his people" (Ps 85:8), the distressed and those in need of help, is "your God," "the Holy One of Israel," "your redeemer," "your salvation," and "with you" in even the worst experiences of suffering and oppression.

b. The other type of reason giving a basis for not being afraid or dismayed is a verbal sentence telling of God's intention to help and deliver. "I will help you" is a characteristic form of this announcement.[33] Isaiah 41:10 elaborates this:

> I will strengthen you, I will help you,
> I will uphold you with my victorious right hand.

Similar expressions occur: "I have redeemed you" (Isa 43:1); "I am going to save you" (Jer 30:10). Isaiah 54:6 uses marital imagery to express this intention of God to help:

> For the LORD has called you
> like a wife forsaken and grieved in spirit,
> like the wife of a man's youth when she is cast off,
> says your God.

These declarations are often couched in the perfect tense in Hebrew and thus as completed actions, even if sometimes they are translated with future verbs. God has heard the prayer and has announced an intention to help. It is an accomplished fact, and so the psalmist can declare with certainty—and also often in the perfect tense—that "the LORD has heard my supplication; the LORD accepts my prayer" (Ps 6:9), that "you have struck all my enemies on the cheek; you have broken the teeth of the wicked" (Ps 3:7; my trans.).

As the nominal statements address the fear that God is no longer present with me, so the verbal statements address the issue of the power and willingness of God to help. The prayer that seeks God's presence as a refuge in time of trouble[34] also seeks God's help and deliverance from the pit, the waters, the plots of the enemies, the death that threatens. The one who hopes that God will see the trouble and woe prays further that "you will take it into your hands" (Ps 10:14). Where there has been "no one to help" (Ps 22:11), now God will help.

5. Sometimes the oracle of salvation will *elaborate the ways of helping* in a future tense. We see this in Isa 41:11 in language familiar from the Psalms:

> Yes, all who are incensed against you
>   shall be ashamed and disgraced;
> those who strive against you
>   shall be as nothing and shall perish.

The conclusion of Psalm 6 seems to grow directly out of just such an elaboration of God's way of helping:

> The LORD has heard my supplication;
>   the LORD accepts my prayer.
> All my enemies shall be ashamed and struck with terror;
>   they shall turn back, and in a moment be put to shame.
>   (vv. 9-10)

Isaiah 41:14-16 uses the imagery of a threshing sledge to describe the way the returning exiles will eliminate obstacles on their journey home, and in 43:5-6 God announces that the deliverance will bring all the offspring of Israel home.

In all of these instances, the oracle from God elaborates in detail and with poetic imagery how the help that is sought in prayer will come to those who cry out.

Not every oracle of salvation is formed on the above model. The announcement of salvation to Baruch, Jeremiah's scribe, is really quite different, focusing upon the specific situation and God's punishment of the people as well as assuring Baruch of his personal deliverance in that situation (Jer 45:4-5). As we shall see, the divine response comes in different forms fairly frequently in the prose accounts of prayer, reflecting the contextual character of those prayers. But the basic form of the divine response as we have described it on the basis of Second Isaiah's prophecies is significantly enough reflected in psalm, prose, and prophetic prayers that we can identify it as representative of what is generally characteristic of God's way of responding to human prayer. The extent to which that is the case is further indicated by the ubiquity of this type of divine address to those who pray, not only in Scripture but also among Israel's neighbors. There, such oracles are no more completely uniform or identical to the biblical oracle of salvation than those in Scripture are exactly alike. But the similarity is clear.

Salvation Oracles outside the Bible

Oracles of salvation as a response to prayer are found in some of the Assyrian royal inscriptions of the first millennium in Mesopotamia. In the first of a series of oracles to the king Esarhaddon,[35] the goddess Ishtar addresses him by name, "Esarhaddon, king of the lands," and says immediately, as is often the case in the biblical oracles, "Fear not!" As in the case of Isa 41:8-13, that basic word of assurance is repeated at the end of the oracle, where the king is addressed with reference to his prayer and lament, that is, in terms of his situation of distress: "Fear not! You who are paralyzed (saying), 'Only in crying Woe can I either get up or sit down.'" The goddess identifies herself in first-person sentences that serve to assure the king of the continuing presence of the goddess and of help against his enemies: "I am Ishtar of Arbela! I shall lie in wait for your enemies, I shall give them to you. I, Ishtar of Arbela, will go before you and behind you." Like the other oracles in this series, a note at the end identifies the one through whom the oracle was given, in most of the instances a named woman.

A second oracle, mostly untranslatable, begins: "O king of Assyria, fear not! The enemy of the king of Assyria I will deliver to slaughter." The following oracle addresses the king once more with the basic word of assurance, "Fear not, Esarhaddon!" repeated once more near the end of the oracle. The grounds for that assurance are given in the announcement that "sixty great gods are standing together with me and protect you." If the translation is correct at this point, the king is further reassured in language reminiscent of Second Isaiah: "When you were small, I chose you."[36] A theme from the prayers for help of the Psalms appears in the admonition: "Do not trust human beings!"[37] And twice the goddess indicates what should be the response of the king to the word of assurance: "Praise me!"

An oracle gives the basis for not fearing by echoing the fears of abandonment and shame that are so prominent in the prayers and by offering help to the king: "Fear not, O king! Because I have spoken to you (in an oracle), I will not abandon you. Because I have encouraged you, I shall not let you come to shame. I will help you."

Yet another oracle of salvation was given to Esarhaddon by the god Ashur and indeed is called an "(oracle of) well-being." It shows some of the diversity of this type of speech in that there is no "fear not" assurance here, but the king refers to Esarhaddon's prayer and promises to come and help:

> You (Esarhaddon) opened your mouth. Now I, Ashur, have heard your distress cry. From the gate of heaven I soar down (?). I will surely overthrow (them); I will surely have fire consume them. You can stand securely among them.[38]

It concludes with a call for the praise of those who see the destructive power of the god in Esarhaddon's behalf.

On the occasion of an invasion by the Elamites, the later Assyrian king Ashurbanipal prayed to the goddess Ishtar a lengthy and formal prayer in the sanctuary and received an oracle of salvation from her when she appeared to him in a theophany at night.[39] The king describes in detail his approach to the image of the goddess, how he stood in front of it and then crouched down at the feet of the statue, praying and crying:[40] "I kneeled before her, prayed to her, and wept."[41] The king reports:

> The goddess Ishtar heard my anxious sighs and said, "Fear not!"
> and gave me confidence, (saying) "Since you have lifted your hands
> in prayer and your eyes have filled with tears, I have had mercy."

The context provided by the text confirms what we see in various ways in the Bible: that the oracle of salvation is a word of assurance in response to a prayer for help by one in great distress ("anxious sighs," "tears"). Its effective character is demonstrated here as in the Psalms and other prayers. The king explicitly states that the "Fear not!" spoken by the goddess "gave me confidence." The oracle to the king, quoted above, is quite brief. The more extended elaboration of what the deity will do to help is then given in a separate "nocturnal vision" to a priest or seer.[42]

One other instance from Mesopotamia should be mentioned. In the didactic literary text *ludlul bel nemeqi* (I will praise the lord of wisdom),[43] the afflicted speaker describes himself at length in the kind of lamenting language of a psalmic prayer for help, referring to tears and weeping, disintegration of the self, the nearness of death, abandonment by friends and family, as well as persons who slander and tell lies about the suffering noble and plot against him. The turning point in the account is when the suffering speaker has a dream in which there appears "a remarkable young woman of shining countenance,... equal to a god." He continues: "She spoke my deliverance... 'Fear not,' she said, 'I [will... you].'... She said, 'Be delivered from your very wretched state.'" The "young woman," apparently an emissary from the god Marduk, gives the basic word of assurance and then a reason for it in terms of what she will do, most of which is no longer preserved in the text. The text goes on in the immediately following lines to say that Marduk "received my prayers" and gave him prosperity or well-being. The medium of the oracle of salvation is both dream vision and the tablet of an incantation priest. The rest of the poem details all that Marduk did to restore him and concludes with words of praise and thanksgiving as well as sacrifice. The text as a whole recounts the move from lament to oracle to praise in much the same way as the biblical structure of prayer, moving from prayer to oracle to praise and thanksgiving.

That same movement is found in an Egyptian context in a speech of Ramesses II in the Literary Record of the Battle of Kadesh. There the Egyptian king reports his prayer to the god Amun and the response of the deity:

> Now I made prayers from the ends of foreign countries, while my voice circulated throughout Southern On. I found Amun had come when I called to him. He placed his hand with mine while I had rejoiced, for he had called behind me, "Do not fear, forward! I am with you, I am your father, my hand is with you. I am more beneficial than myriads of men. I am a Lord of Victory who loves valor."[44]

The human prayer is followed by the divine oracle of salvation. The heart of the deity's response to the cry for help is again the words, "Do not fear." And again the reason for that assurance is found in a series of first-person statements by the deity about the continuing relation between the one who prays, the king, and the deity Amun. The central grounding is exactly what we hear again and again in the Bible, "I am with you." But that is underscored by other similar statements, such as, "I am your father." The repeated reference to the deity's hand being with the king is similar to the claim in the oracle of salvation in Deutero-Isaiah that "I will uphold you" (Isa 41:10) or "I hold your right hand" (Isa 41:13). The god Amun thus answers the Egyptian king in the same manner as does the Lord of Israel in responding to the prayers of God.

The Greek historian Herodotus also reports an oracle of salvation in a dream to "Sethos" or Seti in a battle against the Assyrian king Sennacherib:

> Afterwards, therefore, when Sennacherib, king of the Arabians and the Assyrians, marched his vast army into Egypt, the warriors one

and all refused to come to his (Sethos') aid. Upon this the monarch, greatly distressed, entered into the sanctuary and, before the image of the god, bewailed the fate which impended over him. As he wept he fell asleep, and dreamed that the god came and stood at his side, bidding him to be of good cheer, and go boldly forth to meet the Arabian host, which would do him no hurt, as he (the god) himself would send those who should help him. Sethos then, relying on the dream, collected those of the Egyptians who were willing to follow him who were none of them warriors, but traders, artisans and market people; and with these marched to Pelusium, which commands the entrance into Egypt, and there pitched his camp. (Herodotus 2.139)[45]

The oracle of salvation appears in yet other contexts. It occurs in Hittite dream reports, telling of the appearance of a deity with a reassuring word to the king.[46] Two examples closer to the biblical world should be mentioned particularly. One of these is reported in a ninth- or eighth-century Aramaic inscription on a stele set up by Zakir, king of Lu'ash and Hamat, commemorating his battle with a coalition of Syrian and Anatolian kings.[47] At the beginning of the inscription, the king says: "I am Zakir,[48] king of Hamat and Lu'ash. A humble ['nh] man am I. Be'elshamayn [helped me] and stood by me." Here the king describes himself in the same terms as the psalmist in Ps 34:6, the text we have identified as setting forth in its simplest form the structure of biblical prayer.[49] The "humble" man is the same self-designation as used by the psalmist in the song of thanksgiving, "this poor soul" ('ny), a faithful servant of God in distress. The text is broken in the next line, but the proposal to read "Be'elshamayn [helped me/saved me]" or the like is surely correct and corresponds to the second half of Ps 34:6:

> This poor soul cried, and was heard by the LORD,
> and was saved from every trouble.

That a prayer for help is in view is then confirmed further on in the inscription. Zakir describes at length the siege preparations made against him by the coalition of kings, a royal and national equivalent of the enemies surrounding and hemming in like wild beasts the afflicted suppliant—which is exactly the position in which Zakir finds himself. Facing this massive threat, the king says:

> But I lifted up my hand to Be'elshamayn, and Be'elshamayn heard me. Be'elshamayn [spoke] to me through seers and through diviners. Be'elshamayn [said to me]: Do not fear, for I made you king, and I shall stand by you and deliver you from all [these kings who] set up a siege against you. [Be'elshamayn] said to me: [I shall de-

stroy] all these kings who set up [a siege against you and made this moat] and this wall which...[50]

The explicit reference to Zakir's praying—"I lifted my hand to Be'elshamayn"—is followed by the one other element of the paradigm found in Ps 34:6: "Be'elshamayn heard me." Because this is in the form of the song of thanksgiving, we have already heard in the first lines that the deity helped Zakir and stood by him. Now he reports not what his god did for him, but the word of salvation Be'elshamayn spoke to him, that is, the oracle of salvation. As in the Assyrian texts, the oracle is transmitted through a priestly or prophetic figure, the latter in this case. The basic word of assurance, "Fear not," is the first and primary word. It is then grounded in reasons, like the biblical oracle. They are a series of verbal sentences, the first of which reaffirms the relationship between king and deity: "I made you king." The other two are stated in a future tense and declare the deity's intention to stand with the king and deliver him. The expression "I will stand with you" is reminiscent of the many biblical affirmations of God, "I will be with you," but in this instance an active verb is used that appears frequently in the psalm prayers in the petition to God to "rise" or "rise up" (*qûm*) in behalf of the persecuted psalmist and against her or his enemies.[51] The idiom in this instance is different and points to an action toward the petitioner rather than against the enemy. In fact, of course, it is both. The final basis for the king's confidence before the enemy is the deity's assurance, "I will deliver you." The verb used in this expression, *ḥlṣ*, "deliver/save/rescue," appears in the Bible almost exclusively in the psalm prayers for help[52] and the songs of thanksgiving[53] that grow out of them, either as pleas for God's deliverance or reports of its happening. In two instances, the verb actually appears in divine oracles within the Psalms. Psalm 81:7 is a divine word to the people recalling God's response to their prayers in the past:

> In distress you called, and I rescued [*ḥlṣ*] you;
> I answered you in the secret place of thunder.

The structure of prayer is set forth in God's own speech, similarly to that of the grateful petitioner in Ps 34:4-6. People in distress cry out to God in prayer. God answers and delivers. The second divine speech with the verb *ḥlṣ* is a general salvation oracle at the end of Psalm 91 (see below):

> When they call to me, I will answer them;
> I will be with them in trouble,
> I will rescue [*ḥlṣ*] them and honor them. (v. 15)[54]

There follows then a much more detailed spelling out of just what Be'elshamayn will do in this instance, corresponding to the form of the

oracle of salvation we have seen in Second Isaiah in the elaboration of
the way God will help and deliver: "I shall destroy all these kings, etc."[55]
The biblical forms and idioms are thus echoed in very pronounced ways
in Zakir's stele, and the oracle of salvation, as in the other Near Eastern texts examined, is set forth as a response to the prayer for help of
a person in trouble.

Finally, we return to the cave at Khirbet Beit Lei outside Samaria in
the early sixth century and the prayers carved roughly on the walls by
those who hid there.[56] Along with the prayers, there is the following
inscription:

> ['n(k)y] yhwh 'lhykh . 'rṣh
> 'ry yhdh wg'lty yršlm
> [I am] the LORD your God.
> I will accept the cities of Judah;
>   I will redeem Jerusalem.

If the inscription is read correctly—and its reading is somewhat problematic[57]—it is an oracle of salvation in response to the prayers for help
inscribed elsewhere on the walls, though in this case the usual mediation
of a priest in the sanctuary would seem to be ruled out. The language
and form are very reminiscent of the salvation oracles of Second Isaiah.
We do not find the typical assurance, "Fear not," but the reasons for
that assurance appear in the usual form of: (1) a nominal sentence identifying the deity and in terms of an affirmation of the relationship to
those who pray; and (2) two verbal sentences announcing what God is
going to do in behalf of the suppliant(s). The former, "I am your God,"
occurs also in the salvation oracles of Second Isaiah, as we have seen (Isa
41:13). The latter are also echoed in the Isaianic oracles of salvation in
Isa 43:2: "Do not fear, for I have redeemed you," as well as in the psalm
prayers where the first-person statements of the inscription appear in a
somewhat variant form as third-person statements:[58]

> For God will save Zion [i.e., Jerusalem]
>   and rebuild the cities of Judah. (Ps 69:35)

The comparison to the biblical Psalms is important because, as we
have noted,[59] one of the brief prayers on the wall of the cave—"Save,
O Lord!"—is virtually identical to the opening line of the prayer in
Psalm 69: "Save me, O God."[60] The petition at the beginning of Psalm
69 is answered in an oracle of salvation, not preserved in the psalm itself but alluded to in the verse quoted above (Ps 69:35). The apparent
incongruity between a *personal* and *individual* prayer being answered
by a salvation oracle referring to *Jerusalem* and *the cities of Judah* is at
least alleviated in the recognition that such an association occurs both in
biblical prayer and in extrabiblical prayers contemporary with those in

Scripture. The help and assurance given to the individual in trouble encompass the larger community that has undergone woe and trouble. The oracle of salvation inscribed in the cave is still addressed personally—"I am the Lord *your* [sing.] God"—even though the salvation announced involves the larger community. In the early sixth century, individual and personal distress clearly overlapped under the threat and conquest of the Babylonian army and its outcome in destruction of Jerusalem and Judah as well as the exile of many of the citizens.[61] Furthermore, Second Isaiah's salvation oracles, addressed to the community of Israel, are also couched in second-person singular terms, appropriate in response to the individual prayer for help.

While other examples of the salvation oracle in extrabiblical texts could be cited, the texts discussed above, ranging from Ramesses II and Esarhaddon to Herodotus and from Egypt and Anatolia to Syria-Palestine, are sufficient indication of the widespread presence of this form of divine speech. Even as the biblical prayers echo the prayers of Israel's neighbors, so also the divine response to human prayer is characteristically the same, further suggesting an underlying universality of form and experience in the structure of prayer and faith as well as confirming the intimate relation of the oracle of salvation to the prayer for help. A further look now at the biblical prayers themselves will help cement that connection and reinforce the central claim of these pages, that what is most sought and received when those in trouble cry out to God is the word of assurance found in the oracle of salvation.

The Oracle of Salvation in the Context of Prayer

While the discussion of the oracle of salvation in Second Isaiah has already pointed to its echoes in the psalm prayers and particularly the songs of thanksgiving after God has heard and responded, this basic word of assurance is so widely present, either directly or indirectly, as God's response to the cry for help that we need to look more closely at its occurrence in the context of prayer. Not every instance of prayer reveals a salvation oracle in response, though a divine word of some sort is often the outcome of prayer in the prose texts, as we have seen earlier in this chapter. Nor is every salvation oracle tied to a previously uttered prayer, though in some instances prayer may have preceded the oracle even if no longer preserved. The widespread use of the word of assurance, "Fear not," in the context of war and preparation for war probably reflects some form of prayer to God or inquiry of God even when that is not reported in the text.[62] Elements of the salvation oracle also appear as divine speech in the context of commissioning prophets and leaders. Here also there may be an association with prayer in that the words of assurance usually come in response to an objection or fear of the one standing under commission.[63] At least, there is the common denominator of divine speech of assurance in response to human address to God expressing fear and anxiety.

Prose and prophetic texts. Our particular interest, however, is the numerous occurrences of this divine word where prayer seems clearly in view and the oracle is at the heart of God's response. A number of prose and prophetic texts show us this association of prayer and oracle of salvation.

The two—prayer for help and salvation oracle—are "narrativized" in Gen 15:1-6, one of the stories of the promise of posterity to Abraham. That is, they are both present but now as a narrative structure. The oracle of salvation is given at the beginning of the text: "Do not be afraid, Abram, for I am your shield; your reward shall be very great" (v. 1). The primary word of assurance, "[Y]ou don't have to be afraid," is addressed personally and directly to Abram and is rooted in nominal sentences establishing and confirming God's protecting relationship and promising a future. While some may read this as a response to the preceding chapter, it is really a narrative "reordering" of the prayer and oracle. The oracle now anticipates the prayer, which is a complaint, "What will you give me, seeing that I continue[64] childless? . . . " repeated in the next verse. The basis for the assurance not to fear, "[Y]our reward shall be very great," is an apparently general promise of how God will help. But in this instance it is clearly a specific response to the plight of Abraham, which is the lack of an heir, a situation of suffering that evokes a number of prayers in the Old Testament[65] as well as in the contemporary world. In verses 4-5, the Lord goes on to elaborate specifically how Abraham will be helped or delivered—in the promise of a son and posterity as numerous as the stars of the heaven. The text concludes with an aspect of the structure of prayer that we shall take up in the next chapter, the response of trust when the word of assurance comes, even when the actual deliverance is yet to take place and the certainty of God's help is only there in the divine word of assurance.

There are two salvation oracles growing out of prayers for help that should be mentioned in this context because they also are requests concerning children. But because they are also prayers of women, we shall look at them more closely in relation to other women's prayers in chapter 6. In this context, it is sufficient to call attention to the presence of the oracle of salvation following after the prayer. Sent out by Abraham into the wilderness with her son Ishmael and dying of thirst, Hagar, the Egyptian slave-girl who had borne a son to Abraham when it appeared his wife Sarah could not, cries out in despair, "Do not let me look upon the death of the child" (Gen 21:16). In response to her lament, she receives an oracle of salvation from God: "Do not be afraid, for God has heard the voice of the boy where he is."[66] A promise of future greatness for Ishmael is then given, and water is provided to save their lives. In somewhat different fashion, a barren and "deeply distressed" Hannah prays with anguished weeping for a son and receives a word of assurance from the priest Eli that God will hear and answer her petition (1 Sam 1:9-18).[67]

There is no recorded oracle of salvation following Jacob's prayer for help out of his fear of meeting Esau (Gen 32:9-12). Instead the narrative tells of the struggle with the "man" at the ford of the Jabbok. But the prayer reveals that he is afraid (v. 11), that human situation toward which the heart of the salvation oracle is directed. Furthermore, the narrative does, at a later stage, place on Jacob's lips a report of God's positive response and in language reminiscent of the oracle: "Come, let us go up to Bethel, that I may make an altar there to the God *who answered me* in the day of my distress and *has been with me* wherever I have gone" (Gen 35:3). Jacob has received an answer to his prayer of distress—in whatever fashion the answer may have come—and affirms the reality of that assurance so persistent in the salvation oracles, "I am with you."[68] Jacob knows that God has been with him, not only in the day of distress and prayer, but throughout his journey. The fundamental assurance of the prayer is seen to have a larger character and defines his whole journey. Rather than seeming to point away from the specificity of the oracle of salvation in relation to a particular prayer, this suggests that the reason this word of assurance, "I am with you," is so frequently a part of the divine word is that it is definitive of God's continuing help. Thus at the end of Jacob's journeys—in actuality, only the apparent end—that divine promise is placed over the whole story as characteristic of Jacob's experience all along the way, an important clue to the centrality of this promise as the primary basis for alleviating human fear and distress (see below).[69]

Two texts present us with complaint prayers that are channeled through human beings who give salvation oracles but with quite different results. They are further related in that the "prayer" in both cases is part of the complaints or murmuring of the people of Israel in the wilderness. The first occasion is in the exodus from Egypt when the Israelites are at the sea and see the Egyptian army advancing upon them (Exod 14:10-14). While the questions of complaint are directed to Moses, "Was it because there were no graves in Egypt that you have taken us away to die in the wilderness?" (vv. 11-12), they are preceded by the report that "in great *fear* the Israelites cried out to the LORD" (v. 10).[70] Their questions are really a prayer of complaint, and Moses' response is an oracle of salvation assuring them of the Lord's help and deliverance: "Do not be afraid, stand firm, and see the deliverance that the LORD will accomplish for you today; for the Egyptians whom you see today you shall never see again. The LORD will fight for you, and you have only to be still" (vv. 13-14). The human situation in this moment is what it has been seen to be time and again, fear before the forces of oppression and persecution that threaten to do in the small and the weak. In that situation of despair when no mortal help can suffice, two things happen or may happen. The reality and power of God are questioned at their roots, and the presence and power of God are the only possible hopes, a court of last resort. As we have seen, these two possibilities may be present in a single prayer. So they are here. The cry of the people is described as a prayer to God in the Priestly tradition (v. 10b) but is articulated in the narrative whole as a complaint against Moses that in effect rules out God (vv. 11-12). But the presence and power of God are affirmed in the word of salvation as the basis for the disappearance of fear. Where no human force can help, the weak may "see" or look to the power of God to deliver. The warrior imagery functions precisely at this point to indicate that the one who hears the prayers of the suffering and the oppressed and responds with compassion and help is *able* to deliver the goods: The Lord will fight for you.[71] And so the word of assurance is fulfilled in the mighty act of God at the sea, and the "fear" of the people in the face of the mighty Egyptian army—after all they knew the oppressive power of the Egyptians quite well—is removed and transformed into the "fear" of the Lord and trust "in the LORD and his servant Moses" (Exod 14:30-31).

But the complaint to Moses that takes no account of God is ominous. The complaining prayer is always on the edge of distrust, which is why the expressions of confidence play such a major role in the psalm prayers for help. The anger and fear and questions about God can be uttered at the deepest level, but only if they are on the lips of trusting creatures who will not let go of that trust even when the facts of the case call in question to them as well as to others the presence of God and God's power to deliver. The stories of the wilderness are all too often stories of complaint without trust, and the prayers are more often prayers of intercession by the leader for a faithless people. So we encounter an oracle of salvation given by Joshua (Num 14:9) that does not have its outcome in the people's deliverance because it is addressed to complaints of the people against Moses and Aaron that are not authentic prayers, however much they may be accompanied by weeping and great fear (Num 14:1-4). The people have listened to the unfavorable reports of some of the spies, who speak of a land of giants, rather than to the reports of Caleb and Joshua of the goodness of the land. Joshua is well aware that his oracle of salvation is only that insofar as the people receive it in trust and confidence that the Lord will deliver them. So while he assures them that "the LORD is/will be with us; do not fear them [i.e., 'the people of the land']" (v. 9), he has already qualified that promise of deliverance with the caveats, "if the LORD is pleased with us," and "only do not rebel against the LORD" (vv. 8-9). The effective power of the words "Fear not" is always qualified by the trust of those who hear them. Where the cry for help is uttered in trust, even doubting and questioning trust, these are words of assurance that can turn weeping into laughter. Where they are words of complaint without the fundamental confidence in God's perduring compassion and protection, the "Fear not" becomes an exhortation and a warning rather than a word of assurance. It becomes that in the case of Joshua's words to the people when in response to his assurance that "the LORD is with us; do not fear them," the text immediately tells us "the whole congregation threatened to stone them" (vv. 9-10). The word of assurance has no effect, and the Lord receives the complaints as acts of faithlessness to which God responds in anger, evoking Moses' own prayer of intercession and mediation in behalf of a complaining and untrusting people (Num 14:13-19).

At a later point in the story of Israel's beginnings, the people cry out in the face of the Midianite threat (Judg 6:7). The response of God to the threat and the fear it evokes is the commissioning of Gideon as a deliverer of the people. This takes place in response to a prayer of complaint by Gideon and is both a commissioning of the leader and an oracle of salvation promising deliverance for the people: "Go in this might of yours and deliver Israel from the hand of Midian; I hereby commission you" (v. 14). As in the case of the calling of Moses and Jeremiah, the one called raises an objection to the call on the basis of inability to carry out the task, and the Lord responds here as in those other call stories: "But I will be with you, and you shall strike down the Midianites" (v. 16). The clear indications of a call narrative should not obscure the fact that the call story, in this instance, blends with prayer for help or complaint and the divine response. The help that the Lord gives is precisely the calling of an effective leader. The affirmation of the continuing relation of God to the people is there in the reassurance of Gideon, "I will be with you," and the intervention of God to help takes place through the calling of Gideon, the agent of God's deliverance of the people.

The oracle of salvation may take other forms. At the beginning of this discussion, we noted in Ps 85:8 the explicit announcement of a divine word or oracle in the following way:

> Let me hear what God the LORD will speak,
> for he will speak *peace* to his people.

There are two occasions when that word of *peace* (*šālôm*) is expressly the word of assurance that eliminates the fear and transforms the distress into joy. One of these is the response of the priest, Eli, to Hannah's prayer, when he says to her, "Go in peace; the LORD will grant your petition" (1 Sam 1:17). The other occasion is God's response to Gideon's lamenting prayer, "Ah Lord GOD! For I have seen the angel of the LORD face to face!" (Judg 6:22). "Peace be to you," says the Lord, "do not fear, you shall not die" (v. 23). All of these texts suggest that another fundamental form of the divine word of assurance to prayers out of fear and distress is the promise of peace and well-being.[72] *Šālôm* is one of the most inclusive and broadest terms for good in the whole of Scripture. It is God's announcement that the distress has been turned into ease and tranquility; the troubled soul may be at rest. Gideon's fear that he would die because he had seen the face of the angel of the Lord, that is, the face of God,[73] is taken away and his fearfulness laid to rest with the word of peace and the assurance of God that he will not die.

The account of Hezekiah's reign contains three prayers followed by salvation oracles. Two of these vary from the primary model we have noted in the texts to this point. The first, however, is consistent with the basic form.[74] Confronted with the invasion of the Assyrian king Sennacherib and fearing for the safety of Jerusalem, Hezekiah, king of Judah, sends emissaries to the prophet Isaiah, asking him to "lift up your prayer for the remnant that is left" (2 Kgs 19:4). The distress and anguish of the king are revealed in his tearing his clothes, covering himself with sackcloth, and going into the house of the Lord. We may assume that the king himself has already prayed for help and now asks Isaiah to pray also. Neither prayer is recorded, but Isaiah's transmission of a salvation oracle is reported:

> Say to your master, "Thus says the LORD: Do not be afraid because of the words that you have heard, with which the servants of Assyria have reviled me. I myself will put a spirit in him, so that he shall hear a rumor and return to his own land; I will cause him to fall by the sword in his own land." (vv. 6-7)

The fear of the king is addressed in the familiar words, "Do not be afraid," and a reason is given justifying the reassurance and promising the Lord's help. Whereas a salvation oracle addressed to a more generalized psalm prayer, one that may be used again and again, speaks in basic and general terms of God's help and deliverance, the oracle directed to a specific situation like this couches the promise of help in concrete form related to the situation. The oracle of salvation here focuses therefore on the elaboration of what God will do to help rather than on the general ground of reassurance: I am with you; I will help you.

The same thing is true in the second of the prayers arising out of the threat of Assyria. It is Hezekiah's own prayer later in the chapter (2 Kgs 19:14-19)[75] and like the first occasion is evoked by the arrogant and mocking words of the Assyrian king, delivered by his messenger the

Rabshakeh. Indeed the second prayer and oracle seem to be a variant of the first.[76]

Isaiah's response (vv. 20-34) includes a long first-person oracle against Assyria, typical of prophetic, and indeed specifically Isaianic, speech (vv. 21-28). Around that oracle is set an oracle of salvation directed particularly at this situation (vv. 20, 32-34). In it the Lord says, "I have heard your prayer concerning King Sennacherib of Assyria," and then promises that he shall not come into the city, "for I will defend this city to save it, for my own sake and for the sake of my servant David" (v. 34). There does not appear the familiar assurance, "Do not be afraid." But, as in other announcements of salvation, the promise of God to save is explicitly stated. Like most of the prose prayer accounts, including the immediately preceding one, the word of God in response is a promise of deliverance directed toward the need that has been lifted up in the prayer. The petition of Hezekiah was "*Save* us from his hand." The divine response is "I will defend this city to *save* it." Furthermore, the prayer is permeated with motive clauses appealing to God's reputation before the world.[77] In fact, except for the brief petition at the end, the whole prayer is an obvious effort to move God to action on the grounds that Sennacherib has mocked the living God and destroyed other nations and their gods, a point made by Hezekiah's emissaries to Isaiah before the first salvation oracle. Even the petition is "Save us, so that all the kingdoms of the earth may know that you, O LORD, are God alone" (v. 19). So the Lord promises to save the city "*for my own sake* and for the sake of my servant David." The reputation of God is at stake in this moment as is the Lord's promise to preserve Zion and the Davidic line. The word of salvation is in behalf of the king and Jerusalem. At the same time, it is a defense of the claims of the Lord of Israel to be in control of history and faithful to the divine promise.[78]

Immediately after this incident, Hezekiah is taken ill and prays for healing (2 Kgs 20:2-3). Again, the prophet Isaiah brings a response from God (vv. 5-6). It lacks the assuring words, "Fear not," but the Lord says, "I have heard your prayer, I have seen your tears." Then the first-person announcement is made, directed toward the specific need: "I will heal you." That promise of salvation is elaborated in the further words, "I will add fifteen years to your life." The oracle of salvation goes on to say, "I will deliver you and this city out of the hand of the king of Assyria,... " but this part of the oracle may be a carryover from the previous one in chapter 19.[79]

One of the clearest examples of a salvation oracle in response to prayer is found in 2 Chronicles 20. In the face of an impending attack by Moabite and Ammonite armies, the people of Judah assemble "to seek help from the LORD" (vv. 3-4). Jehoshaphat's lengthy prayer is followed by an oracle of salvation uttered by a Levite upon whom the spirit of the Lord had come while "all Judah stood before the LORD" (vv. 13-14). He says:

> Thus says the LORD to you: "Do not fear or be dismayed at this great multitude; for the battle is not yours but God's. Tomorrow go down against them; they will come up by the ascent of Ziz; you will find them at the end of the valley, before the wilderness of Jeruel. This battle is not for you to fight; take your position, stand still, and see the victory of the LORD on your behalf, O Judah and Jerusalem." Do not fear or be dismayed; tomorrow go out against them, and the LORD will be with you. (vv. 15-17)

The primary word of assurance, "Do not be afraid," in the face of a terrible threat ("this great multitude") is grounded in the claim that "the LORD will be with you." The specific way in which God will save Judah—so Jehoshaphat's petition (v. 9)—is elaborated in the middle of the oracle in much the same way as the elaboration in the salvation oracles of Second Isaiah and elsewhere. The prayer is heard and answered by the Lord. God's response is once more the assuring declaration that the people need not fear because the Lord is with them and will help them in their present need.

After the Babylonian destruction of Jerusalem, Jeremiah is approached by those fleeing to Egypt that he might pray to the Lord to find out what they should do (Jeremiah 42). The request is, in fact, both a prayer for guidance and a plea for help. They ask Jeremiah to "let the LORD your God show us where we should go and what we should do" (v. 3), that is, to give divine direction. But they also say to Jeremiah, "Pray to the LORD your God *for us, for all this remnant*" (v. 2). Their words, therefore, are also a plea for help by people in distress, "the few of us left out of many" (v. 2), those "intending to go to Egypt because of the Chaldeans; for they were afraid of them" (41:17-18). Jeremiah's prayer is not reported, but the Lord responds in a lengthy oracle of salvation, which Jeremiah transmits to the people. The heart of it is as follows:

> Do not be afraid of the king of Babylon, as you have been; do not be afraid of him, says the LORD, for I am with you, to save you and to rescue you from his hand. I will grant you mercy, and he will have mercy on you and restore you to your native soil.
> (vv. 11-12)

The familiar notes are heard once more. A fearful people are reassured: Don't be afraid, for I am with you; I will save you.

In this case, however, the divine speech goes on to say that God's help is contingent upon their remaining in the land. The Lord will not be with them if they continue to flee to Egypt. On the contrary, should

they do so, God's wrath will come upon them because they have disobeyed. Here is where the prayer for deliverance out of distress and the
prayer for direction come together but in a serious tension. The salvation is real. The people do not have to be afraid for God will help them.
But the effectiveness of God's promise is contingent upon obedience to
God's instruction. Once again we see how the promise of deliverance
in the oracle of salvation calls for an attitude of profound trust that is
open to the words of assurance in the midst of great trouble. That trust
is not present, and so the words of assurance are ineffective. The people
respond to this word from the Lord by denying it is really that. They
accuse Jeremiah of lying, incited by the scribe Baruch to hand them over
to the Babylonians to be killed or taken into exile (43:2-3). The assuring
word of the Lord that one does not have to be afraid is not a magical
incantation automatically creating the reality it bespeaks. It is still possible to hear such words and be afraid, to resist the promise that sounds
in such unpromising circumstances. The prayer for direction turns out
to be a faithless prayer, and so the people continue afraid.

Two personal oracles of salvation as response to prayer are reported
in Jeremiah. One is addressed to Jeremiah himself in response to one
of his prayers for help, his complaint over his "unceasing pain" and
"incurable wound" (Jer 15:15-18). The Lord responds with words of
encouragement and promise in a salvation oracle:

> And I will make you to this people
>   a fortified wall of bronze;
> they will fight against you,
>   but they shall not prevail over you,
> for I am with you
>   to save you and deliver you,
>   says the LORD.
> I will deliver you out of the hand of the wicked,
>   and redeem you from the grasp of the ruthless. (vv. 20-21)

Those promises that run as a thread through so many of the oracles of
salvation are repeated here: I am with you; I will deliver you. The Lord's
intention to help is spelled out in more detail in the preceding part of the
oracle of salvation where God promises to make Jeremiah as a fortified
wall against which the people who threaten Jeremiah shall not prevail
(cf. Jer 1:18-19).

Jeremiah's scribe, Baruch, also receives a word of assurance from
God when he complains, "Woe is me! The LORD has added sorrow to
my pain; I am weary with my groaning, and I find no rest" (Jer 45:3).
The Lord answers, first in the language of Jeremiah's call, "I am going
to break down...and pluck up" (v. 4; cf. 1:10), and then with an assur-

ance to Baruch, "I will give you your life as a prize of war in every place to which you may go" (v. 5).[80]

A final example from the prophets, Joel 2:19-22, begins to take us back toward the psalm prayers. For here, in partially poetic form, an account is given of an assembly of the people who offer, through the weeping voices of their priests, a typical community prayer:

> Let them say, "Spare your people, O LORD,
>   and do not make your heritage a mockery,
>   a byword among the nations.
> Why should it be said among the peoples,
>   'Where is their God?' " (v. 17)

Then come the words:

> In response to his people the LORD said:
>   I am sending you grain, wine, and oil,
>   and you will be satisfied;
> and I will no more make you
>   a mockery among the nations.
> I will remove the northern army far from you,
>   and drive it into a parched and desolate land,
> its front into the eastern sea,
>   and its rear into the western sea;
> its stench and foul smell will rise up.
>   Surely he has done great things!
> Do not fear, O soil;
>   be glad and rejoice,
>   for the LORD has done great things!
> Do not fear, you animals of the field,
>   for the pastures of the wilderness are green;
> the tree bears its fruit,
>   the fig tree and vine give their full yield. (vv. 19-22)

The poetic character of this oracle accounts in part for its differences from other such oracles, for example, its address to soil and animals. But it is set explicitly as God's response to the people's prayer of complaint. It includes the assurance that you don't have to be afraid and the first-person divine promises to deliver by removing the "northern army"[81] and replenishing the earth. The prayer of the people is met with a divine word like the many other oracles evoked by cries for help.

Modes of God's help. We should not leave these narrative texts as they tell us about God's response of presence and power without taking note of some of the specific ways in which that power and presence are worked out as answer to prayer. The acts of help and deliverance are manifold. Children are born to barren parents (Abraham and Sarah and Hannah). God causes water to appear in the desert or from a rock to save the lives of those dying of thirst (Hagar, Samson, and the Israelites in the wilderness). Plague destroys the Assyrian army and Hezekiah and the Judaeans are saved while other kings and people accomplish military victories or see the power of God overcome the enemy (Asa, Jehoshaphat, and the Israelites at the sea). The sick are healed (Miriam, Hezekiah, the son of the widow who kept Elijah, the father of Publius,[82] and the suppliants of the Psalms), the dead resuscitated (the son of the Shunammite woman[83] and Tabitha after Peter's prayer),[84] and those in fear of death preserved alive (Gideon, Baruch, and often in the Psalms). The natural world is the scene of divine activity in response to prayer by the people at the exodus and the sailors on Jonah's ship. While Paul and Silas pray in prison—though we are told nothing of the content of their prayer—an earthquake opens all the prison doors and unfastens everyone's chains (Acts 16:25-26).

But the response to prayer involves other types of divine working, sometimes of a broader and less momentary sort. So Samson is given strength and Solomon wisdom to carry out tasks, Samson to pull down the temple of Dagon in a moment, Solomon to rule wisely over many years. Leaders are appointed and commissioned in answer to prayer (the seventy elders and Joshua in the wilderness). Instruction and guidance are given (Manoah for Samson), and God exercises providential guidance of the affairs of people and nations.[85] And frequently the response to prayer is a nonact in the sense that judgment is withheld in favor of forgiveness.

Not all these ways of answering prayer and providing help and deliverance are on the same level. Some belong to stories and legends (e.g., Elisha and Jonah) whose facticity is doubtful or excluded. But historicity is problematic in many of the biblical narratives, while even in the stories one may gain clues to the working of God in response to prayer. They are indicative of an understanding of the interrelation of prayer for help and divine response whatever their actuality. The highly miraculous event, seemingly unexpected and without antecedent causes, is God's response to prayer in a number of stories (fire on the altar, water from the rock, blind eyes opened). Alongside such "inexplicable" events are natural and historical occurrences that may be perceived as miraculous, precisely because they conform to petition and are interpreted as answer to prayer. The birth of children to barren women, the evoking and stilling of the forces of nature, and victory over enemies may be at one level ordinary events, but they are understood and interpreted as the hand of God helping the afflicted in response to their cries and prayers. That is true also of other kinds of providential direction, as in the case of Eliezer's prayer for help in finding a wife for Isaac, the defeat of Ahithophel's counsel, the giving of wisdom to Solomon and a dynasty to David, and the amelioration of hostilities between Jacob and Esau. Even Samson's ability to pull down the pillars of the Dagon temple is understood to arise out of the fact that his hair has grown long again.

It is also the case that, even when an oracle of salvation comes in response to prayer, human acts and agencies may be directly involved. In the Gideon story, the announcement of deliverance in the form of a salvation oracle is at the same time the calling of Gideon as Israel's leader and deliverer, the means by which the Lord liberates the people from Midianite oppression. God promises healing to a sick and dying Hezekiah. But the oracle of salvation is followed immediately by the words: "Then Isaiah said, 'Bring a lump of figs. Let them take it and apply it to the boil, so that he may recover'" (2 Kgs 20:7). The promise of help in the salvation oracle does not rule out therapy for the illness. Isaiah's methods may seem primitive to the modern mind, but they ring true as a mode of healing. That is much less the case with regard to the examples of healing wrought by God in response to the prayers of Elijah and Elisha, but there, too, ritual acts accompany and contribute to the restoration of the children.[86]

Two narratives of prayer for help are particularly suggestive in regard to the interaction of human act and divine help. One is on the occasion of Nehemiah's efforts to rebuild the walls of Jerusalem (Nehemiah 4). When that enterprise was proving successful, it stirred the anger and resistance of the enemies of the returned exiles, Sanballat, Tobiah, the Arabs, the Ammonites, and the Ashdodites (v. 7). Nehemiah reports that they became very angry, "and all plotted together to come and fight against Jerusalem and to cause confusion in it" (v. 8). He then reports: "So we prayed to our God, and set a guard as a protection against them day and night" (v. 9). Further problems lead to Nehemiah's strategic placing of defenders and a speech of encouragement to them that is reminiscent of the oracle of salvation: "Do not be afraid of them. Remember the LORD, who is great and awesome, and fight for your kin, your sons, your daughters, your wives, and your homes" (v. 14). Prayer is followed not by an oracle of salvation but by the sensible act of setting up a guard for protection. Yet Nehemiah's words serve as a substitute word of assurance that simultaneously points to the Lord's help ("Remember the LORD, who is great and awesome") while indicating that *the people* should fight for their families. A summary note at the end, however, interprets what happened as God's intervention: "When our enemies heard that their plot was known to us, and *that God had frustrated it,* we all returned to the wall, each to his work" (v. 15). This synergism of divine and human action is reiterated in a later word of Nehemiah to the people: "Rally to us wherever you hear the sound of the trumpet. Our God will fight for us" (v. 20). Prayer and divine response, plea for protection and precautionary and defensive measures, human words of encouragement that sound like divine response to prayer, announcement of God's help and call for human strategies—all are interwoven into a single whole in the narrative.

Analogously, David, fleeing Jerusalem in tears before the rebellion of his son Absalom and hearing that his counselor, Ahithophel, has joined the conspirators against him, prays to God, weeping: "O LORD, I pray you, turn the counsel of Ahithophel into foolishness" (2 Sam 15:31). No oracle of salvation or any other divine response is given at this point. But the prayer is followed immediately by a stratagem that David sets in place to trick Absalom. He plants Hushai the Archite among Absalom's staff as a presumed convert to Absalom's cause but in fact as an opposing voice to Ahithophel's counsel, which David knows is excellent and, if followed, could lead to his defeat. The human scheme works perfectly, as the next two chapters indicate at length. But just at the moment Absalom agrees to Hushai's counsel in preference to Ahithophel's, the narrative reports in straightforward fashion: "For the LORD had ordained to defeat the good counsel of Ahithophel, so that the LORD might bring ruin on Absalom" (2 Sam 17:14). The prayer is answered and David is saved. A savvy piece of human planning and subterfuge is the explicit answer to prayer, and the human stratagem is understood as a divine "command" (*ṣiwwâ*) although no such command is reported in the narrative, only the sort of scheme that one would expect from the seasoned veteran David.

Finally, it is appropriate in this connection to call attention to a narrative that *lacks* the prayer for help—the story of Joseph (Genesis 37–50). Like Abel, he is assaulted by his brothers. Like Jeremiah and the lamenters whose voice is heard in the Psalms, Joseph is cast into the pit and left for dead. What is interesting about this story is that his situation is supremely a presentation of the circumstances in which lament and the cry for help customarily go up to God. But in this instance, there is no prayer for help on the lips of Joseph.

The clue to this strange absence of prayer is found in the character of the story and in other words that Joseph utters. Instead of a prayer for help, he interprets the human situation and makes it clear that, in some strange way, his suffering was a part of the purpose of God. So, when he reveals himself to his brothers after having become Pharaoh's second-in-command, he says to them:

> God sent me before you to preserve for you a remnant on earth and to keep alive for you many survivors. So it was not you who sent me here, but God.... I will provide for you. (Gen 45:7-8a, 11a)

And after his father's death when his brothers approach him in great fear of his revenge, he says once more:

> *You* intended to do harm to me; *God* intended it for good, in order
> to preserve a numerous people, as he is doing today. So do not fear;
> *I* will provide for you and your little ones. (Gen 50:20-21a)

Joseph's role in this story is not primarily as victim of human oppression, though he is clearly that, but as interpreter of what is going on. As his suffering does not evoke the prayer for help, so the brother's petition (Gen 50:17) does not evoke either human or divine forgiveness. God has dealt with their evil/wrong in another way, in the mystery of divine providence, a mystery that Joseph points to but does not explain. He simply identifies the place of each of the actors (the brothers, God, and himself) in the story.[87]

Other forms of God's response. Before leaving the narrative accounts of God's response to prayer for help and the interaction of human elements in that response, we must recognize that there is also on occasion a *divine resistance* to such human agency. The most obvious instance is Abraham's effort to follow up his prayer of complaint and God's promise of help via an oracle of salvation (Genesis 15) by his and Sarai's effort to secure the promise of offspring through the use of Hagar to provide a child for them (Genesis 16). The maneuver is explicitly rejected as the way of God's answering the prayer and providing help (Gen 17:19).

In this regard, the *divine silence* on another occasion of prayer may, in fact, speak volumes. The tribal war against Benjamin because of the rape and murder of the Levite's concubine results in the decimation of the Benjaminite tribe. That outcome results from an enterprise endorsed by the Lord (Judg 20:26-28) in a process of lament, sacrifice, inquiry, and positive response by the Lord. But faced, then, with the prospect of the loss of a whole tribe, the people pray to the Lord once more, again with tears, lament, and sacrifice (Judg 21:3-4). In this instance, however, we are given no indication whatsoever of God's response. No word of assurance or promise of help is forthcoming. Instead, the narrative tells a sordid tale of calculated murder, kidnapping, and rape on the part of the Israelites to repopulate the tribe of Benjamin. The silence of the text about God's response cannot be ignored. The claims of a divine and human synergism as an answer to prayer cannot be made in this instance. There is only the final verdict on the whole episode: "In those days there was no king in Israel; all the people did what was right in their own eyes" (Judg 21:25).

Alongside such implicit negative responses from God, there are accounts of occasions when *God's no to the prayer for help* is quite explicit. At the beginning of Deuteronomy, Moses recounts the fearfulness and rebellion of the people who did not trust the Lord enough to go up against the inhabitants of the land that God had promised to them (Deut 1:19-45). When the Lord became angry with the people, they then decided to go up and fight even though they had now been forbidden to do so and had been told that the Lord would not be with them if they went. The account concludes with Moses' words:

> The Amorites who lived in that hill country then came out against you and chased you as bees do. They beat you down in Seir as far as Hormah. When you returned and wept before the LORD, the LORD would neither heed your voice nor pay you any attention.

The weeping of the people is clearly in the context of the community prayer for help in the face of the defeat of the enemy. The two verbs referring to the Lord's unwillingness to listen (*šāmaʿ* and *heʾĕzîn*) occur frequently in the Psalms with reference to God's answer to prayer.[88] But on this occasion, the Lord refuses to listen. What is clear from the narrative is that the critical element of *trust* is missing from the community. If one is uncertain how important that element is in the prayer for help, this narrative clarifies the matter. The people who did not trust in the Lord's power to deliver them against a mighty foe cannot now get a hearing. Their prayer is not answered.

At the conclusion of Samuel's "antimonarchical" speech warning the people, at the Lord's behest, of the dangers of kingship, he says:

> And in that day you will cry out because of your king, whom you have chosen for yourselves; but the LORD will not answer you in that day. (1 Sam 8:18)

The people's insistence on a human king is a manifestation of lack of trust in the power of the Lord to be king over them and against their foes. This rejection of God's rule by the people (v. 7) is underscored in the verse that follows: "But the people refused to listen to the voice of Samuel" (v. 19). So the structure of faith that is manifest in the prayer for help and the divine response breaks down. As one interpreter puts it:

> The central practice of covenantal faith is nullified. The most fundamental covenantal connection binding Yahweh attentively to Israel has been broken. In a perfect situation of covenantal attentiveness, Yahweh will answer before Israel speaks (Isa 65:24). Now that possibility is forfeited. The monarchy substitutes human power for the availability of Yahweh. There are certain circumstances in which Yahweh will not function. In choosing monarchy, Israel chooses a desperate autonomy that finally can lead only to futility, abandonment, and eventually death.[89]

The prayer for help in times of trouble is rejected ahead of time in Jer 11:11-14. There the Lord promises that an apostate people cannot expect that God will listen and save. They have gone after other gods, so the Lord will punish them. Their cry will not be heard because their suffering is itself the Lord's response to their faithlessness. Such a prayer, in fact, has been voiced already at the close of the immediately preceding chapter, drawing upon the language of Pss 6:1 and 79:6-7.

> Correct me, O LORD, but in just measure;
>   not in your anger, or you will bring me to nothing.
> Pour out your wrath on the nations that do not know you,
>   and on the peoples that do not call on your name;
> for they have devoured Jacob;
>   they have devoured him and consumed him,
>   and have laid waste his habitation. (Jer 10:24-25)

"It is appalling to see traditional words used to justify irresponsibility," comments one scholar,[90] and the chapter that follows makes it clear that such a prayer will have no effect upon the deity. Even the prayer of the intercessor, Jeremiah, will be to no avail: "As for you, do not pray for this people, or lift up a cry or prayer on their behalf, for I will not listen when they call to me in the time of their trouble" (Jer 11:14). In sarcastic tones, the Lord says that the cities of Judah and the inhabitants of Jerusalem "will go and cry out to the gods to whom they make offerings, but they will never save them in the time of their trouble" (v. 12). The gods they worship cannot hear their prayer and cannot save them. Once again, human faithlessness has undermined the structure of faith reflected in the prayer–response dialogue. There are times when the intercessor can gain God's ear (see chap. 8, below), but not always. This dialogue between the human creature and the Creator is not a fixed and monolithic structure. It is fluid, complex, and open.

God's response to human prayer, however, is not always as positive or negative as the above discussion might suggest. If questions play a large role in the complaint to God in the prayer for help, it is also the case that there are a number of places where the divine response is itself set in terms of *God's questions to the complainant.*

Job is a particularly telling example. The way in which that book is structured along the lines of the lament or prayer for help has been worked out in some detail by Claus Westermann.[91] The lament, with its obvious weight upon the complaint against God, makes up much of the Job speeches.[92] But there are also wishes and petitions,[93] protestations of innocence, and even expressions of confidence and trust.[94] And in the final analysis, literally, God does respond with acts of deliverance and blessing as they are recounted in the prose epilogue. But in the dialogues themselves, where the lament character of the book is most evident, the prayer for help with its complaints against God is met, not with words of assurance and expectations of deliverance, but with questions thrown back at the sufferer who cries out. As Westermann puts it:

> Considered from the standpoint of its form, God's answer [i.e., chaps. 38–41] is a disputation speech. It is expressly introduced as such (38:2-3 = 40:1, 2, 6, 7). Although expanded and varied in many ways, it is couched as *a grand question* to Job ("I will question you, and you shall declare to me!" [38:3b]), and a question it remains to the very end. Even the imperatives which occur are meant as interrogatives. For example, "deck yourself with majesty and dignity" (40:10a), says in effect, "Are you perchance adorned with...?"[95]

In a similar fashion, the prayers for help or laments of the exiles are met in Isa 40:12-31 with a whole series of questions that, like the Lord's questions to Job, are rooted in creation theology. That these questions, in this instance from the mouth of the prophet, are responding to implicit and explicit prayers for help and complaints against God is seen in verses 27-31 where the final part of this divine-prophetic speech begins with a quotation from the prayers of the people in exile that is itself enclosed within a question and then responds to it with two rhetorical questions:

> [27] Why do you say, O Jacob,
>   and speak, O Israel,
>   "My way is hidden from the LORD,
>   and my right is disregarded by my God"?
> [28] Have you not known? Have you not heard?
>   The LORD is the everlasting God,
>   the Creator of the ends of the earth.
>   He does not faint or grow weary;
>   his understanding is unsearchable.
> [29] He gives power to the faint,
>   and strengthens the powerless.
> [30] Even youths will faint and be weary,
>   and the young will fall exhausted;
> [31] but those who wait for the LORD
>   shall renew their strength,
>   they shall mount up with wings like eagles,
>   they shall run and not be weary,
>   they shall walk and not faint.

In both Isaiah 40 and God's answer to Job in chapters 38–40, the rhetorical questions of the deity are aimed at identifying the power and creative work of the great God that makes complaint of little force. As the complaints are a challenge to God, they are in part met by God's defense and challenge back to the ones who complain.

It is significant, however, that here, in contrast to the divine no of the passages discussed immediately above, the questions of God serve to give positive affirmation to the one who cries out for help. Isaiah 40:28b-31 is an answer to the questions: "Have you not known? Have you not heard?" These verses, however, not only answer the question about God; they also show how the answer is a word of assurance to the people who have cried out in complaint (vv. 29-31). There follows immediately, then, in Isaiah 41, a series of oracles of salvation and proclamations of salvation that provide the heart of God's answer to these weary and defeated exiles. In similar fashion, it is clear from Job 42:1-6 that God's questions back to Job have served in some way as a genuine response to Job's complaint. He is at a different point than before the answer comes. Job's lament has turned into an acknowledgment of his place as creature before the Creator. And beyond the spoken answer in divine questioning, there is a restoration of Job to his former state and even more. God's question to the one who prays is not a way of not responding. It is a response that is appropriate to the questioning challenge of the sufferer. And it is on the way to God's deliverance.

Jeremiah is also full of rhetorical questions directed by God to the people. At least some of these seem to be a response to prayer, that is, to their prayers of complaint (e.g., Jer 14:7-9, 19-22, which are almost entirely questions addressed to God). Jeremiah 2 is full of the questions of God back to the people whose prayers are reflected in verses 27 ("But in the time of their trouble they say, 'Come and save us!' "), 29 ("Why do you complain against me?"),[96] and 35 (protestations of innocence). In this case, the questions are a rejection of the prayers. The apostasy of the people cannot be overcome by prayers. The suffering they are to endure is the judgment of God (see above). The answer of God is once more a question, but there is no hope in these divine judgments. They make the case, not for God, as in Job and Isaiah 40–41, but against the people.[97]

Oracles in the Psalms. While referring briefly to the Psalms at the beginning of this discussion of the way God responds to prayer, we have focused primarily on the oracles of salvation in the ancient Near East and the narrative and prophetic texts of the Old Testament. The psalm prayers generally lack any context for informing us about the particular circumstances or the response of God to the prayer. Specific acts of deliverance—whether or not they involved the miraculous, hidden providence or human agency—are, in the nature of the texts, not described except in very general terms. These prayers do, however, give other indications that they were often answered by God's assuring promise of salvation and the alleviation of fear. Allusions to salvation oracles occur, or their transmission in the liturgy may be inferred.[98]

We have already identified the request for a salvation oracle in Ps 35:3, "Say to my soul, 'I am your salvation,' " and the individual prayer in Lam 3:57, which refers to a previous prayer when the lamenting one who called on God received the assurance, "Do not fear." It is clear that that same word is what is sought and needed in the present moment. These examples tie the oracle of salvation to the psalm-type prayers in a very explicit way. Precisely because those kinds of words appear so often in response to the narrative prayers and are explicitly identified in these two contexts as the response received or desired in answer to prayer, we can be confident that such words of assurance, the promise of God's presence and help, were understood to be the typical way in which God answered prayer and delivered people from their distress and their fears. There are other places, however, where divine oracles are referred to in the Psalms. Only some of these are oracles of salvation,[99] but those are the ones relevant to this discussion. Psalm 91:14-16 seems to be a divine promise of salvation:

> Those who love me, I will deliver;
>   I will protect those who know my name.
> When they call to me, I will answer them;
>   I will be with them in trouble,
>   I will rescue them and honor them.
> With long life I will satisfy them,
>   and show them my salvation.[100]

This is a generalized salvation oracle indicating that when God is called upon (in prayer), God will answer. The further assurance is given in language typical of the oracle of salvation: I will be with them, I will rescue them. Now appearing in the context of a didactic psalm about God's protection to those who take refuge in the Lord, the oracle does not address a specific situation. So it is couched in the basic—and crucial— terms that underlie all such divine assurances, the promise of presence and protection and the announcement of intention to help.

Other oracles in the Psalms vary more from the form we have encountered so often. In Ps 12:5, the Lord speaks a word of assurance:

> "Because the poor are despoiled,
>   because the needy groan,
> I will now rise up," says the LORD;
> "I will place in safety [or 'salvation']
>   the witness[101] in their[102] behalf."

The prayer is a plea for help against the oppression and persecution of those who lie, particularly to do in the poor. It is a prayer against social oppression effected in large part out of the manipulation of the system of justice[103]—false witness, slander, and the like. The promise of the Lord to "rise up" echoes a number of petitions for help that call for God to "rise up" against the enemy.[104] A number of prayers arise out of just such situations where the powerful use mendacity to do in the poor or become powerful out of such mendacity. If the prayers of Israel are any indication, lying is one of the fundamental social crimes and at the root of much evil. It may often be shady and semilegal, or it may be as overt as the trumped-up charges against Naboth so that royalty might extend its territory and build bigger vegetable gardens over Naboth's dead body (1 Kings 21). The commandments against false witness and coveting are not a petering-out of the Decalogue or a movement to lesser crimes after the large ones have been dealt with. It is precisely false witness and coveting that produce the murder, adultery, and theft addressed in the other commandments. So in this instance, the divine word of assurance is a promise to keep secure the truthful witness, the one who tells the truth in court in behalf of those who are being done in by the lies, the *con*ceits as well as the *de*ceits, of the, truthfully named, "evildoers" in the community. That promise is a word of salvation to the needy and the poor.

The prayer of the community in Psalm 60 contains a unique oracle of salvation (vv. 6-8), repeated in Ps 108:7-9. It lacks any of the more typical sentences of that form of speech. Instead, God speaks in a series of first-person statements claiming ownership of territories in the sphere of the Northern Kingdom and Transjordan as well as the rule of certain foreign nations often at odds with Israel—Moab, Edom, and Philistia. The particular force of the oracle in the psalm is difficult to discern. One must assume that parts or all of Northern Israel had been taken over by foreign powers, and the salvation oracle is God's promise to take them back but also to take possession of nations that have oppressed Israel and Judah.[105] The community prayer is answered by a promise of salvation that speaks to the national situation broadly but appropriate to the petition that precedes it:

> Give victory [or "save"] with your right hand and answer us,
>   so that those whom you love may be rescued. (v. 5)

Other oracles of salvation may be present in Pss 21:8-12 and 27:14, but these are less certain. We have already alluded to the signs that such a word is spoken in the context of prayer in Ps 85:8-13. It is also atypical in form, but its character is indicated in the opening description of "what God the LORD will speak" (v. 8). "He will speak *peace* to his people." We have already encountered that word within other salvation oracles, and here it signals a divine promise that is a broad description of the peace and well-being God will give to a defeated people:

> Steadfast love and faithfulness will meet;
>   righteousness and peace will kiss each other.
> Faithfulness will spring up from the ground,
>   and righteousness will look down from the sky.
> The LORD will give what is good,
>   and our land will yield its increase.
> Righteousness will go before him,
>   and will make a path for his steps. (vv. 10-13)

The word of assurance to the people is a vision of peace in their midst, harmony and good in a land where God will richly provide what is needed.

Finally, one should include, in this look at the Psalms, those places where no oracle appears at all but the petitioner declares that God has heard the prayer and turns from sorrow and complaint to joy, praise, and thanksgiving (e.g., Ps 6:8-10 and Ps 22:21bff.). The claim that God has heard the prayer (Pss 6:8-9; 22:21b, 24) is so sure and the reversal of the psalm so sharp that one can account for all of that only on the premise that a word of assurance and salvation has been received from the Lord, an oracle of salvation. A clue to its presence in Psalm 22 may be found also in the editing of the Psalter. For immediately after this psalm, there appears the text that has surely been the most widely used affirmation of trust and confidence in the Lord, Psalm 23. At its heart are the words:

> Even though I walk through the darkest valley,
>   I fear no evil;
> for you are with me;
>   your rod and your staff—
>   they comfort me. (v. 4)

Embedded within those words is an oracle of salvation, not now a word sent from the Lord but placed on the lips of one who has heard them and knows they are true. The "darkest valley" points back to that terrible despair and anguish we hear so often in the prayers, and nowhere more poignantly than in the preceding psalm. But the words, "Do not fear," have been heard and taken to heart, and for just the reasons given again and again when God speaks compassionately to those who cry out for help: because "you are with me, and because you will help and protect me" (the rod and staff of comfort).

CONCLUSION

As Psalm 23 suggests and many have discerned, we are here as close to the heart of God's good news as one can get. The repetition of the words, "Do not be afraid, for I am with you," should not dull one's mind to their impact and significance. On the contrary, their constant appearance as God's response to prayer suggests that here we find most clearly what it is people seek in prayer and what God provides. Prayers for help, as we have seen them in the Scriptures, often arise out of the most desperate of human situations—terror, pain, fear, despair, the threat of death. What is it they seek and how does God respond in those situations of varying degrees of human need?

The oracle of salvation is our best indication. There where the human condition is at its worst and no mortal can sufficiently help, where people are terribly frightened, God speaks the only word that matters: you don't have to be afraid. That is not a word that can ever be given with any finality by human beings except as mediators of the divine assurance. For it is not simply a word of consolation. It is rooted in the reality of God's presence and God's power: I am with you; I will help you.

With these divine words of assurance, we are not only at the center of what is going on in prayer in the Bible. We are at the center of the whole structure of faith to which it bears witness. From the first words that ever went up to God—Abel's blood crying out to God from the ground—through the cries of the victims of Sodom and Gomorrah, the groans and cries of affliction of the people in slavery in Egypt and later defeated or under oppressive rule again and again, to the individual prayers of Abraham and Hagar, Hannah, David, and Hezekiah, and all the prayers for help in the Psalms, the biblical story has at its center the experience of human pain and suffering, trouble and woe, that is given voice in the prayer for help and heard in the oracle of salvation.[106] It may seem anachronistic to say so, but it is nevertheless profoundly true that in these words we hear the "gospel," God's good news, declared and enacted. The Bible is not unclear about what that is or what it is God does in response to prayer. The underlying fear is taken away as one is found to be no longer alone or without help.

That we are dealing with something that is not only central to prayer but to the very nature of God is suggested by the salvation story par excellence of the Old Testament, the exodus. It is in that event that God's name and identity are revealed. While we cannot fully grasp what it means when God says 'ehyeh 'ăšer 'ehyeh in response to Moses' request to know the name of God (Exod 3:14), the narrative setting gives two clues to the meaning of the name. One is in the immediate context of the giving of the name when God says in response to Moses' fear of going before Pharaoh to bring the Israelites out of Egypt, 'ehyeh 'immak, "I will be with you" (Exod 3:12). The enigmatic word of the name is placed in a sentence that serves to interpret it. The name of this God is a declaration to those in fear: I will be with you; you do not have to be afraid. The larger narrative of the exodus then tells us more. When the people cry out in their affliction, God says, "I have heard their cry.... I know their sufferings, and I have come down *to deliver them*" (Exod 3:7-8). The rest of the exodus story is a confirmation that the one who is "with you" will also help and deliver. Whatever else they may be, chapters 3–14 of Exodus are a narrativized form of the oracle of salvation in response to the prayers for help of an oppressed people. If these chapters are paradigmatic for our understanding of God's way with God's people, this is how that is so. They are as much as anything a story of prayer. As we have seen, what they tell us about prayer and about God is repeated again and again in the Bible. One further story serves to confirm the point, even as it seems to challenge it. It does not have to do with prayer, apparently, but one needs to be careful about assuming that.

The story begins with the words: "When the house of David heard that Aram had allied itself with Ephraim, the heart of Ahaz and the heart of his people shook as the trees of the forest shake before the wind" (Isa 7:2). The fear of Ahaz and the people is palpable in this story. There is no record of any prayer by Ahaz, and that is important to the story. But Isaiah is still sent by the Lord to the king with an oracle of salvation: "Take heed, be quiet, do not fear, and do not let your heart be faint because of these two smoldering stumps of firebrands, because of the fierce anger of Rezin and Aram and the son of Remaliah" (v. 4).[107] The basis for being unafraid, "I am with you," apparently is not present, but there, too, the text is deceptive (see below). Then in the following verses, the oracle spells out what the Lord is going to do to these kings. The king is offered a sign as well, as happens in other instances of the announcement of salvation.[108]

But the fear of the king does not erupt into a cry for help, and the divine assurance of deliverance does not evoke a royal response of confidence and trust in the power and presence of God. Ahaz refuses to ask for a sign to confirm the promise of deliverance. We have seen throughout the prayers for help that they are human words arising out of trust in God even when God seems absent. The possibility that the assuring words of God can effectively remove fear and transform the human situation is tied to the mode of faith out of which prayer arises. For if there is no conviction that God's presence and power can help in the darkness of existence when the heart shakes like "the trees of the forest ... before the wind," then even divine speech cannot accomplish what it otherwise does so profoundly.

Ahaz is given a sign anyway, the sign of Immanuel, "God is with us." It is one of the poignant ironies of Scripture. For what is elsewhere the principle word of assurance to persons caught in fear and despair is for this fearful king an announcement of judgment. But the deeper word of promise that is in that name perdures and becomes an intimation of the larger promises of God to be present with God's people, indeed with the larger community of humankind. Even before this episode is over, the word "Immanuel" is a word of hope, and the assuring "Fear not" is sounded once more (Isa 8:9-15). And in the unfolding of the whole biblical story, the name Immanuel is a confirmation of the name of God revealed in the exodus, "I am with you." When the New Testament tells us this is the name of the promised child, we are not at all surprised, any more than we are to hear that he bears another name, "Jeshua/Jesus," which means, "He will *save* his people." The names could be no other if that child was indeed the answer to "the hopes and fears of all the years," the good news to all who cry out to God for help, God's incarnate oracle of salvation and word of assurance to a troubled world. That certainly was the claim of the angel who brought to the frightened poor and weak (called "shepherds" in the story) an oracle of salvation: "Do not be afraid; for see—I am bringing you good news of great joy for all the people: to you is born this day in the city of David a Savior, who is the Messiah, the Lord. This will be a sign for you: you will find a child wrapped in bands of cloth and lying in a manger" (Luke 2:10-12).

It is, therefore, no accident that when the New Testament interprets the meaning of the death and resurrection of Jesus Christ, it turns to Psalm 22. For the constant reference to that psalm, beginning with the cry of despair on the lips of Jesus, "My God, my God, why have you forsaken me?" is a clear declaration that Immanuel is true, that "God is with us" in the midst of whatever suffering and trouble comes upon human beings.[109] All the cries for help, all the prayers of those in trouble, are taken up by the one "who became flesh and dwelled among us" (John 1:14).[110] In Jesus came God's enduring word of assurance, the declaration once and for all that you do not have to be afraid, for I am with you, I will help you. The resurrection is God's saving help confirmed for and through Jesus Christ.

Finally, this "thread" of prayer and salvation oracle, running through the whole of Scripture and one of the clearest indicators of its unity as the revelation of God, carries through to the end. In the vision of the new Jerusalem at the conclusion of the book of Revelation, anticipated in Old Testament prophecy (Isa 65:17-19), a voice proclaims the final oracle of salvation, and we hear the sounds of all the human cries for help and God's final word over the whole story:

> Behold, the dwelling of God is with humankind.
> God will dwell with them as their God;
> they will be God's peoples,
> and God will be with them;
> God will wipe every tear from their eyes.
> Death will be no more;

> mourning and crying and pain will be no more,
> for the first things have passed away. (Rev 21:3-4)

The story that began with a victim's cry for help ends with a divine word of assurance: God will be with them. It has been effective throughout that story, and it is so finally: death will be no more; mourning and crying and pain will be no more. The structure of prayer and divine response identified in these chapters is more than an isolated topic of biblical faith. It is the very structure of faith itself. The good news underlying everything else is in these oft-repeated words, "Do not be afraid; for I am with you, I will help you."

The dialogue of prayer is not over at that point, however, as we have noted along the way. If we are truly onto the very shape of prayer, and indeed of faithful existence *coram Deo,* it is not yet complete when the divine response is given to prayer. There are other human words in this conversation. They are found in the hymns of praise and thanksgiving and the songs of trust and confidence. To them, we now must turn.

5

"O Give Thanks to the Lord"

DOXOLOGY AND TRUST

❧

When one is addressed in the most personal way by the gracious power that undergirds all that is, the transcendent God, and promised a companioning presence in the face of whatever trouble may beset and a liberating saving power over the forces that threaten and destroy, more is not only expected,[1] it is required and, at least sometimes, irresistible. Vows of praise and thanksgiving have been uttered, and they will be kept. Tears have been wiped away and the threat of danger removed, so joy ensues. The deliverance may not yet be realized, but faithful trust waits in expectation and confidence that God is at work and help is at hand. Prayer has received a "perfect-tense" response. If God's help has not already happened, as it often has in the stories and psalms, it is on its way. The promises of God are sure and certain. Such confidence expresses itself in words of praise and trust. These are the matters we need to take up now. For they are a part of prayer, the structure of faith, the continuation of the conversation and dialogue with the Lord of the universe, the helper of those who have no help.

In the previous chapter, we noted that Ps 34:4-6 provides a kind of paradigm of the structure of prayer in Scripture and shows how the cry for help, the prayer of an afflicted one, initiates a movement of response from the God who hears the prayer. That same psalm, a song of thanksgiving, carries the paradigm further as its opening verses show the continuation of the dialogue that prayer effects:

> I will bless the LORD at all times;
>> his praise shall continually be in my mouth.
> My soul makes its boast in the LORD;
>> let the humble hear and be glad.
> O magnify the LORD with me,
>> and let us exalt his name together. (vv. 1-3)

The delivering response of God to the outcry of the suffering one has led to a new articulation on the part of the one who prayed. The sounds are no longer those of tears and groans but those of joy and exultation. The verses above identify two aspects to that new and different voice of the praying one. The first is a personal and continuing address to God, but now in the mode of *blessing and praise* (vv. 1-2a). The second is a *testimony* to the salvation of God that is set before others and elicits from them a similar and supporting expression of praise and joy.

In Psalm 40, where we also saw the movement from prayer to divine response (vv. 1-2), that song of thanksgiving, too, goes on to the next stage in the structure of faith in dialogue with God (v. 3):

> He put a new song in my mouth,
>   a song of praise to our God.
> Many will see and fear,
>   and put their trust in the LORD.

The dimensions of praise and testimony before others, identified above, are present here also. But they are given a particular nuance that we must attend to in looking at the prayer of the redeemed, of those who have been heard and attended to by the Lord of the universe. One of those nuances is the identification of praise with *song and music*. The other is the testimony that evokes not only praise and exaltation of God (so Ps 34:1-3), but also *trust and confidence in the Lord*.

In these prayers of thanksgiving, therefore, we encounter the primary elements of the prayers of those God heard and delivered, prayers of praise and trust. Their exploration is the primary aim of this chapter.

PRAISE AND THANKSGIVING

Prayers of Thanksgiving

Blessing. Our starting point for discerning the character of thanksgiving and praise[2] is the term *bĕrākâ*, "blessing," and the verbal forms associated with the noun. They have a specialized usage to refer to expressions of thanksgiving in interpersonal relations and in thanksgiving to God.[3] In the latter instance, it is especially in the expression, "Blessed be the Lord...," followed by a description of what God has done, that human beings express their thanks to the Lord.[4] In various psalms, especially songs of thanksgiving or at the beginning or end of prayers for help, this expression of thanksgiving occurs.[5] In some instances, God is specifically blessed or thanked for having heard the prayer.[6] Typical of such thanksgiving are Pss 18:46-48 and 31:21:

> Blessed be my rock,
>   and exalted be the God of my salvation,

> the God who gave me vengeance
>   and subdued peoples under me;
> who delivered me from my enemies. (Ps 18:46-48)

> Blessed be the LORD,
>   for he has wondrously shown
>   his steadfast love to me
>   when I was beset as a city under siege. (Ps 31:21)

So also in narrative texts, various people give thanks to God with such a prayer, or it is reported that they did so.[7] The report of Jehoshaphat's battle with the people of Ammon, Moab, and Mount Seir in 2 Chronicles 20, which begins with prayer and the receipt of a divine oracle of salvation, concludes as follows:

> On the fourth day they assembled in the Valley of Beracah, for there they blessed the LORD; therefore that place has been called the Valley of Beracah [Blessing] to this day. Then all the people of Judah and Jerusalem, with Jehoshaphat at their head, returned to Jerusalem with joy, for the LORD had enabled them to rejoice over their enemies. They came to Jerusalem, with harps and lyres and trumpets, to the house of the LORD. (vv. 26-28)

The act of "blessing" in this case is clearly a joyful expression of thanks to God for the victory wrought by divine miracle (see vv. 22-23).

From the early story of Israel, such a prayer of thanks is recorded in Genesis 24. After Eliezer has prayed to God for help in finding a bride for Isaac and has successfully accomplished the mission, he prays:

> Blessed be the LORD, the God of my master Abraham, who has not forsaken his steadfast love and his faithfulness toward my master. As for me, the LORD has led me on the way to the house of my master's kin. (Gen 24:27; cf. v. 48)

The notion of "blessing" in whatever particular form it may take as an expression of gratitude suggests a kind of reciprocity, a verbal gift in return for the divine (or human) gift that has elicited the expression of thanks. On the human level, this becomes in effect a way of saying thanks by verbally seeking good, or blessing, that is, the tangible and intangible goods of wealth, long life, posterity, and the like, for the one who has extended good toward the one who has been helped. In some sense, less rational or tangible, the same notion carries over to the idea of "blessing" God. That is, the grateful recipient of divine help now ascribes, not glory (as in the notion of praise, see below), but blessing. The tangibility of that blessing, as it is normally experienced in human life, disappears, but the wish for good for God is analogous to the wish

for glory or honor or greatness for the Lord and the Lord's name, a
frequent aspect of praise and thanksgiving.[8]

The way in which "blessing" serves as thanksgiving offering to God
has been illumined by Sheldon Blank. He notes: "Blessing has a quality
that praise does not share. A blessing is a giving, a gift, an offering.
To 'bless' the Lord is to bring Him an offering. It is right to say we
'offer' a blessing."[9] He notes further that there are several places where
the "words of the mouth," song and prayer, are compared with other
offerings that are brought to God in praise and thanksgiving. So in Hos
14:2, we read:

> Take words with you
>   and return to the LORD;
> say to him,
>   "Take away all guilt;
> accept that which is good,
>   and we will offer the fruit [or "bulls"] of our lips.

The textual witnesses differ as to whether the offering is "fruit" or
"bulls" of the lips. But in both instances, it is an offering of the lips that
is being given to God. So also in Ps 69:30-31, the psalmist concludes
the prayer for help with a vow that plays on the words *šîr,* "song," and
šôr, "ox":

> I will praise the name of God with a song [*šîr*];
>   I will magnify him with thanksgiving.
> This will please the LORD more than an ox [*šôr*]
>   or a bull with horns and hoofs.

Rather than the offering of an animal as a gift of gratitude, the psalmist
offers a song of thanksgiving. In a similar way, the petitioner in Psalm
141 asks:

> Let my prayer be counted as incense before you,
>   and the lifting up of my hands as an evening sacrifice. (v. 2)

In this instance, it is the prayer for help that is offered up, but as before,
it is seen as comparable to a sacrifice to God. All of this leads with some
cogency to the conclusion that "the words of a blessing are material and
ponderable like incense and animals."[10]

Prose prayers of thanksgiving. To return to the prayer of Eliezer, as a
way of looking more broadly at the prayer of thanksgiving, its character as such a prayer is seen further in the way it reflects Eliezer's earlier
prayer for help (Gen 24:12-14) and shows how God has responded to
his need. He had prayed for God to show steadfast love (*ḥesed*) to his
master Abraham and grant him (Eliezer) success. Now he gives thanks

for the "steadfast love and faithfulness toward my master" and because God has led him on the way. Eliezer specifically identifies God's help as consonant with his earlier prayer. In so doing, he points us to what is at the heart of the prayers of praise and thanksgiving, the praise of God's goodness as demonstrated in steadfast love and faithfulness.[11] The help God renders, God's ḥesed in the less-afflicted situation of an Eliezer and in the deep suffering of Hezekiah or Hannah or one of the tormented souls who cry to God in the psalmic prayers for help, is the gracious turning toward those with whom God lives in perduring relationship. The faithfulness God shows toward Abraham is the persistence of this grace and kindness, the maintenance of the promise and blessing God offered to Abraham at the beginning. "Steadfast love and faithfulness" are really two ways of saying the same thing, that God's way is gracious and reliable, that those in the deepest trouble can count upon the help of God. That is again and again the basis for praise, so much so that the paradigm of thanksgiving becomes a call to give thanks or praise because God's steadfast love and faithfulness are forever (see below). Psalm 107 well illustrates this as it sets forth four situations of human need that elicit a cry or prayer to God—wandering hungry and thirsty in the desert, sitting in prison, sickness, and being caught in stormy seas—and tells of God's specific manner of deliverance in each situation: pointing the way, breaking the bonds, healing, and stilling the storm. At the conclusion of each of these very particular situations of human distress and need that evoke a human cry and God's response, there comes the call:

> Let them thank the LORD for his *steadfast love,*
> for his wonderful works to humankind.

To speak of God's "steadfast love and faithfulness" is to encapsulate all the particularities that are borne witness to in the various prayers of thanksgiving encountered in Scripture (see below). In this instance, the particularity is in the narrative. There we learn what God's steadfast love and faithfulness are for Abraham. Here, therefore, in a spontaneous prayer unrelated to the context of worship and set in the early story of Israel, the nature of thanksgiving is indicated as well as its close relation to the prayer for help.

Similar to Eliezer's prayer of thanksgiving is that of Moses' father-in-law, Jethro, when he hears of the marvelous deliverance of the Hebrews from the Egyptian army. The text reads:

> Then Moses told his father-in-law all that the LORD had done to Pharaoh and to the Egyptians for Israel's sake, all the hardship that had beset them on the way, and how the LORD had delivered them. Jethro rejoiced for all the good that the LORD had done to

Israel, in delivering them from the Egyptians. Jethro said, "Blessed be the LORD, who has delivered you from the Egyptians and from Pharaoh. Now I know that the LORD is greater than all gods, because he delivered the people from the Egyptians, when they dealt arrogantly with them."[12] And Jethro, Moses' father-in-law, brought a burnt offering and sacrifices to God; and Aaron came with all the elders of Israel to eat bread with Moses' father-in-law in the presence of God. (Exod 18:8-12)

This conversation between Jethro and Moses contains the most fundamental dimensions of thanksgiving. It arises out of the confessional, narrative report of the marvelous, saving work of God ("Moses told his father-in-law..."). The recounting of the deeds of the Lord is a testimony to others that elicits their own thanksgiving ("Blessed be the LORD who has...") and confession, even that of those outside the community, such as Jethro. In fact, in this instance the prayer of thanksgiving and the confession accompanying it ("Now I know that the LORD is greater than all gods...") recorded in the text are those of the outsider who has heard the story.[13] The confession rendered by Jethro is also an act of praise, reminding us of the intricate connection between praise and thanksgiving. Finally, the thanksgiving and praise carry over into expressions of joy (v. 9) and sacrifice (v. 12).

With these texts, we are very much at the heart of thanksgiving as an act of prayer to God. On several occasions, we are told of prayers of thanksgiving and praise following upon a prayer for help and, in some cases, the oracle of salvation that God addresses to the praying one. So Hannah sings—or "prays," as the text says—her powerful song of thanksgiving for God's positive response to her prayer for a son (1 Sam 2:1-10).[14] The people give thanks for healing in the Chronicler's report of Hezekiah's passover (2 Chr 30:21-22), and the sailors on Jonah's boat fear the Lord and offer sacrifices and make vows when God stills the storm (Jonah 1:16). Jonah's own prayer becomes, in its narrative context, a song of thanksgiving in anticipation of the Lord's deliverance (Jonah 2). Both the song that Miriam and the women dancers sing when God delivers the Hebrews from the Egyptian army (Exod 15:1-21) and Deborah and Barak's song in Judges 5 are victory songs praising and thanking God for help rendered in response to prayer (Exod 14:10; Judg 4:3). The usual order of prayer is stood on its head in 2 Chr 20:21-22 when Jehoshaphat appoints singers to lead in praise and thanksgiving as the army goes *out* to battle. What is clear, however, from the narrative is that the matter is already settled. An oracle of salvation has been received (vv. 15-17). God has announced victory for Israel. So when, in fact, they return victorious, they come with joy and music (vv. 27-28).[15]

The shape of thanksgiving. The extended thanksgiving prayers of the Psalter confirm what we see in the prayers of thanksgiving by Eliezer and Jethro, as well as those of Hannah (1 Sam 2:1-10), Hezekiah (Isa 38:10-20), and Jonah (2:2-9).[16] Psalm 107:21-22 offers a kind of paradigm, indicating what belongs to acts of thanksgiving:[17]

> Let them thank the LORD for his steadfast love,
>   for his wonderful works to humankind.
> And let them offer thanksgiving sacrifices,
>   and tell of his deeds with songs of joy.

Four characteristic features are evident in this text and in the songs of thanksgiving to which it points. They serve to define the nature of thanksgiving in ancient Israel and thus set the agenda for our discussion of this type of prayer. (1) The most obvious feature is the presence of expressions and declarations of praise and thanksgiving on the part of the one who has been delivered (Ps 107:21). In the prayers themselves, as we shall see, these occur most often in first-person form as address to God. Praise and thanksgiving are also called for on the part of others, an exhortation that arises out of the third feature listed below. (2) The thanksgiving songs tend to show a close connection to the prayer for help (see Ps 107:19). (3) Other persons in the community and beyond are addressed and told of God's deliverance (Ps 107:22b). (4) Finally, there is a direct association with an act of worship, usually sacrifice, that takes place in company with others (Ps 107:22a).

Psalm 22:22-31 places the song of thanksgiving of a person in the closest relation to the prayer for help—the song comes immediately after the prayer and within the same psalm. The transition is in verse 21, where one presumes the psalmist refers to an oracle of salvation (see chap. 4, above). Certainly something has happened in the midst of verse 21, so to speak, that has turned things totally around and transformed this despairing and anguished psalmist into a proclaimer of God's greatness and a singer of praise to the Lord. Specific reference back to the prayer and to what God did that has turned things around is there in verse 24 where the psalmist reports:

> For he did not despise or abhor
>   the affliction of the afflicted;
> he did not hide his face from me,
>   but heard when I cried to him.

In these verses also are the first-person declarations of praise and payment of vows (v. 25), apparently in an act of worship but certainly before others:

> In the midst of the congregation I will praise you. (v. 22)
>
> My vows I will pay before those who fear him. (v. 25)

The declarations of praise are themselves acts of praise and thanksgiving. They may as well be translated in the present tense as in the future, expressing in the moment of their speaking the praise of the psalmist and the payment of the vows.[18] Of course, the whole of these verses serves as an act of thanksgiving and praise as the psalmist declares that praise shall come to the Lord from an ever widening circle that reaches throughout space and time. The praise and thanks of the psalmist evoke a chorus of unending and unbroken praise. That it is because of what God has done, and so an expression of thanksgiving, is signaled once more at the end, literally:

> They will proclaim God's deliverance [*ṣidqātô*]
> to a people yet unborn, *that the* LORD[19] *has acted!* (v. 31)

The explicit reporting or telling of God's deliverance to a wide audience, therefore, is one of the most noticeable features of this song of thanksgiving. Indeed there is an unending echo of reporting and proclamation to others. It begins in the midst of the community to which the psalmist belongs, among "my brothers and sisters,"[20] "in the midst of the great congregation," among those who fear the Lord (vv. 22, 25). But others hear, and, like Jethro in Exod 18:10, they join in the praise and thanksgiving:

> All the ends of the earth
> shall remember and turn to the LORD. (v. 27)

Future generations shall hear about what God has done and pass it on to other generations, all of whom shall serve the Lord (vv. 30-31). The song of thanksgiving in this psalm places at its center the report of God's response to the prayer for help, which becomes a kind of converting testimony, as others join in both the confession of what God has done and the praise and worship appropriate to that marvelous redemptive power at work.

The power of God's answer to prayer to evoke confession of faith, praise, and thanksgiving *even on the part of those not already worshipers of the Lord* is not confined to the song of thanksgiving. Frequently, the Bible reports such an event. When Elijah on Mount Carmel prays to the Lord to send fire on the altar, and the Lord sends fire, all the people, who had been inclined to follow the god Baal, now fall on their faces and say: "The LORD indeed is God; the LORD indeed is God" (1 Kgs 18:39). The Chronicler's report of Jehoshaphat's prayer before battle, the receipt of an oracle of salvation, and the miraculous deliverance bracketed by praise and thanksgiving has its final outcome in the note: "The fear of God came on all the kingdoms of the countries when they heard that the LORD had fought against the enemies of Israel" (2 Chr 20:29). So also in the tale of Jonah, the "pagan" sailors (see Jonah 1:6) become worshipers of the Lord and make vows of thanksgiving when the Lord answers their prayer and stills the raging sea: "Then the men feared the LORD even more, and they offered a sacrifice to the LORD and made vows" (1:16). Their fearfulness before the power of God in the storm (v. 10) becomes a reverential, worshiping fear of the Lord. In Psalm 126, such testimony of the nations to what the Lord has done actually *precedes* the testimony of Israel:

> Then they will say among the nations,
>   "The LORD has done great things for them."
> The LORD has done great things for us;
>   we are those who rejoice. (vv. 2-3)

As we shall see, such incorporation of a larger circle into the praise of God is a significant feature of the hymns of praise as well as of these songs and occasions of thanksgiving.

Psalm 22:21-32 has provided a proper starting point for looking at the songs of thanksgiving because of its intimate connection to the paradigmatic prayer for help in the first half of the psalm. But that connection and the other features of thanksgiving identified above are present in other prayers of thanksgiving.

Expressions of praise and thanksgiving. The first-person declarations of praise and thanksgiving are usually directed to God in the second person but sometimes speak of God in the third person:

> I will extol you, O LORD, for you have drawn me up,
>   and did not let my foes rejoice over me.
> . . . .
> O LORD my God, I will give thanks to you forever.
>   (Ps 30:1, 12)

Or in the procession liturgy of Psalm 118, when the one giving thanks has entered the gates of the temple, expressions of thanksgiving are made to the Lord:

> I thank you that you have answered me
>   and have become my salvation.
> . . . .
> You are my God, and I will give thanks to you;
>   you are my God, I will extol you.
>   (Ps 118:21, 28)

Jonah speaks of making his sacrifice "with the voice of thanksgiving" (Jonah 2:9), and Psalm 138 begins with the personal expression of thanks and praise by one whose prayer has been answered:

> I give you thanks ['*ôdĕkā*], O LORD, with my whole heart;
>   before the gods I sing your praise;
> I bow down toward your holy temple
>   and give thanks ['*ôdeh*] to your name
>   for your steadfast love and your faithfulness;
>   for you have exalted your name and your word
>   above everything.[21]

Sirach 51:1-12 begins and ends with the personal address of thanks to God (vv. 1, 11a, 12b).

Sometimes, the expression of thanks in the song of thanksgiving addresses or speaks of God in the third person.[22] But the intention to praise and thank is still the case:

> I will bless the LORD at all times;
>   his praise shall continually be in my mouth.
> My soul makes its boast in the LORD;
>   let the humble hear and be glad. (Ps 34:1-2)

Psalm 40:1-3 also incorporates the personal praise of God in the third-person references to what God has done. The brief song of thanksgiving at the end of Psalm 52, however, addresses the expression of thanks directly to God:

> I will thank you forever,
>   because of what you have done. (v. 9a)

In all of these cases, where the text gives any indication, the thanksgiving is, as we see in the immediately preceding example, because of what God has done (cf. Ps 30:1). That may be expressed with specific reference to hearing the prayer (Ps 118:21) or more generally with reference to the steadfast love (*ḥesed*) and faithfulness God has rendered (see above).

The connections between song of thanksgiving and prayer for help. These connections are made in two ways: (1) a brief statement about the prayer having been uttered and heard;[23] and (2) a more extended report of the situation of distress and need, the cry for help, and God's deliverance.[24] The simple report of answered prayer is sufficient to ground the thanksgiving and the call for the praise of others:

> I thank you that you have answered me
>   and have become my salvation. (Ps 118:21)

> I love the LORD because he has heard
> my voice and my supplications. (Ps 116:1)

> On the day I called, you answered me,
> you increased my strength of soul. (Ps 138:3)

> I called to the LORD out of my distress,
> and he answered me;
> out of the belly of Sheol I cried,
> and you heard my voice. (Jonah 2:2)

The more extended reports are essentially elaborations of the basic confession contained in the statements above and in some cases are, in fact, elaborations in the same psalm, as for example, in Psalms 116 and 118. They are a sort of narrative account of all that happened: the distress and affliction that elicited prayer, the cry to God, and the way in which God heard the prayer and delivered the sufferer. Psalm 30:6-12 comprises such an account:

1. The situation of affliction (vv. 6-7):

> As for me, I said in my prosperity,
> "I shall never be moved."
> By your favor, O LORD,
> you had established me as a strong mountain;
> you hid your face;
> I was dismayed.

2. The prayer for help (vv. 8-10):

> To you, O LORD, I cried,
> and to the LORD I made supplication:
> "What profit is there in my death,
> if I go down to the Pit?
> Will the dust praise you?
> Will it tell of your faithfulness?
> Hear, O LORD, and be gracious to me!
> O LORD, be my helper!"

3. God's deliverance from distress (vv. 11-12):

> You have turned my mourning into dancing;
> you have taken off my sackcloth
> and clothed me with joy,
> so that my soul may praise you and not be silent.
> O LORD my God, I will give thanks to you forever.

The situation of distress is described in the simplest of terms. The prosperity that was seen as a divine gift disappeared and the psalmist was undone. "Dismayed" may be a rather mild term. It is the same word (*bāhal*) translated as "terror" in the cry of affliction in Psalm 6. Elsewhere, the affliction is elaborated at greater length, as, for example, in the depiction of the nations surrounding the psalmist in Ps 118:10-12 or the way Ps 116:10-11 picks up again the description of affliction already set forth in verses 3-4. Sirach 51:2-7 develops the description of distress in an almost baroque fashion, laying out many of the modes and images of affliction that occur throughout the prayers for help: the trap of lies and slander, grinding teeth that devour, choking fire, being surrounded by enemies, and imminent death. This last affliction, the nearness of death, is especially prominent in the reports of distress. The king who gives thanks in Psalm 18 (‖ 2 Samuel 22) describes his plight:

> The cords of death encompassed me;
>> the torrents of perdition assailed me;
> the cords of Sheol entangled me;
>> the snares of death confronted me. (vv. 4-5)

The affliction recalled in Ps 116:3 is similar:

> The snares of death encompassed me;
>> the pangs of Sheol laid hold on me;
> I suffered distress and anguish.

In other thanksgiving psalms, the experience is depicted as one of the dissolution of the self and the body as if sickness unto death were the plight that evoked the prayer for help.[25]

In all these instances, the close tie of the prayer of thanksgiving to the prayer for help is very evident. It is alluded to and often quoted. In Psalm 30 and elsewhere, we hear complaints and laments, petitions, motivation sentences, and forms of address to God very similar to those that are so common in the prayers for help.[26] The sense of the dialogue of prayer is firmly indicated, and the songs of thanksgiving are not generalized thanksgiving but prayers and acts that give thanks to God for quite specific prayers that were heard and particular moments when the Lord's delivering help was received and felt. This tie to earlier prayers for help is also felt in the way that thanksgiving in these songs is seen as planned and anticipated but also unrestrained and unavoidable. For these songs and acts were promised or vowed by the one who prayed in deep distress:

> I will come into your house with burnt offerings:
>> I will pay you my vows,
> those that my lips uttered
>> and my mouth promised when I was in trouble.
>>> (Ps 66:13-14)

But they also come forth as joyful expressions of gratitude (see Ps 30:11) because the help for which one prayed has been received and has transformed distress and suffering into health and well-being:

> You have turned my mourning into dancing;
>   you have taken off my sackcloth
>   and clothed me with joy. (Ps 30:11)

Report of God's deliverance to other persons. The report of what happened, however, is not primarily a part of the actual expression of thanks to God. Thanks and praise are addressed to God. The report of the distress and God's response, however, is an act of proclamation addressed to others, particularly members of the community or congregation but extending beyond that immediate context in some instances, as we have seen in Psalm 22. In the account in Job 33 of the movement from prayer to acceptance to thanksgiving, it is said:

> That person sings *to others* and says,
>   "I sinned and perverted what was right,
>   and it was not paid back to me.
> [God] has redeemed my soul from going down to the Pit,
>   and my life shall see the light." (vv. 27-28)

The song of thanksgiving is thus a song of testimony to the steadfast love and faithfulness of God, who hears and answers prayer. Psalm 22 rings the changes on this, making the testimony to the community and beyond to all the people past, present, and future the central feature of the act of thanksgiving. But this is a regular feature of the thanksgiving prayer:[27]

> I will thank you forever,
>   because of *what you have done;*[28]
> *in the presence of the faithful*
>   I will hope for[29] your name, for it is good. (Ps 52:9)

> Come and hear, all you who fear God,
>   and I will tell *what he has done for me.* (Ps 66:16)

> I will pay my vows to the LORD
>   *in the presence of all his people.* (Ps 116:14, 18)

> I shall recount *the deeds of the* LORD. (Ps 118:17)

In these verses, two things stand out: the presence of the people and what God has done. Testimony before others of the wonderful deed of God to deliver the sufferer or the afflicted is at the heart of the thanksgiving prayer. In two other instances, Ps 22:31 and Isa 38:15, thanksgiving prayers refer to the proclamation of "what God has done" or "that God has acted." The tradition of the mighty acts of God in the Old Testament has a double rootage. It is those wonderful, impossible saving acts that created and preserved and delivered Israel, and it is those equally concrete and specific acts of deliverance that individuals experienced in moments of sickness, oppression, barrenness, pain, and fear. In both cases, the outcome is prayer of praise and thanksgiving. In both cases, it is also testimony in and before the whole community and all who will listen in.

The report *qua* testimony or proclamation is well indicated in Ps 40:9-10:

> I have told the glad news of deliverance
>> in the great congregation;
> see, I have not restrained my lips,
>> as you know, O LORD.
> I have not hidden your saving help within my heart,
>> I have spoken of your faithfulness and your salvation;
> I have not concealed your steadfast love and your faithfulness
>> from the great congregation.

The first line is indicative. The Lord's salvation of the afflicted one is good news to be proclaimed and shared. It is like the report of victory in battle that is brought back to the people at home. It is almost sermonic in character. It is certainly a kind of momentary confession of faith in which the one who has been helped declares before others what he or she has experienced of God's nature and way with humankind. So in this particular thanksgiving prayer, the psalmist heaps up the terms that customarily represent the central attributes of God. He or she speaks of "your deliverance" and "your saving help," both of which are translations of *ṣedeq* or *ṣĕdāqâ,* usually translated as "righteousness." The redemptive experience of the one afflicted in answer to prayer is indicative of God's righteousness. It is the way that God is in the perduring relationship with God's people. That way, now demonstrated quite concretely in the hearing of the prayer of the afflicted and the deliverance wrought, whether it is healing, vindication in the courts, victory over enemies, deliverance from death, or the gift of a child, is further characterized as "your faithfulness," "your salvation," and "your steadfast love." This confession is highly experiential in its grounding. It is not a matter of rote. It is what the one who prayed in distress has come to know about God's way, God's order. And, like all proclamation and testimony, it is set before others that they also might hear, rejoice, and fear the Lord:

> Many will see and fear,
>> and put their trust in the LORD. (Ps 40:3b)

> You who fear the LORD, praise him!
> All you offspring of Jacob, glorify him;
>   stand in awe of him, all you offspring of Israel!
> For he did not despise or abhor
>   the affliction of the afflicted. (Ps 22:23-24a)

The deliverance of *one* of God's afflicted is cause for rejoicing by *all*. It is not only the thanks of the one saved. This act is a pointer to the way that God always acts. The salvation of one who cried out creates a community of praise and thanksgiving, of worship and the fear of the Lord. The voice of one becomes a choir of many. And as Psalm 22 makes clear, there is no end to that community of thanksgiving and praise. It reaches to the ends of the earth and the ends of time. The song of thanksgiving in Psalm 138 makes the same point:

> All the kings of the earth shall praise you,[30] O LORD,
>   for they have heard the words of your mouth.
> They shall sing of the ways of the LORD,
>   for great is the glory of the LORD.
> For though the LORD is high, he regards the lowly;
>   but the haughty he perceives from far away. (vv. 4-6)

The activity of the one delivered in giving thanks (vv. 1-2) is echoed now in the voices of "all the kings of the earth" as they "praise" or "give thanks." The elements of praise, thanks, and confession or proclamation that are all a part of the verb *hôdâ* and lead us to use all of those English words at different times (or even at the same time) to translate it are present in its usage in verses 1-5. The word[31] and event of the psalmist's deliverance are such a marvelous work of salvation that even the great rulers of the earth will join in praise and thanksgiving to this God. The meaning of this part of the song of thanksgiving in Psalm 138 is so well stated by Hans-Joachim Kraus that his words bear quoting in this context:

> The "kings of the earth" are brought into the psalmist's song of thanksgiving. Amazed and prayerfully they are to recognize the salvific power of the word of Yahweh. . . . Such expectation is naturally to be understood in the first place as applied to a king. The descendants of David are destined "to be the greatest among the kings of earth" (Ps 89:27). They are the representatives of the might of Yahweh and thus witnesses to the universal claim of lordship of the God of Israel. But the universal expectations also enter the mouth of simple members of the OT people of God (cf. Pss 22:27f.; 47:1; 66:8; 67:3, 5; 68:32; 96:7). Yahweh's salvation is for the whole world. What takes place in Israel has universal validity. The miracle of the condescension of "God Most High" to

the lowly (v. 6; cf. especially Isa 57:15), when it is beheld in one single case as an example, draws all the mighty as witnesses to join in the praise and thanksgiving. The psalmist submits his own experience as an example.[32]

It is this dimension of the thanksgiving prayer that opens up the whole tradition of exhortation to praise and thanksgiving that is so prominent in the Psalms as well as in Isaiah 40–55 and manifests itself in the plural imperatives, "Sing!" "Give thanks!" "Praise!" Those who are gathered to hear the report of the wonderful deed of God in response to a cry for help are called to join in the praise and thanksgiving now being uttered by the one redeemed. So the psalmist who has been delivered calls to the congregation:

> Sing praises to the LORD, O you his faithful ones,
>   and give thanks to his holy name.[33] (Ps 30:4)

> Be glad in the LORD and rejoice, O righteous,
>   and shout for joy, all you upright in heart. (Ps 32:11)

> Praise the LORD! (Ps 116:19b)

Psalm 118 most dramatically sets this exhortation in the context of liturgy around the sacrifice and prayer of thanksgiving. The report of the deliverance and the confession that goes with it—including a possible echo of the oracle of salvation in verse 6—is bracketed by calls to the congregation at the beginning and end to give thanks:

> O give thanks to the LORD, for he is good;
>   his steadfast love endures forever! (Ps 118:1, 29)

This call to give thanks is then elaborated in two ways. First, it is developed into a call to the various elements that make up the congregation—the laity, the priests, and the proselytes[34]—each to give thanks by saying, "His steadfast love endures forever" (vv. 2-4). Second, the people make their own confession and report, expressing in a self-exhortation the call to praise and rejoice. And their confession is a response to the psalmist's own summary statement of deliverance. So the psalmist gives thanks as follows:

> I thank you that you have answered me
>   and have become my salvation. (v. 21)

Then the people respond with their own praise and confession:

> The stone that the builders rejected
>   has become the chief cornerstone.
> This is the LORD's doing;
>   it is marvelous in our eyes.

> This is the day that the LORD has made;
> let us rejoice and be glad in it. (vv. 22-24)[35]

The summons to thanks and praise that begins and ends the psalm becomes in the Old Testament a kind of definition of what it means to praise and give thanks. There is a sense in which all the songs of thanksgiving and indeed all the praise of God can be caught up in—not reduced to—the words, "O give thanks to the LORD, for he is good; for his steadfast love endures forever." In the books of Chronicles, when praise and thanksgiving are referred to as taking place, this brief call to give thanks, or some part of it, is often quoted to indicate what it is the people are doing:

> It was the duty of the trumpeters and singers to make themselves heard in unison in praise and thanksgiving to the LORD, and when the song was raised, with trumpets and cymbals and other musical instruments, in praise to the LORD,
>> "For he is good,
>> for his steadfast love endures forever" . . .
>>> (2 Chr 5:13)
> The priests stood at their posts; the Levites also, with the instruments for music to the LORD that King David had made for giving thanks to the LORD—for his steadfast love endures forever—whenever David offered praises by their ministry. (2 Chr 7:6)[36]

In the account of Jehoshaphat's prayer and victory over Ammon, Moab, and Mount Seir in 2 Chronicles 20, it is said that Jehoshaphat

> appointed those who were to sing to the LORD and praise him in holy splendor, as they went before the army, saying,
>> "Give thanks to the LORD,
>> for his steadfast love endures forever." (v. 21)

Elsewhere in the Old Testament, this brief song of thanksgiving is repeated again and again.[37] When the Lord sends word to Jeremiah announcing the future restoration of the fortunes of the land after the exile, God says that in this present wasteland, there shall be heard again

> the voices of those who sing, as they bring thank offerings [*tôdâ*] to the house of the LORD:
> "Give thanks to the LORD of hosts,
>> for the LORD is good,
>> for his steadfast love endures forever!" (Jer 33:11)

Here, therefore, we are given implicit instruction about the fundamental character of praise and thanksgiving and a kind of model of thanksgiving that can function as does the Lord's Prayer in the New Testament. The community of faith carries this prayer with it on into the future. Here is what it means to give thanks, and this is how it is done. The community is summoned to thanksgiving, joining in the praise of God either because of the testimony of one who has been delivered, as in Psalm 118 and other songs of thanksgiving, or because of its own experience of deliverance, as in 2 Chronicles 20 and the return from exile (Jer 33:11). All the particular experiences of salvation are caught up in the causal clauses, "for he is good; for his steadfast love endures forever." The goodness and steadfast love of God are among the broadest terms in the Old Testament to describe the fullness of God's benevolent activity in behalf of those in trouble and distress, the covenantal faithfulness of God that can be counted upon in every situation. As we have seen, in the first of all the thanksgiving prayers of Scripture, Eliezer's prayer of blessing and gratitude for success in his mission to find a wife for Isaac (Gen 24:27) was for God's steadfast love and faithfulness. Now we see that particular prayer becomes the definitive prayer of thanks. In its use, two things about thanksgiving prayer become clear.

One is that the experience of salvation reported in the more extended prayers is there only as a pointer to the enduring goodness and steadfast love of God. It is possible to praise and thank without ever identifying particular experiences, for they all say the same thing about God. Or more accurately, every particular experience points in the same direction, and Israel captured that in this brief prayer. The very particular prayers of thanksgiving are illustrative of the Lord's goodness and steadfast love; and that way of God's being with God's people, succinctly set forth in the brief, paradigmatic prayer of thanks, "O give thanks to the LORD, ... " is demonstrated in all these particular moments of deliverance to which the songs of thanksgiving testify.

The other thing we hear in this brief prayer is, of course, the communal character of praise and thanksgiving. The one who begins declaring "I give thanks" calls on the rest of the community to "Give thanks." Thanksgiving takes place in community and by the community. It is an act of solidarity in joy and response. If the prayer for help is a highly individual act, uttered often in isolation or out of the experience of loneliness and separation, the prayer of thanksgiving by one who has been helped is itself the primary indicator of the restoration of community. The one who was outside the circle now stands at its center but only as the community has become a circle of thanksgiving to God. If human frailty, wickedness, and neglect have contributed to the isolation, it is divine goodness, love, and help that have created the new community of praise and worship. This community of worship is not only there in the hearing of the report of deliverance. It is created also by the last feature of these songs to be lifted up in our study of thanksgiving prayer.

Vows of sacrifice in the sanctuary. The prayer of thanksgiving takes place in the context of the worship of God expressed customarily in sacrifice and apparently in the presence of God and the community in the sanctuary. Psalm 107:22 says:

> Let them offer thanksgiving sacrifices,
>   and tell of his deeds with songs of joy.

The report to others of God's help is joined with the sacrifice of thanksgiving to God as central features of the act of giving thanks. Both take place in the presence of others, and the sacrifice, at least, is in the sanctuary:[38]

> I will offer to you a thanksgiving sacrifice [*zebaḥ tôdâ*]
>   and call on the name of the LORD.
> I will pay my vows to the LORD
>   in the presence of all his people,
> in the courts of the house of the LORD,
>   in your midst, O Jerusalem.
> Praise the LORD! (Ps 116:17-19)

> But I with the voice of thanksgiving
>   will sacrifice to you;
> What I have vowed I will pay. (Jonah 2:9)

The response of the one delivered is not only words of thanksgiving; it consists also of acts and gifts of thanks:

> What shall I return to the LORD
>   for all his bounty to me?
> I will lift up the cup of salvation
>   and call on the name of the LORD,
> I will pay my vows to the LORD
>   in the presence of all his people. (Ps 116:12-14)

In this respect, sacrifice and the accompanying words of thanks are like the *běrākâ,* the blessing, that is offered to God. Only here words *and gifts* are given over to God: the verbal expressions of thanks—"I thank you, O LORD"—and the slaughtered animal(s).[39]

As the prose prayers have indicated, it is possible for thanksgiving to take place spontaneously and apart from formal sacrifice in the sanctuary. Though even there, one finds numerous indications of similar sorts of cultic acts and expressions of thanksgiving, suggesting they were the norm. The songs of thanksgiving belong to such occasions, as is indicated by Hannah's story, where a prayer for help went up and God heard and answered. When the question of Ps 116:12 arises in this instance—"What shall I return to the LORD for all his bounty to me?"—the answer is given in Hannah's song of thanksgiving (1 Sam 2:1-10) offered to God along with sacrifice and the child she had vowed to give over when she uttered her bitter complaint and plea for help. Jethro's prayer of thanksgiving for the salvation of the Hebrews from the Egyptian army is accompanied by sacrifices and a communal meal with Aaron and the elders of Israel (Exod 18:12). The sailors on Jonah's boat who prayed for help in the storm make vows and sacrifice when God saves them (Jonah 1:16).

In other instances, an altar is built in response and gratitude to God for having heard a prayer for help and responded. Although it is commanded by God, Jacob's altar at Bethel is interpreted by him to the family as an act of thanksgiving.[40] No prayer or song of thanksgiving is given in the account of Gideon's lament upon seeing the face of God and the oracle of salvation that follows, but the narrative does report the building of an altar. Once again a cult legend is also a story of thanksgiving. The name of the altar is the same as the words of the oracle of salvation.[41] It is an act of thanksgiving as much as it is the establishment of a shrine. So also Samuel's cry to the Lord for help against the Philistines, which is heard and answered, is followed by the building of an altar named "Ebenezer," which means "stone of help" or, as the narrative says, "Thus far the LORD has helped us" (1 Sam 7:12). The altar is a testimony to God's response to the cry for help.[42]

The sacrifice of thanksgiving, which seems to have included both animals and grain offerings,[43] is the setting out of which comes the Hebrew term for this song of thanksgiving, *tôdâ*, and the verb for giving thanks, *hôdâ*, in its various conjugated forms. In the songs of thanksgiving themselves (Ps 116:17) as well as in the Levitical laws (Lev 7:11-15; 22:29), we hear of "sacrifice(s) of thanksgiving" (*zebaḥ/zibḥê tôdâ*). *Tôdâ* is the occasion when one who has received help from the Lord in time of trouble comes into the sanctuary and offers sacrifice while declaring "I thank you, O Lord." The address, "I thank you" (*'ôdĕkā*), is what constitutes this particular sacrifice, which may be a sacrifice of well-being (*šelem*) or a burnt offering (*'ōlâ*), as a "sacrifice of thanksgiving."[44] That occasion seems to have been an act of worship and a meal of fellowship[45] as others are told the good news of God's deliverance and join in the expression of thanksgiving. It may well have been a part of a larger celebration. That is, the vow of the delivered sufferer was paid or fulfilled at the time of a regular sacrificial feast, as the story of Hannah (1 Samuel 1) suggests. It may have taken place, however, on a separate occasion. So the term *tôdâ* is rooted in this complex of address to God as sacrifice is offered and proclamation before other people, who share in the thanksgiving, both the words and the meal. Thanksgiving in the Old Testament is word and act, song and sacrifice, address to God and proclamation to others, performed by an individual but in the presence of other people, lifting up the experience of a human being but only to point to the God who has redeemed, bearing witness to the salvation of a single individual or group but calling for thanksgiving by a chorus much larger than the one(s) delivered. It is thanks, confession, and praise all wrapped up in a single reality.

Spiritualizing thanksgiving. Within the history of thanksgiving in the Old Testament, however, questions are raised about the appropriateness of sacrifice as a response to God's deliverance, and a tension is created between the word of thanksgiving and praise and the act of sacrificing. Two psalms that are not themselves songs of thanksgiving and one that is raise these questions. In Psalm 50, the attitude of the people in bringing their sacrifices comes under divine judgment. While the text gives some appearance of a blanket condemnation of sacrifice as a whole and a rejection of it by God, a closer look suggests that it is not sacrifice itself that is rejected. Indeed, God says, "Not for your sacrifices do I rebuke you; your offerings are continually before me" (v. 8), and speaks of "my faithful ones who made a covenant with me *by sacrifice*" (v. 5). The issue, as verses 8-14 indicate, is more the tendency of the people to view sacrifice as a gift to sustain the deity and thus necessary for God's sake. "Yahweh is expected to accept (*lqḥ*, v. 9) the animal, recognize the value of the sacrifice, satisfy his hunger (v. 12), and enjoy it. In other words, the idea is to purvey strength to Yahweh, make an impression on him, allay his wrath, and achieve a favorable disposition."[46] The *effects* of the sacrifice seem to be the primary point of criticism.

But in that criticism, there is a tendency toward what might be called a "spiritualizing"[47]—not a pejorative term—of the act of thanksgiving, a move already noted and discussed with regard to the vow of praise in the prayer for help (see chap. 3, above). Twice in the psalm, specific reference is made to sacrifice and thanksgiving. But the binding of the two, indicated in the genitival construction "sacrifice(s) of thanksgiving" (*zebaḥ/zibḥê tôdâ*), is broken. Instead of "make a sacrifice of thanksgiving to God," the divine instruction[48] here is to "make thanksgiving your sacrifice to God" (*zebaḥ lē'lōhîm tôdâ* [v. 14]). The text goes on to say:

> Call on me in the day of trouble;
> I will deliver you, and you shall glorify me. (v. 15)

The issue is not feeding or nurturing the deity but glorifying in praise and thanksgiving. The point is reiterated at the end of the psalm with the final piece of God's instruction: "Sacrificing/offering thanksgiving [*zōbēaḥ tôdâ*] glorifies me" (v. 23). Thanksgiving, *tôdâ*, is what is to be "sacrificed." Because the *tôdâ* included sacrifice, it cannot be ruled out that what is meant here is the whole of the *tôdâ*—thanksgiving, proclamation, sacrifice. But the formulation is moving toward the words of thanksgiving *replacing* the sacrifice of thanksgiving as the appropriate response to God when complaints and laments have been prayed and heard.

That direction is carried further in one of the penitential prayers for help, Psalm 51. It includes a vow (v. 13), but in this instance it is not a vow to give thanks and sacrifice:

> Then I will teach transgressors your ways,
>   and sinners will return to you.

Such a vow is not inconsistent with the song of thanksgiving's proclamation to others of God's steadfast love and goodness, but that sacrifice of animals and other foods is not meant is indicated by what follows in verses 15-17:

> O LORD, open my lips,
>   and my mouth will declare your praise.
> For you have no delight in sacrifice;
>   if I were to give a burnt offering,
>   you would not be pleased.
> The sacrifice acceptable to God is a broken spirit;
>   a broken and contrite heart, O God, you will not despise.

Sacrifice is replaced by praise and the petitioner's own stance of submission and contrition is offered in place of food offerings. These are the appropriate gifts of gratitude.

Inscribed prayers of thanksgiving. Within the songs or prayers of thanksgiving themselves, a similar understanding is present in Ps 40:1-10. In every respect but one, the character of thanksgiving as we have unfolded it from the thanksgiving prayers is evident in this text. Praise is offered to God (in the third person), and the "glad news" of God's deliverance is proclaimed "in the great congregation." But we read also these words:

> Sacrifice and offering [of grain] you do not desire,
>   but you have given me an open ear.
> Burnt offering and sin offering you have not required.
> Then I said, "Here I am;[49]
>   in the scroll of the book it is written of me.
> I delight to do your will, O my God;
>   your law is within my heart." (vv. 6-8)

Sacrifice is understood not to be the gift desired by the Lord in gratitude. Four different sacrifices, any one of which apparently could be used as a thank offering, are set aside in this instance. Instead, a quite different gift is offered—a book! What is "written of me," that is, of the one praying, is probably an inscribed account of what is customarily given verbally: a report of the situation of distress, the prayer, and God's response of deliverance.[50] One may assume that the account was what we now find in verses 1-4, or at least something similar.[51] Again, therefore, the "sacrifice" is the thanksgiving itself, or more particularly here, the proclamation to others of what God has done in behalf of the one who prayed for help.

The notion of an inscribed prayer of thanksgiving, or at least the report of distress, outcry, and deliverance, is given greater justification by the clear evidence for such inscribed prayers or reports among Hebrew, Aramaic, and Phoenician inscriptions of the first millennium, contemporaneous with the period in which most of the prayers discussed here were composed. But such inscribed prayers of thanksgiving are not confined to that period or the Syro-Palestinian sphere. In chapter 1, we called attention to the thirteenth-century prayer of Neb-Re, which gives thanks to Amon for delivering him from illness and near death. Neb-Re speaks in the first person, offering praises to the deity in second-person or third-person address. He reports about calling to God in distress and being rescued. He also calls for testimony to the power of Amon on a universal scale, across generations, and including the elements of nature.

In the previous chapter, we looked at the eighth-century inscription of Zakir, the Aramaean king of Lu'ash and Hamat.[52] There the king inscribes on a stele his account of the coming of a coalition of kings against him and how "I lifted up my hands to Be'elshamayn, and Be'elshamayn answered me, and Be'elshamayn spoke to me... 'Do not fear... I will rescue you....'" The king then goes on, apparently, to recount what Be'elshamayn did for him, though the text is too broken and incomplete to fill out. This inscription has already been properly called a "song of thanksgiving," for it is essentially the public report of the deity hearing the prayer and rescuing the one in trouble who prayed. One may assume that the stele being set up is part of the vow contained in the prayer for help.

That is explicitly the case in another Aramaean royal inscription on a stele, this one by a ninth-century king known from the Bible, Ben-Hadad. It reads as follows:

> The stele which Bir-hadad, son of Tabramman son of Hadyan, king of Aram, set up for his lord Milqart because he had prayed [nzr] to him and he had hearkened to his voice.[53]

The causal clause may better be translated "to whom he had vowed and who had heard his voice." While nzr in this instance can certainly be translated as "prayed," and it is clearly the prayer for help that is intended, the more common translation of nzr as "vowed" probably refers to the vow part of the prayer, which is the reason why the stele has been set up. We have already noted with regard to Hannah's prayer for a son that only the vow of that prayer is present in the text (1 Sam 1:11), because the vow is what is crucial to the story. So also with regard to the stele, the vow is what is crucial. In any event, once more we have an inscribed report of prayer and its hearing by the deity, suggesting how common it would be to write down a thanksgiving, as Psalm 40 suggests.[54]

Kings were not the only persons who set up or inscribed thanksgiving prayers. One has been discovered from eighth-century Judah at Khirbet el Qôm. It was inscribed on a stone pillar in a tomb and reads as follows:

> (For) Uriyahu the rich: his inscription.
> Blessed is Uriyahu by Yahweh;
> Yea, from his adversaries by his asherah he has saved him.
> (Written) by Oniyahu.[55]

The occupant of the tomb, Uriyahu, has had a scribe, Oniyahu, carve a memorial that is a kind of permanent inscription of the public testimony to what the Lord did in rescuing him from all his adversaries, expressing gratitude for the Lord's deliverance of him from trouble.[56] Such inscribed thanksgiving is suggested also by the beginning of Hezekiah's prayer of thanksgiving in Isaiah 38, where it is called "a writing of King Hezekiah of Judah, after he had been sick and had recovered from his sickness" (v. 9).

All of these instances, therefore, suggest that in addition to sacrifice as an act of thanksgiving, or instead of it, as Psalm 40 suggests, a public inscribed record of the distress, the prayer, and the divine deliverance could be a part of the thanksgiving to God.

Thanksgiving and credo. What we have encountered in these thanksgiving prayers or songs is echoed elsewhere in a quite different context, that is, in the Deuteronomic provision for thanksgiving at the great pilgrimage festivals, particularly the harvest festival, the feast of weeks (Deut 16:9-12). At the conclusion of the code of Deuteronomy, in chapter 26, the people are instructed to make a thanksgiving offering. Upon coming into the land, each Israelite is to take some of the first fruits of the harvest to the sanctuary and offer it to the priest, who places it before the altar of the Lord. Then the Israelite recites the familiar credo:

> A wandering Aramean was my father; he went down into Egypt.
> ... [W]e cried to the LORD, the God of our ancestors; the LORD heard our voice and saw our affliction, our toil, and our oppression. The LORD brought us out of Egypt with a mighty hand and an outstretched arm, ... and he brought us into this place and gave us this land, a land flowing with milk and honey. (vv. 5-9)

At the conclusion of the report of God's deliverance, the Israelite addresses the Lord: "So now I bring the first of the fruit of the ground that you, O LORD, have given me" (v. 10). The offerer is then instructed to leave the gift at the altar and "you, together with the Levites and the aliens who reside among you, shall celebrate with all the bounty that the LORD your God has given to you and to your house" (v. 11).

The Deuteronomic instruction includes those matters that we have seen belong to the acts and prayers of thanksgiving on the part of individuals who have been delivered from distress by God. A sacrifice is brought to the sanctuary. The one whose prayer was heard reports/ confesses/proclaims—it is all of that—what God did in behalf of the afflicted. As in the thanksgiving songs, this includes description of the situation of distress, the cry to the Lord, and God's positive response of deliverance. The public character of the report is implicit in its being offered at the sanctuary, apparently at the harvest festival, and in the fact that at the conclusion of the offering, the one who gives it is to celebrate with others in a meal.[57] Along with the address to others, there is the explicit address to God in the handing over of the offering (v. 10).[58]

Deuteronomic law, psalmic prayer, and narrative reports out of the story of Israel coalesce in a single understanding of thanksgiving arising out of God's hearing of prayers of need. Thanksgiving, proclamation, joy, and gifts or offerings of gratitude are the ingredients of thanksgiving. It is a very personal act that takes place before God. But it is also a public act that creates a community of restoration and praise, a community that joins with the one who has been in trouble and shares with him or her in the joy of deliverance. If trouble and woe have broken community and set people in lonely situations of need and suffering, the thanksgiving that arises out of God's hearing and responding to prayer re-creates that community and draws people together in gratitude to God and joy over the deliverance.

The presence of the "credo" as the report of God's deliverance in the celebration of thanksgiving makes us even more aware of what is readily discernible in the songs of thanksgiving themselves. In the biblical context, confession of faith is rarely done as an act in and of itself. While elsewhere it may be catechetical (e.g., Deut 6:20-25) or part of the enactment of covenant (e.g., Josh 24:1-13),[59] in this context such confession arises out of the experience of God's goodness and steadfast love and is both an expression of gratitude and a testimony to others. Its aim is more sermonic, even "evangelistic," and doxological than it is theological. Rather than serving narrowly to define a group of believers, it seeks to draw in and incorporate a larger community. Rather than serving to mark out the parameters of belief, confession here expresses gratitude for the very specific manifestations of the grace of God. Rather than being a generalized statement of belief, it is an account of a per-

son's trouble and God's help. All of those other things may accrue to
the setting forth of a credo, but they are not what is operative in these
many proclamations in the songs of thanksgiving and the Deuteronomic
liturgy of thanksgiving.

Confession of faith is thus not, in this instance, a matter of stating
the things one believes. It is testimony to what God has done in one's
own life and experience. Thanksgiving in the Old Testament is where
prayer and creed are joined. That for which one gives thanks to God is
declared before others. The aim of both prayer and creed is the praise
of God. Its outcome, if one can take at all seriously the song of thanksgiving in Psalm 22, is the conversion of the whole world to the praise
and worship—the fear—of God.

Community prayers of thanksgiving? In the Deuteronomic liturgy,
however, we are also sharply aware that the trouble reported there
by the one who brings the gift, while it begins in the first-person singular—"a wandering Aramean was *my* father"—shifts into the plural
"*we.*"

The thanksgiving of an individual who, in this instance, brings his or
her particular gift grows out of a situation of distress that afflicted the
community *as a whole.* In our discussion of thanksgiving, we have actually been dealing almost entirely with prayers of thanksgiving by or for
individuals whose prayers for help were heard and answered. Jethro's
prayer of thanksgiving is for God's deliverance of the Israelites from
Egyptian oppression, but it is the prayer and testimony of an individual.
Clearly, however, within the Bible, the affliction of the community is as
prominent as that of individuals, and the experience of God's goodness
and steadfast love is as centrally prominent in the great events of Israel's
deliverance as it is in those moments of personal or individual help from
God. Are there, then, prayers or songs of thanksgiving by the community, and are they the same as these prayers of individuals who cried out
to God and were answered?

There are indeed such prayers, but they are less clearly defined than
the thanksgiving prayers of individuals that have occupied our attention
to this point and less directly tied to prayers for help. They also take us
closer to that other very common form of prayer in response to God's
goodness, the hymn of praise. We have said little to this point about
Hannah's song (prayer) of thanksgiving because while the context is so
clearly the same as we have seen for thanksgiving by an individual who
prayed for help, the prayer itself is more like the hymn of praise. At least
logically, the hymn of praise is an outgrowth of the song of thanksgiving
of an individual. Indeed it is in such songs of thanksgiving as the brief
model prayer we noted earlier "O give thanks to the LORD for he is
good..."—that the form of praise takes shape and through which we

become even more aware of the intimate connection between praise and thanksgiving (see below). A brief look at two psalms that seem to be instances of the community in thanksgiving for God's answering their prayers and delivering them will take us into a closer examination of the hymn of praise, which was the primary way in which the community gave thanks to God.

Two psalms particularly, Psalms 124 and 129, have been regarded by many as community songs of thanksgiving. Psalm 124 is clearly an expression of thanksgiving by the community. The psalm is dissimilar from the songs of thanksgiving discussed above in lacking the kind of direct address to the Lord, such as, "We thank you, O Lord," and gives no indication of a previous prayer or of sacrifices and vows to be performed. But it does contain a recounting of the distress and God's help (vv. 1-5, 7) as well as an expression of thanks to God (v. 6). So some of the features we have identified with the word and act of thanksgiving are present, but it is uncertain what particular setting or circumstance provided the context for this prayer. Indeed it is in some ways more instructive than it is an actual prayer of thanksgiving. Psalm 124 has some affinities with Psalm 129 (see vv. 1-2), which has been regarded by some as a community song of thanksgiving. That happens primarily by the phrase, "[L]et Israel now say" (v. 1). Otherwise it seems more like an individual prayer for help or a song of trust, the latter particularly if verses 5ff. are read as a declaration, that is, "All who hate Zion will be put to shame...," as these verses may be translated. Its only real affinity with the prayers of thanksgiving we have encountered so far is in the report of the speaker(s) about the distress encountered (vv. 1-3) and God's help (v. 4).[60]

These psalms, therefore, may have served the community as a way of expressing thanks to God. They do not seem, however, to be definitive of the nature of communal thanksgiving or typical of the prayer, the address to God, that belonged to occasions of national deliverance. Other psalms that are more apparently communal thanks are so much like the hymn of praise, itself a form of thanksgiving, that we need to turn to that mode of prayer to see both the community in gratitude for God's salvation and the further expressions of the praise of God.

Hymns of Praise

The shared ground of praise and thanksgiving. We have noted above that there is a kind of model brief prayer of thanksgiving that occurs in part or whole a number of times in the Old Testament:

> O give thanks to the LORD, for he is good;
> for his steadfast love endures forever.[61]

In those several places in Chronicles and Ezra where this prayer is alluded to in the context of a narrative, two verbs are used to characterize what the ones praying or singing this song are doing. In 1 Chr 16:41, the verb is, as we would expect, *hôdâ:*

> With them were Heman and Jeduthun, and the rest of those chosen and expressly named to *render thanks* [*lĕhôdôt*] to the LORD, for his steadfast love endures forever. (cf. 7:3)

So also, in Jer 33:11, this song is sung as people bring thank offerings (*tôdâ,* from the verb *hôdâ*) to the sanctuary. Elsewhere, however, when this song is quoted or referred to, the texts speak not only of "thanks," *hôdâ/tôdâ,* but also of "praise," *hillēl/tĕhillâ.* The singers in 2 Chr 5:13 "make themselves heard in unison *in praise and thanksgiving*" (*lĕhallēl ûlĕhôdôt;* cf. v. 13, "in praise"). At the consecration of the temple, as recorded in 2 Chr 7:6, reference is made to the priests and Levites having "the instruments for music to the LORD that King David had made *for giving thanks* [*lĕhôdôt*] to the LORD—for his steadfast love endures forever—whenever David *offered praises* [*bĕhallēl*] by their ministry." The two verbs are also used together in Ezra 3:10-11 as a way of describing what the Levites were doing when they sang, "[F]or he is good, for his steadfast love endures forever." And in both 2 Chr 7:6 and Ezra 3:10-11, the text speaks either at the beginning or the end of this activity simply as "praise" (*hillēl*), as is the case when the model prayer of thanks is quoted in 2 Chr 20:21-22.

Two different words, therefore—"thanks" and "praise"—are used to describe a single act or a single prayer. We have already described this as the model prayer of *thanksgiving.* But now we must also say that in some respects the prayer, "O give thanks to the LORD, for he is good, for his steadfast love endures forever," is also the model prayer of *praise.* Nothing demonstrates more clearly how closely these two activities are related. All thanksgiving to God becomes a form of praise. And much of the praise of God is an expression of gratitude.[62] The prayer, "O give thanks...," arises out of the song of thanksgiving and the call to others to give thanks. But the form of that prayer exemplifies the basic character and form of praise as it is manifest in the hymn. And while it may be possible to identify the basic features or characteristics of the song of thanksgiving (see above) or the basic form of the hymn of praise (see below), they come together not only in this model prayer of thanksgiving but also in other psalms and prayers.[63]

The shape of praise. The form of the hymn of praise is simple in its basic character and rich in its various and diverse manifestations. (1) It begins with *a call to praise* the Lord, for example, "Praise the Lord," "Sing to the Lord," "Rejoice in the Lord," "Bless the Lord."[64] This is most commonly a plural imperative form of address to an audience usually identified with a vocative, for example, "all the earth."[65] Sometimes the call may take the form of a first-person singular or plural declaration or self-exhortation to praise, for example, "I will extol you, . . . I will bless you, . . . I will praise you";[66] "I will sing to the LORD";[67] "[M]y heart exults in the LORD" (1 Sam 2:1); "I will sing of your steadfast love, O LORD" (Ps 89:1); and "Come, let us worship and bow down."[68] (2) The hymn then continues with the expression of praise itself in a causal clause, usually beginning with *kî*, "for," "because," that gives *a reason for praise* in some characteristic or activity of God.[69]

This structure is seen in the model prayer of thanksgiving, "O give thanks to the Lord [imperative call to praise], *for he is good* . . . [reason for praise]," which is why praise and thanks may be seen to overlap in this particular example. But this structure and its logic—calling for praise and justifying the appropriateness of that act—are found commonly in the hymns of the Psalter and elsewhere.[70] An excellent succinct example is the shortest of all the psalms, Psalm 117:

> *Praise the* LORD, all nations!
> Extol him, all you peoples!
> *For* great is *his steadfast love* toward us,
> and the faithfulness of the LORD *endures forever.*
> Praise the LORD!

In the italicized words, one sees both the hymn of praise in its simplest form and also the way in which the model song of thanks ("O give thanks . . . ") is reflected in this hymn, particularly the italicized words of the second verse.[71] Its paradigmatic character for the community of faith rests not only on its content but also very much on the way it is a model of both the song of thanksgiving and the hymn of praise. It gives us, in effect, the "shape" of praise. As we have seen its elaboration in a thanksgiving song, such as Ps 118:1-4, so we shall see it repeated and developed again and again in the hymns of praise.

One such hymnic elaboration is Psalm 100. Along with Exodus 15, it provides an appropriate starting point for moving from the song of thanksgiving into examples of hymns of praise. The frequent use of this hymn as a call to worship in contemporary church gatherings is rooted in two aspects of the form and setting of the psalm. One is its heightening or elaboration of the call to praise in *seven* imperatives in verses 1-4. Such heaping up of commands to sing, rejoice, praise, bless, and the like are found elsewhere in hymns of praise, for example, Psalms 96 and 98. Two things happen in such elaborations of the imperatives.

1. They tend to turn the call to praise into the act itself. That is, one cannot really see the praise as only in those things that are attested to or confessed and declared in the *kî* causal or reason clauses. As Psalm 150

indicates by its character at the end of the Psalter as a concluding extended call to praise without reasons given, the uttering of the command is the expression of praise itself. And that is even more the case when the call is elaborated in various and different forms. The same thing happens when the hymn is reduced to a single "Hallelujah!" or "Praise the Lord!" It assumes the grounding, the reasons for praise, but the simple call to praise is itself praise. One hears this in the "Hallelujah Chorus" of Handel's *Messiah*. The words are a classic hymn of praise with the call to praise, "Hallelujah," followed by the reason for praise, "for the Lord God omnipotent reigneth." But anyone who hears or sings that chorus knows that the repeated Hallelujahs, sounded again and again in the music, are themselves powerful expressions of praise.

2. Such elaborated calls to praise also accent the notes of jubilation, joy, and singing. Invariably, the more extended the imperative the more these notes are sounded. As the imperatives, when heaped up, are an expression of praise, so their heaping up is the way in which the joy and music of praise are let loose. There is something about the expression of praise and thanksgiving that requires song and music. It seems to be found in the joy that comes out of the experience of God's marvelous acts. Thanksgiving and praise, when they are authentic, cannot finally be contained. Their breaking forth is in song and dance and music. The place where that is particularly manifest in the doxologies and songs of thanksgiving is in the calls to sing and shout and make a joyful noise.

The other sign of the appropriate locus of Psalm 100 in the calling of the congregation to worship is the indication in verses 2 and 4 that its setting is the entrance into the sanctuary for worship. The purpose of the hymn, to elicit from the community gathered for worship the praise of God, is sharply identified in these few verses. Praise is a public act; it is an act of worship; and it is a corporate act. In the song of thanksgiving, the focus is on the individual's act of thanks in the midst of the people to whom that one bears witness. Its outcome in a corporate act of praise by the community in worship is what we find in the hymn of praise. The two are clearly merged in this hymn in several ways: the parallelism of thanksgiving (*tôdâ*) and praise (*tĕhillâ*) in verse 4; the concluding emphasis upon thanksgiving in the final two imperatives, which are calls to "give thanks" and "bless" (i.e., thank—see above); and the superscription at the beginning of the psalm that calls this a psalm of "thanksgiving" (*tôdâ*).

The primary grounding of the calls to praise in Psalm 100 is the familiar reason: the goodness of the Lord and the enduring steadfast love and faithfulness of God (v. 5). Once more we see *ḥesed,* "steadfast love," and *ṭôb,* "good," encapsulating or summarizing the way that God has been with the people. Here is the reason for praise, that the community—both in the individual experiences of persons who have prayed for help in time of distress and in the corporate experience of being helped in trouble and being kept at all times—is sustained by the grace of God. The mercy and love of God can be counted upon. The many oracles of salvation and deeds of help and deliverance that have answered the prayers of the people are a testimony to the goodness and love of God. Psalm 98 shows this grounding of the praise of the people in the steadfast love and faithfulness of God as the summary statement at the conclusion of a description of the Lord's salvific acts:

> O sing to the LORD a new song,
>   *for* he has done marvelous things.
> His right hand and his holy arm
>   have gotten him victory.
> The LORD has made known his victory;
>   he has revealed his vindication in the sight of the nations.
> He has remembered *his steadfast love* [*ḥesed*] and faithfulness
>   to the house of Israel.
> All the ends of the earth have seen
>   the victory of our God. (Ps 98:1-3)

When Israel gives thanks or praise for God's steadfast love and faithfulness, it is just such acts of salvation and vindication, such "marvelous things," as this psalm attests that are in mind. The hymn in Ps 89:1-18 begins with a self-declaration, "I will sing of *your*[72] *steadfast loves* [plural][73] forever, O LORD," and then goes on in the next verse to say, "for *your steadfast love forever* is established." The plural of *ḥesed,* especially, has in mind the many particular manifestations of God's goodness and love.[74] It occurs again at the end of Psalm 107 (v. 43)[75] to refer back to all the different kinds of deliverance and liberation that God has wrought and for which people are to give thanks according to the psalm. And in Isa 63:7, the *ḥasdê yhwh,* the "steadfast loves," or, as the NRSV translates, "the gracious deeds of the LORD," are recounted and the term is placed in parallel with *tĕhillōt yhwh,* "the praises of the LORD," or, "the praiseworthy deeds of the LORD." So praise and thanksgiving are "called for"—in the literal and idiomatic sense. They are both required or commanded, and they are appropriate.

There is another grounding of the call to praise in Ps 100:3 that is less typical of the hymns but not unique to this one. It is present also, for example, in the hymnic section of Psalm 95. The community is called to acknowledge a double reality, that (1) the Lord of Israel is God—the primary claim of Scripture and of Israel's faith—and that (2) the one who is God is "our" God (cf. 95:6-7), the God who created this people and to whom they belong—the secondary claim of Scripture but the primary experience of Israel. The confessional language of the individual in the song of thanksgiving, who reports what the Lord has done, is transformed in this hymn of praise to a confessional language of the people that asserts the most basic claims of all about the God who is praised. Such call to confessional praise can take a more specific or concrete form, as we see in the hymn of praise in Ps 66:1-12 preceding the individual song of thanksgiving in verses 13-20:

> Come and see what God has done:
>> he is awesome in his deeds among mortals.
> He turned the sea into dry land;
>> they passed through the river on foot.
> There we rejoiced in him,
>> who rules by his might forever. (vv. 5-7a)

> Bless our God, O peoples,
>> let the sound of his praise be heard,
> who has kept us among the living,
>> and has not let our feet slip.
> For you, O God, have tested us;
>> you have tried us as silver is tried. . . .
> You let people ride over our heads;
>> we went through fire and through water;
>> yet you have brought us out to a spacious place.[76]
>> (vv. 8-10, 12)

There are two plural imperative constructions, "Come and see" and "Bless our God," which are then grounded, although in different ways. The first is a call to see the act of God in the deliverance at the sea,[77] and the second is a reason for blessing or giving thanks, which is a report of how God tested the people by their enemies but in the end saved them. In each case, there is a kind of report or confessional declaration of what God has done in a specific act of deliverance or perhaps series of saving acts (as is the case in such hymns as Psalms 105 and 135). This is a reason for praise and thanksgiving, and indeed, as in Psalms 100 and 117, for the praise of all the earth or the peoples of the earth. Even as the song of thanksgiving in Ps 22:21ff. moves out from the immediate community into the nations of the earth to call all of them to praise God for the deliverance of the one who now testifies that God heard and helped, so the hymns of praise quite directly and frequently call all the earth to praise what God has done in and for Israel.[78]

The oldest of all the hymns, which occurs in Exodus 15 in two forms, a short incipit in verse 21 and the longer poem in verses 1-18, is analogous to what we find in Ps 66:1-13. In the short form of verse 21, it is very typical in structure:

Call to praise: "Sing to the LORD,

Reason for praise: for he has triumphed gloriously;
                    horse and rider he has thrown into the sea."

The longer form of this hymn of praise is similar except that it is couched as a first-person, individual declaration of praise, and the elaboration of the reason is extended through many verses. They become, in effect, a kind of narrative report in hymnic form of how God delivered the Israelites from the Egyptians and led them into the promised land. Like the song of thanksgiving, this hymn spells out in detail what God did to deliver the people in trouble. The prayer for help is not explicitly to the fore as in the songs of thanksgiving. The hymn, whether couched in individual first-person form or as a summons to the community, stands on its own terms, without reference back to the prayer that initiated God's response of deliverance. The same is true for the song of Deborah and Barak (Judges 5). But the prayer for help is in the background of both of these hymns, even if it is not alluded to. The cry of the people in Egypt to the Lord and to Moses (Exod 14:10-12) and the cry of the people to the Lord in the time of the Judges (Judg 4:3) lie behind these hymns. They grow out of acts of redemption in response to the prayer of people and individuals. The language and structure of the conclusion to the prose report of the deliverance that precedes this hymn are echoed in the allusion to the song of thanksgiving in Ps 40:1-3:[79]

> Thus the LORD *saved* Israel that day from the Egyptians; and Israel *saw* the Egyptians dead on the seashore. Israel *saw* the great work that the LORD did against the Egyptians. So the people *feared* the LORD and *believed* [*'mn*] in the LORD and in his servant Moses. (Exod 14:30-31)

> > He *drew me up* from the desolate pit,
> >   out of the miry bog,
> > and set my feet upon a rock,
> >   making my steps secure.
> > He put a new song in my mouth,
> >   a song of praise to our God.
> > Many will *see* and *fear,*
> >   and put their *trust* [*bṭḥ*] in the LORD.
> >   (Ps 40:2-3)

The very particularized language of Exodus 15—and of Judges 5 as well—serves to offer praise to God because of particular gracious deeds by the Lord.

Even as "I give thanks...," when said upon presentation of the thanksgiving offering, is an act of thanksgiving, so the "I sing to the

LORD..." (Exod 15:1) is an act of praise. The fact that we have duplicate forms of the introductory part of the hymn—in Exod 15:1 and 21—helps us see how the imperative, "Sing to the LORD..." (v. 21), is just as much an act of praise as the self-declaration, "I will sing to the LORD..." (v. 1). One is the voice of an individual becoming the expression of praise of the people;[80] the other is the call of an individual (Miriam) to the community. But they speak about the same event and have the same intention—to render praise to God.

That praise takes shape in a variety of ways, of which Exodus 15 is a typical complex. Prominent are the kinds of sentences describing an act of the Lord, such as one sees in the causal "for" clauses of verses 1 and 21. In the longer form of this hymn, such *magnalia dei* sentences are brought together in two sequences, the first describing all that the Lord did in defeating the Egyptian army at the sea (vv. 1b, 4-5, 6b-10), and the second recounting the way the Lord led the people through the wilderness and against the threats of the hostile neighbors into the promised land. As the salvation oracle often responded to the prayer for help with an explicit indication of what the Lord would *do* to help, and as the thanksgiving songs regularly declared that "the LORD has *done* it" (e.g., Ps 22:31), so the hymn of praise declares in very expansive ways what the Lord *did* in the act of deliverance. Psalm 66 exemplifies the same focus on what God has done when it explicitly calls for the people to

> Come and see what God has *done* [*mip'ălôt*]:
> he is awesome in his *deeds* [*'ălîlâ*] among mortals.
> He turned the sea into dry land;
> they passed through the river on foot. (vv. 5-6; cf. v. 3)

The centrality of such sentences about the mighty acts of the deity in the praise of the people is attested beyond the confines of Israel's praise. At the entrapment of their hated enemy Samson, the Philistines praised their deity, Dagon, in the same way. They

> gathered to offer a great sacrifice to their god Dagon, and to rejoice; for they said, "Our god has given Samson our enemy into our hand." When the people saw him, they praised their god; for they said, "Our god has given our enemy into our hand, the ravager of our country, who has killed many of us."
>
> (Judg 16:23-24)[81]

Along with these sentences grounding praise and effecting praise in *the report of what the power of God has wrought* in delivering the afflicted, there are other expressions that tend to render praise by *describing God* or *ascribing to God characteristics* that are reflected in the way God has been present to help and save. So Moses and the Israelites declare:

> The LORD is a warrior;
>> the LORD is his name. (Exod 15:3)

> Your right hand, O LORD,
>> glorious in power . . . (Exod 15:6)

Such claims are a way of saying that the events of the sea have shown who this God is and the power the Lord of Israel exercises in the world over the forces of tyranny and oppression. The whole exodus story began out of the question of power (Exodus 1–2) and the question of who it was, or who this God was, who confronted and challenged the power of Pharaoh over Hebrew slaves. Now the answer to those questions is clear, and the answer becomes a form of praise.[82]

In some cases, such descriptive and ascriptive sentences are analogous to those divine affirmations of the sureness of God's relationship to the afflicted one(s) that occur so regularly in the oracle of salvation, for example, "I am with you." The reflection of the divine assertions in human affirmations is present in Exod 15:2:

> The LORD is my strength and my might,
>> and he has become my salvation;
> this is my God, and I will praise him,
>> my father's God, and I will exalt him.

All of these expressions of praise attest to the perduring and sure relationship between the one who sings and the God who has heard and answered the prayer(s).

A third type of hymnic sentence is found in verse 11. It is a comparative statement, often couched, as here, in the form of a rhetorical question. Such questions as, "Who is like you, O LORD, among the gods?" assert *the incomparability of the Lord* vis-à-vis other gods or heavenly beings.[83] God is praised as like no other and so exalted, glorious, worthy of praise.

Thematic notes in the music of praise. Finally, the praise of God in Exodus 15 concludes with a ringing affirmation, "The LORD will reign forever and ever!" (v. 18). With this declaration, one of the major *themes* of the hymns of praise is sounded: *the enduring rule of the Lord over Israel, the nations, and the world.* There is a sense in which all the particular acts of God, the various manifestations of God's steadfast love to individuals and to the community, serve the purpose of pointing to the sovereignty of the God of Israel. That is certainly the case for the powerful victory of God over the Egyptians, a victory Exodus

15 ascribes to no human help at all. Whether such an understanding of God as ruler of all is desirable is not an issue. Its appropriateness is clearly indicated by all that has happened. In its praise, Israel does not ask whether one may or ought to think of God as ruler. It bows before the Lord who has "prevailed over it."[84]

A number of hymns, particularly those commonly called "enthronement hymns," have this theme at their center.[85] They are hymns whose aim is to declare the rule of God over the gods of the heavens and the peoples of the earth.[86] The praise of God takes its most political and universal turn as it places this declaration to the fore. And the act of praising is both the response of a people to the love and goodness of God and a claim about the way the world is ordered and where power lies. The claim at the end of Exodus 15 that "the LORD will reign forever and ever" is set over against the claim of the Egyptian pharaoh to sovereignty over Egyptians and Hebrews alike. The exodus story has demonstrated that Pharaoh has power over neither. Israel's praise of the Lord as king, therefore, is not to be understood as an empty phrase or a theological choice. It is testimony to the reality they have encountered, that the power at work in the world is of a particular sort and exercises sway not only over them but over all the other claimants to power in heaven and earth—the gods of heaven and the kings of the earth. The incredible audacity of Israel time and again to demand of the peoples and nations and rulers of the earth their praise of the Lord of Israel is rooted in this experience of ruling and controlling power whose character is constantly perceived as good (*ṭôb*) and gracious (*ḥesed*). The nations are to give praise to the Lord because they have heard and seen the saving and liberating power of this deity (Pss 98:3; 126:2) and because the mighty acts of God have demonstrated the Lord's control of nature and history. The Lord is friend and maker of Israel but king of the world, whose homage is first heard in Israel's praise, which itself calls the whole earth to bow before this ruler. And this, of course, in the face of similar claims on the part of other deities. So Israel, in its praise, is making a political decision about how the world is governed and where it is going to line up its allegiance. Beyond that, it dares to make a political decision for others. When, in the New Testament, the universal lordship of Jesus Christ is affirmed and the New Testament closes with the same hymnic praise, "Hallelujah! For the Lord our God the Almighty reigns" (Rev 19:6), it carries forward that audacious political claim of the Old Testament. The political character of such praise is well indicated by its capacity to create martyrs of those who make that claim in the face of the claims of other human and divine rulers.

The hymn, therefore, is a form of praise and thanksgiving where the accent is on the praise. Because it is not so directly tied in its formulation to a previous prayer for help, it provides a form of prayer that can praise God for very specific moments and deeds of help, but it can also, more expansively, praise God for the creation and for all sorts of ways that God has shown steadfast love and manifested glory. The song of Hannah is more of this style even though it is placed in the context of prayer for help and thanksgiving. That is, the particular occasion of this hymn of praise is contextually set as Hannah's thanksgiving to God for the gift of a son when she was barren and beset by a rival wife who had many children. The hymn authenticates this connection of event and praise in one important way. It sets as one of the grounds of praise:

> The barren has borne seven,
> but she who has many children is forlorn. (1 Sam 2:5)

In its context, the verse attests to the power of God to give fertility where there was barrenness, as in Hannah's case. In its formulation, it moves even closer to the actual story itself in two ways. First, it speaks, in poetic fashion, of the barren woman bearing seven children. The number is obviously a kind of hyperbole to underscore God's power, not simply to provide a single child but to turn things around completely: the totally barren one is now richly fertile. The story of Hannah actually makes that point itself when it reveals eventually that she bore six children altogether. Second, the verse also points indirectly to the "enemy" of Hannah, Peninnah, her rival wife who taunted her for her barrenness. While the story of Hannah in 1 Samuel 1 tells us nothing of Peninnah's reaction or fate after Hannah bore a child, it clearly portrays her as Hannah's enemy who is undone by God's deliverance of Hannah from her distress. She sees the one child move to a favored position in the service of the Lord in the sanctuary, and she sees Hannah receive the blessing of Eli the priest and deliver one child after another.

So by its literary context, the song/prayer of Hannah is, like the songs of Miriam and Moses,[87] an act of praise that arises out of a particular event in which Hannah's prayer for help was heard, and the Lord's gracious and steadfast love was manifest to her in the birth of a child. There is not, as is the case also in Exodus 15, and for that matter in Judges 5, a specific reference to the preceding prayer for help, a frequent feature of the song of thanksgiving. Even more, however, in the case of Hannah's song of praise and thanksgiving, the particular event has receded more into the background, and the hymn is a more generalized exaltation of God for acts of goodness and power. While a removal of Exodus 15 or Judges 5 from their contexts would not keep the reader from discerning the events about which they praise God, that is not the case with 1 Sam 2:1-10. It anticipates another prayer with a different but similar context (Luke 2:46-55) and sounds notes that we hear in other hymns.[88] Here, the hymn of praise, while still overlapping with the song of thanksgiving in being connected to the prayer for help, God's deliverance, and acts of thanksgiving in the sanctuary, moves out into a broader horizon. The particular event is less the focus of the psalm. It is simply and importantly one illustration of a larger reality, one that we find in some of the other hymns. While we hear again the notes of divine incomparability (v. 2), and the song is permeated with statements about what God does, the particular *theme* that is sounded in this hymn, and echoed in others, is *the activity of God in behalf of the weak and needy,* described in this poem as a reversal of fortunes—sweeping the mighty, the rich, and the well-fed from their positions of control and satisfaction and giving to the feeble, the hungry, the barren, and the poor and needy honor, provision, and power. The political character of Israel's praise is heard again in "Hannah's" claim that the activity of the Lord is, literally, a revolutionary one, turning things upside down in the most radical way possible, accomplishing the impossible in the socioeconomic world of that time and, indeed, of any time.[89] Hannah's story is a small attestation of a larger reality about this God that is once more the ground of praise and exaltation. At a later time, the Lord's revolutionary power lifts up another humble woman, Mary, and evokes from her the same song of praise for the wonderful reversal of the ordinary way things are and are expected to be. So she, like Hannah, praises the Lord (Luke 1:46-55) in a hymn that has become one of the most often sung hymns of praise in the world, the Magnificat.

Psalm 113 picks up this same theme and with the dimension of reversal that we find in Hannah's hymn. It begins with the summons to praise and then moves into the praise, first with declarations of God's glory exalted high above all, claims made in part in the form of incomparability sentences:

> The LORD is high above all nations,
>   and his glory above the heavens.
> Who is like the LORD our God,
>   who is seated on high,
> who looks far down
>   on the heavens and the earth? (vv. 4-6)

In the latter part of this section, we encounter another type of sentence characteristic of hymnic praise and found also in Hannah's hymn. It is the participial phrase describing God as "one who does...." In other words, one of the primary ways of ascribing praise to God is to heap up a series of participial descriptive phrases extolling God by showing what God is like. "The Lord is the one who does..." say those who render praise. And we hear a ringing catalogue of claims about God's way. In this instance, the participial phrases grow out of the question of incomparability:

> Who is like the LORD our God,
>> the one enthroned on high,
> the one looking far down
>> on the heavens and the earth,
> the one raising the poor from the dust,...
> the one giving the barren woman a home
>> as the joyous mother of children? (vv. 5-7a, 9)

The thematic focus of the praise is seen in the juxtaposition of the one enthroned and looking down from on high with the one raising the poor from the dust and lifting the needy from the ash heap (v. 7). The exalted Lord, whose throne is above the heavens, is the one who bends down to lift up the lowliest of the earth. It is the enthroned king of all the world who provides for the needy, the poor, and the barren. So—Hallelujah! As in Hannah's hymn, the reversal is not complete. The lowly are lifted up, not in place of the mighty who are cast down, but to *sit with* the princes. The Lord's way is not finally simply a reversal of classes. It is the lifting up of the lowly to join with those who rule and are provided for.

God's care and attention to the weak and lowly and distressed constitute one of the most oft-sounded notes of biblical praise. As Psalm 146 "catalogues" in praise the ways of God, it summons to praise "the one who"

> keeps faith forever;
>> who executes justice for the oppressed;
>> who gives food to the hungry. (vv. 6b-7a)

The participles continue with "the Lord" as a repeated subject in order to underscore the *identity* of the power at work in the world in this way:

> The LORD sets the prisoners free;
>> The LORD opens the eyes of the blind.
> The LORD lifts up those who are bowed down;
>> the LORD loves the righteous.
> The LORD watches over the strangers.

Then the psalm shifts to straight verbal sentences:

> He upholds the orphan and the widow,
>> but the way of the wicked he brings to ruin. (vv. 7b-9)

Finally, and this is crucial to the hymn, the theme of the power of God in behalf of the weak is joined explicitly to the theme of the rule of God as the hymn climaxes by declaring that all these kinds of activities of justice and caring and liberation—activities of God in behalf of the oppressed, the hungry, prisoners, the blind, the bowed down, the innocent or righteous, strangers, orphans, and widows—serve to demonstrate the perduring rule of God: "The LORD will reign forever!" (v. 10). It is not simply victory over Egyptian—and other—tyranny that establishes the rule of God over the world. The care of the weak and the oppressed does the same. But then that, of course, is exactly what God was doing in the exodus, setting free the prisoners, lifting up those who were bowed down with the burdens of slavery, executing justice for the oppressed, watching over strangers and sojourners in Egypt, and bringing the way of the wicked to ruin. The rule of God is demonstrated and established in such acts. And in them, prayers and cries for help are thereby answered, as Psalm 145 makes very explicit:

> The LORD upholds all who are falling,
>   and raises up all who are bowed down....
> *The* LORD *is near to all who call on him*,
>   to all who call on him in truth.
> He fulfills the desire of all who fear him;
>   *he also hears their cry and saves them.* (vv. 14, 18-19)

The hymns of praise confirm that in this way the Lord's reign is established forever:

> All your works shall give thanks to you, O LORD,
>   and all your faithful shall bless you.
> They shall speak of the glory of your kingdom,
>   and tell of your power,
> to make known to all people your mighty deeds,
>   and the glorious splendor of your kingdom.
> Your kingdom is an everlasting kingdom,
>   and your dominion endures throughout all generations.
>   (Ps 145:10-13)

In this hymn, as well as in Psalm 103, the care of the weak and needy (Ps 103:6) is joined with explicit reference to the ancient confessional formula of Exod 34:6 as the ground of Israel's praise:

> The LORD is merciful and gracious,
>   slow to anger and abounding in steadfast love.
>   (Pss 103:8 and 145:8)

We have already seen how this claim, which is so frequent in the Old Testament and seems to belong to the earliest convictions of Israel about the nature and character of its God, was the ground of appeal and motivation in the prayers for help (see chap. 3, above). It is no accident, therefore, that when the people sang their hymns of praise and songs of thanksgiving, they praised God for showing, both in all cases and *in their particular case,* that the claim was true, that the steadfast love of

God could be counted upon and that God's way with the weak and the oppressed, as with the sinful and erring, is truly merciful and gracious.

In the middle of one of the prayers for help, we hear the voice of the afflicted anticipate in a vow the time of deliverance and the prayers of praise and thanksgiving that shall come forth from his or her mouth when that has happened. It places this theme of the care of the weak and afflicted to the fore and joins all the individual prayers for help with these hymns of praise:

> Then my soul shall rejoice in the LORD,
>   exulting in his deliverance.
> All my bones shall say,
>   "O LORD, who is like you?
> You deliver the weak
>   from those too strong for them,
>   the weak and needy from those who despoil them."
>
> (Ps 35:9-10)

The praise of God for the steadfast love and ruling power demonstrated in particular acts of deliverance for the people and for individuals is thus attested both in those specific references to events and mighty acts and in the characterizing of God as one who hears the cries of the afflicted and needy and lifts them up. That praise, however, can and does encompass an even larger horizon of divine activity and glory. When Ps 145:8 cites the credal formula, "The LORD is gracious and merciful ... abounding in *steadfast love,*" it goes on in the next verse to speak of that other divine characteristic that we hear in the model song of thanksgiving, the Lord's *goodness,* in the following manner:

> The LORD is good to all,
>   and his compassion is over *all that he has made* [*ma'ăśāyw*].
> *All your works* [*ma'ăśeykā*] shall give thanks to you, O LORD.
>
> (vv. 9-10)

In Psalm 146, the characterizing of God (in a participial phrase) as "the one who does [*'ōśeh*] justice for the oppressed" (v. 7; see above) is preceded by another participial phrase, "the one who makes [*'ōśeh*] heaven and earth, the sea, and all that is in them" (v. 6). Here we come to a third major *theme* of the hymns of praise: *the power and love of God seen in the creation.* The "deeds/acts" (*ma'ăśîm*) of God, what the Lord "does" that evokes the praise of the people, are not limited to "acts" in behalf of the afflicted. The steadfast love of God is found also in what God has done in the creation. All the elements of heaven and earth are "works" of the Lord. God has "made" them even as God has "made" Israel.[90] God's compassion encompasses them (Ps 145:9) as it does Israel (Ps 103:13). The joining of the "works" of creation and the "works" of righteousness and justice as the ground of praise happens in direct fashion in Psalm 33, a hymn:

> Praise the LORD with the lyre;
>> make melody to him with the harp of ten strings.
> Sing to him a new song;
>> play skillfully on the strings, with loud shouts.
> *For the word of the* LORD is upright,
>> and all his *work* [*ma'ăśēhû*] is done in faithfulness,
> the one loving righteousness and justice;
>> the earth is full of the steadfast love of the LORD.
> *By the word of the* LORD the heavens were made,
>> and all their host by the breath of his mouth,
> the one gathering the waters of the sea as in a bottle;
>> the one putting the deeps in storehouses.
> Let all the earth fear the LORD;
>> let all the inhabitants of the world stand in awe of him.
> For he spoke, and it came to be;
>> he commanded, and it stood firm. (Ps 33:2-7, 9)

Echoes are heard of the Priestly account of creation with its emphasis on everything being made by the decree or word of God. But the first works that are cited in this listing are "righteousness and justice" and "the steadfast love of the LORD." Those who sing God's praise because they have known in their history and in their personal story that justice and that mercy see them as parts of the whole of God's work, the creation itself. So all the earth is called to praise and marvel at all the work of God. The praise of God, therefore, involves the works of creation in two ways. Like Israel and like the afflicted who are lifted up and delivered— these are often one and the same—the things "he has made" (Ps 145:9) in heaven and earth are both the *reason* for praise and *those who are summoned* to praise.

The praise of God because of what the Lord has made is not confined to the hymns celebrating the rule of God and recounting the ways God's steadfast love and goodness are manifest to God's people and to the weak and the needy, those hymns we have been discussing above. There are some that make God's works of creation the central theme of their praise. So Psalm 104 is one long ascription of praise—frequently using the participial phrases—laying out all the "works" of creation God has wrought as testimony to the wonder and power of God. In the middle of the hymn, the psalmist exclaims:

> O LORD, how manifold are your works!
>> In wisdom you have made them all;
>> the earth is full of your creatures. (Ps 104:24)

Psalm 8 begins and ends with the exclamation of praise, "O LORD, our LORD, how majestic is your name in all the earth!" The glory of God that evokes this praise is found in the moon and stars, the heavens, which are the "works" of God's fingers, and even more in the incredible fact that God has paid attention to the human creature in making humanity the crown of creation and the ruler of all the other "works" of God's hands.

But if the works of creation are part of the reason the community exalts the Lord and sings to God's glory, those works also belong to the choir that does the singing. The call to all the earth in some hymns includes the earth itself and not just the inhabitants. In the hymns that anticipate and celebrate the rule of God over the earth, the things of nature are summoned to the praise of God along with the human community:

> Let the sea roar, and all that fills it;
>> the world and those who live in it.
> Let the floods clap their hands;
>> let the hills sing for joy
> at the presence of the LORD, for he is coming
>> to judge the earth. (Ps 98:7-9a; cf. 96:11-13)

The hymns of the prophet of the exile in Isaiah 40–55 echo the hymns of God's rule[91] in calling for the praise of all of nature at the anticipated redemptive event of deliverance of the exiles:

> Sing, O heavens, for the LORD has done it [*ʿāśâ*];[92]
>> shout, O depths of the earth;
> break forth into singing, O mountains,
>> O forest and every tree in it!
> For the LORD has redeemed Jacob,
>> and will be glorified in Israel.
>> (Isa 44:23; cf. 42:10-13)

The ground of praise is the same as always: what the Lord has done. In this case, that deed is, as we see from the whole of Second Isaiah's prophecy, a response to the prayers of the people, their despairing and anguished laments in exile (e.g., Isa 40:27b). When God's help has been given (Isa 41:10, 13), the chorus of those who respond in praise and thanksgiving becomes in the most literal sense possible "universal."[93] Not only the people are redeemed, but all the nations, the coastlands, the desert and its inhabitants, indeed the highest heavens and the depths of the earth—the whole universe shouts in praise to God and gives glory to the Lord of Israel, the ruler of the universe, who hears the cries of the afflicted and helps them:

> Sing for joy, O heavens, and exult, O earth;
>   break forth, O mountains, into singing!
> For the LORD has comforted his people,
>   and will have compassion on his suffering ones.
> (Isa 49:13)[94]

Finally, one notes that it is in the context of praise for God's care of the weak and the needy *and* of God's creation of the world and the natural processes that a further theme of praise is sounded: *God's providential care of all creatures.* The giving of food to the hungry (Ps 146:7) is a manifestation not only of justice for the oppressed but of God's continuing provision for the need of all. So Psalm 145, whose theme is God's graciousness and compassion in and over all his works or deeds, draws together the care of the afflicted or weak and the care of *all* in this way:

> The LORD is faithful in all his words,
>   and gracious in all his deeds.[95]
> The LORD upholds all who are falling,
>   and raises up all who are bowed down.
> The eyes of all look to you,
>   and you give them their food in due season.
> You open your hand,
>   satisfying the desire of every living thing. (vv. 13b-16)

In like manner, Psalm 107, after its four sections describing human situations of need and distress—hunger and thirst, prison, sickness, and storm—in which people cried or prayed to God and were delivered that they might thank the Lord for the steadfast love they had received (vv. 4-32), concludes with praise to God for provision of the needs of life and the blessing of continuity and increase:

> He turns rivers into a desert,
>   springs of water into thirsty ground,
> a fruitful land into a salty waste,
>   because of the wickedness of its inhabitants.
> He turns a desert into pools of water,
>   a parched land into springs of water.
> And there he lets the hungry live,
>   and they establish a town to live in;
> they sow fields, and plant vineyards,
>   and get a fruitful yield.
> By his blessing they multiply greatly,
>   and he does not let their cattle decrease.
> When they are diminished and brought low
>   through oppression, trouble, and sorrow,

> he pours contempt on princes
>> and makes them wander in trackless wastes;
> but he raises up the needy out of distress,
>> and makes their families like flocks. (vv. 33-41)

The particular care of those who have been oppressed or experienced suffering and distress of some sort is all bound up with the provision of place for land, fruitful yield, and the continuity of the generations. In these hymns, one sees the joining of the blessing work and the saving work of God into a single whole as God is glorified in praise.

Psalm 104, however, sets the praise of God for the provision of the creatures as the final word in the praise of God for all the creation and its elements (vv. 27-30). Indeed that provision is already indicated within the catalogue of praise for all the creative acts. The creation of springs in the valleys and grass on the hills is providential by its very character (vv. 10-14).

The binding of all these themes in one grand hymn of praise may be seen in Psalm 147. It begins in praise of "the one who heals the broken-hearted and binds up their wounds" and leads immediately into exalting God as "the one who determines the number of the stars" and names them. That is a sign of the great power and immeasurable understanding of the Lord—which then immediately moves those who praise into exalting the Lord as "the one who lifts up the downtrodden" (vv. 3-6). At this point, the hymn begins afresh with its call to "sing to the LORD with thanksgiving," this time to

> the one who covers the heavens with clouds,
>> preparing rain for the earth,
>> making grass grow on the hills,
> giving to the animals their food,
>> to the young ravens when they cry. (vv. 7-9)

The praise of the creator and protector of the downtrodden has led into praise of God for the provision of food and drink to hungry animals. Then, in the last long stanza of the hymn, the summons to praise is uttered once more, and a long series of participles appears again to extol the Lord as the provider of blessing for all in the human and natural processes and particularly for Israel in the giving of statutes and ordinances to guide their life:

> [The LORD] strengthens the bars of your gates,
>> blesses your children within you,
> the one granting peace within your borders,
>> fills you with the finest of wheat;
> the one sending out his command to the earth,
>> his word runs swiftly;

the one giving snow like wool,
    scatters frost like ashes;
the one hurling hail down like crumbs—
    before his cold, who can stand?
He sends out his word, and melts them;
    he makes his wind blow, and the waters flow,
the one declaring his word to Jacob,
    his statutes and ordinances to Israel. (vv. 13-19)

Conclusion

In all these prayers of thanksgiving and praise, a number of things are evident. One is a kind of logic at work that is evident in the narrative report of the thanksgiving songs and the causal clauses of the hymns: the calling of a community to doxology and thanksgiving and giving reasons or reporting why such praise and thanksgiving are appropriate and irresistible.

Praise, therefore, does not really stand by itself. It is a part of the continuing dialogue that is prayer, the conversation between God and the human creature, the human community. There is some sense in which praise is the end of the conversation. The Psalter itself gives us that clue as it concludes as the book of prayer and praise by a resounding call to everything that has breath to praise the Lord. But that "final" word is rooted in the other stages of the conversation, the cry for help and the response of God. The form and logic of faith are found within this movement, including its end in praise. This is the last word of faith, the last sound in the universe. It is rooted in the cry of one in trouble. It is sounded in the end by all the creation. The loneliness and despair of the afflicted are transformed into a community of praise and joy encompassing all of time and space in its potential.

One needs to recognize, however, that it is only within a particular understanding of the world and all of reality that such acts make sense. If the world is *just* here, then praise makes no sense. If, however, the world is created, then all its inhabitants and all the elements of the world should give praise. If healing is *simply* a matter of the skill of competent physicians and others, then bills should be paid promptly and thank you notes written to all who have helped; but there certainly would be no reason in calling the congregation together to sing Psalm 116. It speaks of sickness and healing but says nothing of doctors and nurses and hospitals, or of whoever were the equivalent of such healers in Israelite society. But if all of that is somehow the hand of God at work, as the healed one of this psalm claims from beginning to end, then, like the psalmist of Psalm 22:

I will tell your name to my brothers and sisters;
in the midst of the congregation I will praise you.

Praise, therefore, assumes and even evokes a world, a world where
the affliction of the weak and the order of the universe are inextricably joined, where the provision of grass for animals and the securing
of justice for one falsely accused are most clearly understood as manifestations of a single reality, the work of God.[96] It is a world where
impossible things become possible, where things too difficult become the
order of the day. We have noted in the hymns of praise the celebration
of God's care of the weak in reversing the way things are, lifting up the
lowly and putting down the mighty, feeding the hungry and giving sight
to the blind, making the barren woman the joyous mother of children.[97]
These are what Walter Brueggemann has aptly called "songs of impossibility,"[98] doxologies celebrating human impossibilities that have become
God's possibilities. The praise of Israel bore witness to transformations
and reversals of condition too wonderful for any human capability to
bring off on its own or even to comprehend.[99] In such reversals, all
human definitions of the way things have to be in this world are challenged and overturned. The freedom and power of God say that what is
laughable from a human perspective—see old Sarah's response to the announcement to Abraham that she would have a child!—is the way things
are going to be when God is at work. In a world that assumes the status
is quo, that things have to be the way they are, and one must not assume too much about improving them, the doxologies of God's people
are one of the fundamental indicators that wonders have not ceased,
possibilities not yet dreamed of will happen, and hope is an authentic
stance. That is ridiculous, of course—unless one has seen the wonders
of God in the past, the overthrow of the mighty and the setting free of
an oppressed people, the gift of life in the face of death, fertility where
there was barrenness. The resurrection truly defies all human categories
and fits no epistemology, no ordinary philosophical, logical, or scientific ways of knowing the truth. Yet Christians gather every Sunday to
give praise to God for the impossible wonder that raised Christ from the
dead. In its acts of doxology, the community of faith says to the world
that all our presumptions about what can happen are overruled by the
wonderful impossibilities that God's freedom and power have wrought.

Such praise, however, as we have already noted, is a powerful political act and, indeed, a subversive one. For it claims to know where
justice and righteousness are to be found in the world, and they are not
necessarily there where the world assumes. Praise declares that the Lord
is turning this world upside down, reversing the order of power, casting
down the mighty from their thrones. Praise of God, as one finds it in
these many prayers of Scripture, is inherently a dangerous act, but al-

ways subject to being domesticated or simply neutralized. That can only happen, however, if the community of faith does not believe its own songs, does not believe that "God has done it!"

If prayer has its focus very much on the human subject who prays in distress or for whom prayer is lifted, thanksgiving and praise shift the focus away from the self in distress as well as from the self in power. In so doing, they undercut all human structures and every human being as pretenders for ultimacy or absolute devotion as well as their claims to be saviors and liberators. The prayers of lament and complaint and petition are very much a move to call God's attention to the human being in need of help. When the dialogue moves to praise, however, it shifts all human attention—indeed the attention of the whole universe—to the God who has helped. Thanksgiving, whether to other persons or to God, is an inherent reminder that we are not autonomous and self-sufficient. By its very character it directs the positive feelings of the individual toward another rather than toward self. Even as the songs of thanksgiving recount the story of the plight of the one delivered, the subject matter is not really the individual but the help of God. The hymns of praise simply expand that movement outward, away from the human creature and the community and toward God. That does not happen, of course, because of any judgment about the unworthiness of the human creature. Quite the contrary, the worth of the one who prayed has been affirmed by the act of the one enthroned on high who looks down on the weak and the afflicted and moves to help. Not human unworthiness but the wonder of God's power and love and grace evokes the adoration of the singers of praise, as one sees the beauty of a flower or hears the beauty of a symphony and is so caught by such beauty that all attention is directed toward the source of that wonder. Gratitude and wonder shift the focus of prayer from those who have prayed in their distress to the one being praised for having helped.

The praises of Israel, therefore, were its most visible expression of obedience to the First Commandment, "You shall have no other gods before me." When Psalm 22 speaks of the Lord as "enthroned on the praises of Israel," it makes the same point. The rule of the Lord—and of no other!—is confirmed in the praises of the people. The community that sings, "The Lord will reign forever," or Psalm 100, cannot give its ultimate allegiance to any other potential recipient. When the Westminster Shorter Catechism declares that the chief end of all human existence is to glorify and enjoy God forever, it says something very similar and sets the praise of God as the goal or "end" of human existence, in much the same way that the hymns concluding the Psalter (Psalms 145–150) make divine praise the end of all creation.

Praise intended to glorify God can also be sung to one's own damnation. Apparently that happened at times in ancient Israel. The political character of praise and thanksgiving is a two-edged sword. There is an unacceptable incongruity in the singing of songs of praise to God "on garments taken in pledge" from a neighbor (Amos 2:8; cf. Exod 22:25-26). Singing "O Lord, our Lord, how majestic is your name in all the earth" (Ps 8:1, 9) in the house of the Lord where one drinks "wine bought with fines" profanes the holy name of God rather than glorifying it (Amos 2:7-8). Bringing a thank offering (*tôdâ*) and giving thanks to God under such circumstances are transgressions against God (Amos 4:5). The conversation that takes place in prayer is not isolated from the one that takes place with the neighbor. The glorification of God cannot be at the expense of the poor. Glorification and gratitude under such circumstances are nullified. The songs of praise are not heard at the heavenly throne. One cannot exalt the power and consistent grace of God that lifts up the weak and the lowly, the afflicted and the needy, and then put down those same weak and afflicted. The corollary of these divine acts is also the putting down of the mighty, the destruction of the wicked (e.g., Pss 145:20; 146:9)—even those who sing praise! The divine rejection of such praise and its incompatibility with injustice and unrighteousness in the human realm are explicitly indicated:

> I hate, I despise your festivals,
>> and I take no delight in your solemn assemblies....
> Take away from me the noise of your songs;
>> I will not listen to the melody of your harps.
> But let justice roll down like waters,
>> and righteousness like an everflowing stream.
>> (Amos 5:21, 23-24)

In marvelously ironic fashion, the book of Amos announces judgment for such damnable and damning praise in part through the interlacing of the prophetic oracles with participial hymns exalting the power of God that will come against those who praise the justice and grace of God in the midst of their own injustice and perversity.[100] Praise of God, therefore, is a dangerous act. It has to do with power in what it says. But its very utterance becomes a matter of power. Under some circumstances, it may get one in trouble with the human powers whose rule is ultimately challenged by such praise. Under some circumstances, it *will* get the singers of praise in trouble with the power that in fact is at work in the world and is glorified in praise. Praise that is a lie becomes an act of self-indictment, and the community of faith risks its own damnation in singing lies.

But sing it must, risk and all. When T. S. Eliot wrote,

> There is no life that is not in community
> And no community not lived in praise of GOD[101]

he claimed an essential connection between *human existence* and *the praise of God.* Such connection he surely learned from the praises of Israel. For them, as for Eliot, the connection, however, was in and through *community.* Both the ancient people of faith and the modern poet perceived that praise is fundamentally a social or communal experience and as such is an anticipation of the universal praise of God. That does not mean that praise to God is impossible as an individual or private act. But in its basic character as we have encountered it in the prayers of Scripture, doxology and thanksgiving are rendered *in community.* Thanksgiving, joy, and praise by their very nature reach out, draw in, encompass, and involve others. Thanksgiving is not a private act. It arises out of relationship and further enhances and strengthens it. It is a declaration of one's gratitude and joy for what someone else has done. That other person then finds the original act completed, enhanced, and carried further in hearing and receiving the word of thanks, whether it is a literal word or some responding gesture or activity that signals thanks. Whatever else may have gone on in the relationship between these persons, they are now drawn together in a positive bond of kindness and gratitude. Such an analysis of the human activity of beneficent act and grateful response identifies, if indirectly and partially, what takes place in the relationship between God and human beings when God has heard the prayer and helped and the objects of God's gracious deliverance have responded in praise and thanksgiving.

It is also clear from human experience that *joy* is a response that does not stay contained. It is an emotion to be shared. Whether its character in any particular instance is gratitude, wonder, or happiness, when joy comes forth from those who have received God's steadfast love in concrete ways, it draws others in. Community is thus created, enhanced, and strengthened in the joy of praise and thanksgiving.

The communal and social character of praise, which we have seen to be consistently the case with both songs of thanksgiving and hymns of praise, is further reflected in the way it opens up a chain of praise that leads to the whole universe praising God. One sees that in particular songs of thanksgiving, as, for example, Ps 22:22-31, which depicts an ever widening circle of praise. At the center of this circle is the petitioner whose prayer for help has been answered. This one's testimony to God's power is proclaimed in the midst of the congregation, which, then, in turn, is called to join in that praise. But the circle does not end with the singer's own group. The testimony reaches out to the far corners of the earth. It evokes the praise and worship of all humanity. The mighty of the earth and the dying and the dead shall join the chorus of praise. Even generations yet unborn shall worship God when they hear of the Lord's deliverance of the one in trouble. The praise of one individual helped by the Lord elicits an astonishingly wide echo of praise.

Such language and expression surely seem to belong to the hyperbole of poetic imagery, the deliverance of one individual evoking the praise of all the earth, the mighty and the lowly, of all the generations past and future! Perhaps so. But once this psalm has become the interpretive clue to the meaning of the death and resurrection of Jesus, as the New Testament so makes it, then there is a profound consonance between the words of this psalm and the outcome of God's answer to the one who cries to God from the cross in utter despair. There has been at least one occasion when the response of God to human pain evoked an unending wave of praise that still sounds forth. So Paul writes, in what one may hear as a kind of commentary on this psalm:

> And being found in human form, he humbled himself and became obedient to the point of death—even death on a cross. Therefore God also highly exalted him and gave him the name that is above every name, so that at the name of Jesus every knee should bend, in heaven and on earth and under the earth, and every tongue should confess that Jesus Christ is Lord, to the glory of God the Father.
>
> (Phil 2:8-11)

Such words come from the letter, written while the apostle himself was in prison, that is one of the clearest expressions in the New Testament of praise and joy in the gospel, the good news of God's deliverance. If it is possible for a letter written to friends to be at its heart thoroughly doxological, perfecting the praise of God and overflowing in the joy of one who in the midst of whatever trouble comes his way knows the assuring word of God, "You do not have to be afraid, I am with you, I will help you," it is Paul's letter to the Philippians, a document that "shows the transformation of an existence taken up into the praise of God."[102]

Trust and Confidence

The apostle Paul is also a prime witness to that other outcome of God's response to prayer, the confidence in God of those who cried out in trust (Ps 22:4-5) and found that trust well placed. Others before him are recorded as having trusted in the God who helped and delivered them. When Abraham complained to God about his childlessness and received the promise of posterity as numerous as the stars in the heavens, the narrator of Genesis reported: "And he believed the LORD" (Gen 15:6). At the Red Sea, as the Israelites stood in mortal fear of death at the hands of the oncoming Egyptian army and "cried out to the LORD," Moses addressed them with these words:

Do not be afraid, stand firm, and see the deliverance that the LORD
will accomplish for you today; for the Egyptians whom you see
today you shall never see again. The LORD will fight for you, and
you have only to keep still. (Exod 14:13-14)

Moses' call for the people to "stand firm" and "to keep still" is a call
to trust in the Lord, to be confident that the Lord will "do" (i.e., accomplish, *ya'ăśeh*)[103] for them. The conclusion of this chapter confirms
Moses' words, indicating that "the LORD saved Israel that day from
the Egyptians," and Israel "saw the Egyptians dead" and "feared the
LORD and believed in the LORD."[104] The next verses, Exod 15:1-21,
then record the hymn of praise by Moses, Miriam, and the Israelites.
The trust of the people was short lived in this instance,[105] but the report
of Exod 14:31 means to hold together the prayer for help, the Lord's
deliverance, and the consequent trust and praise of the people who have
been redeemed. A similar report of God's answer and deliverance leading to confidence in the Lord rather than mortals and princes appears
in Ps 118:6-9.

The continuation of the conversation with God that takes place in
prayer is found not only in the songs of thanksgiving and hymns of
praise but also in the *songs of trust and confidence* scattered throughout
the Psalter.[106] They are less common than the songs of thanksgiving and
hymns of praise and do not appear among the prose prayers. Indeed,
as we have already remarked, the expression of praise and thanksgiving is in a very basic way the assertion of trust in God.[107] The
prayer of Hannah in 1 Samuel 2 is as much a song of trust as it is of
thanksgiving.

In some cases, however, that trust is lifted up as the subject of prayer
as the one who has been afflicted speaks in a very personal way of the
experience of God's care. Because of their close affinity with the assertions of confidence that are regularly a feature of the prayer for help, it
is possible they were a part of the ritual and process of seeking God's
help.[108] Indeed, where such confidence is a part of the prayer for help,
it may in some instances have been an assertion made after receiving an
oracle of salvation or some assurance of God's help.[109] It is such trust, as
it becomes the focus of prayer in the experience and process of responding to God's active help when it has been received, that commands our
attention in this context. In the previous chapter, for example, it was
noted that Psalm 23 presents itself as a prayer of confidence of one who
has been through the kind of affliction and suffering of which Psalm 22
speaks and who has been protected and delivered by God's goodness
and steadfast love.

Such prayers of confidence may include several things, though any
single prayer will not have them all and like all the prayers is always

unique. One will often find in such prayers some indication of the trouble through which the afflicted one has gone. So in Psalm 23, the psalmist refers to the "darkest valley" as well as to "enemies." Even the pursuit of goodness and mercy seems to allude to the pursuit of enemies and oppressors. Psalm 27:1-6 speaks of evildoers assailing the psalmist as well as of adversaries, enemies, and foes. The possibility of war and of a day of trouble is expressed. But none of these has done in the psalmist or can do so because God provides "cover" and protection. As in Psalm 23, the human fear that underlies all the prayers for help and is addressed in the oracle of salvation with its divine assurance, "Do not be afraid," is now negated in the song of confidence (Ps 27:1). Though such fear is real, it is not the final word. In Psalm 121, the smiting of the sun and the evil that threatens are fenced off from the psalmist by the Lord's protection and keeping. Psalm 131, to which we shall turn in chapter 6, tells us nothing of enemies or even of trouble. But verse 2 suggests that there has been a struggle of the soul of some sort through which this one who prays has come to a renewed trust in God.

The prayer of trust, therefore, whether it expands the confidence that is claimed in the midst of trouble or expresses the confirmed confidence of one who has been delivered, is not heedless of the terrors that beset life. It is precisely in and through them that confidence matters. The experience of God's vindication in the past is the basis for the declaration of trust in the present. Confidence in God is not a dimension of prayer apart from suffering and the threat of evil and evildoers. It is because one knows, in the face of those realities, the power of God to deliver that such trust comes to the fore. Where it is present in the prayers for help, it alternates with moments of despair and cries for help. Where it takes over and becomes the whole of the prayer, we are probably hearing the other side of praise and thanksgiving, a renewed confidence in God's steadfast love that can be trusted.

Not surprisingly, one may find in the prayers or songs of trust some allusion to the thanksgiving and praise that now come forth from those who have been helped. In Psalm 23, allusion to thanksgiving and praise is found in the depiction of the table prepared before the enemies, which may have in mind the *tôdâ* sacrifice that was a customary part of the vow of praise in the prayers for help. So also in Ps 27:6, the trusting creature concludes with a vow of praise and thanksgiving, promising sacrifice and songs of joy to the God who removes all fear and enables the worshiper to say in the face of any threat, "I will be confident" (v. 3).

Especially frequent in these songs of confidence is the way they direct themselves to God and to the manifestations of God's wonderful, liberating power and goodness. The pursuit of "goodness [*ṭôb*] and mercy [*ḥesed*]" in Ps 23:6 is explicit allusion to those two divine characteristics that are lifted up in the model hymn/song of thanksgiving: "O give thanks to the LORD, for he is good [*ṭôb*]; his steadfast love [*ḥesed*] endures forever." The one who truthfully expresses trust through the words of this song of confidence has experienced that goodness and love more tenaciously than any enemy's pursuit can equal or withstand. The extended descriptions of the Lord's shepherding care (Ps 23:1-4) that function primarily as statements of trust are also descriptive elaborations of the Lord's way with the creature in need. Psalm 11 praises the righteousness of God on which those who are upright can always count (vv. 5-7). Metaphors of light and stronghold (Ps 27:1), of rock and fortress and refuge (Ps 62:2, 6-8), point to the character of the relationship experienced by the trusting psalmist. The Lord hides the one in trouble or provides a secure place high and away from any threats (Ps 27:5). One hears in these songs of confidence a kind of primal experience, that of *being kept and protected,* as the fundamental ground of trust. With all the varying images of shepherd, host, rock, fortress, refuge, stronghold, shade, keeper, and mother,[110] the prayers of trust root that confidence in the sure certainty of having been kept and protected in all situations, a certitude that is grounded in past experience but is the key to the future as well.

Finally, even as the prayers of thanksgiving call upon others to praise and give thanks, so the prayers of trust may bid others in the community to join with them in a sure confidence in God's protection and care.[111] That is particularly indicated in Ps 62:8:

> Trust in him at all times, O people;
> pour out your heart before him;
> God is a refuge for us.

The ending of Psalm 27 returns from the prayer for help to the song of trust at the beginning (vv. 1-6) and turns what may have been a kind of oracle of salvation[112] into an address by the psalmist to others in the community:

> I believe that I shall see the goodness of the LORD
> in the land of the living.
> Wait for the LORD;
> be strong, and let your heart take courage;
> wait for the LORD! (vv. 13-14)[113]

And the final verse of Psalm 131 turns its words of humble trust into an injunction to the community of Israel to hope in the Lord:

> O Israel, hope in the LORD
> from this time on and forevermore.

The one who prays becomes an implicit model for the rest of the people. This psalm, however, raises other questions to which we now turn but in a quite different context as we look more particularly at prayers that were prayed by women of the Old Testament. Only then can we see the depths of trust expressed in this brief prayer.

6

"Things Too Wonderful"

PRAYERS WOMEN PRAYED

✑

In his treatment of biblical prose prayer, Moshe Greenberg cites nearly a hundred examples of prayers outside the Psalter and another forty-three instances where prayer is mentioned without the prayer actually being quoted.[1] When one adds the 150 psalms, most of which are explicitly addressed to God as either petition or praise, and a few other texts that may be construed as prayers but are not included in Greenberg's list, we have nearly three hundred instances of recorded prayers or allusions to prayer in the Old Testament. Of that number only a few prayers are prayed by women.[2] Whatever the reason for that scarcity of women's prayers, the few that are there merit particular attention both as a small body of prayers indicative of the character of biblical prayer and because of the way they are reflective of the particular situations of the women who prayed them. Not surprisingly, several of them are associated with childbirth. The most familiar of these are Hannah's prayers before and after the birth of Samuel and, in the New Testament, Mary's prayer (Luke 1:46-55), reminiscent of Hannah's song. We have already looked at Hannah's song of praise and thanksgiving (1 Sam 2:1-10) and will look more closely below at her prior complaint over childlessness. There are other, much briefer, prayers and thanksgivings associated with childbirth.[3] So also blessing prayers, both those that bless the Lord in thanksgiving and those that pray for blessing on others, are found on the lips of women named and unnamed.[4] In this chapter, the focus is particularly upon those prayers that arise out of the affliction of women, showing also, more briefly, their connection to the songs or hymns of praise that also come forth from women on particular occasions of God's deliverance, in order to see what goes on in these prayers and how the experience of these women interacts with their address to God. These are prayers of ambiguity and hope, of pain and joy. We may learn from them many things, good and bad. What they teach us, if anything, will have to remain open.

Genesis 21:15-19

The first of these prayers is not mentioned by Greenberg and so may be suspect as an act of prayer. It is part of the story of Hagar, one of those "texts of terror," as Phyllis Trible has so aptly named the several biblical stories where women are done in by male acts and divine legitimation of them.[5] Its conclusion in Gen 21:15-21 is where the prayer occurs.

Hagar, who earlier had fled her mistress, Sarah, after being treated harshly, and then was sent back and told by God to submit to Sarah, has now been put out into the wilderness with her son, Ishmael, because of Sarah's jealousy for her own son, Isaac. Abraham is at first upset by Sarah's demand to throw Hagar and Ishmael out. According to the text, however, he is disturbed only by the threat to his son, Ishmael. Nothing is said about any concern for Hagar. The silence in this case is eloquent. Abraham accepts Sarah's demand only when God tells him not to be distressed but to do whatever Sarah says because God is going to make a great nation of both sons, Ishmael as well as Isaac. So Abraham sends Hagar and the child out to wander aimlessly in the wilderness with only bread and a skin of water. At the conclusion of the story of Hagar and Ishmael, the text reads as follows:

> When the water in the skin was gone, she cast the child under one of the bushes. Then she went and sat down opposite him a good way off, about the distance of a bowshot; for she said, "Do not let me look on the death of the child." And as she sat opposite him, she lifted up her voice and wept. And God heard the voice of the boy; and the angel of God called to Hagar from heaven, and said to her, "What troubles you, Hagar? Do not be afraid; for God has heard the voice of the boy where he is. Come, lift up the boy and hold him fast with your hand, for I will make a great nation of him." Then God opened her eyes, and she saw a well of water. She went, and filled the skin with water, and gave the boy a drink.
>
> God was with the boy, and he grew up; he lived in the wilderness, and became an expert with the bow. He lived in the wilderness of Paran; and his mother got a wife for him from the land of Egypt.

The situation of distress and suffering is clear. It is a near-death experience, such as the psalms of lament often seem to suggest. Both Hagar and "the child"[6] face imminent death. Her putting him under the bush, then moving some distance away, followed by the causal indicator *kî...,* *"for* she said...," as well as the lack of any direct address accompanying her words, such as, "O God," suggest that her only words here are an indication of her anguish that she cannot bear to see her child die.

That is certainly the case. But the form of her brief sentence—"Do not let me look on the death of the child"—suggests something else. It is not a statement but a request. There is only one other comparable sentence in the Bible. It is Moses' words to God in his complaint over the burden of the people that God has thrust upon him: "If this is the way you are going to treat me, put me to death at once... and do not let me see my misery" (Num 11:15). While the address to God that is so typical of laments or complaints (but is not present in Moses' complaint or in some others)[7] is not present here, it is likely that the words of Hagar are the prayer of a sufferer who lifts her distress to God, that distress being the imminent death of her only son. Her weeping is typical of those who cry out to God in affliction.[8]

Such a conclusion is reinforced, if still ambiguously so, by what follows. God hears and delivers the child from death. The specific complaint/petition of Hagar is answered in the way other prayers are answered in the Bible, that is, with an oracle of salvation.[9] The presence of the oracle of salvation has not always been recognized in this text, but the typical components of that type of divine speech are fully there: (1) a direct personal address to the one who laments ("What troubles you, Hagar?"); (2) the allusion to the lament and the condition that precipitates it ("God has heard the voice of the boy *where he is*"); (3) the basic word of assurance, which is always, "Do not be afraid"; (4) a reason for that assurance indicating God's turning toward and affirming the relationship with the suffering one who cries out ("for God has heard the voice of the boy"); and (5) an elaboration of what God is going to do in the future to provide deliverance ("Come, lift up the boy and hold him fast with your hand, for I will make a great nation of him"). The narrative further develops the salvation oracle in two ways. It spells out God's way of deliverance in telling how God opened Hagar's eyes so that she sees a well from which to fill a skin of water for the boy. It also transfers into narrative form one of the primary grounds for the word of assurance not to be afraid that is most typical of salvation oracles: "I am with you." We hear that word of assurance in the narrative report that "God was with the boy" (v. 20).

The story has thus provided an example of one of the primary thematic threads of Scripture—the outcry of an oppressed and afflicted sufferer who complains and pleads to God and the delivering response of God. Nothing is more fundamental to the biblical story or to its understanding of God than this. It is there from beginning to end. It is as central to one Testament as it is to the other. Rarely, however, is it so ambiguous as in this story. The deliverance from death—for Hagar and the child—is clear. For a mother or parent whose child faces certain death and then receives a marvelous deliverance, there is no greater anguish and no greater joy. And, as happens in other oracles of salvation, the immediate deliverance is accompanied by a great promise for the future.

But there are other things in this story that clash abrasively with its positive outcome. The distress of Hagar and her child is brought about by a conflict whose causality in a highly patriarchal and class structure is glaringly obvious in the obsession with a male heir that seems in Scripture to allow anything to happen in its pursuit and frequently sets women antagonistically against each other because, within that structure, bearing children (preferably males) is what largely determines the status of a wife. Moreover, the system of slavery allows a person to be controlled and brutalized by another. Hagar is an abused wife and an abused slave. Further, what is done to Hagar is so morally inexcusable that even Abraham is distressed by Sarah's demand to throw her out. He does so, nevertheless, because he is directed to do so *by God*—the one who, according to the biblical story, also hears the outcries of the oppressed and afflicted—so that Isaac may grow and take his place unthreatened by an Ishmael.

The narrative of God's response seems so confusing that, from the Greek translation onward, the text has often been emended.[10] *Hagar* is the one who cries out or prays, but God hears the voice of the *child*. Immediately, however, the angel of the Lord addresses *Hagar* with the salvation oracle and says God has heard the voice of the *boy*. It is her fear that is removed and her suffering, as well as his, that is alleviated. All of which underscores how inextricably the woman's experience and fate are tied up with her child. It is the weeping of the mother and the crying of the child, the prayer of the mother and the need of the child, all wrapped up together, that elicit a divine response. All that happens to Hagar is an outcome of her motherhood and her connection to this child—as well as her slave status. The prayer is an authentic prayer of a mother. It is heard and she is delivered. Ishmael's name ("God hears") has already been explicitly identified as an indicator that God hears/heeds Hagar's affliction (Gen 16:11). Once more, human suffering has not gone unheard in the divine world, and the faithful and just Lord of Israel has acted in compassion. As that happens, however, we are reminded once more how thoroughly a mother's life is absorbed into that of her children. That their deliverance is her deliverance is a reason for joy but also for tears. Hagar's is in every way a typical prayer of lament and petition of those who suffer and whose cries are heard and dealt with by a compassionate God. And Hagar's experience is in every way typical of women whose life as wife and mother may be as ambiguous as is the compassion of a God who delivers from a suffering that God has ordained.

1 Samuel 1–2

The second woman's prayer is the even more familiar account in 1 Samuel 1 of Hannah's prayer for a "male child" (*zera' 'ănāšîm*).[11] The center of the chapter is the account of Hannah's lament. Although the only part of the prayer recorded is the vow at the end, there is no question that we are here dealing with a prayer for help by an afflicted sufferer. It is reported that while she was at Shiloh with her husband, Elkanah, and her rival wife, Peninnah, she would not eat and wept. Rising from the meal, she went into the sanctuary and, according to the text, "She was deeply distressed and prayed to the LORD and wept bitterly" (v. 10). In her vow, we hear her address the deity and refer to her misery or affliction. The petitions to "look," "remember," and "[do] not forget" are familiar from the many other prayers for help.

Hannah's plight is not the near-death experience that seems to be typical of the prayers for help in the Psalms and was the particular distress in which Hagar found herself with her child. The plight of Hannah is of another sort. It is a woman's barrenness in a world where blessing is rooted in posterity and a woman's place in the eyes of the world is determined by her ability to bear children and especially sons. The suffering of such a condition was not at all unequal to the verbal and emotional anguish of the psalmic prayers for help that speak of the pain of isolation and being cut off from community, of being shamed before others, of enemies who taunt and insult the one who prays in pain.

We have noted how the psalms of lament regularly place the pain of the praying one in relation (1) to the suffering and dissolution of the self; (2) to the God to whom the prayer is directed and who is often seen as having to do with the suffering either by active intervention or passive neglect; and (3) to others who either oppress or reproach and humiliate.[12] Not all of these sources of complaint are present in every lament or prayer for help. They are all present, however, in Hannah's story of suffering and lament even though little of her prayer is preserved. The complaint against self and the undoing of the self are evident in the barrenness and the resultant weeping and failure to eat. But one of the primary points of the narrative is that she suffers under the reproach, the vexation and insults, of others in the community who are set against her, in this case a rival wife who is richly fertile. The text reports Elkanah's other wife, Peninnah, who is dubbed Hannah's rival adversary, "used to vex her [*ki'ăsattâ*] severely to irritate her, because the LORD had closed her womb" (1 Sam 1:6-7).[13] The structure of family and the expected role of women have once again set sister against sister. Hannah's sense of isolation from the community of which she is a part is suggested by the outcome of the story when her prayer is heard. The narrative reports: "Then the woman went to her quarters, ate and drank with her husband, and her countenance was sad no longer" (v. 18).

But the narrative tells us more than once that "the LORD had closed her womb" (1 Sam 1:5-6). Her complaint is also against *God;* her bitter weeping is evoked by God's withholding of her greatest need, and neither the absence of any reason for that nor an a-theological analysis of her sterility could alleviate her suffering. Psalm 6 would have been a lament appropriate for her distress:[14]

> O LORD, do not rebuke me in your anger,
>   or discipline me in your wrath.
> Be gracious to me, O LORD, for I am languishing;
>   O LORD, heal me, for my bones are shaking with terror.
> My soul also is struck with terror,
>   while you, O LORD—how long?
> Turn, O LORD, save my life;
>   deliver me for the sake of your steadfast love.
> For in death there is no remembrance of you;
>   in Sheol who can give you praise?
> I am weary with my moaning;
>   every night I flood my bed with tears;
> I drench my couch with my weeping.
>   My eyes waste away because of vexation [*ka'as*];
>   they grow weak because of all my foes.

So Hannah prays in the sanctuary, as she says to Eli, "out of my great anxiety and vexation [*ka'as*] all this time." And her prayer is heard, her countenance changed from sadness to joy, and she is restored to a normal life in her community. Eli's words ("Go in peace. The God of Israel will grant the petition you have made to him") are in effect an oracle of salvation.

Once again we hear the voice of a woman at prayer and in the typical modes and forms of prayer as we find them generally in Scripture; and, once again, the prayer of a woman is answered by God's provision of the need voiced in the prayer of the sufferer. But here also, in Hannah's story, is all the ambiguity that one sees in Hagar's. Her terrible distress arises because of her inability, although beyond her control, to do what every woman was expected to do—to bear children. That situation makes her vulnerable to the vexation of another woman who has become her enemy, solely over their differing abilities to bear children to a single husband. And the text *may* suggest that her loving husband, like a distressed Abraham, nevertheless discriminates against her because of her failure.[15] This oppressive situation is given only one cause in the Bible—God. Whether or not we believe this, the biblical story understands that the compassionate God of Israel has kept Hannah from bearing children. And when deliverance comes, it is in the form of a male child whom she relinquishes to the Lord who closed her womb.

These, then, are prayers of abused women, abused by men and abused by other women, victims of a patriarchal and family system that measured their worth heavily by their capacity to bear sons, that gave men—and in this case husbands—power and legitimacy to use women for their purposes or to abuse their wives, and that set women in competition with each other and led them to be *abusive of each other*. These are prayers of women whose life is defined by their relationship to men but whose suffering is ordained by God. They are also prayers of women whose only recourse and help in their suffering is—like that of others, male and female—the God who is part of their problem.

One should not read the ending of Hannah's story as unhappy. It ends in joy and thanksgiving. Like the oracle of salvation that Hagar receives, Hannah's prayer of thanksgiving is one of the most powerful testimonies to Israel's understanding of their God and to why they readily and often turned to that God in the face of whatever hurt and pain they encountered. To that prayer of thanksgiving we will turn briefly at the conclusion of this chapter. To appreciate its significance, however, we need to look at one other prayer.

PSALM 131

Psalm 131,[16] referred to at the end of the last chapter, is one of the briefest of all the psalms:

> [1] O LORD, my heart is not lifted up,
>   my eyes are not raised too high;
> I do not occupy myself with things
>   too great and too marvelous for me.
> [2] But I have calmed and quieted my soul,
>   like a weaned child with its mother;
>   my soul is like the weaned child that is with me.
> [3] O Israel, hope in the LORD
>   from this time on and for evermore.

Literally, verse 2 may be translated:

> Like a weaned child on its mother,
> Like the weaned child on me is my soul.[17]

Verse 2 suggests this psalm of trust is from the lips of a woman, a mother.[18] Verse 1, I suggest, is consistent with such an understanding of authorship. In this brief psalm, we hear the quiet voice of a woman expressing to God her sense of utter dependence and humility before God, a way of living before and under God that she has learned from the child who has sought security in trust on her breast and has returned in trust for that security time and time again. This is the weaned child, not the infant, and it is possible that "the child on the mother" refers to carrying the child on the shoulder,[19] but the notion of security and dependency is clearly what is indicated. The particular experience of mother and child has shaped a way of existence before God, one that has not claimed to be able to know and understand God's impossibilities, that is, those things "too great and too marvelous [impossible] for me."

But one also infers from the social setting of women in that time that the experience of submission and humility has been in part a way of living that has been required, forced by her circumstances. She speaks of having calmed and quieted her soul as if that has been necessary, as if there has been a struggle. What happens, however, in this prayer of a woman who does not occupy herself with impossibilities, with things too marvelous, is that her experience, a woman's experience of submission, humility, and motherhood, has become the vehicle for discerning, not the way that human beings relate to each other and live together, but the way that life is to be set before God. Her experience is then offered, implicitly, to the community, not for the way of men and women with each other but for the attitude of the community toward God:

> O Israel, hope in the LORD,
> from this time on and forevermore. (v. 3)

It is customary in the commentaries to understand the reference to the "things too great and too marvelous" (v. 2—*gĕdōlôt* and *niplā'ôt*) with which this praying woman does not occupy herself as indicating personal ambitions and great things for oneself. That is a difficult conclusion to sustain, however. The word *gĕdōlôt*, "great things," occurs a number of times in the Old Testament. With one possible exception (Ps 12:3), it always refers to the great deeds of Yahweh.[20] In five of the instances, all in Psalms and Job,[21] *gĕdōlôt*, "great things," appears in parallel or collocation with *niplā'ôt*, "marvelous things." The latter term occurs some forty times, *always* in reference to God's marvelous wonders. The weight of evidence clearly suggests that it is *God's* wonders, *God's* impossibilities, with which this mother has not occupied herself.

Does this mean, then, that the text suggests an inappropriateness on the part of the woman and mother to care about and bother with theology? Does it mean that this was the *male* task in Israel, so that here once more is an indication of the role restrictions placed upon women in the patriarchal structure of Israelite society? I would infer that such is the case, or at least highly likely to have been so, and that fact has been part of the struggle forced upon the woman of Psalm 131, if struggle may be inferred from the reference to quieting and calming the soul.

Two things further need to be noted, however. First, there are two other instances in the Old Testament where someone speaks of "things too marvelous/wonderful for me" (*niplā'ôt mimmennî*). They are both in the wisdom literature. One is Prov 30:18:

> Three things are too wonderful for me [*niplā'û mimmennî*];
>   four I do not understand:
> the way of an eagle in the sky,
>   the way of a snake on a rock,
> the way of a ship on the high seas,
>   and the way of a man with a girl.

Here the sage, the wise one, sees in the graceful and different kinds of movements of the eagle, the snake, and a ship and in the "inexplicable attraction which draws together the man and the woman"[22] things that are to be marveled but not to be comprehended, even by this intellectual who sets forth a view of the order and character of things in the world. Some things, such as those mentioned, are simply too marvelous for the human mind to understand.

The other place where someone speaks of "things too marvelous for me" is in Job's final speech (42:1-6):

> Then Job answered the LORD:
> "I know that you can do all things,
>   and that no purpose of yours can be thwarted.
> 'Who is this that hides counsel without knowledge?'
> Therefore I have uttered what I did not understand,
>   things too wonderful for me [*niplā'ôt mimmennî*],
>   which I did not know.
> 'Hear, and I will speak;
>   I will question you, and you declare to me.'
> I had heard of you by the hearing of the ear,
>   but now my eyes see you;
> therefore I despise myself,
>   and repent in dust and ashes."

After all the querying, the complaint and accusation to God, in dialogues that many would argue are the most profound part of all of Scripture, Job ends up where the trusting mother of Psalm 131 finds herself. In other words, Job's words at the end of the book are a confession before God that he has occupied himself with things too great and marvelous for him and now repents in dust and ashes, which is a way of saying he recognizes he is human and cannot know the mind of God and will content himself to be the creature. As Gerald Janzen has pointed out, what God does in the divine speeches is not coercive speech but a persuasive rhetoric that undermines Job's assumptions.[23] Job assumes in the order of things that he knows that the sea is to be overcome by God in conflict. Yahweh claims, however, to have handled it a different way, by parental birthing, disciplining, and ordering (38:8-11).[24] The divine speeches, however, are not intended to give Job an intellectual system to replace the existing one. They serve to push, to prod, to subvert, and to illustrate that Job does not understand. A different system operates in God's power, a fact that Job comes to realize when he concludes that he has uttered things he did not understand, "things too marvelous for me which I did not know."

As Job reached his conclusion or end—not understanding—out of his suffering and pain, so the woman who prays in Psalm 131 reaches hers out of the struggle of her soul in her oppressed and often humiliated situation. It is important to pay attention to the *brevity* of this woman's prayer and contrast it with the *length* of Job's dialogues—for the struggle of this woman takes place in the silence of the text. It is, however, equivalent to or analogous to the highly verbal struggle of Job, and both of their struggles arise out of the external situation forced upon them, an oppressive suffering that is in some way allowable by the God in whom they trust.

In some sense, therefore, the point where this trusting woman comes out is the same place where the intellectual tradition of the Old Testament also comes out. As in Job, it is an end that is reached in struggle. For Job, the end happens in theophany and divine address, in revelation. For the woman, it happens in trust that has not required the answering questions of God that Job has needed in order to reach the same conclusion. The human creature is called to trust in the God of the universe, and Job comes to see that as did the woman psalmist. Her submission *to God,* not to other human beings—that is not the issue even if that has taught her how to be submissive—is the mature human stance. It is the point reached by both Job and the woman in their different but similar struggles. In the woman's case, it is offered to the people of God as the way to live: O Israel, hope in the Lord.

One thing further to note about this woman's prayer—and it is the transition also to a briefer attention to two other prayers of women—is that the concern about the things too marvelous or wonderful plays a part in women's stories elsewhere in the Scriptures. Walter Brueggemann has pointed out the trajectory that moves from the angelic query to a skeptical Sarah (assuming old age prevents new birth): "Is anything too wonderful [too difficult—*hăyippālē'*] for God?" (Gen 18:14) to another angelic messenger's words to a skeptical Mary (assuming virginity prevents new birth): "For nothing will be impossible with God" (Luke 1:37).[25] When Mary bears the child and witnesses the human impossibility become possible with God, she sings a song of praise and thanksgiving that is derivative of an earlier song of thanksgiving prayed under similar circumstances, the song of Hannah. In these two songs of thanksgiving by two women of low estate, as humble and humbled as the one who prays in Psalm 131, we discover through their experience of God's marvelous deliverance what those things are that are too wonderful for us but not for God: lifting up the lowly and putting down the mighty, feeding the hungry and giving sight to the blind, making the barren woman a joyous mother of children, God's power and intention to reverse those structures and realities of human existence that seem impossible to break. What we see in the prayers of thanksgiving of Hannah[26] and Mary is that they have become, not investigators of the secrets of the universe, of God's order and power as manifest in nature and history (that is, the marvelous things), but *testifiers* to the impossibilities and wonders that cannot be figured out (Job 41:6; Prov 30:18; and Ecclesiastes) and were witnessed but all too often forgotten by "our fathers/ancestors" (Pss 78:11, 32; 106:7).

It is just such testimony to the marvelous things of God that we encounter in the two other women's prayers of praise, the songs of Miriam (Exodus 15)[27] and Deborah (Judges 5). They are both victory songs that celebrate the power of God to bring about wonders and impossibilities in behalf of an oppressed people, to overturn the expected order of things (the military might of Egyptian and Canaanite armies) so that the mighty are brought down and the lowly are raised up.[28] Here, we do not encounter the prayers of barren mothers caught in a constricting and often oppressive familial and patriarchal system but leaders of the people, women unidentified with marriage and family, exercising leadership and power in a male-dominated social structure.

Among these women of Israel, however—those who cry out in affliction and those who praise God for their victory—the song or prayer remains the same. It is a testimony to things too marvelous that God has done in this world—oppressive power made weak, oppressed ones set free, fertility where there was barrenness, life where there was death, and confidence in the power and compassion of God. They are songs of power and liberation but only as they praise the wonders of what God can do. There are indeed some things that are too marvelous for us. What cannot be comprehended, however, is nevertheless experienced by those who trust in the marvelous power of God and can be celebrated and proclaimed.

7

"We Have Sinned"

PRAYERS OF CONFESSION
AND PENITENCE

The structure of faith and the structure of prayer, as we have discussed them in the preceding pages, are essentially the same. The trusting creature cries for help, is heard and responded to by God, and then, in turn, sings forth in praise and thanksgiving as well as confident trust to the God who has heard and delivered the one in need. Such a structure is not meant to restrict the data or to rule out the diversity that we have seen is clearly present from one prayer to another, from one hymn to another. But all of the examples are a demonstration that prayer is the speech that belongs to the dialogue of faith and that that dialogue has a certain character to it—forms, content, moods, expectations, and responses that are discernible and instruct us in the school of prayer.

Within that structure or dialogue found in the prayers of the Bible, there are particular aspects of prayer that belong to the continuum from petition to praise—and so are implicitly and explicitly included in the earlier discussion—but merit special attention on their own. One of these is the prayer of confession or the confession of sin.

The Occasion of Confession

It is no surprise, in light of the biblical story, to discover that confession of sin is a fairly widespread form of prayer in the Bible. It is not the dominant form of supplication or petition in the prayers for help of the Psalter, but it is there in formulaic parts of complaint psalms and in whole psalms. Confession of sin takes place in both interhuman relationships—as Greenberg well illustrates with the confessions of sin that Saul and Shimei make to David and the one that, *mirabile dictu*, Hezekiah makes to the Assyrian king, Sennacherib[1]—and in the dialogue with God.[2] Indeed, the form of human confession to another that one has done wrong and the form of confession to God are one and the same: "I/we have sinned," or "I/we are guilty [or 'have erred']." Confession of sin before God occurs also in both individual and communal contexts. The essential character of the confession, however, is the same whether it is an individual before God or the whole community.

The situations and occasions of sinful activity that bring forth confession are varied. Individuals make confessions in the following contexts: Pharaoh for his sin against the Lord and against the Hebrews for stubbornly refusing to let the people go serve the Lord; Balaam, the Mesopotamian diviner, for not seeing that it was the Lord who stood in his way and in the path of his donkey; Achan for stealing the treasure of Jericho that had been devoted to the Lord; Saul for disobeying the command of the Lord in the battle against the Amalekites; and David for adultery and murder and for taking a census of the people.[3] The case of David in the Bathsheba affair (2 Samuel 11–12) is particularly instructive, for there the sin is clearly against Bathsheba and Uriah, not apparently against God. But the confession is equally explicit and clear: "I have sinned against the LORD" (2 Sam 12:13). The sin against the brother or sister is viewed as sin against the Lord and an occasion for confession before God and the seeking of divine forgiveness. Such a confession warns against an easy division of the commandments into those that have to do with God and those that have to do with the neighbor. For in David's case, the sins of adultery and murder, sins of the second table of the Decalogue, are not admitted as sins against the neighbor, which they most assuredly were, but as sins against God.

Communal confessions take place as a consequence of various types of disobedience. For example, the people confess their sin and guilt for not trusting the Lord and not being willing to go up against the enemy at God's command as well as for serving other gods.[4] Aaron confesses his and Miriam's sin for challenging Moses' authority as God's spokesman and leader.[5] What is in some ways the paradigmatic confession of the people is found in Solomon's prayer at the dedication of the temple:

> If they sin against you—for there is no one who does not sin— and you are angry with them and give them to an enemy, so that they are carried away captive to the land of the enemy, far off or near; yet if they come to their senses in the land to which they have been taken captive, and repent, and plead [*hithannan*][6] with you in the land of their captors, saying, "We have sinned, and have done wrong; we have acted wickedly"; if they repent with all their heart and soul in the land of their enemies, who took them captive, and pray to you toward their land, which you gave to their ancestors, the city that you have chosen, and the house that I have built for your name; then hear in heaven your dwelling place their prayer

[*tĕpillâ*] and plea [*tĕḥinnâ*], maintain their cause and forgive your people who have sinned against you, and all their transgressions that they have committed against you and grant them compassion in the sight of their captors, so that they may have compassion on them. (1 Kgs 8:46-51a)

The prayer of Solomon—or of the Deuteronomistic editor who prays through the voice of the earlier king—lacks the specificity of the other occasions mentioned above. Instead it generalizes in two ways. For one, it asserts the universality of sin that Paul later lifts up to prominence in his letter to the Romans.[7] More importantly in this context, the prayer catches up all the sins of the people that result in divine punishment through exile. The generalizing and heaping up of confessional statements without specifying the particular sins are appropriate in a prayer that may come from the exilic period or later but in its present setting cannot claim to know the future sins but can only anticipate exile, a fairly common fate in those days. The use of three different terms for confession of sin—"We have sinned and have done wrong; we have acted wickedly"—serves to emphasize the sense of sin and earnestness of repentance as well as echoing the catchall category of the confession by incorporating all the standard ways of making confession (see below). In various ways, the confession in Solomon's prayer is comparable to the several confessional and penitential prayers in Ezra and Nehemiah as well as Daniel 9 (see below).[8]

THE NATURE AND CHARACTER OF CONFESSION

Sin and Calamity

Confession of sin in the Old Testament is characteristically for specific sinful acts—though they may be recurring or prolonged sinful acts—rather than for a general condition of sin.[9] That is related to the fact that sin was seen as directly connected to calamity. Or perhaps one should say the reverse: when calamity happened, it was understood to be in some sense the judgment or punishment of God for sins of some sort. This, of course, is what Job's friends argued as the reason he suffered so much. The point of Job's dialogues is in large part to challenge such an assumed connection between calamity and sin. But such an assumption is more often the norm in Scripture. It is reflected in a number of the prayers of confession. For example, Pharaoh's confession takes place in the face of the plagues, which he rightly sees as the punishment of God. The sins of idolatry in the books of Judges and Samuel are regularly confessed in the face of a national oppression identified as the judgment of God aroused against the national apostasy.

The story of Job makes one immediately aware that such a connection between calamity and sin is too simple if perceived as a one-to-one correlation in every case. That awareness is confirmed by our own human experience that denies an immediate connectedness between "bad things" and "bad people," to play on Harold Kushner's phraseology.[10] One needs to be careful, however, about throwing the baby out with the bath water in assuming that there is *never* any connection. Even in Scripture the connection may be seen as the evil deed that organically brings about consequences that are bad, the bad seed sown that comes to fruition and undoes us.[11] Yet, where such a "synthetic" or organic notion of the connection between deed and consequence is articulated or implicit in various images, the power and purpose of God are still what shape events and make the organic or synthetic whole. Retribution is not a meaningless notion in the Bible even if its outworkings are more mysterious and complex than we can grasp, and tragic events can have other causations than our immediate sins.[12] Further, it must be kept in mind that when sins were confessed in the face of disaster, not only was the disaster real but the sins were real. One did not have to dream up a sinful act to account for the calamity at hand. It was sharply present. Nor is the connection between sin and the punishment of God that is experienced in human existence an assumption confined to the Old Testament. It is, of course, a significant dimension of the Christ-event in the New Testament.

This assumed connection between personal or corporate disaster and sin meant, therefore, that in Israel, as in the ancient Near East generally, the act of confession as an approach to God was specifically designed to ward off the wrath of God, to pacify an angry deity and turn God's wrath away that new blessings and deliverance might take place. So Solomon says in his prayer, "If they sin against you . . . and you are angry with them and give them to an enemy . . . " (1 Kgs 8:46). Reminding the people on the plains of Moab of the making of the golden calf and of his intercession in their behalf, Moses says, "Even at Horeb you provoked the LORD to wrath, and the LORD was so angry with you that he was ready to destroy you" (Deut 9:8; cf. v. 7). And the confession of the people in Judg 10:15 arises because "the anger of the LORD was kindled against Israel, and he sold them into the hand of the Philistines and into the hand of the Ammonites" (v. 7).

The notion of the wrath of God is not a pleasant one. Indeed the modern consciousness resists it mightily. Jonathan Edwards's sermon "Sinners in the Hands of an Angry God" is cited often, but only for negative and antiquarian reasons, that is, as an example of a time and a theology that are long gone. Again, however, a dismissal of this notion may be simplistic and reflective of a tendency to cut the moral nerve of our theology. The wrath of God is a metaphor, an anthropomorphic figure, to express the conviction that there is in the universe a moral connection, that the love and mercy of God are not apart from or understandable without the justice of God. Sin is not finally, and in the Bible never actually, an abstract notion. It is a warp in the divine order, a breakdown in the nature of relationship, a moral breach that always has consequences, however small they may be, and damages the way things are meant to be among ourselves and with God. The wrath of God is a figure of thought that personalizes and confirms all that. And the prayer of confession is clearly understood as an act that contributes to straightening out the warp, restoring the relationship, repairing the breach. God's response to such confession must never be misunderstood as a need to satisfy a divine appetite or appease the deity unless it is understood that to speak of the anger of God being appeased is to claim that there is a moral reality that undergirds all our finite experiences of moral reality, and that reality seeks moral perfection,[13] not simply a kind of satisfaction unrelated to what we know as good and right and just. Indeed when Solomon prays to God to forgive the people when they sin, he not only assumes that God will be angry at the sin but also believes that when confession comes forth and the people repent, God will hear their prayer and "maintain their cause/justice" (*mišpāṭ*) (1 Kgs 8:49).[14] Setting things right in the created and moral world God made happens in penitence as much as in judgment. It is not a divine *appetite* that confession seeks to satisfy, but a divine *nature* that is just and insists that the universe reflect that justice. That order and the reciprocal relation between human sin and divine wrath are suggested in a quite specific way in the context of confession of sin in Lev 26:40-41:

> But if they confess their iniquity and the iniquity of their ancestors, in that they committed treachery against me and, moreover, that they continued hostile to me—so that I, in turn, continued hostile to them and brought them into the land of their enemies...

The judgment of God is a verbal reflection ("continued hostile") of the sin of the people.[15] So also in Baruch's prayer of confession in the apocryphal book ascribed to him, this sense of the righteousness of God as the source of the calamity that befalls the one who sins is elaborated in full scope:

> The Lord our God is in the right, but there is open shame on us and our ancestors this very day. All those calamities with which the Lord threatened us have come upon us. Yet we have not entreated the favor of the Lord by turning away, each of us, from the thoughts of our wicked hearts. And the Lord has kept the calamities ready, and the Lord has brought them upon us, for the Lord is just in all the works that he has commanded us to do. (Bar 2:6-9)

The theology expressed in these texts and the moral order they imply are reflected in a significant way in the confessional and penitential prayers where they expressly acknowledge the justice and righteousness of God in judgment (see below).

The calamity that arises from God's judgment for sin and that sometimes evokes a penitent confession has another mode of expression in Scripture in addition to the familiar language of the wrath or anger of God. In at least two instances, the effect of the sin of the people is the negation of the "Immanuel" character of God's assurance that is so central to the oracle of salvation. The one who responds to the prayer for help with the words that are indicative of the very nature of God,[16] "Do not be afraid, for I am/will be with you," responds to the sin of the people in Joshua 7 with the words: "I will be with you no more, unless you destroy the devoted things from among you" (v. 12). In Deut 1:41, the people who had been too fearful to go into the land and then had rushed ahead with a quick confession, "We have sinned against the LORD," and an all-too-sudden willingness to fight now that they were in danger of losing the land because of their timidness hear the divine word: "Do not go up and do not fight, for I am not in the midst of you; otherwise you will be defeated by your enemies" (v. 42). Authentic confession of sin seeks to avert the wrath of God and to make real and true once more the assurance that undergirds all other assurances and is the primary answer to prayer: I am with you.

The Act of Confession

If we ask more specifically after the *form* and *content* of the prayers of confession, we find, as might be expected, both a consistency and an individuality in their various expressions. That has been the case with all the forms of prayer we have examined. Indeed the first thing to be said about the form and setting of prayers of confession is what was noted briefly at the beginning, that confession of sin may be set as a part or dimension of a more general complaint or lament in a prayer for help, as, for example, in Ps 41:4:

> As for me, I said, "O LORD, be gracious to me;
> heal me, for I have sinned against you."

Often, however, as one sees in narrative texts as well as in some of the penitential psalms, the confession of sin is the primary focus of the prayer.

Typically, the individual or the community of the Old Testament made *general* confession for *specific* acts or sins. The sin is generally clear if there is a narrative context. It is not clear if there is not, because the confession is more generalized and available as prayer for different persons or groups in different circumstances. So Psalm 51 has a quite general and universal character until a superscription is given to it that identifies it as David's confession with Bathsheba. Its power as a prayer is in no small degree precisely because of its ability to serve as the voice of anyone who comes in penitence before God while also seeming exceedingly appropriate for the context to which it was assigned in the superscription (see below).

Primary formulation. A perusal of all the accounts of people confessing their sins reveals that such confession has a simple basic formulation: "I/We have sinned"[17] or "I/We have sinned against the Lord."[18] This statement, in long or short form, is like the basic assurance at the heart of the oracle of salvation, "Do not fear." As that assurance is meant to address every situation of human distress and outcry to God, so this simple declaration, "I/We have sinned," is the heart of the matter in confessional prayer and identifies what needs to be said in every case of wrong doing. Three things may be noted about this basic formulation.

1. The act of confession is the same whether it is of a sin against God or the acknowledgment of a wrong done to another. Shimei, who cursed David during the time that he was fleeing from Absalom, says to David, "I have sinned," the same words uttered by Saul to David because of his hostile actions toward him. We even encounter an Israelite king (Hezekiah) saying the same thing to an Assyrian overlord (Sennacherib), suggesting that the structure of treaty relationships was subject to violation in the same sort of way as were human relationships and the relationship with God. One may translate the basic formulation, "I have sinned," "I have erred," or "I am guilty." Other ways of making the primary confessional statement were available. But all mean the same thing, and the reality is one and the same on the human plane and on the theological. One deals with God in the face of the reality of sin in the same way that one deals with human beings, and vice versa.

2. This simple confession is often a public statement. While confession did take place in more private ways, for example, Saul to Samuel and David to Nathan, like thanksgiving, it could, and often did, involve public declaration and sacrifice or symbolic acts.[19] The provision for confession of iniquity and guilt in the law codes serves that end. Both Leviticus and Numbers testify to the conjoining of sacrifice and confession.[20] In Lev 16:21, Aaron is instructed to confess all the transgressions and sins of Israel as he places his hands on the goat who is sent away into the wilderness bearing the iniquities of Israel on his head. Here, public declaration and symbolic act in the strongest sense join in the act of confession. In what seems to be a public and sacral assembly, Joshua tells Achan, who stole the devoted things at Jericho, to confess his sins before God. The long confessional and penitential prayers of Ezra in

Ezra 9 and Nehemiah 9 are set in the context of an assembly of the people. Baruch 1:14 sets the act of confession in the context of the festivals in the house of the Lord.[21] Even the confession of one individual to another is a form of public declaration. It is not a silent confession kept within the inner heart and unexpressed to the one against whom the sin was enacted.

All of this suggests that the reconciliation that is sought, the turning away of the wrath of the other, does not happen without open and straightforward declaration that I or we have done wrong. The confession of sin "tries to clear the past in the presence of the just God who sees everything."[22] That is also, of course, what happens on the human level—a clearing away of the injustice, the wrong that has been done, so that the relationship between the two parties may be renewed afresh.

3. In Psalm 32, one of the penitential psalms, which, to quote Gerstenberger again, "is not a private meditation, as some authors insist, but a story of pardon to be witnessed by the congregation,"[23] we clearly hear that the failure to open up and declare one's sin affects the self:

> While I kept silence, my body wasted away
>   through my groaning all day long.
> For day and night your hand was heavy upon me;
>   my strength was dried up as by the heat of summer.
> Then I acknowledged my sin to you,
>   and I did not hide my iniquity;
> I said, "I will confess my transgressions to the LORD,"
>   and you forgave the guilt of my sin. (Ps 32:3-5)

After his census of the people, David "was stricken to the heart" and confessed: "I have sinned greatly in what I have done" (2 Sam 24:10). Such personal anguish as reflected in these texts is clearly in part because God's judgment is felt. But there is also something else quite fundamental here. The weight of the sin undoes the psyche and "does in" the guilty one. Acknowledging one's errors, whether these are sins before God or against others, and being pardoned is a healing and renewing enterprise. Reconciliation is restorative from both ends of the line, the one who has erred and injured and the one erred against. We speak of a sin or an injury festering like a sore. That metaphor suggests the undeclared and unreconciled sin has its effects that continue beyond the act itself, affecting both parties. In a theological sense, those effects may be judgment or abandonment by God—so Jesus says to those who have wronged another to be reconciled before bringing their gifts to the altar—but also a sickness of the heart within the one who has sinned without confessing it, a malady of the soul no therapy can overcome that does not open up the moral and theological dimensions creating the distress.

The primary confessional formulation of Scripture has been appropriately carried over as a basic and universal mode of confessing in the general prayer of confession in the Anglican Book of Common Prayer, as it begins: "We have erred and strayed from thy ways like lost sheep." Indeed the verb that appears in the Hebrew formulation, "I/We have sinned," means "to miss the way." This general confession from the Anglican liturgy—and one that is often used in Christian worship among other communions—is modeled on the form of confessional prayer we see in the Old Testament in its very general character, in its tone, and in the fact that it goes on to *petition* to God. The first line of the petition is almost identical to the first line of Psalm 51: Have mercy on me, O God.

Elaboration of form. The heart of the prayer of confession and penitence, therefore, is the simple declaration that I/we have sinned (against God). If that is developed further, it can have several other elements in its elaboration.[24] There may be a *repetition of the basic confession in other terms.* Several times we hear the confessors say, "We have sinned; we have done wrong; we have acted wickedly."[25] Such repetition gives emphasis to the contrition and penitence inherent in the basic confession and underscores the sense of sin on the part of those who confess.

Elaboration of the basic confession may take place also by a *petition* for God's mercy, restoration, healing, or forgiveness, for example:

> As for me, I said, "O LORD be gracious to me;
> heal me, for I have sinned against you." (Ps 41:4)

The people who respond to Samuel's indictment with the confession, "We have sinned because we have forsaken the LORD, and have served the Baals and the Astartes," then plead to the Lord, "but now rescue us out of the hand of our enemies" (1 Sam 12:10).

Relatively common also are *motivation* clauses and expressions of *renunciation,* in which the one praying gives a reason for God to grant forgiveness and relief, which may include renouncing the sin that has been committed. There may also be an elaboration of the confession in which the sinner, in Greenberg's terms, *acknowledges the folly of the sin,* as Saul did to David (1 Sam 26:21). More often, however, one finds an *acknowledgment of the justice of God* in the prayer of confession. The moral dimension of the prayer rests, therefore, not only on the acceptance of culpability but also on the acceptance of judgment as appropriate and just or right (*ṣaddîq*). The confession of sin matches the blame of the sinner with the blamelessness of the divine judge.

Examples of such elaborated confessions are numerous. Pharaoh *confesses,* "This time I have sinned." Then he expands his confession with an *acknowledgment of the right or justice of God,* "the LORD is in the right and I and my people are in the wrong." There follows his *petition,* "Pray to the LORD!" and then a *motivating reason,* "Enough of God's thunder and hail!" and finally a *renunciation* of the sin, "I will let you go; you need stay no longer" (Exod 9:27-28).

Balaam follows his *confession,* "I have sinned," with a *motivation* for God's forgiveness, "for I did not know that you were standing in the road to oppose me." There then follows a *renunciation* of the wrong action: "Now therefore, if it is displeasing to you, I will return home" (Num 22:34).

So also David, "stricken to the heart because he had numbered the people," prays:

> I have sinned greatly in what I have done. [*confession*]
> But now, O LORD, I pray you, take away the guilt of your servant;
>   [*petition*]
> for I have done very foolishly. [*acknowledgment of folly*]
>
> (2 Sam 24:10)

In Jer 14:20, one hears first the *confession* of sin in the primary formulation but with *repetition* that incorporates a dimension found in the later confession of sin in Ezra 9, a solidarity in sin with previous generations:

> We acknowledge our wickedness, O LORD,
>   the iniquity of our ancestors,
>   for we have sinned against you.

A *petition* is uttered:

> Do not spurn us (v. 21a),

followed by several *motivating clauses* that function in the same way as other such clauses in prayers for help generally:

> for your name's sake;
>   do not dishonor your glorious throne;
>   remember and do not break your covenant with us. (v. 21bc)

Sometimes the basic form of confession and petition is elaborated by a more detailed and *specific explication of the sin.* This is found, for instance, in the Deuteronomistic prayer of confession in Judg 10:10, where the people (who are here really the voice of the Deuteronomists) elaborate their sin of idolatry, and, similarly, in 1 Sam 12:10. Such spelling out of the sin in greater detail seems to be more characteristic of the communal confessions of the later period, the long prose prayers of the postexilic period (see below).

SOME PRAYERS OF CONFESSION

Most of the prayers of confession and penitence we have discussed are relatively short and their form simple and concise. But there are some confessional prayers that are much more extended and elaborate. They tend to come from the later literature of the Old Testament. A presentation of confessional and penitential prayer would not be complete without some examination of such prayers. We shall look first at Psalm 51, whose date is quite uncertain although in its final form it seems to be exilic or postexilic and probably from the time of Nehemiah (see v. 18),[26] and then turn to the prayers of Ezra, Nehemiah, and Daniel.[27]

Psalm 51

The superscription, which attributes this psalm to David "when the prophet Nathan came to him, after he had gone in to Bathsheba," gives concreteness and particularity to the undefined sins that are confessed in the psalm itself. Like the primary confessional formulation, "I/We have sinned (against the Lord)," the psalm itself does not identify any particular sins. It is universal, a general confession available as a prayer by any who have sinned and come penitently before God. The superscription says that such a prayer, with its appealing sentiments, belongs on the lips of murderers and adulterers. It may function for all sorts of other sins also because there is a common denominator: we have sinned against the Lord. The moral culpability is more important than any calculus of value or hierarchy of greater and lesser sins.

The psalm begins with the basic *petition* of the confession of sin: have mercy on me.[28] But the petition is elaborated in three successive supplications, all directed toward removal of the sin and guilt and expressed in the language and imagery of wiping off and cleansing.[29] The three terms for sin ("transgressions," "iniquity," and "sin") and the call for cleansing and purifying not only express the fundamental petition; they also are an *acknowledgment of the sins* that have been committed. That acknowledgment is extended in verses 3-5. Here we encounter the *confession* proper in its typical form: "Against you, you alone, have I sinned" (v. 4). As Gerstenberger and others have observed, there is an escalation in verses 3-5: sin and guilt are acknowledged and confessed; the pure confession of sin thereafter completely exculpates God and *acknowledges the justice of God's judgment;* and the penitent is ready to accept whatever God may decide.[30] The climax of the confession is the assertion of the all-pervasive character of sin in verse 5: "Indeed I was born guilty, a sinner when my mother conceived me." This is not meant to be a dogmatic statement about original sin. It is rather an expression of an intense awareness on the part of the praying one that the sin is so great that he or she feels that one's very life began in that moral culpability. It may well be that in this hyperbolic language are to be found the literary and actual roots of the later-developing notion of a truly pervasive sinful condition as over against intensely and often repeated sinful acts.

The petition is resumed in verses 6-12, and the main thematic petition is reiterated, that is, the cleansing. Along with that are the more familiar petitions of the prayers for help: to experience the presence of God and the powerful salvation of God that evoke praise and joy. The remaining verses then express the vow of praise and sacrifice typical of the prayers for help in the Psalms. In verses 16-17, the sacrifice is spiritualized in a way that we have noted earlier, but when these verses are placed alongside the last two verses of the psalm the result is a more complex understanding of the relation of sacrifice to penitence. Verses 16-17 and 18-19 are often seen as contradicting one another. Whether or not the final verses were added from a later time and whatever the motivation for such an addition, when juxtaposed with the call for the sacrifice of a broken heart in preference to burnt offering, they serve to identify the intimate relation between the spirit of contrition and the actual sacrifices to God. Such sacrifices are twofold: the sacrifice of the heart and the symbolic sacrifice on the altar.

Late Prose Prayers

In the late literature of the Old Testament, there is a group of long narrative prayers of confession that share various characteristics and reflect features of confessional prayer that have been identified above. They are Ezra 9:6-15, Neh 1:5-11 and 9:6-37, Dan 9:4-19, as well as the apocryphal prayer in Bar 1:15—3:8.[31] While generally the prayers of confession are short and their form simple and concise, when they develop into longer prayers they still seem to reflect a formal genre with similarities in the midst of their particularities.[32] In all of these prayers, unlike the shorter prayers discussed above, the ones praying are specifically characterized in the frameworks of the prayers as "confessing" or "making confession."[33] Typically, they are marked by extensive acts of contrition and humbling oneself, such as weeping and fasting, and the tearing of garments.[34] The fact that these prayers occur in both priestly (Ezra and Nehemiah) and apocalyptic literature is important because the literatures from those spheres of interest are "often thought to be antithetical to each other in social origin and theological outlook."[35] The act of confessing sins cut across one of the deep theological and social divides in the community of Israel and was shared by persons whose analysis of what was happening and what God desired and would do was radically different.

The prayers as a whole bear some resemblance to the community prayers for help or laments in that they are communal prayers rising out of distress and often calling God to remember the covenant promises.[36] But they lack the strong element of complaint, the questioning of God's actions. On the contrary, the acknowledgment of God's justice is a persistent theme, and confession of sin has replaced the complaint against God. It has been suggested that in this late period the prayer and service of penitence have taken over the role of the community prayers for help.[37] If that was the case, then one may see in this move a significant stage in the transition from complaint and lament to confession of sin as the context for supplication that is so characteristic of contemporary community worship and prayer.

In a fashion not generally characteristic of prayers for help, most of these prose prayers of penitence begin with an ascription of praise.[38] The primary form of that ascription is Deuteronomistic in character and alludes to God's covenant-keeping as the context for confession and the ground for the appeal, for example:

> O LORD God of heaven, the great and awesome God who keeps covenant and steadfast love with those who love him and keep his commandments . . . (Neh 1:5)[39]

A sense of solidarity with the people on the part of the ones who pray and with their predecessors on the part of the people is common to these prayers. So Ezra, Nehemiah, and Daniel all begin with a first-person singular mode but move in the course of their prayers to first-person plural.[40] The sense of continuity with the sins of the ancestors is most marked in the long historical retrospect of Neh 9:7-31, but it is a feature of the other prayers also.[41] In this respect, one should also compare Psalm 106, which is similar to Neh 9:6-37 in its long historical recounting of the sins of the people in the past. While it begins and ends in praise, it is as much a confession of sin with petition for help as it is hymnic.[42]

The primary confessional formulation occurs in each of these prayers except Ezra 9, sometimes repeatedly.[43] While it is lacking in Ezra 9, that is the one prayer in this group that confesses *specific* sin, the sin of intermarriage against the command of God. The others make confession in terms of the basic formulation, "We have sinned/done wickedly," and by reference to breaking the commandments. In all of the prayers, the confessional dimension is heightened by a heaping up of declarations of sin and guilt:

> Our iniquities have risen higher than our heads, and our guilt has mounted up to the heavens. (Ezra 9:6)

> We have been deep in guilt. (Ezra 9:7)

We have forsaken your commandments.
>   (Ezra 9:10; cf. Neh 1:7; 9:34; Dan 9:5, 11)

We have offended you deeply. (Neh 1:7)

We have rebelled. (Dan 9:5, 9)

We have not obeyed the voice of the LORD our God by following
his laws, which he set before us by his servants the prophets.
>   (Dan 9:10; cf. Ezra 9:11; Neh 9:34; Bar 1:18-19, 21; 2:10)

Specific *petitions* are present in every case except Ezra 9. Nehemiah prays for success in his enterprise at the conclusion of his penitential prayer. The Levites in Neh 9:32 pray simply, "Do not treat lightly all the hardship that has come upon us." In a more extended petition, Daniel prays that God will turn away the divine wrath and forgive the people (Dan 9:15-19). The petition of Daniel is lengthened in part by a congeries of motivational clauses to encourage God's forgiveness. These include reference to God having brought "*your* people out of the land of Egypt with a mighty hand and made *your name* renowned to this day," as well as allusion to "your city Jerusalem," "your holy mountain," "Jerusalem and your people," and "your desolated sanctuary," all of which serve to ground the appeal implicitly in the relationship between God and the people, Zion, and the temple. Like other prayers for help, especially the community laments, this one asserts a connection between the fate of the people and God's reputation or name. The point is made quite explicit at the end of the prayer:

For your own sake, O my God, because your city and your people
bear your name. (v. 19).

A similar motivational claim is made in Neh 1:10:

They are your servants and your people, whom you redeemed by
your great power and your strong hand.

There is no explicit statement of *renunciation* in these prayers, but in the one prayer where a specific sin is lifted up, Ezra's prayer of confession of sin in the mixed marriages of the people, renunciation takes place in an act, rather than a verbal statement, as the people separate themselves from the peoples of the land and from the foreign wives (Ezra 10).

Theologically, the heart of these prayers is to be found in their juxtaposition of a clear *acknowledgment of the justice and rightness of God's judgment* with an *appeal to the mercy of God*. Except for Neh 1:5-11, each of the prayers explicitly recognizes that God's judgment for the sin of the people is "right" or "just" (*ṣaddîq*):[44]

O LORD, God of Israel, you are just [*ṣaddîq*]. (Ezra 9:15)

You have been just [*ṣaddîq*] in all that has come upon us.
(Neh 9:33)

Righteousness [*haṣṣedāqâ*] is on your side. (Dan 9:7)

Indeed, the LORD our God is right [*ṣaddîq*] in all that he has done.
(Dan 9:14)

These prayers, therefore, recognize in the judgment of God for the sins confessed that moral order that lies behind the wrath of God evoked by human disobedience. But they also see in the way of God's dealings with Israel a pattern of mercy, steadfast love, and forgiveness that is also operative in "all that he has done." That is, the ancient liturgical credo that we have seen so prominent in the prayers for help is central to these prayers also:

The LORD, the LORD, a God merciful and gracious, slow to anger and abounding in steadfast love and faithfulness, keeping steadfast love for the thousandth generation, forgiving iniquity and transgression and sin, yet by no means clearing the guilty...
(Exod 34:6-7)[45]

Ezra refers to the "favor" that "has been shown by the LORD our God," even if only for a brief moment (Ezra 9:8). Nehemiah's petition is that God may "grant him mercy" in the sight of Artaxerxes, the Persian king (Neh 1:11). In the prayer of the Levites in Nehemiah 9, the Exodus formulary is abundantly present in the historical retrospective:

But you are a God ready to forgive, gracious and merciful, slow to anger and abounding in steadfast love, and you did not forsake them. (v. 17)

... and according to your great mercies you gave them saviors.
(v. 27)

Many times you rescued them according to your mercies. (v. 28)

Nevertheless, in your great mercies you did not make an end of them or forsake them, for you are a gracious and merciful God.
(v. 31)

... the great and mighty and awesome God, keeping covenant and steadfast love... (v. 32)[46]

Daniel also prays out of the same conviction:

To the LORD our God belong mercy and forgiveness. (Dan 9:9)

We do not present our supplication before you on the ground of our righteousness, but on the ground of your great mercies. (v. 18)

The justice and mercy of God are complexly interrelated in the way in which the Lord deals with a sinful people. These prayers of confession and penitence express the community's trust in both features of the divine activity.

CONCLUSION

From all of this it is possible to identify some fundamental aspects of confession and penitential prayer. There is, first of all, a generalized statement that is at the heart of the confession, long or short. It is unequivocal in declaring that what has happened, whatever the particulars may be, is that a wrong has been done, a sin has been committed. There are particulars in virtually every case. But they are not the focus. The focus is on the actuality that what has happened is a sin, an error, a wrong. It is that universal formulation that keeps constantly before us the moral dimension and identifies what is constant in all the acts and in the face of whatever social and cultural relativities one may identify. They are sins/wrongs against God or another person, or against both. That is what protects against the tendency to explain in another way, against the tendency to which one of T. S. Eliot's characters refers, to regard one's errors or sin as bad form, psychological, or mental kinks.[47]

It is in this context also that one must understand the protestations of innocence where they occur, for example, Pss 7:3-5 or 26:4-6. Such protests are not general statements of an original innocence or a perfection of the moral life. They are a claim that the one praying has not done specific sins, hurts, or injustices that might seem to justify the present experience of suffering as the judgment of God.

The corollaries of these protestations of innocence are the common acknowledgments in the confession of sin that God has properly punished because "We have sinned." Here is a further significant element in penitential prayer. Like the acknowledgment of one's folly, the recognition of the "rightness" of God's wrath against the sin means the reality of the sin and its significance are not covered over by the one who has sinned. What has happened is real and wrong and has negative consequences. The sinner does not beg that question or try to explain it away. As the righteousness of God can be appealed to by the one in trouble and distress who cries for help, so it cannot be denied by the one who has sinned against God. In the penitential prayer, the wrath of God is not explained away or protested. It is acknowledged as "right."

There is further a renunciation that serves as a formulation of repentance, a turning away from the activity that has been done. That is not always present because sometimes the act is complete, and confession indicates one's awareness and remorse. But where continued manifestation of the sin is a real possibility, renunciation, the will to sin no more, is expected as an act of repentance.[48]

The prayer of confession is also petitionary. It seeks God's forgiveness or mercy even as it recognizes the justice of God's wrath. In such supplication, the penitential prayer is seen to be, like other prayers for help, an open conversation with God that includes what those other prayers contribute to the dialogue—reasons and motivations that ground the grace of God in the reality of God's goodness, the relationship that exists between the praying one and God, the faithfulness of God to the covenant, even the very reputation of God before the world.

In the New Testament, confession of sin continues as an act of prayer, and the connection between sin and calamity so prominent in the Old Testament does not disappear. In the letter of James, confession is called for and related to the prayer for healing of the sick:

> The prayer of faith will save the sick, and the Lord will raise them up, and anyone who has committed sins will be forgiven. Therefore confess your sins to one another, and pray for one another, so that you may be healed. The prayer of the righteous is powerful and effective. (Jas 5:15-16)

The association of healing and forgiveness that is at the center of Jesus' healing of the paralyzed man[49] is carried over into the prayer life of the community and becomes a part of intercession and mutual support.

At the same time, the picture shifts to some degree. The protestation of innocence that is fairly common in the Old Testament diminishes, and the tying of calamity and suffering to sin is not as pronounced, except in one crucial way. It is *Christ's* calamity as the large consequence of human sin that becomes the focus of attention. So confession of sin does not diminish. What happens is that there is a move toward confession of *general* unworthiness as well as unworthy and sinful acts since "all have sinned and fall short of the glory of God" (Rom 3:23), or as Jesus said to those who would stone the woman caught in adultery: "Let anyone among you who is without sin be the first to throw a stone at her" (John 8:7).

It is out of this understanding of sin as a part of the human condition that there is a move in Christian liturgy toward regularizing the confession of sin, although this appears to be a largely post–New Testament development. In the Old Testament, such confession takes place on the occasion of the sinning, and that form of confession does not disappear. But confession as a regularized activity comes into play when there is a sense within the community of a general condition of sin that always needs forgiveness and must be cleansed before the community can rightly come before the holy Lord. The tendency toward a specifying of the sins in a general confession may have something to do with the fact that the occasion of the confession is a regularized confession of sin rather than an immediate sinful act, as it would be when in the Old Testament the community makes the general confession, "We have sinned." Where the particular sins are not immediately obvious—and the letter of James as well as numerous stories in the Gospels and Acts indicate that they often were obvious—then it may be necessary to identify them for the community. There is certainly some of that in the confessions of sin prayed by leaders in the Old Testament. Most often, however, people are aware of their sins and make confession because of them.

The sacrificial ritual that is a part of the confessional process in the Old Testament is taken up in Christ's sacrifice, which certainly in the letter to the Hebrews and elsewhere is understood as a sacrifice for human sin. The theology that sees penitence accompanied by acts to take away the judgment of God does not disappear. It is indicated in the New Testament, however, that while the one who prays confesses and is penitent, God's blotting out is not through any sacrifice made by the community or individual who sinned but through God's own sacrifice in behalf of a sinful world.

8

"Intercession for the Transgressors"

PRAYER FOR OTHERS

◆

THEY MADE INTERCESSION

In Jer 15:1, the Lord says to the prophet, "Though Moses and Samuel stood before me, yet my heart would not turn toward this people. Send them out of my sight, and let them go!" The verse is indicative of what happened (historical event) and of what was supposed to happen (role function). That is, the stories of the Old Testament attest to occasions in which Moses and Samuel prayed to God in behalf of the people (event), and their position as leaders is what evoked those prayers (role). Put the other way, one may say that intercession in the Old Testament seems to belong primarily to figures who were leaders of family, tribe, and community or who, in some fashion, represented God to the people. Their standing before the people in behalf of God was matched by a standing before God in behalf of the people.[1]

It is no accident that Moses and Samuel are cited in Jeremiah 15 as examples of mediators whose prayers God would be least likely to resist. The biblical stories tell us often of the intercessory activity of these two leaders, and especially of Moses. The latter is so identified with praying for the people in order to avert the divine wrath at their sin that Psalm 90 came to be ascribed to him, presumably because he was one whose prayers were able to turn away that wrath.[2] There are other such figures, however, some of whom shared characteristics with Moses and Samuel that place them in the role of intercessor and mediator for others.

Tribal and clan leaders prayed to God in behalf of others, and not necessarily the members of their own family group. The Deuteronomic law instructs the *elders* of the community to pray for God's absolution of the people when a murder has been committed and the murderer is unknown (Deut 21:8). Abraham's prayer of intercession for Abimelech, the king of Gerar, brings healing and an averting of the divine wrath for him and all in his household (Genesis 20) even as his fervent intercession for Sodom and Gomorrah has a quite ambiguous outcome—at least in terms of Abraham's prayer, though not in terms of the fate of those wicked cities (Genesis 18–19). The patriarch Job also intercedes for his friends when they are threatened with the divine wrath for the folly of their counsel to Job (Job 42).

In this instance, God calls Job *"my servant"* four times, a relational term that is also applied to Abraham and Moses on more than one occasion.[3] The association suggests the intercessory role of the one who stands as the Lord's servant, the responsibility, capacity, and opportunity of those in the human community who function as agents and servants of God, in one capacity or another, to pray effectively for God's positive inclination toward others. Confirmation of the intercessory activity of God's servants is found in the concluding words about the suffering servant of the Lord in Isa 53:12:

> Yet he bore the sin of many,
> and made intercession for the transgressors.[4]

In the context of Abraham's prayer for Abimelech, however, he is called by God a *prophet,* and his intercessory activity is particularly associated with that role:

Now then, return the man's wife; for he is a prophet, and he will pray for you and you shall live. (Gen 20:7)

While it is a commonplace to speak of the prophets as messengers and announcers of God's word of judgment or salvation, their mediatorial function worked both ways. They were spokespersons to God in behalf of the people and prayed for God's mercy upon them as well as for God's healing upon individuals.[5] Most of the figures who "prayed in behalf of"[6] others, the community as a whole or individuals within it, were prophets or were regarded as such by the tradition. These included not only Abraham,[7] Moses,[8] and Samuel,[9] but also Elijah, Elisha, Isaiah, Jeremiah, Ezekiel, and Amos, as well as unnamed prophets.[10] While on occasion a king, such as David or Hezekiah,[11] prayed effectively in behalf of the people, the intercessors of Israel were primarily the prophets,[12] that group of the Lord's agents who were particularly designated "my servants."[13]

The strong connection between the prophetic office and the act of intercession is suggested by several texts.

1. Jeremiah shows this quite clearly, not only in the words of the Lord quoted above, indicating that not even Moses or Samuel could "turn" God's heart toward the disobedient people, but also in other places where God is resistant to even the possibility of intercession. Three times, the Lord forbids Jeremiah's intercession in behalf of the people—and does so in very strong terms:

As for you, do not pray for this people, do not raise a cry or prayer on their behalf, and do not intercede with me, for I will not hear you. (Jer 7:16)

As for you, do not pray for this people, or lift up a cry or prayer on their behalf, for I will not listen when they call to me in the time of their trouble. (Jer 11:14)

The LORD said to me: Do not pray for the welfare of this people. Although they fast, I do not hear their cry. (Jer 14:11-12)

Implicit in these strong words to the prophet is an expectation that—even in the terrible situation in which Jeremiah prophesied, one that evoked his own terrible cries for help and calls for destruction of those who threatened him—he will in fact pray for the life of the people, interceding to avert the divine wrath that will lead to their doom.

2. Such intercession is just what Amos did, apparently in connection with his call and the beginning of his prophetic activity. In the vision reports that seem to be the presupposition and ground of his prophecy, four times he sees a vision of judgment. In the first two instances, he immediately intercedes with a poignant cry to God, the first time to seek forgiveness of the people and then the second time to persuade the Lord to stop the pending judgment (Amos 7:2, 5). The message of unrelenting doom that so characterized his prophecy was rooted in the reality of a situation so bad that eventually Amos could only stand mute before further visions of divine judgment, no longer able even to pray in behalf of the people (Amos 7:7-9; 8:1-3). But the announcement of divine judgment by the prophet comes only after his fervent prayer in their behalf.

Ezekiel also cried out on two occasions essentially the same prayer of intercession for the people:

While they were killing, and I was left alone, I fell prostrate on my face and cried out, "Ah Lord GOD! will you destroy all who remain of Israel as you pour out your wrath upon Jerusalem?"
(Ezek 9:8; cf. 11:13)

On several occasions, we hear of persons, often representatives of the people or their leaders, coming to a prophet to ask him to intercede for them. Twice, Jeremiah was asked to "pray for us," though the request seems to have been aimed as much at inquiry to determine God's intention as it was to seek a change in the divine purpose.[14] Isaiah also received emissaries from King Hezekiah asking him to "lift up your prayer for the remnant that is left" (2 Kgs 19:4).

A prophet also could be expected to intercede in behalf of an individual sick or near death. Parallel accounts of such an incident appear in both the Elijah and Elisha cycles of prophetic legends.[15] At the death of her son, the Shunammite woman with whom Elisha lodged immediately set out to get Elisha, who prayed to the Lord and lay upon the body of the child to resuscitate him.[16] The prophet is portrayed in these stories as a miracle worker, but the prayer of intercession is a part of that miraculous activity. Prayer and ritual acts combine to bring about healing and restoration to life.

All of these stories and texts confirm that intercession in ancient Israel was primarily a mediatorial function associated with those who represented the people before God or spoke the word of the Lord to the people. Those "servants of the Lord" who were called to lead or proclaim, especially the prophets but also kings, clan leaders, and elders, whose leadership was less a calling than a responsibility within the social structures,[17] found their position or role involved them in representing the people through prayer or carrying out their "service" of the Lord by speaking to God in behalf of others.[18] The stories and laws and legends of Israel reveal a kind of inherent responsibility on the part of such persons to exercise their leadership in prayer. If intercession was associated primarily with such positions, it seems indeed to have *belonged* to them, whether legislated, as in the case of the elders in Deuteronomy 21, or inherent within the prophetic burden. The prophets seem to have spoken to the Lord in behalf of the people with as much fervor as they did to the people in behalf of the Lord. The anguish of an Ezekiel or an Amos at the vision of destruction awaiting the people in whose midst they were set like a plumb line bore no resemblance to the calculating and unswerving determinism of such a measuring line. That the Lord's judgment and response to these prayers were themselves hardly such mechanical determinations as that imagery from the visions of Amos suggests is well indicated below as we look at the divine response to the intercessions of the prophet. But the voice of the prophet who saw the people under threat or actuality of doom was real and heartfelt. The prophets did not announce the word of the Lord to those for whom they did not also pray. We do not have evidence for every prophet, but it is so consistently a part of the prophetic stories that we can only assume that such prayers for the people were as much a part of their being God's servants as their speaking the word of the Lord.

OCCASIONS OF INTERCESSION

If intercession in the Old Testament is notable by its general restriction to prophets or other representative figures,[19] it is also noteworthy that the circumstances precipitating such prayer were limited in character. There are a few cases of prayer for others who are barren or ill or oppressed in which no presumption is made about the cause of their particular circumstance. Thus Isaac prayed for his barren wife Rebekah, and the Lord gave her a child (Gen 25:21). In stories that are "variations on the same legend,"[20] Elijah and Elisha prayed for a child who was dead or near death, and the child was restored to life and health.[21]

By far the great majority of occasions, however, where intercession for others took place were situations in which individuals or, more often, the people as a whole were under threat or actuality of divine judgment. The whole purpose of the intercession was to avert the divine judgment and remove the present or pending disaster, which was God's punishment for the sin of the people or of the individual. The context of intercession in the Old Testament, therefore, is the reality of judgment. While such prayer might occur under other circumstances, the prayers of the servants of the Lord in behalf of others were most often lifted to try to avert the divine wrath that was upon them or at hand.

Time and again Moses prayed to the Lord to take away judgment from the people, sometimes at their request and sometimes out of his own sense of solidarity with the people he led. So he several times acceded to Pharaoh's request to pray to the Lord to remove the plagues upon Egypt.[22] On other occasions, he prayed to avert God's powerful wrath upon the people, and Aaron in particular, for the making of the golden calf,[23] as well as to take away the divine fire and the poisonous serpents that the Lord had sent upon the people in anger at their complaining.[24] Repeatedly, Moses had to intercede for the people in the wilderness as the Lord became angry again and again for the complaints and disobedience of the people.[25] On one occasion he prayed for healing for Miriam, but the leprosy or skin disease that had overcome her was the explicit punishment of God for her challenge to Moses' authority.[26]

The example of Moses is repeated in the stories of the prophets as they prayed to the Lord not to punish the people for their sin or to take away the harsh punishment they had received.[27] Abraham, David, Hezekiah, and Job also prayed to avert the divine wrath that had come upon others or was about to.[28] The prayer the elders are instructed to pray in the face of a murderer who has not been found is to remove "the guilt of innocent blood," which could bring down the Lord's judgment on the land (Deut 21:8).

Except for the piece of legislation just described, all the prayers of intercession to stop God's wrath and judgment are recounted in narratives from Israel's past history. Only one reference to intercession is set in the future, but it is an important one. It is the poem of God's suffering servant who was despised but bore upon himself the judgment due to others (Isa 52:13—53:12). The problem that is addressed in that account of an unknown figure who suffers vicariously for others is undeniably the problem of human sin. Regardless of how one identifies the servant, whether as an individual or a community, the mission of this particular servant of the Lord, whose future vindication and exaltation are because of a silent and faithful acceptance of God's will and purpose to make "his" life an offering for sin, was to bear the iniquities of others. The final word of the poem is that "the righteous one, my servant, ... bore the sin of many, and made intercession for the transgressors" (vv. 11-12). Even as the identity of the servant is open, so is the circle of those for whom intercession is made. They are described only as transgressors, an identity that is characteristic of those for whom intercession is made. They are also "many."

THE CHARACTER OF INTERCESSORY PRAYER

While the confession of sin in the Bible regularly centers in the declaration, "We/I have sinned," there is no common form for intercessory prayer. Sometimes we have only the report that it happened.[29] It can be as brief as Moses' plea for Miriam, "O God, please heal her" (Num 12:13), or as long as the extended prayer for forgiveness of the people that is reported two chapters later (Num 14:13-19). There is not a significant difference in form between the prayer of intercession and the prayer for help or lament. It may be heavily complaint in character[30] or primarily petition, as, for example, the prayer for Miriam mentioned above. On occasion, the intercession is in the context of extended confession of sin, as is the case in Daniel's prayer (Daniel 9).

Because there is no single form or shape that may be exemplified by a particular intercessory prayer, one can gain a sense of its character best by looking at some of the different prayers. We shall take examples from three representative figures whose prayers are recorded at some length: Abraham, Moses, and Amos. Other prayers will have varying features, but they are not sharply different in character from these three.

Genesis 18:23-32

The first of these intercessions is Abraham's plea for the innocent who might be found in the wicked cities of Sodom and Gomorrah. It is not called a prayer in the text. In form it is a dialogue between Abraham and God. But its character as intercession is unmistakable. It anticipates the prophetic intercession of Abraham for Abimelech and his household in Genesis 20. Rather than keeping this from being a prayer, the form of the prayer transforms it into a genuine dialogue or conversation with God. There is give-and-take, pleading and response. The one who prays for the sinful people will not let the matter go quickly. And the one who listens is patient and willing to attend to the intercession. There is a real sense in which the human praying and the divine listening both go to extremes in this intercession, as happens again in Amos (see below). Ostensibly, the prayer is for the innocent, and we know that Lot is in the background here, though unnamed by Abraham.[31] But the plea for the few righteous or innocent is couched in the form of a prayer for *forgiveness of the whole,* the wicked with the righteous, as over against a destruction of the whole, the righteous/innocent with the wicked. The prayer could have been a plea to remove the innocent from the punishment, a tack that in fact is taken by the Lord before the story is over (Gen 19:29). Instead it is a persistent plea for forgiveness of the whole wicked city, for the sake of the innocent, a plea to which the Lord is responsive (Gen 18:26).

In this conversation with God, therefore, the intercessor Abraham is importunate. He will not be put off easily and presses God to the limit. There is a profound mix of audacity and humility in his stance before God. The audacious pressure of Abraham is suggested even in the ancient tradition that understood verse 22 to say that "the LORD remained standing before Abraham," as if the deity were petitioning the creature rather than the reverse. But it is particularly seen in verse 25 with the repeated "Far be it!" of Abraham and his direct challenge to the Lord, "Shall not the Judge of all the earth do right?" Such daring thrusts in the prayer are matched, however, by the humility and sense of creatureliness before the transcendent God that are found in other remarks of Abraham, his self-definition, "I who am but dust and ashes," that is, a mere mortal, and his recognition that he may be pushing the limits of the relationship when he says as he makes his fourth and sixth petitions, "Oh do not let the LORD be angry if I speak."[32] This is not just a general conversation. Persistent and daring as it may be, it is a prayer to the Judge of all the earth! What happens in other prayers in the prostration of the petitioner or the lifting of the hands is manifest in Abraham's words. The human creature dares to speak in behalf of other creatures to the Almighty, the Judge of all the earth, but the creature remains just that. It is prayer from earth to heaven, from dust and ashes to the one who is enthroned above the universe. Can dust and ashes push the Creator? As Job did it in his prayer for help, so Abraham does it in his prayer for the forgiveness of Sodom and Gomorrah. In this case, at least, intercession is a daring act, even when carried out by one who knows his true place in the order of things.

The intercession of Abraham, like many of the prayers for help, grounds its petitions and its insistent pressure on the deity in the very character of God. Contextually, this is emphasized by the immediately preceding verses where God carries on a kind of interior dialogue as to whether to let Abraham in on what God is about to do. The decision to inform Abraham is rooted in God's election of him to charge his children and household "to keep the way of the LORD by doing righteousness and justice" (v. 19). The first instance of Abraham and his family doing that is now set forth, quite surprisingly, by Abraham calling for God, in effect, to "keep the way of the LORD by doing...justice [*mišpāṭ*]." "Shall not the Judge of all the earth do justice [*mišpāṭ*]?" says Abraham. The appeal of this intercessory prayer is to God's own way of being and acting in the world, the way of justice and righteousness. The question appeals to the character and reputation of God, to press the Lord to be and act according to the divine intention and nature. Such an appeal is not uncommon in the intercessory prayers of the Bible.

In this case, one uncovers in the nature of God a revision of the usual calculus that the wickedness of some brings judgment or disaster upon many. That is something very evident in human affairs. Here the revision suggests that the innocence of a few can overcome the move to judgment upon the many, a word that carries through the Scriptures in the intercessory role of the suffering servant and in the cross. There it is the innocent taking the suffering that belongs to others, but Isa 53:12 sees in this act an intercession in behalf of the many others. Intercessory prayer, therefore, arises here out of the assumption that God is bent toward mercy, grace, and deliverance, that judgment is subordinated to the merciful disposition of God.[33] The stopping of the conversation and the pleading at the number ten mean nothing literally. The dialogue as a whole indicates that God will go as far as God can in behalf of the innocent even if that means pardon and forgiveness of the wicked.[34]

But the city was destroyed! What does that mean for the prayer of intercession and the openness of the deity toward extravagant forgiveness? One response to that question is to see in the narrative that follows a different kind of theological voice, an older traditional voice that is in conflict with the more radical voice of the intercessory prayer and the dialogue that it effects. Certainly such a tension in the narrative is possible. That is not the only way of viewing the whole, however. One must keep in mind how this story of judgment begins, in the divine self-command:

> How great is the outcry against Sodom and Gomorrah and how very grave their sin! I must go down and see whether they have done altogether according to the outcry that has come to me; and if not, I will know. (Gen 18:20-21)

That "outcry" is the prayer for help of the victims of oppression and injustice. We have noted its character as one of the thematic threads of Scripture.[35] The openness of the ears of God to hear and respond to that outcry of those in suffering and trouble is as persistent as the cry itself. The judgment of Sodom and Gomorrah is as much an act of God to deliver the victims from oppression and violence as are the plagues upon Egypt and the destruction of the Egyptian army.

Finally, we have to take account of Gen 19:29:

> So it was that, when God destroyed the cities of the Plain, God remembered Abraham, and sent Lot out of the midst of the overthrow, when he overthrew the cities in which Lot had settled.

The intercession of Abraham was efficacious to save the innocent, or at least to save Lot and his family. Nothing is said, in fact, about the righteousness or innocence of Lot. We hear simply that "God remembered Abraham." What that "memory" was we are not told. It may have been a remembrance of his promise to Abraham and his posterity. But it surely included the prayer of intercession. The outcome of Abraham's prayer rested less in his persuasion of God that there were innocent to be saved than it did in the fact that he prayed it. As one interpreter has put it cogently and simply, "By the new mathematics of 18:22-33 (and 19:29), *one* is enough to save (Rom 5:15-17)."[36]

The Prayers of Moses

We have already, to some extent, looked at Moses' prayers as prayers for help. But a number of them are particularly intercessory for the people.[37] They form the largest block of intercessory prayers from a single context, in this case, the wandering of the Hebrews in the wilderness under the leadership of Moses. Several features stand out when they are examined as a whole.

As in the case of Abraham's prayer for Sodom and Gomorrah, all of these prayers arise out of the pending or actual judgment of God because of the sins of the people. That sinfulness is not hidden or covered over in the prayers. It is fully acknowledged:

> Alas, this people has sinned a great sin. (Exod 32:31)

> Pay no attention to the stubbornness of this people, their wickedness and their sin. (Deut 9:27)

The intercession is for mercy and forgiveness that are cognizant of the persistent disobedience and sin of the people. The people rebel often, and each time Moses stands before them as a shield of prayer seeking to avert the divine wrath and the consequent destruction of the people.[38] That is true even though the rebellion is as much against the leadership of Moses as it is against the God who led them out of Egypt. The prayers of Moses echo those of Abraham, not in any particular content but in the fact that they are prayed in the context of repeated sin—of a different sort than those in the cities of the Plain—and themselves reflect a persistence and a willingness to push and prod the deity, to do whatever is possible in the vehicle of prayer to turn away the divine wrath and evoke the mercy and compassion that are known to be so characteristic of the Lord of Israel.[39]

Again, the intercessor appeals to various aspects of the Lord's character and nature as a motivating factor to evoke a positive response. This is most explicit in Num 14:13-19, where Moses quotes the familiar confessional or liturgical formula:

> The LORD is slow to anger, and abounding in steadfast love, forgiving iniquity and transgression, but by no means clearing the guilty, visiting the iniquity of the parents upon the children to the third and fourth generation. Forgive the iniquity of this people *according to the greatness of your steadfast love.*

As Abraham had appealed to the justice and righteousness of the Lord as a basis for forgiveness, so Moses now appeals to the steadfast love of God to elicit the same response. In this same prayer, Moses finishes the petition cited above by referring to the fact that God has "pardoned this people from Egypt even until now" (v. 19). The story of repeated rebellion and persistent prayer is also one of continuing pardon. That must be kept in mind when one encounters instances where God resists the prayer and brings judgment (Exod 32:33-34; see below).

The appeal touches also on other factors. Moses pleads for the forgiveness of the people on the grounds of the longstanding relationship between this people and their God. He reminds God of the promise or oath to the ancestors, Abraham, Isaac, and Jacob/Israel, to multiply their descendants and give to them a land and a home, knowing that God's faithfulness will not allow a breaking of the divine oath.[40] Moses also recalls God's special election of this people, with references to "your people" (Exod 32:11-12) and "the people who are your very own possession."[41] Again the prayer of intercession assumes that God's faithfulness and purpose will overcome the will to judgment, that the order of divine purpose is tilted by those realities. There is an assumption here that in the undescribed but clearly assumed struggle within the heart and mind of God the love and faithfulness of God toward this people control the justice and judgment sufficiently that they may be appealed to as a basis for counteracting the move to judgment and punishment. The same is true of the appeal to God's redemptive work and purpose in Israel.[42] It is as if Moses says to the Lord, "Do not bring to nothing the work you have already done in this people. Do not nullify your deeds of loving-kindness and redemption." Once more, the servant of the Lord who stands before a wicked people in prayer is daring and willing not only to "take it to the Lord in prayer" but to do so with a vigor and audacity that are sometimes surprising when viewed in the light of our assumptions about the humility of prayer, a humility that is in fact also present in the stance of those who speak to God in behalf of a people whose case before the Lord is not very strong.

As in many prayers for help, Moses' pleas for the people contain an appeal to the reputation of the Lord's power and purpose in the world, an appeal that, except for the communal prayers for help in the Psalter, is more pronounced in these prayers than anywhere else in the Bible:

> Now if you kill this people all at one time, then the nations who have heard about you will say, "It is because the LORD was not able to bring this people into the land he swore to give them that he has slaughtered them in the wilderness." (Num 14:15-16)

> Otherwise the land from which you have brought us might say, "Because the LORD was not able to bring them into the land that he promised them..." (Deut 9:28)

> Why should the Egyptians say, "It was with evil intent that he brought them out to kill them in the mountains, and to consume them from the face of the earth"? (Exod 32:12)

In such appeals, one hears an implicit, but no less clear call for the vindication of God's power and purpose, a claim that the divine judgment would be seen by others as a reflection of God's inability to do what God wills or a terrible misunderstanding of what the exodus was all about.

In the light of the discussion to this point, there are three other matters to note in Moses' prayers of intercession. One is the way in which he and Aaron, in the prayer for the people who supported Korah's rebellion, reverse the "mathematics" of Abraham's plea while appealing to the same sense of divine justice that Abraham invoked:

> Shall one person sin and you become angry with the whole congregation? (Num 16:22)

If the innocent few can be a means by which God's judgment can be stopped, then how much more an appeal to the innocent many. That the people are not that innocent—see verse 19—simply underscores how far Moses is willing to go in appealing to the Lord, even to stretching the facts if doing so will touch a divine nerve.

The second point is apparent in what has just been said, and that is the similarity to Abraham in the daring and persistent manner in which Moses carries on an intercessory dialogue with God. In his case, the dialogue is carried on over a long period of time, and all of these prayers need to be looked at together as an ongoing intercession of a leader for a people who continually rebel and disobey. The theological significance of this ongoing dialogue has been stated aptly in the following words:

[T]his text reveals *an amazing picture of God,* a God who enters into genuine dialogue with chosen leaders and takes their contribution to the discussion with utmost seriousness. It is a God who works at the level of possibility, but it is not a God who is indecisive or vacillating, filled with uncertainties. It is a God who chooses not to act alone in such matters for the sake of the integrity of relationships established. God chooses to share the decision-making process with the human partner, in the interests of honoring the relationship with Moses and a final determination that is the best for as many as possible. This is a God who remains genuinely open to the future for an extended period of time. . . .

We do not know what God would have done if Moses had not entered into the discussion as he did. But the picture that finally emerges from this chapter is that Moses is responsible for shaping a future other than what would have been the case had he been passive and kept silent. This text lifts up the extraordinary importance of human speaking and acting in the shaping of the future. Simply to leave the future in the hands of God is something other than what God desires. Simply to leave the future in the hands of the people is not a divine desire either. That leaves chosen leaders in an uncomfortable position—between God and people, but to such they are called.[43]

Finally, the line between this early servant of the Lord who interceded again and again for a transgressing people and the later and future unidentified servant of the Lord who did so also with equal success (Isa 52:13—53:12) is even sharper if one looks at Moses' prayer in Exod 32:31-32. For there Moses offers himself "to make atonement for your sin." So, in his prayer, he asks the Lord for forgiveness for the people, "but if not, blot me out of the book that you have written against me." God's way in this instance is not as it comes to be in Isaiah 53. Moses cannot stand in their place. But his intercessory role anticipates that of the suffering servant in opening the possibility that such intercession, such standing before the Lord in behalf of the people, may involve more than prayer. It may end in a taking of the place of those upon whom the divine judgment is sure to come. That such a possibility opens up in the biblical portrayal of Moses is indicated also in Deuteronomy where, three times, Moses tells the people that his inability to go with them into the promised land is because "the LORD was angry with me *on your account.*"[44] A model of intercession that requires more than prayer, indeed the very offering of self in behalf of others, begins to take shape in the prayers of Moses. It breaks forth ever stronger in the figures of Jeremiah and Ezekiel and reaches its sharpest profile in the suffering servant. The New Testament claims that such intercession reaches its fullest expression in the person and work of Jesus Christ.

Amos 7:1-6

The intercession of Amos is a brief moment in the prophetic activity ascribed to him. It stands outside the various oracles of judgment and somewhat at odds with them. That is, the voice of doom that echoes so relentlessly in the book is turned into a voice of pleading. The "outsider" from the south who goes north at the command of God to announce judgment upon the people there is found praying for them with an anguish that bespeaks one who fears his own folk are threatened rather than a foreign country with which he has no connections. But this is one of those servants of the Lord whose place as one called to speak the word of the Lord does not mean he cannot speak the word of the people to the Lord, even when they do not know the word they need. On the contrary, there seems to be something in that prophetic burden that calls forth a word in behalf of a people too blind to know their danger and their need, too confident and secure in their human accomplishments and achievements, and especially their prosperity and well-being, to perceive the Damoclean sword suspended so precariously above their heads.

So the one who speaks the word of judgment to the people who are not his own speaks first a word in their behalf. Two visions of judgment are given to Amos. The first is of a locust plague consuming the fertile growth of the field, the second of a judgment or rain of fire[45] that was devouring the sea and eating up the land. The meaning of these visions is transparent to the prophet. They are words of judgment. His response in each instance is immediate and succinct: an address ("O Lord GOD"), a simple, one-word petition, and a brief single reason or motivation. The petition at first is "Forgive!" and then, as if that is too much to ask a second time, simply "Cease!" The point of the prayer is unmistakable. It is once more a plea to God to lift up and pardon the sin of the people or, if that is really too much, then at least to hold back the judgment, a divine decision that would carry an implicit pardon. Amos thus stands in the line of Abraham, Moses, and the other representative figures who dared to interpose themselves between the people and the Lord's decision to punish. God's intention and its appropriateness are undeniable in each case. But it is precisely *God's* representative or servant who risks a resistance to that intention with all its justice.

The ground for such a plea, as we have noted earlier, is subtle but clear. "How can Jacob stand? He is so small." The prophet knows the nature of this God who has called him. The one whose power is everywhere apparent is prone to act in behalf, not of the powerful, but of the weak. Identifying Jacob among the insignificant and weak is to draw God's positive attention because the story of Israel and the lesson of its torah are that there is a special place in the heart and will of God for the weak ones of the community. If in the eyes of God—if certainly not in their own eyes—they can be seen to be small and insignificant, then the powerful God of the powerless may look down in mercy and protect rather than destroy them. Such is the implicit but no less clear logic of Amos's appeal. And it works—at least for a time.

THE OUTCOME OF INTERCESSION

What happens when intercession in behalf of others takes place? Do such prayers have any effect? We begin to answer those questions with a caveat regarding the emphasis we have placed on the audacity of these intercessors who push and press the deity, even in the face of the divine wrath that could consume the intercessor together with the people. We have suggested also that there seems to be a sense in which such intercession belongs to the burden of being the servant of the Lord, of taking up the responsibility of representing God to the people. Whatever audacity may seem to be expressed, however, in the way these figures come before the deity in prayer, there is a countering *expectation* on the part of God that they will in fact stand forth in behalf of the people and against the anger of God's judgment. It has to do with what was noted above about the intention of God to act in the light of the dialogue that intercessory prayer establishes, expecting to take account of the human partner in the conversation and what he or she has to say in behalf of those who have sinned.

The encounter of Abraham with Abimelech of Gerar concludes with an account of a prayer of intercession of Abraham for Abimelech, his wife, and his female slaves:

> Then Abraham prayed to God; and God healed Abimelech, and also healed his wife and female slaves so that they bore children. For the LORD had closed fast all the wombs of the house of Abimelech because of Sarah, Abraham's wife. (Gen 20:17-18)

This intercession happens, however, because God told Abimelech to ask Abraham to pray for him: "Return the man's wife; for he is a prophet, and he will pray for you and you shall live." (v. 7). It is God who has come to Abimelech to tell him of his unwitting sin and God who has shut the wombs of the women. But he requires the intercession of his prophet Abraham to bring about the healing of Abimelech and the fertility of the women. The intercession of God's prophet is a part of the divine activity to forgive and heal.

We have noted Moses' powerful intercession in Exod 32:11-13. Prior to this prayer, the Lord has anticipated Moses' intervention and its capacity to effect the outcome, the divine decision. For God says to Moses: "I have seen this people, how stiff-necked they are. *Now let me alone* so that my wrath may burn hot against them and I may consume them; and of you I will make a great nation" (Exod 32:9-10). Precisely because of the divine expectation that the servant-leader Moses will intercede and that God will take account of it, God seeks to put Moses off. This time God does not want to be affected by such intercessions. The intercessory prayer initiates a true dialogue that has the capacity to affect the divine intention, as the response to the prayer in verse 14 makes very clear (see below).

A similar divine resistance to intercession occurs in the three similar texts from Jeremiah cited at the beginning of this chapter (Jer 7:16; 11:14; 14:11). The conversation there between God and the prophet suggests that God expects to be affected by the intercession of Jeremiah and staves it off before it can come. This is a time of judgment, and God has no intention of holding back. Because the divine activity is indeed responsive to and incorporates the intercession, God does not allow the prophet to move in that direction.

The point being made with reference to these several texts becomes explicit when we come to Ezekiel. In Ezek 22:23-31, the Lord recounts at length the sins of the leaders of the people. These include the political leaders and officials and the religious leaders, that is, the priests and prophets, as well as the "people of the land," or landowners. At the conclusion of this broad and vigorous condemnation, God says:

> And I sought for anyone among them who would repair the wall and stand in the breach before me on behalf of the land, so that I would not destroy it; but I found no one. Therefore I have poured out my indignation upon them; I have consumed them with the fire of my wrath; I have returned their conduct upon their heads, says the Lord GOD. (vv. 30-31)

The meaning is clear. It is at the heart of the dialogical character of these intercessory prayers. God *expects* a prophetic voice to stand forth and plead for the people.[46] There is a divine openness to the intercession of "his servants the prophets" and an expectation that that intercession will have impact, will help to shape the future, will affect the divine decision. If such intercession seems at times audacious from a human point of view—as these mediators press the deity again and again not to bring judgment—from God's point of view it is just what is expected. Nor is that expectation perfunctory, as if such intercession were merely a duty but not of any significance. To the extent that we may take our clues from Ezekiel, it is the one thing that can change

things, or at least change God's mind. The will to justice that is so prevalent in the prophetic announcements of God's judgment is malleable and
self-consciously vulnerable to the pleas of human representatives. Those
pleas are what can alter the future, at least as far as God is concerned: "I
sought for anyone among them who would . . . stand in the breach before
me on behalf of the land, *so that I would not destroy it.*"

Such words go far to account for the outcome of the prayers of
Moses and Amos and take us directly into the matter of whether or not
prayer changes things. From the biblical perspective, that is not quite
the way to put the issue. One would not make the general statement
that prayer changes things. For one of the things that prayers for help
depend upon in the biblical story is the consistency of the nature and
character of God. Those who pray seek a change in the present situation because God's faithfulness can be counted upon, which means that
God will be present and will help. The one place where there is explicit
reference to "change" is right at the point of these intercessory prayers,
and it is not a matter of generally changing things but of changing God's
mind. If one asks that question (i.e., Can God's mind be changed?), then
these prayers and the contexts in which they take place answer a firm
and repeated yes. Prayer can change God's mind. The words of the Lord
in Ezek 22:30-31 indicate God expects that to be the case, and the narrative contexts of several of the intercessory prayers state quite explicitly
that "the LORD changed his mind"[47] or "the LORD relented concerning
this and said, 'It shall not be.' "[48]

So the notion of prayer actually affecting God and effecting change is
very much there in the accounts of prayer in the Bible, but it is confined
to the intercessory prayer. More specifically, the Lord's relenting or not
relenting, God's changing of mind or not changing it, is in relation to
acts of punishment or judgment, not to acts in general. At least, where
there is explicit indication that the Lord's mind was or could be changed,
it is either because the people have changed or could change their ways[49]
or because one of God's servants has interceded to avert the divine wrath
when the community has sinned.[50] One begins to understand Samuel's
words to the people:

> [F]ar be it from me that I should sin against the LORD by ceasing
> to pray for you. (1 Sam 12:23)

The intercession of the servant-representative is so crucial to the divine decision and action when the community has sinned that failure
to pray for the community would itself be a sin on the part of the
prophet-servant.

It is no accident that on three occasions where the Lord "relents"
and has a change of mind, there is explicit reference to the confessional
formula of Exod 34:6-7, so often encountered as a ground of appeal

to God. Jonah's anger at the Lord is because God has acted toward Nineveh precisely according to that ancient characterization:

> [F]or I knew that you are a gracious God and merciful, slow to anger, and abounding in steadfast love, and *ready to relent [nḥm] from punishing.* (Jonah 4:2; cf. 3:9-10)

The call to repentance and the hope of God's "relenting" and withholding judgment in Joel 2:12-14 are rooted in the same understanding of God's nature that so frustrated Jonah:

> Return to the LORD, your God,
>   for he is gracious and merciful,
> slow to anger, and abounding in steadfast love,
>   and relents [*nḥm*] from punishing.
> Who knows whether he will not turn and relent...?
> (vv. 13b-14a)

And Moses' prayer of intercession in Num 14:13-19, seeking God's forgiveness instead of the announced intention to "strike them with pestilence and disinherit them," achieves that divine forgiveness as it quotes Exod 34:6-7, or the tradition that produced it, in detail. In other words, the changing of God's mind is rooted in the character of God. What seems to be a change, and in a fundamental way is that, is also a shift that is fully consistent with who and what God has chosen to be and the way God has demonstrated throughout the biblical story.

Perhaps what is going on in all these intercessions can be indicated best by the following quotation:

> [T]he Scriptures persistently testify that the heart of God is moved by the importuning prayers of chosen servants and that a dimension of the divine consistency is precisely the continuing inclination of God toward a merciful dealing with humankind, and especially those who are God's people. What is clear from the motivating appeals of Moses is that the prayer is not for an arbitrary or inconsistent action on God's part. It is a prayer for the divine will and purpose as it has been manifested over and over again—a faithful, redemptive, forgiving purpose grounded in perduring relationships and constantly being vindicated before the public audience of peoples and nations. The prayer, with all its appeals and as it pushes God, is precisely in tune with who God is and how God acts. It anticipates later prayers in behalf of a sinful humanity ("Father, forgive them...""—Luke 23:24) and the hearkening response of God that will withhold appropriate judgment in favor of mercy, yea, even take the judgment for the sake of mercy ("Truly this was the Son of God!"—Matt 27:54).[51]

It would be a mistake to assume that intercession by God's representative figure always leads to pardon and forgiveness. Things are not that simple in the biblical story, much less in the mind and purpose of God. That story reveals a complex interaction of mercy and judgment shaped by prayer that may be seen in *particular moments,* such as Abraham's intercession for Sodom and Gomorrah—a sure testimony to the complexity of that interaction—or in *more extended periods,* such as the numerous prayers of intercession of Moses during the wandering of the people in the wilderness and the two prayers of Amos that must be viewed in relation to the following vision reports where there is no intercession and no changing of the mind of God. In that connection, one notes also God's explicit indication, several times in Jeremiah (and contrary to what we have seen in Ezek 22:30 and 1 Sam 12:23), that intercession will not be heard and is not to be allowed. If there is testimony to God's relenting, there is also indication of occasions when that did not happen.[52] And in Jeremiah, God speaks of being weary of relenting (Jer 15:6) and unmoved even if Moses or Samuel were to intercede (v. 1).

These words of judgment resistant or even opposed to intercession for mercy are not the primary note that is sounded. As the stories of the wilderness wandering and the vision reports of Amos reveal, there can be a continuing divine relenting in the face of the sin of the people that finally runs its course. So Amos eventually ceases to pray, but only after praying again and again and hearing again and again God's acceptance of the prayer, declaring that the judgment shall not be. The ancient confessional formula speaks not only of God being "slow to anger and abounding in steadfast love, forgiving iniquity and transgression," but also of a justice that will "by no means clear the guilty."[53] As the people wander through the wilderness, their repeated rebellions evoke the fervent and pushy prayers of Moses again and again. And he himself testifies that the Lord has "pardoned this people *from Egypt even until now*" (Num 14:19). On that occasion pardon comes again. But as judgment is tempered over and over again with mercy, so it is also true that mercy is stiffened by judgment when persistent disobedience erodes the possibility of forgiveness. So in Exod 32:31-34, the sin of the people does not lead to a destruction as God had planned, but the generation that rebelled and disobeyed over and over is not allowed to enter the land. Failure to take account of the interaction of mercy *and judgment* woven into the story of these prayers would be equal to ignoring the same interaction in the crucifixion of Jesus, a strange but inescapable revelation of the mercy *and judgment* of God.

CONCLUSION

The responsiveness of God to human intercession suggests an openness within the nature and work of God that raises some problems for our theological conceptuality but is consistently what we encounter in the Scriptures, that is, that God is not a way of speaking about a determined or deterministic universe where everything is forever fixed. While reality is a whole, and the nexus of cause and effect is not something that one can claim for a while and then let go willy-nilly, intercessory prayer, as we find it in the Bible, suggests there is some freedom and openness within God's providence, which is nevertheless reliable and not capricious. Indeed, that is demonstrated by what we find with intercessory prayer in that it seems to have its effect on God as it makes its petitions consistent with the nature and activity of God.

The freedom of God is unlimited except by the presence of what and whom God has created; that is, there is a self-limiting dimension in God brought about by God's creative activity. God responds to human activity in countless ways, often in overcoming human resistance to God's purpose and work. What the human creature does is taken and incorporated into what God is doing even if that incorporation involves a resistance to, a denial of, or an overcoming of what humanity does. But that taking of human words and deeds can also be an incorporation of what the human creature does faithfully. We speak of participating in the work of God, so that in some fashion the work of God is mediated through human creatures. That participation can also take the form of prayer, so that God incorporates human prayers into the dynamic, nonstatic, purposive divine activity.

That may mean that at times it appears as if prayer is changing God's mind. As we have seen, the biblical prayers do just that, according to the story. But if there is a responsiveness, what happens is within the larger purposes of God, and the prayers of the leaders, the servants, and also of the people are part of the stuff with which God shapes the future. Nowhere is it more apparent than in these prayers of intercession that prayer is a genuine dialogue and makes a difference.

9

"The Lord Bless You"

BLESSING AND CURSE

๛

We now come to two kinds of prayers that are obviously related but also exist in a kind of tension, certainly for the contemporary community of faith. The blessing as a prayer is one of the most familiar and easiest of prayers to comprehend. There are many persons for whom public prayer is not an easy matter, and perhaps never done, but who may say "God bless you" to a departing family member with relative ease. In like manner, the blessing that comes at the close of virtually every occasion of public worship, the benediction, while not said by everyone, is familiar to all who have participated in worship services with any regularity in their lifetime.

Curse, on the other hand, is not only generally unfamiliar to the contemporary religious community as a prayer; it also seems to have no legitimate place in its life of prayer. No religious community engages in any kind of frequent or regular prayer for God to bring harm or trouble to others. And most persons would reject such prayer on any occasion. A curse prayer is theologically unacceptable and psychologically nearly impossible to utter—except under certain occasions, which may be a clue to what is going on in such prayers. They do occur in Scripture, however, and so need some attention in this context. They also have an obvious relation to blessing in that blessing is a prayer for good or well-being while curse is a prayer for evil or trouble. But blessing and curse are not simply two sides of the same coin. The larger place of blessing in biblical and contemporary prayer requires a primary focus upon it before asking about curse and its place or possibility in prayer.

THE OCCASIONS OF BLESSING

A significant clue to what blessing is all about is the fact that most of the prayers of blessing in Scripture take place in the context of the *family,* including clan and tribe, and its ongoing life within the community of which it is a part. Blessings are spoken at times of parting when members of the family separate or go forth on a journey. So Isaac blesses Jacob when he sends him to Paddan-aram, and Naomi blesses her daughters-in-law when she seeks to send them back to their "mother's house."[1] Jonathan blesses David when they are about to separate for good (1 Sam 20:13). The parting that takes place at the end of a life also evokes blessing within the family, as we see in Isaac's blessing of Jacob and Esau, Jacob's blessing of Joseph and his sons, and the long blessings of the tribes by Jacob and Moses.[2] In this context, that is, the leave-taking within the family or clan circle, the blessing prayer could be a simple prayer for the Lord's presence with the one who leaves—"May the LORD be with you,"[3] a prayer that was appropriate, of course, on any occasion and reflected that definition of the primary human need identified in the oracles of salvation: I am with you. Such blessings often had to do with the ongoing welfare of the one on whom the blessing was pronounced or for whom the blessing was invoked. We see this in both of Isaac's blessings of Jacob, the one that he places upon his son because of his old age and impending death and the blessing as Jacob leaves home:

> May God give you of the dew of heaven,
>   and of the fatness of the earth,
> and plenty of grain and wine. (Gen 27:28)

May [God Almighty] give to you the blessing of Abraham, to you and to your offspring with you, so that you may take possession of the land where you now live as an alien. (Gen 28:3)

The prayer for blessing often has to do with the growth and continuity of the family represented in the ones who go off on a journey or are the bearers of the family name and heritage in the next generation(s):

> May you, our sister, become
>   thousands of myriads;
> may your offspring gain possession
>   of the gates of their foes. (Gen 24:60)

May God Almighty bless you and make you fruitful and numerous, that you may become a company of people. (Gen 28:3)

Now therefore may it please you to bless the house of your servant, so that it may continue forever before you. (2 Sam 7:29)

God's protection during the time of absence and separation may be the point of the blessing prayer:

The LORD watch between you and me, when we are absent one from the other. (Gen 31:49)

The blessing of the father in old age has much to do with insuring both the continuity and the well-being and prosperity of the family. It is also a way of shaping and directing the future in terms of family relations, seeking to create a particular order of relationships, especially among brothers, among whom the leadership and prosperity of the family are worked out.[4] Those about to be married receive blessings to secure for the couple a good future and especially children.[5]

Within the family, blessing is most often pronounced or prayed by family heads,[6] though it is not an act reserved to them or even only to males. There are blessings spoken by mothers and brothers upon their sons and daughters.[7] Generally family blessings are placed upon males or sons as prospective family heads responsible in a crucial way for the family's welfare. Those blessings invoked upon women usually have to do primarily with their fertility and the generational continuity that mothers provide for the family.[8]

One should not presume that blessing is only a family matter or restricted to certain persons. The ordinary give-and-take of a day's activities and encounters with other people could lead to blessings uttered by anyone. That is beautifully illustrated when Boaz is seen walking among the reapers in the fields and they greet each other:

Just then Boaz came from Bethlehem. He said to the reapers, "The LORD be with you." They answered, "The LORD bless you." Then Boaz said to his reapers... (Ruth 2:4-5; cf. 1 Sam 15:13)

The public worship of the community is also an occasion for blessing, though in this instance it is a blessing placed upon the community as a whole and not simply upon individuals or family groups.[9] We shall look at this setting for blessing more closely in taking up the Aaronic benediction below.

PRAYER OR MAGIC?

More than with any other dimension of prayer, the blessing takes us into the question of the power of words to affect and effect reality. While that issue arises with regard to other forms of prayer, the change in reality effected by such prayers is as God responds to them and changes what had previously been the divine intention. Much prayer is designed in some sense to touch the heart of God and bring about a response that will affect the way things are. But in the case of blessing, some instances seem to reflect a kind of power to shape the future in the very speaking of the words. Is it prayer or is it magic? We may not be able to give a simple answer to that question. But the effort to do so takes us more deeply into the *form and theology of blessing.*

The majority of recorded blessings are examples of prayer in what is sometimes called a prayer-wish form.[10] That is, they are often—not always—addressed to a human being in the second person and God is spoken of in the third person [jussive forms], for example, "May the LORD, the God of your ancestors, increase you a thousand times more" and "May [the LORD] bless you," which are blessings that Moses says over the tribes as they are about to enter the promised land (Deut 1:11), or "May the LORD be with you," Jonathan's parting blessing to David (1 Sam 20:13). The verbal forms in Hebrew are usually jussive, expressing the wish notion, "May [or Let] such and such happen/be so."[11] The blessing may not refer explicitly to the deity, as is the case, for example, in the blessing of Rebekah's mother and brother when she leaves home to become Isaac's wife (Gen 24:60). Most often it does, however, and when that is not the case, Yahweh as the source of the blessing may be assumed.

The possibility that the very speaking of the words of blessing has some power in it apart from the activity of God in responding to the prayer-wish is indicated less from the form of the blessing itself and more from the context in some instances. These are virtually all blessings of the patriarch upon the next generation. The familiar story of Isaac's blessing of Jacob and Esau is a good example. Here is a form of ritual occurring near death when the father, before he dies, passes on to the son the power of life so that the next generation may live and thrive. The story suggests that there is only one blessing, that it cannot be taken back or annulled, that it really will give Jacob something that Esau cannot have. While the blessing bestowed upon Jacob is a prayer-wish for God's blessing, in the narrative describing this act there is nothing theological, only the report of Isaac's violent trembling when he learns that it was Jacob he blessed and not Esau. He exclaims: "Who was it then that hunted game and brought it to me, and I ate it all before you came, and I have blessed him?—*and blessed he shall be!*"[12] Esau manages eventually to get another blessing from Isaac. In the words of that blessing there is no reference to God at all. Esau believes that the power for life in its abundance that Isaac could bestow has in fact gone to Jacob, and he hates him. In the narrative context of the story, therefore, and in the Esau blessing, there is no sense of prayer or of God at work. There is a sense of some power that the father has to bestow upon a son that takes effect in a way outside human control but not necessarily as a divine activity.

What do we make of this incident and other such stories of patriarchal blessings that seem to be a kind of magical control of the future apart from God's initiative? Several things may be suggested.[13] The first is that we are dealing here with the oldest concept of blessing, a notion of blessing in which it is understood as an effective power let loose in the act of blessing, whatever the words may contain. The tradition preserves that.

That story, however, and others like it in the tradition of the mothers and fathers of Israel, what we customarily call the patriarchal stories, have now been placed in the context of and in the service of the larger story of *God's* way of blessing. That larger story is especially the theme of the Yahwist's account of Israel's beginning. It provides the theological foundation for understanding the notion of blessing and the prayer for blessing. All the particular older stories of family blessing in Genesis, which is where we encounter this more magical notion of a blessing power, are pieces now in the warp and woof of the story that the Yahwist weaves.[14] From the pieces and the whole we learn about the substance and theology of blessing.

The Yahwist's story of God's blessing begins with the call of Abraham.[15] In the book of Genesis, it identifies the way that God is going to work out the problem of sin and judgment or curse that arises as the human condition in Genesis 1–11. The Yahwist tells that story in what is, in effect, a kind of sermon that lays a claim on the people and addresses them in their later history. The basic point of this long sermon is that through Abraham's faithful obedience to the divine command to go forth to the land that God will show him, his posterity shall be blessed (Gen 12:2-3a) and he and his seed shall be the means by which all the families of the earth find blessing (v. 3b).[16] The way out of the *curse* that came upon humankind because of its varied sin and wickedness— as described in the Yahwist's history of beginnings in Genesis 1–11—is through God's *blessing*. The universality of the curse shall be replaced by the universality of the blessing. As the human creature brought divine curse, so that same creature, in the form of Abraham and his people, shall bring divine blessing. This promise of universal blessing through Abraham is thematic in the Yahwist's narrative.[17] It is the fundamental point of that particular pentateuchal stratum.

The character of that blessing and how it shall be manifest in the life of this family and the larger community are then illustrated in the stories of Abraham and his descendants in the rest of Genesis. The "families of the earth are to be found" among the peoples Abraham and his seed encounter, some of whom are seen as kinfolk, for example, the Moabites and Ammonites (Abraham's nephew Lot)[18] and the Aramaeans (Jacob's uncle Laban).[19] The interaction of Abraham and his descendants with the other peoples is told in the Genesis stories and demonstrates the working out of the divine blessing through Abraham's family. So the promise of universal blessing through Abraham is mentioned in the story of Abraham's intercession for Sodom and Gomorrah, "the cradle of the Moabites and Ammonites." While it did not succeed in this instance, Abraham's intercession, which opens up both divine forgiveness and God's willingness not to destroy one of "the nations of the earth" (Gen 18:18b), illustrates one of the ways that this family can bring blessing to other peoples. In Genesis 26, the promise of blessing to the nations through Abraham appears again (v. 4). Here Isaac encounters the Philistines and demonstrates the way of blessing by being willing to deal with the Philistines peacefully rather than belligerently when they take his wells. He is recognized by the Philistine king Abimelech as blessed by God, and the two establish a covenant to live together in peace (v. 31).[20] Jacob, too, is given the promise of blessing for himself and through him and his seed for "all the families of the earth" (Gen 28:14). That promise comes, significantly, just prior to his stay with his Aramaean uncle Laban. For his stay there becomes the means by which Laban (the Aramaeans) increases his wealth. Laban states that quite directly and Jacob confirms it:

> But Laban said to him, "If you will allow me to say so, I have learned by divination that the LORD has blessed me because of you; name your wages, and I will give it." Jacob said to him, "You yourself know how I have served you, and how your cattle have fared with me. For you had little before I came, and it has increased abundantly; and the LORD has blessed you wherever I turned." (Gen 30:27-30a)

Hans Walter Wolff summarizes the way the divine blessing is wrought out in these stories—stories that are meant to demonstrate the role(s) that Israel is to play later among the nations—as follows:

> [T]he Yahwist expounds his kerygma through the patriarchal narrative. He deals with "all the families of the earth" using as examples the Moabites, Ammonites, Philistines, and Arameans. How are they to find blessing *in Israel?* By Israel's intercession with Yahweh on the example of Abraham; by readiness for peaceful agreement on the pattern of Isaac; by economic aid on the model of Jacob. Yahweh created the prerequisite by fulfilling the promise of increase and expansion. In what way is *blessing* found through all this? Blessing is found in annulment of guilt or punishment, in community life without strife, in effective material aid.[21]

As one continues to read in the Yahwist's "sermon," the same message unfolds. Joseph brings the Lord's blessing, in terms of prosperity, upon Potiphar's house when he serves as overseer of it (Gen 39:5). Eventually he brings blessing, manifest in the preservation of life, upon all Egypt, one of the "nations of the earth," as well as upon his brothers and their families, that is, upon Israel. In the exodus from Egypt, the possibility of blessing through Abraham's descendants, even upon this oppressor nation, is indicated as Pharaoh asks Moses to effect the blessing for him that he and the Hebrews have obviously received from the Lord (Exod 12:31-32).[22]

Throughout the whole story, with all its varying episodes and the different ways the Abrahamic family encounters different nations of the earth, we gain an understanding of both the substance of divine blessing and the way that this people is to effect that blessing. Its content is found in the blessing of fertility and growth in the family, as well as in the flocks and herds whose multiplying brings prosperity to the family as it grows. Land and a place to live in peace and to prosper are a part of God's blessing. Peaceful existence, in well-being and without threat and hostility, comprises God's blessing. Health and long life are not lifted up in the stories looked at above, but they, too, manifest the divine blessing. Preservation of life and provision for its continuity, in good times and in bad, are part of God's blessing of human existence, for the Abrahamic seed and for the nations of the earth.

This look at the substance of God's blessing as that is demonstrated in the story the Yahwist tells in the Pentateuch is the context for thinking once more about the power of the father's blessing in the narratives of the ancestors. We noted that is especially indicated in the story of Isaac's blessing of Jacob, which cannot be duplicated for Esau. The older notion of blessing as effective power is present in the narrative, and as such we seem to be closer to a magical notion of words than in other blessings where the character of blessing as prayer-wish is more evident. But we need to keep in mind that even this sort of "accomplishing speech" is not uncommon in other spheres. There is a kind of performative and declarative speech in which the speaking of the words brings something into effect. In contemporary life we experience this, for example, in such things as the declaration of marriage in a wedding ceremony. The declaration itself makes legal and real the marriage of the couple. In the Old Testament, the various Deuteronomic statements of the Lord, "I am hereby granting/giving you the land which I swore to your fathers to give to you," are a kind of declarative or performative speech that hands the land over to the people and gives it a religio-legal claim upon the land. The notion of effective power in blessing is not far from this kind of performative speech.

Even more important, however, in the case of Isaac's blessing of Esau and Jacob is the way in which the older form or notion of blessing has been incorporated into the Yahwist's history of blessing and thus made a part of the activity of God to effect blessing among the nations. That happens in four ways:

1. The most obvious indicator that this old blessing is not simply a

magical pronouncement apart from God's control is the explicitly theological character of the blessing itself. That is apparent in an indirect way in Isaac's words about Jacob smelling like a field "that the LORD has blessed" (Gen 27:27b). But it is quite directly set forth in the first part of the blessing with the words, "May God give you of the dew of heaven" (v. 28). The jussive prayer-wish form is present in the verb, "may he give" (*wĕyittēn*). Isaac's words are, in fact, a prayer for God's blessing upon Jacob. They are not simply human words that take effect on their own.

2. The final part of Isaac's blessing of Jacob is:

> Cursed be everyone who curses you,
> and blessed be everyone who blesses you!
> (Gen 27:29b)

This is a formula that appears first in a slightly different form in the call of Abraham as a part of the promise to bless Abraham and to effect blessing through him. In both cases, it is blessing for the recipient, Abraham/Jacob, and also indicates that blessing shall come upon others as they come into relation with Abraham/Jacob. The formula also opens up the possibility of curse (or judgment, as we see from the use of curse in Genesis 1–11) for the one who curses or seeks ill for the one who is given this blessing. The use of the formula in Abraham's call, however, which is programmatic and definitive, makes the blessing and cursing/judging that others receive vis-à-vis Abraham clearly a *divine* activity: "I will bless," "I will curse" (Gen 12:3a). One may infer, therefore, that the blessing of Isaac upon Jacob, which lacks the explicit reference to divine agency, assumes it and is controlled by the way the blessing is worked out in the whole story. Confirmation of that is found in the other use of this formula in Num 24:9b. It occurs as a part of the oracle of Balaam and is identical in form to Gen 27:29b except that the blessing is placed before the curse:

> Blessed is everyone who blesses you,
> and cursed is everyone who curses you.

What is significant for our purposes in this final occurrence of the formula is that the context of its use in the oracle is explicitly the divine blessing (vv. 4, 8) and that the introduction to Balaam's words tells us that Balaam saw that the Lord was going to bless Israel and that his oracle is a result of the coming of the spirit of the Lord upon him. Once more, therefore, the formula is a vehicle for God's blessing/curse upon those who come into relation with Israel, depending upon how they respond to or treat the chosen people.

3. A further way in which Isaac's blessing of Jacob participates in the

Yahwist's sermon about God's blessing upon the nations through Israel is as it makes explicit reference to those peoples and nations:

> Let peoples serve you,
>   and nations bow down to you.
> Be lord over your brothers,
>   and may your mother's sons bow down to you.
>   (Gen 27:29a)

Nothing is said here about blessing per se, but a structure of relationship between Israel/Jacob and the nations of the earth is given. It is only in the rest of the Yahwist's narrative that one learns that the subservient structure does not mean an oppressive domination of the other peoples, but a relationship that brings blessing upon those who serve or bow down.

4. That the Yahwist has just this in mind comes to the surface in a quite direct way in the report of the encounter between Esau and Jacob at the end of the Jacob cycle. The two brothers meet again after all the years and their separation in hostility, Jacob having "stolen" Esau's blessing (Genesis 33). In direct contrast to the presumably effective blessing, it is Jacob who bows down to his brother and not the reverse (v. 3). And the conversation that takes place between the two brothers is almost entirely about the blessing that God has showered upon them both. At Esau's query, Jacob identifies the people with him as "the children whom God has graciously given your servant" (v. 5).[23] But when he tries to give his present to Esau, the latter responds, "I have enough, my brother; keep what you have for yourself." Nothing is said about the source of this "enough," but in the context of the story we are to see that Esau has been richly blessed with wealth and family. He even brings four hundred men to meet Jacob (v. 1)! Even so, his encounter with Jacob brings him yet more of the goods of life as blessing. Note the extent of the blessing that Jacob presses upon Esau until he takes it (v. 11):

> [H]e took a present for his brother Esau, two hundred female goats and twenty male goats, two hundred ewes and twenty rams, thirty milch camels and their colts, forty cows and ten bulls, twenty female donkeys and ten male donkeys. (Gen 32:13-15)

To be able to give away such a large gift implies that Jacob is a man of considerable wealth. Together with his large family, this demonstrates the degree that he has been the recipient of God's blessing. But his extravagant gift now enriches Esau yet more. The relation with Esau, who is the ancestor and thus representative of the nation Edom, has been a tricky one, literally. Its ending is one of blessing manifest for both Jacob and Esau, Israel and Edom. The one who seemed closed out of the blessing once it had been given unwittingly by Isaac to Jacob and whose own blessing was both ambiguous and nontheological in its formulation is found at the end to have received blessing in his own life as well as through Jacob's gift at the end of the story.

One may understand the blessings of Jacob upon his sons (Genesis 49) and Moses upon the tribes (Deuteronomy 33) in a manner similar to this analysis of the blessings in Genesis 27. They have to do with the security and well-being of the brothers/tribes, their relations to one another and to others, and fertility of human beings and animals. In one or two cases, they are more negative and thus fall more into the curse category, that is, words of judgment upon a tribe for the sin of its ancestor (Gen 49:3-7). Ronald Clements has characterized these prayers well in his comment on Jacob's blessing of his sons in Genesis 49:

> [T]he prayer of Jacob is truly remarkable, since it begins with a frank and full recognition of the characteristic features of each of Jacob's sons. They are what they are so that, if God is to bless them, it will have to be done in and through the personalities with which each of them is endowed. In this sense, far from Jacob's "blessing" being a typical instance of vagueness in prayer, it is quite the opposite. It is a careful asking of God to make the divine power known in the life of each son, as he really is![24]

In Deuteronomy 33, as Clements notes, the petitions or blessings express a yearning and longing that each of the tribes might come to realize its full potential.[25] Sometimes that is linked to the particular geographical setting of the tribe, as in the case of Zebulun and Issachar, while in the case of Levi, it is its vocation as a priestly tribe that is the focus of the blessing. There is a kind of realism in these blessings that does not see or expect that all of the brothers/tribes will reach their potential or find a fullness of blessing in the same way. In some instances, for example, the blessing of Reuben, the prayer is a modest but important petition that the tribe will at least make it, that it will survive.

RUTH: A STORY OF BLESSING

Two texts, one long and one short, place the prayer(s) of blessing very much at the center of human life and religious life. A close look at them may serve to flesh out the understanding of blessing as prayer that has been laid out above.

The first of these is the book of Ruth. If one reads that short book closely, one will discover people again and again expressing blessings toward one another. They are offered in all sorts of contexts and give us a kind of collection within a single story of most of the possibilities of blessing discussed above.

The story begins with a parting, or, better, with a famous attempted parting, when the Judaean widow, Naomi, decides to return home from temporarily dwelling—ten years or more—in Moab. On the way, she urges her also-widowed Moabite daughters-in-law, Orpah and Ruth, to go back to their own homes in Moab, each of them to her mother's house. At their parting—although only Orpah eventually leaves—Naomi prays a blessing upon them:

> May the LORD deal kindly with you,[26] as you have dealt with the dead and with me. The LORD grant that you may find security, each of you in the house of your husband. (Ruth 1:8-9)

At a time of separation, Naomi commits the lives and futures of her two daughters-in-law to God. The prayers are general, seeking God's kindness or steadfast love and security or rest and comfort for each of them. The specificity of the prayer is implicit in the reference to "the house of your husband." The possibilities for a good and secure life for these women rest in their finding the security and care that come from a married relation. In the social context in which they lived, that was imperative. To live as widow was to place them in the situation of insecurity and threat that made the widow a category, together with the orphan and the poor, on the margins of society. All three of these groups needed special protection because the social structures did not provide it.[27] Here the prayer of Naomi seeks from the Lord just that provision for life that was needed for the two women who would leave her.

Blessing as prayer occurs next in the story of Ruth in the context of meeting and greeting rather than separation and parting. When Boaz encounters his reapers in the field, they exchange blessings that are virtually paradigmatic for this prayer. He says to them, "The LORD be with you." And they answer, "The LORD bless you" (Ruth 2:4). This is not a situation of trouble that would evoke an urgent petition or intercession. These people are carrying on their normal daily lives. But *in the midst of life* as it goes on quite ordinarily, they seek for the other party the continuity of that life and of God's involvement in it. In the oracle of salvation as the basic response of God to those who cried out in trouble, we saw that the fundamental assurance lay in hearing the words, "I am with you." Here that assurance is sought in ordinary life as it is in crisis. In like manner, the reciprocal prayer seeks for Boaz the continued blessing of God, the manifestation of God's good in his life in prosperity, well-being, and security. All of life is placed under God's care in such blessings. As people come together and as they part, their relation is given that context by a prayer of blessing.

The first encounter between Ruth and Boaz results also in blessing, though this is not the blessing of meeting or parting. It is Boaz's specific prayer for Ruth's well-being because of her faithfulness to Naomi:

> May the LORD reward you for your deeds, and may you have a full reward from the LORD, the God of Israel, under whose wings you have come for refuge! (Ruth 2:12)

The prayer is comparable to intercession, as in some sense is true of all blessing. Boaz lifts up in prayer the young woman and seeks God's good for her. There are no specifics to this prayer. It is simply for God to enrich her life. Like Naomi's prayer for Ruth and Orpah,[28] the prayer incorporates a sense that human faithfulness merits God's good. Or more accurately, human faithfulness evokes a *prayer* for the good of the faithful one. That faithfulness of Ruth to her mother-in-law is fundamental to the story. There is a counterpart to it in the prayer of blessing for the faithful one. Such fidelity to relationship evokes on the part of those who receive or witness it a prayer for the well-being of the one who has maintained such human loyalty.

That the narrative is woven in large part around this interplay of faithfulness evoking the prayer for blessing is seen in Ruth 3:10 when Ruth daringly steals up to the sleeping Boaz and lies down at his feet to seek his acting for her as next-of-kin, that is, to assume responsibility for her protection and well-being. His response to this act is similar to his earlier response:

> May you be blessed by the LORD, my daughter; this last instance of your loyalty is better than the first; you have not gone after young men, whether poor or rich.

The "father figure" or next-of-kin invokes blessing upon the woman who has come to him. And her act is seen as a manifestation of loyalty (*ḥesed*), not simply self-interest in seeking a husband, even though that is what Naomi is about in sending Ruth to Boaz at night. Confirmation of that interpretation is found at the end of the story when, after Ruth and Boaz are married and have a child, the women say *to Naomi,* "Blessed be the LORD, who has not left you this day without next-of-kin" (Ruth 4:14). Here we encounter blessing as *thanksgiving,* the other form of blessing we noted in chapter 5. The exclamation of the women is a prayer of thanksgiving to God for having dealt well with Naomi. That has all happened, of course, through Ruth's acts, which have been as much for Naomi's well-being as her own.

The line between blessing as thanksgiving and blessing as petition is sometimes narrow. One can see how the single notion of blessing can bridge these two forms of prayer in Ruth 2:19-20. There we find Naomi's reaction to Ruth's first return from the barley fields with a good supply of the grain:

Her mother-in-law said to her, "Where did you glean today? And where have you worked? Blessed be the man who took notice of you.... Blessed be he by the LORD, whose kindness [*ḥesed*] has not forsaken the living or the dead."

Naomi's words are a blessing prayer like the others we have noted. They invoke God's blessing upon Boaz in the prayer-wish (jussive) form.[29] At the same time the spontaneous blessings are also expressions of gratitude to Boaz not dissimilar from the thanksgivings, "Blessed be the Lord...," that we noted in looking at the forms of thanksgiving prayer. One seeks God's good for the person who has been helpful. So petition and thanksgiving come together in a single expression. The particular form of thanksgiving in this case is not a word directed to the one being thanked but a prayer for God's blessing upon him.

The final blessing of the story of Ruth is found in the words of the people of Bethlehem when they witness the proceedings in the gate or court whereby Boaz claims the property of Elimelech and the hand of Ruth in marriage. The people all say:

> We are witnesses. May the LORD make the woman who is coming into your house like Rachel and Leah, who together built up the house of Israel. May you produce children in Ephrathah and bestow a name in Bethlehem; and, through the children that the LORD will give you by this young woman, may your house be like the house of Perez, whom Tamar bore to Judah. (Ruth 4:11-12)

Here we have a typical prayer of blessing seeking one of the primary manifestations of God's good or God's blessing that could come upon persons in the course of their lives, the provision of children and the building up of the household of a man and woman. The story of Ruth began with her widowhood and the absence of the security or rest that could be found in a "husband's house" (Ruth 1:9). Now the story is over, and she has found that which Naomi's blessing prayer sought for her. The prayer of the people is that Ruth and Boaz may now have a large family, a prayer that is answered in the closing verses of the book.

Ruth is a story of family, of the concerns of widowhood, the possibilities of marriage, the response of the next-of-kin to the straits of a widow and her mother-in-law, a story of kindness (*ḥesed*) among members of a family and of the Lord's kindness (*ḥesed*) to that family. It has to do with the provision of security (Ruth 1:9) and children (Ruth 4:11-12), fundamental concerns of the family and of human life in general. The book ends with the notation that this large family that grew out of the blessing of God in response to the blessing prayers of family and community was the family from which came David.

The Aaronic Benediction as Paradigm of Blessing

While the family and its life as well as the ordinary enterprises of human existence are one of the primary matrices of the blessing prayer, it is not confined to that. Indeed, it is clear that blessing is also sought in the context of worship. On several occasions we encounter blessing prayers in the context of more formal situations of worship. It is reported that when David brought the ark of the covenant to Jerusalem and set it in its place, he offered various kinds of sacrifices and "blessed the people in the name of the LORD" (2 Sam 6:18). At the dedication of the temple, Solomon's long prayer includes blessing, at the beginning and at the end. He blesses the assembly of Israel at the beginning in a prayer of blessing that opens with the words, "Blessed be the LORD," and is a form of thanksgiving. At the end, he blesses the assembly once more with the words, "Blessed be the LORD," but this time the prayer is petition growing out of thanksgiving:

> Blessed be the LORD, who has given rest to his people Israel according to all that he promised; not one word has failed of all his good promise, which he spoke through his servant Moses. *[May] the LORD our God be with us,* as he was with our ancestors; *may he not leave us or abandon us,* but incline our hearts to him, to walk in all his ways, and to keep his commandments, his statutes, and his ordinances, which he commanded our ancestors. *Let these words of mine,* with which I pleaded before the LORD, *be near to the LORD our God* day and night, and *may he maintain the cause* of his servant and the cause of his people Israel, as each day requires; so that all the peoples of the earth may know that the LORD is God; there is no other. (1 Kgs 8:55-60)

Couched very much in Deuteronomistic language, the prayer includes several blessings that center around the prayer for God's presence with the people[30] and God's continuing attention to the prayer of the king to maintain the right of the king and the people whenever they pray. Psalm 118:26 suggests that blessing took place when persons entered the house of the Lord, and several blessings are couched in different psalms.[31]

Particular responsibility for blessing the people in the name of the Lord is given to the priests and Levites. That is a part of the Deuteronomic instruction in Deut 10:8 and 21:5, where the chief functions of the Levites are defined as carrying the ark, serving (*šrt,* that is, conduct of worship), and blessing in the name of Yahweh. Priestly tradition also assigns this blessing responsibility to the priests. At the service of ordination of Aaron and his sons as priests (Leviticus 8–9), when the sacrifices are over and the service ended, Aaron blesses the people and then Moses and Aaron bless them again when the two of them come out of the tent of meeting (Lev 9:22-23).

The clearest and most explicit assignment of the blessing to the priests, however, is in Num 6:22-27, where the Lord instructs Aaron and his sons to bless the Israelites and gives them the words that they are to say.[32] This blessing has had a wide impact in the Bible, as we have noted in earlier chapters. Its language occurs again and again.[33] It also has been found engraved twice on silver amulets from the seventh or sixth century B.C., testimony to its influence and importance in ancient Israel.[34] Furthermore, this ancient blessing has been prayed down through the centuries in Jewish and Christian worship. For all of these reasons, it stands as a kind of model or paradigm of the blessing prayer and so merits a more detailed consideration.

The LORD spoke to Moses, saying: Speak to Aaron and his sons, saying, Thus you shall bless the Israelites: You shall say to them,

> The LORD bless you
>   and keep you;
> the LORD make his face to shine upon you,
>   and be gracious to you;
> the LORD lift up his countenance upon you,
>   and give you peace.

So they shall put my name on the Israelites, and I will bless them.

The blessing proper consists of three poetic lines, generally parallel in form and content. Each has two jussive clauses or petitions of the prayer-wish type, "May the Lord . . ." The first clause is the longer of the two in each case. Yahweh is the implicit subject of the first clause, the implicit subject of the second one. The relationship between the clauses in each verse has been described in various ways. The interpretation of J. L. Mays is most accurate: "The first part of each line invokes God's personal act upon his people. . . . The last part of each line states the reality or content of the blessing invoked."[35] Such relationship can clearly be seen in verses 25 and 26. It is less clear in verse 24. The prayer asking for God to bless in verse 24 is different from and more sweeping than the shining of the face or the lifting of the face. The reason for that difference, however, probably lies in the fact that the initial prayer, "The Lord bless you," is the basic, all-inclusive petition. Not only the following clause, but the following verses also, are an explication or specification of the prayer for blessing. With this clarification of the opening clause, therefore, we may recognize a simple structure: the first clause of each line invoking the Lord's movement toward the people, the second clause, God's activity in their behalf.

Two particular characteristics of the blessing as a whole should be noted. The singular second-person pronouns "you" express the intimate and personal character of the relationship between the Lord and the recipients of the blessing. Furthermore, as *singular* forms in distinction from the third-person *plural* suffixes referring to the people in the framework of the blessing, these pronouns open up the objects of blessing to include or allow for either individual or collective blessings. The blessing is invoked upon the community as a whole and upon each individual that is a part of it.[36]

Even more significant is the thorough-going emphasis on the divine name. "The Lord" is repeated as the subject of each line in the blessing despite the fact that it is not syntactically necessary. The intention is clearly to give emphasis to the fact that it is *the Lord* who dispenses blessing. It is only through the Lord that the blessing may occur. But it may indeed occur there. It is God's doing, which rules out the priest or any other deity as an effective agent. Here there is no sense of a word that is effective in itself apart from the divine agency. Quite the contrary. The emphasis on the Lord as the source of blessing is confirmed in the conclusion (v. 27). In the Hebrew, the subject of the final clause is emphatic: "So shall they put my name on the Israelites, and *I* will bless them." The character of the blessing as a prayer or petition to the Lord is nowhere more evident than in this blessing.[37]

The formal blessing to be pronounced by the priests begins with the basic and comprehensive prayer, "The Lord bless you" (v. 24). As we have seen, this is a prayer for God's good gifts of posterity, possessions and wealth, and fertility, health, and victory.[38] Deuteronomy 28:1-14 is a fairly complete summary of the blessings of God. All these things are fundamental dimensions and requirements of human life. The first petition of the Aaronic blessing assumes all of them in a comprehensive way, beseeching that God may move toward the people (or the individual Israelite) in all the richness of divine blessing.

As an immediate outgrowth of the priest's petition for God's continuing blessing upon the worshiping community, there follows the prayer, "The LORD keep you," or "May the LORD watch over you." This is a prayer for God's protection in the face of whatever difficulties, misfortunes, or enemies the worshipers may encounter. As Paul Riemann has pointed out, in the Old Testament only God "keeps" persons.[39] Perhaps the most extended theological statement of what this petition is about is Psalm 121, which from beginning to end is both a prayer and an affirmation that God's protecting care from evil, God's preservation of life in the face of its countless threats and vicissitudes, is unceasing. When the psalmist asks help of the ultimate source and of the one who preserves him or her in the face of all trouble, it is the Lord who can be counted upon. The Psalms echo over and over the prayer that God will keep the worshiper safe in God's loving care. To utter that prayer is not only to seek the protection and assistance of God; it necessarily carries with it a clear affirmation that as Lord of the world, God is the one who rules and controls the lives of those who stand under God's care.

In the second line of the blessing, the leader in worship prays for the Lord's face to shine upon the worshipers. We have in these words one of the most common examples of the anthropomorphic imagery of the Old Testament. The face of the Lord indicates the presence of God, but the shining countenance is an emphatically positive presence for help and favor, a sign of the friendly and well-wishing nearness of God, the gracious and helping turning of God to human beings.[40] This prayer for God's turning and deliverance and favor is then in order that the Lord may be gracious. The graciousness of God is in granting divine favors, usually in bringing about redemption from enemies, evil, and sin. Again, the liturgical prayer of the Aaronic benediction is not infrequent in the language of the Psalms where one finds petitions for God to be gracious in the face of sin (Ps 41:4), as well as in the face of affliction (Pss 4:1; 9:13). When David's servants inquire why he fasted and wept for his child while he was alive and then rose and ate food when he was dead, the king replies:

> While the child was still alive, I fasted and wept; for I said, "Who knows? The LORD *may be gracious* to me, and the child may live."
> (2 Sam 12:22)

The second line of the blessing, then, is a prayer to the Lord to turn in favor to the people and deal with them in their ongoing life out of God's great mercy and grace, forgiving sin and delivering them from all affliction.

The third line of the blessing is similar to the second in that it begins with a prayer for the positive presence and favor of God, but it concludes the line and the blessing as a whole with a prayer for God's peace or *šālôm*. This concluding petition is as comprehensive as the initial petition for the blessing of God. *Šālôm* is well-being, with a heavy emphasis on the material character of one's welfare.[41] It can indicate not only cessation of conflict but bodily health.[42] For the nation, *šālôm* means prosperity in the land or place God has given, the absence of conflict with its neighbors. For individual and community alike, the *šālôm* God gives means safety and contentment. Although the term itself is not used, one finds a description of the *šālôm* or peace God wills for the nations of the earth and the individuals that make up those communities in Mic 4:1-4 (‖ Isa 2:1-4), with its picture of the nations transforming their weapons of war into the implements of peace and everyone, safe from enemies, enjoying the benefits of one's own vineyard and fig tree.

The nature of blessing, then, as we see it from this paradigm and, indeed, from all the blessing prayers we have examined, is such that it is not a prayer for things that belong to just one time and place, for example exodus deliverance from enemies. Rather, the blessing persons seek from God and God promises to provide belongs to all times and places, to the continuity of life (birth, fertility, health, peace, prosperity, the presence and favor of God, a place to live, means of life, protection, and care). The blessing of God sought in this prayer is broad and comprehensive, but not vague nor even primarily spiritual (though those dimensions are there). It is concrete and related to this world. We are dealing here, not with some ancient magical sphere, but with the *providence of God*. The function of the prayer is to lift up to God the hope (and the confidence) that God's ongoing provision for humankind will continue. In more systematic terms, the benediction is an expression of the continuing prayer that in the natural and human spheres, God will provide order, process, and grace as the matrix of existence.[43] Albert Outler uses these categories in speaking of providence as the presence of God in history and nature, in and with community and individuals. That presence has been identified more often with miracles, angelic visitations, and episodic interventions than with the constant presence of God to provide the possibilities for life and the context in which human action and freedom in response to God may be worked out.[44] This latter understanding, Outler has suggested, is a more appropriate way of understanding God's relationship to the world and to God's people both from the perspective of the biblical tradition and in terms of a sensible modern cosmology:

> It is tempting, of course, to find the signs of a special providence in history in its odd turns and "accidents"—or to look for it in the gaps that dot the historian's story. But if God is anywhere at all, it must surely be in his provision for the whole: in continuity and discontinuity, in the routine and the extraordinary, in the systolic-diastolic rhythms of crisis and perdurance.[45]

Such an understanding of the provident presence of God is consonant with what we have discerned in the blessing prayers of the Old Testament, whether it is the provision of continuity in the prayer for children in the next generation for the one upon whom the blessing is laid or the prayer of the Aaronic benediction for fruitfulness, protection, mercy, sustenance for life, and well-being. In all of this, "we are trying to point to God's provision for the processes and prospects of the human enterprise."[46]

The blessing of the people committed to the priests or ministers of Israel in Num 6:22-27 concludes with the word of promise that whenever they put the name of the Lord upon the people in this fashion, the Lord will indeed bless them. As the things of blessing are not a one-time occurrence, so the prayer for the Lord's blessing is not a one-time utterance. The same blessing is to be repeated over and over in changing times and circumstances. Indeed it was that way and continues so to be, as it has been repeated throughout the history of the church and the synagogue. The blessing prayer has continual, permanent, lasting character and meaning. This is the prayer for God's providential care of the community, which is always one and the same, and always responsive to the human situation. The role of the priest or minister is explicitly set forth in the text. But it is functional and representative. He or she enacts nothing. The provider of these dimensions of life is the God who is worshiped in the service. And the worshiping community does not assume that the blessing of God comes in some automatic fashion but is a part of God's continuing loving response to the prayers of the people through God's ministers.

In the context of worship, the blessing belongs very much, though not exclusively, to the closing of and going out from worship. That is not unimportant, for it means that the benediction serves as a bridge from the sacral act of worship in the sanctuary to the life of the individual and the community outside the service of worship. It is not so much the end of the worship as it is the connection of the service to the ongoing life of the worshiping people beyond the sanctuary. In benediction, the community says that the one whom they move apart to worship is the one who goes with them as they go from the sacral gathering to guide their life and provide its context. The final prayer of the service moves the people out in the confidence and hope that God will care for their lives in all the basic dimensions of human existence.

The blessing prayers of the New Testament are not distant from these blessing prayers of the Old Testament. We encounter them there especially at the beginning and end of letters to other members of the Christian community, that is, in greeting and parting. They are again words that seek God's benevolent and providential care upon those from whom one is separated. In parting, or as that is reflected in the close of a letter, the apostle lifts up the church and its well-being, its continuing enjoyment of all God's good gifts through Jesus Christ in prayer to God (see chap. 10, below).

> Now may the Lord of peace himself give you peace at all times in all ways. The Lord be with all of you. (2 Thess 3:16)

WHAT ABOUT CURSE?

The corollary of blessing is curse.[47] But the positive connotations of the former are matched by the negative attitude toward curse—at least as far as the topic of prayer is concerned. But the Bible speaks of God's curse as well as of God's blessing. That we have already seen in the Yahwist's story of the judgment of curse dealt with by the promise of blessing. The Psalms speak of "those blessed by the LORD" and "those cursed by [the LORD]" (Ps 37:22). Deuteronomy 28 recounts the curses that shall come upon a disobedient Israel at much greater length than it does the blessings. And within the prayer of blessing itself, a prayer of curse may be embedded.[48] While such curse prayers, or imprecations, as they are sometimes called, do not seem to be as numerous as the blessings, they are present, most noticeably within the Psalms.

In form, they are similar to the blessing. That is, the curses are a prayer-wish, usually jussive in form, "May the Lord do..." The content, however, is a prayer for disaster of some sort to fall upon another individual or group. David utters typical curse prayers after his lieutenant Joab murders Abner, the commander of Saul's army:

> May the guilt fall on the head of Joab, and on all his father's house; and may the house of Joab never be without one who has a discharge, or who is leprous, or who holds a spindle, or who falls by the sword, or who lacks food! (2 Sam 3:29)

> The LORD pay back the one who does wickedly in accordance with his wickedness! (2 Sam 3:39)

The prophet Malachi expresses a prayer of curse for anyone who profanes the sanctuary and worship of the Lord of Israel:

> May the LORD cut off from the tents of Jacob anyone who does this—any to witness or answer, or to bring an offering to the LORD of hosts.[49] (Mal 2:12)

As with the blessings, the Lord is not always mentioned in the curse, but the divine agency is to be assumed and frequently made explicit. That is especially the case with the imprecations that appear as part of laments or prayers for help in the Psalms and elsewhere.[50] There they occur in prayers explicitly addressed to God. The third-person form of the imprecation does not mitigate against its being a part of the prayer to the Lord, for example:

> Let them be put to shame and dishonor
> who seek after my life.
> Let them be turned back and confounded
> who devise evil against me.
> Let them be like chaff before the wind,
> with the angel of the LORD driving them on.
> Let their way be dark and slippery,
> with the angel of the LORD pursuing them. (Ps 35:4-6)

In Psalm 139, the address to the deity becomes explicit in the curse:

> O that you would kill the wicked, O God,
>   and that the bloodthirsty would depart from me—
> those who speak of you maliciously,
>   and lift themselves up against you for evil. (vv. 19-20)

The substance and the tone of this last prayer are what make the curse so disturbing or problematic as a prayer, at least to a contemporary reader of these prayers. They do not seem, however, to have been as problematic to the Israelites and others who prayed them at later times. They belong as much to the discussion of the form and theology of prayer in the Bible as does the blessing, even though the latter is a more dominant theological theme in the Scriptures as a whole. On occasion they are to be found in the New Testament[51] although they are far more prominent in the Old Testament. The tension between their obvious presence in biblical prayer and the resistance to their use in contemporary prayer, or even their very presence in Scripture, requires that we examine both the biblical use and the contemporary resistance in order to see what is at stake.

To start with the latter, the critique of the curse or imprecatory prayer rests largely in its tension with the clear thrust of the Bible's instruction to the community of faith—from biblical times to the present—to express love toward the neighbor and seek his or her good. That seems quite incompatible with these prayers seeking God's destruction or some sort of evil and disaster to come upon another person, whether inside the community or without. Within the Psalms, particularly, the imprecations are focused on enemies and ask God to deal with the enemies of the praying one in a way that undoes them or does them in.

The New Testament, however, gives another word about how persons in the community that worships the Lord are to relate to their enemies. It is a word uttered by Jesus and echoed by Paul. Jesus' instruction is quite specific and contrary to the prayer of imprecation against enemies: "Love your enemies and pray *for* those who persecute you" (Matt 5:44). The curse prayer is a prayer *against* "those who persecute you." The teaching of Jesus and his example undercut all such prayers and instruct the community about a quite different way of dealing with enemies in prayer. Among his final words from the cross is the prayer, "Father, forgive them; for they do not know what they are doing" (Luke 23:34). Paul speaks quite directly to the issue at hand when he counsels the Roman Christians, "Bless those who persecute you; bless and do not curse them" (Rom 12:14). Here the prayer of imprecation is specifically rejected as an alternative for the Christian community. Christian resistance to such prayer is fed by such instruction, which is itself reinforced when Paul quotes Proverbs and says, "[I]f your enemies are hungry, feed them; if they are thirsty, give them something to drink; for by doing this you will heap burning coals on their heads. Do not be overcome by evil, but overcome evil with good" (Rom 12:20-21). The curse prayers of Scripture sound very much like being overcome with evil. They seem to express a violence within the human heart that needs the transforming power of God to turn it into love.

That being the case, several things may be said about these prayers as we encounter them in the Bible. Most important is the recognition that such prayers are a form of prayer for *the justice of God*. While it is possible that hatred is the emotion that evokes such prayer, that is not to be assumed. David's curse prayer on Joab, regardless of how cynically one may interpret it, is a prayer for Joab to be punished for the crime of murder, for God to deal justly with the murderer. Indeed the second of his curse prayers is explicitly a prayer for retributive justice (2 Sam 3:39).[52] Malachi's prayer is also for God's punishment of infidelity and faithlessness. The imprecations of the Psalms sometimes express an emotion and a desire that seem so unrestrained as to demand implicit criticism and rejection. That is true, for example, of the prayer quoted above, "O that you would kill the wicked, O God" (Ps 139:19). The lines that follow, however, are revealing of what lies behind the prayer. The parallel line to the one just quoted is, "and that the bloodthirsty would depart from me." As we have noted in chapter 3, the prayer is at one and the same time against "the wicked," those who resist the way of the Lord and stand against it, and also against those who are oppressing the one who prays. It is both a prayer for justice and a prayer for deliverance. In the next verse, the psalmist recognizes what the Bible shows from beginning to end, to wit, that *God has enemies,* those who set themselves against the loving and merciful and just purposes of God, "those who speak of you maliciously, and lift themselves up against you for evil" (v. 20). The one praying so strongly in Psalm 139 goes on to say:

> Do I not hate those who hate you, O Lord?
>   And do I not loathe those who rise up against you?
> I hate them with perfect hatred;
>   I count them my enemies. (vv. 21-22)

Abhorrent as such words sound to the contemporary reader and emotion-laden as they may become when expressed by someone done in by oppression, the "hate" of this verse is less a term of emotion than it is an indication of firm opposition against those who are opposed to God. It is the same verb that appears in the Decalogue when the Lord speaks of "those who reject [i.e., hate] me" and promises a punishment for them. The psalmist "rejects" those who "reject" the Lord. Their rejection of the Lord is seen, at least in part, in the way they treat the psalmist, in their oppressive conduct toward a member of the community. There is a freedom in these prayers that is willing to identify the injustice one has received from another as injustice, period. That is, the experience of oppression is not simply one's own suffering; it is hostility toward the God who upholds all who are falling and supports the weak and afflicted, whose way is one of blessing for the families of the earth.

Such prayers as these imprecations, therefore, belong to the ethics of justice more than to the ethics of love. They are subject to the critique of the latter but not to a dismissal. They have to do more with the theology of judgment—whose reality is cemented in the cross, not undercut—than with the theology of salvation. But we need to keep in mind what judgment is all about in the Old Testament and how it is worked out in the New Testament. It is a way of maintaining God's just and merciful way, of correcting the instrument, of straightening things out. So in one of the vivid images of judgment in the Old Testament, the Lord speaks of setting a plumb line in Israel,[53] to show the "wall" is out of plumb and the house must come down because it is not "true." God will have to start again. The plumb line is a line of justice and righteousness (Isa 28:17), and the imprecatory prayer is a strange kind of call for the setting of that plumb line in the human situation. In a similar fashion, the Lord speaks of wiping Jerusalem clean as one wipes a dish, setting it aside until it can be used afresh (2 Kgs 21:13).

What must not be missed in these prayers is that they turn the issue of justice over to God rather than taking vengeance into our own hands. They are in some sense "liberating" in that they release the anger and fear of the oppressed as well as the, at times, quite unemotional desire to take justice and judgment into one's own hands and hand all that over to God. The curse prayer is a prayer for God's vengeance. When God says, "Vengeance is mine," we need to remember that really is the case and also that what is meant by that term is vindication, the bringing to fulfillment of all God's purposes even in the face of all that would oppose them. The ultimate act of divine vengeance/vindication is in the cross where God receives the world's hatred and overcomes it. The mode of overcoming, God's self-giving and suffering love in Jesus Christ, means that the curse prayers do not finally teach us how to pray or stand as models of prayer for us. They may give expression to the thoughts and words and feelings that we cannot let go except as they are let go to God in prayer.[54]

10

"Teach Us to Pray"

THE FURTHER WITNESS
OF THE NEW TESTAMENT

⪼

We are near the end of this study of biblical prayer. But we are not quite there. The large focus of the previous discussion has been the Old Testament, even though we have taken account of the New Testament both formally and theologically at a number of points. It remains to be asked, however: What further witness does the New Testament have to give us about prayer?[1] The operative word in that question is "further." There is no attempt in this context to survey everything that is said about prayer directly or indirectly in the New Testament. Rather, we are asking: What further does the New Testament have to tell us beyond what we have already taken account of in earlier chapters? But we are also inquiring about a further witness in the sense of how the New Testament *extends* the witness of the Old. To what extent does the New Testament stand in continuity and carry forward those directions set in the Old Testament? In what ways does it point us in other directions? That is: How does it underscore the witness of the Old while also opening up other perspectives?[2]

A CONTINUING TRADITION

In many ways, the forms and traditions of Israelite and Jewish prayer that precede the career of Jesus and the formation of the early Christian community carry forward into the New Testament. That, at least in part, is why it has been possible to draw upon the New Testament in earlier chapters when dealing primarily with Old Testament prayer. Prayer took place in the temple, as one would expect, but also away from places of worship and in solitude as well as in homes or other places and in the face of crises of various sorts. Paul assumes the prayer of thanksgiving at a meal (Rom 14:6;[3] 1 Cor 10:30). The hours of prayer that had become a part of daily piety in the Jewish community and are first attested in Dan 6:10 are observed, apparently by Jesus and clearly by others in the Christian community (see chap. 2, above). As in Daniel's regular occasions when he would "pray to his God and praise him," so the mix of prayers and supplications for help together with thanksgiving, a combination explicitly found in the Eighteen Benedictions of Judaism, reflects the centrality of the prayer for help and the prayer of praise and thanksgiving in the Old Testament generally.

While there are many references to prayer in the New Testament, we do not have many actual prayers. The most important and best known of these is, of course, the prayer taught by Jesus to the disciples and prayed by all the generations since as the Lord's Prayer.[4] In addition to the prayers from the cross, five of Jesus' prayers are recorded, one by Peter and John, and two by Stephen as he is being stoned.[5] Prayer occupies much of Paul's attention in his letters, but apart from the frequent blessings, most of what we find there is report of his praying.

In all of these, there is much continuity with what we have already encountered. We have noted the similarity between Paul's many blessing prayers and those of the Old Testament. He too seeks God's grace and mercy, peace and well-being, upon those whom he blesses in prayer. Jesus' own prayers are prayers for help and prayers of thanksgiving.[6] While there are some differences in his praying that we need to take account of (see below on "The Will of God and a Theology of the Cross"), we hear in his prayers the voice of an Israelite nurtured in the traditions of Israelite and Jewish prayer.[7] That is certainly the case with his prayers from the cross, where the prayers for help of the Psalter are specifically present in his cry of despair and anguish, "My God, my God, why have you forsaken me?" (Ps 22:1), and his final words, "Father, into your hands I commend my spirit" (Ps 31:5).[8] These prayers create an immediate identity between Jesus and all those who have prayed the despairing complaint of Psalm 22 and the expression of confidence of Psalm 31. The movement between those two, the possibility of such anguish and complaint against God being an expression of a trusting creature and of such confidence permitting the harshest and sharpest of complaints, is at the very heart of the prayers for help of the Psalter (see chap. 3, above). The letter to the Hebrews speaks of Jesus in a way that sets him as a model of the praying Israelite:

> In the days of his flesh, Jesus offered up prayers and supplications, with loud cries and tears, to the one who was able to save him from death, and he was heard because of his reverent submission.
> (Heb 5:7)

The long prayer in John 17 is a piece of Johannine theology, but, as such, it is reminiscent of Solomon's long prayer of dedication at the temple, itself a piece of Deuteronomistic theology (1 Kings 8). It is essentially an intercessory prayer and as such is reminiscent of those prayers of the leaders and prophets of centuries before. Jesus prays for himself (vv. 1-5) but only as God's response in his behalf leads to God's own glorification. Such praying, while it is more abstract in its formulation, is in direct continuity with those prayers for help "for your name's sake" of the Old Testament, a calling on God's help in order that God's own name may be lifted up and glorified. The rest of the prayer is intercessory, first for the community of disciples and then for "those who will believe in me and through their word" (v. 20). The prayer for the disciples is primarily a prayer for their protection (vv. 11-12, 15); the prayer for "those who will believe" is that they all may be one (vv. 20-21). The subject matter is partially different and the long Johannine exposition unique to biblical prayer, but its concerns connect it with the intercession of previous leaders of the community.

The letter of James is instructive in this regard. It contains a section of teaching about prayer as follows:

> Are any among you suffering? They should pray. Are any cheerful? They should sing songs of praise. Are any among you sick? They should call for the elders of the church and have them pray over them, anointing them with oil in the name of the Lord. The prayer of faith will save the sick, and the Lord will raise them up; and anyone who has committed sins will be forgiven. Therefore confess your sins to one another, and pray for one another, so that you may be healed. The prayer of the righteous is powerful and effective. Elijah was a human being like us, and he prayed fervently that it might not rain, and for three years and six months it did not rain on the earth. Then he prayed again, and the heaven gave rain and the earth yielded its harvest. (Jas 5:13-18)

Not only does James illustrate his points about prayer with explicit citation of the Old Testament—although his Scripture texts are not in fact references to prayer except by inference—his instruction is almost a synopsis of some of the main things we learn about prayer from the Old Testament. The suffering pray for help, and those who have experienced God's good gifts sing hymns of praise. These are the two primary human points in the dialogue of prayer as we have uncovered it—the prayer for help of the suffering and the song of praise of the redeemed. The focus upon sickness and the importance of prayer in behalf of others take us back to Abraham's intercession for Abimelech and Moses' prayer to God to heal Miriam. Confession of sin is placed in the prayer life of the community to whom James writes. And "the prayer of faith" and "the prayer of the righteous" take us directly back to those prayers in trust and confidence and those prayers of the righteous or innocent that make up much of the prayers of the Psalter.[9]

If, however, there are large lines of continuity identified above and in previous chapters, there are ways in which the New Testament places us in a somewhat different context and lets us know that the reality of Jesus Christ affects all aspects of our life with God including prayer.

INSTRUCTION ABOUT PRAYER

One of the noticeable differences between the Old Testament and the New Testament on this subject is the significant presence of teaching about prayer in the latter. While there is far more prayer and reporting of people praying, as individuals or as community, in the Old Testament, there is little, if any, instruction in prayer. In the New Testament, the presence of Jesus and his establishment of a new community oriented toward the kingdom of God seem to raise afresh the question of how to pray, a development particularly signified by Jesus teaching the disciples the Lord's Prayer but seen in many other ways, from the teaching of Jesus to the letters of Paul and James. This focus on prayer instruction may be in part because a particular form and content of prayer serve to define a particular community. So one interpreter sees the disciples' request to Jesus, "Lord teach us to pray, as John taught his disciples" (Luke 11:1), as indicating that a particular way of praying was characteristic of different groups at that time, such as the disciples around John the Baptist, and that the request of Jesus' disciples was in effect, "Teach us to pray as those should pray who are already partakers of the coming reign of God."[10] Whatever lay behind this development, each of the Synoptic Gospels as well as different parts of the epistolary literature of the New Testament contain various kinds of instruction about prayer.

Much of this instruction is hortatory, both defining a way or ways of praying and calling for their practice. So Jesus and Paul both exhort their followers to pray for their enemies, to seek blessing for them rather than cursing them.[11] There is clear indication in the text that the community is being taught something new about prayer, that a different way of praying is being offered and required.[12] That is in fact the case. The enemies are frequently in the prayers of the Old Testament (see chap. 3, above), but the prayer is for God's overcoming and putting them down. They are the objects of the curse prayers of the Old Testament. Their defeat is the means whereby God's justice will be manifest and the oppressed helped. Now another kind of prayer is set before the community of faith. The enemies are the recipients of blessing and intercession. They are to be lifted up in prayer rather than put down. A radical new direction in prayer is set forth in these exhortations.

This does not mean that overcoming the enemy and his or her hostility is no longer a goal. In Romans 12, Paul goes on to draw together various Old Testament sayings to make the point that the nonretaliation and the love of the enemy on the part of the Christian become a searing fire that overcomes the enemy by good. While that point is not obvious in Matthew 5, one may assume that there also the instruction to pray for the enemy intends to overcome the enemy.[13]

The coincidence of Paul's teaching with that of Jesus underscores how important this prayer for the enemies is in the New Testament. It gets its further affirmation when such prayers in fact are prayed, as happens on two occasions as persons are dying at the hands of their enemies. In his last words on the cross, Jesus prays, "Father forgive them; for they do not know what they are doing" (Luke 23:34). As he is being stoned, Stephen takes to heart the teaching of his Lord and imitates Jesus' example with his last act—a prayer:

> Then he knelt down and cried out in a loud voice, "Lord do not hold this sin against them." When he had said this, he died.
>
> (Acts 7:60)

One may assume that these two prayers exemplify what Jesus means by praying for the enemies. While other forms of prayer are to be included, for example, typical blessings (Rom 12:14), the fact that the enemies are defined as such by their opposition to those who are at work for the kingdom of God, the righteous and the servants of the Lord, means that the primary prayer in their behalf is for their forgiveness. In these instances of the prayer for the enemies, we see again what is characteristic of the Old Testament, that the enemy is defined by his or her opposition to the will and purpose of God as that is manifest in an oppression of those who are God's righteous ones. The enmity has a moral dimension; it has to do with one's stance vis-à-vis God. And the personal enemies are also God's enemies.[14] But it is not their destruction for which one prays. It is not God's act to remove this instrument of suffering and oppression that is sought in prayer. The release from suffering is not now the primary object of the prayer. It is rather the forgiveness of those who inflict it. Here we see the first sign of the way in which prayer begins to be shaped and reshaped by a theology of the cross. And it is not just a theology of the cross that is at work; there is a cruciform praxis at work here affecting all of life, including, in a most dramatic fashion, the prayer of the suffering and dying.

It is not surprising, therefore, that the New Testament instruction about prayer should place some weight upon forgiveness and the prayer of forgiveness. That is the context in which Matthew places the Lord's Prayer (Matt 6:14-15), though it is more likely the enactment of forgiveness among the members of the community rather than toward those outside and in opposition to it that is in view in the Matthean instruction.[15] It is the prayer for one's own forgiveness and the act of forgiveness toward the brother and sister that are the context of the petition to "forgive us our debts."[16] The prayer for the enemies moves outside the community to make forgiveness not an object of supplication for ourselves, but an act of intercession for others and particularly those who are ordinarily not a subject of prayer except as curse.

The sense of instruction marking off a mode of prayer in distinction from the way others pray or have prayed is indicated in other ways in the teaching about prayer. In the Sermon on the Mount, Jesus calls for private rather than public and ostentatious prayer as well as for simplicity and brevity (Matt 6:1-14). In both cases, he marks his way of praying off from other groups, the hypocrites (v. 5) and the Gentiles (v. 7). Such instruction joins with the model of prayer, the "Our Father," as well as the exhortation to pray for enemies to set before the community the particular style of prayer appropriate to the kingdom. One other feature is a part of the Matthean instruction on prayer. It is the encouragement to ask of God in prayer in the confidence that God will hear and respond:

> Ask, and it will be given you; search, and you will find; knock, and the door will be opened for you. For everyone who asks receives, and everyone who searches finds, and for everyone who knocks, the door will be opened. Is there anyone among you who, if your child asks for bread, will give a stone? Or if the child asks for a fish, will give a snake? If you then, who are evil, know how to give good gifts to your children, how much more will your Father in heaven give good things to those who ask him!
>
> (Matt 7:7-11 || Luke 11:9-13)

Several things are to be noted about such prayer instruction.

1. It suggests, as do other passages,[17] that such exhortation was needed, that there was uncertainty about the divine response and the possibility that prayers would not be answered.

2. One needs to be careful about assuming that such instruction implies that anything is to be prayed for and always to be received. It is no accident that this teaching is directly connected with the Lord's Prayer in Luke 11:1-4. It is such prayer as this—indeed the prayer itself—that one may and should pray in confidence.

3. The series of three verbs, "ask..., search..., knock," followed by verbs of response, "it will be *given* you..., you will *find*..., it will be *opened* for you," is not simply a way of scoring a point and emphasizing it by repetition. The verbs of response are *appropriate* to the petitions. What is asked is given. What is sought for is found. The door upon which one knocks is opened. Jesus indicates to his followers that God responds to the petitions of those who pray and in ways appropriate

to the pleas.[18] That in itself is not at all a new idea or a new reality. It is part of Jesus' encouragement to the disciples to pray as Israel had always prayed, in trust and confidence that God would respond as the need required.[19]

4. These words of encouragement are as much about the nature of God as they are about the possibility of prayer. They are meant to speak to the community about the way God responds, not just *that* God does so. It is a good God who can be counted upon to provide good gifts to those who come in prayer.

5. There are other texts that convey the same notion.[20] In some way, each one makes a slightly different point about prayer. For instance, the Lucan parallel to Matt 7:7-11 with its transitional "So I say to you" continues the important Lucan theme of persistence in prayer that is the subject of the immediately preceding pericope (see below). The saying of Jesus in Mark, to "have faith in God," that "whatever you ask for in prayer, believe that you have received it, and it will be yours," is not a claim that in fact mountains move into the sea by some sort of mind game called prayer.[21] The emphasis is indeed on the call to faith,[22] but this is once again an exhortation to pray in trust and confidence, a feature of prayer that is consistently a part of the prayers for help in Scripture (see chaps. 3 and 5, above). Jesus' words are a reinforcement of that to the disciples, a call to trust in the Lord who hears the prayer of the faithful and righteous. In the Johannine texts that sound this same theme about the sure response of God to prayer, we encounter a matter that we will need to look at more closely below, the will of God. Suffice it to say, at this point, that the open invitation to ask whatever you wish is qualified in a significant way. The clearest instance is 1 John 5:14:

> And this is the boldness we have in him, that if we ask anything *according to his will,* he hears us.

The prayer that is uttered in conformity to the will of God is surely heard. In this case, specific petitions are not indicated. The primary thing, as we shall note more specifically below, is the will of God. A similar perspective is found in Jesus' words in John 15:7:

> If you abide in me, and my words abide in you, ask for whatever you wish, and it will be done for you.

The freedom of prayer and the responsiveness of God are found for those who abide in Christ and in whom Christ's words are at work and controlling.[23] The prayer of such petitioners will, therefore, once more be in accord with the will and word of Christ. It is not a wish list. Those "words" of Jesus, those "specific sayings and precepts,"[24] include all the words about prayer and quite specifically the Lord's Prayer itself. That model is the prayer that will come forth from the lips of those in whom

Christ's words abide. Finally, 1 John 3:21-22 reiterates this point in a different way because of its context. The author says:

> Beloved, if our hearts do not condemn us, we have boldness before God; and we receive from him whatever we ask, because we obey his commandments and do what pleases him.

Doing what pleases God is to bring one's petitions into conformity with God's will. Obedience to God's commandments in this letter centers in obedience to the love commandment. So prayer is open and unrestrained except by the rule of love and the will of God. Whatever is asked from God that way is sure to be received.

There is a further theme in the teaching of Jesus, especially as it is found in Luke's Gospel, and also in the Epistles.[25] It is a note that we have not really heard heretofore as teaching, but we have encountered it in practice throughout the Old Testament. It is also a further dimension of the injunctions of Jesus to "ask, . . . search, . . . knock." This recurring theme is the exhortation to *importunate, persistent prayer.* As we noted above, Jesus in the Gospel of Luke gives the injunctions to "ask, . . . search, . . . knock" as an elaboration of his teaching about persistence in prayer. He tells an illustrative story or parable about a person who asks a friend for some bread and receives it not because of the friendship but because of the persistence in asking (Luke 11:5-8). Immediately after this, Jesus says, "So I say to you, Ask, and it will be given you. . . . " The concern for persistence in prayer is important enough that it becomes the subject of a second parable in Luke, the story of a widow who gets justice from a judge because she "keeps bothering" him (Luke 18:1-8). The parable has its place in the larger concern of Luke's theology.[26] That is indicated by the final verse: "And yet when the Son of Man [or "the Human One"] comes, will he find faith on earth?" (v. 8). The concern is for the possibility of the community resisting both persecution and the temptations of the world until the Human One comes (cf. Luke 22:46). The parable has its own point about God's justice coming "to his chosen ones who cry to him day and night." That claim is fully consistent with the Old Testament and, as we have argued throughout this book, is one of the fundamental themes of the whole of Scripture. Here the particular angle that is given to it is precisely the *persistence*[27] of the cry for help. To those who persist in crying/praying to a just God, justice will come. The parable is an implicit confirmation of Job's insistent and raging cries for justice. In this context, that scriptural theme is drawn into the particular theology of Luke with the transitional sentences, "Will he delay long in helping them? I tell you, he will quickly grant justice to them" (vv. 7b-8a).[28]

The teaching about importuning, persistent prayer is a double one. In its simplest terms, persistence pays off. Or to put it more specifically (for this is not a general rule of human existence), persistent prayer to God will find an appropriate response.[29] One must not "lose heart" (Luke 18:1). Such teaching, and the stories that convey it, are making the point, in spades, that God is responsive to human prayer. The other aspect of this teaching is the continuity between the exhortations to pray persistently and those that exhort to *pray continually*.[30] Jesus joins these as one at the beginning of the parable of the widow and the judge: "Then Jesus told them a parable about their need to pray always and not to lose heart." This is the point of the parable—continual, persistent prayer that does not flag when it seems that God does not hear. God will hear and respond. So the Christian is called to "pray without ceasing" (1 Thess 5:17), which means to keep at it, thus nurturing a discipline of prayer, and not to give up or to lose heart, thus nurturing a confidence and trust in God. If, for Luke, this constant prayer is in order to be able to resist temptation, as Jesus says quite directly to his disciples asleep on the Mount of Olives just before his arrest,[31] it is clear from the other Gospels, as well as the story of the early Christian community in Acts and the Epistles, that such constant prayer was a discipline that belonged to the relationship with God. For Paul it was as much a continual prayer of thanksgiving as it was persistent supplication for help in his troubles[32] or intercession for others (1 Thess 5:16, 18).[33]

It is out of such teaching and praying as these texts reveal that we begin to encounter in the New Testament the sense of prayer as a *spiritual discipline,* that is, as an ongoing and regular part of the relationship with God. That may be implicit in the Old Testament, but there prayer is tied more to a particular occasion and we do not find the frequent injunction to continue constantly in prayer. Certainly there are indications in the Psalter of long prayer vigils, and prayer was a regular part of temple worship. But it is in the late Old Testament literature (e.g., Dan 6:12) and continuing on in Judaism at the time of the New Testament that we begin to find a regular discipline of prayer.[34] The witnesses of the New Testament, in teaching and practice, carry this direction forward.

The Christian life involves prayer as a part of communion with God that belongs to the regularity and ongoing discipline of life as well as to specific moments. Such praying was characteristic of the Gospels, especially Luke, which not only emphasizes constancy and persistence in prayer as a part of Jesus' teaching, but mentions nine prayers of Jesus, usually at pivotal occasions.[35] Luke "depicts Jesus often at prayer, because this is to become one of the ways in which the disciple is to follow him."[36] So we read in Acts 1:14 in reference to the early Christian community in Jerusalem: "All these were constantly devoting themselves to prayer." The community is assiduous in prayer. It "devotes" itself to prayer (*proskarterein*—Acts 1:14; 2:42). Indeed the whole story of the early Christians in Acts indicates that they followed the command of their Lord to pray unceasingly. Such "devotion" to prayer is a part of Paul's instruction to congregations elsewhere.[37] He refers to his own practice of prayer as a regular and constant activity. So he tells the Christians at Rome that "without ceasing [*adialeiptos*] I remember you always [*pantote*] in my prayers" (Rom 1:9), a word he expresses in various ways to other communities.[38] It is not altogether clear exactly what Paul has in mind when he speaks of praying without ceasing or what the "constant devoting" of the early Christians actually referred to in terms of specific practice. Gunther Harder, who sees in these practices a Jewish ideal being taken up by Paul, has suggested that what Paul means is that he does not let any prayer time go by without giving thanks or remembering the people. To "pray without ceasing" means for Paul, in effect, that "at no time do I neglect to pray for this or that goal."[39] With regard to Paul's words about constant prayer in his first letter to the Thessalonians, Gordon Wiles has summed up the matter as follows:

> Yet how literally need his claims be taken when he speaks of unceasing, constant prayer, practised "night and day" (I Thess 3:10)? . . . As Origen pointed out, the apostle who gave instructions to the readers to work with their hands as he himself had done night and day (cf 4:11 with 2:9), could hardly have intended them to be consciously praying at every moment (4:17—*Sir* = 5:17), nor that his own thoughts were uninterruptedly on the readers in prayer. Rather he seems to have believed that their whole life should be lived as if standing prayerfully "before God," but be punctuated by frequent acts of consciously turning back to Him. Indeed, the very structure of the letter illustrates this alternation between unconscious and conscious prayer, by the way in which the prayers are interspersed throughout the epistle (1:1b-3, 2:13, 3:9-13, 5:23f., 28).[40]

Certainly Paul's injunctions to "persevere in" or "devote yourselves to" prayer indicate his judgment that, whether at particular periods, frequently without fixed times, or for long stretches, prayer is a *sine qua non* of the Christian life (Phil 4:6).

It is clear, therefore, that Paul regarded persistent, constant devotion to prayer as a part of the *sanctified life*. That is also the case in the portrayal of the early Christian community in Acts. As such, however, both the experience of prayer and the teaching about it in the New Testament take us deeper into facets of Christian prayer that are particularly evident and central to the New Testament.[41] To those we now must turn.

THE TRINITARIAN CHARACTER OF CHRISTIAN PRAYER

What particularly marks the witness of the New Testament on prayer is its movement toward a trinitarian shape. In some ways, this takes place in direct continuity with Jewish prayer as a trinitarian stamp is placed upon it. One notes, for example, that while Paul refers to the practice of giving thanks at a meal,[42] a custom at home in Judaism, in his words to the Romans he turns that prayer of thanks to God into a confession of faith in Jesus Christ:

> Also those who eat, eat in honor of the Lord, since they give thanks to God; while those who abstain, abstain in honor of the Lord and give thanks to God. (Rom 14:6)

The prayer of thanks, which for Greek-speaking Jews would be *eulogetos kurios,* "Blessed be the Lord," is seen by Paul as in honor of "the Lord," that is, of Jesus Christ. In its very formulation as carried over into Greek, the ancient prayer is directly a Christian prayer. What may seem to be an accident of language and translation is for Paul a very important Christian confession. In other words, the proclamation and confession we have identified as being fundamental to thanksgiving in the Old Testament is recognized here by Paul and is specifically seen as a *Christian* confession.[43]

To God the Father

In various ways, however, this trinitarian context for prayer is made explicit and shapes prayer so that it is peculiarly Christian even as it stands in continuity with the prayers of Israel. That continuity is particularly marked in the degree to which the prayer of the Christian remains prayer *to God.* Clearly, in his praying and in his teaching, Jesus pointed his disciples to God as the one to whom all prayer is addressed and the one who is able to hear and respond. But that did not change with the trinitarian convictions of the early church. Krister Stendahl has correctly said, "Our starting point must be that the object of prayer for Paul is God, not Christ. This also holds for doxologies, thanksgivings, and the very structure of Paul's life of prayer."[44] What is true of Paul is true generally, though not exclusively, of the whole of the New Testament.[45] The *kurios*-Lord terminology opens up the possibility of prayer being directed toward the risen Christ, but that is not characteristic.[46] Nowhere more than in its prayers and its words about prayer does the New Testament demonstrate that it speaks about, from, and to the same central subject of the Old Testament, the God of Israel, Maker of heaven and earth.

So we hear from Paul and others such prayers or prayer-reports as the following:

Thanks be to God through Jesus Christ our Lord! (Rom 7:25)[47]

We give you thanks, Lord God Almighty. (Rev 11:17)

To the only wise God, through Jesus Christ, to whom be the glory forever. (Rom 16:27; cf. Jude 25)

Furthermore, several times Paul speaks of "prayer to God" or "thanks to God" but never of prayer or thanks to Christ.[48] The same is true for the rest of the New Testament except for one or two instances in Acts.[49] It is also clear from many texts that it is to God *the Father* that the prayers are often directed. In the New Testament, the prayer to the Father begins with Jesus.[50] It is his address to God in all but one of his prayers[51] and the way of addressing God that Jesus teaches to the disciples.[52] Such address to God carries over in the prayers and prayer-reports of the rest of the New Testament. So Paul's blessings and thanksgivings are often addressed to or speak of God as Father, either as "the Father," or "our Father," or "the Father of our Lord Jesus Christ."[53] This mode of address marks the trinitarian character of Christian prayer because it arises out of the filial relation of Jesus of Nazareth to the God of Israel. It is Jesus' "sonship" that evokes the address of "Father," the understanding of the relationship between Jesus and God as filial and parental. And from that, Christians, who by the Spirit of Christ are made children of God, "and if children, then heirs, heirs of God and joint heirs with Christ," are able to address God in the same parental-filial way.[54] The Old Testament "people of God" moves into another kind of imagery, one already anticipated in the Old Testament itself where the parental imagery for deity (both mother and father) is to be found also.[55] In the New Testament, the community of faith that has its being in relation to Jesus Christ shares with him a relation to God as child to parent. So the prayer to God the Father bears testimony to our unity with Christ and our relation to God. The significance of the prayer to God the Father is not finally whether or not it was new in Jesus' time but that it characterizes the way in which the Christian community understands it may approach God in prayer, as children of a loving parent whose way with Jesus points to the Father's way with the rest of the family.[56] An image that takes seed in the Old Testament becomes a touchstone for prayer to the trinitarian God of Christian faith.

Through Christ

One cannot claim that there is never prayer to Christ in the New Testament, but it is exceedingly rare. In addition to Paul's apparent prayers to Christ as Lord in 2 Cor 12:8-9, there is at least one clear instance of a prayer addressed to "Lord Jesus." It is the prayer of Stephen as he is being killed after his long sermon: "Lord Jesus, receive my spirit" (Acts 7:59).[57] It is noteworthy, however, that after his sermon and immediately prior to his being dragged out to be stoned, Stephen has a vision:

> But filled with the Holy Spirit, he gazed into heaven and saw the glory of God and Jesus standing at the right hand of God. "Look," he said, "I see the heavens opened and the Son of Man [or the Human One] standing at the right hand of God!" (vv. 55-56)

This vision just before his stoning may have something to do with Stephen's subsequent prayer, "Lord Jesus, receive my spirit." The prayer may be a reflection of the second dimension of the trinitarian character of Christian prayer in the New Testament, that it is prayer to God *through* Christ. The risen Christ, who stands at the right hand of God, is the intercessor through whom access to God takes place. That New Testament claim may be what triggers the prayer of Stephen to "Lord Jesus." In the first chapter, we noted ancient precursors of such a notion. Now in the New Testament, the mediator or intercessor through whom prayers are lifted to God comes once more into the picture.

The prayer through Christ and Christ as intercessor are facets of a single reality, but neither one completely exhausts the other. Christ as our intercessor in prayer is witnessed to in various ways in the New Testament. Especially is that seen in the High Priestly Prayer of Jesus in John 17 where the Lord prays for his disciples and for the world. There the intercession is Christ's own prayer for the world. The letter to the Hebrews picks up this role and lifts it to a high level in its depiction of Jesus Christ:

> Since, then, we have a great high priest who has passed through the heavens, Jesus, the Son of God, let us hold fast to our confession. ... Let us therefore approach the throne of grace with boldness, so that we may receive mercy and find grace to help in time of need.
>
> (Heb 4:14, 16)

The story of one who in suffering and prayer intercedes for others, a story that began with the prophets of the Old Testament and a suffering servant who "made intercession for the transgressors" (Isa 53:12), reaches its climax in the once and continuing intercession of the anointed of God, Jesus Christ. The prayer for mercy and grace is "carried" by Christ.

All of this is metaphoric speech, but it is powerful imagery, a way to speak of the conviction given to Christians that Jesus Christ is there in our behalf, that our prayers are heard because there is one with God who represents us, who knows our human need and our human experience. It is no accident that the writer to the Hebrews sees Jesus' preparation for this role "in the days of his flesh" when he "offered up prayers and supplications, with loud cries and tears, to the one who was able to save him from death" (Heb 5:7). It is *our* loud cries and tears that Jesus now offers up to God. Within the very reality that is God, there is always a voice in our behalf, one that has shared our sufferings and knows our sorrows.

> It is Christ Jesus who died, yes, who was raised, who is at the right hand of God, who indeed intercedes for us. (Rom 8:34)

This ministry of intercession is not confined to the lifting up of our cries and tears to God. Nor can one assume—based on Jesus' prayer for the world and the picture of Christ as intercessor in Paul and Hebrews—that prayer to God can come only through Christ. That is not the point. Paul's conviction and that of other Christians was that it *did* come through Christ.[58] And here is the other dimension of Christ's place in Christian prayer. For Paul, certainly, but apparently for others also, *all* prayer is *through Christ*. Indeed, within Paul's own prayer-reports, it is not with regard to supplication and intercession that we hear of his praying to God through Christ. As we have already noted, it is much more in thanksgiving. Time and again, he says the kind of word that we hear at the beginning of the letter to the Romans: "I thank my God *through Jesus Christ* for all of you" (Rom 1:8).[59] So also Paul's ascriptions and benedictions and those of other New Testament writers were prayers to God through Christ, for example:

> Now to God...—to the only wise God, through Jesus Christ, to whom be the glory forever! Amen.
>
> (Rom 16:25-27; cf. Jude 25)

> Now may the God of peace...make you complete in everything good...working among us that which is pleasing in his sight, through Jesus Christ, to whom be the glory forever. Amen (Heb 13:20-21)

Every benefit, every facet of Christian life, every aspect of God's saving work is through Christ:

> We have peace with God through our Lord Jesus Christ. (Rom 5:1)

> Grace...through justification leading to eternal life through Jesus Christ our Lord...(Rom 5:21)

> Our consolation is abundant through Christ. (2 Cor 1:5)

> Such is the confidence we have through Christ toward God...
>
> (2 Cor 3:4)

All this is from God, who reconciled us to himself through Christ.
(2 Cor 5:18)

Paul an apostle—sent... through Jesus Christ... (Gal 1:1)

[God] destined us for adoption as his children through Jesus Christ. (Eph 1:5)

The harvest of righteousness that comes through Jesus Christ...
(Phil 1:11)

God has destined us... for obtaining salvation through our Lord Jesus Christ. (1 Thess 5:9)

This Spirit is poured out on us richly through Jesus Christ.
(Titus 3:6)

We have been sanctified through the offering of the body of Jesus Christ once for all. (Heb 10:10)

It is the claim of the gospel—and it was the discovery of the early church that that claim is true—that every thing in our relation to God is and happens through Jesus Christ, in virtue of Jesus Christ,[60] that the one who lived and died as God's tabernacling among us (John 1:14) mediates every dimension of our life and death with God. So surely, therefore, is every act of thanksgiving, every prayer of blessing, every supplication for others also *through Christ.*[61]

In the Spirit

The trinitarian shape of New Testament prayer is also evident in the prayer that takes place in or by the Spirit. Paul is quite explicit about the work of the Holy Spirit in the act of prayer.[62] Two times in the New Testament there are injunctions to "pray in the (Holy) Spirit."[63] It is not unimportant that the instruction about praying in the Spirit in each of these instances is not a separate injunction but a qualification or an aspect of "being strong in the Lord" and "standing" (Eph 6:10-20) and of "keeping yourselves in the love of God."[64] That is, "praying in the Spirit" is *a dimension of the Christian life,* of the sanctified life, variously described in these instances as being strong in the Lord and putting on the armor of God or as keeping oneself in the love of God. The prayer with or in the Spirit belongs to a number of features that characterize this life, as both texts indicate. But being strong in the Lord or keeping oneself in the love of God, as a definition of the Christian life, clearly involves prayer, and specifically prayer in the Spirit.

The question remains, however, as to just what it means to "pray in the Spirit." Two possibilities seem to suggest themselves from the texts where the Spirit and prayer are brought into conjunction. One is that prayer in the Spirit means ecstatic prayer, prayer that is uttered by those upon whom the Spirit has descended as a sign of the end time.[65] This is suggested by 1 Cor 14:13-19, where Paul instructs the Corinthians about speaking in tongues, about praying, singing praise and blessing in tongues. Here he speaks specifically about "praying with [or 'in'] the Spirit":

> Therefore, one who speaks in a tongue should pray for the power to interpret. For if I pray in a tongue, my spirit prays but my mind is unproductive. What should I do then? I will pray with the spirit, but I will pray with the mind also; I will sing praise with the spirit, but I will sing praise with the mind also. Otherwise, if you say a blessing with [or "in"] the spirit, how can anyone in the position of an outsider say the "Amen" to your thanksgiving, since the outsider does not know what you are saying? For you may give thanks well enough, but the other person is not built up. I thank God that I speak in tongues more than all of you; nevertheless, in church I would rather speak five words with my mind, in order to instruct others also, than ten thousand words in a tongue.

The reference to "my spirit" in verse 14 suggests that this discussion may have nothing to do with the Holy Spirit but only with Paul's spirit. The NRSV's lack of capitalization tends to confirm that interpretation. But the context of chapters 12–14 indicates that in fact, here too, Paul has the Holy Spirit in mind.[66] It is not just intercessory or petitionary prayer that takes place under the influence of the Spirit and thus in tongues, but hymnody and songs of thanksgiving. Paul has in mind such prayer and thanksgiving in the Spirit, ecstatic prayer and thanksgiving, as an act of corporate worship. But here he, in effect, relegates it to private prayer and thanksgiving. The very fact that he says that *"in church"* he will speak/pray with the mind and not in tongues suggests that while praying/praising in the Spirit may refer to ecstatic prayer, it can have a broader reference. That at least would seem to be the case when one looks at other places where Paul takes up the relation of the Spirit to prayer.

In Romans 8, Paul speaks of the help of the Spirit making prayer possible and particularly appropriate prayer, that is, prayer according to God's will.[67] Romans 8 is Paul's effort to interpret the work of the Spirit in the Christian. It is the presence of the Spirit, which is the Spirit of God and the Spirit of Christ (v. 9), that makes us children of God (v. 14). The indwelling of the Spirit determines whether or not one belongs to Christ (v. 9). Much of Romans 8 seeks to show what the Spirit does or accomplishes in the Christian:

1. The Spirit gives *life* (vv. 10-11, 13). "If *by* the Spirit you put to death the deeds of the body, you will live" (v. 13).

2. The Spirit makes us *children of God* (*huioi theou*). "For all who are led *by* the Spirit of God are children of God" (v. 14).

3. The Spirit is the first fruit of the coming glory of God (v. 23).

4. And finally, the Spirit helps us *pray*. This point joins with the second one in verses 15-17:

> For you did not receive a spirit of slavery to fall back into fear, but you have received a spirit of adoption. When we cry, "Abba! Father!" it is that very Spirit bearing witness with our spirit that we are children of God, and if children, then heirs, heirs of God and joint heirs with Christ—if, in fact, we suffer with him so that we may also be glorified with him.

When we pray, that is, "When we cry, 'Abba! Father!' " it is the Spirit at work within us, "bearing witness with our spirit" that we are children of God. The possibility of crying "Abba" means that we have "inherited" the filial relation that Jesus has with God. We belong to the family.[68] But that possibility comes to reality only by the Spirit of Christ at work within us. So when the Christian cries "Abba," this is the Spirit enabling prayer and testifying to our status as children of God.[69] We do not do this without the Spirit's presence within us, Paul says.[70]

The point about the Spirit's help in prayer is then developed in a different direction in verses 26-27. There, it is specifically the *help* of the Spirit "in our weakness" because we do not know how to pray as we ought, or, more literally, "we do not know for what to pray as is necessary." It is possible to understand this as ecstatic prayer, as in the case of prayer in the Spirit in 1 Corinthians 14.[71] But it is also possible that this is speaking more broadly of the help of the Spirit in prayer, whether that prayer is the prayer of ecstasy or not.[72] The claim seems a strange one in a context where there is much prayer and certainly many models and examples of prayer, not least the model offered by Jesus, precisely in order to teach the disciples what it is necessary to pray for. In this context, the help of the Spirit is related to the groaning of the whole creation (v. 22) and of "ourselves, who have the first fruits of the Spirit" (v. 23) for redemption and the glorious freedom of the children of God (v. 21). And whatever "our weakness" may be, whether a generally human feature, as seems to be the case usually,[73] or an inability to pray, or "the external temptations of Christian existence,"[74] the Spirit is at work to help us in praying, in that the Spirit intercedes for us, does the "groaning" for redemption for us. The critical point Paul makes here is not so much a style or mode of prayer, either the (ecstatic) prayer of the spirit or the (rational) prayer of the mind—to use his way of differentiation in 1 Corinthians 14. The help of the Spirit is precisely with regard to "what we do not know," which is, "to pray as is necessary" (*katho dei*).

But the Spirit's intercession for the saints is "according to God" (*kata theon*, v. 27). In other words what the Spirit does is pray *according to God's will* (so the NRSV translation) or according to God's plan of salvation (vv. 28-30). Such prayer is at one and the same time an act of help to the Christian in a weakness that does not know to pray that way, that is, *katho dei*, and an act of intercession in our behalf. What is *katho dei*, "as is necessary," is precisely *kata theon*, "according to God." Here, therefore, Paul takes us into that crucial dimension of prayer that is to the forefront in the Old Testament, the prayer according to God's will. We must, therefore, turn more specifically to the question of praying according to the will of God.

THE WILL OF GOD AND A THEOLOGY OF THE CROSS

The question of the relationship of the human petition and the will of God is implicit in all petitionary prayer and supplication. In looking at the motivational clauses of the Old Testament prayers, we took note of the way that the one who prays presses his or her case on the deity, claiming that God's help (in various forms) is what should be done (chap. 3, above). Here there is an implicit assumption that the cry for help is appropriate because a priori it is God's will to save the innocent and the righteous. The experience of Israel and others has confirmed that. This assumption is made more explicit when the prayers seek to motivate God by asking for help "for your name's sake" or "according to your steadfast love." That is, the prayer is consistent with the will of God as it seeks something that is consistent with the divine nature.

In the New Testament, we begin to encounter the prayer for help that clearly subordinates the present trouble of the one who prays to the will of God, a somewhat different move from the assumption of the Old Testament prayers that deliverance from trouble is to be expected as the will of God. Several illustrations will help to show how that is the case.

1. "Your kingdom come, your will be done" (Matt 6:10). In the Lord's Prayer, the second and third petitions set the prayer for God's will as the first matter of prayer, and the prayer for the hallowing of God's name, reminiscent of the Old Testament motivation clause, "for your name's sake," is consistent with this starting point. While the prayer for deliverance is there—"deliver us from evil"[75]—the petitions "your kingdom come, your will be done" are prior and controlling. Structurally, therefore, in the movement of the model prayer Jesus taught his disciples, the prayer for the will of God takes priority over all other petitions

even though other and specific petitions are to be expected. As in the prayer that is "according to God" (Rom 8:27), there is an eschatological dimension to such praying. The prayer for the fulfillment of God's purposes is the controlling or initiating petition in the lesson Jesus gives.

2. "Remove this cup from me; yet, not my will but yours be done."[76] The prayer of Jesus in Gethsemane becomes the exemplum of the prayer he teaches the disciples: your will be done. The significance of this petition in the Lord's Prayer is thus underscored, and the community is given the definitive illustration of how to pray that petition when it moves from Jesus' teaching about prayer at the beginning of Matthew and Luke to his own prayer in time of oppression, suffering, and death. Jesus' prayer is for deliverance, but Jesus accepts the possibility that God's will may be otherwise. He subordinates his own will to God's, a dimension of the prayer for God's will to be done that is implicit in the Lord's Prayer but is now made explicit. Matthew's account, which reports Jesus' prayer a second time, takes this submission to the will of God a step further. The first prayer is: "My father, if it is possible, let this cup pass from me; yet not what I want but what you want." The second time Jesus prays: "My father, if this cannot pass unless I drink it, your will be done" (26:42). The prayer for help has become fully a prayer of submission to the will of God.[77]

3. "Father, glorify your name." The Johannine form of the Gethsemane prayer of anguish is found in John 12:27-28:

> Now my soul is troubled. And what should I say—"Father, save me from this hour"? No, it is for this reason that I have come to this hour. Father, glorify your name.

Here the Old Testament tradition of prayer joins with what is found in the Gospels but in a way that the prayer for help and deliverance is explicitly rejected, and the only prayer that is uttered is a prayer that is oriented entirely toward the glory of God. The Johannine Jesus knows what is the prayer for the occasion: "Father, save me from this hour." But such a prayer in this case would not be in conformity with God's will. So he rejects such a prayer and offers another one of a quite different sort. Whereas prayers for help that we have examined before plead for God's saving help "for your name's sake," that is, so that God's name may be magnified in the act of deliverance, that is not possible now. Jesus' deliverance from his suffering ("this hour") is not the purpose and will of God. So Jesus turns the typical motive clause, "for your name's sake," into a prayer, "Your name be glorified." This is not the familiar hymnic or thanksgiving praise of the name of God.[78] It is a petition that is entirely oriented toward God. Jesus in this instance does not even open the possibility of his deliverance in prayer, natural as that may be. His prayer is only for God's glory.[79]

4. "Three times I appealed to the Lord about this" (2 Cor 12:8). In his only report of a personal prayer for help to be delivered from some trouble, Paul's prayer for deliverance is rebuffed three times.[80] Instead the Lord says to him, "My grace is sufficient for you, for power is made perfect in weakness" (v. 9a). Paul prays for divine deliverance, but instead is told that his trouble and suffering, whatever they may be, are where the power of God will be manifest.[81] That is not, however, in a mighty act of deliverance. Paul will endure his suffering by the grace of Christ, and in it will find strength.

As in every case, we encounter here a particular situation. It is not like any of the above, but again the suffering of the praying, faithful petitioner is subordinated to another purpose.[82] The power of God at work in Paul will be made perfect in weakness, that is, in his trouble or suffering. And from this, Paul draws a large conclusion:

> So, I will boast all the more gladly of my weaknesses, so that the power of Christ may dwell in me. Therefore I am content with weaknesses, insults, hardships, persecutions, and calamities *for the sake of Christ;* for whenever I am weak, then I am strong. (vv. 9b-10)

The *appeal for help* "for your name's sake" has moved in Paul to an *acceptance of the trouble* "for the sake of Christ." As he indicates, this becomes a way of life for him. It does not mean that he will not appeal for prayers in his behalf from others. But those prayers are the intercession of the community, which is a different matter (see below), and they are to be prayers seeking God's help in his successful carrying out of his mission.[83] They are "for the sake of Christ" not Paul. Stendahl has penetrated to the heart of the matter when he says:

> But now he has learned to accept his handicap as a divine lesson about how his weakness bars him from self-glory. Thus this insight, won through prayer, becomes a key to his whole theology. Here in the very prayer life of Paul is the root of his famous theology of the cross (cf. 2 Cor 13:4).[84]

In these examples, therefore, Christian prayer begins to be shaped by a theology of the cross. We see that in Stephen's dying prayer, an imitation of Jesus' prayer from the cross: "Lord, do not hold this sin against them" (Acts 7:60). Jesus' drawing of the Old Testament prayers into the cross demonstrates their own cruciform shape and crucifixion context. These Old Testament prayers of the Psalter are now given a narrative context that tells us such prayers belong to the cross and its suffering, anticipated in the experience of Israel, and made normative now, but not simply as human cries of pain, which they truly are. They have become exemplary of Christian prayer as precisely power made perfect in weakness, the subordination of one's trouble and pain to that of the other (see below), and the subordination of one's will and need to God's will and purpose, to the kingdom and will of God. The Spirit praying within us *kata theon*, "according to God," is Christ at work within us to shape our prayers in just this way. Here is what it means to pray *kath dei*, "as is necessary" or "as we ought" (Rom 8:26).[85] All of this means that one has to look at the relation of suffering and prayer in a somewhat different fashion. The Christian community knows that suffering is now not just something that happens and is incomprehensible. The laments still remain as a voice for the cry of despair and suffering, and Job's raging dialogue with God articulates an all-too-human experience from which the Christian is no more protected than any other human being. Christian faith claims, however, that suffering has a different face because the one whom we call Lord has gone through it for us and with us.

Nor is suffering something from which we simply seek deliverance for ourselves. The way of Christ is the way of the cross. Suffering *for the world* as Christ suffered for the world is a part of conformity to the image of Christ. Not all of Christian suffering is automatically a suffering after the example of Christ in behalf of others, but the New Testament in various ways suggests that Christians who follow their Lord as fully as they can should expect to suffer for Christ's sake.[86] As we shall see, Paul seeks the prayers of the community for his deliverance from adversity, but something else than the relief of his suffering is at work there. It is precisely his commitment to the way of Christ that evokes such pleas, not his own well-being.

What this means is that the Christian says to every other person, "Your suffering matters more than my own." Those other persons may be friend or foe, near or far, known or unknown. The way of Christ has identified the suffering of the other as the place where Christ's followers are to be, in prayer and righteous action. The simple but important corollary of that fact is that intercession now takes precedence over the prayer of petition in the dialogue of faith. The prayer for the suffering of others is the paradigm of faithful prayer.

Such a conviction is not the exclusive claim or insight of Christian faith or to be found only by a reading of the New Testament. Josephus said the same thing about the same time but on other grounds:

> Prayers for the welfare of the community must take precedence of those for ourselves; for we are born for fellowship, and he who sets [the community's] claims above his private interest is specially acceptable to God.[87]

Those prayers for others are such a significant part of the New Testament that we must now turn to look at them more closely.

A COMMUNITY OF INTERCESSION

As the prayer of intercession moves to the forefront in the New Testament, it is no longer primarily the prayer of the leaders and prophets. It is now a responsibility of all the members of the Christian community. In one of the early accounts of persecution in the early church, when Peter is jailed by Herod, the writer of Acts reports that "while Peter was kept in prison, the church prayed fervently to God for him."[88] But Paul, especially, lifts up the intercessory activity of the community and encourages the congregations at every place to become "a mutually supportive community of intercession."[89] He frequently invites, indeed urges, a congregation to pray for him. Sometimes it is as simple as, "Pray for us," Paul's words at the conclusion of his first letter to the congregation at Thessalonica (1 Thess 5:25). The mutual support through intercession is well illustrated in this letter, for it begins with his words to the Thessalonians that "we always give thanks to God for all of you and mention you in our prayers" (1 Thess 1:2).[90] At other times the appeal is more elaborate, indicating the particular need for which Paul seeks the prayers of the communities.

> I appeal to you, brothers and sisters, by our Lord Jesus Christ and by the love of the Spirit, to join me in earnest prayer to God on my behalf, that I may be rescued from the unbelievers in Judaea, and that my ministry to Jerusalem may be acceptable to the saints, so that by God's will I may come to you with joy and be refreshed in your company. (Rom 15:30-32)

Here and elsewhere it is apparent that such exhortation to pray in his behalf is directly related to his mission.[91] The prayers are always, either directly or indirectly, a prayer for his success in his mission. Or, as in the case of his request to the Corinthians to "join in helping us by your prayers," he claims the goal of such prayer is the glory of God, that is, "so that *many will give thanks* on our behalf for the blessing granted us *through the prayers of many*" (2 Cor 1:11). The immediate aim is Paul's deliverance, but the ultimate goal is praise to God.[92] A similar correlation of Paul's deliverance and honor to God, or in this case, to Christ, is found in his request for prayer to the Philippians:

> For I know that through your prayers and the help of the Spirit of Jesus Christ this will turn out for my deliverance. It is my eager expectation and hope that I will not be put to shame in any way, but that by my speaking with all boldness, Christ will be exalted now as always in my body, whether by life or by death.
> (Phil 1:19-20)

Paul's own prayers for others are also to be found in the blessings that abound in his letters, especially at the beginning and end. While these belong to a different genre of prayer, they are never more clearly seen as prayer in behalf of others than in these letters.[93]

While Paul sets his exhortations to prayer in his behalf very much in the context of his mission, not all instruction concerning intercession is of that sort. In the letter of James, as we noted earlier, intercession for the sick is enjoined upon the community:

> Are any among you sick? They should call for the elders of the church and have them pray over them, anointing them with oil in the name of the Lord. The prayer of faith will save the sick, and the Lord will raise them up. (Jas 5:14-15a)

Here the community of supportive intercession is readily apparent, as is the conviction that such intercession is heard and answered by God. The structure of faith reflected in biblical prayer is illustrated once more. It is assumed that those who pray in trust and confidence will be heard and delivered.

As the call for intercession by the *elders* in James 5 indicates, however, the community of intercession in the New Testament does not mean that the responsibility for praying for the people is now no longer a matter for the leaders of the community. Quite the contrary. In fact, Paul himself is a classic example of the apostle praying for his people. The account in Acts 6 of the choosing of the Seven is instructive in this regard. For here is the first move to a structure and defined responsibilities in the early church. In this case, a group of seven persons is chosen to tend to the daily service of providing for the needy. What is to be observed in this connection, however, is that the apostles ask for this appointment so that they may devote themselves to "prayer and to serving the word" (Acts 6:4). That is, there is a double task and responsibility for the apostolate: the teaching and preaching of the word and prayer for the people. And the order of Acts 6:4 places prayer first, giving some weight to that responsibility. It is not simply a ministry of preaching that is incumbent upon them. Of equal significance is the act of prayer.[94] So while all are free to pray and called to pray, that is a central aspect of the vocation of those who are set apart to the ministry of preaching and teaching.

The stories of Acts tell us of God's servants, the leaders of the community, praying for healing and forgiveness, and not only for those who are members of the congregations. Stephen in his dying breath prays for forgiveness for those who kill him (Acts 7:60). And Simon Magus asks for the prayers of Peter and John that he might be forgiven and not perish (Acts 8:24). Peter and Paul both pray for healing of the sick (Acts 9:40; 28:8). As we know from James, however, the responsibility for intercession for the sick and the sinful was not alone assigned to the apostles. The elders of the church are enjoined to come and pray for the sick and anoint them.

As Paul's letters demonstrate, the prayers of intercession in the early Christian community are not confined to forgiveness and healing. They speak to various needs. Arland Hultgren, speaking of the New Testament as a whole and not just the prayers of the apostles, suggests there are six particularly prominent objects of intercessory prayer:

> First, there are intercessions for the growth of others in spiritual maturity (Eph 1:16-17; Phil 1:9; Col 1:9). Second, there are those asking that the gospel or the Christian witness may be extended through the ministry of others (Eph 6:18-20; Col 4:3; 2 Thess 3:1). Third, there are petitions and exhortations to pray for the physical healing of others (Acts 9:40; 28:8; Jas 5:13-16). Fourth, there are prayers for the deliverance of others from perilous conditions, such as imprisonment, and for safety in travel (Acts 12:5-12; Rom 15:30-32; Phil 1:19; Heb 13:18-19). Fifth, there are prayers for ruling authorities and for civil order (1 Tim 2:1-2). And finally, there are prayers made, or to be made, for persons outside or even opposed to, the Christian movement: Jesus instructs his followers to pray for their persecutors (Matt 5:44/Luke 6:28)...; and Paul prays that unbelieving Israel might be saved (Rom 10:1).[95]

The range of such petitions is affected by the circumstances of the narratives and letters of the apostles, but they are indicative of those concerns for the well-being of others that are characteristic of Christian prayer. Some of them are particularly characteristic of the apostolic ministry of Paul and his companions. Others are more familiar to us from the whole range of petitions for help in biblical prayers. The final category seems especially to mark Christian prayer, as indeed it does. But even the prayer of Paul for his people, Israel, so apparently a prayer of Christian presumption, is set in the context of Old Testament prophecy and places him in that line of God's servants, the prophets, who prayed for Israel's deliverance. It is so peculiarly a part of an extended and complex argument about Israel and the church that, like other prayers in Paul's letters that are so contingent upon the particular situation, the prayer for Israel's salvation or deliverance (Rom 10:1) may offer itself less as a model of Christian prayer than as a piece of the argument with which the church still wrestles, prayerfully.[96]

THE LORD'S PRAYER

Nothing is more central to the New Testament witness concerning prayer than that brief prayer that Jesus taught his disciples when asked by them to do so. Its exposition has brought forth an untold number of volumes. Here, we shall turn to it primarily to see how it encompasses so much of what we have seen in both the Old Testament and the New about the prayer of faith.

It begins as petitionary prayer customarily begins in the Old Testament with a direct address to God. The "Our Father" echoes the "My God" of Old Testament prayer even as it shifts it in ways that noticeably reflect what we have seen about prayer in the New Testament but that are not inconsistent with the prayers for help of the Old Testament. The critical feature of the address is its invoking of an intimate relationship, in this case seen as a reality (1) experienced in community, and (2) expressed in one of the most relational of all images, the familial and specifically parental metaphor of "father."

The communal context of the prayer of the Christian family is not to be overlooked. It draws in and opens up the prayer to the world. It assumes that our prayers for help are not solitary acts or expressions only of our personal relation to God. They belong to and arise out of a social solidarity with the Christian community and with all humankind so that the prayer is with others and in behalf of all others at one and the same time. Karl Barth has expressed the force of this plural address to God as follows:

> It implies the communion of all humanity praying with Jesus Christ, our existence in the fellowship of the children of God. . . .
>
> This "us" signifies also the communion of the one who prays with all those who are in his or her company and who are likewise invited to pray; with those who have received the same invitation, the same command, the same permission to pray beside Jesus Christ. We pray "Our Father" in the communion of this assembly, of this congregation which we call the church (if we take this expression in the original meaning of ecclesia, the congregation).
>
> But even while we are in the communion of the saints, in the ecclesia of those who are brought together by Jesus Christ, we are also in communion with those who do not yet pray, perhaps, but for whom Jesus Christ prays, since he prays for humankind as a whole. It is the object of this intercession, and we ourselves enter into this communion with the whole of humanity. When Christians pray, they are, so to speak, the substitutes for all those who do not pray; and in this sense they are in communion with them in

the same manner as Jesus Christ has entered into solidarity with sinners, with a lost human race.[97]

The familial or parental imagery in the address to God is something that we have already noted as characteristic but not unique to Christian prayer.[98] We are instructed in such language to address God as the one who has brought us into being, who regards us as the dearest of creatures, whose heart is always affected and moved by our needs, who instructs and teaches, who deals with us lovingly, with a justice that is always shaped and controlled by mercy, who is reliable and can be counted upon always. We address God thus as one who is with us in a manner that we comprehend in part from our own experience as sons and daughters and as mothers and fathers. We judge and comprehend and shape our own experience as sons and daughters and as mothers and fathers by our experience of God as our father and mother.

This last point is important. When we say "Our *Father*," we both know something about God and learn something about ourselves in such roles. The use of the term "Father" in address to God has become problematic in our days. But we, at least, ought to be clear about what the problematic is. It is not, as sometimes suggested, because some people have bad fathers. That may be just the reason why the imagery is necessary or desirable.[99] Further, every human image for the divine is problematic in that it may have negative connotations, strange connotations, or none at all. We would remain mute if all such imagery required perfect human examples.[100] Such imagery is primarily problematic when it is understood as exclusively paternal or male imagery that may be used to express the parental image.[101] But that is a misunderstanding of the force of the image in its original and present context. The issue here is the intimate, caring, relational image of a parent. That is what Jesus teaches when he says, "Pray like this." He teaches the freedom and marvelous possibility of addressing the Lord of the universe as a loving, caring, protecting, providing, disciplining parent, as a father or mother.

When "our Father" is addressed as "in heaven" we hear the claim of divine transcendence that is the presupposition of all prayer in the Old Testament.[102] So Solomon in the prayer of dedication of the temple again and again appeals to God to hear the prayer "in heaven your dwelling place."[103] Nehemiah speaks of fasting and praying "before the God of heaven" (Neh 1:4), and Ezra addresses the Lord as the one who "made heaven, the heaven of heavens, with all their host, the earth and all that is on it, the seas and all that are in them. To all of them you give life, and the host of heaven worships you" (Neh 9:6). Of particular note is the communal confession and petition for help in Isa 63:7—64:11. There the community *three times* says, "You are our father" (63:16; 64:8), and explicitly notes that this is not the case with regard to Abraham and Israel:

> Though Abraham does not know us
>   and Israel does not acknowledge us;
>   you, O LORD, are our father;
>   our Redeemer from of old is your name. (v. 16)

It is the *heavenly* father who is addressed in prayer, not the human "father" of the people. As Westermann puts it:

> Here, however, as the community makes its supplication to God, it says that it cannot put its trust in Abraham or Jacob: they do not know it. The way in which God is the father of Israel is entirely different from that in which Abraham and Jacob are the nation's fathers.[104]

The appeal to the divine parent whose realm is the heavens is made very explicit, however, in this ancient prayer of Israel. Twice the petitioner(s)[105] cry out to God to look down or come down from heaven to deliver them:

> Look down from heaven and see
>   from your holy and glorious habitation. (63:15)

> O that you would tear open the heavens and come down,
>   so that the mountains would quake at your presence. (64:1)

The one who is addressed in the personal and intimate form of "father" is the one whose abode is the heavens, whose response originates in the divine world. It is surely the case that the appeal to "Our Father, who art in heaven," holds together the personal relationship and accessibility with the transcendence and utter otherness of God.[106] But the address to God in heaven is not simply a safeguard of divine transcendence in our praying. Apart from the assumption "who art in heaven," that is, the one to whom human prayer is lifted is the transcendent God, the one in whom all creatures live and move and have their being, then our prayers are fruitless. If prayer is not to the one who is in heaven, beyond human ken, whose throne is above all and whose rule is over all, then our prayers are fruitless. The metaphor of heaven is a way of pointing to the possibility of prayer and to its efficacy. For heaven is the symbol of the divine governance, the rule of the universe. So the prayer assumes that God's will is done in heaven ("on earth as it is in heaven"). That is where God's rule has its origination and primary locus. It is from the heavenly realm that the divine decrees, the divine word that brings into being and effects all things, comes forth. Prayer to any other than the one who is in heaven is a waste of breath.

The three petitions that follow the opening address, the second-person petitions, all belong together and in some sense express a single or the same prayer:

> Hallowed be your name.
> Your kingdom come.
> Your will be done, on earth as it is in heaven.

The intent and effect of these petitions are to subordinate all prayer to the will and purpose of God. The starting point of Christian prayer on this model is the prayer for the effecting of *God's* purpose, not the prayer for our needs. The order is important in that the petitions for ourselves come only after and under the petitions for God to do and be what God will do and be or for God to accomplish through human and divine action the will and purpose that God seeks. We do not begin, according to this model, with the prayer for ourselves, but we place our words to God in the service of the work and purpose of God. Every petition and supplication and intercession is shaped and controlled by the prior prayer for the manifestation of God's rule and the accomplishment of God's will. Here, therefore, Jesus teaches what he clearly practiced at Gethsemane.

Such a starting point is not only consistent with what we have earlier noted about New Testament prayer generally, but it is also the ground for all the motivations of the Old Testament prayers for help and intercessions. When one hears in the Old Testament the prayer of the afflicted for God to help "for your name's sake," we hear an anticipation of the prayer that God's name be hallowed, that in all that we seek, the name of God, the being and reality and character of God, will be demonstrated, confirmed, vindicated. The specific Old Testament background for this petition is found at least partly also in Ezek 36:22-32:

> It is not for your sake, O house of Israel, that I am about to act, but *for the sake of my holy name,* which you have profaned among the nations to which you came. I will *sanctify [i.e., hallow] my great name,* which has been profaned among the nations, and which you have profaned among them; and the nations shall know that I am the LORD, when through you I display my holiness before their eyes. I will take you from the nations ... and bring you into your own land. I will sprinkle clean water upon you.... A new heart I will give you, and a new spirit I will put within you.... I will put my spirit within you, and make you follow my statutes and be careful to observe my ordinances.... *It is not for your sake that I will act,* says the Lord GOD.

All of this that the Lord will do with and among Israel is "for the sake of my holy name," that the Lord's name may be hallowed.[107] The question of whether such hallowing of the name is accomplished by God or by human beings is not an issue. The joining of these two is self-evident in this text as the Lord hallows the divine name by what takes place in and through Israel. So in its acts and in its praise of the name of God in hymns and prayers, the community of faith participates in the vindication and sanctification of the name of God.

The prayer, "Your kingdom come," echoes the Old Testament hymns of praise that celebrate God's rule, the enthronement hymns such as Ps 29:10:

> The LORD sits enthroned over the flood;
> the LORD sits enthroned as king forever.

The prayer sets the accomplishment of God's will and purpose in the context of a political image that does not leave the will of God as a vague, abstract conception but sees that purpose in terms of the establishment of an order, a way, a community that has a particular character. That such a petition has an eschatological dimension cannot be denied, but it is open in its formulation and is thus informed by all that the Scriptures teach us about the kingdom of God and its reality both now and then. The whole story of Israel is a story of God's effort to effect such a rule on earth as it is in heaven. The New Testament sees that rule very much underway in Jesus of Nazareth but still to be sought with prayer and righteous action (Matt 6:33).

The prayer for the doing of God's will "*on earth* as it is in heaven" carries forward the Old Testament placing of God's purpose and the petitions of God's people thoroughly in this world and its needs, problems, and possibilities.[108] All of what is expressed in these petitions to "our Father in heaven" is then carried forward into the life of the disciple in Jesus' further teaching in the Sermon on the Mount:

> Not everyone who says to me, "Lord, Lord," will enter the kingdom of heaven, but only the one who does the will of my Father in heaven. (Matt 7:21)

Here it becomes clear that these petitions are also the prayerful expression of our commitment to the First Commandment, "You shall have no other gods before me," that the beginning of everything we do is obedience to God's way. As Karl Barth has said with regard to these opening petitions, in praying them the community says to God, "Here we are, engrossed in thy cause."[109]

So it is then, to use Barth's language once more, that as the prayer goes on to become now petitions for ourselves, we say, in effect: "Therefore, to thee we hand over our existence—to thee, who has invited and commanded us to pray, to live for thy cause. Here we are. It is now up to thee to concern thyself with our human cause."[110] But as we have seen time and again, the prayers of Israel and the biblical story make clear that these are largely coincident. The human cause *is* God's cause.

"Give us this day our daily bread." Here is the most fundamental prayer for God's blessing and providence. It is like the prayers for God's blessing in the Old Testament, the prayer that God will provide what we need for our lives, keep them going from day to day with all that is needful to sustain them. The term "daily bread" is, of course, important in this regard because it points precisely to the regular provision of life that is the focus of blessing even as blessing is always open to a richness that we may not hear in the term "daily bread" but is always implicit in it. It is a prayer that is both limited and full. Its Old Testament symbol is the manna, God's daily and full provision for life, but not in a way that permits or leads to acquisitiveness, consumerism, and greed.[111]

"And forgive us our debts as we also have forgiven our debtors." In this petition, the confession of sin is regularized in Christian prayer, but it is done in the context of the petitions that we hear in the Old Testament time and time again, the prayers for forgiveness.[112] What the prayer does at this point is remind us that confession of sin has its meaning and place only as the prayer on the way to the plea for forgiveness. Christian prayer, like the Old Testament prayers, may place more weight of words and emphasis on the confession of sin than on the prayer for forgiveness and the assurance of God's pardon, but forgiveness is what the prayer of confession is all about.

This petition also places a focus on the other, the neighbor, though not in intercession. What we hear echoed at that point from the Old Testament is not so much its prayer as its divine word to act with the other as you would act with yourself (Lev 19:18b; Deut 5:14b). In Sir 28:2, however, the admonition is given that directly anticipates Jesus' instruction to his disciples about prayer:

> Forgive your neighbor the wrong he has done,
> and then your sins will be pardoned when you pray.

The prayer of Jesus thus juxtaposes God's dealings with us with the way we deal with others. "This explanation added to the petition is not to be understood as a *do ut des* attitude or as a 'condition'; rather it springs from the realization that God's forgiveness cannot be expected if human forgiveness is withheld."[113]

"And do not bring us into temptation" is a somewhat troubling petition as it suggests the agency and responsibility of God in persons being tempted to wrong actions, whether these are the "temptations which occur in everyday life"[114] or the sin of apostasy.[115] From the perspective of the Old Testament, that is, at least not so surprising. There are instances of explicit divine testing of human beings and even more of implicit testing. So the command to Abraham to sacrifice Isaac is a testing of him by God (Gen 22:1), and the time in the wilderness is a time of testing for the people (Deut 8:2). In other instances, the Lord sets human beings in situations that lead to temptations that may or may not be actual testings of human faithfulness and obedience. The Genesis story indicates that more than once.[116] The snake tempts the primeval couple to disobey God, and the story makes clear that all three are accountable for their sin. But the placing of the tree has created the circumstances in which temptation arises. That becomes even more the case in the Cain and Abel story where the divine response to the sacrifices of the brothers arouses in Cain an anger that may "lead him into temptation," as the deity well recognizes. Indeed this story may provide a clue to what the Lord's Prayer is after. For in the Cain and Abel story, the Lord calls Cain to a kind of self-control in saying, "You are to rule over"[117] the sin that is lying in wait for you. *He* is to deal with the anger and depression that have come upon him at the Lord's favorable response to Abel's sacrifice and not to his.

In the Lord's Prayer, however, we are led to pray that *God* will help us in such situations. The prayer means that the need of God's help is acknowledged in whatever the situation of temptation or testing. Whether it is God's restraining activity that keeps us from such situations rather than letting us be caught in them or the help of God to enable us to resist and "rule over" the situation and the temptation, we are not simply on our own. The Gospel context for this prayer is there in Jesus' words to the disciples in the garden: "Stay awake and pray that you may not come into the time of trial [or 'into temptation']; the spirit indeed is willing, but the flesh is weak" (Matt 26:41). The trial or temptation occasion is at hand. The danger is real. It is time for prayer on the model that Jesus has already taught the disciples. Jesus' own actions throughout the passion events are a demonstration of the human situation of testing and temptation wherein he again and again is faced with the kinds of testing that are explicitly laid at his feet by the temptations of the devil early in his ministry. In his "hour of trial," he prays to God for help, indeed that he may not be led into the time of trial, that the cup may pass from him. Even there, however, the prayer is subordinated to the will of God.

Both the passion story and the other instances we have cited make it clear that this petition cannot be kept separated for long from the one that follows it in Matthew: "But deliver us from evil." To the extent that the temptations that beset the Christian life are to be seen as the work of demonic power, then it is possible that the "evil" spoken of here can be "the evil one." But that is not necessarily the primary meaning of the petition. It is more apparently the basic petition of all the Old Testament prayers for help, the prayer for God's saving grace, God's delivering help in the face of any evil that may befall us—illness, oppression, insolent or evil people (see Ps 19:13), and the like. The Lord's Prayer thus comes at its end to encapsulate all those cries for help that we have seen at the heart of the prayers of the Psalter and the stories of people and communities in distress.

"For thine is the kingdom, the power, and the glory." The three-part doxology to the Lord's Prayer is not in the New Testament forms of it, but it was probably a very early addition to the prayer and so rightly belongs in its use.[118] In two significant ways it brings to expression in the model prayer what we have heard time and again in the biblical prayers. First, in its "for" or "because" we are reminded once more that the prayers for God's help and deliverance are proper because this is the one who has the power to deliver and also because such a response by God is appropriate to God's rule or kingship and a manifestation of or testimony to God's glory.

Finally, we hear again what we expect from the totality of the biblical witness, that the prayer of the Christian family closes in praise. The circle is complete. As the last psalm of the Psalter turns the prayers of Israel into utter praise, so the last word of Christian prayer is always praise. And even as the petitions of the Old Testament anticipate God's response with their vow of praise, so we anticipate God's response to our petitions and the accomplishment of God's kingdom and God's will in our ascriptions of praise.

Hallelujah! For the Lord our God the Almighty reigns.

Appendix 1

A Structural Outline of Prayers for Help and Intercession in Prose Texts

જ્જ

Genesis 15:1-6

OCCASION: An appearance of God to Abraham in a vision after the battle with the kings and the encounter with Melchizedek.

Address	"O LORD God,
Complaint	"What will you give me, for I continue childless....
Petition (implicit)	"You have given me no offspring, and so a slave born in my house is to be my heir."

DIVINE RESPONSE: God promises him offspring as numerous as the stars of the heavens.

Genesis 17:18

OCCASION: Abraham prays that Ishmael might be heir of God's promise.

Address	[none]
Petition	"O that Ishmael might live in your sight!"

DIVINE RESPONSE: God denies the petition.

Genesis 18:23-33

OCCASION: Abraham pleads in behalf of Sodom and Gomorrah.

Address	[none]
Petition	"Will you then sweep away the place and not forgive it? ... [Indirect in terms of different questions]
Motivation	"Far be it from you ... Shall not the judge of all the earth do what is just?"

DIVINE RESPONSE: No immediate response, but see 19:29: "So it was that, when God destroyed the cities of the Plain, God remembered Abraham, and sent Lot out of the midst of the overthrow, when he overthrew cities in which Lot had settled."

Genesis 21:16

OCCASION: Having been sent out into the wilderness and having used up all their water, Hagar puts her child under a bush to die. She lifts up her voice and weeps.

Address	[none]
Petition	"Do not let me look on the death of the child." (Cf. Num 11:15)

DIVINE RESPONSE: "And God heard the voice of the boy; and the angel of God called to Hagar from heaven, and said to her, 'What troubles you, Hagar? Do not be afraid; for God has heard the voice of the boy where he is. Come, lift up the boy and hold him fast with your hand, for I will make a great nation of him. Then God opened her eyes and she saw a well of water" (vv. 17-18).

Genesis 24:12-14

OCCASION: Eliezer, Abraham's servant, seeks God's help in securing a wife for Isaac.

Address	"O LORD, God of my master Abraham,
Petition	"please grant me success today and show steadfast love to my master, Abraham. I am standing here by the spring of water, and the daughters of the townspeople are coming out to draw water. Let the girl to whom I shall say, 'Please offer your jar that I may drink,' and who shall say, 'Drink, and I will water your camels'—let her be the one whom you have appointed for your servant Isaac. By this I shall know that you have shown steadfast love to my master."

DIVINE RESPONSE: The narrative recounts the success of Eliezer's plan, and in verses 26-27 he gives thanks to God.

Genesis 32:9-12

OCCASION: Jacob's prayer before he encounters his brother Esau at the Jabbok.

Address	"O God of my father Abraham and God of my father Isaac, O LORD who said to me, 'Return to your country and to your kindred, and I will do you good,'
Motivation & Praise	"I am not worthy of the least of all the steadfast love and all the faithfulness that you have shown to your servant, for with only my staff I crossed this Jordan; and now I have become two companies.
Petition	"Deliver me, please, from the hand of my brother, from the hand of Esau,

Motivation	"for I am afraid of him; he may come and kill us all, the mothers with the children. Yet you have said, 'I will surely do you good, and make your offspring as the sand of the sea which cannot be counted because of their number."

DIVINE RESPONSE: The divine response is indicated in Jacob's words in Gen 35:3: "Come, let us go up to Bethel, that I may make an altar there to the God who answered me in the day of my distress and has been with me wherever I have gone."

Exodus 5:22-23

OCCASION: Moses complains to God because Pharaoh has increased the Hebrews' burdens.

Address	"O LORD,
Complaint	"*why* have you mistreated this people? *Why* did you ever send me?
Elaboration of complaint	"Since I first came to Pharaoh to speak in your name, he has mistreated this people,
Petition (implicit)	"and you have done nothing at all to deliver your people."

DIVINE RESPONSE: "Now you will see what I will do to Pharaoh. Indeed, by a mighty hand he will let them go" (6:1).

Exodus 17:4

OCCASION: Moses cries out in complaint to God because of the people's murmuring against him for their thirstiness.

Address	[none]
Complaint *Lament*	"What shall I do with this people? "They are almost ready to stone me."
Petition	[implicit]

DIVINE RESPONSE: God tells Moses to strike a rock and water will come forth for the people to drink.

Exodus 32:11-13 (cf. Deut 9:25ff.)

OCCASION: Moses' intercession in behalf of the people after they have made the golden calf.

Address	"O LORD,

Complaint	"why does your wrath burn hot against your people, whom you brought out of the land of Egypt with great power and a mighty hand? Why should the Egyptians say, 'It was with evil intent that he brought them out to kill them in the mountains and to consume them from the face of the earth?'
Petition	"Turn from your fierce wrath; change your mind and do not bring disaster on your people. Remember Abraham, Isaac, and Israel your servants, how you swore to them by your own self, saying,
Motivation (implicit)	" 'I will multiply your descendants like the stars of heaven, and all this land I have promised I will give to your descendants, and they shall inherit it forever.' "

DIVINE RESPONSE: "And the LORD changed his mind about the disaster that he planned to bring on his people."

Exodus 32:31-32

OCCASION: Same as the preceding (*confession* and *intercession*).

Address	[none]
Confession	"Alas, this people has sinned a great sin; they have made for themselves gods of gold....
Petition	"If you will only forgive their sin—but if not, blot me out of the book."

DIVINE RESPONSE: "Whoever has sinned against me I will blot out."

Numbers 11:10-15

OCCASION: Moses complains about the heavy burden of leading the people.

Address	[none]
Complaint	"Why have you treated your servant so badly? Why have I not found favor in your sight, that you lay the burden of all this people upon me? Did I conceive all this people? Did I give birth to them, that you should say to me, 'Carry them in your bosom, as a nurse carries a sucking child,' to the land that you promised on oath to their ancestors? Where am I to get meat to give to all this people?
Lament	"For they come weeping to me and say, 'Give us meat to eat.' I am not able to carry all this people alone,
Motivation	"for they are too heavy for me.
Complaint	"If this is the way you are going to treat me,

Petition	*a.*	"put me to death at once—if I have found favor in your
(Motivation)		sight—
	b.	"and do not let me see my misery."

DIVINE RESPONSE: The Lord says: "I will take some of the spirit that is on you and put it upon them; and they shall bear the burden of the people along with you so that you will not bear it all by yourself" (v. 17).

Numbers 12:13

OCCASION: Moses "cries out" to God to heal Miriam's leprosy.

Address	"O God,
Petition	"please heal her."

DIVINE RESPONSE: The response is ambiguous. Miriam is kept outside the camp for seven days. When she is brought in the march resumes.

Numbers 14:13-19

OCCASION: Moses' intercession to keep God from destroying the people.

Address	"O LORD, [2 times]
Motivation	"Then the Egyptians will hear of it, for in your might you brought up this people from among them, and they will tell the inhabitants of this land. They have heard that you, O LORD, are in the midst of this people; for you, O LORD, are seen face to face, and your cloud stands over them and you go in front of them, in a pillar of cloud by day and in a pillar of fire by night. Now if you kill this people all at one time, then the nations who have heard about you will say, 'It is because the LORD was not able to bring this people into the land he swore to give them that he has slaughtered them in the wilderness.'
Petition	"And now, therefore, let the power of the LORD be great in the way you promised when you spoke, saying,
Motivation	" 'The LORD is slow to anger. . . .'
Petition	"Forgive the iniquity of this people
Motivation	*a.* "according to the greatness of your steadfast love, *b.* "just as you have pardoned this people from Egypt even until now."

DIVINE RESPONSE:
a. The Lord forgives in explicit response to Moses' petition.
b. But none of the present rebellious generation except Caleb shall be allowed to go into the land.

Numbers 16:22

OCCASION: Moses and Aaron intercede for congregation at Korah's rebellion.

Address   "O God, the God of the spirits of all flesh,

Complaint   "Shall one person sin and you become angry with the whole congregation?"

Motivation   [implicit in complaint]
and petition

DIVINE RESPONSE: "And the LORD spoke to Moses, saying: 'Say to the congregation: Get away from the dwellings of Korah, Dathan, and Abiram.'"

Numbers 27:16-17

OCCASION: Moses, forbidden to enter the land, asks the Lord to appoint a leader.

Address   "Let the LORD, the God of the spirits of all flesh,

Petition   "appoint someone over the congregation who shall go out before them and come in before them, who shall lead them out and bring them in,

Motivation   "so that the congregation of the LORD may not be like a sheep without a shepherd."

DIVINE RESPONSE: The Lord tells Moses to take Joshua and commission him as leader.

Deuteronomy 3:23-25

OCCASION: Moses asks the Lord to let him go over and see the land beyond the Jordan.

Address   (extended) "O Lord GOD,

[Praise]   "You have only begun to show your servant your greatness and your might. What god in heaven or on earth can perform deeds and mighty acts like yours?

Petition   "Let me cross over to see the good land beyond Jordan."

DIVINE RESPONSE: "But the LORD was angry with me on your account and did not listen."

Deuteronomy 9:25-29

OCCASION: Moses' intercession in behalf of the people after they have made the golden calf.

Address   "Lord GOD,

Petition	*a.*	"do not destroy the people who are your very own possession, whom you redeemed in your greatness, whom you brought out of Egypt with a mighty hand.
	b.	"Remember your servants, Abraham, Isaac, and Jacob;
	c.	"pay no attention to the stubbornness of this people, their wickedness and their sin,
Motivation	*a.*	"otherwise the land from which you brought us might say, 'Because the LORD was not able to bring them to the land he promised them and because he hated them, he has brought them out to let them die in the wilderness.'
	b.	"They are the people of your very own possession, whom you brought out by your great power and by your outstretched hand."

DIVINE RESPONSE: "And the LORD said to me, 'Get up, go on your journey at the head of the people, that they may go in and occupy the land, which I swore to their ancestors to give them" (Deut 10:11).

Joshua 7:7-9

OCCASION: Joshua complains to God after the Israelites have been defeated by the men of Ai.

Address		"Ah, Lord GOD!
Complaint	*a.*	"Why have you brought this people across the Jordan at all, to hand us over to the Amorites so as to destroy us? Would that we had been content to settle beyond the Jordan.
	b.	"O LORD, what can I say, now that Israel has turned their backs to their enemies!
Lament		"The Canaanites...will hear of it, and surround us, and cut off our name from the earth.
Motivation (implicit petition)	*c.*	"Then what will you do for your great name?"

DIVINE RESPONSE: "Israel has sinned" (v. 11).

Judges 6:13

OCCASION: The Israelites cry to the Lord on account of the Midianites (6:7), and Gideon is here chosen and commissioned to lead the people against them. The angel of the Lord, a surrogate for the Lord in Judges, appears to Gideon with the words of assurance, "The LORD is with you, you mighty warrior" (v. 12). Gideon's response is a prayer of complaint.

Address	"But sir [or LORD],

Complaint	if the LORD is with us, why then has all this happened to us? And where are all his wonderful deeds that our ancestors recounted to us, saying,
(implicit petition)	'Did not the LORD bring us up from Egypt?' But now the LORD has cast us off, and given us into the hand of Midian."

DIVINE RESPONSE: Gideon is commissioned to go and deliver Israel from the hand of Midian.[1]

Judges 6:22

OCCASION: "Then Gideon perceived that it was the angel of the LORD; and Gideon said,

Address	"Help me, Lord GOD.
Lament (implicit petition)	"For I have seen the angel of the LORD face to face."

DIVINE RESPONSE: "But the LORD said to him, 'Peace be to you; do not fear, you shall not die.' "

Judges 10:10, 15

OCCASION: The Israelites confess their sin and cry out for help after being oppressed by the Philistines and the Ammonites.

Address	[none]
Confession	*a.* "We have sinned against you, because we have abandoned our God and have worshiped the Baals.
	b. "We have sinned.
Petition	"Do to us whatever seems good to you; but deliver us this day!"

DIVINE RESPONSE: "So they put away the foreign gods from among them and worshiped the LORD; and he could no longer bear to see Israel suffer."

Judges 13:8

OCCASION: Manoah entreats the Lord for help in what to do with the boy (i.e., Samson) that will be born to him and his wife.

Address	"O LORD, I pray,
Petition	"let the man of God whom you sent come to us again and teach us what we are to do concerning the boy who will be born."

DIVINE RESPONSE: "God listened to Manoah, and the angel of God came again to the woman as she sat in the field" (v. 9).

Judges 15:18

OCCASION: After killing the Philistines with the jawbone of an ass, Samson becomes very thirsty and calls on the name of the Lord.

Address	[none]
Motivation	"You have granted this great victory by the hand of your servant.
Lament-Petition	"Am I now to die of thirst and fall into the hands of the uncircumcised?"

DIVINE RESPONSE: "So God split open the hollow place that is at Lehi, and water came from it. When he drank, his spirit returned, and he revived" (v. 19).

Judges 16:28

OCCASION: In the temple of Dagon, blind Samson prays for strength to pull down the pillars of the temple.

Address	"Lord GOD . . . O God,
Petition	"remember me and strengthen me only this once,
Motivation	"so that with this one act of revenge I may pay back the Philistines for my two eyes."

DIVINE RESPONSE: There is no reference to divine activity here, but Samson grasps the pillars and pulls the temple down.

Judges 21:3

OCCASION: After destroying the Benjaminites, the Israelites lift up their voices and weep bitterly to God.

Address	"O LORD, the God of Israel,
Complaint	"why has it come to pass that today there should be one tribe lacking in Israel?"

DIVINE RESPONSE: None is indicated. The Israelites develop various schemes of rape and destruction to repopulate the Benjaminites.

2 Samuel 7:18-29

OCCASION: David goes in and sits before the Lord after Nathan has reported the divine promise to David.

Address	"O Lord GOD[2] [repeated eight times in the prayer], O LORD you, O LORD of hosts, the God of Israel." [This address grows out of the immediately preceding designation of this as God's name: "Your name will be magnified forever in the saying, 'The LORD of hosts is God over Israel.'"]

Praise	Praise is interspersed throughout the prayer. Verses 18-24 are virtually entirely praise: "Who am I, O Lord GOD, and what is my house, that you have brought me thus far? And yet this was a small thing in your eyes, O Lord GOD; you have spoken also of your servant's house for a great while to come. May this be instruction for the people,[3] O Lord GOD! And what more can David say to you? For you know your servant, O Lord GOD! Because of your promise, and according to your own heart, you have wrought all this greatness, so that your servant may know it. Therefore you are great, O Lord GOD; for there is no one like you and there is no God besides you, according to all that we have heard with our ears. Who is like your people, like Israel? Is there another nation on earth whose God went to redeem it as a people, and to make a name for himself, doing great and awesome things for them, by driving out before his people[4] nations and their gods? And you established your people Israel for yourself to be your people forever; and you, O LORD, became their God.
Petition	"And now, O Lord GOD, as for the word that you have spoken concerning your servant and concerning his house, confirm it forever; do as you have promised.
Motivation	"Thus your name will be magnified forever in the saying, 'The LORD of hosts is God over Israel'; and the house of your servant David will be established before you. For you, O LORD of hosts, the God of Israel, have made this revelation to your servant, saying, 'I will build you a house'; therefore your servant has found courage to pray this prayer to you. And now, O Lord GOD, you are God, and your words are true, and you have promised this good thing to your servant;
Petition	"now therefore may it please you to bless the house of your servant,
Motivation	"so that it may continue forever before you; for you, O Lord GOD, have spoken, and with your blessing shall the house of your servant be blessed forever."

DIVINE RESPONSE: No immediate response. The story of the Judahite monarchy confirms the promise and the blessing.

2 Samuel 15:31

OCCASION: David fleeing before Absalom has gone up the ascent of the Mount of Olives with the people weeping.

Address	"O LORD, I pray you,

Petition   "turn the counsel of Ahithophel into foolishness."

DIVINE RESPONSE: David works out a plan to do this, and when that happens it is reported: "For the LORD had ordained to defeat the good counsel of Ahithophel, so that the LORD might bring ruin on Absalom" (2 Sam 17:14).

1 Kings 3:6-9 ‖ 2 Chronicles 1:8-10

OCCASION: "At Gibeon the LORD appeared to Solomon in a dream by night; and God said, 'Ask what I should give you.'"

Address   "O LORD my God [in the middle of the prayer],

Praise   "You have shown great and steadfast love to your servant my father David, because he walked before you in faithfulness, in righteousness, and in uprightness of heart toward you; and you have kept for him this great and steadfast love, and have given him a son to sit on his throne today.

Motivation   "And now, O LORD my God, you have made your servant king in place of my father David, although I am only a little child; I do not know how to go out or come in. And your servant is in the midst of the people whom you have chosen, a great people, so numerous they cannot be numbered or counted.

Petition   "Give your servant therefore an understanding mind to govern your people, able to discern between good and evil; for who can govern this your great people?"

DIVINE RESPONSE: "It pleased the LORD that Solomon had asked this. God said to him,... 'I now do according to your word. Indeed I give you a wise and discerning mind; no one like you has been before you and no one like you shall arise after you. I give you also what you have not asked, both riches and honor all your life; no other king shall compare with you. If you will walk in my ways, keeping my statutes and my commandments, as your father David walked, then I will lengthen your life.'"

1 Kings 8:22-53 ‖ 2 Chronicles 6:14-42

OCCASION: Solomon's prayer of dedication in the newly built temple.

Address   "O LORD, God of Israel [three times throughout first part of prayer],
"O LORD, my God,...
"O Lord GOD,

Praise	"there is no God like you in heaven above or on earth beneath, keeping covenant and steadfast love for your servants who walk before you with all their heart, the covenant that you kept for your servant my father David as you declared to him; you have promised with your mouth and have this day fulfilled with your hand.
Petition	"Therefore, O LORD, God of Israel, keep for your servant my father David that which you promised him, saying, 'There shall never fail you a successor before me to sit on the throne of Israel, if only your children look to their way, to walk before me as you have walked before me.' Therefore, O God of Israel, let your word be confirmed, which you promised to your servant my father David."

Series of circumstance + petition

General circumstance: "But will God indeed dwell on the earth? Even heaven and the highest heaven cannot contain you, much less this house that I have built!

General petition: "Regard your servant's prayer and his plea, O LORD my God, heeding the cry and the prayer that your servant prays to you today; that your eyes may be open night and day toward this house, the place of which you said, 'My name shall be there,' that you may heed the prayer that your servant prays toward this place. Hear the plea of your servant and of your people Israel when they pray toward this place; O hear in heaven your dwelling place; heed and forgive."

First particular circumstance: "If someone sins against a neighbor and is given an oath to swear, and comes and swears before your altar in this house,

First particular petition: "then hear in heaven, and act, and judge your servants, condemning the guilty by bringing their conduct on their own head, and vindicating the righteous by rewarding them according to their righteousness."

Second particular circumstance: "When your people Israel, having sinned against you, are defeated before an enemy but turn again to you, confess your name, pray and plead with you in this house,

Second particular petition: "then hear in heaven, forgive the sin of your people Israel, and bring them again to the land that you gave to their ancestors."

Third particular circumstance: "When heaven is shut up and there is no rain because they have sinned against you, and then they pray toward this place, confess your name, and turn from their sin, because you punish them,

Third particular petition: "then hear in heaven, and forgive the sin of your servants, your people Israel, when you teach them the good way in which they should walk; and grant rain on your land, which you have given to your people as an inheritance."

Fourth particular-comprehensive circumstance: "If there is famine in the land, if there is plague, blight, mildew, locust, or caterpillar; if their enemy besieges them in any of their cities; whatever plague, whatever sickness there is; whatever prayer, whatever plea there is from any individual or from all your people Israel, all knowing the afflictions of their own hearts so that they stretch out their hands toward this house;

Fourth particular-comprehensive petition: "then hear in heaven your dwelling place, forgive, act, and render to all whose hearts you know—according to all their ways, for only you know what is in every human heart—

    Motivation for fourth petition: "so that they may fear you all the days that they live in the land that you gave to our ancestors."

Fifth particular circumstance: "Likewise when a foreigner, who is not of your people Israel, comes from a distant land because of your name—for they shall hear of your great name, your mighty hand, and your outstretched arm—when a foreigner comes and prays toward this house,

Fifth particular petition: "then hear in heaven your dwelling place, and do according to all that the foreigner calls to you,

    Motivation for fifth petition: "so that all the peoples of the earth may know your name and fear you, as do your people Israel, and so that they may know that your name has been invoked on this house that I have built."

Sixth particular circumstance: "If your people go out to battle against their enemy, by whatever way you shall send them, and they pray to the LORD toward the city that you have chosen and the house that I have built for your name,

Sixth particular petition: "then hear in heaven their prayer and their plea, and maintain their cause."

Seventh particular-complex circumstance: "If they sin against you—for there is no one who does not sin—and you are angry with them and give them to an enemy so that they are carried away captive to the land of the enemy, far off or near; yet if they come to their senses in the land to which they have been taken captive, and repent, and plead with you in the land of their captors, saying, 'We have sinned and have done wrong; we have acted wickedly'; if they repent with all their heart and soul in the land of their enemies, who took them captive, and pray to you toward their land, which you gave to their ancestors, the city that you have chosen, and the house that I have built for your name;

Seventh particular-complex petition: "then hear in heaven your dwelling place their prayer and their plea, maintain their cause and forgive your people who have sinned against you, and all their transgressions that they have committed against you; and grant them compassion in the sight of their captors, so that they may have compassion on them

    Motivation for seventh petition: "(for they are your people and heritage, which you brought out of Egypt, from the midst of the iron-smelter)."

Final general petition and circumstance: "Let your eyes be open to the plea of your servant, and to the plea of your people Israel, listening to them whenever they call to you.

    Motivation for final petition: "For you have separated them from among all the peoples of the earth, to be your heritage, just as you promised through Moses, your servant, when you brought our ancestors out of Egypt, O Lord God."

1 Kings 17:17-24

OCCASION: The son of the widow with whom Elijah lives is near death, and she accuses him of having brought about the illness. Elijah takes the child to his bed and lays him down. He prays once (lit. "cries out") and then stretches himself upon the child three times and cries out to the Lord a second prayer. (Intercession)

FIRST PRAYER:

Address	"O LORD my God,
Complaint	"have you brought calamity even upon the widow with whom I am staying, by killing her son?"

SECOND PRAYER:

Address	"O LORD my God,
Petition	"let this child's life come into him again."

DIVINE RESPONSE: "The LORD listened to the voice of Elijah; the life of the child came into him again, and he revived."

1 Kings 18:36-37

OCCASION: Elijah prays for God to rain down fire on his offering in the contest with the prophets of Baal on Mount Carmel.

Address	"O LORD, God of Abraham, Isaac, and Israel,... O LORD,...O LORD,
Petition	"let it be known this day that you are God in Israel, that I am your servant, and that I have done all these things at your bidding. Answer me, O LORD, answer me,
Motivation	"so that this people may know that you, O LORD, are God, and that you have turned their hearts back."

DIVINE RESPONSE: "Then the fire of the LORD fell and consumed the burnt offering.... [T]hey [the people] fell on their faces and said: 'The LORD indeed is God; the LORD indeed is God.' "

1 Kings 19:4

OCCASION: Elijah on Horeb under the broom tree asks that he might die.

Address	"O LORD,
Petition	"[i]t is enough now, take away my life,
Motivation	"for I am no better than my ancestors."

DIVINE RESPONSE: An angel comes and tells Elijah to get up and eat. Then the word of the Lord comes telling him to go back to the tasks to which God has set him.

2 Kings 6:17-18, 20

OCCASION: Samaria is surrounded by the Aramaean army, and Elisha's servant is frightened.

Address	"O LORD,
Petition	"please open his eyes that he may see."

DIVINE RESPONSE: "So the LORD opened the eyes of the servant and he saw."

v. 18   "When the Arameans came down against him, Elisha prayed to the LORD and said,

Address	[none]
Petition	"strike this people, please, with blindness."

DIVINE RESPONSE: "So he struck them with blindness as Elisha had asked."

v. 20   "As soon as they entered Samaria, Elisha said,

Address	"O LORD,
Petition	"open the eyes of these men so that they may see."

DIVINE RESPONSE: "The LORD opened their eyes, and they saw that they were inside Samaria."

2 Kings 19:14-19 ‖ Isaiah 37:14-20 (‖ 2 Chronicles 32:20)

OCCASION: Hezekiah's prayer upon receiving the message of the king of Assyria at Libnah challenging the power of the God of Israel to keep Jerusalem from being given into the hand of the Assyrian king.

Address and *Praise*	"O LORD the God of Israel, who are enthroned above the cherubim, you are God, you alone, of all the kingdoms of the earth; you have made heaven and earth."
Petition	for a hearing: "Incline your ear, O LORD, and hear; open your eyes, O LORD, and see; hear the words of Sennacherib,

Motivation	(1) appeal to divine reputation	"which he has sent to mock the living God.
	(2) appeal to human need	"Truly, O LORD, the kings of Assyria have laid waste the nations and their lands,
	(3) appeal to divine reputation	"and have hurled their gods into the fire....
Petition	for deliverance: "So now, O LORD our God, save us, I pray you, from his hand so that all the kingdoms of the earth may	
Motivation	(4) appeal to divine reputation	"know that you, O LORD, are God alone."

DIVINE RESPONSE: "Then Isaiah the son of Amoz sent to Hezekiah saying, 'Thus says the LORD, the God of Israel: I have heard your prayer to me about King Sennacherib of Assyria.... He shall not come in this city or shoot an arrow there, come before it with a shield, or cast up a siege-ramp against it" (vv. 20, 32).

2 Kings 20:3 ‖ Isaiah 38:3 (‖ 2 Chronicles 32:24)

OCCASION: "In those days Hezekiah became sick and was at the point of death.... Hezekiah wept bitterly" (vv. 1, 3).

Address	"O LORD, I implore you,
Motivation (implicit *petition*)	"remember now, how I have walked before you in faithfulness with a whole heart, and have done what is good in your sight."

DIVINE RESPONSE: " 'Thus says the LORD, the God of your ancestor David: I have heard your prayer, I have seen your tears; indeed, I will heal you; on the third day you shall go up to the house of the LORD. I will add fifteen years to your life. I will deliver you and this city out of the hand of the king of Assyria; I will defend this city for my own sake and for my servant David's sake.' Then Isaiah said, 'Bring a lump of figs. Let them take it and apply it to the boil, so that he may recover' " (vv. 5-7).

1 Chronicles 4:10

OCCASION: No context is given except the immediately preceding name explanation: "His mother named him Jabez, saying, 'Because I bore him in pain ['ōṣeb].' "

Address   [none]

Petition   "Oh that you would bless me and enlarge my border, and
               that your hand might be with me, and that you would keep
               me from hurt and harm!"

DIVINE RESPONSE: "And God granted what he asked."

2 Chronicles 14:11

OCCASION: King Asa, facing Zerah the Ethiopian in battle, calls to the Lord.

Address   "O LORD,...O LORD our God,...O LORD,

Praise/   "there is no difference for you between helping the mighty
Motivation   and the weak.

Petition   "Help us, O LORD our God,

Motivation   "for we rely on you, and in your name we have come against
               this multitude. O LORD, you are our God; let no mortal
               prevail against you."

DIVINE RESPONSE: "So the LORD defeated the Ethiopians before Asa and before
Judah, and the Ethiopians fled" (v. 18).

2 Chronicles 20:5-12

OCCASION: Moabites, Ammonite, and Edomites come out against Judah. "Jehoshaphat was afraid; he set himself to seek the LORD, and proclaimed a fast
throughout all Judah. Judah assembled to seek help from the LORD; from all
the towns of Judah they came to seek the LORD." Jehoshaphat prays in the
assembly, in the house of the Lord, before the new court.

Address   "O LORD, God of our ancestors,...O our God,...

Praise/   "are you not God in heaven? Do you not rule over all the
Motivation   kingdoms of the nations? In your hand are power and might,
               so that no one is able to withstand you. Did you not, O our
               God, drive out the inhabitants of this land before your people
               Israel, and give it forever to the descendants of your friend
               Abraham? They have lived in it, and in it have built you a
               sanctuary for your name, saying, 'If disaster comes upon us,
               the sword, judgment, or pestilence, or famine, we will stand
               before this house, and before you, for your name is in this
               house, and cry to you in our distress, and you will hear and
               save.'

Lament	"See now, the people of Ammon, Moab, and Mount Seir, whom you would not let Israel invade when they came from the land of Egypt, and whom they avoided and did not destroy—they reward us by coming to drive us out of your possession that you have given us to inherit....
Petition	"[W]ill you not execute judgment upon them?
Motivation	"For we are powerless against this great multitude that is coming against us. We do not know what to do, but our eyes are on you."

DIVINE RESPONSE: Jehaziel, upon whom the spirit of the Lord comes, gives a divine oracle of salvation. The Moabites, Ammonites, and Edomites end up destroying each other after "the LORD set an ambush against the Ammonites, Moab, and Mount Seir, who had come against Judah, so that they were routed" (v. 22).

2 Chronicles 30:19-20

OCCASION: "For a multitude of the people, many of them from Ephraim, Manasseh, Issachar, and Zebulun, had not cleansed themselves, yet they ate the passover otherwise than as prescribed. But Hezekiah prayed for them, saying,

| Address | [none] |
| Petition | "The good LORD pardon all who set their hearts to seek God, the LORD the God of their ancestors, even though not in accordance with the sanctuary's rules of cleanness." |

DIVINE RESPONSE: "The LORD heard Hezekiah, and healed the people."

Nehemiah 4:4-5

OCCASION: Sanballat and Tobiah mock the Jews as they are building the walls of the city. The prayer has no introduction and presumably is Nehemiah's prayer.

Address	"O our God,
Petition	"hear,
Lament and Motivation	"for we are despised;
Petition	"turn their taunt back on their own heads, and give them over as plunder in a land of captivity. Do not cover their guilt, and do not let their sin be blotted out from your sight;
Lament and Motivation	"for they have hurled insults in the face of the builders."

DIVINE RESPONSE: None indicated.

Jeremiah 4:10 (cf. 14:13)

OCCASION: In the immediately preceding verse, God has given an announcement that what is about to happen will utterly demoralize the leadership of Judah.

Address	"Ah, Lord GOD [cf. 14:13; 32:17; Josh 7:7; Judg 6:22],
Complaint	"how utterly you have deceived this people and Jerusalem, saying, 'It shall be well with you,' even while the sword is at the throat!"

DIVINE RESPONSE: None given.

Jeremiah 32:16-25

OCCASION: With the Babylonian army besieging Jerusalem, God has commanded Jeremiah to buy his cousin's field at Anathoth, saying that houses and fields and vineyards shall again be bought in the land. After giving the deed of purchase to Baruch, Jeremiah "prayed to the LORD."

Address	"Ah Lord GOD! [cf. 4:10; 14:13; Ezek 9:8; 11:13; Josh 7:7; Judg 6:22]
Praise	"It is you who made the heavens and the earth by your great power and by your outstretched arm! Nothing is too hard for you. You show steadfast love to the thousandth generation, but repay the guilt of parents into the laps of their children after them, O great and mighty God whose name is the LORD of hosts, great in counsel and mighty in deed; whose eyes are open to all the ways of mortals, rewarding all according to their ways and according to the fruit of their doings. You showed signs and wonders in the land of Egypt, and to this day in Israel and among all humankind, and have made yourself a name that continues to this very day. You brought your people Israel out of the land of Egypt with signs and wonders, with a strong hand and outstretched arm, and with great terror; and you gave them this land, which you swore to their ancestors to give them, a land flowing with milk and honey; and they entered and took possession of it. But they did not obey your voice or follow your law; of all you commanded them to do, they did nothing. Therefore you have made all these disasters come upon them.
Complaint and Lament	"See, the siege-ramps have been cast up against the city to take it, and the city, faced with sword, famine, and pestilence, has been given into the hands of the Chaldeans who are fighting against it. What you spoke has happened, as you yourself can see. Yet you, O LORD God, have said to me, 'Buy the field for money and get witnesses'—though the city has been given into the hands of the Chaldeans."

DIVINE RESPONSE: "The word of the LORD came to Jeremiah: See, I am the LORD, the God of all flesh; is anything too hard for me?"

Jeremiah 45:3

OCCASION: Jeremiah's scribe, Baruch, receives a word of divine assurance (a salvation oracle) after having cried out in complaint to God—much like Jeremiah—for the burden he had had to carry as Jeremiah's scribe (see, e.g., Jer 36:19, 26). The oracle incorporates Baruch's prayer:

Complaint	"Woe is me! The LORD has added sorrow to my pain;
Lament	"I am weary with my groaning and find no rest."

DIVINE RESPONSE: The Lord gives a salvation oracle to Baruch through Jeremiah indicating that his life will be safe ("I will give you your life as a prize of war in every place to which you may go") (v. 5).

Ezekiel 9:8 (cf. 11:13)

OCCASION: Ezekiel sees a vision of the Lord ordering the killing of the people of Jerusalem, young and old. Ezekiel falls prostrate and cries out.

Address	"Ah, Lord GOD! [cf. 11:13; Jer 4:10; 14:13; 32:17; Josh 7:7; Judg 6:22]
Complaint	"will you destroy all who remain of Israel as you pour out your wrath upon Jerusalem?"

DIVINE RESPONSE: The Lord announces that he will not spare or pity.

Amos 7:2

OCCASION: Amos's intercession upon seeing a vision of judgment upon Israel.

Address	"O Lord GOD,[5]
Petition	"forgive, I beg you!
Motivation	"How can Jacob stand? He is so small!"

DIVINE RESPONSE: "The LORD relented concerning this; 'It shall not be,' said the LORD."

Amos 7:5

OCCASION: Same as preceding.

Address	"O Lord GOD,[6]
Petition	"cease, I beg you!
Motivation	"How can Jacob stand? He is so small!"

DIVINE RESPONSE: "The LORD relented concerning this; 'This also shall not be,' said the LORD."

Jonah 1:14

OCCASION: The sailors in the storm call out to the Lord for help.

Address	"Please, O LORD, we pray,
Petition	"do not let us perish on account of this man's life. Do not make us guilty of innocent blood;
Motivation	"for you, O LORD, have done as it pleased you."

DIVINE RESPONSE: The sailors toss Jonah in the sea, the sea stops its raging, and Jonah is swallowed up.

Jonah 4:2-3

OCCASION: Jonah is displeased and angry that God decides not to destroy Nineveh after the people repent. "He prayed to the LORD and said,

Address	"O Lord, . . . O Lord,
Complaint	"[i]s this not what I said while I was still in my own country? That is why I fled to Tarshish at the beginning; for I knew that you are a gracious God and merciful, slow to anger, and abounding in steadfast love, and ready to relent from punishing.
Petition	"And now, O LORD, please take my life from me,
Motivation	"for it is better for me to die than to live."

DIVINE RESPONSE: "And the LORD said, 'Is it right for you to be angry?'"

Appendix 2

The Form of the Hymn of Praise

∝

In his study of the hymn, Frank Crüsemann[1] has claimed that the second part of the hymn of praise, which is customarily introduced by *kî* and which most interpreters understand as a causal clause beginning with the word "for (*kî*)...," should *not* be understood as a reason. Rather it is the actual carrying out of the command to praise. What is called for in the command to praise is uttered or sung in the *kî* clause. It is the praise itself, and the conjunction *kî*, customarily translated in a causal sense, is actually more deictic or emphatic, "surely," "indeed," "yes."

The primary reason for this is first of all the logic of the form. A command to praise is given, and one expects that praise will follow rather than a reason for praise. More important, however, Crüsemann looks at the model prayer, "O give thanks...," and sees that in Psalm 118 and apparently Psalm 136, the second half of the prayer or song, "His steadfast love endures forever," is sung antiphonally by particular groups in response to command. It, therefore, seems to function as response to the command to praise or give thanks rather than as reason for doing so. Further, in several places—Crüsemann mentions only Ezra 3:11, but one should add 2 Chr 5:13 and 7:3—the *kî* sentence of the model prayer of thanks and praise is mentioned by itself when the text speaks of the priests and Levites giving thanks or praise, suggesting again that to repeat the sentence, "For he is good...," is an *act* of praise rather than a *reason* for praise. Further, in Neh 9:5a we have a call to praise whose accomplishment is first described in verse 5b—"They blessed [his] glorious name..." (according to the Hebrew text)—and then in verse 6 carried out in a prayer of direct address to the Lord. Finally, Crüsemann cites several instances where it is clear that what follows the call is what those commanded are to speak, for example, Isa 48:20; Jer 31:7; Ps 66:3-4, even if the *kî* is not present. One could add to his list Pss 35:27; 40:16; 70:4; and 96:10.

Crüsemann's point and argument are impressive here. He has clearly pointed to the character of these statements about Yahweh as praise. Whether he is correct that the *kî* constructions are to be understood only deictically or emphatically and not causally is less clear. The examples where the *kî* sentence is broken off and given as the definition of praise or of what Israel is to say are confined to the use of the model prayer of thanks and praise, "O give thanks..."; this raises the question of whether this brief song has become so much a model that it can be used in different ways. Certainly, in the uses in Chronicles and Ezra, the second half seems at times to have become the way of giving thanks or praise, and not simply a reason for doing so. But even in those instances, what is happening may not be that simple. In some instances, the whole prayer is given, the imperative "O give thanks" as well as the "for" or *kî* clause (2 Chr 20:21; Jer 33:11), and it is clear that what goes on in the act of praising or giving thanks is this whole song. In 2 Chr 7:3 and 6 where the *kî* clause seems to stand alone as the expression of thanks or praise, it is preceded by an infinitival form of the call to thanks, *hôdôt lyhwh,* "giving thanks to the LORD," which obviously triggers the second half of the song. There would be no need to repeat the first part, *hodû lyhwh,* "O give thanks to the LORD." That is already present in the infinitive forms. As for Ezra 3:10-11, cited by Crüsemann, that is more complicated also. First of all, this also may be simply a case, like the ones just mentioned, where the presence of the infinitival clause, *hôdōt lyhwh,* "giving thanks to the LORD," triggers the rest of the song, "for he is good...." Further, one notes that, in this action, the priests and Levites are "responding" or "singing"—the verb is *'ānâ,* which can mean either kind of action but is not necessarily responsive singing—to the action of the builders. The text then goes on to say that "all the people shouted with a great shout" because the foundation was laid. It does not appear in this instance as if the words *kî ṭôb kî le'ōlām ḥasdô,* "(for) he is good, (for) his steadfast love endures forever," are the words of the people but rather the words of the priest and Levites.

Crüsemann's interpretation of the *kî* as deictic has some problems. That there is such a thing as the emphasizing or pointing *kî* in Hebrew seems clear, though it is probably not as widespread as sometimes assumed, and it is used in Ugaritic syntactically in ways that help one identify the emphatic function. One wonders, however, if this is its use in all these instances of the hymnic form, why the versions have not discerned that more clearly. In addition, in the several examples where there is a call to praise and those so called are explicitly told what to say, there is *never,* as far as I can tell, any use of the *kî* particle, except in the use of the stereotyped "for his steadfast love endures forever" (Ps 118:2-4). It seems rather strange that it would be completely absent from those examples that are claimed to be very analogous. But when the text explicitly tells the people what to say in praise, it is missing (Pss 35:27; 40:16; 66:3; 70:4; Isa 48:20; Jer 31:7). In Ps 126:2-3, the psalm reports that the nations will say (or have said): "The LORD has done great things for them." This is then repeated by the people: "The LORD has done great things for us." In neither case does the *kî* appear although the second instance would seem to be a perfect place for an emphasizing *kî.* Here, of course, we are not in a typical hymnic text, but the quotation is typical of the kinds of sentences that occur in the second part of the form, declaring what God has done.

A look at one of the hymns, Psalm 96, helps us to see some of the issues involved in deciding how the *kî* functions. The psalm begins with a series of imperative calls to praise. While, as Crüsemann notes, verse 3 resembles the instruction to heralds, there is no reason not to include it as part of the call to praise. It is not at all unusual with a series of three verbs calling to praise that are the same (*šîrû*) to shift to something quite different for the fourth.

The same thing happens in verses 7-9. Here in verses 1-3, the shift is with the verb *baśśĕrû,* "tell," in verse 2, which is then paralleled by the verb *sappĕrû,* "declare," in verse 3. But all of that is call to praise. In verses 4-6, we have then two *kî* clauses, which could be read simply as the carrying out of the commands to praise. But they make very good sense as causal clauses indicating why praise is appropriate—"for great is the LORD and *greatly to be praised.*" This is as much or more *why* praise is called for as it is *what* that praise is. Now, indeed, the reasons are also statements that give God glory. The reasons for praise indeed become expressions of praise, which is why they can sometimes stand by themselves. The character of these *kî* clauses as reasons is further indicated by the way verses 4b-5 show why one should "declare... his marvelous works among all peoples"—that is, "because [*kî*] all the gods of the peoples are idols, but the LORD made the heavens." Here again the declaration is both reason for praise and praise itself. But the character of the sentences as grounding of the call for praise seems clear.

Crüsemann seems to make a sharp distinction between the *kî* sentences in verses 4-5 and those in verse 13 because of his emphasis on the *kî* sentences as being regularly perfect/imperfect sentences describing the Lord's deeds. But this is too narrow a restriction of their content. Indeed the model prayer of thanksgiving, "O give thanks to the LORD...," consists of nominal sentences quite analogous to what we have in Ps 96:4-5.

In the second part of the hymn, the imperative calls to praise are found in verses 7-8 and 11-12. For Crüsemann, verse 10 can in no way be understood as part of the carrying out of the praise. It is a herald's instruction, and the carrying out of the praise happens only in verse 13. But, elsewhere, he sees the herald instruction used by the prophets as part of their carrying through of the praise.[2] In fact, it is just such examples in Isa 48:20 and Jer 31:7 that provide him with presumed instances of sentences saying what those commanded to praise are to express because the herald instruction occurs in contexts of praise language—exactly as here. Methodologically, it will not work to exclude that understanding from Ps 96:10, which occurs right in the middle of a whole series of calls to praise. The verse, like others, suggests that proclamation of the Lord's deeds belongs to the praise of God or belongs to the grounds for calling the nations to praise. But there is no *kî* before the sentences that are to be said. The whole of verse 10 is basis even as the quotation is also praise.

Verse 13, however, is no less a causal or *Begründung* sentence than verses 4-5. Indeed it may be more so. Here we have the *kî* followed by a perfect verb and then the same verb in the imperfect, which Crüsemann has noted as being typical of this part of the basic hymn form. But after the call to the various aspects of creation to rejoice and sing "before the LORD," the sentence "*kî* [for] he comes to judge the earth" is as likely to express a reason for exulting and singing before the Lord as it is what they are to sing. One notes further that a causal understanding of the *kî* makes better sense of all the verbs except "sing" (*rānan*). The *kî* is more likely to identify the reason for rejoicing than what the rejoicing is to express, though the latter can certainly not be excluded.

Finally, one may note that in the other form of praise in the Old Testament, the song of thanksgiving, the report of what the Lord has done, when addressed to God as, for example, in Psalms 30, 32, and 138, serves very much as a reason for praise and thanksgiving, a reason for the thanksgiving of the one who now says, "I give you thanks, O LORD," and also for those who are called to praise and thanksgiving in the light of what God has done for the one who prayed in affliction. Further, one notes that the use of *kî* clauses indicating the reason for the present expression of thanks is quite common (e.g., Pss 116:1ff.; 138:1 [LXX—so also Crüsemann]). So in Ps 30:1, a verb of praise in the first person is followed by a *kî* clause expressing the reason for the praise/thanks. Here Crüsemann does not hesitate to translate the *kî* as *denn,* "for":

> I will extol you ['*ărômîmĕkā*], O LORD, for [*kî*] you
>   have drawn me up,
>   and did not let my foes rejoice over me.

There is no further indication of what the carrying out of the extolling involves, no information of how one is to do that. It takes place in the whole of the psalm, in the first person declaration of thanks and the reason for that, which may occur in a short sentence as above or may be elaborated, as indeed it is in verses 6ff. So also in the hymnic form, the call to praise, normally in the plural imperative but sometimes taking the form of a first person declaration in early texts (e.g., Exod 15:1; 1 Sam 2:1) and later (e.g., Ps 145:1), together with the reason for praise, become as a whole the expression of praise. In Psalm 150, an exception to the typical form, the call to praise alone can serve to express praise to God.

There are some hymns in which what follows the summons to praise is not introduced by a *kî,* "for," and the sentences seem to function more as expression of praise or the carrying out of praise than a reason for giving praise. Psalm 113 is an excellent example of this as it begins with the call:

> Praise the LORD!
> Praise, O servants of the LORD;
>   praise the name of the LORD (v. 1)

and then follows with words that seem to be a response to the summons:

> Let the name of the LORD be blessed
>   from this time on and forevermore.
> From the rising of the sun to its setting
>   praised be the name of the LORD.
> The LORD is high above all nations,
>   and his glory above the heavens. (vv. 2-4)

Psalm 146 works in a similar way as it moves from the call to praise and first person self-declaration of praise (vv. 1-2) to a recounting of the ways of God in behalf of the weak and needy (vv. 5-10).

A particular hymn, therefore, may give more of an impression of presenting a reason for praise after the summons while another may seem to respond to the summons with an expression of praise. In fact both things are happening.

That the summons itself offers praise rather than just calling for others to do it is nowhere better indicated than the frequent Hallelujahs ("Praise the Lord") that appear at the *end* of hymns, as in the case of Psalms 113 and 146, mentioned above. At that point there is no more possibility of response. In fact, one hears those as flowing out of the preceding sentences about what God has done, shaping them into a reason for repeating the summons once more at the conclusion.

Abbreviations

❧

AB	Anchor Bible
ANET	J. B. Pritchard (ed.), *Ancient Near Eastern Texts*
AOAT	Alter Orient und Altes Testament
BARev	*Biblical Archaeology Review*
Bib	*Biblica*
BibRev	*Bible Review*
BJS	Brown Judaic Studies
BThSt	Biblisch-Theologische Studien
BWANT	Beiträge zur Wissenschaft vom Alten und Neuen Testament
BZAW	Beihefte zur Zeitschrift für die alttestamentliche Wissenschaft
CBQ	*Catholic Biblical Quarterly*
CBQMS	Catholic Biblical Quarterly—Monograph Series
ConBOT	Coniectanea biblica, Old Testament
CurTM	*Current Trends in Theology and Mission*
EvT	*Evangelische Theologie*
FRLANT	Forschungen zur Religion und Literatur des Alten und Neuen Testaments
HAR	*Hebrew Annual Review*
HBC	J. L. Mays, et al. (eds.), *Harper's Biblical Commentary*
HR	*History of Religions*
HTR	*Harvard Theological Review*
HUCA	*Hebrew Union College Annual*
IEJ	*Israel Exploration Journal*
Int	*Interpretation*
JAOS	*Journal of the American Oriental Society*
JBL	*Journal of Biblical Literature*
JCS	*Journal of Cuneiform Studies*

JNES	*Journal of Near Eastern Studies*
JSOT	*Journal for the Study of the Old Testament*
JSOTSup	Journal for the Study of the Old Testament—Supplement Series
KD	*Kerygma und Dogma*
KTU	M. Dietrich, et al. (eds.), *Die keilalphabetischen Texte aus Ugarit*
NCB	New Century Bible
NICNT	New International Commentary on the New Testament
NTF	Neutestamentliche Forschungen
OBO	Orbis biblicus et orientalis
OBT	Overtures to Biblical Theology
OTL	Old Testament Library
OTS	*Oudtestamentische Studiën*
RB	*Revue biblique*
RevQ	*Revue de Qumran*
SANT	Studien zum Alten und Neuen Testament
SBLDS	Society of Biblical Literature Dissertation Series
SBLMS	Society of Biblical Literature Monograph Series
SBLSBS	Society of Biblical Literature Sources for Biblical Study
SBM	Stuttgarter biblische Monographien
SBS	Stuttgarter Bibelstudien
SBT	Studies in Biblical Theology
SNTSMS	Society for New Testament Studies Monograph Series
TBü	Theologische Bücherei
TS	*Theological Studies*
VT	*Vetus Testamentum*
VTSup	Vetus Testamentum, Supplements
WBC	Word Biblical Commentary
WMANT	Wissenschaftliche Monographien zum Alten und Neuen Testament
ZAW	*Zeitschrift für die alttestamentliche Wissenschaft*
ZNW	*Zeitschrift für die neutestamentliche Wissenschaft*
ZTK	*Zeitschrift für Theologie und Kirche*

Notes

CHAPTER 1: "WHAT OTHER GREAT NATION HAS A GOD SO NEAR TO IT?"

1. A detailed comparative study of the Egyptian hymns and prayers and those of the Bible is to be found in André Barucq, *L'expression de la louange divine et de la prière dan le bible et en Égypte* (Institut Français d'Archéologie Orientale, Bibliothèque d'Étude 33; Le Caire: Institut Français d'Archéologie Orientale, 1962). For an extensive collection of Egyptian prayers and hymns, see Jan Assmann, *Ägyptische Hymnen und Gebete* (Der Bibliothek der Alten Welt; Munich: Artemis, 1975).

2. E.g., Sumerian SISKUR, SUB; Akk. *karābum/ikribu, utnennu/unnīnu, suppû, sullû.*

3. So Wolfram von Soden, *Akkadisches Handwörterbuch* (Wiesbaden: Otto Harrassowitz, 1965) 1. 22.

4. For discussion of these terms, see, in addition to the lexicons, Karel van der Toorn, *Sin and Sanction in Israel and Mesopotamia: A Comparative Study* (Assen: Van Gorcum, 1985) 117–20.

5. So Othmar Keel, *The Symbolism of the Biblical World: Ancient Near Eastern Iconography and the Book of Psalms* (New York: Seabury, 1978) 314.

6. Yigael Yadin, "Symbols of Deities at Zinjirli, Carthage and Hazor," *Near Eastern Archaeology in the Twentieth Century: Essays in Honor of Nelson Glueck* (ed. James A. Sanders; Garden City, N.Y.: Doubleday, 1970) 199–231. The interpretation of the symbol is debated. Yadin reads it as a symbol of the moon god and sees the upraised hands as a symbol of that god's consort, Tannit. Frank M. Cross associates the disk and crescent symbolism specifically with the Asherah-Qudshu-Tannit figure, which could mean that both parts of the relief on the stela are Tannit imagery. This would be a modification of Yadin's interpretation but would still view the upraised hands as divine symbol rather than representation of a suppliant. See Frank M. Cross, *Canaanite Myth and Hebrew Epic* (Cambridge: Harvard Univ. Press, 1973) 33–35.

7. See, e.g., the drawings of upraised hands or persons in that posture accompanying the inscriptions from both Kuntillet Ajrud and Khirbet Beit Lei. On the former, see Zeev Meshel, "Did Yahweh Have a Consort?" *BARev* 5 (1979) 26. On the latter, see Joseph Naveh, "Old Hebrew Inscriptions in a Burial Cave," *IEJ* 13 (1963) 74–92.

8. On these various bodily stances and gestures see especially, Keel, *Symbolism*, 308–23.

9. W. G. Lambert, *Babylonian Wisdom Literature* (Oxford: Clarendon, 1960) 104–5, ll. 139–40 (from "Counsels of Wisdom").

10. Ibid., 76–77, l. 73 (from "The Babylonian Theodicy").

11. So ibid., and von Soden, *Akkadisches Handwörterbuch,* s.v. *labānu.*

12. I am indebted to J. J. M. Roberts for pointing out this particular gesture for prayer as well as for the suggestion that it may be reflected in the expression "my mouth has kissed my hand," which may be an act of obeisance to a deity.

13. Keel, *Symbolism,* 313.

14. Ibid.

15. Thorkild Jacobsen, *The Treasures of Darkness: A History of Mesopotamian Religion* (New Haven: Yale Univ. Press, 1976) 15.

16. Ibid.

17. Several of the names cited here are taken from the summary of Wolfram von Soden in his article "Gebet II (babylonisch und assyrisch)," *Reallexikon der Assyriologie* (Berlin: W. de Gruyter, 1957-71) 3.162–63, as well as from the extended presentation and discussion of such theophorus names in both the Old Testament and Mesopotamia in Rainer Albertz, *Persönliche Frömmigkeit und offizielle Religion* (Stuttgart: Calwer, 1978) 49-76 and 101–19, and the volume by Jeaneane D. Fowler, *Theophoric Personal Names in Ancient Hebrew: A Comparative Study* (JSOTSup 49; Sheffield: JSOT, 1988). For a much more extended presentation of prayer names, one should consult the standard editions: Hermann Ranke, *Early Babylonian Personal Names from the Published Tablets of the So-Called Hammurabi Dynasty (B.C. 2000)* (Philadelphia: Univ. of Pennsylvania Press, 1905); Knut L. Tallqvist, *Assyrian Personal Names* (Hildesheim: Georg Olms, 1914); Johann J. Stamm, *Die Akkadische Namengebung* (Leipzig, 1939); Claudio Saporetti, *Onomastica Medio-Assira* (Rome: Biblical, 1970); as well as J. J. M. Roberts, *The Earliest Semitic Pantheon: A Study of the Semitic Deities Attested in Mesopotamia before Ur III* (Baltimore: Johns Hopkins Univ. Press, 1972).

18. Respectively: *Aššur-rabi, Sîn-karābī-išme, Irēmanni-ilī.*

19. Respectively: *Ātanaḫ-ilī, Ilī-wēdāku, Al-ilī, Masiam-Eštar,* and *Adi-māṭi-ilī* (cited by Edward R. Dalglish, *Psalm Fifty-One in the Light of Ancient Near Eastern Patternism* [Leiden: E. J. Brill, 1962] 28 n. 41).

20. There are also names that include penitential elements common to Mesopotamian penitential prayers (see below), names, e.g., that say, "What have I done?" "How have I sinned?" or a name like *Ea-ḫiṭī-ul-īdi,* "Ea, my offense, I know not." See Fowler, *Theophoric Personal Names,* 305–6.

21. Respectively: *Sîn-gimlannī, Nashiram-ilī, Sîn-usuḫ-biltī, Izzizam-ilī, Ayyabāš-ilī, Gamal-Sîn-lūmur,* and *Nabû-tultabši-līšir.*

22. Respectively: *Nabû-alsīka-ul-abāš, Ana-Šamaš-taklāku, Ana-amat-Bêl-atkal,* and *Ibašši-uznī-ana-ili.*

23. Respectively: *Adalal-Sîn,* and *Ludlil-Enlil.*

24. Prayer names are not uncommon among Egyptian names also, as indicated by a perusal of H. Junker, *Die Ägyptischen Personnamen* (Gluckstadt-Hamburg, 1952). Some of these are discussed by François Daumas, "L'éxperience religieuse égyptienne dans la prière," *L'éxperience de la prière dans les grandes religions* (ed. Henri Limet and Julien Ries; Louvain-La-Neuve: Centre

d'Histoire des Religions, 1980) 59–80. For a broad look at other Semitic onomastica, see Fowler, *Theophoric Personal Names,* chap. 4, and the reference
works cited there.

25. William W. Hallo, "Individual Prayer in Sumerian: The Continuity of
a Tradition," *JAOS* 88 (1968) 75. The discussion that follows is heavily dependent upon Hallo's analysis of Sumerian prayer and his comparison with
the biblical Psalms. Other general works drawn upon in the discussion that
follows are: Dalglish, *Psalm Fifty-One;* Erhard S. Gerstenberger, *Der bittende
Mensch: Bittritual und Klagelied des Einzelnen im Alten Testament* (WMANT
51; Neukirchen-Vluyn: Neukirchener Verlag, 1980); Adam Falkenstein, "Gebet
I," *Reallexikon der Assyriologie* (Berlin: W. de Gruyter, 1957–71) 3.156–60;
von Soden, "Gebet II," 3.160–70; Jacobsen, *The Treasures of Darkness;* Marie-
Joseph Seux, *Hymnes et Prières aux dieux de Babylonie et d'Assyrie* (Paris:
Éditions du Cerf, 1976); John H. Walton, *Ancient Israelite Literature in Its Cultural Context: A Survey of Parallels between Biblical and Ancient Near Eastern
Texts* (Grand Rapids: Zondervan, 1989); Adam Falkenstein and Wolfram von
Soden, *Sumerische und Akkadische Hymnen und Gebete* (Stuttgart: Artemis,
1953); van der Toorn, *Sin and Sanction;* J. J. M. Roberts, "Biblical Literature
and the Literature of Antiquity," *HBC* 33–41. While all of these studies do
some sort of categorization, the most detailed organizing of the prayers into
types or genres in English publications is found in the works by Dalglish and
Walton. Other works consulted dealing with more specific topics will be noted
when referred to explicitly.

26. Hallo, "Individual Prayer," 79.

27. Such Mesopotamian letter prayers probably have their best Egyptian
analogy in the letters to dead relatives seeking their help in specific situations.
There are some examples of demotic letter prayers to necropolis deities from a
much later period in Egyptian history. And one demotic letter prayer to Thoth
is a petition to the deity whom the petitioner, Efou, serves, asking help against
extreme persecution at the hands of a fellow worker (George R. Hughes, "A
Demotic Letter to Thoth," *JNES* 17 [1958] 1–12). The prayer contains a brief
address to the deity with appropriate epithets, "Thoth, Twice Great, Lord of
Hermopolis, the great god," an extended recounting of all the ways the petitioner's fellow worker has persecuted him, stealing everything and killing his
servants, and a plea for protection from this destructive colleague. Two things
are worth noting. Like the Sumerian letter prayers, and as one would expect
with regard to the letter form, the name of the petitioner is given. Also the petitioner, Efou, makes the point that he has appealed to Thoth because "I have
no human master." The sentence is sensible in that Efou is a servant of Thoth,
but it suggests, as its editor indicates, that he finds no social structures likely
to provide the help and protection he needs. The appeal to the god explicitly
recognizes the lack of human means of redress or protection, the situation often existing when the Israelite cries out to God in prayer (see chaps. 2 and 3,
above).

28. The prayers seem for the most part to have been written by scribes
and may, therefore, belong to scribal practice. That does not mean, of course,
that they are any less prayers. As Hallo ("Individual Prayer," 78) suggests,

"[T]he scribe found in his own life and circumstances the materials for exercising his stylistic talents." It is worth noting that one or two of these prayers were penned by women scribes, a possibility that needs to be raised when one examines the biblical prayers (see chap. 6, above).

29. For a discussion of lament or complaint prayers organized in terms of Sumerian and Akkadian categories or types, see Dalglish, *Psalm Fifty-One*, chap. 3.

30. The translation is that of Hallo in his article, "Individual Prayer," 85–87. Parts of this prayer have been translated by Jacobsen in *The Treasures of Darkness*, 153–54. Where his translation differs significantly, it will be given in a note so that the reader may compare with that of Hallo.

31. Jacobsen, *The Treasures of Darkness*, 153, translates ll. 16–17 as follows:

> I lie down on a bed of wails and woes,
>   grief cuts me (to the quick);
> my comely frame droops toward the ground,
>   I grovel at (people's) feet.

32. Jacobsen, *The Treasures of Darkness*, 154, translates ll. 21–23 as follows:

> I, a literate person, have been changed
>   from one who knew things into a clod,
> my hand has been stayed from writing,
>   my mouth has had (its power to) discourse lessened,
> I am no oldster, (yet) I have become hard of hearing,
>   my eyesight dim!

33. Jacobsen, *The Treasures of Darkness*, 154, translates ll. 46–50 as follows:

> Today let me take my trespasses to you,
>   snatch me from my foes,
> and when you have seen where I fell,
>   take pity on me,
> When you have turned my dark stretches
>   (of road) into daylight
> let me pass through your gate,
>   which releases from sin and wrongdoing,
>   let me sing your praises,
> let me confess, (roaring) like a bull,
>   my trespasses to you,
>   and let me tell of your greatness.

34. Hallo, "Individual Prayer," 77, interprets the prayer as having to do with scribal problems.

35. Such praise is frequently found also in the petitionary prayers of Egypt, though sometimes the prayer begins with the simple address to the deity by name, as in many of the biblical prayers, e.g., a prayer of a poor person to Amon for help and justice in the law court (*ANET* 380) or another prayer

that begins, "Come to me, Amon, and save me in this wretched year [or perhaps 'year of need']" (Ricardo Caminos, *Late-Egyptian Miscellanies* [Brown Egyptological Studies 1; London: Oxford Univ. Press, 1954] 171). Cf. Gerhard Fecht, "Literarische Zeugnisse zur "persönlichen Frömmigkeit," *Ägypten: Analyse der Beispiele aus den ramessidischen Schulpapyri* (Abhandlungen der Heidelberger Akademie der Wissenschaften, Philosophisch-historische Klasse; Heidelberg: Carl Winter, 1965) 58–62.

36. Henri Limet, *Les légendes des sceaux cassites* (Brussels: Palais des Académies, 1971).

37. Dalglish, *Psalm Fifty-One*, 259.

38. Dalglish, *Psalm Fifty-One*, 44, gives the following summary of the praise of the deity as it is found particularly in the Akkadian *šu-illa* prayers: "*The praise of the deity* devotes itself particularly to the praise of the divine attributes of gentleness and righteousness, by which the worshipper emphasized that the deity possessed the will as well as the ability to help. An analysis of this theme results in disengaging the following strains of thought: the deity emancipates from sin; he regards mankind graciously with his look; he bestows help in social problems; he is like a father and mother; he directs judgment in righteousness; and he protects and assists in the hour of man's need."

39. *ANET* 380. Cf. a similar address to this deity in another prayer in Jan Assmann, *Ägyptische Hymnen und Gebete*, 349, ll. 10–13.

40. Gerstenberger, *Der bittende Mensch*, 97.

41. Dalglish, *Psalm Fifty-One*, 23.

42. E.g., "If my queen is truly of heaven..." (cited by Hallo, "Individual Prayer," 79).

43. Ibid., 77.

44. Werner Mayer (*Untersuchungen zur Formensprache der Babylonischen "Gebetsbeschwörungen"* [Rome: Biblical Institute, 1976] 12 and 68 n. 5) notes that while the lament is frequently a part of the *šu-illa* prayer, a number of such prayers do not contain a lament element.

45. Some of the examples presented here are taken from the discussion of van der Toorn, *Sin and Sanction*, chap. 4, where he puts the sufferings of petitioners in four categories: physical sufferings, social adversity, divine disapproval, and mental discomfort. Such a breakdown is quite legitimate. The combination of physical and mental rests on the fact that they all have to do with the breakdown and dissolution of the self, both body and soul. It is not always easy to tell if the illness language describes a physiological sickness or is metaphorical for another kind of personal distress. Some of the mental discomforts cited by van der Toorn, e.g., headache and loss of appetite, are not easily distinguishable from physical discomforts. In his discussion of both physical and mental discomforts, van der Toorn acknowledges at various points the difficulty of keeping them separate or being able to demarcate in clear fashion physiologically caused and psychologically caused symptoms.

46. Geo Widengren (*The Accadian and Hebrew Psalms of Lamentation as Religious Documents: A Comparative Study* [Uppsala: Almqvist and Wiksell, 1937] 93–257) gives numerous examples of lament expressions in the Mesopotamian prayers compared with similar biblical expressions. The most extended

and systematic discussion of the language and formulas of these laments is that of Mayer, *Untersuchungen zur Formensprache,* chap. 2.

47. Cf. Widengren, *Accadian and Hebrew Psalms,* 104.

48. Cf. ibid., 121.

49. See W. Lambert, "*Dingir.ša.dib.ba* Incantations," *JNES* 33 (1974) 277–78, ll. 98–99, and the discussion of van der Toorn, *Sin and Sanction,* 65.

50. For examples of these symptoms from the *namburbi* and *šu-illa* prayers, see Mayer, *Untersuchungen zur Formensprache,* 72–75.

51. Dalglish, *Psalm Fifty-One,* 25. The references are omitted from the quotation for readability. They may be found in Dalglish, where there are also some alternative translations proposed by Falkenstein in the notes.

52. Although most of the praying ones may have been males, despite the gender reference of Dalglish's quote, it must be remembered that some of the petitioners, as in the Bible, were women.

53. Van der Toorn, *Sin and Sanction,* 64.

54. Ibid., 64–65.

55. Jacobsen, *The Treasures of Darkness,* 153.

56. Cf. Widengren, *Accadian and Hebrew Psalms,* 258–310.

57. Examples given by Hallo, "Individual Prayer," 78–79 include: "[M]ay she remove from my body (interrupt) whatever sickness demon may exist in my body"; "[M]ay Damu your son (oh healing goddess) effect my cure."

58. These specific petitions are found in the letter prayers cited by Hallo, "Individual Prayer," 78–79.

59. These distinctions, not only for the petitions but for other parts of the prayers, are used with regard to the biblical laments by Claus Westermann, *Praise and Lament in the Psalms* (Atlanta: John Knox, 1981) and Craig C. Broyles, *The Conflict of Faith and Experience in the Psalms: A Form-Critical and Theological Study* (JSOTSup 52; Sheffield: JSOT, 1989).

60. Mayer, *Untersuchungen zur Formensprache,* 211–90.

61. Hallo, "Individual Prayer," 79.

62. See van der Toorn, *Sin and Sanction,* 96, for examples.

63. Cf. Lambert, "*Dingir.ša.dib.ba* Incantations," 281, 283:

> Who is there who has not sinned against his god?
> Who that has kept the commandment for ever?
> All of mankind who exist are sinful.

64. Van der Toorn, *Sin and Sanction,* 97.

65. Hallo, "Individual Prayer," 79.

66. See Mayer, *Untersuchungen zur Formensprache,* 165–66.

67. Cf. the alternative translation of Jacobsen in n. 33 above.

68. Mayer, *Untersuchungen zur Formensprache,* 340–41.

69. Ibid., 327–34.

70. Ibid., 310–15. Cf. the expression from the Psalms:

> For in death there is no remembrance of you;
> in Sheol who can give you praise? (Ps 6:5)

71. Hallo, "Individual Prayer," 79. For other examples, see Mayer, *Untersuchungen zur Formensprache,* 317–19.

72. Note the example cited by Hallo, "Individual Prayer," 79: "Perhaps the most persuasive offer that the petitioner can dangle before the deity's eyes is to endow him or her with yet another epithet, based on their latest kindness: 'When I have been cured, I will rename my goddess the one who heals(?) the cripples.' "

73. Jacobsen, *The Treasures of Darkness*, 147–64, associates this development with the rise of personal religion and the influence of the personal god in second millennium Mesopotamian religion. This includes a close personal relation with the deity, expecting help and guidance in one's personal life, divine anger and punishment when one sins, but divine compassion and forgiveness when there is penitence. Cf. Hallo, "Individual Prayer," 81–82.

74. On this category of prayers and bibliography on them, see Piotr Michalowski, "On the Early History of the Ershahunga Prayer," *JCS* 39 (1987) 37–45 and n. 10; and Stefan M. Maul, *"Herzberuhigungsklagen": Die sumerisch–akkadischen Eršaḫunga–Gebete* (Wiesbaden: Otto Harrassowitz, 1988).

75. See especially Marie-Joseph Seux, *"šiggayon = šigû?" Mélanges bibliques et orientaux en l'honneur de M. Henri Cazelles* (ed. André Caquot and Mathias Delcor; AOAT 212; Neukirchen-Vluyn: Neukirchener Verlag, 1981) 419–38.

76. The primary treatment of the *dingiršadibba* prayers is Lambert's study, *"Dingir.ša.dib.ba* Incantations," 267–327. For helpful discussion of both *dingiršadibba* and *šigû* prayers, see van der Toorn, *Sin and Sanction*, 117–38.

77. Mayer, *Untersuchungen zur Formensprache*, 14–17.

78. The Sumerian word *er-ša-ḫun-ga*, which means "lament for appeasing the heart," i.e., the heart of the deity, points to its character as a prayer having to do with sin and seeking the deity's favorable attention rather than his or her anger because of the sin.

79. Michalowski, "On the Early History of the Ershahunga Prayer," 44.

80. Dalglish, *Psalm Fifty-One*, 26.

81. So Jacobsen, *The Treasures of Darkness*, chap. 5, and Hallo, "Individual Prayer," 81–82.

82. The penitential emphasis of many Mesopotamian prayers is not generally duplicated in Egyptian prayers. This does not necessarily mean that there was little sense of sin among the Egyptians. It may be that the various claims of innocence on the part of the deceased found in chap. 125 of the Book of the Dead suggest quite the contrary (so Siegfried Morenz, *Egyptian Religion* [London: Methuen, 1973] 130–33; for a translation of chap. 125 see *ANET* 34–36). Further, Dalglish, *Psalm Fifty-One*, 15, notes other places in the Book of the Dead where penitential prayers are in fact present. There is in the late Egyptian Empire a small group of hymns and prayers that reflect an attitude of submission before the deity, confession and penitence for things done wrong. They either pray for the deity's mercy or give thanks for its occasion. A brief discussion of these may be found in Dalglish, *Psalm Fifty-One*, 8–17. Examples of such prayers may be found in *ANET* 379–81; and Miriam Lichtheim, *Ancient Egyptian Literature: A Book of Readings*, vol. 2: *The New Kingdom* (Berkeley: Univ. of California Press, 1976) 104–10.

83. Jacobsen, *The Treasures of Darkness,* 163.

84. For more elaborate detail see Mayer, *Untersuchungen zur Formensprache,* chap. 5; Gerstenberger, *Der bittende Mensch,* 64–112; van der Toorn, *Sin and Sanction,* appendix; and Dalglish, *Psalm Fifty-One,* passim.

85. Hallo, "Individual Prayer," 79 and n. 74.

86. Mayer, *Untersuchungen zur Formensprache,* 179–80.

87. Ibid., 177–79.

88. Ibid., 179. The similarity to the notion in 1 Kings 8 of praying toward the temple where the name of God dwells so that God in heaven may hear and forgive is obvious.

89. Gerstenberger, *Der bittende Mensch,* 78–93.

90. Jacobsen, *The Treasures of Darkness,* 159–60.

91. A. Leo Oppenheim, "Analysis of an Assyrian Ritual (KAR 139)," *HR* 5 (1965/66) 261–62.

92. Mayer, *Untersuchungen zur Formensprache,* 231, 234. Cf. Oppenheim, "Analysis," 261–62.

93. Oppenheim, "Analysis," 263.

94. Mayer, *Untersuchungen zur Formensprache,* 236.

95. Oppenheim, "Analysis," 263 n. 51.

96. Morenz, *Egyptian Religion,* 101–2.

97. Ibid., 102. For further examples of Egyptian intercessory prayer, see Deborah Sweeney, "Intercessory Prayer in Ancient Egypt and the Bible," *Pharaonic Egypt* (ed. Sarah Israelit-Groll; Jerusalem: Magnes, 1985) 212–30.

98. For an extended study of the Sumero-Akkadian city laments in relation to the biblical communal laments, see Paul Ferris, *The Genre of Communal Lament in the Bible and the Ancient Near East* (SBLDS 127; Atlanta: Scholars Press, 1992); cf. Walter C. Bouzard Jr., "Psalms 74, 79 and the Sumerian City Laments," paper presented at the 1992 annual meeting of the Society of Biblical Literature in San Francisco.

99. Hallo, "Individual Prayer," 75.

100. "The lament for Ur was written as part of efforts by the early kings of the dynasty of Isin to rebuild the former capital. It aims to calm the disturbed, turbulent, suffering soul of Nanna, the god of Ur, so that he can regain his composure and think of rebuilding his destroyed home" (Thorkild Jacobsen, *The Harps That Once...Sumerian Poetry in Translation* [New Haven: Yale Univ. Press, 1987] 447). On these congregational laments, cf. Piotr Michalowski, *The Lamentation over the Destruction of Sumer and Ur* (Winona Lake, Ind.: Eisenbrauns, 1989) 1–15.

101. Raphael Kutscher, *Oh Angry Sea (a-ab-ba hu-luh-ha): The History of A Sumerian Congregational Lament* (New Haven: Yale Univ. Press, 1975) 152.

102. Jacobsen, *The Harps That Once,* 474.

103. Jacobsen, *The Treasures of Darkness,* 164. Cf. the discussion in Walton, *Ancient Israelite Literature,* 160–63.

104. *ANET* 383; the translation is by Ferris J. Stephens.

105. Hallo, "Individual Prayer," 74, compares those hymns that end with prayers to the king with the royal psalms of the Psalter. Such comparison may be noted, but the focus of such hymns is less on the king and more on the deity.

106. Hermann Gunkel, *Einleitung in die Psalmen* (Göttingen: Vandenhoeck und Ruprecht, 1933) 285–86.

107. H. L. Ginsberg, "Psalms and Inscriptions of Petition and Acknowledgment," *Louis Ginzberg: Jubilee Volume on the Occasion of His Seventieth Birthday* (ed. A. Marx; New York: American Academy for Jewish Research, 1945) 166–67.

108. The translation is basically the one found in *ANET* 380, with slight modification to make the language inclusive.

109. Ibid.

110. Ibid.

111. Hallo, "Individual Prayer," 74.

112. See, e.g., the texts referred to by Ginsberg, "Psalms and Inscriptions of Petition and Acknowledgment," 159–71, and, as an example, the inscription of Ben-Hadad of Damascus in *ANET* 501.

113. Jonas Greenfield, "The Zakir Inscription and the Danklied," *Proceedings of the Fifth World Congress of Jewish Studies* (ed. Pinchas Peli; Jerusalem: World Union of Jewish Studies, 1972) 174–91.

114. *ANET* 655.

115. Ibid., 143–44.

116. For translation and discussion see Patrick D. Miller Jr., "Prayer and Sacrifice in Ugarit and Israel," *Text and Context: Old Testament and Semitic Studies for F. C. Fensham* (ed. Walter T. Classen; Sheffield: JSOT, 1988) 139–55.

117. The inscriptions from the cave at Khirbet Beit Lei are an important primary source for our knowledge of prayer in ancient Palestine, but because these are Israelite inscriptions, they are taken up in the following chapters where relevant.

118. Roberts, "Biblical Literature and the Literature of Antiquity," 35.

119. *ANET* 383–85.

120. In the short prayers on Cassite seals as well as in other prayers where the address is brief, the focus may be more upon the attribute of the deity that is the basis for calling on him or her for help.

121. Roberts, "Biblical Literature and the Literature of Antiquity," 35.

122. Westermann, *Praise and Lament in the Psalms*, 42.

123. One may see this difference reflected in Israelite hymnody where the atypical Psalm 29, which may be a Canaanite Baal hymn brought over into Yahwism, calls the gods to praise the Lord while the more typical Psalm 96 uses similar language to call the "families of the peoples" to praise.

124. Roberts, "Biblical Literature and the Literature of Antiquity," 35.

125. Ibid.

126. Ibid.

CHAPTER 2: "WHENEVER WE CALL"

1. A good but not exhaustive list of references to prayer or occasions of prayer in the Old Testament is found in Moshe Greenberg, *Biblical Prose*

Prayer as a Window to the Popular Religion of Ancient Israel (Berkeley: Univ. of California Press, 1983) 59–60 n. 3. For discussion of prayer terminology, in addition to the standard dictionary articles, see Samuel E. Balentine, "The Prophet as Intercessor: A Reassessment," *JBL* 103 (1984) 161–73.

2. Num 14:13 (Moses); 16:22 (Moses and Aaron falling on their faces to God); 22:34 (Balaam in confession of sin to the angel of the Lord); Judg 6:39 (Gideon); 10:15 (Israelites in confession); 21:3 (Israel); 1 Sam 7:6 (Israel in confession); 2 Sam 15:31 (David); 24:10, 17 (David in confession); 1 Kgs 3:6 (Solomon); 1 Kgs 8:23 (Solomon); 1 Kgs 18:36 (Elijah); 2 Kgs 6:20 (Elisha); Amos 7:2, 5 (Amos); Ezra 9:6 (Ezra); 2 Chr 20:6 (Jehoshaphat); Luke 11:2 (Lord's Prayer); John 17:1 (Jesus).

3. The following discussion is heavily indebted to the detailed study of these verbs by Claus Westermann, "Die Begriffe für Fragen und Suchen im Alten Testament," *KD* 6 (1960) 2–30. Reprinted in Claus Westermann, *Forschung am Alten Testament: Gesammelte Studien Band II* (TBü 55; Munich: Chr. Kaiser, 1974) 162–90.

4. See 2 Chr 7:12-14; 20:4ff.; and Ezra 8:21-23.

5. Cf. Westermann, "Die Begriffe für Fragen und Suchen," 170–71, and for a more extended discussion Gerhard von Rad, *Der Heilige Krieg im alten Israel* (Göttingen: Vandenhoeck und Ruprecht, 1952).

6. Cf. 2 Kgs 3:9-20.

7. See 2 Kgs 22: 13-20; Jer 21; 37:6-10; Ezek 14:1ff.; 20:1ff.

8. Westermann, "Die Begriffe für Fragen und Suchen," 184. Cf. 1 Chr 28:9; 2 Chr 15:12; 22:9; 31:21; Ps 119:2, 10. Other examples of *biqqēš* and *dāraš* being used in parallel relation may be found in Isa 65:1; Zeph 1:6; Pss 24:6; 105:3-4.

9. Cf. 2 Chr 14:4.

10. Cf. Westermann, "Die Begriffe für Fragen und Suchen," 188–90.

11. Westermann refers to Isa 34:16 ("Seek and read from the book of the Lord") as well as to John 5:39 and the frequent use of *dāraš* or other verbs for seeking the Lord in reference to the study of prayer in Philo, the Rabbis, as well as the Qumran Manual of Discipline ("Die Begriffe für Fragen und Suchen," 185 n. 19).

12. Ibid., 190.

13. E. A. Speiser, "The Stem *PLL* in Hebrew," *JBL* 82 (1963) 301–6.

14. This point is made at some length with reference to Jeremiah's prayers, or confessions, as they are more commonly called, by Sheldon H. Blank, "The Confessions of Jeremiah and the Meaning of Prayer," *HUCA* 21 (1948) 331–54. On this understanding of the root *pālal* and the noun *tĕpillâ*, see especially 337–38 n. 12.

15. Hans-Joachim Kraus, *Psalms 1–59* (Minneapolis: Fortress, 1988) 50.

16. It may be that the parable of Jesus encouraging persistent prayer uses the imagery of appeal to a judge because of the association of prayer with the laying out of a case (Luke 18:1-8). So Asher Finkel, "Prayer of Jesus in Matthew," *Standing before God: Studies in Prayer in Scriptures and in Tradition with Essays in Honor of John M. Oesterreicher* (ed. Asher Finkel and Lawrence Frizzell; New York: KTAV, 1981) 160 n. 19.

17. Other instances of the verb *pallēl* used for the prayer of intercession may be found in Gen 20:17; Num 11:2; 21:7; 1 Sam 7:5; 12:19; 2 Kgs 4:33; Jer 29:7; 37:3; 42:2, 4, 20.

18. Judg 13:8; Job 22:27; 33:26.

19. Gen 25:21; 2 Sam 21:14; 24:25; Isa 19:22; 1 Chr 5:20; 2 Chr 33:13, 19; Ezra 8:23.

20. Note that the granting of the prayer by God is also indicated by the Niphal conjugation of *'ātar.*

21. Exod 8:8-9, 28-30; 9:28; 10:17-18.

22. Here is one of the instances where "seeking" (*biqqēš*) refers to a particular act of prayer in distinction from its more common general usage in reference to the relationship to God.

23. There is cognate evidence suggesting that the root meaning of the word *'ātar* may have to do with slaughtering for sacrifice.

24. See the discussion of *zā'aq/ṣā'aq* and "crying out" below and in the next chapter.

25. For the Deuteronomistic material, see Deut 3:23; 1 Kgs 8–9. In Jeremiah, see Jer 3:21; 31:9; 36:7; 37:20; 38:26; 42:2, 9. For the Chronicler, see 2 Chronicles 6 and 33:19. In Job, see Job 8:5; 9:15. For the Psalms, see Pss 6:9; 30:10; 55:1; 119:170; 142:1; 143:1; and in the idiom "voice of supplication," 28:2, 6; 31:22; 86:6; 116:1; 130:2; 140:6. This is exclusive of the frequent petition, *ḥannēnî,* "Be gracious to me." For Zechariah, see Zech 12:10.

26. See 1 Kgs 8:28, 30, 33, 38, 45, 47, 49, 52 [2x], 59; 9:3 [2x]. The parallel uses in 2 Chronicles 6 are vv. 19, 21, 24, 29, 35, 37, 39.

27. Dan 9:3, 17, 18, 20, 23.

28. E.g., Deut 3:23; Jer 36:7; and Pss 6:9 and 130:2 (penitential psalms).

29. The basic stem of the verb *ḥānan* frequently has to do with God showing compassion and mercy (or refusing to do so) upon a sinful people (e.g., Amos 5:15; Isa 27:11; 30:18-19; 33:2).

30. See 1 Sam 13:12; Ps 119:58; Zech 7:2; 8:21-22.

31. Exod 32:11; 1 Kgs 13:6 [2x]; 2 Kgs 13:4; 2 Chr 33:12; Jer 26:19; Dan 9:13; Mal 1:9.

32. E.g., Pss 3:4; 4:1, 3; 17:6; 18:3, 6; 22:2; 27:7; 28:1; 30:8; 31:17; 34:6; 55:16; 56:9; 57:2; 61:2; 86:3, 7; 88:9; 119:145, 146; 120:1; 130:1; 141:1 [2x].

33. While there are some differences in the usage of these two roots, they are etymologically and semantically closely linked. They occur interchangeably in contexts discussed here, e.g., Judg 10:10, 12, and 14; Ps 107:6, 13, 19, 28.

34. See the fundamental work of Richard Boyce, *The Cry to God in the Old Testament* (Atlanta: Scholars Press, 1989).

35. Gen 18:21; 19:13.

36. Exod 2:23; 3:7, 9.

37. Judg 3:9, 15; 4:3; 6:6, 7; 10:10, 12, 14. Cf. Walter Brueggemann, "Social Criticism and Social Vision in the Deuteronomic Formula of the Judges (Judges 3:12, 4:1-2, 6:1; Deuteronomy 32)," *Die Botschaft und die Boten: Festschrift für Hans Walter Wolff zum 70 Geburtstag* (ed. Jorg Jeremias and Lothar Perlitt; Neukirchen-Vluyn: Neukirchener Verlag, 1981) 101–14.

38. Exod 22:23, 27.

39. Pss 22:5; 34:17; 77:1; 88:1; 107:6, 13, 19, 28; 142:1, 6.

40. Matt 27:46; Mark 15:34.

41. For the imagery of God listening to these cries see, e.g., Exod 3:7; 22:23, 27; and chap. 3, above.

42. Job 19:7 ‖ *zāʿaq*; 24:12; 29:12; 30:20, 28; 35:9; 36:13, 19; 38:41.

43. Pss 5:2; 18:6, 41; 22:24; 28:2; 30:2; 31:22; 34:15; 39:12; 40:1; 88:13 (‖ *tĕpillâ*); 102:1 (‖ *tĕpillâ*); 119:147; 145:19.

44. E.g., Exod 2:23 (‖ *zāʿaq*); Jonah 2:3; Hab 1:2 (‖ *zāʿaq*); Lam 3:8, 56; Isa 58:9.

45. Job 7:11, 13; 9:27; 10:1; 21:4; 23:2.

46. Pss 6:6; 55:2, 17; 64:1; 102 [superscription] (= "poured out his complaint before the LORD"); 142:2.

47. The above discussion leaves out some of the terms for prayer that are closely related to the ones discussed here (e.g., *rinnâ*, Jer 7:16; 14:12). Others, however, are much less common and do not add to the understanding gained from the ones presented here.

48. Pss 63:6; 77:3, 6, 12; and 143:5.

49. Vv. 15, 23, 27, 48, 78, 148.

50. Pss 63:6; 77:6.

51. Pss 63:6; 77:3.

52. Pss 77:12; 119:27; 143:5; 145:5.

53. Ps 119:15, 23, 48, 78, 97, 99; cf. Ps 1:2 and Josh 1:8.

54. On meditation in the Psalter, cf. Harold Fisch, *Poetry with a Purpose: Biblical Poetics and Interpretation* (Bloomington: Indiana Univ. Press, 1988) 107–9. Fisch associates this activity with the compositions of psalmic song and poetry.

55. The theological character of such praying is developed in chap. 3, above.

56. See Leslie Allen, *Psalms 101–150* (WBC 21; Waco, Tex.: Word, 1983) 218, for the possibility that the Feast of Tabernacles is in mind here, a possibility suggested indirectly also by Isa 30:29.

57. Cf. Pss 22:2; 77:2.

58. Pss 6:6; 77:6; 119:55, 148.

59. See Pss 46:5; 90:14; 143:8. Cf. Joseph Ziegler, "Die Hilfe Gottes 'am Morgen,'" *Alttestamentliche Studien: Friedrich Nötscher zum sechzigsten Geburtstage, 19 Juli, 1950* (Bonn: Hanstein, 1950) 281–88; and Bernd Janowski, *Rettungsgewissheit und Epiphanie des Heils: Das Motiv der Hilfe Gottes "am Morgen" im Alten Orient und im Alten Testament*, vol. 1: *Alter Orient* (Neukirchen-Vluyn: Neukirchener Verlag, 1989).

60. Acts 10:3, 30. For evidence indicating that Jesus observed the hours of prayer as well as praying at other times, see Joachim Jeremias, *The Prayers of Jesus* (SBT, n.s., 6; London: SCM, 1967) 73–76.

In Judaism of the first century and later, the prayer used at the hours of prayer was the *Tephilla*, a hymn consisting of eighteen benedictions (usually) and thus called the "Eighteen Benedictions." One's private petitions could be added to that. The benedictions themselves, each of which ends with a benediction of praise and thanksgiving (see chap. 5, above), "Blessed are you, O Lord, who...," include various kinds of petitions modeled directly and indirectly on biblical petitions for deliverance, protection, healing, forgiveness, blessing, and the like. On the three hours of prayer, see Jeremias, *Prayers*, 69–72.

61. Erhard S. Gerstenberger, *Der bittende Mensch: Bittritual und Klagelied des Einzelnen im Alten Testament* (WMANT 51; Neukirchen-Vluyn: Neukirchener Verlag, 1980) 151–53.

62. E.g., 2 Kgs 4:17-37; Isa 38:1; Acts 9:40; 28:8.

63. Cf. Num 12:11ff.; 1 Kgs 17:17ff.; 2 Kgs 4:30ff.; 5:8ff.; 20:1ff.

64. E.g., Psalms 27; 42–43; and 84 (so Gerstenberger).

65. On praying in the temple: Acts 3:1; in places of prayer: Acts 16:13; in homes: Acts 9:11; 10:30; by sickbeds: Acts 9:40; 28:8; in prison: Acts 16:25.

66. E.g., 1 Kgs 17:21; 2 Kgs 4:32-37; Acts 28:8.

67. This tendency seems to increase as one moves in the Bible from the experience of ancient Israel toward the practice of Judaism in the Second Temple and the early Christian community.

68. If Hagar's weeping in Gen 21:16 can be interpreted as praying, as probably should be the case, then here is another instance of the praying one sitting. In each of these cases, however, sitting does not seem to be a part of prayer in any expected sense but is more a part of the particular circumstances, in one case the coming of a king into the sanctuary and the other a woman utterly exhausted in the wilderness.

69. E.g., 1 Sam 1:26; 1 Kgs 8:22; 2 Chr 20:5, 13; Matt 6:5; Mark 11:25; Luke 18:11, 13.

70. E.g., Gen 24:26, 48; Exod 34:8; Num 16:22; Deut 9:25; Josh 7:6; Ezek 9:8; 11:13; 1 Chr 29:20; Matt 26:39.

71. E.g., 2 Chr 7:3; 20:18.

72. As to the bowed head, see, e.g., Gen 24:26; 1 Chr 29:20; 2 Chr 29:30; Ps 35:13(?). As to kneeling, see 1 Kgs 8:54; 2 Chr 6:13; Ezra 9:5; Dan 6:10; Luke 22:41; Acts 7:60; 9:40; 20:36; 21:5; Eph 3:14.

73. See chap. 1, above.

74. Cf. Exod 5:22; 32:31.

75. Cf. chap. 7, above.

76. Pss 30:11; 35:13; 69:11-12.

77. Joseph Heinemann notes that in later Jewish prayer, "the worshiper does not address God forcefully in language which could be considered too direct and presumptuous." He notes, however, that in fact there is the mix of persistence and humility that is not unlike what we find in Job: "Even though one attitude is reflected in sentences like, 'However much you bother Him, the Holy One, blessed by He, will receive you' (Palestinian Talmud Berakhoth IX, 13b), and 'However much Israel presses Him..., He is pleased' (ibid.), yet another attitude prevails: 'The worshiper must humble himself' (Numbers Rabbah IV) and approach God with awe and reverence" (Joseph Heinemann, "The Background of the Lord's Prayer," *The Lord's Prayer and Jewish Liturgy* [ed. Jakob J. Pethuchowski and Michael Brocke; New York: Seabury, 1978] 84–85).

CHAPTER 3: "THEY CRIED TO YOU"

1. Claus Westermann, *Praise and Lament in the Psalms* (Atlanta: John Knox, 1981) 11–12 and passim.

2. Confession of sin is not infrequently a part of the cry for help. That will be seen in the prayers discussed in this chapter, but confession of sin is the specific focus of chap. 6, above.

3. The basic form-critical study of the Psalms remains the original and influential work of Hermann Gunkel and Joachim Begrich, *Einleitung in die Psalmen: Die Gattungen der religiösen Lyrik Israels* (Göttingen: Vandenhoeck und Ruprecht, 1933). Their work has been summarized and developed by many other scholars, and few treatments of the Psalms are not heavily influenced by their analysis. Among those works in English that make the results of form-critical study of the Psalms readily accessible are Claus Westermann, *The Psalms: Structure, Content, and Message* (Minneapolis: Augsburg, 1980); idem, *Praise and Lament in the Psalms*; Bernhard W. Anderson, *Out of the Depths: The Psalms Speak for Us Today* (rev. ed.; Philadelphia: Westminster, 1983); Erhard S. Gerstenberger, "Psalms," *Old Testament Form Criticism* (ed. John Hayes; San Antonio: Trinity Univ. Press, 1974). Most commentaries also work with these form-critical categories and discuss them in their introductions.

4. Prayers that look least like prayers out of distress include Gen 24:12-14; Num 27:16-17; Judg 6:36-37, 39; Judg 13:8; 2 Sam 7:18-29.

5. See below, "Address to God."

6. The sense that the prayer arises out of crisis and need is suggested in the following comments by Katharine Sakenfeld: "The person in need is Abraham—the continuity of his line (and of God's promise to his descendants) is at stake in this mission.... In this instance as with Joseph in prison the initial step in the sequence of human actions which leads to deliverance from the dilemma is Yahweh's action of *hesed*" (*The Meaning of Hesed in the Hebrew Bible* [Missoula, Mont.: Scholars Press, 1978] 103–4).

7. Two other royal prayers should be mentioned in this context. Solomon's conversation with God at Gibeon involves an explicit petition for wisdom and understanding to govern (1 Kgs 3:6-9 ‖ 2 Chr 1:8-10). This is, in effect, a prayer for help that does not reflect a situation of trouble or suffering. One should note, however, that in the context it is set as a dream, i.e., more of an incubation type experience than ordinary prayer.

Solomon's prayer of dedication to the temple is in 1 Kgs 8:22-53 (‖ 2 Chr 6:14-42). This is as much a piece of Deuteronomistic theology and interpretation of the place of the temple as it is a prayer. It obviously does not take place in a setting of threat, but most of its petitions are anticipatory of such situations and seeking God's help and forgiveness when the pleas for help will come in the future.

8. There is a brief prayer inserted into a genealogy in 1 Chr 4:10: "Jabez called on the God of Israel, saying, 'Oh that you would bless me and enlarge my border, and that your hand might be with me, and that you would keep me from hurt and harm!' And God granted what he asked." The prayer seems a general one and without context to suggest a setting of distress. But it is

preceded by the word that his mother gave him the name Jabez "because I bore him in pain [*'ōṣeb*]." The fact that in the next sentence Jabez prays that God will keep him from harm or pain (*'ōṣeb*) suggests that this prayer is in fact fundamentally about pain and suffering, that such belongs to Jabez's destiny, and the prayer arises out of the fact that he comes out of and belongs to pain.

9. While they are not set specifically as prayers, the cry of "Violence" in Jer 20:8; Hab 1:2; and Job 19:7 may be understood as exclamatory cries or prayers for help, such as the Akkadian cry *aḫulap* (see chap. 1, above). Perhaps the best example of a succinct formal prayer is the cry of Moses that God would heal Miriam: "O God, please heal her" (Num 12:13).

10. With reference to *prose* or nonpsalmic prayer, Moshe Greenberg states: "The formulated prayers follow a simple pattern, consisting basically of address, petition, and motivating sentence, with freedom to add and subtract elements" (*Biblical Prose Prayer as a Window to the Popular Religion of Ancient Israel* [Berkeley: Univ. of California Press, 1983] 17). Anneli Aejmelaeus makes a similar judgment with regard to petitionary prayers in the *Psalms* as well as prose prayers: "The pattern of traditional prayer, when employed in its most simple form—one imperative, one address, and one motivation clause—was found to represent one of the most basic modes of speech in Hebrew" (*The Traditional Prayer in the Psalms* [BZAW 167; Berlin: Walter de Gruyter, 1986] 88).

11. See, e.g., Claus Westermann, *The Psalms: Structure, Content, and Message,* 38–41.

12. One may refer also to Greenberg's *Biblical Prose Prayer* for helpful discussion and examples of the prose or narrative prayers.

The psalm prayers are not included in appendix 1 both because there are too many of them to present and because there are various resources that provide extensive analysis of psalm types, including the lament or complaint prayers of the Psalter. For representative examples, see Westermann, *The Psalms: Structure, Content, Message;* Anderson, *Out of the Depths;* Aejmelaeus, *The Traditional Prayer in the Psalms.* The psalm prayers are included in the discussion that follows in this chapter.

13. E.g., Gen 17:18; Exod 17:4; Num 11:10-15.

14. E.g., Psalms 11; 14; 53.

15. E.g., Psalms 3; 5; 6; 25; 26; 30; 35; and especially 86 (ten times!).

16. E.g., Num 12:13; Ps 16:1.

17. E.g., Exod 5:22; 1 Kgs 19:4; Ps 17:1.

18. E.g., Deut 3:24; 9:26.

19. "Most High": see, e.g., Pss 9:2; 56:2; cf. 57:2. "God/Lord of Hosts": e.g., 1 Sam 1:11; Ps 59:5. "The Holy One of Israel": e.g., Ps 71:22; cf. Isa 5:19, 24; 37:23; 41:16. "God of Israel": e.g., 2 Kgs 19:14; Ps 69:6; cf. 59:5.

20. E.g., Pss 3:7; 5:2; 7:6 [LXX]; 22:1, 2; 25:2; 40:8, 17; 59:1; 71:4, 12, 22; 86:12; 102:24; 109:21, 26; 140:7; 141:8; cf. 1 Kgs 3:7; 8:28.

21. E.g., Ps 18:2, 6, 29, 46.

22. In both of the instances cited, Pss 22:9 and 31:14, we have adversative *kî* or the *waw* adversative followed by the personal pronoun ("yet it was *you*" and "but *I*") that Westermann has called attention to as indicative of the

turning of the prayer in confession of trust or praise or certainty of a hearing. The claim of the deep personal relationship that has been confirmed again and again in experience is a fundamental ground of that turn. It may be expressed in many ways other than "my God," but that is one of its primal expressions.

23. The claim, "You are my God," i.e., the ground of appeal, is precisely the confession that is then made in thanksgiving by those who have been heard and delivered, as Ps 118:28 confirms.

24. The Hebrew for "strength" is different from what appears in v. 1, but the idea is the same.

25. See n. 14.

26. "My rock": Pss 19:14; 28:1; cf. 42:9. "God of my salvation": Pss 27:9; 88:1. "My help": Ps 22:19. "My strength": Ps 59:9, 17. "God of my right": Ps 4:1; cf. "O righteous God" in Ps 7:9. "Faithful God": Ps 31:5. "Our shield": Ps 59:11.

27. "My God": Ps 83:13. "Our God": Jer 14:22. "God of our salvation": Pss 79:9; 85:4.

28. See 1 Kgs 8:23, 25, 26.

29. J. Jacob Milgrom, *Numbers (Ba-midbar): The Traditional Hebrew Text with the New JPS Translation* (JPS Torah Commentary; Philadelphia: Jewish Publication Society, 1990) 135.

30. Ibid., 234. On one occasion, the Lord addresses Jeremiah, "I am the LORD, the God of all flesh" (Jer 32:27).

31. Gen 32:10; Deut 3:24; Judg 15:18 [?]; 2 Sam 7:18-24; 1 Kgs 3:6; 8:23-24; 2 Chr 14:11a; 20:6b-9.

32. Here and in other prayers, e.g., 2 Sam 7:18-29 and 1 Kings 8, Deuteronomic or Deuteronomistic elements will be present. They are not to be ignored or discounted in favor of some earlier form of the text or earlier form of prayer. Indeed they contribute to the character of prayer but not in a fashion that is in tension with other expressions of prayer.

33. E.g., Exod 15:11; Pss 18:31; 35:10; 76:7; 89:6-8.

34. Cf. Deut 33:26; Ps 86:8; Jer 10:6-7.

35. The Hebrew of the statement might best be conveyed, if more freely, by something like: "There is no difference for you between helping the one with many and the one without strength." The reference is to the mass of army poised against Judah and Benjamin.

36. The question of whether or not the praise elements of this prayer are a later expansion is a debated matter. For arguments in favor of the expansionistic character of it, see Claus Westermann, *Genesis 12–36: A Commentary* (Minneapolis: Fortress, 1985); for arguments in favor of its essentially Yahwistic character, see Gerhard von Rad, *Genesis* (Philadelphia: Westminster, 1972).

37. See the discussion in John Bright, *Jeremiah: A New Translation with Introduction and Commentary* (AB 21; Garden City, N.Y.: Doubleday, 1965) 288ff., and William L. Holladay, *Jeremiah 2: A Commentary on the Book of the Prophet Jeremiah, Chapters 26–52* (Minneapolis: Fortress, 1989) 202-20.

38. Cf. 2 Sam 7:18-24; 1 Kgs 3:6-7; 8:23-24.

39. 2 Chr 14:11; 20:5ff.

40. The extent to which praise is regularly a part of the address of psalms and the relation of this to patterns of prayer in Mesopotamia are subjects of debate. For summary and bibliography of different positions see Aejmelaeus, *The Traditional Prayer in the Psalms*, 54–59; and Erhard S. Gerstenberger, *Der bittende Mensch: Bittritual und Klagelied des Einzeln im Alten Testament* (WMANT 51; Neukirchen-Vluyn: Neukirchener Verlag, 1980) 128–30.

41. Note the summary comment of Hans-Joachim Kraus (*Psalms 60–150: A Commentary* [Minneapolis: Fortress, 1989] 71): "Psalm 71 belongs to the category of prayer songs....Worth noting is the fact that the psalm is very heavily pervaded by expressions of trust and by exulting cries. An analysis of the structure presents the following picture: vv. 1-8, petitions and expressions of trust which in v. 8 conclude with a song of exultation; vv. 9-16, descriptions of distress and petitions which in vv. 14-16 change to a song of praise; vv. 17-24, a vow of praise which is shot through with petitions."

42. Vv. 6, 8, 14, 16, 17, 18, 22, 23.

43. See Exod 34:6-7; Num 14:18.

44. Praise elements are found also in Jeremiah's lament prayers, functioning in similar ways to those described above. In Jer 11:20, the prophet expands the address that leads into the petition with the words:

> But you, O LORD of hosts, who judge righteously,
>   who try the heart and mind...

The participial constructions serve to render praise, ground the petition in the character of God, and express the confidence of the prophet in God's righteous judgment. The petition, "[S]ave me, and I shall be saved," in Jer 17:14 is followed by a *kî* clause, "for you are my praise."

45. Aejmelaeus, *The Traditional Prayer in the Psalms*, 57, agreeing with Joachim Begrich, "Die Vertrauensausserungen im israelitischen Klagelied des Einzelnen und in seinem babylonischen Gegenstuck," *ZAW* 46 (1928) 221–60.

46. Westermann, *Praise and Lament in the Psalms*, 42.

47. Note that Greenberg (*Biblical Prose Prayer*, 59–60) does not even include lament or complaint as a regular form of the prose prayer. He sees address, petition, and motivating factors as the regular components of such prayers. In that these are the primary features, he is correct. But the presence of complaint elements in prose as well as psalmic prayer, and certainly in a number of the prophetic prayers that he lists, indicates that this dimension of prayer extends beyond the Psalter.

48. This triangular relationship of self, God, and others has been lifted up as central to the lament psalms in the work of Claus Westermann. See, e.g., *Praise and Lament in the Psalms*, 169–70, 267–69; and *The Psalms: Structure, Content, and Message*, 39–41.

49. As shall be observed in the discussion of motivation below, it is not always easy to distinguish the lament part of the prayer for help from the motivational part. Clearly the description of one's plight can serve as a basis for urging God's intervention and action.

50. E.g., Craig C. Broyles, *The Conflict of Faith and Experience in the Psalms: A Form-Critical and Theological Study* (JSOTSup 52; Sheffield: Academic, 1989).

51. With reference to the plight of the people, see, e.g., Exod 5:22-23; 32:11-13; Num 16:22. In reference to a person in the community, see, e.g., 1 Kgs 17:4.

52. Psalms 6; 9–10; 13; 22; 35; 39; 42–43; 44; 60; 74; 77; 79; 80; 85; 88; 89; 90; 102. These include all of the communal laments but only a minority of the individual laments, if one follows Gunkel's listing.

53. Broyles, *The Conflict of Faith,* chap. 2.

54. The above discussion makes clear why in this chapter we are using the more general term "prayer for help" to talk about all of these prayers. Lament and complaint are dimensions of the prayer for help, but the variation and complexity of the way in which they are present and function in these psalms suggest the difficulty of using either term as the primary, all-inclusive designation of the prayers of those who seek God's help in some sort of distress or trouble (cf. pp. 55–57).

55. On the question to God as a major part of the complaint against God, see Westermann, *Praise and Lament in the Psalms,* 176ff.; Broyles, *The Conflict of Faith,* 80–82; and Samuel E. Balentine, *The Hidden God: The Hiding of the Face of God in the Old Testament* (New York: Oxford Univ. Press, 1983) 116–35.

56. See note 52.

57. As to the prose prayer texts, see Exod 5:22-23; 17:4; 32:11-13; Num 11:10-15; 16:22; Josh 7:7-9; Judg 15:18; 1 Kgs 17:20; Ezek 9:8; 11:13; Jonah 4:2-3. Only Jer 4:10; 14:13; and 32:16-25 among the prose texts have complaint components without questions directed to God. As to the poetic complaint prayers of the prophets, see, Jer 12:1-4; 14:7-9; 19-22; 15:15-18; 18:19-23; Hab 1:2-4, 12-17. Only Jer 11:18-20 and 20:7-12 lack the interrogative form anywhere in the lament.

58. So Terence E. Fretheim, *Exodus: Interpretation* (Louisville: Westminster/ John Knox, 1991) 155. The text is a conflate of JE (complaint to Moses) and Priestly (cry to the Lord) traditions accounting for the "channeling" effect of the final form of the text.

59. In this instance, one should note that the complaint of the people is challenged by the Lord: "Why do you cry out to me?" In some sense, the prayer of complaint in this instance is not accepted as an appropriate complaint. This narrative begins the series of complaints in the wilderness that are directed against Moses but are really against the Lord. They are finally not judged as acceptable complaint, but acts of faithlessness. The stories of the complaining in the wilderness are interesting in this regard because the Lord's response is partially an answer to the prayer and partially judgment for the faithlessness of the people.

60. Broyles, briefly noting such quotations (*The Conflict of Faith,* 40), does not see them playing any role in the God lament because they may be followed by petitions for help or confessions of help. This ignores the fact that that is just as true of most of the God laments he cites where questions are used to complain to God. His dismissal of these quotations of others as a serious type of complaint against God may be because their presence in psalms that he does not see as complaint psalms muddies his sharp distinction between psalms of

complaint and psalms of plea. But the clear presence of psalms that have a large dimension of complaint against God does not mean that it cannot be present in milder or less direct form in other psalms.

61. The quotations from Psalm 10 are all in the singular in the Hebrew. The NRSV has translated them collectively, primarily to avoid a gender distinction that would be present in the English. The collective may be the best way to understand the Hebrew in any event.

62. The RSV translation ("the wicked does not seek him") indicates the possibility of reading the subject of the verb "seek" (*dāraš*) as the wicked rather than God. The almost identical quotation in v. 13, however, which is literally, "You will not seek [*dāraš*]," strongly pushes the reader toward understanding v. 4a as a quotation of the wicked.

63. The Hebrew is somewhat ambiguous as to whether the one who thinks these words is the wicked one or the psalmist. Most interpreters agree with the NRSV at this point that the quotation is like the rest of the ones in the psalm, the expression of the wicked's sense of impunity before divine impassivity. If the quotation is the thought of the victim who prays, then its character as complaint is even sharper.

64. Pss 59:7; 64:5-6; 73:11; and 94:7.

65. Cf. the questions in the complaint part of Psalm 119, vv. 82 and 84.

66. For an extended discussion of such expressions, see Balentine, *The Hidden God*, 136–57; and Broyles, *The Conflict of Faith*, 61–80.

67. The Hebrew here is very uncertain and the translation a guess.

68. Although it may be a literary doublet, Abraham's question of complaint in Gen 15:2 is also followed up by an assertion that makes the same point: "You have given me no offspring, and so a slave born in my house is to be my heir" (v. 3).

69. Pss 74:10, 18, 21; 79:4, 11.

70. Pss 42:3, 10; 79:10; 115:2; cf. Joel 2:17. See Patrick D. Miller Jr., "Psalms and Inscriptions," *Congress Volume, Vienna 1980* (ed. J. A. Emerton; VTSup 32; Leiden: E. J. Brill, 1982) 324–27.

71. While no prayer of any sort is recorded, note that when the Lord tells Samuel, "I regret that I made Saul king," the text reports that "Samuel was angry; and he cried out to the LORD all night" (1 Sam 15:11b). One may assume that the prayer was a prayer of complaint by one who felt betrayed and frustrated at God's change of mind after having instructed Samuel to anoint Saul as king earlier. The anger of Samuel is probably typical of some of the situations of complaint, people crying in anger to and against God.

72. E.g., Pss 6:6; 22:2.

73. Pss 6:6; 39:12; 69:3; 80:5; 102:9.

74. As to the estrangement from others, see Pss 22:6-8; 25:16; 38:11; 69:8; 88:8, 18; 102:6-7; 142:4; Jer 15:17; 20:7. As to weariness, see Pss 6:6-7; 69:3.

75. Broyles, *The Conflict of Faith*, 104.

76. Pss 6:2, 7; 22:14-15; 31:11; 38:7-8, 10; 102:3-5.

77. Pss 6:2; 38:3, 5; 41:3-4; Jer 15:18; 17:14.

78. Pss 22:15; 39:10, 13; 102:10-11, 23-24; 143:7.

79. Pss 7:1-2; 13:4; 22:12-18 (both God and the enemies bring death near); 31:13; 35:4, 7; 38:12; 40:14; 55:2-5; 63:9; 143:3.

80. Broyles, *The Conflict of Faith,* 91–92.

81. Psalms 6; 32; 38; 51; 102; 130; and 143.

82. E.g., Pss 39:11; 40:12; 41:4.

83. "The enemies": e.g., Psalms 3; 5; 6; 7. "The wicked": Ps 10:4, 13, 15. "Evildoers": Pss 10:15; 22:16. "Those who hate me": Ps 9:13. "Workers of evil": Ps 6:8.

84. On the enemies as wild animals: Pss 7:2; 17:12; 57:4; 58:4-6; 59:6-7. On being surrounded and hemmed in: Pss 3:6; 17:9, 11; 31:21.

85. Pss 4:1; 18:19, 36; 31:8; 66:12; 118:5; cf. Exod 3:8.

86. Pss 7:15; 9:15; 25:15; 31:4; 35:7-8; 57:6; 142:3.

87. Pss 4:2; 5:6, 9; 10:7; 12:2-4; 31:18, 20; 38:12; 52:2; 55:21; 58:3; 59:7, 12; 62:4; 64:3-4; 69:1, 19-20; 140:3.

88. Pss 7:14; 10:8-9; 52:1-2; 64:2-6; 140:2.

89. Pss 42:3, 10; 79:10; 115:2; Joel 2:17.

90. On this text, see also chap. 6, above.

91. "As a poetic creation, the psalm takes up the experiences of many different people and gives expression to them, while, as a vehicle for worship, it becomes the well-tried means of expression for ever fresh experiences" (Claus Westermann, *The Living Psalms* [Grand Rapids: Eerdmans, 1989] 14).

92. Ibid., 13–16.

93. Ibid., 13.

94. Greenberg, *Biblical Prose Prayer,* 6–7.

95. The prophetic prayers fall somewhere in between these two categories, or overlapping them, and shall be looked at where appropriate under one or the other of the two primary categories.

96. For a summary statement listing the various petitionary aims of the prayers of the Apocrypha and Pseudepigrapha, see Norman B. Johnson, *Prayers in the Apocrypha and Pseudepigrapha: A Study of the Jewish Concept of God* (Philadelphia: Society of Biblical Literature and Exegesis, 1948) 7–37.

97. Elijah's repeated prayer, "Answer me, answer me," in the conflict with the prophets of Baal on Mount Carmel belongs in this context (1 Kgs 18:37). That is also the prayer of the prophets of Baal: "Answer us" (1 Kgs 18:26).

98. On this text, see also chap. 6, above.

99. The parallel passage in Deut 1:9-18 actually has Moses working out his own plan for a system of shared leadership.

100. Cf. Pss 35:4; 38:12; 40:14; 54:3; 63:9; 70:2; 86:14.

101. Joshua 7:7-9 contains no petition, but the circumstances indicate that the leader's complaint is because they are about to be destroyed by the Canaanites, having been routed by the men of Ai.

102. A wish form of this sort of petition occurs in the conversation between David and Saul in 1 Sam 24:12-15. David says: "May the LORD judge between me and you. May the LORD avenge me on you." The wish is that the Lord may judge, i.e., vindicate the right or establish David's right/innocence vis-à-vis Saul and so avenge/vindicate David. The wish is then elaborated in extended form in v. 15: "May the LORD therefore be judge and give sentence between me and

you. May he see to it, and plead my cause, and vindicate me against you" (cf. Gen 31:53).

103. The somewhat similar situation and appeal in Num 14:13-19 should be noted in this connection. While the petition is explicitly for forgiveness of the people, Moses calls to mind what God has done for the people in the past and suggests that God's power will be questioned by the nations if the people are destroyed in the wilderness. So he prays: "[L]et the power of the LORD be great *in the way you promised when you spoke....*"

104. On these prayers, see now Fredrick Holmgren, "Remember Me; Remember Them," *Scripture and Prayer* (ed. Carolyn Osiek and Donald Senior; Wilmington, Del.: Michael Glazier, 1988) 33–45.

105. Cf. Samuel's praying to the Lord in 1 Sam 8:6, which seems to be a prayer for instruction or direction about whether or not to set up a king for Israel. The prayer itself is not reported.

106. E.g., Ps 22:21b (see NRSV, note z).

107. On the taunts of the enemies, see the discussion of the complaint against God in pp. 77–79.

108. The petitions of the Psalms have been studied in detail by Aejmelaeus in *The Traditional Prayer in the Psalms*. Her work in collecting and organizing the data has been very helpful in the following analysis. The fundamental work in this regard remains that of Hermann Gunkel (Gunkel and Begrich, *Einleitung in die Psalmen*). Erhard Gerstenberger includes an extended discussion of the petition in his monograph on the prayers of the individual (*Der bittende Mensch,* 119–27). He gives his own grouping into categories with examples but does not elaborate them in much detail (p. 120): (*a.*) introductory petitions (for a hearing); (*b.*) petitions to avert something, to be spared; (*c.*) petitions for removing or destroying enemies; (*d.*) petitions for help and salvation; and (*e.*) petitions for particular gifts, specific accomplishments.

109. "Hear" (*šm'*): Pss 4:1; 17:1, 6; 27:7; 28:2; 143:1; etc. "Give ear" (*h'zynh*): Pss 5:1; 17:1; 39:12; 54:2; 55:1; 140:6; etc. "Attend = heed" (*hqšybh*): Pss 5:2; 17:1; 55:2; 61:1; 86:6; 142:6. "See" (*r'h*): Pss 9:13; 25:18, 19; 59:4; 119:153; 142:4. "Consider" (*hbyth*): Pss 13:3; 142:4; 80:14 (communal prayer for help).

110. See pp. 87–88.

111. Pss 4:1; 13:3; 27:7; 55:2; 60:5 (communal prayer); 69:13, 16, 17; 86:1; 102:2; 108:6; 119:145; 143:1, 7.

112. Pss 4:1; 13:3; 27:7; 55:2; 86:1; 102:2; 143:1, 7.

113. Aejmelaeus, *The Traditional Prayer in the Psalms,* 31.

114. Pss 4:3; 5:3; 6:8-9; 10:17; 18:6; 22:24; 28:6; 31:22; 34:6; 40:1; 55:17, 19; 65:2; 66:19; 69:33; 94:9; 116:1; 145:19.

115. Pss 3:4; 17:6; 38:15; 86:7; 119:26 (prayers for help). Pss 34:4; 65:5; 118:5, 21; 138:3 (songs of thanksgiving). Cf. Ps 99:6, 8.

116. Ps 65:2; cf. 94:9. The verb in this instance is *šām'a* = "hear" rather than *'ānâ* = "answer."

117. E.g., Pss 6:8-9; 22:21 (read "answered" with NRSV note z), 24; cf. chap. 4.

118. Pss 6:4; 25:16; 69:18; 86:16; 119:132. In Ps 6:4, the verb is *šûb;* in all other instances, it is *pānā.* The verb *šûb,* "return," also occurs twice as a petition in communal laments (Pss 80:14; 90:13). Its use in these instances is consistent with the discussion above.

119. A similar movement is seen in the preceding verses (13-15) as the psalmist first sets the prayer before God and asks for an answer (v. 13), then lays out in more detail the particular ways God needs to help and save (vv. 14-15).

120. See the discussion of the words "prayer" (*tĕpillâ*) and "supplication" (*tĕḥinnâ*) in chap. 2, above.

121. The point being made here is similar to Gunkel's suggestion about initial cries for help that prepare the way for other substantive requests (Gunkel and Begrich, *Einleitung in die Psalmen,* 221). Aejmelaeus (*The Traditional Prayer in the Psalms,* 28) has rightly noted that they may not be actually initial even if logically they are. The petitions seeking contact with God may appear anywhere in the prayer. They are, however, logically—and often actually—preparatory, coming either at the beginning or immediately before a specific petition for help. Aejmelaeus, in argument with Gunkel that the initial plea for a hearing or answer is not "merely preparatory" (her language), which of course it is not, points out that the only explicit petitions in Psalms 88 and 130 are for a hearing. Those examples, however, are less persuasive against Gunkel's basic point. Psalm 130 clearly has implicit petitions having to do with redemption and forgiveness that need to be taken into account when asking what the prayer is for. Psalm 88 is often noted as the one prayer that never moves to any point of hope or confidence in God's response. Its relentless focus on the cry for attention and hearing is consonant with its character as a prayer of one who feels utterly abandoned by God and bereft of God's consideration except in a most negative way. There are implicit petitions in this psalm also, but it remains initial or preparatory in very profound ways. While it may not be the only exception, it is indeed exceptional as a prayer for help, and this is one of the ways that is so.

122. Pss 35:2; 44:26; 59:4.

123. Pss 7:6; 9:20; 10:12; 17:13; 59:5; 74:22; 80:2; 94:2.

124. Such calls for God to rise up or awake are rooted in the experience of holy war when such exhortations were directed toward God, the divine warrior, and toward the warriors (Judg 5:12). The song of the Ark when it went out with the people to battle began: "Arise, O LORD, let your enemies be scattered" (Num 10:35; cf. Pss 68:1; 132:8; Isa 51:9).

125. "To my help": Pss 22:19; 38:22; 40:13; 70:1; 71:12. "To me": Pss 70:5; 141:1.

126. Note in Ps 138:6, the psalmist in a song of thanksgiving rejoices over the fact that God *is far* from the haughty.

127. The words *'ĕyāl* and *'ĕyālûtî* both seem to be *hapax legomena* and so must be translated with some hesitancy.

128. In this instance, one notes that the petition is prior to the complaint, which occurs later, indirectly, as a quotation of the enemies.

129. Complaints to God about hiding (without reference to the face) occur also in Pss 10:1; 55:1; 89:46.

130. As is the case with other complaint/laments and petitions, the correspondence carries over into expressions of confidence and within the same prayer: "He does not forget the cry of the afflicted" (Ps 9:12); "For the needy shall not always be forgotten" (Ps 9:18).

131. Here, as in some other examples, the petition is anticipated in lament aspects, i.e., against enemies or over self, as well as in complaint against God (e.g., Ps 4:2).

132. Pss 35:4, 26; 40:14, 15; 70:2; 71:13; 86:17; 109:29; etc.

133. On the correspondence of sin and judgment, see Patrick D. Miller Jr., *Sin and Judgment in the Prophets: A Stylistic and Theological Analysis* (SBLMS 27; Chico, Calif.: Scholars Press, 1982).

134. Here again the correspondence carries over into an expression of trust and confidence: "Salvation [*hayšû'â*] belongs to the LORD" (v. 8; my trans.).

135. Once more there is also a corresponding expression of confidence: "But you do *see!*" (Ps 10:14).

136. The song of thanksgiving that flows out of this prayer for help in vv. 21b-31 begins with the confident claim of the suppliant: "You have answered me" (v. 21b).

137. Cf. Aejmelaeus, *The Traditional Prayer in the Psalms*, 47.

138. Pss 35:7-8; 57:6; 140:5; 142:3.

139. Pss 4:1; 6:2; 9:13; 25:16; 26:11; 27:7; 30:10; 31:9; 41:10; 56:1; 57:1; 86:3, 16.

140. Cf. Num 14:18; Neh 9:17; Jer 32:18; Jonah 4:2. An alternate form of the confession, presumably quite ancient, is found in the divine self-presentation: "I will be gracious to whom I will be gracious, and I will show mercy to whom I will show mercy" (Exod 33:19).

141. Pss 86:15; 103:8; 111:4; 116:5; 145:8. The first example cited here, Ps 86:15, is followed in the next verse by the plea, "Be gracious to me." In other words, the association of the petition with the confessional formula is made explicit in the text. While Aejmelaeus is probably correct in seeing an association of this petition with the clause in the Priestly Blessing of Num 6:25, "The LORD be gracious to you," the more basic connection is with the confessional formula of Exod 34:6, as the psalmic references above indicate, particularly Ps 86:15-16.

142. This plea, grounded in the confessional claim about the Lord's way of mercy and compassion, is not confined to the use of the root *hnn* in various forms. One sees this confession lying behind a petition such as the following, which uses three words or roots from it:

> Do not, O LORD, withhold your *mercy* [*rahameyka*] from me;
> let your *steadfast love* and your *faithfulness*
> keep me safe forever. (Ps 40:11; cf. Ps 79:8)

The petition is both a plea to God to act according to the character revealed in the exodus and throughout the people's history (v. 11a) and a petition for the Lord's protection (v. 11b; see below).

143. E.g., Pss 6:2; 25:16 (cf. v. 18); 41:4; 51:1; 86:3 (cf. v. 5a).

144. So also Aejmelaeus, *The Traditional Prayer in the Psalms*, 23.

145. The interpretation depends in part upon whether v. 21 is read as referring to the psalmist's "integrity (or blamelessness) and uprightness," so that the prayer concludes with a protestation of present innocence, or the verse is understood as referring to the integrity and uprightness of God that will keep the psalmist despite sins committed and persecutions inflicted.

146. Psalm 39:8 may contain a plea for forgiveness if the Hebrew text reflected in the NRSV translation is correct: "Deliver me from all my transgressions." Some translations and interpreters, however, would emend the text to read: "Deliver me from all who transgress against me."

147. In this connection, one should note also that the plea to God, "Do not rebuke me in your anger" (Pss 6:1; 38:1; cf. 27:9), may be understood as an implicit plea for forgiveness because the anger of God is understood to be manifest in response to the sin of the people. Only in Psalm 38 are sin and guilt the expressed distress, and even here the petitions are for help and salvation rather than forgiveness, though the latter is implied. Psalm 32, a song of thanksgiving, certainly assumes petitions for forgiveness in the prayer that lies behind it because it gives thanks to God for forgiveness.

148. Joseph Naveh, "Old Hebrew Inscriptions in a Burial Cave," *IEJ* 13 (1963) 74–92; Frank Moore Cross, "The Cave Inscriptions from Khirbet Beit Lei," *Near Eastern Archaeology in the Twentieth Century* (Garden City, N.Y.: Doubleday, 1970) 299–306; André Lemaire, "Prières en temps de crise: Les inscriptions de Khirbet Beit Lei," *RB* 83 (1976) 558–68; Miller, "Psalms and Inscriptions," 311–32.

149. Other prayers from this cave are discussed in chap. 4, above.

150. Primarily forms of the following Hebrew roots: *yšʿ, nṣl, pdh, plṭ, ʿzr, gʾl, ḥlṣ, mlṭ.*

151. E.g., Pss 6:4; 7:1; 22:19-21; 31:1-2, 15-16; 40:13; 44:26 (communal prayer for help); 59:1-2; 69:18; 71:2-3; 109:26.

152. Ps 70:1 and Pss 79:9; 80:2 (communal prayers).

153. See, e.g., Pss 14:7 ‖ 53:6; 80:2-3, 7, 19.

154. *yšʿ:* Pss 3:7; 6:4; 12:1; 28:9; 31:16; 35:2; 54:1; 69:1; 71:2; 86:2, 16; 60:5 ‖ 108:6 (community prayer); 109:26; 119:94,146; cf. 106:47; 118:25. (This verb is usually translated as "save" or "deliver" except in 12:1, where it is "help," and 60:5 ‖ 108:6, where it is "Give victory.")

nṣl: Pss 31:2; 71:2; 79:9 (community prayer); 109:21; 119:170. (Usually translated as "deliver" but is "rescue" in Ps 31:2.)

ḥlṣ: Pss 6:4 ("save"); 119:153 ("rescue").

pdh: Pss 25:22; 26:11; 44:26 (community prayer); 69:18 (translated as "redeem" except in 69:18, where it is "set me free").

plṭ: Pss 31:1 ("deliver"); 71:2 ("rescue").

mlṭ: Ps 116:4 ("save").

gʾl: Pss 69:18; 119:154 ("redeem").

ʿzr: Pss 20:2; 22:19; 30:10; 38:22; 40:13; 44:26 (community prayer); 60:11 ‖ 108:12 (community prayer); 70:1; 71:12; 79:9 (community prayer); 109:26; 119:86. (All of these texts involve some verbal or nominal form of "help.")

The quotations of petitions that speak of deliverance from something or somebody, cited in the text, involve various verbs out of the list above, especially *yš'* and *nṣl,* except in the case of 25:17 and 142:7, where the verb *hôšî'* is used.

155. Pss 54:4; 60:11 ‖ 108:12; 94:17.

156. Pss 16:1; 17:8; 20:1; 25:20; 40:11; 59:1; 64:1-2; 69:29; 79:11 (community prayer); 86:2; 140:1, 4; 141:9.

157. Ps 64:2; Ps 40:11-12.

158. God as rock and fortress: Ps 31:2-3; God as hiding place: Ps 64:2; God as a bird under whose wings one may take refuge: Ps 17:8; 57:1; 91:4.

159. Pss 16:1; 17:7-8; 25:20; 64:1-2 (see v. 10); cf. 57:1; 141:8-9.

160. "Preserve those doomed to die": Ps 79:11; cf. 102:20. "Preserve my life": Pss 86:2; 143:11. See the repeated use of *ḥayyēnî,* "preserve my life," "give me life," in Psalm 119 (vv. 25, 37, 40, 88, 107, 149, 154, 156, 159).

161. Pss 40:14; 41:5; 88:10-12, 15; 102:3-5, 11. See the discussion on pp. 79–84.

162. See my suggestion (p. 85) of the possible association of Psalm 6 with the story of Hannah's suffering in 1 Samuel 1.

163. Cf. Othmar Keel, *Feinde und Gottesleugner: Studium zum Image der Widersacher in den Individualpsalmen* (SBM 7; Stuttgart: Katholisches Bibelwerk, 1969).

164. E.g., Ps 3:1, 6.

165. Pss 7:1; 35:3.

166. E.g., Pss 10:2-11; 52:1-4.

167. In Ps 27:12, "my adversaries" are "false witnesses" (*'ēdê šeqer*), the same term as used in the Decalogue, and "witnesses of violence" or "malicious witnesses" (my trans.; see Dennis Pardee, "YPḤ 'Witness' in Hebrew and Ugaritic," *VT* 28/2 [1978] 204–13). This latter description of the enemies appears also in Ps 35:11.

168. E.g., Pss 10:2; 35:8.

169. See Miller, *Sin and Judgment in the Prophets.*

170. Pss 6:2; 41:4; cf. 102:24; Jer 17:14.

171. E.g., Psalms 38; 41; 102. On these prayers for recovery from illness, see Klaus Seybold, *Das Gebet des Kranken im Alten Testament: Untersuchungen zur Bestimmung und Zuordnung der Krankheits- und Heilungspsalmen* (BWANT 5/19; Stuttgart: W. Kohlhammer, 1973).

172. On the acknowledgment of sin: Pss 38:3-4; 41:4; cf. 32:5. On illness and the judging hand of God: Pss 38:1-2; cf. 6:1.

173. E.g., Psalms 7; 17; 26; 35; and 139. Particular such petitions may be found in Pss 7:8; 17:2; 26:1; 35:24; 43:1; 54:1; 119:84.

174. On these prayers of persons accused, see Hans Schmidt, *Das Gebet der Angeklagten im Alten Testament* (BZAW 36; Giessen: A. Töpelmann, 1928); Lienhard Delekat, *Asylie und Schutzorakel am Zionheiligtum* (Leiden: E. J. Brill, 1967); and Walter Beyerlin, *Die Rettung der Bedrängten in den Feindpsalmen der Einzelnen auf institutionelle Zusammenhänge untersucht* (FRLANT 99; Göttingen: Vandenhoeck und Ruprecht, 1970).

175. E.g., Pss 7:3-5; 17:1, 3-5; 26:1-7, 11a; 139:23-24.

176. E.g., Pss 17:2; 26:1; 35:24; 43:1; 54:1.

177. A possible procedure for dealing with false accusations by bringing them into the sanctuary before God is suggested in 1 Kgs 8:31-32: "If someone sins against a neighbor and is given an oath to swear and comes and swears before your altar in this house, then hear in heaven, and act, and judge your servants, condemning the guilty by bringing their conduct on their own head, and vindicating the righteous by rewarding them according to their righteousness." Cf. Exod 22:7-8 and Deut 17:8-13 for other indications of a judicial decision in a religious setting, calling upon God for a judgment.

178. Pss 27:12; 35:11. Literally, "witnesses of violence," those who witness for or in behalf of violence.

179. Ps 26:10; cf. Isa 1:23; Deut 10:17; 16:19.

180. "The God who judges is glorified as the legal helper of the ṣaddîq [righteous] and as the perpetual punitive agent for the rešā'îm [wicked]" (Hans-Joachim Kraus, *Psalms 1–59: A Commentary* [Minneapolis: Fortress, 1988] 173).

181. The petition is uttered twice—once negatively—in Ps 25:6-7, which is an individual prayer, but it is an acrostic literary composition and therefore more artificial in form than other prayers. The plea to God to "remember" in Ps 89:47, 50 is also in that part of the psalm for the king that is an individual prayer for help for the king who has been defeated.

182. For the former, see Pss 74:2, 22; 79:8; 89:47, 50; 137:7; cf. Jer 14:21. For the latter, see Pss 20:3; 89:47, 50; 132:1.

183. Pss 74:18, 22, cf. v. 23; 89:50; 137:7; cf. Jer 15:15.

184. Ps 74:18, 22; 89:50.

185. Cf. Jer 14:21, where the people call upon God to "remember and do not break covenant with us."

186. One should add Lamentations 5, where the people appeal to God to remember them, but they do so by describing themselves, in effect, as "your poor," "your afflicted":

> Remember, O LORD, what has befallen us;
>   look, and see our disgrace!
> Our inheritance has been turned over to strangers,
>   our homes to aliens.
> We have become orphans, fatherless;
>   our mothers are like widows. (Lam 5:1-3)

187. See Exod 22:21-27; Deut 10:18.

188. Pss 3:8; 28:9; 29:11; 67:1, 7; 115:12-13; 134:3. The exceptions are Pss 109:28 and 128:5.

189. On this text, see chap. 9, above, as well as Patrick D. Miller, Jr., "The Blessing of God: An Interpretation of Numbers 6:22-27," *Int* 29/3 (July 1975) 240–51; David Noel Freedman, "The Aaronic Benediction," *No Famine in the Land: Studies in Honor of John L. McKenzie* (ed. James W. Flanagan and Anita Weisbrod Robinson; Missoula, Mont.: Scholars Press, 1975); and Klaus Seybold, *Der aaronitische Segen: Studien zu Numeri 6/22–27* (Neukirchen-Vluyn: Neukirchener Verlag, 1977).

190. See Michael Fishbane, "Form and Reformulation of the Priestly Blessing," *JAOS* 103 (1983) 115–21. An inscribed form of this blessing has now been found on silver amulets from around the end of the seventh century B.C.

191. Pss 3:8; 28:9; 109:28 (cf. v. 26).

192. The analysis of the relation between salvation and blessing is especially the contribution of Claus Westermann. Cf., e.g., Westermann, *Elements of Old Testament Theology* (Atlanta: John Knox, 1978).

193. In Pss 5:8 and 27:11, the prayer to be taught and led is "because of my enemies."

194. Kraus, *Psalms 60–150*, 414.

195. See now William Michael Soll, *Psalm 119: Matrix, Form and Setting* (CBQMS 23; Washington, D.C.: Catholic Biblical Association, 1991).

196. See Patrick D. Miller, *Deuteronomy* (Louisville: Westminster/John Knox, 1990) 56–57.

197. For a later reflection of the same theological understanding, see 1 Macc 3:48: "And they opened the book of the law to inquire into those matters about which the Gentiles consulted the likenesses of their gods." In reference to this text and in contrast to Mesopotamian practice, William W. Hallo comments: "For many purposes, the Torah replaced the divine image" ("Texts, Statues and the Cult of the Divine King," *Congress Volume Jerusalem 1986* [ed. J. A. Emerton; VTSup 40; Leiden: E. J. Brill, 1988] 64).

198. See Miller, *Deuteronomy*, 57.

199. The oft-noted ambiguity in Ps 23:3 is related to this understanding of prayer and law. "He leads me in paths of *ṣedeq*." Is that "paths of righteousness," meaning that God helps the psalmist keep the law and live a righteous life? Or is it "right paths" in the sense of the proper path that leads to deliverance or the path of God's *ṣedeq* that will protect the psalmist? The ambiguity is not to be dissolved. The statement of trust would be clear to the one who prays Psalm 119. The paths of righteousness, of God's instruction, provide the guidance that keeps one on the safe way, even in the darkest valley.

200. Cf. Gunkel, *Einleitung in die Psalmen*, 130–32, 231–232; Greenberg, *Biblical Prose Prayer*, 9–18; Gerstenberger, *Der bittende Mensch*, 40–42; Aejmelacus, *The Traditional Prayer in the Psalms*, 59–84; and Johnson, *Prayer in the Apocrypha and Pseudepigrapha*, 38–61.

201. It may also serve to bolster the trust of the psalmist as memory of God's faithfulness becomes a ground for hope in the present. The same is true of vv. 9-10.

202. Greenberg (*Biblical Prose Prayer*, 11) has well described the function of the motivational element in biblical prayer: "The pray-er needs a good that only God can bestow. He appeals to God on the basis of an established relation with him, which he invokes in several ways: by aptly chosen epithets and descriptive attributes, and especially in the motivating sentence. In the motivation, the pray-er appeals to a common value, some identity of interest between him and God, some ground on which he can expect God's sympathy and a demonstration of solidarity. Thus all the elements surrounding the petition, before it and after it, aim at establishing a bond between the pray-er and God, an identity of interest—a primary aim of prayer rhetoric."

203. For psalm prayers explicitly identifying God's justice or righteousness as a ground for God's acting to help, see Pss 5:12; 35:24; cf. 31:1; 71:2; 143:1, 11.

204. A similar appeal to God's keeping promises appears in another Mosaic prayer, Exod 32:13, under similar circumstances.

205. E.g., Pss 6:4; 25:7; 31:16; 44:26; 51:1; 69:13, 16; 86:5, 15; 109:21, 26; 143:12.

206. Pss 106:1; 107:1; 118:1; etc.; cf. chap. 5, above.

207. Cf. Ps 94:1; Nah 1:2.

208. Greenberg, *Biblical Prose Prayer*, 13.

209. Ibid.

210. Other examples may be found in Pss 71:18; 79:13; 80:18; 86:11; 142:7.

211. See the discussion of the vow of praise and thanksgiving below.

212. Pss 25:11; 31:3; 79:9 (communal prayer); 109:21; 143:11; Jer 14:7, 21 (communal prayers); cf. Pss 54:1; 83:16.

213. A similar move is made more implicitly in the individual prayer for help in Psalm 69; cf. Ps 109:27.

214. The motivation clause is conditional in Matthew and Luke and so functions quite differently.

215. See 2 Kgs 19:14-19. For further discussion of the appeal to God's reputation in this prayer and in God's response, see chap. 4, pp. 158–59, above.

216. See 2 Kgs 19:34; see chap. 4, p. 159, above.

217. Cf. Pss 44:25 (community prayer); 69:1; 70:5; 88:3; 102:3ff.

218. Pss 7:2; 13:3b; 28:1; 143:7b.

219. Pss 5:8-10; 27:11; 35:7, 20; 54:3; 56:1-2; 71:10; 109:2; 143:3.

220. Ps 38:2; cf. 39:12-13.

221. Cf. Ps 119:141 as well as the discussion of 2 Chr 14:11 in chap. 3, p. 64, above.

222. See the discussion of Judg 16:28 on p. 93, above.

223. Pss 16:1; 25:20-21; 31:4; 43:2; 57:1; 61:3; 143:8-10; cf. Ps 86:2. Aejmelaeus (*The Traditional Prayer in the Psalms,* 72) calls such clauses expressions of confidence in God. They are, of course, exactly that, but the implicit character of the expression of confidence as a reason for God's action becomes explicit in such constructions.

224. Exod 19:5-6; Deut 7:6; 14:2.

225. Cf. Begrich, "Die Vertrauensausserungen im israelitischen Klagelied"; Gunkel, *Einleitung in die Psalmen,* 232–36; Westermann, *Praise and Lament in the Psalms,* 71–75.

226. As in the Mesopotamian prayers. Cf. chap. 1, above, and the discussion of praise in the address to God in this chapter.

227. Cf. Westermann, *Praise and Lament in the Psalms,* 74.

228. E.g., Psalms 11; 16; 27:1-6, 62.

229. E.g., Pss 3:3; 5:7; 13:5; 17:15; 22:3, 9; 31:14; 38:15; 52:8; 55:16, 23a, 23b; 59:8; 64:7; 71:14; 73:23; 86:15; 102:12; 141:8; cf. 54:4.

230. E.g., Pss 16:2; 22:10; 31:14; 63:1; 86:2. The relation of the expression of confidence to other parts of the prayer is evident in the carryover of

this assertion into the direct address (e.g., Ps 22:1) and the motive clauses (Ps 143:10).

231. "My shield": Ps 7:10; cf. 3:3. "My help": Pss 40:17; 54:4; 70:5. "The help of the helpless": Ps 10:14; cf. vv. 17-18. "My rock" or "strength": Ps 73:26. "Merciful and gracious": Ps 86:15. "The one who lifts up my head": Ps 3:3. "The upholder of my life": Ps 54:4.

232. God's salvation: Pss 3:8; 31:5; 40:17; 55:16; 57:3. Deliverance in the past: Pss 4:1; 22:3-5, 9-10; 44:1-8; 74:12-17; 77:11-20.

233. On the former: Pss 5:4-6; 55:23; 59:10. On the latter: Pss 12:7; 31:19-20; 59:9; 60:12; 64:7-8.

234. E.g., Pss 3:5-6; 7:1; 25:2; 31:14; 38:15; 55:23; 56:3-4, 10-11; 71:14a.

235. In turn, Eliezer's prayer of thanksgiving in Gen 24:26-27 gives thanks to God for not forsaking God's "steadfast love."

236. Cf. Psalms 42–43.

237. Cf. Gunkel, *Einleitung in die Psalmen*, 247–50; Westermann, *Praise and Lament in the Psalms*, 75–81.

238. Gen 24:26-27; Isa 38:9-20. After their prayer is heard, the sailors on Jonah's ship offered sacrifice to the Lord and made vows. The primary point is their obedience, indeed conversion, to the Lord over against Jonah's disobedience. When Samuel and the people were delivered from the Philistines after Samuel cried out to the Lord, the narrative reports that Samuel raised a stone and named it Eben-ezer because "thus far the LORD has helped us" (1 Sam 7:7-12). Here is the report of what would seem to have been a vow being performed.

239. The technical language of vow is actually used in some instances (Pss 22:25; 56:12; 61:5, 8) while in other instances the vow is simply made without designating it as such. In the songs of thanksgiving, sung after God has responded to the cry for help (see chap. 5, above), reference is also made to the payment of vows (Pss 66:13; 116:14, 18).

240. Pss 7:17; 9:1-2; 13:6; 22:22-31; 26:12; 27:6; 28:7; 31:7; 35:9-10, 18; 43:4; 51:14-15; 52:9; 54:6; 56:12-13; 57:7-11; 59:16-17; 61:5, 8; 63:3-5; 69:30; 71:14-24; 79:13; 86:12; 109:30; 144:9. For the possibility of the vow of praise in other forms in some of the prayers, see Westermann, *Praise and Lament in the Psalms*, 75 n. 24.

241. Only in Ps 79:13 does the vow of praise come to clear expression in a community prayer.

242. Pss 7:17; 9:1-2; 26:12; 28:7; 35:18; 43:4; 51:15; 52:9; 54:6; 57:9; 63:3-5; 69:30; 71:14; 79:13; 86:12; 109:30.

243. Pss 22:22; 26:12; 35:18; 52:9; 109:30.

244. Gerstenberger, *Der bittende Mensch*, 156ff.

245. On singing and music: Pss 7:17; 9:2; 13:6; 27:6; 28:7; 51:14; 57:7-9; 59:16-17; 61:8; 69:30; 71:22. Cf. the discussion of this dimension of praise in chap. 5, above. On offerings and sacrifices: Pss 27:6; 54:6; 56:12; cf. the songs of thanksgiving, Ps 66:15; 116:17. On God's deeds: Pss 9:1; 22:22; 71:15-18.

246. Pss 40:6-8; 50:8-13; 51:16-17; 69:30-31.

247. See, e.g., F. Stolz, *Psalmen in den nach-kultischen Raum* (Zurich: Theologischer, 1983).

248. Cf. chap. 5, above, on the spiritualizing of thanksgiving.

249. See God's condemnation of the music and songs of worship as well as the various sacrifices and offerings (Amos 5:21-23), a condemnation that occurs because of the lack of justice and righteousness in the community.

250. On the *do ut des* character of the vow and the act of praise, see chap. 5, above.

251. E.g., Psalms 39; 88.

CHAPTER 4: "DO NOT BE AFRAID"

1. The translation of v. 5 is from an emended text. The verse reads literally:

> They looked to him and were radiant;
> so their faces were not ashamed.

It is possible that is the correct text and it is meant to be a generalized statement of which the particular petitioner is an example. Verse 6 is entirely in the active voice in the Hebrew, literally:

> This afflicted one cried and the LORD heard,
> and delivered him from all his troubles.

2. See v. 18:

> The LORD is near to the brokenhearted,
> and saves the crushed in spirit.

3. See chap. 2, above.

4. The NRSV adds "the righteous" with the Septuagint in order to clarify that the ones crying out are the righteous of v. 15 and not the sinners of v. 16. For discussion, see Hans-Joachim Kraus, *Psalms 1–59* (Minneapolis: Fortress, 1988) 382–83.

5. See chap. 2, pp. 44–48, above.

6. Pss 18:6, 16-19; 40:1-2; 116:1, 8; 118:5, 21; 138:3.

7. The NRSV, like other translations, translates the infinitive absolute + finite verb construction as "waited patiently." Such waiting may be patient in the modern sense, or it may be prolonged and intense. The construction is emphatic, but the particular nuance of that emphasis is vague.

8. In this connection, see Solomon's prayer in 1 Kgs 8:27-30.

9. E.g., Ps 69:1ff.

10. Cf. Ps 118:5.

11. Pss 6:8-9; 22:24; 28:6; 31:22.

12. The perfect-tense verbs here are to be translated as accomplished acts. The translation of verbs generally in the Psalter is a notoriously tricky and difficult matter. Psalms 36:12 and 57:6b contain verbs in perfect tense that also may reflect declarations of the one praying that God has defeated the evildoers and persecutors against whom the psalmist has sought help. But the verbs there are less certain, especially the key verb *nāpal* ("lie prostrate" or "fall"), which may have a present-action sense in the perfect or *qtl* form.

13. "The perfect tense *hwšyʿ* establishes an event that is to be awaited as sure" (Kraus, *Psalms 1–59,* 281).

14. Gen 35:3 (with reference to Gen 32:9-12); Exod 32:11-14; Judg 10:10-16; 13:8-9; 1 Kgs 17:17-24; 2 Kgs 6:17-18, 20; 1 Chr 4:10; 2 Chr 14:11-12; 30:18-20; Amos 7:2-3, 5-6. For the specific texts, see appendix 1, above.

15. Gen 15:1-6; 17:18-19; Exod 5:22-6:1; Num 11:10-17; 14:13-23; 16:20-24; 27:16-21; Judg 6:22-23; 1 Kgs 3:6-14; 2 Kgs 19:14-20, 32; 2 Chr 20:5-18; Jer 32:16-27, 42-44; cf. Neh 4:14; Amos 7:2-3, 5-6. For the specific texts, see appendix 1.

16. Exod 17:4-7; Deut 10:10-11 (with reference to 9:25-29); Judg 15:18-19; 16:28-30; 2 Sam 7:18-29 (in the story of the Judahite monarchy); 17:14 (with reference to 15:31); 1 Kgs 18:36-38; Neh 4:6-22 (with reference to Neh 4:4-5); Jonah 1:14-15. For the specific texts, see appendix 1.

17. Gen 4:10-12; 18:21-22; 20:7-17; 25:21; 30:6, 22; Exod 2:23-24; 3:7-8; 9:29, 33; 10:16-19; 14:10-18; 22:23, 27; Num 11:2; 20:16; 21:7-9; Deut 26:7; Judg 3:9; 4:3-23; 1 Sam 1:10-17; 7:7-11; 8:6-9; 12:8, 17-18; 1 Kgs 13:6; 2 Kgs 4:32-36; 1 Chr 5:20; 21:26; 2 Chr 33:12-13; Ezra 8:23; Dan 2:18-19; Jonah 2:1-10.

18. Num 14:13-24; Deut 3:23-26; Josh 7:7-11; 2 Sam 12:15-18; Ezek 9:8-10; cf. Deut 1:45; 1 Sam 8:18; 12:19-25.

19. Cf. Josh 7:7-11, where Achan's clan is punished so that Israel may go on.

20. Pss 18:6 (2 Sam 22:7); 34:15; cf. 2 Chr 6:40; 7:15.

21. Thus the cries of the Hebrews against Egyptian oppression.

22. So, many psalms and the laws of Exod 22:23, 26.

23. So, Abel's blood crying out (Genesis 4) and Hannah's bitter prayer in the sanctuary at Shiloh (1 Samuel 1).

24. On the matter of accompanying ritual and liturgy, cf. note 86.

25. The basic study of this type of speech is Joachim Begrich, "Das priesterliche Heilsorakel," *Gesammelte Studien zum Alten Testament* (TBü 21; Munich: Chr. Kaiser, 1964) 217–31. The following discussion draws particularly on this work and the introduction of Claus Westermann, *Isaiah 40–66: A Commentary* (Philadelphia: Westminster, 1969); cf. Thomas M. Raitt, *A Theology of Exile: Judgment and Deliverance in Jeremiah and Ezekiel* (Philadelphia: Fortress, 1977) 128–73. This book, while critical of Begrich's position, includes a helpful summary of it (pp. 152–54).

26. Cf. Isa 41:14; 43:1; 44:1-2; cf. Jer 30:10.

27. The same thing may apply to the second colon of this verse if *mty yśr'l* is to be read *rmty yśr'l,* "maggot, Israel." The word *rimmâ* appears in two other instances parallel to *tôlaʿat* (Job 25:6; Isa 14:11), as would be the case here with the correction. The example from Job is another instance of the imagery applied to human beings to indicate their low estate.

28. Other references to the plight and self-description of the afflicted one appear in Isaiah 40–55, if not in direct relation to the oracle of salvation, e.g., "one deeply despised, abhorred by the nations" (cf. Pss 22:6; 119:141) or the complaint in Isa 49:14-15:

> But Zion said, "The LORD has forsaken me,
> my Lord has forgotten me."
> Can a woman forget her nursing child,
> or show no compassion for the child of her womb?
> Even these may forget,
> yet I will not forget you.

29. In Second Isaiah and the salvation oracles of that period, see Isa 41:14; 43:1, 5; 44:2; 54:4; cf. Jer 30:10 = 46:27; 46:28.

30. Pss 3:6; 23:4; 27:1, 3; 56:3-4, 11; cf. Jer 30:10 ‖ 46:28.

31. These reasons may or may not be directly connected to "Do not fear" by a "for" (*kî*) conjunction.

32. E.g., Isa 41:10; 43:2, 5; cf. Jer 30:10-11 ‖ Jer 46:28.

33. Isa 41:10, 13, 14; 44:2.

34. See Ps 46:7, 11.

> The LORD of hosts is with us;
> the God of Jacob is our refuge.

35. See *ANET* 605; the translation is by Robert D. Biggs.

36. See Isa 41:9; 44:1-2.

37. See Pss 118:8-9; 146:3.

38. The text is K2401, edited in part by S. A. Strong, *Beiträge zur Assyriologie* (1894) 2.627–33, 637–43, and copied in full by J. A. Craig, *Assyrian and Babylonian Religious Texts,* 1.22–25 (with a list of corrections in vol. 2). The translation here is that of Herbert Huffmon, based on a collation of the tablet in the British Museum (private communication).

39. *ANET* 606 (translation by Biggs).

40. This information is derived from the study of this text by A. Leo Oppenheim, *The Interpretation of Dreams in the Ancient Near East* (Transactions of the American Philosophical Society, n.s., 46/3; Philadelphia: American Philosophical Society, 1956) 200; and Jonas C. Greenfield, "The Zakir Inscription and the Danklied," *Proceedings of the Fifth World Congress of Jewish Studies* (ed. Pinchas Peli; Jerusalem: World Union of Jewish Studies, 1972) 189–90.

41. The translation is that of Greenfield, "The Zakir Inscription," 190.

42. So Greenfield, "The Zakir Inscription," 190. He cites other examples from Mesopotamia of "Fear not" as a divine response to prayer.

43. See *ANET* 596–600 (translation by Biggs).

44. The quotation is taken from Scott Morchauser, "The Speeches of Ramesses II in the Literary Record of the Battle of Kadesh," *Perspectives on the Battle of Kadesh* (ed. Hans Goedicke; Baltimore: Halgo, 1985) 150–51.

45. The translation comes from Oppenheim, *The Interpretation of Dreams,* 252.

46. See Greenfield, "The Zakir Inscription," 186. He notes the similarity to Isa 41:10 when Ishtar says "Fear not" to Hattushilish III and then is described by the king as holding his hand.

47. For translation, *ANET* 655–56 (translation by Franz Rosenthal).

48. The pronunciation of the name of this king is now known to be Zakur rather than Zakir, but the more familiar spelling is used here because of its

long history of use. See Mordechai Cogan and Hayim Tadmor, *II Kings* (AB 11; Garden City, N.Y.: Doubleday, 1988) 144.

49. The comparison of the Zakir stele to the biblical song of thanksgiving has been made by Greenfield, "The Zakir Inscription." Further comparison with biblical prayer and the salvation oracle is found in the helpful essay by Hans-Jürgen Zobel, "Das Gebet um Abwendung der Not und seine Erhörung in den Klageliedern des Alten Testaments und in der Inschrift des Königs Zakir von Hamath," *VT* 21 (1971) 91–99, as well as in James F. Ross, "Prophecy in Hamath, Israel, and Mari," *HTR* 63 (1970) 1–28.

50. The translation is that of F. Rosenthal in *ANET* 655.

51. See Pss 7:6; 9:19; 10:12; 17:13; 74:22; and chap. 3, p. 99, above.

52. Pss 6:4 ("Save my life"); 119:153 ("Rescue me"); 140:1 ("Deliver me").

53. Pss 18:19 ‖ 2 Sam 22:20 ("delivered"); 34:7 ("delivers"); 116:8 ("delivered").

54. The Hebrew actually has the pronouns in the singular, as is customary for the oracle of salvation.

55. The text is quite broken at this point, and most of the specifics of the elaboration are lost.

56. See chap. 3, p. 103, above.

57. For a detailed justification of this reading, see Patrick D. Miller Jr., "Psalms and Inscriptions," *Congress Volume, Vienna 1980* (ed. J. A. Emerton; VTSup 32; Leiden: E. J. Brill, 1982) 320–22. The reading is along the lines first proposed by Frank M. Cross ("The Cave Inscriptions from Khirbet Beit Lei," *Near Eastern Archaeology in the Twentieth Century* [Garden City, NY: Doubleday, 1970] 74–92), but it is a result of my own independent and prolonged study of the inscriptions in the Israel Museum in Jerusalem.

58. Cf. Ps 77:7, where the verb *rṣh* of the second line of the cave salvation oracle appears in questioning complaint to God:

> Will the LORD spurn forever,
> and never again accept [or "look with favor"—*rṣh*]?

59. See chap. 3, p. 104, above.

60. Cf. Ps 86:2, where the similar petition, "Save your servant," is followed by a statement of trust equivalent to the first line of the Khirbet Beit Lei oracle of salvation: "You are my God."

61. The associations of the inscriptions with Psalm 69 are even more extensive, for the petitioner in this psalm also asks the Lord to "redeem [*g'l*] me." Furthermore, the primary theme of the lament in this prayer is the taunts and insults of others, including "the insults of those who insult you [*ḥôrĕpeykā*]," and the cave inscriptions include a curse prayer of the same sort: "Cursed be the one who insults you [*ḥôrĕpāk*]."

62. E.g., Num 21:34 (cf. Deut 3:2); Josh 8:1 (cf. Josh 7:5-9); 10:8. Following up the suggestion of von Rad, that this call to trust and not be discouraged had its roots in the holy wars of Israel (Gerhard von Rad, *Holy War in Ancient Israel* [ed. Marva J. Dawn; Grand Rapids: Eerdmans, 1991] 42–45), Edgar Conrad has suggested that the word of assurance, "Fear not," is entirely a word addressed to warriors and leaders going into battle (*"Fear Not, Warrior!" A Study of 'al tîrā' Pericopes in the Hebrew Scriptures* [BJS 75; Atlanta: Scholars

Press, 1985]). In this case, the claim is overdone. The context of war is certainly a frequent locus for this word, but prayers quite unrelated to war and battle received this word of assurance.

63. See, e.g., the elements of the oracle of salvation in response to Moses' objections to the divine call (Exod 3:12; 4:11-12) and to the objection of Jeremiah (Jer 1:8, 19).

64. The idiom here may mean "go to my death."

65. E.g., Gen 24:60; 25:21; 30:6, 17, 22; 1 Sam 1:10-11.

66. For more detailed analysis of this oracle, see chap. 6.

67. Cf. chap. 3, p. 85, above, and chap. 6. In this instance, the form of the salvation oracle is different from those that center around the assurance, "Fear not," and reminds us that the divine word of salvation may vary in particular settings.

68. On this expression, see the study of all its occurrences in the essay by Horst Dietrich Preuss, "...ich will mit dir sein!" *ZAW* 80 (1968) 139–73.

69. It should be noted that there are other places in addition to those discussed in these pages where the assurance "I shall be with you" occurs, some of them salvation oracles or words of encouragement centering in the call to "fear not," where prayer is not the precipitating factor, but the frequency further reinforces the importance of this divine address (e.g., Gen 26:3, 24; 28:15; Deut 20:3; 31:8; 31:23; Josh 1:9; 3:7; 7:12; Judg 6:12, 16; 1 Kgs 11:38; 1 Chr 28:20; 2 Chr 32:8; Isa 40:9-10; Hag 1:13; 2:4-5; Zech 10:5). Cf. Preuss, "...ich will mit dir sein," for further instances of this expression as a wish or a third-person statement that "God is/will be with you/us."

70. The text is a classic case of the conflation of different documents or strata of tradition, in this case the JE account being found in the report of the complaint to Moses and his response in the oracle of salvation while the Priestly tradition gives the report of the people crying out to God and God's response to Moses in vv. 15-18. But in the present form of the narrative, the texts have been brought into a single whole, not without its rough spots in terms of the consistent flow of the narrative. The discussion of this prayer and its response is built upon the integrated narrative as a testimony to the complaint of a people in fear and the response of God through a prophetic-priestly spokesman.

71. Cf. Patrick D. Miller Jr., "The Sovereignty of God," *The Hermeneutical Quest* (ed. D. G. Miller; Pittsburgh: Pickwick, 1986) 129–44.

72. The term "peace" so well characterizes the divine word of assurance that we find in Jeremiah a whole group of prophets who bring such positive words of assurance that their message is characterized by the one word "peace" (*šālôm*; Jer 6:14; 8:11), or "it shall be well [*šālôm*] with you," and "no calamity shall come upon you." The people in their community prayer say, "We look for peace" (Jer 14:19; cf. 8:15). Such prophetic mediators of divine words of assurance, i.e., salvation oracles, are also found in 2 Kings 22. The only problem is that in the circumstances behind these texts, the prophets are not in fact bringing a divine word. The word of the Lord in those circumstances was in fact calamity and not peace. But because the transmission of the announcement of *šālôm* is so expected and so often received as God's word of assurance to people in the face of threats to their existence and well-being, the refutation of

these false oracles and the conflict with these prophets are major features of the book of Jeremiah.

73. Cf. Exod 33:20; Deut 5:24-26.

74. All three of these prayers betray the language and themes of the Deuteronomistic Historian, as is true of the prayers of David and Solomon. The aim of this study is to look at the prayers of Scripture as they are found there without trying to strip them of particular ideological components or peel them back to earlier or original layers. Both then and now, prayer is often a reflection of the theological perspective of those who compose the prayers, hardly an astonishing fact. In these pages, both the similarities and the variations are given attention. The analysis is formal and theological rather than historical. On the Deuteronomistic character of these prayers, see Steven L. McKenzie, *The Trouble with Kings: The Composition of the Book of Kings in the Deuteronomistic History* (VTSup 42; Leiden: E. J. Brill, 1991) 105–9. For a perceptive analysis of the way the second prayer of Hezekiah (2 Kgs 19:15-19) combines "traditional cultic patterns" or the "basic structure of prayer" with "the style of the Dtr. historian," see Brevard S. Childs, *Isaiah and the Assyrian Crisis* (SBT; London: SCM, 1967) 99–100.

75. The parallel accounts are in Isa 37:14-20 and 2 Chr 32:20.

76. The complexity of the Kings account of Sennacherib's invasion is well known. See, among other works, Childs, *Isaiah and the Assyrian Crisis;* Ronald E. Clements, *Isaiah and the Deliverance of Jerusalem* (JSOTSup 13; Sheffield: JSOT, 1980); Cogan and Tadmor, *II Kings;* and McKenzie, *The Trouble with Kings,* 103–6. Most commentators understand 2 Kgs 19:9b-35 as a variant of the account in 2 Kgs 18:17-19; 9a+36-37, both of these being alternate accounts of the event referred to in 2 Kgs 18:13-16. Some would see two campaigns referred to in these variants.

77. See chap. 3, pp. 120–22, above.

78. One should note here the parallel account in 2 Chronicles 32 where, prior to the account of Hezekiah's prayer, which is a three-verse summary of the praying and God's deliverance (vv. 20-22), Hezekiah recruits the people to build up defenses for the city and encourages them with words identical to the divine oracle of salvation: "Be strong and of good courage. Do not be afraid or dismayed before the king of Assyria and all the horde that is with him; for there is one greater with us than with him. With him is an arm of flesh; but with us is the LORD our God, to help us and to fight our battles" (vv. 7-8). The central word of assurance, "Fear not," is uttered and grounded in the claim that "God is with us" and will "help us." Furthermore, the speech addresses the people in full acknowledgment of their plight ("the king of Assyria and the horde that is with him"). While this is not a divine speech, the words of assurance are effective in just the same way as the salvation oracle: "The people were encouraged by the words of King Hezekiah of Judah."

79. The fairly precise duplication of 1 Kgs 19:34, the differences in the Hebrew and Greek of the parallel text in Isa 38:5-6, and the irrelevance of the response to the particular need and Hezekiah's prayer call in question the pertinence and the originality of the last part of the oracle in 1 Kings 20.

80. On this verse, see the interpretation of P. A. H. de Boer, "Jeremiah 45, Verse 5," *Selected Studies in Old Testament Exegesis* (ed. C. van Duin; *OTS* 27; Leiden: E. J. Brill, 1991) 122–28.

81. Probably the locust plague.

82. Acts 28:8.

83. 2 Kings 4.

84. Acts 9:40.

85. 2 Sam 7; 17:14; Jeremiah 32; 42.

86. See 1 Kings 17 and 2 Kings 4. The frequent involvement of human agents, intermediaries, in the instances discussed here, as well as the transmission of oracles by priest and/or prophet, raises the whole question of the role of ritual or liturgical "experts" or officials in the process of prayer and response for those in distress. The determination of such roles or of the ritual and ceremony accompanying prayer is a difficult matter about which there is much debate. For that reason, we have not felt it desirable to elaborate various hypotheses about possible ritual accompanying prayer. Failure to do so should not suggest that there was no such ritual and that prayer was a purely individual enterprise between the petitioner and God in private. Quite the contrary. Biblical and extrabiblical evidence suggests there often were accompanying acts and the involvement of "third" parties. But figuring out what this involved in terms of any clear and consistent pattern of practice is quite difficult. The presence of a priestly or prophetic figure in the transmission of the divine response is frequently indicated and so assumed in this discussion. The larger role of an external party is also suggested in such stories as those of Elijah and Elisha healing or Moses praying for Miriam's healing as well as in Job 33:14-30, which points to the involvement of a "mediator" in the sequence of suffering, prayer, response, healing, and thanksgiving. There are many indications of prayer for help being offered in the sanctuary, but it is not excluded that it could be offered in a quite different situation. Indeed there are a number of instances of such circumstantial prayer outside the sanctuary.

For extended discussion of possible ritual ceremony accompanying prayer for help, see, among other works, E. Gerstenberger, *Der bittende Mensch: Bittritual und Klagelied des Einzelnen im Alten Testament* (WMANT 51; Neukirchen-Vluyn: Neukirchener Verlag, 1980); Klaus Seybold, *Das Gebet des Kranken im Alten Testament: Untersuchungen zur Bestimmung und Zuordnung der Krankheits- und Heilungspsalmen;* idem, *Sickness and Healing* (Nashville: Abingdon, 1981); Sigmund Mowinckel, *The Psalms in Israel's Worship* (New York and Nashville: Abingdon, 1962), vol. 2; James F. Ross, "The Phenomenology of Lament," *JBL* 94 (1975) 38–46.

87. A prayer for help attributed to Joseph has now been found among the Qumran texts. A narrative introduction includes the statement "and he cried out and called [aloud] to God Almighty to save him from their hands and he said..." There follows a fairly typical prayer for help as we have described that form in chap. 3, above. It happens, however, that this late prayer does not seem to be set in the context of his brother's hostility. The fragments include narrative material that refers to Joseph being "cast into lands he did not [know]" and "[given] into the hands of foreigners." But the actual prayer seems to have

him joined with his brothers who are together under the threat of others. See Eileen M. Schuller, "4Q372 1: A Text about Joseph," *RevQ* 14 (1990) 349–76; and idem, "The Psalm of 4Q372 1 within the Context of Second Temple Prayer," *CBQ* 54 (1992) 67–79.

88. E.g., Pss 5:1; 17:1; 39:12; 54:2; 55:1; 77:1; 80:1; 84:8; 86:6; 140:6; 141:1; 143:1. The *Hebrew and English Lexicon of the Old Testament* (ed. F. Brown, S. R. Driver, and C. A. Briggs) lists Deut 1:45 as the one other instance of the verb *he'ĕzîn* referring to God hearing prayer.

89. Walter Brueggemann, *First and Second Samuel* (Interpretation; Louisville: John Knox, 1990) 64–65.

90. William L. Holladay, *Jeremiah 1: A Commentary on the Book of the Prophet Jeremiah, Chapters 1–25* (Hermeneia; Philadelphia: Fortress, 1986) 344.

91. See Claus Westermann, *The Structure of the Book of Job* (Philadelphia: Fortress, 1981).

92. Westermann sees the lament particularly in 6:4-7; 7:1-21; 9:17-31; 10:1-22; (12:13-25); 13:20—14:22; 16:6—17:16; 19:7-20, 23, 27 (*Structure of Job*, 31). For the complaint against God, see the discussion in Westermann, *Structure of Job*, 50–59.

93. Westermann (*Structure of Job*, 67–68) lists the following four groups of petitions and wishes:

1. The wish to die (3:11-13, 21-22; 6:8-10; 7:15; cf. 10:18b-19)

2. The wish that God would leave Job alone

   a. so that Job might be able to breathe freely (7:16b; 10:20b) or so that humankind might be able to breathe freely (14:6, 13-15)

   b. so that Job might be able to address God (9:34-35; 13:21-22 [and hear God's answer])

3. The wish that Job's cause might be heard and that he might find an advocate despite his death (16:18-22; 17:3; 19:23-24)

4. The wish to encounter God (23:3-12; 31:35-37 [the summoning of God])

94. Protestations of innocent: e.g., Job 9:21; 13:15, 18, 23; 23:7, 10-12; 31:1-34, 38-40. Expressions of confidence and trust: Job 16:19-21; 19:25-27.

95. Westermann, *Structure of Job*, 105; emphasis added.

96. The verb for "complain" in this instance is *rîb*, "contend," a word that often refers to lawsuits.

97. On rhetorical questions in Jeremiah as a part of the Lord's disputation against the people, see now Walter A. Brueggemann, "Jeremiah's Use of Rhetorical Questions," *JBL* 92 (1973) 358–74.

98. On oracles in the Psalms, see Raymond Jacques Tournay, *Seeing and Hearing God with the Psalms: The Prophetic Liturgy of the Second Temple in Jerusalem* (JSOTSup 118; Sheffield: Sheffield Academic, 1992) esp. 160–98.

99. Others may be words of warning and instruction.

100. The third-person plural pronouns in the translation are actually third-person *singular.*

101. For the justification of this translation, see Patrick D. Miller Jr., "*Yāpîach* in Psalm 12:6," *VT* 29 (1979) 495–501, and J. Gerald Janzen, "Habakkuk 2:2-4 in the Light of Recent Philosophical Advances," *HTR* 73 (1980) 53–78. The word *yāpîaḥ* is now recognized from its usage in Ugaritic as a Northwest Semitic word for "witness." There is an incongruity between the plural words for "poor" and "needy," but that incongruity is in the text and present in the NRSV translation as well. While it does not appear that the translations that deal with the text in the manner of the NRSV are correct, the text would still be a salvation oracle. It would be a straightforward promise of salvation of the needy and the poor.

102. Literally, "his."

103. See in this regard Amos 5:7, 10-11.

104. E.g., Pss 3:7; 7:6; 9:19; 10:12; 17:13; 35:2; 44:26; 68:1; 74:22; 82:8; 94:2; 132:8. Cf. the expression of confidence in Ps 102:13: "You will rise up and have compassion on Zion," and chap. 3, p. 99, above.

105. On the possible historical contexts for this psalm, see Hans-Joachim Kraus, *Psalms 60–150* (Minneapolis: Fortress, 1989) 4–5; and Raymond J. Tournay, *Seeing and Hearing God with the Psalms,* 177–82.

106. On the significance of giving voice to pain, see Elaine Scarry, *The Body in Pain: The Making and the Unmaking of the World* (New York: Oxford Univ. Press, 1985).

107. This text is an example of the overlap in function of those oracles of salvation that were a response to prayer and those that were encouragement to the Israelite army as it went out to war. As we have seen, such occasions evoked prayers that received salvation oracles. Here there is no prayer, but the king is given an announcement of salvation that should quiet the fear that shakes his heart and the hearts of the people.

108. E.g., 2 Kgs 19:29-31 ‖ Isa 37:30-31.

109. See in this regard Psalm 14, with particular reference to the depiction of rampant evil and oppression in the first three verses and the claim that is made in v. 5. The relevance of this psalm for the present discussion is hinted at, at least, in Patrick D. Miller Jr., *Interpreting the Psalms* (Philadelphia: Fortress, 1986) 94–99.

110. For this understanding of Psalm 22, see Miller, *Interpreting the Psalms,* 100–111 and the bibliography cited there.

CHAPTER 5: "O GIVE THANKS TO THE LORD"

1. See Luke 17:17-18.

2. Two Hebrew words especially identify the prayers of praise and thanksgiving in the Old Testament. They are *tôdâ,* commonly translated "thanksgiving" or "confession" (of what God has done), and *těhillâ,* "praise." Both words have verbal forms that are extensively used to speak of the act

of praise and thanksgiving. The two terms have considerable overlap in meaning and are often used together and in parallel with each other. They refer to genres or types of prayer that are closely related but capable of being distinguished. Claus Westermann (*The Praise of God in the Psalms* [Atlanta: John Knox, 1965]) has proposed that we speak of declarative (or "narrative") psalms of praise (= *tôdâ*) and descriptive psalms of praise (= *těhillâ*) rather than songs of thanksgiving and hymns of praise. The categories he has in mind are essentially the same as those more commonly understood as thanksgiving and praise, but he is convinced that thanksgiving is not a separate or independent mode of expression in ancient Israel and so keeps everything together under praise. His point about the overall category of praise and exaltation is surely correct, and so we speak of "doxology" here in the title to the chapter. But the dimension of thanksgiving is not missing from this praise and is often sharply present in the so-called songs of thanksgiving, Westermann's declarative psalms of praise. It is also there in numerous references to blessing, on which see Westermann, *The Praise of God in the Psalms,* 27 n. 13 and 87–90.

Westermann's claim that there is no independent concept of thanks is not finally convincing. Clearly the verb *hôdâ* is not simply a matter of expressing thanks and is not used in human intercourse to do that. But as Westermann himself observes, the verb *běrēk,* "to bless," is used in that fashion and carries over into the expression of thanks to God (see below). Further, Westermann's analysis rests upon presumed inabilities of "primitive man" to differentiate thanks as an expression as well as the notion that the differentiation of thanks from praise is an outcome of modern individualistic thought. Both claims are more asserted than grounded. Westermann seeks to identify "those elements which characterize modern thanks, now independent of praise." Each one is highly debatable. They are as follows:

a. "In praise the one being praised is elevated (*magnificare*); in thanks the one thanked remains in his place." On the contrary, the receipt of expressions of thanks is often "elevating," as one can see in those more public expressions of thanks to individuals for contributions and gifts. Of course, praise may be a dimension of this, but not to the exclusion of a quite clear notion of gratitude and specific expression of it.

b. "In praise I am directed entirely toward the one whom I praise, and this means, of necessity, in that moment a looking away from myself. In thanks I am expressing *my* thanks." The expression of *my* thanks, however, does not mean that one does not look away from self and toward others.

c. "Freedom and spontaneity belong to the essence of praise; giving thanks can become a duty." The difficulty with such claims is that their reversal is just as true of experience. Many expressions of thanks are free and spontaneous, while much praise is rendered as a duty and without spontaneity.

d. "Praise has a forum and always occurs in a group; giving thanks is private, for it need concern no one except the one thanking and the one being thanked." Here is where the claim about modern individualism unnecessarily and inaccurately controls the assumption. In human intercourse, praise may occur in a quite private conversation or one-to-one relationship, while thanks is often expressed corporately. Again, there may be elements of praise in such occasions, but it is not the case that the thanks is secondary or individualistic.

e. "Praise is essentially joyful; giving thanks can take on the character of something required. Praise can never, but thanks must often be commanded." This is simply not the case, either in the Bible or in modern life. Praise can be expressed in quite somber ways, although we would argue it is not meant to have that character. But neither is thanks. And in human intercourse, thanks is often expressed with great joy and enthusiasm that can be quite contagious. So it is in the expressions of thanks in the Bible. Further, praise can and is commanded. Certainly that is frequently the case in Scripture. And thanks may be commanded, but it may also come forth quite freely and spontaneously.

f. "The most important verbal mark of difference is that thanking occurs in the speaking of the words, 'thank you,' or in shortened form, 'thanks'; genuine spontaneous praise occurs in a sentence in which the one being praised is the subject, 'thou hast done,' or 'thou art...'" Again the reverse is also true in each instance. "Hallelujah" is just as short and verbal an expression as "thank you." And thanks may take all sorts of expressions in addition to the words "thanks" or "thank you." One may say, e.g., "How good you are to me!" and so point to the one thanked, elevating and exalting that individual.

In this respect, we are following Frank Crüsemann in his extended study of the thanksgiving song. He sees the dimension of "thanks" in the verb *ydh* and the need to make some discrimination from the verb *hll* and "praise." Crüsemann rejects all of the six reasons Westermann gives for saying that "thanks" is unacceptable, but he does not give any explanation of the rejection (Frank Crüsemann, *Studien zur Formgeschichte von Hymnus und Danklied in Israel* [WMANT 32; Neukirchen-Vluyn: Neukirchener Verlag, 1969] 281 n. 6).

For all these reasons, we are using the more traditional categories of song of thanksgiving and praise or hymn while holding to the close interrelationship of the categories and the acts of praise and thanksgiving. The focus is always on the God who is praised/thanked, but the particular experience of the praising and thanking community may evoke the praise/thanks and is not completely separate from it. The disappearance of the dimension of thanks from the praise of God is not finally either an exegetical or theological improvement. In Westermann's presentation, the word disappears but not the reality. Gratitude is taken up in praise, and in that respect he is surely correct.

3. Other modes of prayer that belong under the rubric of "blessing" will be discussed in chap. 9. As to forms of the term used in reference to expressions of thanksgiving in personal relations, see, e.g., Deut 24:13; Ruth 2:19-20; 1 Sam 25:32-33; 26:25; 2 Sam 14:22; Neh 11:2; Job 31:20; Prov 30:11; Zech 11:5.

With regard to thanksgiving to God, see the comment of Sheldon Blank: "Roughly two out of three times when a man blesses God in the Bible he intends thus to express his gratitude to God for a favor God has done him. He means to 'return thanks,' to 'offer thanks.' The proportion may be still higher, exceptions may be rare, but in approximately two-thirds of the examples of such blessings their nature is obvious. They are a return for a favor experienced" (Sheldon Blank, "Some Observations Concerning Biblical Prayer," *HUCA* 32 [1961] 88). The exceptions are indeed rare.

4. That notion has carried through the traditions of Jewish prayer into the present, as some of the most common prayers of thanksgiving begin with "Blessed art thou, O Lord our God." On the shift from "Blessed be the Lord" to "Blessed are you, O Lord," see W. Sibley Towner, " 'Blessed Be Yahweh' and 'Blessed art Thou, Yahweh': The Modulation of a Biblical Formula," *CBQ* 30 (1968) 386–99.

5. E.g., Pss 68:19, 35; 113:2. For songs of thanksgiving, see, e.g., Pss 18:46; 66:20; 124:6. In prayers for help, see, e.g., Pss 28:6; 31:21; 144:1.

At the close of each of the first four books of the Psalter, such a prayer of thanksgiving, "Blessed be the Lord...," occurs (Pss 41:13; 72:18-19; 89:52; 106:48), leading toward the final conclusion of book 5, which is a fulsome call to praise (Psalm 150).

6. Pss 28:6; 31:21; 66:20.

7. Narrative texts: e.g., Ruth 4:14; 1 Sam 25:39; 2 Sam 18:28; 1 Kgs 1:48; 5:7; 8:15; 10:9; Dan 3:28; Zech 11:5. For narrative texts in which people are reported to use such a prayer, see, e.g., 2 Chr 31:8; Dan 4:34.

8. Note in Neh 9:5, the term *běrākâ*, "blessing," is paired with *těhillâ*, "praise," as *tôdâ*, "thanksgiving," is often paired with "praise." The continuing force of such gratitude in the form of blessing is well illustrated by the journalist Ari Goldman, who reports the following habit of his childhood: "My Mother spent my childhood years on *b'racha* patrol, making sure that nothing would pass my lips without thanks to the Almighty properly expressed. After she gave me a cookie, she would watch closely for the mumble. Saying *b'rachas* is a habit that never left me, and it still sometimes looks like I am talking to my food before I pop it in my mouth. It is an involuntary act, and, on those rare occasions when I think about what it is that I'm doing, I kind of like it. In the great scheme of things, it seems only right to give thanks" (*The Search for God at Harvard* [New York: Time Books/Random House, 1991] 15).

9. Blank, "Some Observations Concerning Biblical Prayer," 87.

10. Ibid., 89.

11. Cf. Westermann, *The Praise of God in the Psalms*, 120–22.

12. The translation here follows the NRSV in transposing part of v. 10 to v. 11 for reasons of sense.

13. Judgment here is clouded by the fact that Jethro may have been a worshiper of the Lord, as has often been suggested. Even if that is the case, however, we still have an instance where the recounting of God's help in response to cries of distress evokes in those who did not experience that help joy, thanksgiving, and praise.

14. The strict form-critical assignment of 1 Samuel 2 to the song of thanksgiving genre is a matter of debate. Gunkel and Westermann as well as others see it as belonging to that group (although Westermann uses the terminology of declarative praise rather than "song of thanksgiving"). Crüsemann (*Studien zur Formgeschichte*, 295ff.) regards it as a hymn of the individual. Without trying to settle the matter of genre classification and recognizing some formal differences from other songs of thanksgiving, we would keep it in that general

category for the purposes of this discussion because the song has been given a contextual definition by being set as Hannah's prayer of gratitude to God for hearing her prayer for a son and also by being placed in connection with her fulfilling her vow. Sacrifice and the fulfillment of vows in the sanctuary by the one who has been delivered are characteristic of the songs of thanksgiving. Contextually, the more hymnic song of Hannah has been turned into a song of thanksgiving, illustrating once more the close relation between the categories of hymn and thanksgiving song, of praise and thanks.

15. On the songs of praise of Miriam, Moses, and the Israelites in Exod 15:1-21 and the song of Deborah in Judges 5, see especially the conclusion of chap. 6, above.

16. Among those psalms most often characterized as songs of thanksgiving by individuals are Psalms 18; 22:22-31; 30; 32; 34; 40:1-12; 66:13-20; 116; 118; 138. Psalm 107 fits somewhat broadly in the category, and there are pieces of other psalms that seem to be thanksgiving songs, e.g., Pss 41:11-13; 52:8-9. There are also songs of thanksgiving scattered in other texts where the context does not set them forthrightly as such, e.g., Job 33:26-28; Isa 12:1ff.; and Sir 51:1-12. On Isa 38:10-20 as a song of thanksgiving, see F. Crüsemann, *Studien zur Formgeschichte,* 239–41 (following Begrich).

17. In this connection, we should also call attention to Job 33:26-28, which seems to describe the process of giving thanks after God has heard the prayer of one who suffered:

> Then he prays to God, and is accepted by him,
>   he comes into his presence with joy,
> and God repays him for his righteousness.
>   That person sings to others and says,
> 'I sinned, and perverted what was right,
>   and it was not paid back to me.
> He has redeemed my soul from going down to the Pit,
>   and my life shall see the light.'

The description, while couched in gender-fixed language, should not be understood as simply a description of male acts. Presumably, anyone, male or female, could and did give thanks to God in this way, entering the sanctuary, i.e., "his presence," with words of thanksgiving and joy to God and reporting to others what God has done in his or her behalf (see Hannah, e.g.). What we see here as a description of a process is laid out in other ways in the songs of thanksgiving.

18. Obviously the translation of the verbs as future or present depends upon whether vv. 22-31 are understood as an extended vow to offer thanksgiving in the future or are themselves an expression of that song of thanksgiving as a conclusion to the prayer. A clear-cut decision in this matter is probably not possible in light of the fact that the vow to praise and sacrifice is not infrequently a part of the prayer for help.

19. Greek and Syriac include the divine name. Textually it is uncertain.

20. Literally, *'eḥāy,* "my kin." The term normally translated "brothers" usually has a more inclusive reference in mind.

21. There are textual problems in the latter part of v. 2. The NRSV translation used here is a plausible understanding of the text.

22. Crüsemann, *Studien zur Formgeschichte,* distinguishes sharply an original "you" address to God from a later development of this into a third-person "he." The latter is a carryover from the fact that there is a third-person report of God's deliverance. This two-directional character, an address of praise and thanks to God and a report of God's deliverance to others, is the heart of the song of thanksgiving in Crüsemann's analysis. While this sharp distinction may or may not have been original to the form of the song of thanksgiving, it is clear that in the present corpus of songs a third-person reference to God as the object of praise can function in the same way as the direct address—to express thanks to God on the part of the one who has been heard and delivered.

23. E.g., Pss 22:24; 66:17-19; 138:3. Sometimes, there is a brief summary proclamation that God heard the prayer preceding or following a more extended report of what happened, e.g., Pss 30:1-3; 116:1; 118:21; Jonah 2:2. Psalm 34:4 and 6 also seem to be this more summary type of report, as we have suggested earlier. Cf. Westermann, *The Praise of God in the Psalms,* 103–8.

24. E.g., Pss 18:4-19; 30:6-11; 32:3-5; 40:1-2; 116:3-11; 118:5-18; Sir 51:2-10, 11b-12a.

25. E.g., Pss 30:3; 32:3; Isa 38:10-11, 17-19.

26. On complaints and laments, cf., e.g., Ps 32:3-4 with Ps 31:9-10. On petitions, cf., e.g., Ps 30:10 with Pss 27:7 and 22:19. On motivation sentences, cf., e.g., Ps 30:9 with Ps 6:5. Forms of address to God are, e.g., "O Lord," "O Lord my God."

27. As in other instances, the imperfect tense of the verbs for thanking and the like, which are usually translated in the NRSV as future, may better be translated as present tense. At least they refer in all likelihood to the present act of praying and giving thanks.

28. The sentence perhaps should be translated:

> I will give thanks forever
> that you have acted [or "that you have done it"].

The second colon, *kî 'āśîtā,* is similar to the final two words of Psalm 22 as well as the expression *hû' 'āśâ,* "he has acted" or "he has done it," in the thanksgiving prayer of Isa 38:15. In other words, in all of these cases we probably have reference to the testimony of what God has done that is central to the act of giving thanks. This is why some would translate the verb *hôdâ* in the first colon as "I will confess."

29. The verb *qāwâ,* "await" or "hope," is sometimes emended here to *'ăhawweh,* "to proclaim" (so NRSV). In that case, the proclamation to the congregation is more evident. But the proposal remains a conjecture. While it would involve the assumption of only a single letter error (qof for het), a more likely original text would be *'ôdeh,* particularly in light of the line in Ps 54:6 that reads *'ôdeh šimkā yhwh kî ṭôb,* "I will give thanks to your name, O LORD, for it is good," as well as the frequency of the paradigmatic song of praise and thanksgiving, "O give thanks to the LORD, for he is good" (see below).

30. The verb here is *yôdûkā.* It could be translated as "give you thanks" or "confess you."

31. The "words of your mouth" in v. 4 as well as "your word" in v. 2 probably refer to the salvation oracle by which help was conveyed to the suf-

ferer (so Hans-Joachim Kraus, *Psalms 60–150* [Minneapolis: Fortress, 1989] 507). There is an interesting addition to the text of v. 1 in the Greek, which reads: "I give you thanks, O LORD, with my whole heart, *because you have heard the words of my mouth.*" This obvious anticipation of v. 4b, whether it is original or not, probably refers to the prayer for help even as the "words of your mouth" refer to the salvation oracle by which the Lord answered the prayer.

32. Kraus, *Psalms 60–150,* 508.

33. Literally, "to the remembrance of his holiness," but *šēm,* "name," and *zeker,* "remembrance," occur in parallel and close synonymity in other contexts, e.g., Exod 3:15 and Ps 135:13.

34. These same groups are identified in Pss 115:9-11 and 135:19-20. The identification of those who "fear the Lord" as a group of converts in distinction from the Israelites who belong to the community of faith by birth and generation is found also in the Acts of the Apostles (10:2, 22; 13:16, 26; 16:14; 18:7). Cf. 1 Kgs 8:41-43 and Isa 56:6.

35. Kraus (*Psalms 60–150,* 400) notes that the hearing of this text in the New Testament as a "prophetic witness to the passion and resurrection of Jesus Christ" is "implicitly intelligible on the basis of the intention of the OT text." For it has to do with one who was despised being given honor (v. 22) and one who was consigned to death being allowed to see life (v. 17).

36. Cf. v. 3 and Ezra 3:10-11.

37. E.g., Pss 100:5; 106:1; 107:1; 136:1; Jer 33:10-11.

38. The whole prayer, including the report to others of the deliverance, may be in the sanctuary. It has been suggested, however, that Psalm 118 indicates the report is before entering the sanctuary where the *tôdâ* sacrifice with its words "I thank you, O Lord," is offered. See Crüsemann, *Studien zur Formgeschichte,* 217–23.

39. On the association of praise and sacrifice in Mesopotamian texts, see Hans Jürgen Hermisson, *Sprache und Ritus im altisraelitischen Kult: Zur "Spiritualisierung" der Kultbegriffe im Alten Testament* (WMANT 19; Neukirchen-Vluyn: Neukirchener Verlag, 1965) 53–54.

40. That we may have here, as well as in Genesis 28, a cult legend undergirding the sacredness of the Bethel shrine does not in any way undercut the story's understanding of this act as a response to divine guidance and help, prayed for at an earlier time.

41. Oracle of salvation = "Peace be to you"; name of the altar = "The Lord is Peace" (Judg 6:23-24).

42. The text also tells of a sacrifice made, but this is in connection with the prayer for help, as the story is told, and takes place as God routs the Philistines. So it is uncertain if this was meant to be a thank offering (1 Sam 7:9-10).

43. See in this regard Exod 18:12; Lev 7:11-15; 1 Sam 1:24; Ps 66:15.

44. Cf. Crüsemann, *Studien zur Formgeschichte,* 270–84.

45. Cf. Exod 18:12; 2 Chr 30:21-22; cf. Ps 22:26. On Ps 22:26 as a possible reference to the thanksgiving meal, see Hans-Joachim Kraus, *Psalms 1–59* (Minneapolis: Fortress, 1988) 299–300.

46. Kraus, *Psalms 1–59,* 493.

47. On this phenomenon in psalmic and other literature, see Hermisson, *Sprache und Ritus.*

48. Probably transmitted through a prophetic or Levitical figure in the cult.

49. Or "See, I am come/enter." The reference is probably to the entrance into the sanctuary to offer *tôdâ.*

50. Cf. the comment of Hermisson, *Sprache und Ritus,* 45: " 'In the scroll of the book it is written of me' then means: In the written scroll is recorded what I have done, what I have suffered, and how Yahweh rescued me. But that is nothing but a written form of the song of praise that people were accustomed to present orally in the sanctuary—which in this case probably takes place additionally. Then the praise here formulated in writing and presented in a scroll takes the place of the offering" (translation from Kraus, *Psalms 1–59,* 426).

51. It is also possible to read Psalm 40 as a unity with vv. 1-10 prefatory to the lament and referring to an earlier occasion when one in trouble cried out, was delivered, and carried out *tôdâ,* only without sacrifice because the Lord had so commanded, an explanation being necessary precisely because such sacrifice was customary. Now a new situation of need has arisen, and the one praying does not understand how that could be since he or she had fulfilled the ordinary requirements for thanksgiving properly (so Crüsemann, *Studien zur Formgeschichte,* 258–63). This scenario is not implausible and serves to give a rational explanation for the psalm as a unity. Even so, the rejection of sacrifice in favor of the written account of the psalmist's report is still to be noted.

52. See pp. 150–52, above, for a translation.

53. The translation is that of Harold Louis Ginsberg, "Psalms and Inscriptions of Petition and Acknowledgment," *Louis Ginzberg: Jubilee Volume on the Occasion of His Seventieth Birthday* (ed. A. Marx; New York: American Academy for Jewish Research, 1945) 160. Cf. *ANET* 655.

54. See Ginsberg, "Psalms and Inscriptions of Petition and Acknowledgment," 162–71 for Palmyrene, Phoenician, and Egyptian inscriptions analogous to these thanksgiving reports. The Egyptian thanksgiving inscription of Neb-re is especially like Psalm 30.

55. For this translation and discussion of this text and other matters relating to Hebrew inscriptions of prayers, see Patrick D. Miller Jr., "Psalms and Inscriptions," *Congress, Volume Vienna 1980* (VTSup 32; Leiden: E. J. Brill, 1981) 311–32.

56. The meaning of "by his asherah" in this inscription is a much-debated matter. While some have suggested we have here a reference to a consort of Yahweh, it is more likely that it refers to a cult object of the deity, in this instance in a kind of parallelism to "Yahweh" or "Lord," much as one often sees the divine name paralleled by some feature or aspect of the deity such as "his hand," "his soul," "his name," etc. in the Psalms.

57. The eating together is not specifically indicated in chap. 26, but it is mentioned several times in connection with the bringing of the offerings and rejoicing together (Deut 14:23, 26, 28).

58. For further discussion of this text and its similarity to the thanksgiving song, see Patrick D. Miller, *Deuteronomy* (Louisville: John Knox, 1990) 178–83.

59. The character of this as divine speech makes it something quite other than the reports of persons who cried out in trouble and then received a divine response and help.

60. The difficulties with seeing either of these psalms as community songs of thanksgiving have been laid out by Crüsemann, *Studien zur Formgeschichte,* 160–74. For a summary of his treatment of Psalm 124, see Kraus, *Psalms 60–150,* 440–41. Crüsemann makes a case for seeing Psalm 124 being composed out of formal and language elements that originate out of the prayer, or even profane speech, of an individual and have become secondarily a psalm of the community by the formula, "Let Israel now say." This does not rule out the possibility that the psalm found some use in the worship of Israel (p. 167).

61. See 1 Chr 16:34, 41; 2 Chr 5:13; 7:3, 6; 20:21; Ezra 3:10-11; Pss 100:4-5; 106:1; 107:1; 118:1-4, 29; 136; Jer 33:11. Cf. Sirach 51 (Heb. addition); 1 Macc 4:24.

62. Here, therefore, is where one feels the cogency of Westermann's press to keep these two closely together as well as the sense that the overarching category is praise of God. Form and language, however, suggest that within that overarching category, there is a sense of ways of expressing gratitude in quite specific situations, and so we have held on to the language and notion of thanksgiving.

63. E.g., 1 Sam 2:1-10; Psalms 92; 111; 145. On Psalm 92 as a mix of hymn and song of thanksgiving, see Crüsemann, *Studien zur Formgeschichte,* 283 n. 1.

64. "Praise the Lord": Ps 117:1; etc. "Sing to the Lord": E.g., Ps 96:1. "Rejoice in the Lord": Ps 33:1. "Bless the Lord": e.g., Ps 103:1.

65. Pss 96:1; 100:1.

66. Ps 145:1. Note the cohortative forms here to indicate the self-command.

67. E.g., Exod 15:1. Again a cohortative form, *'āšîrâ,* is used.

68. Ps 95:6. Psalm 95:6-7 is to be compared with Ps 100:1-3, the former using first-person cohortatives, the latter plural imperatives. Both texts have the same aim and much the same structure and language.

69. See appendix 2, above.

70. E.g., Exod 15:1, 21; Ps 117:2; Isa 44:23; etc.

71. The parallelism of this particular verse is an example of the simple complexity that one often finds in parallelism. The word *ḥasdô,* "his steadfast love," in the first (A) colon is paralleled in the second (B) colon by *'ĕmet yhwh,* "the faithfulness of the Lord." *Ḥasdô* also participates in *two* cases of the breakup of stereotyped phrases, i.e., words that occur regularly in juxtaposition, in this single verse. One often finds the expression *ḥesed we'ĕmet,* "steadfast love and faithfulness," in juxtaposition as well as in parallel, as in this instance. But, as we have seen, the suffixed form of *ḥesed* that we have here, *ḥasdô,* is also regularly a part of another frequent collocation, *ḥasdô + lĕ'ôlām,* "his steadfast love endures forever." The verse is deceptive in its artfulness and the way in which sameness and difference come together in the parallelism: (1) although the NRSV translation does not make it clear, a verbal clause in colon A is balanced by a nominal clause in colon B; (2) a suffixed form, "his steadfast love" is matched by a construct or genitival form, "the faithfulness of the Lord"; and

(3) "steadfast love" and "faithfulness" are different words but close enough in meaning that when they occur together, they are a virtual hendiadys. So in the two cola of v. 2, the *same* thing is said in a *different* way, and the hearer/reader perceives, perhaps quite unconsciously, the intermingling of equivalence and contrast in a single entity. Cf. Patrick D. Miller, "The Theological Significance of Biblical Poetry," *Language, Theology, and the Bible: Essays in Honor of James Barr* (Oxford: Oxford University Press, 1994), 213–30.

72. Reading with the Septuagint and Theodotion.

73. The plural clearly has in mind a plurality of manifestations of God's goodness and love in the history of Israel.

74. The reference to *ḥasdê dawīd,* "the steadfast loves [or 'gracious deeds'] for David," in Isa 55:3 suggests that the reference to *ḥasdê* in Ps 89:2 may also have particularly in mind all the gracious deeds God has wrought for David (note vv. 3-4).

75. The NRSV singular "steadfast love" does not reflect the plural of the Hebrew, which can be translated as a plural with the older term "mercies" or else something like "acts of steadfast love."

76. The correction of *rĕwāyâ,* "saturation," to *rĕwāḥâ,* "wide space" or "relief," reflecting the ancient versions, has been widely accepted.

77. It is possible, as Kraus has argued, that the imperative is a call to see a present cultic reality, the reenactment of the miracle at the sea and the crossing of the Jordan in Israel's later festival worship (Hans-Joachim Kraus, *Psalms 60–150: A Commentary* [Minneapolis: Fortress, 1989] 37).

78. See, e.g., Pss 66:1; 67:4; 96:1, 3, 7; 97:1; 98:4; 99:3; 148:13.

79. As pointed out to me by J. G. Janzen.

80. "Then Moses and the Israelites sang this song to the LORD."

81. This example is one of the better ones to argue Crüsemann's case, disputed here (see appendix 2), that the praise is really in these sentences that speak about what God has done. There are no imperatives or first-person declarations of praise, only the sentences that customarily belong to the grounding of the praise.

82. On the force of the warrior imagery as a dimension of divine sovereignty, see Patrick D. Miller Jr., "The Sovereignty of God," *The Hermeneutical Quest: Essays in Honor of James Luther Mays* (ed. D. G. Miller; Pittsburgh Theological Monograph 4; Allison Park, Pa.: Pickwick, 1986) 129–44.

83. Pss 89:5-8; 113:5; cf. Pss 18:31; 35:10; 40:5.

84. Psalm 117:2a is properly translated: "[F]or his steadfast love has prevailed over us."

85. Psalms 47; 93; 95–99; cf. Psalms 24; 29; 68; 145; 146; Isa 52:7-10.

86. On God's rule over the gods of heaven: Pss 95:3; 96:4; 97:9. On God's rule over the peoples of the earth: Pss 47:2, 7-9; 98:3-6; 99:2.

87. While originally the song at the sea may have been Miriam's, we are assuming in this study the presence of two forms of the song on the lips of two individuals or groups. There is, in other words, a double tradition about the song, and both hymns, though doublets, are properly the focus of attention.

88. E.g., Psalms 113; 146; 147.

89. On this note of reversal and God's doing the impossible, see the essay by Walter Brueggemann, "'Impossibility' and the Epistemology in the Faith Tradition of Abraham and Sarah (Gen 18:1-15)," *ZAW* 94/4 (1982) 615–34, and on 1 Samuel 2, see his treatment in "1 Samuel 1: A Sense of Beginning," *Old Testament Theology: Essays on Structure, Theme, and Text* (ed. Patrick D. Miller; Minneapolis: Fortress, 1992) 219–34, as well as in his commentary *First and Second Samuel* (Louisville: John Knox, 1990).

90. Pss 95:6; 100:3; 149:2.

91. The so-called "enthronement hymns": Psalms 47; 93; 95–99.

92. Cf. Pss 22:31; 52:9; Isa 38:15.

93. The comment of Claus Westermann (*Isaiah 40–66* [Philadelphia: Westminster, 1969] 144) is to the point: "Here God's act of deliverance and salvation and the activity of the Creator are regarded as identical. The result is that an answer, a reaction on the part of the created universe, is not simply connected as in the psalms which speak of creation (e.g., 148) with the fact of its having been created, but with a saving act of God on behalf of his people. This gives God's saving activity a far wider horizon than the human race (as in Gen 12.1ff.); the whole cosmos shares in it....How wonderfully Deutero-Isaiah expresses the connection between the central point of the divine action and its farthest horizon, and also, the mighty arch which, *sub specie Dei,* unites the destiny of the chosen people not only with that of the human race, but also, over and beyond it, with that of the entire created universe."

94. While it is less typical of the summons to the creation, in one of the last hymns of the Psalter, Psalm 148, all the elements and parts of the creation and all the natural processes are called to the praise of God because they have been created. Like Israel, they are to render praise to the one who made them.

95. This verse is supplied from the Greek and Syriac as well as the Qumran Psalter scroll.

96. On the world-making character of praise, seem Walter Brueggemann, *Israel's Praise: Doxology against Idolatry and Ideology* (Philadelphia: Fortress, 1988).

97. E.g., 1 Sam 2:1-10; Psalm 113.

98. Brueggemann, "Impossibility."

99. See chap. 6, above.

100. Amos 4:13; 5:8-9; 9:5-6.

101. T. S. Eliot, "Choruses from the Rock," *The Complete Poems and Plays, 1909–1950* (New York: Harcourt, Brace & World, 1952) 101.

102. Daniel W. Hardy and David F. Ford, *Jubilate: Theology in Praise* (London: Darton, Longman and Todd, 1984) 25.

103. Cf., e.g., Ps 22:31.

104. Cf. Ps 40:1-3.

105. See Numbers 14, where the Lord does not allow the people who complained to enter the land because they refused to trust the Lord and the good report of the spies.

106. Among the songs of trust, one may include Psalms 11; 23; 27:1-6; 62; 121; 131; and possibly 14 ‖ 53 and 73.

107. Cf. Westermann, *Praise and Lament in the Psalms,* 74.

108. That would seem particularly the case with Psalms 11; 14; 62; and 27:1-6, as it prefaces the prayer for help that follows.

109. Westermann, *Praise and Lament in the Psalms,* 74.

110. Pss 23:1-4, 5 (cf. 73:23-24); 27:1; 62:2-8 (cf. 73:28); 121; 131:2.

111. The confession and acknowledgment of *others* when God answers prayer, including persons and communities beyond the bounds of Israel, are found a number of times in the Old Testament: e.g., Deut 4:6-8 (the nations); Exod 18:10 (Jethro); 1 Kgs 18:37 (the people confess); 2 Chr 20:29 (fear of God coming on all the kingdoms); Jonah 1:16 (the sailors); Psalm 126 (the nations). On the interpretation of Deut 4:6-8 in this connection, see now Norbert Lohfink, "Poverty in the Laws of the Ancient Near East and of the Bible," *TS* 52 (1991) 46.

112. So, e.g., Kraus, *Psalms 1–59,* 332, and A. A. Anderson, *The Book of Psalms,* vol. 1: *Introduction and Psalms 1–72* (London: Oliphants, 1972) 226–27.

113. The verbs are couched in the singular, possibly reflecting their original character as words addressed to the psalmist. The first-person character of the rest of the psalm, however, has converted those words in an address to an unidentified audience of hearers.

CHAPTER 6: "THINGS TOO WONDERFUL"

1. Moshe Greenberg, *Biblical Prose Prayer as a Window to the Popular Religion of Ancient Israel* (Berkeley: Univ. of California Press, 1983) 59–60 n. 3.

2. Gen 21:16-17; 25:22; 29:35; 30:24; Exod 15:21; Judg 5:1-31; Ruth 1:8-9; 4:14; 1 Sam 1:10, 12-15; 2:1-10; 1 Kgs 10:9; Psalm 131.

3. Gen 25:22; 29:35; 30:24; Ruth 4:14. The first of these is too brief and enigmatic to say much about.

4. Prayers that bless the Lord: Ruth 4:14; 1 Kgs 10:9; see chap. 5, pp. 179–81, above. Prayers for blessing on others: see Ruth 1:8-9; see chap. 9, above.

5. Phyllis Trible, *Texts of Terror* (Philadelphia: Fortress, 1984) 9–35.

6. Trible's claim that the story intends to create a distance between Hagar and her child by always referring to him as "the child/boy" and never "her child" or "her son" is not fully convincing. While it is clear that elsewhere in Genesis 21 Isaac is often referred to as "his son" or "my son," the use of a definite rather than pronominal phrase to designate a person's child is also quite standard, particularly when the child is not named. That even happens twice in Genesis 22 (vv. 5 and 12), where there is otherwise strong emphasis on the relationship of father and son. In the story of Hannah and the birth of Samuel (see below), Samuel is four times called "the child" or "this child" by Hannah or the narrator and only once "her son."

7. See chap. 3, above.

8. See, e.g., Hannah's weeping bitterly as she prays in 1 Sam 1:10.

9. See chap. 4, above.

10. In v. 16, the Septuagint reads, "[L]ifting up his voice the child cried."

11. On this chapter see now Walter Brueggemann, "1 Samuel 1: A Sense of a New Beginning," *ZAW* 102 (1990) 33–48 (reprinted in *Old Testament Theology: Approaches to Structure, Theme, and Text* [ed. Patrick D. Miller Jr.; Minneapolis: Fortress, 1992] 219–34).

12. Cf. chap. 3, above, and Claus Westermann, *The Psalms: Structure, Content, and Message* (Minneapolis: Augsburg, 1980) 56–61; idem, *Praise and Lament in the Psalms* (Richmond: John Knox, 1981) 169–94, 267–69.

13. As Hagar had done to Sarah.

14. Patrick D. Miller Jr., *Interpreting the Psalms* (Philadelphia: Fortress, 1986) 56–57.

15. The attitude of her husband is ambiguous in the text as preserved. His affection is indicated in v. 8. Verse 5 is textually uncertain and may indicate that he shows a special care for her even though she is barren (NRSV) or that he gives her less because she does not have sons and daughters (RSV). The latter seems more likely. For arguments in favor of the former, see P. K. McCarter, *1 Samuel* (AB 8; Garden City, N.Y.: Doubleday, 1980) 51–52.

16. The most extended recent treatment of this psalm is the detailed monograph of Walter Beyerlin, *Wider die Hybris des Geistes: Studien zum 131. Psalm* (SBS 108; Stuttgart: Katholisches Bibelwerk, 1982). While the interpretation presented here departs significantly from his analysis, it is also much indebted to his careful discussion of the issues. Particularly with regard to v. 2, I have followed more the lines of interpretation laid out by Gottfried Quell, "Struktur und Sinn des Psalms 131," *Das ferne und nahe Wort: Festschrift L. Rost* (BZAW 105; Berlin: A. Topelmann, 1967) 173–85, and Klaus Seybold, *Die Wallfahrtpsalmen: Studien zur Entstehungsgeschichte von Psalm 120–34* (BThSt 3; Neukirchen-Vluyn: Neukirchener Verlag) 53ff., and idem, *Introducing the Psalms* (Edinburgh: T & T Clark, 1990) 159–60.

17. For this translation, see also Quell, "Struktur und Sinn," 173; Seybold, *Introducing the Psalms*, 159–60; and idem, *Wallfahrtpsalmen*, 37, 93. It should be noted, of course, that '*ālay* in v. 2b can be read with *napšî*, and a number of translations so read it. The idiom *napšî 'ālay* or '*ālay napšî* occurs elsewhere, as do *lēb* and *rûaḥ* + *nepeš* + pronominal suffix. Such a translation, "my soul within me" (so RSV and NRSV note), is possible, but it is less likely in this instance. Ordinarily, but not always, there is a verb with the construction *nepeš* + '*al* + suffix, and ordinarily, but not always, the experience attested to by the construction is a negative one. Psalm 131:2 might be one of the exceptions. The decision in part is a matter of being guided by an idiom found elsewhere or by the parallel colon. The latter is the closest, most immediate context. The construction *kaggāmul 'ālay* is precisely parallel in word order, syntax, and meaning to *kegāmul 'ălê 'immô*, except for the indefinite ‖ definite character of the first word. But that is best explained in terms of the parallel and the movement implied in it. In effect, the one who speaks says, "My soul is like a weaned child with/on its mother; indeed, it is like the weaned child on/with me." The point of the simile is not just "like a/the weaned child" but "like a weaned child *on/with its mother*." That point is vitiated if the simile is shortened in the second colon of the line, and the move from the indefinite

to the definite noun is less intelligible. The exact position of the weaned child vis-à-vis its mother suggested by the preposition *'al* is not altogether clear. For discussion, see Quell, "Struktur und Sinn," 178–80.

A poetic tricolon with a similar form may be found in Ugaritic in the Baal cycle:

> Like the heart of a cow for her calf,
> Like the heart of a ewe for her lamb,
> So's the heart of Anath for Baal. (*ANET* 140)

This analogy has been noted by Walter Beyerlin, *Wider die Hybris des Geistes*, 50 n. 11, but without recognizing its significance for the translation of Ps 131:2.

18. So also Quell, "Struktur und Sinn"; Seybold, *Die Wallfahrtpsalmen*, 37; and idem, *Introducing the Psalms*, 159–60; and Kathleen Farmer, "Psalms," *The Women's Bible Commentary* (ed. Carol A. Newsom and Sharon K. Ringe; Louisville: Westminster/John Knox, 1992) 142–43.

19. This is the suggestion of Quell on the basis of Egyptian reliefs of Syrian prisoners ("Struktur und Sinn," 178–79).

20. Deut 10:21; Jer 33:3; Pss 71:19; 106:21; 136:4; Job 5:9; 9:10; and 37:5, plus one reference to the great things Elisha did—2 Kgs 8:4.

While Jer 45:5 has been translated often in a way that suggests *gĕdōlôt* refers to Baruch's ambition for personal greatness or reward, that is not a correct reading. The verse has been well treated by P. A. H. de Boer, "Jeremiah 45, Verse 5," *Selected Studies in Old Testament Exegesis* (ed. C. van Duin; Leiden: E. J. Brill, 1991) 120–28. He recognizes that *gĕdōlôt* "is not used in the Old Testament to indicate high social positions or great rewards" (p. 125) and questions whether even Ps 12:4 can be so read. He translates Jer 45:5 and comments as follows:

> "And you ask for mighty acts?—do not. Though, behold, I am bringing disaster upon everybody—says Yhwh—I will let you capture your life as a prize wherever you go."
> Based on this translation, Baruch must be acquitted from selfishness. He is not out for personal advancement. Neither the scanty evidence elsewhere in the book of Jeremiah, nor that which is related about him in chap. 45 give reason to regard him as an egocentric personality. In the oracle the immutability of God's decision to destroy the country is expressed. Baruch's complaint is interpreted by God, or by Jeremiah as Yhwh's prophet, as a penetrating plea for a favourable change. It is clear that the oracle presupposes that Baruch has called upon God, who can do "great and unsearchable, mysterious things", marvels in favour of his people. But his God keeps this side of his being hidden. He rejects the plea. Baruch's attempt to intercede with God who had pronounced his sentence is in vain. Yhwh will reveal himself as devastator." (pp. 127–28)

21. Pss 106:21; 136:4; Job 5:9; 9:10; 37:5; cf. Ps 86:10.

22. William McKane, *Proverbs: A New Approach* (Philadelphia: Westminster, 1970) 658.

23. J. Gerald Janzen indicates this generally in his commentary *Job* (Atlanta: John Knox, 1985) and more specifically in a paper, soon to be published,

entitled "On the Moral Nature of God's Power: Yahweh and the Sea in Job and Second Isaiah."

24. Janzen, "On the Moral Nature of God's Power."

25. Walter Brueggemann, " 'Impossibility' and Epistemology in the Faith Tradition of Abraham and Sarah (Gen 18:1-15)," ZAW 94 (1982) 615–34.

26. While it is not of crucial moment in understanding the song of thanksgiving itself, one notes that the text explicitly speaks of it as an act of prayer: "Hannah prayed and said..." (1 Sam 2:1).

27. While Exod 15:21, a variant of the first verse of the longer poem ascribed to Moses in vv. 1-18, is explicitly said to be sung by Miriam, scholars as diverse as Frank Cross, David Noel Freedman, and Phyllis Trible have pointed out that the longer poem was probably originally ascribed to Miriam, who was replaced in the tradition by the more dominant figure of Moses. See Frank M. Cross Jr. and David N. Freedman, *Studies in Ancient Yahwistic Poetry* (SBLDS 21; Missoula, Mont.: Scholars Press, 1975) 45; and Phyllis Trible, "Subversive Justice: Tracing the Miriamic Traditions," *Justice and the Holy: Essays in Honor of Walter Harrelson* (ed. Douglas A. Knight and Peter Paris; Atlanta: Scholars Press, 1989) 102.

In all of these cases, of course, the ascription of the prayer or song to an individual is a part of the traditioning fact and cannot be assumed to be an indication of actual authorship. They speak, therefore, of the role that women played in the tradition of prayer in ancient Israel.

28. For a more extended explication of the ways in which the songs of Miriam, Hannah, and Mary "provide the substance for a hermeneutic and theology of liberation" see Gail O'Day, "Singing Women's Song: A Hermeneutic of Liberation," *CurTM* 12 (1985) 203–10.

CHAPTER 7: "WE HAVE SINNED"

1. Saul and Shimei's confession: 1 Sam 26:21 and 2 Sam 19:20. Hezekiah's confession: 2 Kgs 18:14.

2. Moshe Greenberg, *Biblical Prose Prayer as a Window to the Popular Religion of Ancient Israel* (Berkeley: Univ. of California Press, 1983) 24–30.

3. Pharaoh's confession: Exod 9:27; 10:16-17. Balaam's confession: Num 22:34—a similar sin to that of Pharaoh. Achan's confession: Josh 7:20. Saul's confession: 1 Sam 15:30. David's confession for adultery and murder: 2 Samuel 12. David's confession for the census: 2 Samuel 24.

4. Num 14:40; Deut 1:41; Judg 10:10; 1 Sam 7:6; 12:10.

5. Num 12:11.

6. On this term for supplication, see chap. 2, above.

7. Rom 3:23; 5:12; cf. 1 John 1:10.

8. Ezra 9:6-15; Neh 1:5-11; 9:6-37; Dan 9:4-19.

9. That is true even with regard to the generalized or universal statement cited above in 1 Kgs 8:46.

10. See the title of his widely read book, *When Bad Things Happen to Good People* (New York: Schocken, 1981).

11. For a presentation of this notion in detail, see Klaus Koch, "Gibt es ein Vergeltungsdogma im Alten Testament?" *ZTK* 52 (1955) 1–42. The article has been translated in abbreviated form as "Is There a Doctrine of Retribution in the Old Testament?" *Theodicy in the Old Testament* (ed. James L. Crenshaw; Philadelphia: Fortress, 1983) 57–87. It has been reprinted with a number of related and responding essays in Klaus Koch, ed., *Um das Prinzip der Vergeltung in Religion und Recht* (Darmstadt: Wissenschaftliche Buchgesellschaft, 1972). A summary presentation of Koch's views and a critical discussion of them that points to a greater dimension of genuine retribution in prophetic speech may be found in Patrick D. Miller Jr., *Sin and Judgment in the Prophets: A Stylistic and Theological Analysis* (SBLMS; Chico, Calif.: Scholars Press, 1982).

12. For a discussion of retribution and its relation to other aspects of judgment, see Miller, *Sin and Judgment,* chap. 4, "The Judgment of God."

13. Cf. Lev 19:2; Matt 5:48; Col 1:22; 1 Thess 3:13; 5:23.

14. In a similar way, the lamenting people in exile complain,

> My way is hidden from the LORD,
> and my right [*mišpāṭ*] is disregarded by my God. (Isa 40:27)

15. This repetition of the idiom "continue hostile" (lit. "go with X in a hostile fashion"—*hālak* + *'im* + suffix + *b* - + *qerî*) is confined to this chapter but occurs there several times (vv. 21, 23–24, 27–28). It is an example of the verbal or linguistic correspondence of human sin and divine judgment that I have delineated at length in the prophets (see Miller, *Sin and Judgment*).

16. See *'ehyeh 'immāk,* "I will be with you," in Exod 3:12 as a contextual illumination of the meaning of the name of God in v. 14: *'ehyeh 'ăšer 'ehyeh,* "I will be who/what I will be" and the sentence in v. 15: *'ehyeh šělāḥānî,* " 'I will be' has sent me." Cf. chap. 4, pp. 174–75.

17. *ḥāṭā'tî/ḥāṭā'nû:* Exod 9:27; Num 22:34; Judg 10:15; 1 Sam 12:10; 15:30; 2 Sam 24:10; 1 Kgs 8:47; Ps 106:6; Dan 9:5; Neh 1:6. Cf. Bar 2:12.

18. *ḥāṭā'tî/ḥāṭā'nû lyhwh/lāk:* Exod 10:16; Deut 1:41; Judg 10:10; 1 Sam 7:6; 2 Sam 12:13; 19:20; Jer 14:7, 20; Pss 41:4; 51:4; Neh 1:6. Cf. Bar 1:13, 17; 2:5b; 3:2.

19. Even as the English term "confession" functions in a dual sense to refer to both confession or declaration of one's sin and confession or declaration of one's faith, so the Hebrew root *ydh* in verbal and nominal forms can refer not only to the public declaration of what God has done in the act of thanksgiving but also to the confession of sin(s) (Lev 5:5; 16:21; 26:40; Num 5:7; Josh 7:19; Ezra 10:1, 11; Neh 1:6; 9:2–3; Ps 32:5; Prov 28:13; Dan 9:4, 20; cf. Ps 38:18 [*higgîd*]).

Something of the same thing happens in the New Testament where *exomologounai* is regularly the root for speaking of confession of sins and *homologein* the root for confession of Christ. The former refers to confession of Christ at least twice when the Septuagint is being quoted (Rom 15:9; Phil 2:11), and the latter refers to confession of sin on one occasion (1 John 1:9).

20. Lev 5:5–6; Num 5:5–10.

21. The gestures and acts associated with confession of sin and penitence and their significance are discussed in more detail in chap. 2, above.

22. Erhard S. Gerstenberger, *The Psalms: Part I with an Introduction to Cultic Poetry* (Forms of Old Testament Literature 14; Grand Rapids: Eerdmans, 1988) 13.

23. Ibid., 141–42.

24. The discussion here is significantly indebted to Greenberg's *Biblical Prose Prayer*, 22–30 but with some additions to his analysis of the elements of elaboration or development of the confession.

25. E.g., 1 Kgs 8:47; Ps 106:6; Dan 9:5; Bar 2:12. Cf. 2 Sam 24:17 (and the Qumran text).

26. The influence of Jeremiah, Ezekiel, and Third Isaiah is apparent in various ways in the psalm. Cf. Hans-Joachim Kraus, *Psalms 1–59* (Minneapolis: Fortress, 1988) 501, and Carroll Stuhlmueller, "Psalms," *HBC* 457.

27. Baruch 1–2 also belongs in this category and will be referred to where appropriate.

28. Cf. Ps 41:4 and the general confession of the Book of Common Prayer referred to earlier.

29. Such imagery comes to have a significant force in the understanding of Christian baptism as a cleansing and regeneration.

30. Gerstenberger, *The Psalms,* 213–14.

31. Among the studies of these prayers that are particularly helpful, in addition to the commentaries, are B. N. Wambacq, "Les prières de Baruch (1.15-2.19) et de Daniel (9.5-19)," *Bib* 40/1 (1959) 463–75; André LaCocque, "The Liturgical Prayer in Daniel 9," *HUCA* 47 (1976) 119–42; Maurice Gilbert, "La place de la Loi dans la prière de Néhémie 9," *De la Tôrah au Messie: Études d'exégèse et d'herméneutique bibliques offertes à Henri Cazelles pour ses 25 années d'enseignement à l'Institut catholique de Paris (Octobre 1979)* (ed. J. Dore, P. Grelot, and M. Carrez; Paris: Desclée, 1981) 307–16; and Henning Graf Reventlow, *Gebet im alten Testament* (Stuttgart: W. Kohlhammer, 1986) 275–86.

32. In all of the prayers, one recognizes allusions and quotations from other literature. The Deuteronomistic style, vocabulary, and content are prominent in Neh 1:4-11 and Ezra 9:6-11. Similarities to Solomon's prayer in 1 Kings 8 are evident. But prophetic and pentateuchal language, as well as that of the Deuteronomistic Historian, is prominent in these prayers.

33. Forms of the verb *hitwaddeh*—which occurs only in late Old Testament literature—are used in each instance: Ezra 10:1; Neh 1:6; 9:2-3; and Dan 9:4, 20. Cf. Bar 1:14.

34. Ezra 9:5; 10:1; Neh 1:4; 9:1; Dan 9:3.

35. W. Sibley Towner, *Daniel* (Interpretation; Atlanta: John Knox, 1984) 130.

36. Note, e.g., the plea to remember the promise to Moses in Neh 1:8 and the description of the present plight of the people in Neh 9:36-37. Some of the motivating clauses, like those in Jer 14:20-21, which is both confession of sin and community lament, appeal to the relationship between God and people, a common feature of the community prayers for help.

37. Claus Westermann, *The Psalms: Structure, Content, and Message* (Minneapolis: Augsburg, 1980) 31. Cf. H. G. M. Williamson, *Ezra, Nehemiah* (WBC; Waco, Tex.: Word Books, 1985) 167–68.

38. Neh 1:6; 9:6; Dan 9:4b.

39. Cf. Dan 9:4 and Neh 9:32. In the latter case, this ascription occurs after the long historical retrospective of God's mercy and the people's sins that occupies most of the prayer and just before the confessional and penitential prayer proper in vv. 32-37. If, therefore, one brackets the historical retrospective in Neh 9:7-31, that prayer is even more like the other ones in this group.

40. While the NRSV inserts "And Ezra said" at the beginning of the prayer in Neh 9:6-37, following the Greek translation, that emendation is not to be accepted. The Greek is secondary at this point. There is no move from singular to plural in this prayer because, like the prayer of the Levites (v. 5), it is plural from the start. For discussion, see H. G. M. Williamson, *Ezra, Nehemiah*, 304.

41. It is least prominent in Neh 1:5-11 where reference is made only to "the sins of the people of Israel" along with Nehemiah and his family.

42. Note especially the primary confessional formulation in Ps 106:6, whose heaped up expressions are identical to the formulation in 1 Kgs 8:47, Dan 9:5, and probably Bar 2:12.

43. Neh 1:6; Dan 9:5, 8, 11, 15; Bar 2:12. Nehemiah 9 does not have the common "We have sinned" (*ḥāṭā'nû*), but it has the parallel expression, "We have acted wickedly" (*hiršaʿnû*) at the point in the prayer where it moves from retrospect to the confession of the community praying (v. 33).

44. For the extended acknowledgment of God's righteousness in judgment in the prayer of Baruch, see above, pp. 248–49.

45. See chap. 3, above.

46. Psalm 106, to which this prayer has been compared, also includes reference to the mercy of God as the ground for the final petition after the confession of the sins of Israel's history has been made:

> Nevertheless he regarded their distress
>   when he heard their cry.
> For their sake he remembered his covenant,
>   and showed compassion
>   according to the abundance of his steadfast love.
> He caused them to be pitied [or "let them find mercy"]
>   by all who held them captive. (vv. 44-46)

47. So Celia Coplestone in "The Cocktail Party." See T. S. Eliot, *The Complete Poems and Plays, 1909–1950* (New York: Harcourt, Brace & World, 1952) 361.

48. Such renunciation, sadly, does not necessarily indicate that the sin will never be committed again. Pharaoh's renunciation turned out to be hollow, and David certainly did not have much conviction about the authenticity of Saul's promise never to harm him (1 Sam 26:21); he flees to the Philistines in the next chapter, saying, "I shall now perish one day by the hand of Saul" (1 Sam 27:1).

49. Matt 9:2-7 ‖ Mark 2:1-12 ‖ Luke 5:17-26.

Chapter 8: "Intercession for the Transgressors"

1. On intercessory prayer in the Old Testament, see Henning Graf Reventlow, *Gebet im Alten Testament* (Stuttgart: W. Kohlhammer, 1986) 228–64. He includes extensive bibliography and discussion of critical issues arising from the texts.

2. See Ps 90:13 and the discussion of the attribution of this prayer to Moses by David Noel Freedman, "Who Asks or Tells God to Repent?" *BibRev* 1/4 (1985) 56–59.

3. Abraham is called "my servant" in Gen 26:24 and "his servant" in Ps 105:6, 42. Moses is called "my servant" (Num 12:7-8; Josh 1:2, 7; 2 Kgs 21:8; Mal 4:4), "your servant" (Exod 4:10; Num 11:11; 1 Kgs 8:53; Neh 1:7, 8; 9:14; cf. Bar 2:28), "his servant" (Exod 14:31; Josh 9:24; 11:15; 1 Kgs 8:56; Ps 105:26; Isa 63:11; cf. Bar 1:20), and "the servant of the Lord/God" (Deut 34:5; Josh 1:1, 13, 15; 8:31, 33; 11:12; 12:6; 13:8; 14:7; 18:7; 22:2, 4, 5; 2 Kgs 18:12; 1 Chr 6:49; 2 Chr 1:3; 24:6, 9; Neh 10:29; Dan 9:11; cf. Heb 3:5; Rev 15:3).

4. For the use of the verb *pāgaʿ* as "intercede," see Jer 7:16.

5. On the prophet as intercessor, see Samuel E. Balentine, "The Prophet as Intercessor: A Reassessment," *JBL* 103 (1984) 161–73 and the bibliography in n. 2 of that article; Edmond Jacob, "Prophetes et intercesseurs," *De la Tôrah au Messie: Études d'exégèse et d'herméneutique bibliques offertes à Henri Cazelles pour ses 25 années d'enseignement à l'Institut catholique de Paris (Octobre 1979)* (ed. J. Dore, P. Grelot, and M. Carrez; Paris: Desclée, 1981) 205–17; and Reventlow, *Gebet,* 228–46, with bibliography.

6. In Hebrew, the typical expression is *hitpallēl* + *beʿad* + person(s) prayed for, e.g., Gen 20:7; Num 21:7; Deut 9:20; 1 Sam 7:5; 12:19, 23; 1 Kgs 13:6; Job 42:10; Jer 7:16; 11:14; 14:11; 29:7; 37:3; 42:2, 20. Cf. Exod 8:28; 1 Sam 7:9; 2 Kgs 19:4; 2 Chr 30:18; Job 42:8.

7. For Abraham as prophet, see Gen 20:7. For his intercessory activity, see Gen 18:23-32; 20:7, 17.

8. For Moses' designation as prophet, see Deut 18:15, 18; 34:10; cf. Sir 46:1. For his intercessory activity, see Exod 5:22-23; 8–10 (passim); 14:10-15; 32:11-13, 30-32; Num 11:2; 12:13; 14:13-19; 16:22; 21:7; Deut 9:20, 25-29; and possibly Exod 15:22-25. In light of Exod 17:1-7, the crying out of Moses in 15:25 may have been a complaint. Cf. Lothar Perlitt, "Mose als Prophet," *EvT* 31 (1971) 588–608; Reventlow, *Gebet,* 230–37; and Wesley Furst, "Moses as Intercessor," *Scripture and Prayer* (ed. Carolyn Osiek and Donald Senior; Wilmington, Del.: Michael Glazier, 1988) 5–19.

9. Samuel is called prophet or seer in 1 Sam 3:20; 1 Chr 9:22; 26:28; 29:29; 2 Chr 35:18; cf. Sir 46:13; 1 Esdr 1:20; Acts 13:20. His intercessory activity is referred to in 1 Samuel 7 and 12. Cf. Reventlow, *Gebet,* 237–39.

10. On Elijah, see 1 Kgs 17:20-21. On Elisha, see See 2 Kgs 4:33-34. On Isaiah, see 2 Kgs 19:3-4. On Jeremiah as a prophet, see Jer 37:3; 42:2, 4, 20. On Ezekiel as a prophet, see Ezek 9:8; 11:13. On Amos as a prophet, see Amos 7:2, 5. On unnamed prophets, see 1 Kgs 13:6; Isa 53:12 (?).

11. See 2 Sam 24:17, 25; 2 Chr 30:18.

12. It is worth noting that there is little indication of an intercessory role on the part of the priests, except in regard to blessing the people (on which, see below). Aaron is once cited alongside Moses as praying for the people (Num 16:22). Here it is less his priesthood that is in view than his role as coleader (and prophet! see Exod 7:1) with Moses. Phinehas, the priestly descendant of Aaron, is said to have prayed for the people (Ps 106:30), but the story referred to in that text, Numbers 25, does not speak of an intercession or prayer, but rather of an aggressive act of destruction that becomes the basis for his priesthood. There is one occasion where Isaac prays for his barren wife, Rebekah (Gen 25:21), but there we are dealing with both a patriarchal figure and the husband of the barren woman.

13. "My servants the prophets": 2 Kgs 9:7; 17:13; Jer 7:25; 26:5; 29:19; 35:15; 44:4; Ezek 38:17; Zech 1:6. Cf. 1 Esdr 1:32; 2:1; Rev 10:7. "His servants the prophets": 1 Kgs 14:18; 2 Kgs 14:25; 17:23; 21:10; 24:2; Jer 25:4; Dan 9:10; Amos 3:7. Cf. Rev 22:6. "Your servants the prophets": Ezra 9:11; Dan 9:6. Cf. Bar 2:20, 24; 1 Esdr 8:82; Rev 11:18.

14. Jer 37:3; 42:2 (cf. 42:4, 10).

15. 1 Kgs 17:17-24; 2 Kgs 4:18-37.

16. 2 Kgs 4:32-37.

17. In Deuteronomy, at least, some of the responsibilities of the elders, including the prayer for absolution of the people in the face of an unsolved murder that threatens to bring guilt upon the land, are incorporated in the divine instruction given in the Mosaic law. The social structure and the consequent intercessory role are legitimated in a way different from the prophetic call, but it is still a divine legitimation.

18. As the above discussion indicates, intercession on the part of the prophet was more extensively a part of prophetic activity than is indicated by Balentine ("The Prophet as Intercessor"). His approach depends too heavily on a terminological analysis and does not recognize all the examples of "prayer on behalf of someone else" (his—correct—definition of intercession) or give sufficient weight to the designation of Abraham and Moses as prophets. The issue is not whether every prophet saw his or her role as including intercession but that such activity was frequently and primarily associated with such individuals.

19. An exception to this is Jeremiah's letter to the exiles in Babylon with God's instruction to "seek the welfare of the city where I have sent you into exile, and pray to the LORD on its behalf, for in its welfare you will find your welfare" (Jer 29:7). The call for intercession here is exceptional both by its assignment to the people generally and by the absence of an explicit situation of calamity or disaster that provokes divine judgment.

20. Richard D. Nelson, *First and Second Kings* (Interpretation; Atlanta: John Knox, 1987) 171.

21. One might add to these examples, the occasions in Exod 5:22-23 and 14:10-15 where Moses prays to the Lord for the people when they are under the oppression of Egyptian slavery or frightened before the onslaught of the Egyptian army. The former is as much a complaint—because the people are blaming Moses—as it is an intercession, but then the complaint character of other Mosaic intercessions is evident also. The latter may not even be an exam-

ple of intercession. It is the account of a complaint of the people who would rather have stayed in Egypt than die in the wilderness. But in Exod 14:15, the Lord speaks to Moses as if the preceding complaint has been in fact his cry (cf. Num 11:2). However the voices are to be related to each other, this is hardly a typical case of intercessory prayer by a mediator.

22. Exod 8:8-9, 28-31; 9:28; 10:16-17.

23. Exod 32:11-13, 30-32; Deut 9:20, 25-29.

24. Num 11:2; 21:7.

25. Num 14:13-19; 16:22. Cf. Deut 9:7, 22.

26. Num 12:13. Cf. 1 Kgs 13:6.

27. See 1 Sam 7:5, 8-9; 12:19, 23; Jer 37:3; 42:2-4, 20; Ezek 9:8; 11:13; Amos 7:1-6. Only when Isaiah is appealed to by Hezekiah to pray for the people in the face of the Assyrian army of Sennacherib is there no reference to the Lord's judgment as an imminent or precipitating factor. In fact, in that instance the only allusion to sin is Hezekiah's confession to the Assyrian king, Sennacherib, "I have done wrong" (2 Kgs 18:14), and the only prayer that is explicit in the narrative is Hezekiah's own prayer for help. It receives a positive response by the Lord but without reference to any taking away of divine wrath or punishment.

In this connection, however, one should take note of Jer 26:19, which seems to point to a prayer by Hezekiah that averted the disaster that was to come upon them according to Micah's prophecy. Hezekiah's entreaty led the Lord to "change his mind" (see below).

28. Gen 18:23-32; 20:7, 17; 2 Sam 24:17, 25; 2 Chr 30:18-20; Job 42:7-10.

29. E.g., Gen 25:21; Num 11:2; Deut 9:20; 1 Sam 7:5-11; 1 Kgs 13:6; Job 42:8-10.

30. E.g., Exod 5:22-23; 32:11-13; Num 16:22; 1 Kgs 17:20; Ezek 9:8; 11:13.

31. See Gen 13:12-13.

32. See the discussion of Job's final words to God at the end of chap. 2, pp. 53–54.

33. For particular examples of this see Gen 12:3a and the discussion of the text in P. D. Miller, "Syntax and Theology in Genesis 12:3," *VT* 34 (October 1984) 472–76, and Ps 30:5.

34. See the comment of Walter Brueggemann (*Genesis* [Interpretation; Atlanta: John Knox, 1982] 172): "One might insist, if we were calculating mathematicians, that that ending shows there must be ten and that nine will not do. But, one would fail to see the point. Rather, the conversation breaks off because the point is established that the power of righteousness overrides evil. The dramatic explanation need not be carried further."

35. See chap. 2, p. 45, above.

36. Brueggemann, *Genesis,* 173.

37. These include the prayers of Moses on the occasion of the making of the golden calf (Exod 32:11-13, 31-32; Deut 9:25-29) as well as two other prayers in the wilderness by Moses (Num 14:13-19) and then by Moses and Aaron (Num 16:22). These prayers are all given in appendix 1. On Moses as intercessor, cf. Samuel E. Balentine, "Prayer in the Wilderness Traditions:

In Pursuit of Divine Justice," *HAR* 9 (1985) 53–74; and Erik Aurelius, *Der Fürbitter Israels: Eine Studie zum Mosebild im alten Testament* (ConBOT 27; Stockholm: Almqvist Wiksell, 1988).

38. Cf. Num 21:7 and the intercessions for Miriam (Num 12:13) and Aaron (Deut 9:20).

39. Cf. Exod 33:19; 34:6-7.

40. Exod 32:13; Deut 9:27.

41. Deut 9:26, 29; cf. Exod 19:5-6; Deut 7:6.

42. Exod 32:11; Num 14:13; Deut 9:26, 28, 29.

43. Terence E. Fretheim, *Exodus* (Interpretation; Louisville: John Knox, 1991) 291–92.

44. Deut 1:37; 3:26; and 4:21.

45. For discussion of the textual difficulties and possibilities in Amos 7:4, see D. Hillers, "Amos 7,4 and Ancient Parallels," *CBQ* 26 (1964) 221–25.

46. That the expectation is for a prophetic intercessor is indicated by the similar language in Ezekiel 13 where the Lord accuses the prophets of not having "gone up into the breaches, or repaired a wall for the house of Israel" (v. 5).

47. Exod 32:12, 14; Jer 26:19. The verb is *nḥm*. Cf. Num 14:20.

48. Amos 7:3, 6; cf. 2 Sam 24:16, 25 ‖ 1 Chr 21:15. Again the verb is *nḥm*.

49. E.g., Jer 18:8, 10; 26:3, 13; Joel 2:13-14; Jonah 3:9-10; 4:2.

50. Exod 32:12, 14; Num 14:20; 2 Sam 24:16, 25; Jer 26:19; Amos 7:3, 6.

51. Patrick D. Miller Jr., *Deuteronomy* (Interpretation: Louisville: John Knox, 1990) 123–24.

52. Ezek 24:14; Zech 8:14.

53. Exod 34:7; Num 14:18.

Chapter 9: "The Lord Bless You"

1. Gen 28:1-5 and Ruth 1:8-9. Cf. Gen 24:59-61; 31:49-50, 55; 2 Sam 13:25.

2. Gen 27:1-5, 27-29, 39-40; 48:8-22; 49:1-28; Deut 33:1-29. The blessings of Moses upon the tribes reflect the family context also, only in this case it is the leader of the family community "Israel," not an actual father or family head.

3. E.g., 1 Sam 20:13.

4. Gen 9:25-27; 27:29, 40; 48:17-21; 49:3-12, 26; Deut 33:16, 24.

5. Gen 24:60; 28:1-5; Ruth 4:11-12.

6. E.g., Isaac (Gen 27:27-29, 39-40; 28:1-5), Jacob (48:8-21; 49), and David (2 Sam 6:20; 7:29).

7. Gen 24:60; Judg 17:2.

8. Gen 24:60; Ruth 4:11-12; 1 Sam 2:20.

9. Num 6:22-27; 2 Sam 6:18; 1 Kgs 8:14, 55.

10. Klaus Seybold has collected a number of blessing prayers from the ancient Near East that demonstrate a similarity to the form of such blessings in ancient Israel (*Der aaronitische Segen: Studien zu Numeri 6/22–27*

[Neukirchen-Vluyn: Neukirchener Verlag, 1977] 30–34). These include blessings at the beginning and end of letters, sometimes as simple as "May the gods bless you," equivalent to the common Old Testament blessing, "May the Lord bless you." A sample blessing from the Amarna Letters is analogous in form and content to blessings in the Old Testament: "May the gods of Burra-Buriyas accompany you" (translation of William L. Moran, *The Amarna Letters* [Baltimore: Johns Hopkins, 1992] 24). Other epistolary blessings from Near Eastern and Jewish sources may be found in Ernst Lohmeyer, "Probleme paulinischer Theologie, I. Briefliche Grussüberschriften," *ZNW* 26 (1927) 158–73.

Blessings similar to the Aaronic benediction and other Old Testament blessings are to be found in the ritual of the Babylonian New Year's festival and in a ritual for a house dedication (Seybold, *Der aaronitische Segen,* 32, 33). In the Syro-Palestinian sphere, we find blessing greetings invoking the Lord's blessing in the Arad Letters and among the inscriptions from Kuntillet Ajrud, "I will bless you by the Lord. . . . " For examples from Arad, see Dennis Pardee et al., *Handbook of Ancient Hebrew Letters* (SBLSBS 15; Chico, Calif.: Scholars Press, 1982) 48, 57, and 64. For examples from Kuntillet Ajrud, see Klaas A. D. Smelik, *Writings from Ancient Israel: A Handbook of Historical and Religious Documents* (Louisville: Westminster/John Knox, 1991) 159–60. See especially the blessing at Kuntillet Ajrud, "May he bless you and may he keep you and may he be with my lord. . . . " (Smelik, *Writings from Ancient Israel,* 159).

A particularly good example in a non-Yahwistic inscription is found at the conclusion of the inscription of Yehawmilk of Byblos from the fifth or fourth century B.C.: "May the Lady of Byblos bless and preserve Yehawmilk, king of Byblos, and prolong his days and years in Byblos, for he is a righteous king. And may [the mistress] the Lad of Byblos, give [him] favor in the eyes of the gods and in the eyes of the people of this country and (that he be) pleased with the people of this country" (*ANET* 502). Cf. the similar blessing in the tenth-century inscription of Yehimilk of Byblos (*ANET* 499).

11. See the forms *yōsēp,* "may he increase," (Deut 1:9) and *wîhî,* "may he be" (1 Sam 20:13).

12. Or: "Surely he will be blessed!"

13. Here I am indebted to Claus Westermann, *Blessing in the Bible and the Life of the Church* (OBT; Philadelphia: Fortress, 1978) and the seminal essay of Hans Walter Wolff, "The Kerygma of the Yahwist," in Walter Brueggemann and Hans Walter Wolff, *The Vitality of Old Testament Traditions* (Atlanta: John Knox, 1975) 41–66 (Originally published in *Int* 20 [1966] 131–58).

14. The blessings of Moses upon the tribes are a part of Deuteronomy. But in their context and in their particulars they are given a much heavier theological character. They are consistently a way of calling upon and describing God's blessing upon the tribes. Both these blessings in Deuteronomy 33 and the blessing of Jacob in Genesis 49 as well as the song of Deborah in Judges 5 preserve an ancient and probably common tradition of tribal blessings.

15. The analysis of the Yahwist stratum of the Pentateuch and its theology, particularly in the book of Genesis, is taken directly from Wolff's study "The Kerygma of the Yahwist."

16. I am is still persuaded by the arguments that place the Yahwist early in Israel's history, around the tenth century. But the thematic character of the divine blessing, growing out of the key transitional text, Gen 12:1-4a, is clear whenever the Yahwist is to be dated.

17. Gen 12:3; 18:18; 22:18; 26:4; 28:14; cf. 27:29; 22:6.

18. See Gen 19:30-38.

19. See Gen 28:5.

20. "How does he effect blessing? Here the answer is: by concluding a solemn covenant (*běrît*) with the Philistines in spite of their former hostility. In what way is the blessing worked out? *Shalom* is established (vss. 29 and 31) in the promise to do one another no harm" (Wolff, "The Kerygma of the Yahwist," 58).

21. Ibid., 59.

22. Wolff notes that the way Israel is to bring blessing upon this nation under curse or judgment is already suggested by the several times that Pharaoh earlier asked Moses to pray to the Lord to forgive him (Exod 8:8, 12, 28-29; 9:28; 10:17). Wolff writes: "The manner of conveying the blessing is thus similar to Genesis 18—intercession and forgiveness! The effect of the blessing is to be the removal of the curse of judgment. And because Egypt was both a world power and Israel's overlord, the Yahwist's narrative becomes particularly pointed for his contemporaries: in spite of all the suffering received at her hands, Israel is appointed to bring even Egypt under the blessing. It is no wonder that this facet of his kerygma was thought about again in succeeding centuries, when Israel once again saw herself subjugated by world powers" (ibid., 61).

23. See the use of the verb *ḥānan*, "deal graciously," in the Aaronic blessing (Num 6:25) and the discussion of that benediction below.

24. Ronald E. Clements, *In Spirit and in Truth: Insights from Biblical Prayers* (Atlanta: John Knox, 1985) 36.

25. Ibid., 51–58.

26. Literally, "Do steadfast love [*ḥesed*] with you."

27. This was true of the ancient Near East generally although Israel lifted the protection of the widow, the orphan, and the poor to a special place as a measure of the justice without which a society could not exist.

28. See the conclusion of the blessing: "as you have dealt with the dead and with me" (1:8b).

29. The translation of the first blessing could be, "May the one who took notice of you be blessed."

30. See above on Ruth 2:4.

31. Pss 29:11; 67:1, 7; 115:14-15; 134:3. The blessing at the beginning of Psalm 67 is derived from the Aaronic blessing in Num 6:24-26.

32. For a more extended treatment of this benediction, a treatment from which the following discussion is drawn, see Patrick D. Miller Jr., "The Blessing of God: An Interpretation of Numbers 6:22-27," *Int* 29/3 (1975) 240–51. Cf. Klaus Seybold, *Der aaronitische Segen* and the bibliography cited there. For more recent treatments of the blessing as well as of its use in Scripture, see David Noel Freedman, "The Aaronic Benediction," *No Famine in the Land:*

Studies in Honor of John L. McKenzie (ed. James W. Flanagan and Anita Weis-brod Robinson; Missoula, Mont.: Scholars Press, 1975); and Michael Fishbane, "Form and Reformulation of the Biblical Priestly Blessing," *JAOS* 103/1 (1983) 115–21.

33. See Leon J. Liebreich, "The Songs of Ascent and the Priestly Blessing," *JBL* 74 (1955) 33–36, and Fishbane, "Form and Reformulation."

34. Gabriel Barkay, *Ketef Hinnom: A Treasure Facing Jerusalem's Walls* (Jerusalem: Israel Museum, 1986) 29–31. Cf. Marjo C. A. Korpel, "The Poetic Structure of the Priestly Blessing," *JSOT* 45 (October 1989) 3–13; Ada Yardeni, "Remarks on the Priestly Blessings on Two Ancient Amulets from Jerusalem," *VT* 41 (1991) 176–85.

35. James Luther Mays, *The Book of Leviticus; The Book of Numbers* (Layman's Bible Commentary; Richmond: John Knox, 1963) 79.

36. There is, of course, an analogy to this in the Decalogue. It is given to the people assembled together, but the commandments are formulated in the second-person singular, thus addressing each individual Israelite.

37. It is of interest to note that in the effort to decipher the silver amulet with the Aaronic benediction on it, it was the presence of the name of the Lord, YHWH, three times in the text that gave the clue to what was written on the scroll of silver.

38. On God's good gifts of posterity: e.g., Gen 28:3; Deut 1:11. On posses-sions and wealth: e.g., Gen 24:35. On fertility, health, and victory: e.g., Deut 1:11; 7:12-16; Ruth 4:11-12.

39. Paul A. Riemann, "Am I My Brother's Keeper?" *Int* 24/4 (1970) 482–91.

40. Pss 31:16-17; 67:1; 80:3, 7, and 19.

41. Judg 19:20; 1 Sam 16:5; 2 Sam 18:28.

42. Note in this connection its relationship to *rāpāʾ*, "to heal,"; e.g., Isa 53:5; 57:18-19; Jer 6:14; Ps 38:3.

43. Albert Outler, *Who Trusts in God: Musings on the Meaning of Providence* (New York; Oxford Univ. Press, 1968) 72ff.

44. Ibid., 62.

45. Ibid., 81.

46. Ibid.

47. On the question, "What about curse?" see also the discussion "Pe-titions against the Enemy" in chap. 3, above. On the curse generally, see Herbert C. Brichto, *The Problem of "Curse" in the Hebrew Bible* (SBLMS 13; Philadelphia: Society of Biblical Literature, 1963).

48. E.g., Gen 9:25; 27:29.

49. The text and meaning of this verse are problematic at points. The word "witness" is not in the Hebrew but is read by the NRSV and others as a trans-lation of the Hebrew consonantal text lying behind the Greek text. Its character as a curse, however, is clear.

50. E.g., Pss 35:4-6, 8, 26; 58:7-8; 69:22-28; 109:6-19; 139:19; 140:9-11; Jer 18:21-22.

51. E.g., 1 Cor 16:22; Gal 1:8-9.

52. On this theme and its relation to the correspondence between a sin and its punishment, see Patrick D. Miller Jr., *Sin and Judgment in the Prophets. A Stylistic and Theological Analysis* (SBLMS 27; Chico, Calif.: Scholars Press, 1982).

53. See 2 Kgs 21:13; Amos 7:7-9.

54. It is interesting that the most authentic prayers of imprecation that I have heard have been those lifted by persons in behalf of others, i.e., as prayers of intercession that are also prayers for God's justice to stand against the rapist, the murderer, etc. who has attacked or threatened another person.

CHAPTER 10: "TEACH US TO PRAY"

1. An extended bibliography on prayer in the New Testament has been prepared by Mark Harding for the Society of Biblical Literature Consultation on New Testament Prayer in Historical Context, New Orleans, 1990. This work is forthcoming under the title "Prayer Texts from the Greco-Roman Era," in a volume edited by James Charlesworth (Philadelphia: Trinity).

2. The assumption underlying this book is that there is a continuing, unresolved, and proper tension between, on the one hand, the sense of the canon as a single whole whose unity is a given in its witness to the God who speaks and acts within it and whose words and deeds are one and, on the other hand, the reality of the double witness, the Old and the New, the effect of the Christ-event on our understanding of those words and deeds. The Old Testament and the New Testament are both one and two. Thus we have dealt with them as one and now deal with them as two. Theologically, we can and must assume their interrelatedness, while we also receive them both as distinctive testimonies. On this issue, see most recently R. W. L. Moberly, *The Old Testament of the Old Testament* (Minneapolis: Fortress, 1992) 155–66; and Brevard S. Childs, *Biblical Theology of the Old and New Testaments: Theological Reflection on the Christian Bible* (Minneapolis: Fortress, 1992).

3. For the way in which Paul understands such typical Jewish prayer to be a Christian confession, see below.

4. Matt 6:9-13 ‖ Luke 11:2-4.

5. The prayers from the cross: Matt 27:46 ‖ Mark 15:34 (Ps 22:1); Luke 23:46 (Ps 31:5; cf. Acts 7:59). The five prayers of Jesus: Matt 11:25-27 ‖ Luke 10:21-22; Matt 26:39 ‖ Mark 14:36 ‖ Luke 22:42; John 11:41-42; 12:27-28; 17:1-26. The prayer of Peter and John: Acts 4:24-30. Stephen's prayer: Acts 7:59-60.

6. Jesus' prayers for help: Mark 14:36 ‖ John 12:27-28. His prayers of thanksgiving: Matt 11:25; John 11:41. On Jesus at prayer, cf. John Koenig, *Rediscovering New Testament Prayer* (San Francisco: Harper, 1992) 15-19.

7. Whether these prayers contain the actual words of Jesus or Gospel tradition, the issue at hand is their continuity with the traditions of prayer in Scripture and Judaism.

8. For the prayer from Ps 31:5, cf. Acts 7:59. Jesus' words to his disciples when he prays in Gethsemane are not a prayer, but they do draw upon one of

the characteristic prayers for help of the Psalter (Matt 26:38; Mark 14:34; cf. John 12:27a and Ps 42:6). On these prayers, see Donald Senior, "Jesus in Crisis," *Scripture and Prayer* (ed. Carolyn Osiek and Donald Senior; Wilmington, Del.: Michael Glazier, 1988) 117–30.

9. For an extended presentation of the influence of the Septuagint Psalter on Paul's prayers and prayer-reports, see Gunther Harder, *Paulus und das Gebet* (NTF 10; Gutersloh: Bertelsmann, 1936) 64–79.

10. Joachim Jeremias, *The Prayers of Jesus* (SBT, n.s., 6; London: SCM, 1967) 77.

11. Matt 5:44; Luke 6:27-28; Rom 12:14.

12. See the prefatory, "But I say to you...," in Matt 5:44 and Luke 6:27. In Matthew, Jesus' words are explicitly set over against Old Testament instruction and what he understands to be the current way of relating to the enemy.

13. I am indebted to Ulrich Mauser for helping me see the continuities between the Old Testament and the New at just this point where there are significant differences.

14. See the discussion of Psalm 139 in chap. 9, above, and the treatment of the petition against the enemies in chap. 3, above.

15. See Krister Stendahl, "Prayer and Forgiveness: The Lord's Prayer," *Meanings* (Philadelphia: Fortress, 1984) 115–25.

16. Cf. Matt 18:35; Mark 11:25.

17. Mark 11:23-24; John 15:7; 1 John 3:22; 5:14.

18. Cf. the comment of Joseph Fitzmyer: "Three human modes of petition are mentioned (asking, searching, knocking at a door), and each is promised a reward (gift, discovery, welcome). They are not to be allegorized as human endeavor resulting in progress, but express rather the kinds of simple petition the Christian disciple is to present to the heavenly Father" (Joseph A. Fitzmyer, *The Gospel according to Luke X–XXIV* [AB 29; Garden City, N.Y.: Doubleday, 1985] 914).

19. Cf. Jas 5:15-16. Stendahl sees this emphasis upon trust in God and the righteousness of the praying one as the primary point of James's teaching ("Prayer and Forgiveness," 121).

20. Mark 11:22-24; John 15:7; 1 John 3:22; 5:14.

21. Mark 11:22-23 ‖ Matt 21:21-22; cf. Mark 9:23-29.

22. Note the triple use of the verb *pisteuo* or the noun equivalent, *pistis*, in the pericope (vv. 22, 23, 24).

23. See the comment of C. K. Barrett with regard to John 15:7: "The prayer of a truly obedient Christian cannot fail, since he can ask nothing contrary to the will of God" (*The Gospel according to St John: An Introduction with Commentary and Notes on the Greek Text* [London: SPCK, 1956] 396).

24. Barrett, *The Gospel according to St John*, 396.

25. E.g., Rom 12:12; Eph 6:18; Col 1:9; 4:2; 1 Thess 5:17.

26. For the way in which these parables fit into the theology of Luke, see Wilhelm Ott, *Gebet und Heil: Die Bedeutung der Gebets-paranese in der Lukanische Theologie* (SANT; Munich: Kosel, 1965).

27. Fitzmyer notes that "Luke's Greek word for 'persistence' is really 'shamelessness' " (*Luke X–XXIV,* 910).

28. On this text and the particular emphasis on prayer in Luke, see Allison A. Trites, "The Prayer Motif in Luke-Acts," *Perspectives on Luke-Acts* (ed. Charles H. Talbert; Perspectives in Religious Studies; Danville, Va.: Association of Baptist Professors of Religion, 1978) 168–86.

29. The passive form of this sentence is consistent with the theological passive that appears in Matt 7:7-11 and Luke 11:9-13: "[I]t will be given you.... [I]t will be opened for you." That is, God will give you and God will open for you. Cf. Fitzmyer, *Luke X–XXIV,* 915.

30. Luke 18:1; Rom 12:12; Eph 6:18; Col 4:2; 1 Thess 5:17.

31. Luke 22:40, 46; cf. 21:36.

32. Note his statement that "three times I appealed to the Lord" that his "thorn in the flesh" would leave him (2 Cor 12:8). On this text, see below.

33. Except in his greetings and benedictions at the end, there is very little actual prayer in Paul's writings. But the concern for prayer and the reality of prayer in his life and apostolic mission pervade his letters. Note the comments of Stendahl with reference to Paul's "prayerful language" that the "primary mood and mode is that of thanksgiving" and that "Paul speaks a language that constantly borders on prayer and doxological confession" ("Paul at Prayer," *Meanings* [Philadelphia: Fortress, 1984] 152–53).

34. That such discipline could also be practiced by Gentiles is illustrated by the story of the Italian centurion, Cornelius, who "was a devout man who feared God with all his household; he gave alms generously to the people and *prayed constantly to God*" (Acts 10:1), though the point here may be a Lucan one rather than a reflection of Gentile practices.

35. Luke 3:21; 5:16; 6:12; 9:18, 28; 11:1; 22:32, 41-42. This depiction is not confined to the Gospel of Luke. Cf. Mark 1:35; 6:46; 14:32, 35, 39. On the prayers of Luke and Acts, see now Steven F. Plymale, *The Prayer Texts of Luke-Acts* (New York: Peter Lang, 1991).

36. Joseph A. Fitzmyer, *The Gospel according to Luke I–IX* (AB 28; Garden City, N.Y.: Doubleday, 1981) 244. Note that there are some differences in the teaching about persistence. While Luke places the Lord's Prayer in the context of importuning prayer in Luke 11, Matthew takes a different tack. He warns of heaping up "empty phrases, as the Gentiles do, for they think they will be heard because of their many words. Do not be like them, for your Father knows what you need before you ask him. Pray then in this way, 'Our Father...' " (Matt 6:7-9). Matthew's words, of course, are not against persistence in prayer. They are a separation of Jesus' prayer from hypocritical and ostentatious prayer. The model prayer is given as an example of simplicity. But in the context the issue of persistence is subdued. Neither Luke's Jesus nor Paul has any idea of heaping up empty phrases in persistent, constant, importuning prayer. But Matthew's Jesus has a greater concern with simplicity than persistence.

37. Rom 12:12; Col 4:2; cf. 1 Thess 5:17. In this text, his injunction is "pray without ceasing [*adialeiptos*]."

38. Phil 1:4; Col 1:3; 1 Thess 1:2; 2:13; 2 Thess 1:11; Philemon 4; cf. "night and day" in 1 Thess 3:10. Paul's formulations in these contexts are very similar to that in a letter of the high priest Jonathan to the Spartans in 1 Macc 12:11: "We therefore remember you constantly on every occasion, both at our festivals and on other appropriate days, at the sacrifices that we offer and in our prayers, as it is right and proper to remember brothers." Such assurances of constant remembrance in prayer are "closely related to a well-attested conventional letter style" (Wiles) attested not only in Maccabees but also in earlier times in Near Eastern and Jewish letters from Assyria, Amarna, and Elephantine, as well as in a number of Greek papyrus letters. See chap. 9, n. 10, above, and Gordon P. Wiles, *Paul's Intercessory Prayers: The Significance of the Intercessory Prayer Passages in the Letters of St Paul* (SNTSMS 24; Cambridge: Cambridge Univ. Press, 1974) 158–59 and the bibliography cited there; Harder, *Paulus und das Gebet*, 8–9. Harder develops the Jewish background of Paul's prayer at some length in his first chapter. He also seeks to set Paul's forms and notions of prayer in the context of the ancient Gentile world while also identifying those things he sees as marking Paul's prayer as Christian prayer. On the last, see the discussion in the next section, below.

39. Harder, *Paulus und das Gebet*, 10, 15.

40. Wiles, *Paul's Intercessory Prayers*, 182.

41. A judgment is being made here that some of Paul's teaching about prayer is less directly about that and also less central to the New Testament witness, e.g., his words to the Corinthians about whether men and women should have something on their head when praying (1 Cor 11:4-5, 13).

42. Rom 14:6; 1 Cor 10:30.

43. It is worth noting in relation to this text that the shift in academic and ecclesial practice from "the Lord" to "Yahweh" in reference to the God of Israel breaks the continuity that Paul recognizes and affirms so explicitly. While it may be the case that the *kurios* terminology of the early church grew out of "the cultic acclamation of Hellenistic Christianity," and only later became fixed as the translation of "Yahweh" in the Septuagint, *kurios* as a translation of the divine name in the Greek translation of the Old Testament and as a title for Jesus in the language of the New became a very important bridge between the Testaments, opening up, as Stendahl says, "mighty theological avenues" (Stendahl, following Bultmann and others, in "Paul at Prayer," 157). As with the shift from "Old Testament" to "Hebrew Bible" in some Christian reference to the first part of the Christian canon, the shift from "the Lord" to "Yahweh" serves to pull the Testaments apart and dissociate one Testament from the other. On this subject, see now Moberly, *The Old Testament of the Old Testament*, 155–66.

44. Stendahl, "Paul at Prayer," 156.

45. On the question of whether Paul addressed prayers to Jesus, see the bibliography cited in Wiles, *Paul's Intercessory Prayers*, 55 n. 3.

46. On this, see Stendahl, "Paul at Prayer," 156–58.

47. Cf. Rom 1:8; 1 Cor 15:57; 2 Cor 2:14; 8:16; 9:15.

48. Rom 6:17; 10:1; 14:6; 15:30; 1 Cor 1:4; 14:18; 2 Cor 13:7; Eph 5:20; Col 1:3; 3:17; 1 Thess 1:2; 2:13; 3:9; 2 Thess 1:3; 2:13; Phlm 1:4.

49. See note 55, below.

50. There is no need in this instance to go into the vexed and debated question as to whether prayer to God as Father was common in Judaism at the time of Christ. In the biblical witness, there is a marked development in this direction from the Old Testament to the New that is rooted in the particular relation between Jesus of Nazareth and the God of Israel. Even if such address in prayer was a feature of Judaism at that time, it still remains the case that, as Wiles—who argues the title "our Father" is to be found in traditional Jewish prayers—says, "the extraordinary new profundity and vividness with which Paul used the name Father must also be given the fullest attention.... To invoke God as Father in prayer was to call on the aid of one whose purpose to bless was beyond all description" (Wiles, *Paul's Intercessory Prayers*, 55). Cf. Ulrich Luz, *Matthew 1–7* (Minneapolis: Fortress, 1989) 375–77, and Georg Schelbert, "Sprachgeschichtliches zu 'abba,'" *Mélanges Dominique Barthelemy* (ed. Pierre Casetti; OBO 38; Göttingen: Vandenhoeck und Ruprecht, 1981) 395–477. Critical argument with the supposedly unique use by Jesus of Abba and "Father" in addressing God in prayer may be found in Mary Rose D'Angelo, "Theology in Mark and Q: Abba and 'Father' in Context," *HTR* 85 (1992) 149–74 and the bibliography cited in n. 4.

51. Matt 11:25-26 ‖ Luke 10:21; Matt 26:39 (cf. 42, 53) ‖ Mark 14:36 ‖ Luke 22:42; Luke 23:34, 46; John 11:41; 12:27-28; 17:1, 5, 11, 21, 24, 25. The only exception is the cry from the cross, "My God, my God, why have you forsaken me?" a quotation of Psalm 22.

52. Matt 6:6, 9 ‖ Luke 11:2.

53. E.g., in blessings: Rom 1:7; 1 Cor 1:3; 2 Cor 1:2; Gal 1:3; Eph 1:2; 2:18; Phil 1:2; Col 1:2; 1 Thess 3:11; 2 Thess 1:2; 2:16; cf. 1 Tim 1:2; Titus 1:4; and in thanksgivings: 2 Cor 1:3; Eph 1:3; 5:20; Col 1:3, 12; 3:17.

54. Rom 8:14-17; cf. below.

55. Cf. Adrian Schenker, "Gott als Vater—söhne Gottes," *Text und Sinn im Alten Testament: Textgeschichtliche und bibeltheologischen Studien* (OBO 103; Göttingen: Vandenhoeck und Ruprecht, 1991) 1–53.

56. Two things need to be added to the above discussion. One is to affirm with Stendahl that the address to the Father, to God the Parent, does not mean "informality and emotional warmth" (Stendahl, "Paul at Prayer," 156) and with many others that the "Father" terminology must not be understood as saying something about gender and God. It says something about parent-filial relationship as a way of experiencing and claiming the relation to God. Whatever is indicated by that imagery is carried by the maternal-parental image as well as the paternal one. Contemporary liturgy and theology need to appropriate in rather widespread ways the maternal language and imagery along with the paternal imagery to break the restriction to the masculine that the exclusive use of the "Father" term forces upon us. (See further below on the Lord's Prayer.)

57. A second prayer follows that also may be addressed to the risen Lord: "Lord, do not hold this sin against them." Other prayers occur in Acts that are addressed to the "Lord" (Acts 1:24; 4:24; 8:22, 24). The reference may be ambiguous, but it is likely that they are addressed to God.

58. Stendahl, "Paul at Prayer," 156–58.

59. Cf. Rom 7:25; 1 Cor 15:57; 2 Cor 2:14; Col 3:17; cf. Eph 5:20.

60. So Ernst Käsemann for the *dia* of the "through Christ" thanksgiving formulations (*Commentary on Romans* [ed. Geoffrey W. Bromiley; Grand Rapids: Eerdmans, 1980] 17).

61. A particular fixed form of this prayer through Christ is found in the benedictions at the beginning of most of the Pauline letters: "Grace to you and peace from God our Father and the Lord Jesus Christ" (Rom 1:7). The formulation is somewhat different, "from God … and the Lord Jesus Christ." But the benediction is consistent with the other prayers "through Christ." That is best seen in the theological grounding of this conventional blessing, found in Rom 5:1-2: "Therefore, since we are justified by faith, we have *peace* with God *through our Lord Jesus Christ,* through whom we have obtained access to this *grace* in which we stand." The grace and peace from God are through Jesus Christ. In this connection, see the argument of Klaus Berger that the benediction indicates not only that God in Christ is the source of grace and peace, but also that the letter itself is the concrete form or manifestation of God's grace and peace as it discloses God to the recipients of the letter ("Apostelbrief und apostolischer Rede/Zum Formular frühchristlicher Briefe," *ZNW* 65 [1974] 190–231).

62. Rom 8:15, 26-27; Gal 4:6.

63. Eph 6:18; Jude 20.

64. Jude 20. The form in both instances is a participle, *proseuchomenoi.* In Eph 6:18, this may be a case of a concluding imperative participle after a series of participles (in vv. 14-16—*perizōsamenoi,* "girding [oneself]"; *endusamenoi,* "putting on"; *hupodēsameno,* "putting on [shoes]"; *analabontes,* "taking up"), as appears to be the case in 5:21 (see F. F. Bruce, *The Epistles to the Colossians, to Philemon, and to the Ephesians* [NICNT; Grand Rapids: Eerdmans, 1984] 383 n. 78 and 411 n. 86). But it is also possible, and I think more likely, that v. 18 continues the line of thought begun in v. 14 and that this participle modifies the injunction "stand" in v. 14, as do the participles mentioned above, or, more likely, it modifies the immediately preceding imperative, *dexasthe,* "take" (v. 17). Thus the text would be understood as: "Take the helmet of salvation … praying in every time in the Spirit … keeping alert. …" Even understood thus, the verb "praying" has an imperative force, allied with the other imperatives that govern the unit, reaching back to v. 10.

The same analysis belongs to the Jude passage, only here the imperative comes after the participles: "But you beloved, building yourselves up …, praying in the Spirit, keep yourselves in the love of God. …"

65. Harder (*Paulus und das Gebet,* 171) sees the prayer in the Spirit as always referring to ecstatic prayer except for the "spiritual songs" of Col 3:16.

66. See the comment of Gordon Fee (*The First Epistle to the Corinthians* [NICNT; Grand Rapids: Eerdmans, 1987] 670): "In the present context the difficult wording 'my spirit prays' seems to mean something like 'my S/spirit prays.' On the one hand, both the possessive 'my' and the contrast with 'my mind' indicate that he is here referring to his own 'spirit' at prayer. On the other hand, there can be little question, on the basis of the combined evidence

of 12:7-11 and 14:2 and 16, that Paul understood speaking in tongues to be an activity of the Spirit in one's life; it is prayer and praise directed toward God in the language of Spirit-inspiration. The most viable solution to this ambiguity is that by the language 'my spirit prays' Paul means his own spirit is praying as the Holy Spirit gives the utterance. Hence 'my S/spirit prays.' " Cf. Rom 8:16: "that very Spirit bearing witness with our spirit."

67. It should be noted that there has been considerable debate among interpreters of this chapter as to whether the references to the Spirit helping in prayer point to ecstatic prayer, as in 1 Corinthians 14 (e.g., Käsemann), or more general help in our inability to pray (e.g., Black and Stanley). See Käsemann, *Romans*, 239–43 (where various interpretations are discussed); Matthew Black, *Romans* (NCB Commentary; Grand Rapids: Eerdmans, 1973) 123; and David M. Stanley, *Boasting in the Lord: The Phenomenon of Prayer in Paul* (New York: Paulist, 1973) 127–35.

68. On this see Paul J. Achtemeier, *Romans* (Interpretation; Atlanta: John Knox, 1985) 137–41.

69. It is possible that in speaking of crying "Abba" Paul had in mind an acclamation in worship and not an act of prayer (so, e.g., Käsemann, Stendahl). And indeed, it is the Spirit that enables the Christian to say both "Abba, Father" and "Jesus is Lord" (1 Cor 12:3). But the use of the "Father" address in such contexts as the Lord's Prayer and Mark 14:36 presses one toward the sense that such "crying" has also to do with prayer. The particular intention of Paul is debated. The testimony of the New Testament and the early church, however, is that that term is an address, i.e., directed toward God, and thus prayer. In that sense, it is somewhat different from "Jesus is Lord" as a declaration. Käsemann and Stendahl would connect these, as well as *maranatha*, "Our Lord, come!" (cf. "Come, Lord Jesus!" in Rev 22:20), because of their short exclamatory character. They are surely all liturgical, but not necessarily all with the same function. The homologion, "Jesus is Lord," is not the same as the eschatological prayer, "Our Lord, come!" or "Come, Lord Jesus!" Nor is "Abba" or "Father" the same as that. It is known as an address to God in prayer and surely functioned primarily that way. In other words, whether or not the particular force of Paul's usage can be finally determined, the New Testament context clearly carries Paul's claim into the sphere of prayer where Christians then and now cry "Father" in prayer (see Käsemann, *Romans*, 228; Stendahl, "Paul at Prayer," 155–56). It should be noted that the term *krazō*, "cry" is ambiguous, having only one other use in Paul and that with reference to a prophecy of Isaiah (Rom 9:27). It can refer to acclamation or prayer although it does not generally refer to either.

70. So also Gal 4:6.

71. It seems rather strange that Paul would give such weight to the help of the Spirit in prayer in the sense of glossolalia when he has specifically relegated that to a secondary position in the community's worship in his letter to the Corinthians. Käsemann comments here: "In tongues at worship there sounds forth in a singular way, and in such a manner that we do not ourselves comprehend the concern of the Spirit who drives us to prayer, the cry for eschatological freedom in which Christians represent the whole of afflicted creation.... By its

ecstatic cries prayer is made for the whole of enslaved and oppressed creation" (Käsemann, *Romans,* 241). That "the intercession of the Spirit coincides with the cries of those who speak in tongues" seems to be a far cry from the direction of Paul's thought in his comments toward the Corinthians. Even allowing for the contextual difference in the problems in the Corinthian church, Paul's elaboration of the gifts of the Spirit, of which "various kinds of tongues" is only one of a long list (1 Cor 12:1-11), makes it difficult to restrict the help of the Holy Spirit "in our weakness" to ecstatic prayer. Furthermore, Eph 6:18 speaks of praying "in the Spirit at all times."

72. Two representative positions briefly stated may be found in the following comments: "[W]hen we do not know how or what to pray, then the Spirit comes to our help, interceding for us in nonverbal groans; but God, who searches the hearts, knows the mind of the Spirit. Here Paul understands glossolalia as the Spirit praying in us. In a typically Pauline manner he sees this phenomenon not as a sign of high spiritual achievement, but as God's antidote to human weakness" (Stendahl, "Paul at Prayer," 155). "Praying 'in the Spirit' means praying under the Spirit's influence and with his assistance.... [T]here are prayers and aspirations of the heart that cannot well be articulated; these can be offered in the Spirit, who, as Paul says, 'himself intercedes for us with sighs too deep for words' (Rom 8:26)" (Bruce, *Colossians, Philemon, Ephesians,* 411).

73. The word *astheneia* seems to refer to human weakness as represented by human frailty, suffering, or trouble (e.g., 1 Cor 2:3; 2 Cor 11:30; 12:9; 13:4; cf. Heb 5:2; 7:28). It does not seem to refer to the effects of sin and rebellion (but see 1 Cor 11:30).

74. Käsemann, *Romans,* 240.

75. Or "from the evil one" (v. 13); cf. Matt 13:19.

76. Luke 22:42 ‖ Matt 26:39 ‖ Mark 14:36. The Matthean and Marcan forms are "yet not what I want but what you want" and are probably original. There is no significant difference in meaning. The Matthew prayer is probably dependent upon Mark. In its second formulation (26:42; not in Mark or Luke), the prayer in Matthew is brought into direct conformity with the Lord's Prayer. Luke's form of the prayer, cited above in the text, is also similar to the Lord's Prayer, but as it occurs in Matthew and not in Luke's own Gospel. The formulations may be compared:

Matt 6:10—*genēthētō to thelēma sou* (your will be done);

Mark 14:36—*all' ou ti egō thelō alla ti su* (not what I want but what you want);

Matt 26:42—*genēthētō to thelēma sou* (your will be done);

Luke 22:42—*plēn mē to thelēma mou alla to son ginesthō* (yet not my will but yours be done).

The saying in John goes still further but is not a part of a prayer: "Am I not to drink the cup that the Father has given me?"

77. That will is in this case, of course, the salvific purpose of God at work in the death and resurrection of Jesus Christ.

78. E.g., Pss 7:17; 9:2.

79. Cf. Friedrich Heiler, *Prayer: A Study in the History and Psychology of Religion* (New York: Oxford Univ. Press, 1932) 267.

80. On this passage, see Stanley, *Boasting,* 52–60.

81. Stanley notes that this is indeed perceived by Paul as a response by God. The rebuff is to the particular petition, but his prayer does not remain unanswered (ibid., 57).

82. Stanley appropriately sees in this experience of Paul's "a certain resemblance to Jesus' prayer and struggle in the garden as that incident came to be interpreted in the New Testament" (ibid., 58).

83. Even in these cases, Paul may be specific about setting such prayers in the context of God's will, e.g., Rom 15:32.

84. Stendahl, "Paul at Prayer," 154.

85. It is important to recognize that the direction New Testament prayer takes from its Old Testament roots, as described above, may be comparable to the shape of prayer in other communities of faith. It also may be given quite different value judgments. So Heiler in his classic work, quoting the philosopher Höffding, says of Jesus' prayer on the Mount of Olives that it is "the highest moment in the history of prayer, the most profound word in religion that has ever been uttered" (*Prayer,* 123). A quite different point of view is offered by Joseph Heinemann: "When the Jewish petitioner surrenders his wish to the will of God, he nevertheless does not abandon it altogether. His request still stands, and, if it remains conditional upon God's will, this is only because he trusts that it shall, indeed, be God's will to grant the request. We do not have here the same categorical surrender in which the petitioner's request is completely given up. If Jesus' conception represents the 'highest moment in the history of prayers,' then it also seriously undermines the value of prayer. For if, from the very outset, the petitioner has already abandoned all hope of his request's being granted if it does not conform to the will of God, why is he praying at all? For Rabbinic Judaism, prayer only exists to be heard and answered. There is simply no point to a prayer which is not nourished by a sense of assurance that it is not being offered in vain. There is unquestionably an element of paradox in all prayer, and this element is certainly not lacking in the Jewish view of prayer. But the outlook which is expressed in the prayers of Jesus reduces the very possibility of prayer to absurdity, and it is not shared by Rabbinic Judaism" ("The Background of Jesus' Prayer in the Jewish Liturgical Tradition," *The Lord's Prayer and Jewish Liturgy* [ed. Jakob J. Petuchowski and Michael Brocke; New York: Seabury, 1978] 86–87).

86. The comment of Douglas J. Hall elaborates this point as follows: "No doubt it is a human thing to wish to avoid suffering and to regard the lack of suffering as a mark of special favor, or at least good fortune. Conversely, it is also a human and a healthy thing to eschew unnecessary suffering, and to be skeptical of those who go out of their way to find crosses to bear! But once the church confesses faith in a God who through sacrificial identification with a suffering creation heals its brokenness from within, it commits itself to a life in which suffering will have considerable prominence.... The object [of such suffering] is to identify oneself with the suffering that is already there in one's world, to let oneself be led by the love of Christ into solidarity with those who suffer, and to accept the consequences of this solidarity in the belief—the *joyful* belief—that in this way God is still at work in the world, making a conquest of

its sin and suffering" (*God and Human Suffering: An Exercise in the Theology of the Cross* [Minneapolis: Augsburg, 1986] 144–45).

87. *Against Apion* 2.196. The translation is that of the Loeb Classical Library edition. For the reference, I am indebted to Arland J. Hultgren, "Expectations of Prayer in the New Testament," *A Primer on Prayer* (ed. Paul R. Sponheim; Philadelphia: Fortress, 1988) 28.

88. Acts 12:5; cf. v. 12.

89. Stendahl, "Paul at Prayer," 159.

90. See the comment of Gordon Wiles: "At the beginning of the letter Paul has assured his readers of the unceasing prayers of thanksgiving and supplication made for them: now at the end he invites them to complete the intercessory circle of mutual responsibility. The whole letter and the crisis that lies behind it are again drawn into the network of mutual prayers" (*Paul's Intercessory Prayers,* 263).

91. Cf. Col 4:3; 2 Thess 3:1; Philemon 22.

92. Wiles, *Paul's Intercessory Prayers,* 274. In Paul's letter to the Romans, virtually all activity is understood as giving glory to God. The fundamental human sin is the failure to honor or glorify God and to give thanks, a stance that constitutes humankind's basic idolatry as it exchanges the glory of God for idols. Abraham's faith consists in trusting God's promise, i.e., in giving glory to God (Rom 4:20). Harmony in the church and the welcome of one another in the Christian community are for the glory of God. Prayer, therefore, joins with all other human activity in carrying out what the Westminster Shorter Catechism sees as our chief end as human beings, "to glorify God."

93. One also finds on two or three occasions that Paul pronounced curse formulas (1 Cor 5:3-5; 16:22; Gal 1:8-9). These take place in the context of his struggles with various elements in these congregations and his "intense feelings about the special emergencies that had arisen" (Wiles, *Paul's Intercessory Prayers,* 155). Once more, it is necessary to note that such curse prayers are a peculiar minority in the prayer for others, whereas intercession and blessings for others are frequent and constant phenomena in Paul. The curse can hardly be regarded as a typical prayer form. It is an extreme measure pronounced by the apostle as a kind of priestly, prophetic figure exercising control over wayward congregations or individuals. On the curse prayers of Paul, see Wiles, *Paul's Intercessory Prayers,* 116–55.

94. See the comment of Fitzmyer: "Note the order of the terms here: Luke clearly suggests that prayer is as important for the life of the Christian apostle as 'the ministry of the word,' i.e. the preaching of the Christian message" (*Luke I–IX,* 246).

95. Hultgren, "Expectations of Prayer," 28.

96. On Romans 9–11 and the vexed issues it raises, see now *The Church and Israel: Romans 9–11* (supplementary issue, no. 1, [1990] of the *Princeton Seminary Bulletin*).

97. Karl Barth, *Prayer* (ed. Don E. Saliers; Philadelphia: Westminster, 1985) 43–44.

98. See above, pp. 314–15.

99. See Diane Tennis, *Is God the Only Reliable Father?* (Philadelphia: Westminster, 1985).

100. For this reason, of course, some would propose the elimination of all such images in our religious discourse, but the incarnational reality that is at the heart of Christian faith suggests that there is something truthful and real, if also indirect and illusive, in such imagery.

101. This is the serious and fatal flaw in the insistence of Roland M. Frye ("Language for God and Feminist Language," *Int* 43/1 [1989] 45–57) that the father image is of another order than the maternal in that it is a metaphor and not a simile, as is the case with regard to the biblical references to God as mother. He is certainly correct about the maternal imagery occurring in simile form rather than metaphor, but his effort to regard the metaphor as a predication that has a reality in the way that the simile does not is highly questionable. There are frequent instances of images that appear in both simile and metaphorical form in Scripture. Frye takes as his prime example of a simile and the way it operates "in a more restricted way" the imagery of God as warrior in Isaiah 42:13. He comments: "The prophet is careful here not to identify the Lord with a war god, even a supreme war god. Instead by a formal comparison God is said to 'go forth' and 'to stir up his fury' *like* a man of war" (pp. 52–53). The major problem with his example is that this imagery is frequently applied to the deity in Scripture in a quite direct and metaphorical way. For example, the song of Moses exclaims, "The LORD is a man of war!" (Exod 15:3). This is as clearly an example of a predicating metaphor as the others that he cites.

It is just such literalizing or predicating of metaphors that Susan Handelman attacks with such force in her book *The Slayers of Moses: The Emergence of Rabbinic Interpretation in Modern Literary Theory* (Albany: State Univ. of New York Press, 1982).

102. The phrase "in heaven" is not in Luke. For discussion of the differences in the traditions at this point, see Fitzmyer, *Luke X–XXIV,* 896–901.

103. See 1 Kgs 8:30, 34, 36, 39, 43, 49.

104. Claus Westermann, *Isaiah 40–66: A Commentary* (OTL; Philadelphia: Westminster, 1969) 393. Cf. Nicholas Ayo, C.S.C., *The Lord's Prayer: A Survey Theological and Literary* (Notre Dame, Ind.: Univ. of Notre Dame Press, 1992) 30. Ayo calls attention to Matthew's use of the expression "your heavenly Father" immediately before (6:1) and after the Lord's Prayer (6:14) but also to Jesus' instruction in Matthew: "Call no one your father on earth, for you have but one Father—the one in heaven" (23:9).

105. The prayer moves from first-person singular to first-person plural. It, therefore, has something of the character of prophetic intercession. But its primary features align it with the community lament or prayer for help. See the discussion in Westermann, *Isaiah 40–66.*

106. E.g., Ayo, *The Lord's Prayer,* 31.

107. Cf. Helmut Merklein, "Die Einzigkeit Gottes als die sachliche Grundlage der Botschaft Jesus," *Jahrbuch für biblische Theologie,* (1987) 2.13–32, esp. 16–20 and nn. 8–10. Merklein notes the joining of the hallowing of God's name and the rule of God in the Jewish Qaddish prayer.

108. Cf. the notion in various Rabbinic interpretations that God's rule in heaven is distinct from the rule on earth, the kingdom coming or God's rule taking place on earth in the call of Abraham (Sifre 313, on Deut 32:10), or in the people's acclamation in Exod 15:2 and 18 (Sifra on Lev 18:1ff.). For example: "Until Abraham came into this world, the Holy One, blessed be He, reigned, if one dare say such a thing, only over the heavens, as it is said, 'The LORD, the God of heaven, who took me' (Gen 24:7); but when Abraham came into the world, he made Him king over both the heaven and the earth, as it is said, 'And I will make thee swear by the LORD, the God of heaven and the God of the earth' (Gen 24:3)" (Sifre 313, quoted from *Sifre: A Tannaitic Commentary on the Book of Deuteronomy*, trans. by Reuven Hammer [Yale Judaica Series 24; New Haven: Yale Univ. Press, 1986] 319).

109. Barth, *Prayer*, 7.

110. Ibid.

111. See Prov 30:8-9:

> Give me neither poverty nor riches;
>   feed me with the food that I need,
> or I shall be full, and deny you,
>   and say, "Who is the LORD?"
> or I shall be poor, and steal,
>   and profane the name of my God.

112. E.g., Pss 25:11; 51:1-2, 9; 130:3-4.

113. Fitzmyer, *Luke X–XXIV*, 899.

114. Luz, *Matthew 1–7*, 384.

115. Fitzmyer, *Luke X–XXIV*, 899.

116. Cf. God's permission to the Satan to place Job into a situation of testing/temptation.

117. It is not necessary in this instance to resolve the question as to whether the *timsol* of Gen 4:7 is "You must rule" or "You may rule." The divine word may be directive or permissive.

118. See the comment of Luz, *Matthew 1–7*, 385: "The three-member *doxology*, which is usual in our services, is missing in the best manuscripts. But 2 Tim 4:18 and the doxology in *Did.* 8:2 which, according to the custom of the Didache (10:5) has two members, show that the Lord's Prayer was prayed in the Greek church from the beginning with a doxology." Cf. the text-critical comment of Bruce Metzger: "The absence of any ascription in early and important representatives of the Alexandrian (B), the Western (D and most of the Old Latin), and the pre-Caesarean...types of text, as well as early patristic commentaries on the Lord's Prayer (those of Tertullian, Origen, Cyprian), suggests that an ascription, usually in a threefold form, was composed (perhaps on the basis of 1 Chr 29:11-13) in order to adapt the Prayer for liturgical use in the early church" (*A Textual Commentary on the Greek New Testament* [London: United Bible Societies, 1971] 16–17).

APPENDIX 1

1. On Judg 6:13 as an example of early prayer, see Claus Westermann, *Praise and Lament in the Psalms* (Atlanta: John Knox, 1981) 200.

2. Literally, "my lord, Yahweh," although the Masoretic *Qere* indicates the last word is to be read as "Elohim" or "God."

3. McCarter plausibly proposes to read for the sentence, whose meaning is uncertain, "and shown me the generation to come" (P. Kyle McCarter, *II Samuel* [AB 9; Garden City, N.Y.: Doubleday, 1984] 232–33).

4. Possibly restore "whom he redeemed for himself from Egypt."

5. See n. 2.

6. See n. 2.

APPENDIX 2

1. Frank Crüsemann, *Studien zur Formgeschichte von Hymnus und Danklied in Israel* (WMANT 32; Neukirchen-Vluyn: Neukirchener Verlag, 1969) 32–35.

2. Ibid., 34, 54–55.

Index of Scriptural References

❧

OLD TESTAMENT

Genesis

3:24	398
4	395
4:7	438
4:10-12	395
4:10	45, 55, 87
9:25-27	423
9:25	426
12:1-4	412, 425
12:2-3	285
12:3	288, 422, 425
13:12-13	422
15	166
15:1-6	154, 337, 395
15:2	70, 383
15:3	383
15:6	228
16	166
16:11	236
17:18-19	139, 395
17:18	32, 337, 379
17:19	166
18	91, 425
18–19	263, 269
18:1-15	412
18:14	242
18:18	286, 425
18:20-21	269
18:21	87, 375
18:22-33	270
18:22	268
18:23-32	267–70, 420, 422
18:23-33	33, 337
18:23	90
18:25 26	118
18:25	90, 268
18:26	268
19:13	375
19:29	268, 270
19:30-38	425
20	262, 267
20:7-17	395
20:7	263, 275, 420, 422
20:17-18	275
20:17	375, 420, 422
21	413
21:15-19	234
21:16-17	413
21:16	79, 88, 154, 338, 377, 413

21:17-18	338
21:20	235
22:1	334
22:5	413
22:6	425
22:12	413
22:18	425
24	33, 56, 180
24:3	438
24:7	438
24:12-14	56, 181, 338, 378
24:12	32, 61, 130
24:14	130
24:26-27	32, 338, 393
24:26	377
24:27	56, 61, 180, 195
24:31	286
24:35	426
24:48	180, 377
24:59-61	423
24:60	282, 284, 398, 423
25:21	42, 266, 375, 395, 398, 421, 422
25:22	413
26:3	398
26:4	286, 425
26:24	420
26:29	425
26:31	425
27	290
27:1-5	423
27:27-29	423
27:27	288
27:28	282, 288
27:29	288, 289, 423, 425, 426
27:39-40	423
27:40	423
28	408
28:3	282, 426
28:5	425
28:14	286, 425
28:15	398, 423
29:35	413
30	9
30:6	395, 398
30:17	398
30:22	395, 398
30:24	413
30:27-30	286
31:49-50	423